THE PRINCELY
COURTS OF
EUROPE

THE PRINCELY COURTS OF EUROPE

Ritual, Politics and Culture
Under the Ancien Régime *1500-1750*

Edited by
JOHN ADAMSON

WEIDENFELD & NICOLSON
LONDON

First published in the United Kingdom in 1999
by Weidenfeld & Nicolson

Distributed in the United States of America by
Sterling Publishing Co., Inc.
387 Park Avenue South, New York, NY 10016-8810

A CIP catalogue record for this book is available from the
British Library

ISBN 0 297 83653 6

Designed by Peter Butler
Edited by Celia Jones
Picture Research by Jenny de Gex
Typset in Bembo
Printed and bound in Italy

Weidenfeld & Nicolson
Cassell & Co.
The Orion Publishing Group
Wellington House
125 Strand
London WC2R 0BB

Endpapers: *Orazio Scarabelli*, The *Naumachia* at the Pitti
Palace *(1589)*.

Half Title page: *The courtier's routes to success: an allegory of
aulic life, from the 'Hortus Regius', a series of notes and drawings
compiled by the Swedish courtier, Schering Rosenhane, during
the 1640s.*

Title page: *The itinerant court: the entourage and royal pavilion of
Philip III of Spain at his meeting with Louis XIII on the Bidasoa
River, the boundary between the French and Spanish kingdoms, in
1615 (a detail of the painting reproduced on page 39).*

CONTENTS

Introduction

THE MAKING OF THE ANCIEN-RÉGIME COURT
1500–1700

JOHN ADAMSON

O F ALL THE INSTITUTIONS AFFECTING THE POLITICAL, RELIGIOUS and cultural life of early modern Europe, there was probably none more influential than the court. Certainly, no influence assumed a greater diversity of forms. For in the period between the Renaissance and the French Revolution, 'the court' defined not merely a princely residence – a lavish set of buildings and their pampered occupants – but a far larger matrix of relations, political and economic, religious and artistic, that converged in the ruler's household.[1] This was a milieu in which, in almost every corner of Europe, the monarch was personally the source of secular authority and the principal dispenser of offices and honours. His court, accordingly, was the prime locus of decision-making affecting Church and state, the major clearing house for preferment, the setting for the daily rituals of rule. Yet, the court was never a single entity, nor did it offer a single route to patronage or power. In reality, the separate households of the ruler's consort, his heir, even those of powerful ministers, could operate to qualify or sometimes eclipse the authority of the ruler.[2] Courtly practice usually belied the rhetoric of 'absolute' princely power.

The early modern court thus fulfilled a series of multiple and sometimes opposing functions. On the one hand, it provided a means of protecting and enclosing the prince, by limiting access to him to a select and favoured entourage. On the other, it served as a means of connecting the ruler to 'the larger political universe' that lay beyond his palace gates.[3] Courts usually encouraged the attendance of local magnates and aristocratic grandees, and

The sacredness of rule: Rubens's painting of Marie de Médicis's debarkation at Marseilles in 1600 celebrates her transition from princely status, as a daughter of the Grand Duke of Tuscany, to royal rank as the queen consort of Henri IV of France. The waiting processional canopy (right) symbolizes the quasi-sacred quality that attached to royalty, while the figure of Fame, with her twin trumpets, announces the alliance to the world.

through contacts and the distribution of offices fostered a series of subordinate patronage networks that linked courtiers to the localities. They bonded the 'centre' with the 'periphery'. Moreover, the sixteenth and seventeenth centuries saw a major expansion of the range of attractions that the ruler's household could offer to draw the élites to court, not least the number of perquisites that lay within the monarch's and his courtiers' gift.

Changes in the conduct of warfare, the costliest sport of kings, did much to augment this portfolio of courtly patronage. In the course of the sixteenth and seventeenth centuries, the frequency of wars and the general expansion in the size of armed forces across Europe brought a commensurate increase in the opportunities for military service. With senior courtiers (and especially the court nobility) tending to retain a virtual monopoly of the higher military commands well into the eighteenth century, they enjoyed a corresponding influence over the award, or sale, of commissions.[4] The noble (and lucrative) business of war was rarely far from the concerns of the court. Tapestries celebrating famous victories; the ubiquitous images of Mars and Hercules; the gilded trophies adorning guard-chambers, the Baroque palace's first 'room of parade': each attests to the centrality of the military system to the function and ethos of the court.[5]

Nor was the court's importance simply the result of its importance to affairs of state. Almost invariably, it was the principal cultural and social centre of the realm. Wherever the court resided, the demands of housing, provisioning and entertaining this increasingly sophisticated élite created unparalleled opportunities for artists and craftsmen of every variety: hydraulic engineers who created fountains, painters, architects, goldsmiths, musicians, jewellers, furniture- and tapestry-makers. Even ballistics experts were hired to create fireworks that turned night into day.[6] For the élites that this army of craftsmen delighted and entertained, the court was also often the principal marriage market of the realm. The Duc de Saint-Simon's memoirs, for example, record by name more than one thousand persons whose marriages had been arranged, contracted and inevitably gossiped about, at Louis XIV's court.[7] To scholars and men of letters, too, the court offered its slippery ladder towards advancement.

Largesse could be provided either informally, through the support of princes and members of their households, or, increasingly from the second half of the seventeenth century, through 'academies' either located within, or closely associated with, the court. While literary men – Erasmus and Sir Thomas More, Leibniz and Voltaire – frequently excoriated courtly vices, they were seldom absent from the court's 'rooms of parade', and often proved themselves as adept at the arts of flattery as the most practised and toadying of courtiers.[8]

However, perhaps the most striking, and least noticed, transformation in the role of the court affected its influence on the religious life of the realm. The Protestant Reformation and, to a lesser extent, the Catholic Counter-Reformation redefined, and in most cases profoundly enhanced, the authority of the monarch *vis-à-vis* the Church. Of course, the idea that the princely court might be a forum where lay control or 'guardianship' might be exercised over the Church had a long pedigree, going back via late-medieval European monarchy to Charlemagne and Constantine. The famous principle of *cuius regio, eius religio* (that each ruler had the right to determine the confessional allegiance of his realm), enunciated in the 1555 Peace of Augsburg, erected a *de facto* 'royal supremacy' over the Church in almost every principality of the Holy Roman Empire. During the following century and a half, the tendency to vest extensive ecclesiastical jurisdiction in the prince – above all, jurisdiction over clerical patronage – was a feature of most early modern European monarchies and major principalities.

Nor was there anything exclusively Protestant about this trend. Between the 1480s and the 1530s 'Caesaro-Papism' – the principle that the prince had quasi-papal rights over the Church within his own realm – became a defining axiom of monarchy, even in many of the most staunchly Catholic of courts. In France, under the 1516 Concordat of Bologna, the Valois kings extracted from the papacy the right to nominate to all the major benefices in France.[9] And in the Iberian kingdoms, largely as a result of the efforts of Ferdinand II of Aragon (1479–1516) and Carlos I (1516–56), the future Charles V of the Holy Roman Empire, the crown had obtained by 1523 the right to nominate to all bishoprics in Spain – powers that were further enhanced by the 'Caesaro-Papist programme' of Philip II.[10] Joseph Bergin's observation, that with the increase in royal jurisdiction over the Church in France, 'the role of the court as a clearing house for the disposal of church patronage naturally grew accordingly', has an almost Europe-wide application.[11] In Catholic realms in particular, courtiers and court ecclesiastics devoted much of their time to the pursuit of benefices, and success in obtaining them became an important gauge of a courtier's effectiveness and status. The real loser in all of this was the papal court at Rome. The process of attrition was a long one, but by the end of the eighteenth century, the pope appointed less than one sixth of the diocesan bishoprics of the Roman Church. Most of the remainder were to be had at the princely courts of Catholic Europe.[12]

This convergence of the secular with the ecclesiastical imposed new priorities on, and expectations of, the functions of the sixteenth- and seventeenth-century courts. Of course, the piety of the prince and his household had long been extolled as an ideal of virtuous kingship; but at the court of a monarch who was simultaneously quasi-pope within his own realms, the 'sanctification of the court' acquired an altogether heightened urgency. It was a theme that resounded as forcefully in the Catholic sermons of Bossuet before Louis XIV as it did in the Protestant rhetoric of the 'godly magistrate'.[13] It followed, therefore, that a central aspect of the 'representative' function of the court was as a theatre of piety, a place where the religious devotion of the prince and his entourage might be publicly staged and edifyingly displayed.

How, then, has this protean institution fared at the hands of historians? Such a diversity of functions, it might be thought, would have guaranteed it a measure of prominence in the historiography of early modern Europe. Yet, except for its artistic dimension, the study of the pre-French Revolution court has been, until recently, virtually an academic taboo. To the nineteenth-century champions of liberalism and democracy, the *ancien-régime* courts were, at best, paternalist and authoritarian; at worst, despotic and corrupt. Likewise, attempts by nineteenth-century nationalist historians to enlist 'court history' in the service of a crudely jingoistic chauvinism merely served to discredit the subject in the eyes of their post-1918 successors. The court history of Brandenburg-Prussia, for instance, still lies in the

shadow cast by the age of Kaiser Wilhelm II and the *Hohenzollern-Jahrbuch*, Wilhelmine Germany's 'yearbook' dedicated to representing the seventeenth- and eighteenth-century Berlin court as the lodestar of German political and cultural life.[14]

To the two great intellectual schools that have dominated the writing of history in the twentieth century, Marxism and liberalism, the court has also been an obvious target for censure. In so far as it has received attention, it has been as the agent and expression of monarchical 'absolutism': a 'transitional phase' – an institutional adolescence, disagreeable but unavoidable – in the progress towards modernity.[15] In Norbert Elias's highly influential and superficially subtle interpretation of 'the court society' (a work in gestation from the 1930s but only published in full in 1969), the court was a sophisticated instrument of autocracy. Louis XIV's 'authoritarian' Versailles provided the paradigm. Early modern courts inculcated habits of deference and provided monarchs with the means to subordinate and 'tame' their once belligerent noble class. Real power was transferred from the old nobility, the traditional governing caste – so the argument runs – to a newly emergent bureaucracy, immediately beholden to the prince.[16] Despite recent scholarly assaults on the cruder aspects of the absolutist theory, Elias's influence on court history lingers still. The *ancien-régime* court continues to be seen as the 'stage for absolutism' (*Bühne des Absolutismus*), an evolutionary link between the world of medieval Europe – feudal, decentralized, hierarchical – and the modern liberal state – democratic, centralized, egalitarian.[17]

This combination of absolutist teleology and partisan disdain has also left its mark on the 'cultural' history of the court. Ever since Burckhardt and Berenson, there has been a tendency to disengage the manifestations of court culture from the ideologically suspect milieu that created them. Instead, 'connoisseurship' – the consideration of the visual arts in terms of their abiding aesthetic qualities – has provided an alternative frame of reference, one that largely exonerates the art historian from the need to consider the social and political circumstances that brought these art-objects into being. With a very few honourable exceptions, much of what still passes as art history continues to be written in terms of the development of 'taste' and 'style', criteria that owe more to Hegelian aesthetic theories and the preoccupations of present-day museum curators than to the social realities of artistic patronage in early modern Europe.[18] In consequence, certain forms of courtly art – notably easel paintings – have been 'privileged' and singled out for intensive study. Others – such as tapestry, armour, gold and silver plate – have been relegated to an inferior status as merely 'decorative arts', and consigned to comparative neglect.[19]

Conversely, where attempts have been made to relate the material culture of the court to its contemporary political environment, a quite separate series of anachronisms has been brought into play. Despite the occasional plea for caution, the trend has been to define both the objects in question and the rationale behind their creation in terms of the dissemination, through coded symbols, of political 'messages' aimed at convincing a public audience of the reality of the ruler's power.[20] Conveniently, this 'functionalist' interpretation of the various forms of court culture, from architecture to etiquette, can be made to cohere neatly with an interpretation of early modern politics cast in terms of autocratic monarchy and the 'rise of the state'.[21] 'Propaganda' has become the cultural stablemate of courtly 'absolutism'.

These essays attempt to offer an alternative view of the politics and culture of the early modern court. Their authors are in general sceptical of attempts to represent court history in terms of the 'development of the modern state'. Where one recent survey has claimed that the court was the means by which political affinities and local clientage networks were integrated 'into *one all-embracing system* of patronage centred around the king and his court', many of these essays question whether the early modern court was ever such a monolithic institution, exploited by monarchs to centralize their authority and to emasculate their rivals' power.[22] Indeed, many of these essays question whether the modern secular concept of the 'state' has much relevance when it comes to analyzing the political world of sixteenth- and seventeenth-century Europe – a world where the defining unit of politics and diplomacy was the dynasty, and in which sovereign power was as much sacred as secular.

A similar challenge is offered to the prevailing approaches to court culture. While these authors do not deny that aulic culture had its 'public face', or that

it might be concerned with enhancing the monarch's prestige, they nevertheless question the applicability of 'propaganda', with its automatic assumption that almost all court art was aimed at persuading or indoctrinating a broad and biddable 'public'. The alternatives to this approach will be considered in the penultimate section of this introduction. Before turning to these interpretative questions, however, we need first to focus more closely on what exactly contemporaries meant by the idea of 'the court'. Viewing the *longue durée* between the Reformation and the French Revolution, was there, despite the many differences between the various early modern dynastic realms, something loosely recognizable as an *ancien-régime* court?

I. THE COURT AND ITS VARIETIES

Surveying the dozens of royal and princely households that ruled the German-speaking realms midway through the eighteenth century, the antiquarian, Friedrich Carl von Moser, believed that he could list with confidence the defining attributes of a contemporary court. There were three main criteria. A residential court was, first, 'the regular constant dwelling of the ruler'; second, the place where the 'actual seat of the court and the departments of government are [to be found]'; and, finally, the venue where the ceremonial and ritual that surrounded the prince could be properly observed.[23]

For all Moser's confidence, however, at the time he was writing, in the 1750s, this standardized 'Baroque court' was in fact a relatively recent invention. Of course, there had been some non-itinerant courts since at least the early Middle Ages, notably in small principalities, often ecclesiastical states: the court at Würzburg, for example, had been 'resident' since the eighth century. But in the case of the larger sovereignties, the adoption of a 'regular constant dwelling [-place]' for the ruler's household had only generally become a regular feature of European government since the mid-sixteenth century, and in many realms far more recently than that. This shift from an itinerant princely household to one located primarily, if not exclusively, at a single 'seat', was a necessary (if not, on its own, a sufficient) condition for the creation of Moser's *ancien-régime* court. Its implications form one of the major themes of this book.[24] For the change affected almost all aspects of the relationship between the monarch's household and the business of rule, from the size of the monarch's retinue to the possibilities for 'representational display' – the affirmation, through architecture and iconography, clothing and ceremonial, of the status of the prince and of the élites on whom he relied to rule. Above all, for much of the 'long seventeenth century' between the Reformation and the Enlightenment, the adoption of a permanent 'seat' located most major European courts in an urban architectonic setting. In the 'court city' (what in the Empire became known as the *Residenzstadt*), the prince's residence often stood in close and sometimes uncomfortable proximity to the urban palaces of his leading courtiers and the prosperous city élites.[25]

The chronology of this transition was an extended one, with the courts of the Italian peninsula being precociously in the vanguard. In Rome, after the disruptions of the Great Schism, an increasingly elaborate papal court was more or less continuously in residence from the 1420s, and it served as an influential model – if by no means the only one – for many aspects of court culture elsewhere in Europe well into the late 1600s.[26] Similarly, resident courts had been established by the Gonzaga at Mantua, the Este at Ferrara (later at Modena), and the Montefeltro at Urbino, among others, well before the end of the fifteenth century. The trend was seemingly inexorable. By the end of the sixteenth century, from England to Poland, most major European sovereigns had acquired a permanent urban base for their households.[27] Nevertheless, old habits died hard. The ever-travelling Emperor Charles V (1519–56) typified the older attitude with his blunt statement that 'kings do not need palaces';[28] and in France it was not until the end of the religious wars and the accession of Henri IV (1589–1610) that the court came to acquire a more or less permanent base in the Paris Louvre (later at Versailles).[29] Even into the eighteenth century, the royal household of Brandenburg-Prussia divided its time between three urban seats in the various constituent parts of the realm, in Berlin, Königsberg and Cleves.

Thus, for much of the period between about 1500 and 1750, the 'Versailles model' of the court – the court as a self-contained, free-standing, architecturally

harmonious palace-city, distanced from the metropolis, and accommodating both royal household and administration – was the exception rather than the rule. At least until the end of the seventeenth century, most courts chose as their principal residence an established urban environment, usually the major city of the realm. Moreover, 'court space' within this urban setting was a diverse and polycentric phenomenon, encompassing the town residences of the royal apanages and courtier nobility, and even the churches that fell within the social or ceremonial orbit of the court.

This shift from peripatetic to residential court profoundly realigned contemporary attitudes towards what 'a court' actually was. In a formal sense, 'the court' was, by definition, wherever the prince happened to take up residence. Once the ruler's household had acquired a regular residential base, however, it came to be identified far more closely with its urban and architectonic setting. Only a fraction of the total number of courtiers was ever actually housed in the ruler's palaces. 'The court' included not only the palace buildings, but also the personnel of the household and many of the functions of government, within a single portmanteau meaning. Philip II's move to Madrid in 1561 provides a telling instance of the shift in usage. The Venetian ambassador noted that 'the court' now existed in the city even when the monarch himself was not present: it was the ruler's 'residual authority', not his actual presence, that was the prerequisite of a court.[30]

This urban setting often provided a highly competitive environment for 'representational display'. The palaces of great nobles, 'princes of the blood' (cadet lines of the ruling house) and royal dowagers, often sought to equal, or even outshine, the glamour of the monarch's residence. And it was by no means always the monarch who emerged triumphant from the contest. In seventeenth-century Vienna and Westminster, for example, the splendour of the town palaces built by high-ranking courtiers – ironically, buildings often financed from the profits of successful court careers – far outshone what seemed the relatively dowdy and antiquated seats of the ruler's household, the Hofburg and Whitehall.

Ostentation, of course, has never been a reliable index of power. Nevertheless, this architectural competitiveness directs us to a more substantial point.

'The court' was rarely a unitary body in which a single household provided, monopolistically, the only route to favour and patronage. Besides the sovereign's household, there was normally a sequence of subsidiary courts that could act as rival foci of policy and patronage: in the case of kingdoms, the courts of the ruler's consort, the heir to the throne, the cadet branches of the royal line who ranked as princes of the blood royal and, in addition in Catholic realms, the courts of cardinals as 'princes of the Church'.[31] The court of the heir frequently became the rallying point for a 'reversionary interest', a group often at odds with the policies of the monarch's household, and eagerly looking forward to the time when the new monarch would come into his own. To this list of 'subsidiary courts' should probably also be added the households of the great court office-holders, which were often to be found in the immediate environs of the ruler's residence. While, obviously, these did not enjoy the formal status of courts, they too functioned, albeit at one level down, as rival 'points of access' to patronage and favour, and as venues for representational display. This diversity acts as a further check on the Versailles-inspired model of the centralized *ancien-régime* court. Far from being a monolithic body, 'the court' at any one time was a polycentric entity (and here, in fact, even Versailles was no exception).

Perhaps the most obvious effect of the shift from peripatetic entourage to residential court was its impact on the size of the monarch's household. Even if we confine our analysis to salaried officers, there is a clear trend in almost all of the major European courts towards steady expansion in the two centuries after 1500. The Munich household establishment (Hofstaat) of the Wittelsbach Dukes of Bavaria, for example, burgeoned from a mere 162 in 1508 to 866 in 1571. By the late seventeenth century, it stood at well over a thousand, making it the second largest in the Holy Roman Empire and one of the largest in Europe.[32] The Medici ducal household at Florence rose from some 168 in 1564 to a peak of 792 in 1695, before reducing in scale in the early eighteenth century. And in the most extreme case of courtly elephantiasis, the court of France, the royal household increased from some one thousand salaried servants under François I (1515–47) to somewhere between eight to ten thousand under Louis XIV. As service was in most

cases 'by term' – usually three months on, nine months off – the number of individuals actually involved in household service in the course of the year may be multiplied accordingly. To this figure we need further to add the court guard (which could vary in size from a few dozen to several thousand), and those not formally part of the household establishment who, nevertheless, formed part of the social world of the court: noblemen and gentlemen of fashion who 'gave attendance'; actors and musicians hired for major celebrations; tailors and flower-sellers who plied their trade on the fringes of the prince's palace.

In the absence of reliable statistics for many periods between 1500 and 1750, any generalizations about the size of the European princely courts must be provisional. However, while there are doubtless numerous exceptions, a very rough general pattern can be detected. Extensive growth in the size of the major princely households from the early to mid sixteenth century reached an apogee in the last decades of the seventeenth and at the turn of the eighteenth centuries; this, in turn, was followed in many cases by substantial retrenchment in the early eighteenth century – partly in response to the Enlightenment critique of the pomp and 'artificiality' of the Baroque court. Only after the French Revolution does there seem to have been a return – notably in France, Austria, Prussia and Russia – to the large and highly ceremonious households that had characterized the *ancien-régime* courts at their height.[33]

Particularly among the ranks of senior courtiers, the distinction between the 'household' (serving the ruler) and the 'bureaucracy' (serving the government of the realm) tended to be blurred, and this overlap of functions is reflected in the actual spatial configurations of many courts. At Tudor Whitehall, for example, far from there being a separation between the ceremonious and noble-dominated world of the 'household' and the administrative sphere of 'government' – as was once supposed – the two were intimately connected, and physically housed under the same roof. When the new Privy Council was given formal existence in 1540, its meeting room was located in the very heart of the monarch's private apartments (the Privy Lodgings), only a few steps from the king's bedchamber.[34] Similarly, in the

*Court diplomacy: François d'Orbay's escalier des ambassadeurs, or ambassadors' staircase (1674–80),
at Versailles enabled the status of diplomats and other guests to be registered precisely, according to how far
the monarch or his representative descended the staircase to greet them. Similar double staircases already
existed in the Alcázar in Toledo and at El Escorial: as often, Versailles was not the innovator, but followed
and developed existing courtly practice.*

Spanish kingdoms, Mia Rodríguez-Salgado has concluded that to make a division between the administration and those attendant on the king's person 'is not only difficult, it is false'.[35]

The interconnection between these two spheres should come as no surprise. For in a system where the monarch was in theory, and usually in practice, the ultimate source of authority within the realm, a large part of the business of government was determined by the 'politics of intimacy'.[36] To ambitious courtiers, proximity to the monarch – or, better still, the ability to control access to his private apartments – was one sure way of building a power-base at court. And even where ministers had built very different power-bases through the 'great offices of state' in the ruler's administration, they frequently sought to consolidate their authority by acquiring positions within the household that guaranteed them immediate access to the prince.[37]

These preoccupations, in turn, helped shape the forms of palace architecture. As Hugh Murray Baillie pointed out in a highly influential article, the planning of Baroque palaces both gave expression to, and simultaneously helped to define, the very political structures that it housed.[38] Space was a hierarchical and politically charged commodity; and although each court adopted different solutions to its allocation, certain general principles tended to prevail. Palaces consisted of a series of 'thresholds', each requiring higher degrees of status (or the monarch's favour) before they could be crossed. Court gate, guard chamber, Presence Chamber: each interposed barriers between the outside world and the court's inner sanctum, the private apartments of the monarch. In this regard, the arrangements in later Valois and Bourbon France were something of an exception, with most of the palace – including the king's bedchamber – relatively accessible to those attending at court, and the monarch living out virtually all his waking hours under his courtiers' gaze.

Elsewhere, however, there was usually a clear division between the 'public' and 'private' areas of the palace; and it was a distinction that dealt the monarch an important trump card. Control of entry to his private apartments enabled the prince to establish an *ad hominem* hierarchy of personal favour that stood quite separately from, and sometimes in rivalry with, the hierarchies of noble and other ranks that largely determined precedence within the palace's 'public' domains.[39] Even at the Bourbon court, a series of *de facto* 'inner' private apartments came into being after the death of Louis XIV in 1715. In other households that had adopted the 'French' model of court protocol – the Orange court in The Hague from the 1630s, and later at Berlin – the distinction seems to have been made even earlier. Nor were these merely chance parallels. In terms of its culture and personnel, the courtly milieu was cosmopolitan and imitative. Exchanges between courts – of information and objects, craftsmen and architects, artists and musicians, and, above all, of dynastic brides – were frequent and numerous. Contacts were further facilitated through the establishment, intermittently from the early 1500s and regularly by the mid-seventeenth century, of a series of resident embassies in the major European court cities, almost invariably headed by a prominent courtier nobleman as the 'representative' of the foreign sovereign.

Perhaps unsurprisingly, then, in the period between roughly 1550 and 1700 there was what might be termed a 'standardization of expectations' as to the features that a properly constituted court was expected to possess. They were expected to be 'magnificently' housed, hierarchically ordered and administered through departments responsible variously for supply, ceremony, recreation and the hunt. These, in turn, were to be governed respectively by a series of nobly born 'great officers'. Clearly codified protocol was expected to regulate their social and religious arrangements. Piety was to be demonstrated by the regular public observance of a calendar of ecclesiastical solemnities and festivals. And, by the early seventeenth century, the sponsorship of specialist manufactories, working primarily or exclusively for the court, also came to be regarded as

an almost essential badge of the monarch's patronage of the arts. Hence the establishment of a series of workshops devoted to the production of luxury items for consumption by the court, notably tapestry (as at Mortlake, Brussels, Gobelins and Aubusson), goldsmiths' work (as in Florence, Augsburg and Stockholm), tournament armour (as at Milan and Greenwich), and *pietre dure* (or inlaid stonework, as in Florence). These were followed in the eighteenth century by the establishment of royal porcelain factories at Meissen (1710, by the Saxon court), Vienna (1719, by the imperial court), Vincennes-Sèvres (1738 by the French), and Nymphenburg and Fürstenberg (1747, by the Bavarian court). At most courts, a musical establishment of singers and instrumentalists served both the liturgy of the household chapel and the secular entertainment of the court.[40] Likewise, no court could be without an extensive establishment devoted to the hunt, and, later, a further department responsible for theatre and opera – the art that in the eighteenth century came to be regarded as the quintessential courtly entertainment.

Of course, at least some of these attributes can be identified in earlier royal households. What is perhaps the most distinctive aspect of the late sixteenth- and early seventeenth-century court culture was the gradual acceptance of all, or almost all, of the items on this checklist as being virtually *de rigueur* for any sovereign court that aspired to be taken seriously by its peers. In this regard, studies of new courts are particularly revealing, whether they relate to newly elevated princes, such as the Medici (Chapter 10) or the Vasa (Chapter 11), or to courts 'reinvented' after a relocation or period of abeyance, such as the Sabaudian court after its transference from Chambéry to Turin in 1563 (Chapter 9). The thoroughness with which these newcomers acquired the 'correct' courtly amenities reveals more than a pattern of copying and emulation. It effectively itemizes what contemporaries regarded as the defining features of a sovereign court.

It was not, however, for the excellence of their tapestries or the baubles on show in their rooms of parade that courts enjoyed such prominence in the life of the *ancien régime*. They were, above all, centres of power. Yet, if the court was not a single monolithic institution, but composed of a series of separate and potentially competing 'foyers of patronage', where did power actually lie? What, then, of the familiar claim that the early modern court served to augment the authority of the prince at the expense of the traditional ruling élites, above all the 'old nobility'?

II. THE COURT AND THE ELITES

'The transformation of the nobility from a class of knights into a class of courtiers', Norbert Elias once famously declared, was one of the prime examples of what he termed the 'civilizing process'.[41] Fifteenth-century monarchs had gone about in fear of their great magnates. But by 1700, so the argument runs, the magnates' independent military power had been obliterated. Their old belligerence had been sublimated into the relatively peaceable game of court faction. From the early sixteenth century, a Europe-wide 'revolution' in military technology, now requiring much larger forces, centrally mobilized and supplied, had made redundant the old 'feudal', small-scale, noble-led armies of retainers.[42] What was left to this old military caste was merely the honorific and ceremonial sphere of the ruler's household. Real power, meanwhile, was transferred elsewhere: to the domain of the councils, dominated by a new bureaucratic cadre, the *noblesse de robe* and their ilk: *arrivistes* who had acquired their noble status through service of 'the state'.[43]

There is certainly no doubting that many early modern princes would have been delighted with such an outcome. However, the extensive research devoted to the European nobilities over the last two decades has transformed our understanding of their place in early modern politics. Noble influence, both in political and cultural spheres, now appears to have been far more adaptive, resilient and extensive than was formerly supposed. The high nobility[44] remained a prominent, sometimes dominant, presence in royal councils, well into the eighteenth century. They were often to be found presiding over the burgeoning 'bureaucracy', particularly the high-spending naval and military departments, which also tended to offer the most extensive opportunities for patronage.[45] In the Empire, for example, the interconnections between household and administration were intimate. The imperial household's senior officer, the *Obersthofmeister*, invariably a senior nobleman, not only ruled the emperor's domestic arrangements (he was the equivalent of the English lord steward or the Castilian *mayordomo mayor*), but also served as chairman of the Privy Council (the *Geheimer Rat*), a body that advised on all matters of state.[46] Even at the court of Louis XIV, where Saint-Simon's description of the slippage of power from the *noblesse d'ancienne extraction* to the new *robe* nobility contains more than an element of truth, the separation of administrative *pouvoir* from aristocratic *grandeur* was never wholly achieved.[47] Similarly, at most courts, the supposedly hard-and-fast social distinctions between 'new' and 'old' families – in which erstwhile warrior nobles condescended towards the civil-servant *arrivistes* – were attenuated in practice by the natural tendency of success to ally with success. Prickly grandees might well have muttered against the promotion of 'parvenus'; but those *robe* office-holders who prospered were admitted readily enough into the social world of the 'old nobility', and rapidly assimilated themselves to its ethos. The contributors to this book broadly confirm this impression of the resilience of the higher nobility's power. Far from being the cause of the nobles' ensnarement, as was once supposed, service at court generally appears to have been one of the principal means by which aristocratic authority and influence were maintained.[48]

Where, then, does this leave the monarch? It may be reasonably objected that, as the ultimate source of authority, the ruler was always the maker and breaker of courtiers' careers. Exponents of absolutism have suggested that the monarch's ability to create a competitive market for his favour was decisive in making the court into a pliant instrument of rule. By playing off one magnate or faction against another, the ruler could bolster his own authority while neutralizing any potentially competing (and, above all, aristocratic) sources of power. Even revisionist historians, generally sceptical of notions of absolutism, have partly endorsed these views, stressing the extensiveness of the prince's personal authority within his court.[49]

Yet, while the paramount status of an adult monarch was rarely in question (regencies were another matter), the extent of a monarch's personal authority varied, and with it so did the relative value of 'access'. Some of the variables that affected the standing of the prince *vis-à-vis* the court are obvious enough – considerations of age, intellect, stamina, capacity for work – and would be conceded even by proponents of the 'absolutist' model of the court. Many of the contributions to this book, however, go considerably further. They suggest that it was not merely the personal failings of the prince, but the court itself, that imposed limitations on the authority and effectiveness of the crown. This was partly a matter of expectation and tradition. From vice-regal Dublin to 'imperial' Moscow, the court was embedded in a culture that esteemed custom and convention at least as much as it did the sacred rights of kings. Entrenched conventions governing appointments to court office; inherited perks and privileges; deeply ingrained attitudes towards 'proper' aristocratic conduct and honour: all these served to circumscribe the monarch's freedom of manoeuvre, fencing him in with a series of principles that were difficult, if not impossible, to break.

Thus, while authority tended to become more centralized in almost every European realm during the sixteenth and seventeenth centuries, it did not follow that this resulted in a straightforward transfer of power from the nobility to the crown.[50] To take the question of appointments to court office: in theory, it was usually the monarch's right to dispose of places as he saw fit. Once an office had been granted, however, it was often extremely difficult to remove a sitting tenant, even where the office-holder had long since ceased to enjoy the ruler's favour. In realms where court office was regarded as private property, which could be sold by its holder for occupancy or in reversion (*survivance*), as in England or France, the practice further limited the crown's ability to control the appointment or dismissal of those who served at court.[51] Even in that quintessentially 'absolutist' monarchy, France, the crown's influence over appointments had attenuated by the 1750s to 'a point where existing institutions and interest groups severely limited the development and execution of the central will'.[52]

Although the monarch might theoretically be free to dismiss his court officers at will, when it came to the higher nobility the practical obstacles were often well-nigh insuperable. The headmasterly ways of the third Duke of Alba, *mayordomo mayor* and the most senior officer of Philip II's household, were a constant source of irritation to his royal master. Yet removing

him from his post for any offence short of high treason was virtually unthinkable. High court office involved more than an individual's prestige; it entailed the 'honour' of an entire aristocratic dynasty. Indeed, as Roger Mettam has observed of Bourbon France, 'many offices held by the [*noblesse d'épée*]…were *de facto* hereditary within a noble House'. For the king to have given their places to other families would have been 'a slight upon the reputation of the whole kinship network'.[53]

Where a major aristocratic grandee was concerned, deposition from court office was usually only an option *in extremis*, and even then at a heavy cost to the crown in 'collateral damage'. On the occasions when there was a major breach with members of the nobility, as during a rebellion, the monarch was usually at pains to patch up amicable relations with the offending noble dynasty's next generation once order had been restored. The relations between the emperor and the great noble families within the Habsburg hereditary lands (the *Erblande*) – among them the Liechtensteins, Auerspergs, Schwarzenbergs, Lobkovices – illustrate the point.[54] These aristocratic dynasties, with 'one foot in the provinces, the other in court service', owed their promotion to the emperor. But once the emperor had turned them into regional magnates, he could ill afford to alienate those he had elevated, and did so at his peril. When, in the 1670s, Leopold I dismissed his *Obersthofmeister* – the head of the Lobkovice clan, Václav Eusebius (1609–77), Duke of Sagan and president of the War Council – there was an anxious moment when the dynastic fortune seemed under threat of confiscation. By the next generation, however, the Lobkovices had been again restored to royal favour, and the family emerged with its estates and regional influence intact.[55] So it was not only at the level of sovereigns that court politics was premised upon considerations of 'dynastic interest'. 'The basic unit was always the family', Robert Evans has stressed in the context of the sixteenth- and seventeenth-century Habsburg monarchy, 'and the family did not suffer even if an individual fell from grace'.[56] The wholesale destruction of a magnate dynasty – such as the Tudors' ruthless campaign against the de la Poles – was the rare exception that proved the rule.

This is not to undervalue the significance of the monarch as arbiter of favour and promotion, still less

The majesty of death: the funeral rites of princes and senior members of their families were among the most ostentatious instances of courtly display, as much concerned with affirming the continuity and power of the dynasty as with any rite of Christian piety. Here, the gigantic canopy constructed over the catafalque of Prince Francesco de' Medici in Florence in 1614 overawes not only the mourners, but also the high altar itself.

to suggest that crown and nobility were in some sense mutually antagonistic interests at the early modern court.[57] Of course there were periods, particularly in the century following the Reformation, when relations between monarch and élites were acutely strained, at times to the point of armed rebellion and civil war. In general, however, it was Montesquieu's aphorism, 'no crown, no nobility; no nobility, no crown', that remained the watchword for relations between the two.[58] For all the 'magnificence' of the *ancien-régime* courts and the hyperbole extolling the sacred authority of kings, once rulers left the rarefied world of Versailles, Whitehall or the Buen Retiro, they were confronted by a blunt reality: that the effective exercise of their authority remained in large measure dependent on the regional élites – and above all on the higher nobility.[59]

'The court' thus had to register a more diversified series of power relations than merely the supremacy of the ruler's person. In place of the view of the *ancien-régime* court as primarily the manifestation of the monarch's preferences and desires, these essays offer a more complex and politically nuanced entity. Rather than being a centralized institution in which power 'radiated' from the person of the prince, they suggest that influence and, in some cases, formal authority as well, emanated at court from a variety of subsidiary sources: entrenched office-holders, noble magnates, senior prelates, major army commanders, not to mention the satellite courts of the royal apanages. Even within the monarch's own household – the principal court of the realm – its leading officers were often in a position to build up clienteles and powers of patronage that enjoyed a large measure of *de facto* autonomy from interference by the prince.[60] This, in turn, demands a subtler analysis of court politics; not as a series of responses to monarchical fiats, but as a process in which the carapace of autocracy concealed a diversity of partly complementary, partly competing, 'foyers of power'. Of course, court politics remained at one level a politics of access, and the monarch, almost invariably, continued to be the one to whom access was most keenly sought. But he was not the sole focus of courtiers' attentions or the only agent through whom business could be done. The courtier's firmament, to adapt a favourite trope of Baroque rhetoric, contained a constellation, not a single blazing sun.

The disintegration of the monolithic 'absolutist' model of the court has brought in its train a fundamental reassessment of the intellectual and ethical culture that defined relations between the various members of aulic society. Where the cult of deference towards the monarch was once discerned almost all-pervasively by historians – in ceremonial, 'propaganda', and in the courtly obsession with rank and hierarchy – recent research has identified a far more variegated range of moral and ethical values on offer at the early modern court. For while the court was notoriously the cockpit of competition, that contest

was governed by a code of conduct that was premised upon a far more complex series of ethical imperatives: considerations of honour and chivalric duty, or familial and religious obligation. These values set patterns for courtly deportment that might qualify, or even subvert, the monarch's demand for unswerving loyalty to a 'sacred' crown.

III. Honour and Obligation

Perhaps the central element of this milieu was the court's veneration of the 'cult of honour', a model for behaviour that found expression in a rich variety of cultural forms: chivalric, classical, even liturgical. At one end of its broad spectrum, 'honour' was barely distinguishable from a courtier's *amour propre* and sense of pique.[61] Disputes about precedence inevitably centred on questions of 'personal honour', and were endemic at every European court; and while feuds between rival bands of retainers had largely been curbed by the end of the sixteenth century, levels of intra-aristocratic violence, including duelling to death, remained high throughout the period.[62] More benignly, the honour cult promoted, and was reflected in, the preoccupation with courtly chivalry in all its guises: from jousts and tournaments, to portraiture and the literature of the knightly romance.[63] At the other end of this spectrum, 'honour' was effectively a political imperative, dictating that any equitable distribution of office and the ruler's bounty should generally correspond with a hierarchy founded on lineage, title and inherited social rank. In this context the contemporary fascination with genealogy and heraldry, which reached its peak in the seventeenth century, was not mere antiquarianism but had a practical purpose. Heraldic quarterings established, quite literally, an individual's credentials for public life.[64]

'Honour in all parts of Europe will be ever like itself', the Earl of Northampton observed as early as 1610;[65] and recent studies of this 'honour culture' have tended to confirm this view of its pan-European currency. The élites of sixteenth- and seventeenth-century Europe were the inheritors of a shared late-medieval political ethic that defined their responsibilities in terms of a threefold series of moral duties: to serve the king; to offer counsel; and to defend the realm against enemies without and tyranny within. Nor did this duty depend on any royal mandate for its moral sanction. 'The unique feature of the nobility as a political institution', one historian of later-Valois France has observed, 'is the nobles' claim to political power by virtue of their personal identity.'[66] By the mere fact of honour and inheritance, so this claim implied, the ancient nobility, the *noblesse d'ancienne extraction*, had a right to a dominant place in the king's counsels. They were rightfully the 'eyes and ears of the king', one courtier's chaplain argued in the 1630s, and through public service they enjoyed a corresponding entitlement to the fruits of office.[67] In reality, this 'validating past', the distant world where these precepts supposedly had once been dutifully observed, was little more than myth. Even as a fiction, however, it retained a powerful prescriptive force well into the seventeenth and eighteenth centuries.

Its antithesis was the court 'favourite', the parvenu-turned-power-broker, whose promotion violated the axioms of the aristocratic honour code. Though contemporaries used terminology promiscuously – referring to the 'favourite', *valido*, or *privado*, almost synonymously – the phenomenon occurred in a variety of distinct types: from 'minister-favourites' such as Richelieu or Olivares; sexual favourites who also exercised ministerial power, such as James I's erstwhile lover, the Duke of Buckingham; even kinsman-favourites, such as the *nipoti* of Renaissance popes.[68] For all their diversity, however, the popular stereotype of the court favourite remained strikingly consistent in form, from the sixteenth through to the eighteenth centuries.[69] Whether in plays, ballads, histories or

Sacred chivalry: the foundation of the order of the Saint-Esprit by Henri III of France in 1578 was one of the series of creations or re-institutions of chivalric orders that reached its apogee in the second half of the sixteenth century. Admission to the Saint-Esprit was a religious rite, with the new knight swearing his loyalty on the Gospels, being robed with a mantle embroidered with tongues of fire (emblems of the Holy Spirit) and invested with the order's collar – a chain with pendent cross (left).

learned treatises, the characteristics remain the same: a manipulative *arriviste*, 'basely born', who usurps powers of patronage that should rightfully go to the hereditary grandees, and exploits office, not for the good of the realm, but in order to feather his own nest. Warranted or not, most of the 'new men' who acquired extensive influence as a consequence of personal royal favour – from Wolsey to Mazarin – found themselves assimilated to this opprobrious stereotype.

From the monarch's perspective, however, the promotion of a favourite could be seen in a very different light. As was noted by the French commentator on the court, Refuge, Monsieur de Eustache (d.1617), monarchs had an obvious motive for elevating their own creatures. To promote those who were 'born great' (as members of the hereditary nobility) to high office risked enhancing the authority of men who were already powerful, and who might use that power to oppose the crown. The loyalty of a lowly born or parvenu favourite was thought to be doubly assured. Not only were they inherently more grateful for their promotions, but they also knew that if they ever forfeited the monarch's favour, there was usually a posse of hostile court grandees ready and waiting for the moment to bring them down. 'Only let the Prince turn his back upon [the favourite]', wrote Eustache, 'or abandon him to the great ones (who for the most part look with envy upon such), and he is lost.'[70]

Thus, whatever the type of *valido* who received the monarch's favour, the mere fact of his elevation had a powerful emblematic force. He symbolized before the court the ruler's (theoretically absolute) freedom of action as the 'fount of honour' against the rival aristocratic ethic that presumed to dictate how the ruler's powers of patronage should be used.[71] As such, the promotion of a favourite can be seen almost as a calculated affront on the part of the prince to the prescriptive, and potentially 'king-yoking', aspect of the aristocratic honour code. Moreover, favourites were highly useful. The *privado*, like the cardinal-nephew at the Roman court, provided a means of placing distance between the monarch and the other power-brokers within the princely household. For all the vehement hostility that favourites attracted, they nevertheless seem to have provided 'a mechanism of mediation between the monarch and the even broader range of vested interests with which [the ruler] found

himself confronted at court'.[72] Where the favourite was once seen as yet another manifestation of monarchical absolutism, his role now seems to have a more double-edged aspect: simultaneously managerial, but also distancing and defensive.

The charge of monopolizing control of court offices, a recurrent element in the rhetoric of anti-favourite complaint, highlights another major facet of the courtier's honour code: the belief that the value of an office could never be gauged in exclusively financial terms. Beyond its monetary value, its worth lay as much in the prestige derived from its possession as from the opportunities it provided for the distribution of patronage. On such things depended the whole family's *reputatio*; 'a great family's standing', William Doyle has argued, 'was reflected by its share in the spoils of court life.'[73] Given the enduring expectation among the 'old nobility' that the major officers of the household and the council should be chosen from within its ranks, there was an equally strong sense that the promotion of parvenus to these places 'dishonoured' them collectively as a noble caste.[74] Lineage, office, and honour were thus intimately intertwined.

So, despite the hyperbole of unswerving allegiance to the prince, the courtly rhetoric of deference coexisted with an inherited value-system that posed the obligation of allegiance in far more conditional terms. Numerous instances might be cited; but let us take, by way of example, the political culture of the French court, so often held up as the cynosure of authoritarian monarchy. Recent studies of the cult of 'honour' in Valois and early Bourbon France, most notably by Arlette Jouanna, have pointed to the resilience of an aristocratic code that extolled the 'ancient rights' and political independence of the higher nobility. When necessity required, this code even extended to the point of prescribing a 'duty to revolt'. There was a solemn obligation, laid upon the *noblesse d'epée*, to resist the regime when the proper ordering of government was perverted, whether by corrupt regents, over-powerful favourites or, unwittingly, by weak and manipulated kings.[75] For all the attempts of Valois and early Bourbon kings to define the cultural ethos of the court in terms of unswerving devotion to the monarch, they never wholly supplanted this value-system of aristocratic honour that sanctioned, *in extremis*, the nobles' right of revolt.

Similar attitudes have been identified among the nobilities in Spain, England, Scotland and the Empire, at least as late as the mid seventeenth century.[76] The virtual disappearance of armed aristocratic revolt across Western Europe from around the 1660s no longer appears merely another instance of rulers' success in emasculating their élites. On the contrary, it points to the increasing effectiveness of the court, not merely as a 'point of contact', but as a forum where the potentially rival, and intermittently belligerent, interests of crown and the landed élite could be reconciled to the advantage of all concerned.[77]

Of course, the sixteenth and seventeenth centuries did see major refinements in the élite's habits of personal conduct and deportment. Courtly *politesse* became ever more refined, with a bewilderingly large lexicon of rules governing every aspect of behaviour, from the peeling of peaches to the precise form of greeting due to a marquess's younger son.[78] Courtiers had read their Castiglione and the plethora of other handbooks on etiquette that disseminated courtly ways to a fashionable readership well beyond the confines of the ruler's household.[79] But while seventeenth-century courtiers may well have seemed models of decorum beside their Valois or Tudor forebears, this did not preclude 'a very powerful attraction to various forms of illegitimate [or self-legitimized] violence' – from duelling to full-scale revolt.[80] Indeed, perhaps the most important aspect of the duel, as François Billacois has argued, was its almost 'mythic function' as an instance of the nobleman's power of self-definition: his ability to assert his honour and identity by means that were independent from, and often expressly forbidden by, royal authority and 'the state'.[81]

Perhaps the most striking instance of European princes' attempts to co-opt, and hence to neutralize, these potentially subversive elements in aristocratic culture is their promotion of the cult of chivalry at court as a specifically monarch-centred rite. The sixteenth and seventeenth centuries were the heyday for the foundation or reinvention of chivalric orders: besides the Burgundian *Toison d'Or* (the order of the Golden Fleece, 1430), that had already been revamped in the fifteenth century, there was, among a host of others, the Garter revived by Henry VII and Henry VIII of England in the early sixteenth century, and the newly created orders of Santo Stefano in Tuscany (1562) and the Saint-Esprit in France (1578).[82] Often specifically reserved to the higher nobility, the rituals of these chivalric orders affirmed the 'holiness' of regal power and the sacredness of the bond of loyalty between monarch and subject. Likewise, for monarchs faced with realms composed of diverse cultural, ethnic and linguistic groups, appointments to these orders also served as a means of integrating the leading members of disparate local nobilities into a single, supra-regional, court-defined élite. In the case of mid-sixteenth-century Savoy, for example, the re-foundation of the Annunziata afforded a powerful means of 're-knitting loyalties' to the newly restored duke, Emanuele Filiberto (1533–80), after a period of political disorder and exile (Chapter 9).

This redirection of the court's chivalric life into a cult of personal allegiance to the prince can be represented, of course, as one of the signal successes of the *ancien-régime* monarchies. Yet, as so often with aulic culture, the values that the courtly orders of chivalry endorsed were never quite so unambiguous as this assessment would suggest. By promoting, and in many cases revivifying, the values of the old aristocratic honour culture, while seeking to overlay them with a cult of allegiance to the prince, monarchs invested the older chivalric ethic with a new lease of life. In this 'traditional' honour culture, allegiance to the prince was qualified by the knight's overriding duty to act for the wider good of the realm.[83] There was therefore no

Following page: The biblical archetype: the court of David, King of Israel, depicted as a 'modern' Renaissance court of the age of François I or Henry VIII, with formal gardens and an outdoor tennis-play. This elision of ancient and modern affirms a familiar courtly topos: the continuity between David, Israel's prophet-king, and the divinely ordained monarchs of contemporary Christendom. Heavenly sanction, however, did not preclude earthly vice. Here, David (lower right), who has committed adultery with Bathsheba (lower left), gives a letter to her husband Uriah, ordering him into a battle that will result in his death. A page carries the train of the king's ermine-trimmed mantle.

DAVID PVIA BAR
SVRA ATVLENV
ORBIS MATT [V]A
AB HOSTIBVS
OCCVBENDV EN
PR ELIV M TIV
ANNO 15 6

incongruity, despite their protestations of unswerving loyalty to their rulers, that knights of the Golden Fleece were prominent in the court *coup d'état* that deposed the Emperor Rudolf II in 1612, or that in 1642 four knights of the Garter went to war against Charles I. Viewed as an exercise in inculcating obedience, the monarch-centred chivalry of these Renaissance knightly orders was at best only a qualified success.

The recovery of this 'honour culture' goes part of the way to re-establishing the intellectual milieu of the early modern court. Honour afforded one of a series of cultural points of reference – among them classicism, neo-Stoicism, and appeals to precedents from the 'gothic' past – by which early modern rulers and courtiers could define their sense of identity and invest their actions with moral authority. To the modern observer, however, perhaps the most elusive element of aulic culture is its religious dimension; for the court located itself as part of a hierarchy of power that was not merely secular, but also divine. As monarchs were 'God's lieutenants', the custodians of a power that literally derived from heaven, it followed that their courts were the point at which earthly and celestial authority met. It is to this intersection of the worldly and the numinous that we must now turn. What was the place of religion at court, and how did it impinge upon the wider constituency of the realm?

IV. GODLINESS AND COURTLINESS

At first sight, 'courtly piety' may seem a contradiction in terms, for the topos of the court as a seminary of vice has a long and lurid pedigree.[84] Often contrasted with the wholesome rustic virtues of the 'country', it was a literary cliché that the court's many temptations – vanity and worldly pomp, luxury and idleness, together with most of the more interesting of the other Deadly Sins – were likely to ensnare the steeliest of souls. Later historians have tended to take critics of the court's morality at their word. Moreover, with the historiography of the court dominated by a tendency to analyze it either in political terms (as a seat of secular power and faction) or in cultural terms (as a locus of artistic patronage and conspicuous consumption), the question of

religion at court has fallen between the two.

Yet, for all the peccadilloes of princes and their courtiers, religion was at the very centre of aulic life – a centrality that was re-emphasized by the consequences for the court of the upheavals that redrew the confessional map of sixteenth-century Europe. As revisionist historians of that 'long century' of European Reformation – from the 1520s to the 1650s – have stressed, interventions 'from above' were frequently decisive in imposing religious change, often against the will of the ruler's subjects. In almost every European state, the question of the doctrinal orientation of the church was a matter at least powerfully influenced, and often finally determined, by the preferences of the prince and his immediate entourage. The court, therefore, became the principal forum where rival confessional groups contended for influence over 'the conscience of the king'.[85] Even in Catholic realms, major policies governing the enforcement of religious doctrine and practice were invariably mediated through, or obstructed by, the court. The councils of the rulers of France, Castile-Aragon, Bavaria and of the Holy Roman Emperor, nominally the most devoted 'sons of the Church', frequently pursued policies that were at variance with the policies of the papacy. Philip IV's celebrated *privado*, the Count-Duke of Olivares, was not the only pious Catholic to conclude that 'the evil intentions of His Holiness [the Pope] towards us who are defending the faith…have become a detestable and universal scandal'.[86] Even at Catholic courts, filial obedience to Rome was often far from complete.

As court antiquarians helpfully pointed out, this phenomenon of a religiously interventionist princely household was nothing new. What changed decisively in the post-Reformation order, however, was that the court's influence over the governance of the Church acquired a much more sharply focused confessional identity.[87] Henceforth, it had to be pious *in contradistinction* to its external enemies and to the doctrinal errors they held. The implications of this 'confessionalization' of the court were far-reaching. In diplomacy, it prescribed that alliances between realms (and their ruling dynasties) ought to be concluded on strictly denominational lines. Far from being polar opposites, considerations of religious piety and *raison d'état* were often regarded as being the same. This did not necessarily preclude diplomatic treaties, or even dynastic marriages, across the confessional divide; but such alliances were always vulnerable to denunciations from the pulpit, and those who proposed them almost invariably laid themselves open to the charge of apostasy or betrayal. Confessionalization also focused public attention on the doctrinal orthodoxy and religious zeal of the courtiers themselves. Some courts – notably Emperor Maximilian II's in the 1560s, or Elector Friedrich III's in Berlin in 1690s – were conspicuously irenicist and ecumenical in tone; but these were the exceptions. In most of the major princely households the court's public piety acquired an exemplary, indeed almost talismanic, quality: guaranteeing divine protection for the realm, and simultaneously defining the identity and character of the regime.

This exemplary piety took a variety of forms. With few exceptions, the first call on the court's public duties was the ceremonious observance of the great cycle of holy days of the Christian year. With various local variations, these usually included, in addition to Sunday observances, the major feasts of the Church. All Saints (1 November), Christmas (25 December), Easter, and Pentecost (and, in Catholic realms, Corpus Christi as well), were usually marked out for particularly elaborate commemoration. Then came the numerous patronal festivals, dedicated to national or dynastic saints – such as Bavaria's St George or Tuscany's St Stephen – and days devoted to the religious ceremonies of the chivalric orders. What emerges from these essays is, not least, the sheer amount of time that these pious observances entailed. At the major Catholic courts (Paris-Versailles, Madrid, Munich, Innsbruck, Vienna-Prague, Rome, Modena, Turin, Florence), and at the Orthodox Russian court before the early eighteenth-century reforms of Peter the Great, the scrupulous observance of the church calendar involved the court in lengthy ecclesiastical rituals as frequently as every two to three days. At the court of the Austrian Habsburgs, the imperial household's *dévot* piety, the so-called *pietas Austriaca*, came to be an essential part of the dynasty's self-image.[88]

Catholicism placed at the disposal of the court the whole panoply of saintly invocation and protection: office-holders in the court celestial were naturally expected to uphold the interests of their earthly delegates. Central among these developments was the association of the dynasty with the tutelary power of particular sacred images or relics – the Medici dukes' miracle-working painting of the Virgin at the Annunziata, for example, or the Sabaudian rulers' prize possession, the Holy Shroud – and the integration of the churches and chapels that housed them into the circuit of courtly ceremonial. Again, if the origins and the intellectual underpinnings of such practices were medieval or earlier, the prominence that these devotions acquired within the early modern court's calendar was for the most part largely new. Such charismatic objects not only served to protect the palace and its inhabitants; they also acted, in Peter Brown's phrase, as 'holy fixatives', conferring an aura of divinity on their earthly possessors.[89] They were the means by which divine power, almost as a form of numinous electricity, was plugged into the ruling house.

In Catholic Europe, the activities of religious confraternities also offered opportunities, both for nurturing courtiers' private piety and for promoting the public identification of the ruler's household with eucharistic devotion. In Habsburg Naples, for example, by 1641 the court had all but taken over the Congregation of the Holy Sacrament, which was headed by the Holy Roman Emperor Ferdinand III (1637–57), together with the viceroy, and the city's cardinal-archbishop.[90] Its annual celebration of the octave of Corpus Christi, the Feast of the Four Altars, was a major event in the court calendar. The viceroy (later, under Borbón rule, the king) led the court in procession through the city streets behind a monstrance bearing the 'Body of Christ' in the form of a consecrated host. Reading the symbolism of such displays of aulic devotion poses a series of paradoxes. As T. A. Marder has argued in the context of papal Rome, the parading of the monarch's and the court's humility before the sacrament may seem to undermine the concept of an all-commanding temporal power. In fact, in so far as such ceremonies endowed 'the secular ruler's stature with the piety of a holy man', they actually served to reinforce it.[91] For although the ostensible focus of the Corpus Christi procession was the Body of Christ, 'the real sign vehicle' was the body of the ruler, whose political identity became merged with the charismatic symbols of eucharistic devotion.[92]

Since kings could be represented as quasi-priests, so clergy could be turned into courtiers. From the early sixteenth century, members of religious orders constituted a substantial presence in most of the major courts across Catholic Europe: not merely the much demonized Jesuits, but also Capuchins, Augustinians, Barnabites – even, in Florence, the austere Trappists.[93] They served not merely as preachers and confessors, but also as librarians, organizers of court education, promoters of scholarship, and sometimes (as in Turin) as architects and theatrical designers. Regardless of their personal devoutness, Catholic princes were well attuned to the merits of investing their courts with the cachet of Counter-Reformation devotion.[94] As royal confessors, members of religious orders probably enjoyed a degree of intimacy with the prince equalled only, in their rather different ministrations, by royal mistresses. Confessors such as Guillaume Lamormaini, the Jesuit confidant of Emperor Ferdinand II (1619–37), or Father Petre, another Jesuit and the trusted adviser of James II of England (1685–88), acquired an influence that was reputed to extend well beyond the confessional.[95] While their detractors no doubt exaggerated their influence, the custodian of the prince's conscience was inevitably a figure of major importance at court.

With the manifestation of piety forming a central element of the court's *raison d'être*, it comes as no surprise that the model of the monastery exercised a powerful influence on contemporary attitudes towards the 'ideal court'. As early as the 1540s, Rabelais had conceived of his model court as a secular monastery, a place where a humanist synthesis of the active life and the contemplative could be finally achieved. In architectural terms, the ideal found concrete expression in the phenomenon of the palace-monastery, the court residence and conventual house of prayer combined, of which the earliest and by far the most influential example was Philip II's act of thanksgiving for victory in battle, San Lorenzo del Escorial. Begun in 1563 to designs by Juan Bautista de Toledo, the Escorial was conceived as an ostentatious act of piety, a gesture calculated to enhance the godly *reputación* of the royal house. Though never intended as the principal seat of the court, it was here, from the second half of Philip II's reign, that the king kept all the major feasts of the Church, accompanied by a scaled-down travelling court. Both architecturally and

practically, El Escorial located the monastic ideal of the religious retreat from the world at the centre of the conspicuously secular preoccupations of the monarch and his immediate entourage.[96]

Its emulators were numerous.[97] Most ambitious of all, however, were the plans of Emperor Charles VI (1711–40), formulated around 1730, but only partially executed before his death, for a vast palace-monastery at Klosterneuburg. There, both court and monastic community were expected to live a life of exemplary piety in surroundings whose scale was intended to dwarf even the Escorial.[98] In Portugal, a similar spirit of competitiveness, both pious and architectural, inspired Mafra, the ambitious monastery–residence built by King João V (1706–50) that William Beckford described as resembling 'the palace of a giant'.[99] Conversely, many of the equally gargantuan monasteries of the Empire were remodelled around the turn of the seventeenth and eighteenth centuries to incorporate palace-like accommodation for the emperor and his travelling entourage, notably Melk (rebuilt from 1702), Göttweig (remodelled from 1719, and also heavily influenced by the Escorial); and Klosterneuburg itself. The provision of formal secular state apartments in a monastic setting, such as the spectacular *Kaisersaal* (or imperial audience hall) at Melk, articulated the intimacy of the links between crown and Church, their engagement in a common enterprise of godly rule.

Nor did Catholic courts have a monopoly on public 'godliness'. Many Protestant courts exemplified their pious virtue through a no less rigorous calendar of household and public devotions: through the attendance at prayers and sermons, the keeping of public fasts and days of thanksgiving, and the promotion of 'godly' divines and their works.[100] In Protestant England, the court itself became the venue for public sermons for a century after 1540, with the construction by Henry VIII of a substantial pulpit in the north (or chapel) court of Whitehall Palace, used primarily for the series of court sermons delivered during Lent. Able to accommodate an auditory of several thousand, these 'preaching-place' sermons before the royal household and the monarch, who listened from the open Council Chamber window, were a Protestant *auto da fé*, identifying the court with the dissemination of pure doctrine against the errors of Rome. The

Venetian ambassador reported some 5,000 present to hear a vehemently anti-papal sermon in Lent 1559.[101]

The princely household was thus expected to be an inculcator of precepts and attitudes for the realm as a whole. Indeed, the 'holy court' could be a source of moral reformation, argued the Jesuit Père Nicolas Caussin, a confessor to Louis XIII. In a work that was extensively circulated, both in French and in translation, he called on the aulic nobility to exert the influence that 'example can exercise over the hearts of men'.[102] While, in reality, the holiness Caussin sought from his aristocratic readership was generally in short supply, his injunctions nevertheless invite consideration of the court's role as a cultural exemplar more generally. Even where the patronage and juridical powers mediated by the court might be relatively limited, the 'exemplary' effect of the monarch's household could be disproportionately large. The case of 'counter-reforming, aristocratic Austria', Robert Evans has suggested, provides a clear example 'of how a set of values conspicuously embraced by the aulic entourage of the sovereign could create a set of responses in society at large'.[103] While these 'values' were primarily religious in tone and emphasis, they also served simultaneously as the conduit for a more extensive series of court-derived cultural influences: artistic, architectural, literary and philosophical.[104] Moreover, the court's role as a pious *exemplum* also had its overtly political applications. In a system based on the ruler's 'divine right' (or *ius divinum*) to rule, few things signalled the legitimacy of the regime more strongly than public evidence that the monarch's relations with the deity continued on cordial terms.[105]

None of this is to gloss over the obvious tension that existed between the temptations of worldliness, which the court notoriously offered in abundance, and the image of godliness that the princely household tried to project to itself and to the outside world. Many of the sharpest denunciations of this gap between pious rhetoric and worldly practice came from *within* the court, often thundering from the pulpit of the chapel royal, or more subtly encoded – as Kevin Sharpe has argued persuasively – in the texts of plays and masques.[106] Nor is it to suggest that all courts of the *ancien régime* set about their devotions with equal fervour. Court piety took its tone, above all, from the prince; and the degree to which

devotional practices were enforced, beyond what convention and decency demanded, depended in large part on his predilections. Yet, at least until the end of the seventeenth century, in almost every European realm, religion was at the very centre of courtly life. The court, in turn, was the prime focus for the religious politics of the realm.

Reinstating this religious element to the daily practices and preoccupations of the court prompts a re-evaluation of other aspects of court life; above all, of the areas where religious symbolism and practice impinged most directly: in court ritual and ceremonial.[107] To the older generation of court historians – to Elias and his acolytes – court ceremonial was primarily moulded by a secular agenda: the definition of power-relations within the court, the subordination of courtiers, and the exaltation of the prince. From this perspective, even the tendency to 'sacralize' the monarch – to invest his person and office with attributes that were quasi-divine – was merely another instance of the 'propaganda' whereby, manipulatively, authoritarian rulers sought to validate their 'absolutist rule'.[108] How, then, are we to 'read' the ceremonies of the court? Whom was it intended to impress?

V. THE EUCHARISTIC PRINCE: COURT RITUAL AND ITS MEANINGS

It is now a commonplace theory that the early modern court spoke to its members, and to the wider world, primarily in the language of gesture. The courtier lived a 'semiotic existence', dealing daily with coded and symbolic meanings.[109] Some were mere matters of etiquette, a term we shall use in its narrow sense of the rules governing courtly *politesse* – when to wear or remove a hat, how to bow or use a napkin – and were largely concerned with the deportment of the individual courtier. Court ritual, on the other hand, was always a collective – and, at its most solemn, a corporate – act. It involved groups of courtiers performing precisely assigned functions, often imbued with strong historical or customary associations. In the daily routines of the ruler's household, two aspects of aulic life tended to be the most heavily endowed with ritual gesture: the procedures for the prince's dining, and the arrangements for his public worship of God. The study of this repertory of gesture, however, is still in its infancy. An entire art-historical industry has grown up devoted to the iconography of images, to decoding the meanings and associations of visual symbols, whether in tapestries or tournament emblems, portrait miniatures or Raphael cartoons.[110] On the other hand, despite some pioneering studies, principally by anthropologists, relatively little attention has been paid by historians to the iconography of gesture: to understanding the symbolism of formalized actions, and to analysing the relation between ceremonial objects and places and their ritual use.[111]

Where ceremonial has been considered, this too has tended to be slotted into a 'functionalist' framework of explanation. Court ceremonial glorified the monarch while inculcating healthy habits of deference and subordination in even his greatest subjects.[112] The genealogy of the 'ceremonious' *ancien-régime* court, has traditionally been traced back to the fifteenth-century court of Burgundy (the then sovereign duchy whose territories very roughly correspond to the modern-day Netherlands and Belgium), and from there to the 'absolutist' courts of sixteenth- and seventeenth-century Europe. The 'etiquette of modern royal courts', so the argument ran, 'developed in the milieu of the dukes of Burgundy, [was] inherited by Charles V, and transmitted by Philip II to the Escorial, [whence] it returned to France and the Versailles of Louis XIV'.[113] In reality, the lines of transmission were far less direct than this genealogy allows. As Werner Paravicini has demonstrated through a meticulous analysis of household ordinances, the assumption that European courts had to learn their etiquette by copying Burgundy rests on the shakiest of ground.[114] Comparing the relevant texts, he has noted that almost everything that was supposed to be the 'Burgundian' practice of the court of Philip II had been anticipated in the fourteenth-century Castilian court ordinances, which in turn derived from the 1337 *Leges Palatinae* (or Palace Regulations) of the minor Aragonese court of Jaume II of Mallorca.[115] Medieval Europe, it is clear, offered a larger number of models for courtly ceremoniousness than merely the court of Burgundy.

However, while this discovery may puncture one false assumption, it merely highlights the presence of another. As Redworth and Checa point out in Chapter One, while two sets of Castilian household ordinances, two hundred years apart, may well have looked similar on paper, by the early sixteenth century the actual practice of the Castilian court had diverged substantially. Collections of household ordinances, as Aloys Winterling has pointed out in a pioneering study of the electoral court at Cologne, are often only an imperfect guide to the actual daily ceremonial practice of princely courts.[116] And even in the cases where court ritual is described in detail, it is often difficult to establish with any precision exactly when particular ceremonies came into use; more difficult still to establish from which foreign court, if any, they derived. In other cases, such as the courts of Würzburg, Ansbach and Dresden, even the broad outlines of the court ceremonial remain uncertain. A recent scholarly survey taking in these courts in the early eighteenth century was unable to determine whether their court ceremonies followed the 'Spanish' ceremonial forms practised in Vienna, or the 'French' forms then current in Berlin and Bonn, as well as at Versailles.[117]

If the exact lines of transmission of many court ceremonies await further research, at least some general trends are becoming relatively clear. Perhaps the most striking is the tendency towards the 'sacralization' of the prince. With an intensity rarely matched either before or since, in the period between the mid fifteenth century and at least the end of the seventeenth most of the major European courts chose to express the elevated status of the prince in gestures and symbols that resemble, and were often derived from, religious liturgical practice. Of course, the rituals surrounding religious and secular magistracy had never been wholly distinct, and medieval emperors and kings had long been considered *personae sacrae*, either by consecration and anointing or (as with the coronation-less Castilian kings) by the mere fact of inheritance. From the mid fifteenth century, however, there was a marked increase in the number and frequency of these religious appropriations: in Professor Paravicini's phrase, 'a quantitative change, which ultimately produced a qualitative one'.[118]

Court ceremonial throughout Europe made a clear distinction between mere sovereign princes (who were styled 'excellency' or 'highness'), and the far more elevated order of anointed kings. In the case of *regal* ceremonial, monarchs were not merely treated as 'sacred persons'; during the course of the sixteenth and seventeenth centuries royal rituals increasingly emphasized the ruler's sacrality by appropriating many of the accoutrements of eucharistic devotion and applying them to the personal veneration of the king – a process that probably had its origins in medieval papal and imperial court usage.[119] The late-medieval cult of the Corpus Christi, in particular, dedicated to the adoration of the Body of Christ in the form of the consecrated communion wafer, provided a rich source for ritual borrowings. Perhaps the most overt example of the influence of this Corpus Christi ceremonial is provided at the Castilian court, at least from the adoption of 'Burgundian' usage in 1548. In the religious ceremonial of the Real Alcázar at Madrid, the principal royal residence in the capital, the king heard mass from a small covered and curtained booth, situated to the left of the high altar, known as the *cortina* (from the 'curtain' which was drawn at solemn moments to reveal the king within). The *cortina* was in effect a tabernacle where the king 'dwelt', present but mostly unseen, during the course of the mass. Just as Christ 'dwelt' in the tabernacle of the altar under the species of the eucharistic bread, so the royal *cortina* housed its earthly equivalent, the 'sacred person' of the king.[120] This same arrangement was in use at the Portuguese court by the eighteenth century at the latest, and probably long before.[121]

Although it has gone virtually unnoticed, from at least the reign of Henry VII (1485–1509) until the later Hanoverians, the English court also employed a similar arrangement, 'curtaining' the king while in church within a tabernacle-like area called the 'traverse'. This was usually placed in the raised tribune or gallery at the end of the chapel, which further elevated and concealed the king. On the four Household Days when the monarch received communion in public, however, the royal traverse was placed in the presbytery, immediately adjacent to the altar, in a manner that bore close similarities to Castilian chapel usage.[122]

Conversely, on Good Friday and Holy Saturday, the days of Christ's death and burial, the power of the monarch as God's lieutenant was regarded as being symbolically in abeyance. Just as the mass could not be celebrated and the eucharistic tabernacle itself stood empty and un-curtained, many Catholic courts marked the Christ-derived nature of regal power by a corresponding suspension during these days of the normal emblems of sovereignty. [123] In Castile-Aragon, Good Friday was the only day of the year when the king progressed to church *without* a canopy; nor did he use the *cortina*, which, like the eucharistic tabernacle itself, stood unoccupied.[124] Similar arrangements prevailed in Rome, where from the mid fifteenth century the court usage of the Vicar of Christ took on increasingly monarchical forms.[125] The audience hall of the Vatican Palace, the Sala Regia, was stripped of the canopy over the papal throne (the traditional symbol of lordship) on Good Friday. On that day the pope sat only on a footstool (the *scabellum*), leaving his throne empty and without a canopy, and 'neither gives so much as one blessing nor admits anybody to kiss his foot or his hand'.[126] All these symbols of sovereignty were gloriously restored two days later in a blaze of cloth of gold at Easter, when Christ was resurrected, and with Him the powers of His earthly lieutenants.[127]

Likewise, almost ubiquitous throughout European courts by the mid sixteenth century, was the use of processional canopies to mark out the monarch's presence, of a type identical to those carried over the consecrated host in the Corpus Christi day procession.[128] From the early sixteenth century, processional canopies seem to have been used with increasing frequency as a means of designating the sacral status of royal persons and their representatives. In Madrid, a dozen courtiers were deputed to carry the vast canopy over Philip IV and his guest, Charles, Prince of Wales, on their ceremonial entry to the city in 1623.[129] In post-Reformation England, where canopies were no longer permitted to the consecrated communion wafer after 1548, the design of the processional canopy for the consecrated prince became progressively more elaborate in the century after the break with Rome. Henry VIII (1509–47) was content with four knights to carry the canopy; Elizabeth I (1559–1603) had six canopy-bearers; by the reign of Charles I (1625–49), they were 'increased to double that number'.[130] It is revealing; for the canopy was not merely an emblem of regality and rank, but also a symbol of the 'sacredness' of the person it so conspicuously marked out.

Presence-chamber or 'throne-room' ceremonial was equally overlaid with overtly religious symbolism.

In addition to the use of the canopy, many of the major courts (among them Rome, Madrid, London, Innsbruck, and Vienna) adopted the 'triple reverence', the thrice-repeated bow, or genuflexion, with its obvious Trinitarian symbolism, as the standard form of obeisance towards the monarch. Rome seems to have been the court that adopted the practice earliest; at least from the fifteenth century, the ritual there took the form of courtiers and visitors kneeling three times as they approached and withdrew from the papal throne. At each of the three obeisances, the pontiff raised his hand in blessing in the name of the three persons of the Trinity.[131] A variant of this Trinitarian reverence had been adopted at the Castilian court by the reign of Philip II, and roughly contemporaneously, it also seems to have become the practice of the imperial Habsburg court – where it was known as *das Spanische Kompliment*, a deep bow on bended knee, thrice repeated.[132] A similar triple bow had become the usage of the English court by the reign of Henry VIII at the latest. Like so much other 'Popish' English court ritual, it survived the Reformation even though its supposedly idolatrous implications attracted the censure of seventeenth-century Puritans.[133]

In most of the royal courts of western Europe, both the setting and the ceremonial of the king's table unashamedly expropriated liturgical practices and eucharistic symbolism derived from the much older conventions of the mass. Of course, the frequency with which monarchs 'dined in state' in public varied, from as infrequently as three or four times a year in later sixteenth-century Madrid to as often as weekly in early Stuart England. When the king dined in state alone, however, he broke bread at his table in silence, like a priest at his altar.[134] The end of the room where his table was placed (the Ritterstube in imperial and Bavarian usage, the antechamber when the French king dined *au grand couvert*) became, as it were, the liturgical 'east end', set apart from the main body of the room. It was generally railed off or marked out by a carpet, raised on a dais, and covered by a canopy, just as a Catholic altar was similarly elevated and surmounted by a *baldacchino*. Servers approached the royal majesty as they would the eucharist, with genuflexions and 'reverences' (bowings) towards the table. Dining was preceded by a washing of the monarch's hands, which, well beyond being a mere exercise in personal

hygiene, became an elaborate purification ritual closely modelled on the priestly *lavabo* that preceded the canon of the mass.[135] None of this, of course, should necessarily surprise. In a world built on theories of divine right monarchy, Robin Briggs has observed, 'religious rituals naturally formed the central symbolic expression of these same values'.[136] Nor were these practices necessarily confined to specifically royal courts; some sovereign princely courts, such as grand-ducal Florence and electoral Munich, had adopted dining rituals by the 1560s that treated the ruler as if he were a *persona sacra*. In the great swathe of Catholic Europe, what made such 'sacral' gestures so potent was not that they were somehow exceptional, but that they conveyed their 'meanings' in a symbolic language that was reassuringly familiar. The repertory of courtly gesture constituted, in the words of an Italian scholar, a 'semantic system deeply rooted in the structures and values of the collectivity':[137] in the liturgy of the mass, and the well-established traditions of the Corpus Christi cult.[138]

In the non-Catholic courts, the effect of this repertory of 'eucharistic' (or at least religiously derived) imagery is, if anything, more emphatic. While further research is required on the ceremonial differences between Lutheran and Calvinist house-holds, many Protestant courts (among them those of England, Denmark, and, under King Friedrich I, Brandenburg-Prussia) employed a repertoire of quasi-religious gesture towards the monarch that would often have been condemned as 'popish' had it been seen at the communion table. The use of processional canopies; the 'triple reverence' before the throne; bowing or even genuflexion towards the royal table when the monarch dined in state: many, and sometimes all, of these practices either survived the Reformation or were reinstated relatively soon thereafter. Court usage exemplified a phenomenon that John Bossy has helpfully termed the 'transmigration of the sacred': the transference of sacral power from things ecclesiastical to things monarchical. 'Respectable Christian opinion [placed] kings and their office within the sacred circle erased from so many other points of the social landscape.'[139] Many Protestant princes who cheerfully excised 'Catholic' liturgy from the ecclesiastical sphere had few qualms about retaining ritual practices

In the great public eucharistic processions associated with the Catholic courts – such as the Festival of the Four Altars in Naples, depicted here by Antonio Joli around 1757 – the piety of ruler's household was conspicuously on display. Adoration of the Corpus Christi (carried under the canopy at the back of the square, far left) tended to be syncretized with veneration of the prince.

derived from it within the ceremonies of their courts. Courts, accordingly, became the centre of that 'sacred circle'. Indeed, in many, the reverence given to the monarch exceeded that accorded, in Catholic contexts, to the eucharist. Where the faithful 'visited' the Host reserved in a church they were permitted, after a single genuflexion, to turn their back towards the tabernacle on leaving. In papal Rome, Habsburg Madrid and Vienna, Bourbon Paris-Versailles, and eventually in London, anyone received in audience by the monarch was expected to face the throne continuously, and was obliged to walk out of the Presence Chamber backwards, performing the 'triple reverence' as he went.[140]

Of course, the business of divining 'meanings' in such ceremonials needs to be approached with great caution. In particular, whether the 'sacralization' of the crown effected a substantial increase in the political authority of the monarch (as exponents of the 'absolutist' interpretation would wish to believe) must remain for the moment an open question. Already, however, it is apparent that key elements in the

The sacred table: Charles II, dining in state at the Garter Feast in St George's Hall, Windsor Castle, in the 1660s. The arrangements depicted here replicate those for presence-chamber dining in state: the king dines alone, attended by servants on bended knee, with all the ritualized formality of a mass – his table raised on a dais and separated from the body of the hall by a balustrade.

traditional interpretation need to be cast in a very different mould. First, the recovery of the liturgical element in aulic ceremonial, largely pioneered by Italian scholars,[141] has fundamentally modified the older analyses of household ritual in terms of 'theatre' and 'propaganda'.[142] We are dealing with rituals where the 'message' is so deeply embedded in the 'medium', to borrow Clifford Geertz's phrase, 'that to transform it into a network of propositions is to risk…both of the characteristic crimes of exegesis: seeing more in things than is really there, and reducing a richness of particular meaning to a drab parade of generalities'.[143] Secondly, where these household practices are concerned, it should be remembered that the daily 'audience' for most court ceremonial was the courtiers themselves. Like the liturgies of the Church, to which it provided a complement, the act of participation in

court ceremonial defined a cadre that shared in the 'holiness' of power. At least until the end of the seventeenth century, when this ritual culture came under fire from a variety of quarters, its repetitiveness, the very antithesis of theatricality, was of its essence. The *officium regale* (the daily ceremonial usages of the court), like the *officium divinum* (the daily prayer of the Church), was an end in itself.

This is not to suggest that courts were indifferent to questions of audience. On those great state occasions when the court went 'out of doors', monarchs and courtiers alike seem to have been acutely aware that the parade of aulic splendour could serve a variety of pragmatic purposes – not least, to enhance the reputation and diplomatic standing of the ruling house. Printed descriptions of major public court ceremonies – the King in Prussia's coronation at

Königsberg in 1701, for example, or the King of Sicily's at Palermo in 1713 – brought the splendours of the court's 'material culture' to a Europe-wide audience. Their *reportage* provided one of the various means by which rulers who had finally achieved royal status could conduct their campaigns for diplomatic recognition.[144] Likewise, developments in engraving and etching during the course of the seventeenth century permitted depictions of great court festivals to be published to a viewing audience incomparably larger than could ever be present at the actual event. Images such as Theodoor van Thulden's etchings of Rubens's designs for the *Pompa Introitus Ferdinandi*, published at Antwerp in 1641, or Jean Le Pautre's depictions of the 1668 *Feste de Versailles* were widely circulated, domestically as well as in foreign courts. Even so, if the publication of etchings and engravings was an obvious vehicle for royal 'propaganda', it is striking – with the exception of royal portraiture – how relatively infrequently most monarchs exploited such media as a means of impressing their subjects.[145] Louis XIV's France is here the exception, as so often; engravings of palace interiors and court celebrations were issued for presentation to ambassadors and, in cheaper versions, for mass sale throughout the reign. By the eighteenth century, however, this policy had been 'completely abandoned'. Printed illustrations of the king's *cabinet* were few, and copies – almost always in the form of royally sponsored de luxe editions – were reserved to those already well connected at court, in Gérard Sabatier's phrase, as 'precious testimonies of [royal] favour'.[146] We are back with practices that belong to the 'politics of intimacy', not to the propaganda of absolutism.

Similarly, once we turn to court ceremonial, it is evident that there is much more going on in the set-piece rituals of chapel and Presence Chamber than simply the aggrandizement of the prince. After the monarch himself, the secondary roles in aulic ritual were almost invariably allotted on the basis of a hierarchy determined by inherited status and rank: witness Alba's lofty place at the court of Philip II. The most prestigious roles in court ceremonial were almost universally reserved, as of right, to the most senior noblemen present.[147] While it was of course open to the ruler to trump existing hierarchies by promoting a 'new man' to great offices and titles, the *arriviste*

recipient of such princely favour usually enjoyed a lonely eminence. In any event, such controversial promotions could generally only modify, and never wholly supplant, a system of precedence founded on custom, rank and dynastic status.[148] With political and religious values so deeply embedded in court ceremonial, attempts to tamper with it were correspondingly controversial. Hostility against the Emperor Charles V's imposition in 1548 of 'Burgundian usage' on his Castilian court smouldered for decades, even though the old *Corte y Casa de Castilla* (the Castilian court and household) was not replaced by the new Burgundian household, but made to co-exist beside it. The attempt by Queen Christina of Sweden, in 1653, to foist the highly sacralized French court ceremonial on to one of the most Protestant courts of Europe contributed materially to the political crisis that only a year later brought about her abdication.[149]

The very reverence that attached to these priestly protocols, and the time that was expected to be devoted to their performance, imposed their own limitations on the monarch's freedom of manoeuvre. The sacralized ruler was always the object of ritual deference, but there was also a sense in which he was simultaneously held captive in the gilded fetters of ceremonial.[150] Obviously, their capacity to bind should not be exaggerated; strong personalities were usually able to break free. During his last years, Philip II of Spain, for example, was notoriously indifferent to the demands of household ceremony, as was Frederick the Great at Sanssouci. At the other extreme, the vignette of Philip IV in 1633, displayed behind glass like a holy relic on the balcony of the Buen Retiro for the veneration of the court, neatly highlights the double-edged consequences of 'sacralizing' the king. At one level, the tableau presented the monarch as an object of religious devotion; at another, it is also an image of imprisonment, with a puppet-like king caught in a web of court conventions from which he was powerless to escape.[151]

VI. The Reinterpretation of the Court's 'Material Culture'

Raising such questions of meaning and audience in relation to the iconography of gesture prompts similar questions when we turn to another aspect of aulic culture, where symbols took more concrete and tangible forms: the art and artefacts that the European princely courts produced in such prodigious abundance. The inventiveness of this 'material culture' took a multiplicity of forms. Some were durable and permanent: buildings, tapestries, paintings and the whole array of art-objects from Benvenuto Cellini saltcellars to Meissen figurines. Others were deliberately ephemeral: temporary triumphal arches; firework displays; the scenery of masques and operas.[152] Confronted with the question, what purpose did all this magnificence serve, traditional accounts have structured their responses around two central ideas: first, that most 'court art' sought to project a 'political' message; and second, that it was therefore primarily concerned with persuading a 'public', which the regime either wanted to, or needed to, impress. Thus Peter Burke's reading of Raphael's fresco in the Vatican Palace, *The Expulsion of Heliodorus from the Temple* (*c*.1511), is as a simple political allegory: Heliodorus represents the Bentivoglio, lords of Bologna, recently driven out of the papal territories; the papacy and its lands are emblematized by the temple. 'Art is here fulfilling the function of propaganda, just like the modern poster.'[153] If few would now see the role of art in quite such mechanistic terms, the influence of the 'propagandist' interpretation of court culture remains pervasive still.

The alternative is not to deny that art and architecture, indeed courtly magnificence in general, could serve functional ends. 'Messages' relating to the business of rule could of course find expression, in visual form as much as in the gestures of courtly ritual. There remains, however, an important distinction to be made between a generalized intention of conveying meanings that relate to the exercise of rule and the deliberately opinion-forming objectives of propaganda. Perhaps the fundamental misreading imposed by the 'propagandist' approach is the assumptions it implies about the audience that the court's material culture sought to address. For the contriver of propaganda, the prime concern is immediate: the audience of the moment, and arguably the larger the better. The early modern court operated upon very different assumptions. Its expectations were profoundly influenced by the classical Roman concept of *fama*, and by the longevity of name and reputation.[154] Personified

as the winged goddess who trumpeted great deeds down the generations, 'Fame' is a recurrent image in the iconography of the court's visual culture. The goddess is to be found broadcasting the renown of the House of Medici in Rubens's great cycle of paintings for Marie de Médicis, just as it adorns innumerable medals and engravings, and perches nimbly atop a thousand tombs and triumphal arches. At the Vatican, one of palace's most important 'court spaces', the entrance to Bernini's Scala Regia – the 'royal staircase' leading to the papal audience chamber – is dominated by gigantic twin figures of Fame. These, rather than mere angels, support the cartouche of Pope Alexander VII's arms crowning the central Serlian arch, their twin trumpets blasting out the 'renown' of the House of Chigi heavenwards and earthwards, respectively.

This gesture towards celestial as well as earthly renown highlights a further dimension that distances early modern attitudes from the modern concept of propaganda. For the quest for *fama* through artistic patronage coexisted with an equally strong and classically derived disdain for the plaudits of the *ignobile vulgus*, 'the common herd'. While courtly magnificence in its various forms might well have its incidental purpose in creating a sense of awe or admiration in the crowds who flocked to see great ceremonies of state, the true measure of their effect was to be gauged in qualitative rather than quantitative terms. This does not mean that rulers were wholly indifferent to their reputations outside the courtly élite. Nor does it mean that great court ceremonies, such as coronations or state funerals, did not have a public dimension intended, in Bossuet's phrase 'to impress on the people a certain respect'.[155] But any enterprise that was solely concerned with courting 'popular opinion', the prime target of the propagandist, would not have escaped courtly censure for long. Within that milieu, 'great men' sought the estimation of their peers and of future memory, not 'popularity', a word that continued to have strongly pejorative connotations well into the eighteenth century. Even when the act of artistic patronage entailed a substantial component of personal aggrandizement or vanity, individual renown more often than not served a larger purpose: the glorification of the dynasty and the enhancement of its 'fame'.

It followed that one of the most important of all

The opulence of the court's material culture prompted a religiously inspired critique that found visual expression in the vanitas, *with its emphasis on the transience of human life and folly of worldly goods. Ironically,* vanitas *paintings, such as this* Allegory of the Transitory c. 1635, *by Antonio de Pereda (1611–78), were themselves worldly goods, and were largely produced for consumption by affluent collectors at court.*

that the inspiration of Louis XIV's great projects lay in his knowledge of the court of his uncle, Philip IV.[156] Hence, also, the huge resources that were lavished upon the business of impressing foreign monarchs through their ambassadors.[157] In the course of his reign, Charles I spent some £74,000 on gold and silver plate, medals and chains, most of it given away to visiting foreign diplomats or courtiers during New Year celebrations. To place this in perspective: notwithstanding Charles's reputation as a major collector of works of art, this sum exceeded the crown's total expenditure on paintings and sculptures throughout the entire reign.[158] Yet both the act of giving and the gifts themselves were seldom witnessed by more than a handful of spectators, almost exclusively drawn from the inner ranks of the donor's and the recipient's courts. Such presentations nevertheless fulfilled two functions of central importance: domestically, impressing the court élite with the monarch's munificence, and, in the context of dynastic diplomacy, maintaining the fame and renown of the ruling house within the competitive company of European princes.[159]

When foreign rulers visited in person, the sums spent on buildings and entertainment could be astronomical. To impress the Elector Palatine of the Rhine and his entourage in 1613, James I of Great Britain spent in a matter of days a sum equivalent to ten years' expenditure on the building and maintenance of all his English palaces combined. Of course, aspects of these entertainments involved forms of display that were accessible to, and presumably impressed, a relatively large metropolitan public: processions, fireworks, pageants and the like. However, even greater importance seems to have been attached to the task of impressing the élite audience of the court and, still more, the foreign delegations that would spread the 'fame' of the dynasty in foreign parts. For fame, too, had its place as an instrument of policy. In a system of European diplomacy, where dynastic alliances continued to be one of the major influences affecting relations between sovereign states, the court's international prestige was a major determinant of the ruling house's standing in the dynastic marriage market.[160]

Such reservations also apply when considering the pictorial art of the court. The portraits and allegorical paintings adorning the interiors of palaces have been frequently interpreted as exercises in 'monarchical

'audiences' for courtly magnificence was the highly select company of the ruler's fellow sovereigns and their diplomatic representatives at court. Monarchs vied with each other in the creation of 'magnificence'; and John Elliott is almost certainly right in suggesting

The trumpeting of fame: the Scala Regia (or royal staircase) of the Chigi pope, Alexander VII (1655–67). Designed by Bernini and built in 1663–6, it provided a spectacular ceremonial route from the narthex of St Peter's Basilica to the papal Presence Chamber, the Sala Regia. Twin angels in the guise of Fame support the vast shield of the Chigi arms.

propaganda'. Olivares' commission for the Hall of Realms at the Buen Retiro, for example, continues to be regarded as an 'entreprise de propagande'.[161] Yet, many of the images supposedly most propagandist in tone were accessible only to a relatively small number of viewers; and in the case of works of art in the monarch's private apartments, access was often confined to an even smaller group, an élite within an élite. Those who gained access to the emperor's private apartments in the Vienna Hofburg or were permitted to see the Hall of Realms at the Buen Retiro in Madrid already belonged to the court's inner circle.[162]

In the case of the celebrated *studiolo* (or private study) of Grand Duke Francesco I de' Medici (1564–87), one of the most richly decorated and furnished apartments in the palace, access seems to have been denied to all but the duke and a 'select few' of his intimates.[163] It is hard to avoid the conclusion that, in so far as this facet of aulic culture sought to inculcate political principles, it was on the whole preaching to the converted.

Similar considerations apply to the goldsmiths' and jewellers' work and other marvels that stocked the *Kunstkammern* and *Wunderkammern* (the 'art-chambers' and 'cabinets of curiosities') that proliferated in the courts of the Holy Roman Empire from the mid sixteenth century and, under different nomenclature, in some French and Italian courts as well.[164] The *Kunstkammer* was an Aladdin's cave of precious objects: besides paintings there were gold and silver-gilt boxes, enamelled caskets set with precious stones, gold-mounted ostrich eggs, jewelled reliquaries, natural 'curiosities' and scientific instruments.[165] And rulers often made these collections available to a relatively wide audience, permitting entry to travellers and scholars, sometimes even to the merely curious, in the expectation that such visits helped to enhance their prestige. Here, too, however, monarchs were often far more concerned with whom, rather than merely how many, they impressed. Collections, such as the celebrated *Kunstkammer* of the Emperor Rudolf II (1576–1612) in Prague, had numerous 'layers', with the quality and value of items increasing as one progressed towards an inner 'core'. Minute gradations of favour and esteem could be expressed by just how much or how little a visitor to the ruler's collections was permitted to see. Thus, the Duke of Savoy's ambassador to the imperial court, Carlo Francesco Manfredi, was first allowed to see the emperor's collection of paintings (the less prestigious items in the collection) in 1604. But he had to wait until the very end of his embassy to be granted permission, as a mark of particular favour, to see the inner rooms of the *Kunstkammer*, including its prized jewelled boxes and its *pièce de résistance*, a two-metre-long 'unicorn's horn' endowed with magical powers.[166] As with the fabled El Dorado itself, the 'hiddenness' of these most prized treasures was an essential element of their mystique. More than any monetary value, however, *Kunst-* and *Wunderkammern* were believed to offer a microcosm of the cosmic macrocosm: they offered a key to universal knowledge. To be granted sight of them was, almost literally, to glimpse the *arcana imperii*: the occult attributes of rule.[167]

Yet it would be naïve to deny that the contents of *Kunstkammern* and great courtly collections also had their pragmatic – even, arguably, their 'functionalist' – aspect. They usually served to enhance the dynasty's 'fame', and the fact of possession brought prestige to the courts that housed them. Hence what appears to have been the general readiness of rulers to permit access to at least part of their collections to travellers

and visitors of gentle rank. In this context, the group affected by these objects extended well beyond the immediate confines of the court. Of course, there were published catalogues of these wonders, and even printed *explications*, as in France, describing the iconography employed in decorative schemes.[168] But in a society that remained in many respects an oral culture as much as a print culture, word travelled within the governing élite far more extensively and effectively than any engraving could be circulated. In this respect, the system of 'service by term' at court probably acted as a highly efficient conduit of information between the centre and the localities. It provided most members of the household with numerous opportunities to return to their country estates and to converse and gossip with their neighbours. The 'audience' for much court art may well have been precisely that: those who had heard tell of the existence of these fabulous treasures.

When we turn to objects invested with a religious potency, we are clearly dealing with a phenomenon that cannot be assessed in purely material terms.[169] In the courts of Catholic Europe, some of the most valuable objects, in both monetary and symbolic terms, were the reliquaries that contained sacred relics – a tradition of acquisition that went back to late antiquity. Many were among the supreme examples of the goldsmiths' and jewellers' art. Those associated with the doge's court in Venice, with the ducal court at Florence, or assembled at Halle in the early sixteenth century by the Archbishop-Elector of Mainz, Cardinal Albrecht von Brandenburg (the *Hallesches Heiltum*), were widely renowned. Such collections of reliquaries not only cost far more than any painting; their sacred contents were endowed with numinous qualities that complemented and reinforced the sacrality of their princely owners. Yet the 'audience' for such objects was again often highly restricted, and generally confined to no more than the prince, his high-ranking guests and favoured members of his immediate entourage.[170]

Possessions of this kind thus fulfilled a subtler and more diversified series of roles than mere propaganda. Indeed, even when works of art were housed in relatively accessible parts of the court, such as the chapel or guard chamber, how far their viewers deduced political implications from their symbolism, assuming they were competent to decode it, remains unclear. As Theodore Rabb has recently suggested, in the relentless desire to detect propagandist meanings in court culture – in *fêtes* and formal entries, allegories and portraits – historians are in danger of overlooking the ludic quality in courtly art: the sense in which many works were 'shows of learning, homages to antiquity, or *jeux d'esprit*'.[171] Such considerations turn on their head the traditional assumption that the artistic culture of the court was remorselessly concerned with display, and with imparting political 'messages' to some broad but unspecified public.

The revisionist attempt to recover contemporary responses to court art has also pointed up the yawning gulf that exists between early modern assessments of the relative value attaching to various art forms and those imposed by modern art-historical scholarship. In the course of the twentieth century, easel paintings have commanded a financial premium and an aesthetic prestige, as against all other forms of the visual arts, that is without precedent. However, as Jonathan Brown has argued, once it is asked what forms of the visual arts contemporaries endowed with the greatest significance, a very different ordering of priorities begins to emerge.[172] In establishing these priorities an obvious, if highly imperfect, measure is the relative monetary values that contemporaries attributed to particular types of artwork. Even within the field of the visual arts, the most costly of easel paintings tended to come relatively inexpensively when compared with tapestries, which remained, well into the eighteenth century, the most prestigious and expensive of all decorative media. The dispersal in the 1620s of the great collection of paintings assembled by the Dukes of Mantua offers a case in point. The eventual purchaser of the bulk of the collection, Charles I of England, paid around £28,000, thereby acquiring a reputation as one of the most munificent and enlightened of English royal patrons. Yet even the value of the Mantuan collection in the 1620s was merely around half what Charles I spent on his tapestry manufactory at Mortlake in the course of his reign (1625–49).[173]

In most courts, expenditure on jewellery and plate had a far higher priority in the claims on monarchs' and courtiers' purses than did the acquisition of pictures. A single item in Cardinal Richelieu's collection of silver, valued at 90,000 livres and described as a *buffet d'argent blanc ciselé*, was worth more than his entire collection of some 250 paintings at the Palais Cardinal.[174] Nor should this be seen merely as another example of courtly 'extravagance'. The gold and silver plate used in court dining provided reserves of precious metals that effectively formed an emergency treasury; in moments of financial crisis, dinner services could be promptly sold or dispatched to the mint for recycling as coinage.[175]

Dinner services of precious metal, jewelled boxes, the gilded and enamelled baubles that filled royal cabinets and *Kunstkammern*: these objects have frequently been used to illustrate the luxuriousness, even the triviality, supposedly characteristic of the *ancien régime* in general and much 'court art' in particular. Yet, with their easily assayable material value and, throughout the seventeenth century, a rising financial value as collectables within an élite market of princely and aristocratic buyers, these objects were in many ways as secure a means of storing capital as monetary reserves held in specie. Similarly, while jewelled reliquaries might not, like dinner services, be able to pay armies, they could easily act as the security for loans, or be exchanged for cash, that would.

Despite the oft-repeated maxim that the magnificence of the court's visual culture was a 'manifestation of power' there was, in fact, little correlation between the opulence of a court's representational culture and the strength of the regime. Throughout the sixteenth and seventeenth centuries, the court of the Holy Roman Empire was arguably one of the most influential in Europe. Yet in 'representational' terms the imperial household was also one of the dowdiest on the continent, with the Hofburg in Vienna and the Hradčany Castle in Prague, its principal winter seats, crammed into relatively constricted medieval sites that offered few opportunities for architectural display. Not until the 1740s did Schönbrunn, the Habsburg Versailles, become the principal seat of the imperial court; and by then imperial authority was already being challenged by the rise of Prussia.[176] In contrast, the 'representational' glamour of the Dresden court created by Elector Friedrich August I of Saxony (1694–1733, from 1697 King Augustus II of Poland) was second to none in its Baroque architecture, stately court ceremonial and the lavish scale of its cultural patronage.[177] Yet, as every courtier knew, the

Dynastic politics: the elaborately choreographed exchange of royal brides between France and Spain in 1615 on the Bidasoa river, the border between the two realms. Louis XIII gave his sister, Élisabeth, in marriage to the ten-year-old Infante Felipe, the future Philip IV of Spain; the Spanish prince gave his sister, the Infanta Anna, to Louis XIII as the new queen of France (then aged fourteen).

idea that 'display' suggested power always contained a substantial element of bluff. In the 1750s, as Saxony was occupied by Prussian troops and its court was left powerless and humiliated, that bluff was called.

VII. A NEW COURT HISTORY

From a variety of perspectives, then, the broad outlines of a new court history are beginning to emerge. In place of the monolithic, 'absolutist' model of the court, there is a stress on the composite character of most European courts and the variety of routes to patronage and preferment that they offered. If courts often provided the sounding-board for a grandiloquent rhetoric of autocracy, their private discourse retailed a subtler and more nuanced language of power. The monarch remained the pivotal figure

within any court, but the durability of aristocratic authority, both within the court and outside it, inevitably imposed constraints on the crown's freedom of manoeuvre. At the most 'absolutist' of courts, the exercise of authority was always in some sense a negotiation founded, in the final analysis, upon the community of interest between the crown and the noble élites. The court, far from being an instrument whereby monarchs could weaken the nobility, as was once supposed, provided the forum in which that compact could be subjected to a regular process of revision and renegotiation. Of course, the religious tensions of early modern Europe – particularly those of the 'long century of Reformation' from the 1520s to the 1640s – often placed that compact under acute strain. Yet, as Jeroen Duindam has noted, once 'the dust of internal uprisings [had] settled in the middle of the seventeenth century, a symbiosis re-emerged'.[178]

The court's ceremonial culture, in turn, gave expression to that *modus vivendi*. The cult of loyalty to the monarchy, enthusiastically promoted by the newly founded chivalric orders, had to contend with the resilience of the aristocratic honour cult, with its insistence on the great nobleman's 'ancient tradition' of independent judgement when it came to determining the good of the realm. It was not just the monarch who could appeal to a mythical 'validating past'.

Yet perhaps the defining characteristic of the new court history is methodological: an attempt to emancipate the study of court politics and institutions from the anachronistic strictures of 'absolutism', and court culture from crudely functionalist modes of analysis and the equally distorting concept of 'propaganda'. In the process, the new court history inevitably calls into question a closely related historical trend: the analysis of European *ancien régimes* in terms of 'state-building', in which the importance of early modern institutions is gauged according to the extent that they 'anticipate' modern structures of bureaucratic power.[179] From this perspective, the monarch's household, doomed to survive into the modern age only as a quaint antediluvian relic, can be almost wholly ignored. In a major recent survey of the 'rise of the state' in early modern Europe, it rates not a single mention.[180]

That is a conclusion with which Lerma or Olivares, or Colbert or Fleury, would have been unlikely to agree. Reconsideration of the court and its culture suggests a very different approach to the sovereignties of early modern Europe. In place of the modern notion of the unitary nation state, with its bureaucratic institutions, clearly defined borders and relatively integrated cultural and linguistic identity, there is the much looser contemporary concept of the 'realm': less a clearly defined territorial entity than the collectivity of subjects owing allegiance to a particular sovereign. Of course, the early modern discourse of *raison d'état*, like the classical political language of the *res publica*, was perfectly capable of conceptualizing kingdoms and principalities in abstract and impersonal terms. But, in so far as the word 'state' was entering common usage in the sixteenth and seventeenth centuries, it still carried with it strong courtly associations. In Germany, the official lists of the court establishment were known as *Hofstaaten*. 'The totality of such personnel', Robert Evans has reminded

us, 'was a prime meaning of *Staat*, or *état*, or "state".' In England, 'the state' had even more directly courtly connotations: it was a synonym for the canopy that stood over the monarch's throne.[181]

Notoriously, early modern sovereignties were often an untidy composite of disparate territories and subjects; they took their coherence, not from territorial boundaries or 'national' identity, but primarily from religious and dynastic allegiance. Bound together by Christian doctrine and an allegiance to a personal monarch (as to a personal God), early modern sovereignties rested on theological as much as political foundations. Except in the Venetian and Dutch republics and the handful of elective monarchies, the dynasty constituted the prime focus of loyalty; it remained the divinely sanctioned source of political obligation within the realm until the rise of 'nationalism' in the eighteenth century.[182] Court ceremonial, accordingly, tended to syncretize the spheres of political and spiritual allegiance, and to express this fusion in secular rituals that self-consciously evoked religious forms.

Contemporary responses to these forms were, of course, never homogeneous. There is always a problem assessing, at any one point, 'how far repetition is effective in implanting fixed ideas, how it may become an empty show performed with tongue in cheek'.[183] Viewed in the *longue durée*, however, it is possible to acquire at least some sense of which of the two was the predominant response. What emerges from these essays is that by the first decades of the eighteenth century, if not earlier, there was an important change in attitudes towards the sacralized and ceremonialist court of the high Baroque, a belief that the old ritual magic was losing its efficacy. Berlin, London and Versailles in the 1710s each exemplifies in different ways what seems to have been a common, if not universal, trend towards the abandonment of the 'ceremonious court'. At the court of Brandenburg-Prussia, after the death of ritual-obsessed King Friedrich I and the accession of Friedrich Wilhelm I, most of the Bourbon-inspired protocol of the Prussian court, complete with *lever* and *coucher*, was summarily abolished, along with most of the household functionaries it had hitherto employed. Similarly, the inauguration of the new Hanoverian dynasty in England in 1714 witnessed the final jettisoning of the ceremony of touching for the 'king's evil', and a move towards a smaller and far less ceremonious court. 'A sovereign of our own times would find the state and ceremony of former times an encumbrance hardly to be endured', wrote the court chaplain, Samuel Pegge, in the 1780s; 'it would be like reverting to the days of Chivalry, when no person of rank could appear without being buckled up in a suit of armour.'[184]

Even at Louis XIV's court, where the image of the eucharistic monarch reached its apogee, there were times when courtly representation veered perilously close to vacuous bombast. A marked change in attitudes was noted from the beginning of the century and was connected by contemporaries with the traumas of the War of the Spanish Succession (1701–14). As Briggs has suggested of French court ceremonial 'it is possible that by 1715 it had imperceptibly gone over the top; certainly neither of [Louis XIV's] pre-revolutionary successors found it appropriate to continue with the same style'.[185] By the 1720s, ceremonies such as touching for the king's evil were being regarded with open scepticism. From Louis XV's coronation in 1722, the formularies for the service quietly dropped the king's overt claims to miraculous healing powers.[186]

However, the reaction was by no means universal. In the ostentation of their architectural setting and the complexities of their rituals, courts such as Maria-Theresa's Schönbrunn in the 1750s or the Neapolitan monarchs' Caserta in the 1760s had arguably moved far closer to the spirit of Louis XIV's Versailles than any of their predecessors had been at the end of the seventeenth century.[187] Elsewhere, however, the old courtly values were coming under fire. The reverse side of the Enlightenment veneration of nature and honesty was its critique of the stagy artificiality and dissimulation to be found at the princely courts. To many monarchs, and to their courtiers, the bourgeois ideal of simplicity and domesticity presented an attractive alternative to the vast households and protocol-dominated lives of their recent forebears.[188] Few went quite so far as George III of England and his consort in their dislike of courtly pomp and in their desire for bourgeois felicity as 'Mr and Mrs King'. But few courts were unaffected by the cult of 'naturalness' espoused by the *philosophes*. In terms of culture and sensibility, the impact of such ideas during the early decades of the

eighteenth century marked a decisive break with many of the values and attitudes that had informed courtly society since the late fifteenth century.[189] At least in this limited sense, the *ancien-régime* court had ceased to exist long before the political convulsions of 1789.

It is these considerations that provide the principal themes, and the chronological boundaries, for the essays that follow. They survey twelve of the major courts of early modern Europe: the three largest courts of western Europe, Madrid, Paris-Versailles and Whitehall; the three most influential courts of the Italian peninsula, the ducal courts at Turin and Florence, and the papal court at Rome; and the two largest courts of the German-speaking lands of the Holy Roman Empire, Vienna and Munich. The Baltic monarchies are represented by Sweden, while Markus Völkel surveys what was in effect the multiple-court of Brandenburg-Prussia, whose 'seats' ranged from the Duchy of Cleves in the west to Berlin and Königsberg in the east. Jonathan Israel examines the predicament of the Princes of Orange, whose court at The Hague enjoyed an intermittently quasi-monarchical status within one of Europe's very few non-monarchical states, the Dutch Republic. Finally, Lindsey Hughes examines Peter the Great's 'invention' of a new form of Russian sovereign court at St Petersburg, a synthesis of Western tradition with the customs of a royal household that was barely a 'European' princely court at all, the court of Muscovy.

Inevitably, there are omissions. An ideal survey would have taken in the courts of Copenhagen, Dresden, Lisbon, Naples, Nancy, Parma and Modena; the greater ecclesiastical courts of the Empire, among them Cologne and Würzburg, not to mention the *Reich*'s numerous smaller secular princely courts. Such encyclopaedic range, however, would have resulted in a book of unmanageable size and, no doubt, equally unmanageable cost. What emerges with clarity, however, even from the limited survey attempted here, is a very different view of the court's pre-eminence in the political and cultural life of early modern Europe: no longer a single monolithic princely household or the stage for an inflexible and immobile 'absolutism', but an entrepôt that accommodated a series of rival foci of authority and influence, where power was traded, and where the decisions taken touched the lives of every subject – before they learnt to be citizens.

PEDACIO DIOSCORIDES ANA

ZARBEO, ACERCA DE LA MATERIA ME-

DICINAL, Y DE LOS VENENOS MORTIFEROS,

Traduzido de lengua Griega, en la vulgar Caste-
llana, & illustrado con claras y substantiales Annotatio-
nes, y con las figuras de innumeras plantas exquisi
tas y raras, por el Doctor Andres de Laguna,
Medico de Iulio III. Pont. Max.

DIVO PHILIPPO, DIVI CAROLI. V. AVG.
FILIO HAEREDI, OPT. MAX.
DICATVM.

EN ANVERS,
En casa de Iuan Latio. Anno,
M. D. LV.

Cum Gratia & Priuilegio Imperiali.

CHAPTER ONE

The Kingdoms of Spain
THE COURTS OF
THE SPANISH HABSBURGS

creation of a ceremonious royal household was but a late arrival on the political scene, in Castile the idea of what constituted the royal court had been the subject of deliberation and definition for hundreds of years. As early as the thirteenth century, King Alfonso the Wise (King of Leon and Castile, 1252–84) had decreed that the court was 'the place where the king is to be found with his vassals and his own officials, who constantly advise and wait on him, as well as the great men of the kingdom who are present'.[1] The court was deemed to be something more than just the king's household. Indeed, included under its wings was much of royal government. By the time the Habsburgs had acceded to the Spanish thrones, this idea had expanded to encompass the notion that 'court' and 'capital' were much the same thing. This point of view was further elaborated in the mid seventeenth century in the writings of that fastidious court commentator Alonso Nuñez de Castro, who argued that only the town of Madrid was properly entitled to play host to the court. Not only did he cite King Alfonso's definition as authoritative, he also answered his own initial question – what exactly was the court? – by enumerating each of the king's many councils to be found in Madrid.[2] These were as much 'the court' as was the immediate household and entourage of the king.

This broad concept of the court could cause confusion, especially for foreign observers. To the Frenchman François Bertaut, who was used to the more monarch-centred households of the Bourbon court, it was hardly a true court at all. Writing after a visit to Spain in the middle of the seventeenth century, he

The language of heraldry gave expression to the dynasty's territorial claims: the title page of the Castilian translation of Dioscorides' De Materia Medica *(1555), from Philip II's library. The shield of arms is subdivided, with the quarterings on the left representing Philip's Iberian possessions; impaling these, on the right side, are the arms of his wife, Mary I of England, whose claim to the crown of France is registered by the three fleurs-de-lis.*

noted that 'the court of the king of Spain cannot properly be called a court, at least in the same sense as the courts of France, England…or other much less powerful European princes. Rather it is a private house of someone who, we would say, had withdrawn from the world'.[3] If we are to do better by the Castilian court, we should consider that it was not just, as in England or France, the place 'where, by definition, the king resided'.[4] From around the second half of the sixteenth century contemporaries understood the Castilian court to comprise not only the city and governmental centre of Madrid but, as we shall see, a specially constructed web of royal palaces surrounding 'the very loyal town and court' – as the city of Madrid to this day styles itself.

The realm that this court was created to rule was of course a composite entity. Strictly speaking, it is a constitutional misnomer to speak of Spain as a united country before the accession of the Bourbon dynasty in 1701. With the marriage of Ferdinand of Aragon and Isabella of Castile in 1469, their two kingdoms – themselves federations of states – came to share the same monarchs, even if the two countries were not administratively united. Despite the self-conscious styling of the future Philip II, while heir to the throne, as the Prince of *Spain*, Castile was indubitably the core-kingdom of the various Spanish realms, and the royal court can justifiably be called Castilian on the grounds that it was there that the monarch and his entourage were nearly always to be found. Though not entirely satisfactory, the terms Castilian court and Spanish court have been used in this chapter more or less interchangeably, although the latter term has generally been preferred whenever the intention has been to stress the court's role beyond a purely Iberian context.

After the marriage of Ferdinand (II of Aragon, 1479–1516, V of Castile, 1474–1504) and Isabella (Queen of Castile, 1474–1504), Castile not only became the dominant power within the peninsula; through a longer and more hesitant process, set in train by the marriage of their daughter Juana the Mad to a Habsburg prince, that kingdom slowly became the heart of a world-wide empire. By the middle of the sixteenth century Castile was the pivotal kingdom of a collection of states under the rule of the Spanish Habsburgs, which encompassed not only much of northern Europe (including the Spanish Netherlands and the Holy Roman Empire), but also extended to the new world of the Americas in the west, and, after Philip II's seizure of the Portuguese throne in 1580, to Brazil, as well as to trading stations in Africa and India and various possessions in the Pacific. An 'extra-territorial' role was thus cast upon the court in Castile. For the historian this poses important questions about how courts functioned in the early modern world. The work of Norbert Elias and his followers among the pioneers of the 'new court history' has emphasized the role of the court as a means of elevating early modern monarchy and of ensnaring the aristocracy in, as it were, a gilded cage. In contradistinction to this, a more recent view has suggested that the court was actually the scene of a historic mediation between 'absolutist' monarchs and their nobles. In Jeroen Duindam's words, 'the splendour of the court was not an expression of the monarch's victory, but of the compromise between monarch and élites'.[5] In fact, both these propositions are true of the Castilian court, as they doubtless are elsewhere – depending, of course, on when and where one looks.

If we are to understand the special role of the court of Castile, then we must also look afresh at the relationship between the court and the representation of the monarchy that it housed. So much has been made of the way in which rulers were represented by their courts to their subjects, and the particular influence of Elias has resulted in viewing this representation largely in terms of an active courtly propaganda impressing an idealized view of monarchy upon a passive audience. Yet this approach will not do justice to the working of the Castilian court, precisely because one of the most distinctive features of the 'imperial court' of Castile was not only the manner in which it sought to create opinion but, no less importantly, because of the way in which it could play to certain pre-existing expectations and assumptions among the monarch's own subjects, particularly among the élite. In this sense, the subject could be as prescriptive about the relations between himself and the court as the monarch was about relations between the court and his subjects. Thus, the organization of the household was too important simply to reflect a sovereign's personal preferences for one set of ceremonies over another. After all, Spanish monarchs at times needed to appeal to different parts of their composite monarchy for support; and the ordering of the court – the institutional manifestation of both monarch and monarchy – was part of nothing less than a ritualistic dialogue between monarch and subjects.

I. THE CASTILIAN COURT AT THE END OF THE FIFTEENTH CENTURY

towns or, ultimately, leading her great crusade against the rump of a Muslim state in Granada. As Christina Hofmann has lamented, her court has left behind documentation in abundance concerning the titles and salaries of her servants, but very little to provide us with a subjective view of what life in the royal household of the Trastámaras was actually like.[6] What we know about in great detail, however, is the organization of the household of Prince Juan, the only son of Ferdinand and Isabella, who predeceased his parents in 1497. Much commented upon at the time for its splendour, the court of this heir to both the Castilian and Aragonese thrones was designed to reflect the twofold message of royal policy: through its opulence it trumpeted the benefits of stability now that the civil wars that had afflicted both Castile and Aragon were at an end, just as it encapsulated the power and prestige that ensued from what the Catholic monarchs liked to portray as a united Hispania.

Detailed understanding of Prince Juan's Castilian court at the end of the fifteenth century comes largely from a single memoir drawn up by a member of the prince's household, Gonzalo Fernández de Oviedo. He had entered Prince Juan's service in 1490, and his description of the court, completed in 1548 after more than a decade of intermittent work, offers observations not merely on the prince's household, but also, by extension, insights into the court of the monarch as well. In a way that perhaps would not have been unfamiliar to Nuñez de Castro in the seventeenth century, Oviedo adjudged the royal court to be more than just a residence for kings and princes. He, too, saw it as an integral part of the governance of the realm: 'as it is commonly said (and it is true), there are six offices in Castile which oversee all the authority and conformity of the kingdom and its royal crown'.[7] The principal officers were first, of course, the monarch himself, followed by the heir to the throne, and then the archbishop of Toledo, the head of the

was not specified by Oviedo, but the position of the office of *mayordomo mayor*, even in the prince's household, was so important as to provide a classic instance of the way in which royal service could subvert the traditional aristocratic hierarchies. Oviedo recalled that he had many times witnessed the *mayordomo mayor* serve the prince at table (always, paradoxically, a responsibility that indicated superiority of rank), even when members of the titled nobility of higher social standing than himself were present.[9] Household office, and the princely favour that its possession indicated, could thus trump the proudest grandee.

There was one office, however, that almost all agreed was even better than that of *mayordomo mayor*, even if supposedly slightly inferior in rank. The *camarero mayor*, or chamberlain, was 'in the opinion of many…the best job in the royal household'. The reason for this was simple: it gave 'the most access and familiarity to the person of the prince', and thus the holder could justifiably be called 'his secret counsellor'.[10] At night the *camarero* would be informed by the prince what he wished to wear the following day; in the morning he would hand the clothes to the prince's valet; and the prince's guards, the *monteros de Espinosa* (who were primarily associated with protecting the sovereigns of Castile), would not leave their posts outside the royal bedchamber until they had heard the *camarero* and the prince in conversation the following morning.[11]

It is apparent, then, that the Castilian court was highly ritualized well before the Habsburgs came to power in Spain with the accession in 1516 of King Carlos I of Castile and Aragon, better known to history as the Holy Roman Emperor Charles V. Conceivably, this degree of Castilian ceremoniousness went some way towards making up for the abandonment of the ceremony of coronation after the Trastámaran usurpation of the Castilian throne at the end of the fourteenth century.[12] For, while Castilian kings were no longer crowned, there was no actual shortage of symbol-laden ritual contrived to exalt the person of the monarch. For instance, water, so redolent of religious purity and of liturgical practice, featured prominently in the life of Prince Juan's court during the 1490s, as it was later to do under the Habsburgs. When the prince was dressing of a morning, it was the *camarero*'s solemn duty to hand him a vessel with water to wash his hands, though he would cede this honorific position to the Constable of Castile (himself the *camarero mayor* of the king and queen) whenever he happened to be present.

This ritualized serving of water also found a place in the formalities of royal dining. The prince's drinking water had to be the best available from the district, and had to be kept preserved from contamination 'under lock and key'. In a particularly elaborate choreography, it was the duty of the cupbearer, or *copero,* to proffer water to the prince on bended knee whenever he required it.[13] When the ewer of water was returned to the buffet it was preceded by a mace-bearer and followed by a page with an axe. The *copero* would hand the ewer to a servant and then turn to face the table, to await the next indication of princely thirst.[14]

Such levels of ceremony were maintained and extended during the subsequent reigns. On Queen Isabella's death in 1504, the throne passed to her daughter Juana the Mad (1504–55), who seems to have maintained a court very similar in form to that of her late brother Prince Juan.[15] Although Juana's Habsburg husband Philip the Fair briefly ruled in Castile (1504–6), and tried to introduce Burgundian court etiquette into his adopted land, the Use of Burgundy was not a prominent feature of Spanish court life until after the accession of the future Charles V as King of Castile in 1516. Again, most of what we understand about Charles's court

ceremonial derives from a single memoir. At the instance of Philip II, the Count of Chinchón asked Joan Sigonney to write down what he could remember of the ceremonial that was employed in the emperor's service in 1545.[16]

This memoir helped inspire a memorable passage by Sir John Elliott in which he pointed out that the organization of a court could undergo 'changes over time far more drastic than could ever be anticipated from the glacial and apparently immobile surface imposed by ceremonial and etiquette'.[17] Sigonney was astonished at how little of pristine Burgundian ceremonial was actually employed by the emperor.[18] He opined that 'it seems to me that his Majesty's household could not be more different from that of the Dukes of Burgundy'. Adulterations, he thought, had crept in with each royal marriage; when the Emperor Maximilian I had married Maria of Burgundy the previous century he had brought with him his German court: 'I understand', noted Sigonney disapprovingly, 'that this was when the Burgundian court began to lose some of its grandeur.' Philip the Fair had further compromised Burgundian ceremoniousness after his arrival in Castile in 1504; and, to cap it all, Sigonney believed that Maximilian had given the young Charles a household quite unlike that once prevalent in the households of the Dukes of Burgundy.

Charles V's attitude will come as something of a shock. When Sigonney asked the emperor why so little of the ritual associated with the Dukes of Burgundy was maintained in his service, he replied that 'just as they had the freedom to choose how *they* lived, then he too wanted the same not to imitate anything unpleasing to him'.[19] As far as Sigonney was concerned, precious little remained intact of Burgundian ritual, apart from the way in which the emperor was served on those occasions when he dined in public.[20] This was indeed the high point of royal ceremonial at the Spanish court for most of the sixteenth century – or at least this was the ritual most commented on by ambassadors and other observers. The room would be prepared for Charles's solemn entrance, usually after he had attended the chapel. The knives on his table would be arranged in the form of a Burgundian cross. On his arrival, the emperor would ritually wash his hands with great ceremony, and, at that precise moment, the dishes would be uncovered so that he could select what he wished to eat. Before the emperor sat down, the dinner would be blessed by the highest-ranking prelate present. When the emperor dined in public on the four great feasts of the Christian calendar – Christmas, Easter, Whitsun and All Saints – it was the duty of the *mayordomo mayor* to be in attendance, as well as on any other occasion when his presence was specifically required. Perhaps these rules were more

The whole pattern of life at the Spanish court, ceremonial and otherwise, underwent a sea-change in 1548. In that year Charles V (1516–56; Holy Roman Emperor from 1519) decided to reorganize the court of his son and heir Prince Philip along Burgundian lines. Don Fernando Álvarez de Toledo, third Duke of Alba (1507–82), one of the greatest Castilian grandees, was instructed by the emperor to oversee the changes. Many weeks of training were required to practise the new rituals, and large numbers of noblemen and servants had to be recruited to staff the new household; but on Assumption Day (15 August), the Prince of Spain dined in public for the first time according to the ceremonial rite accredited to the Dukes of Burgundy.

It is little wonder that the semi-official account of the prince's first visit beyond Spain began with an account of this rite of passage:

Once everything was in order and the household assembled, they began to serve according to the use of Burgundy on 15 August 1548, the Feast of the Our Lady. The Duque de Alba served as *mayordomo mayor*, along with Don Pedro de Avila, Marqués de las Navas, Don Pedro de Guzmán, Conde de Olivares, Gutierre López de Padilla, and Don Diego de Azevedo as *mayordomos* of the prince. All of them were attired in rich and dashing clothes, as were the gentlemen of the table and of the household. The plates were served with regal ceremony and display by kings-of-arms and mace-bearers clad in the royal livery.[21]

Given the obvious superfluity of offices that the new use required, it hardly comes as a surprise that the size of the prince's household doubled to more than 200 above-stairs officials. Where there had been only one chamberlain attending on the prince before, after 1548 the prince had a high steward (the *mayordomo mayor*) and five assistant chamberlains. He also gained over fifty 'gentlemen' with various ceremonial duties.[22]

What, then, of the freshly recruited courtiers who joined this newly augmented household? The

to hand it to the prince at dinner.[23]

At first sight, it is easy to see why such gestures have often been read as suggesting that the nobles who accepted such courtly office were politically domesticated, so to speak, by their personal service upon the monarch. Yet it would be wholly wrong to assume that ceremonial duties diminished the standing of court nobles. Far from it; such matters of precedence went to the heart of the aristocratic honour code. On one occasion, the question of who should proffer the royal napkin almost provoked an international incident. In July 1554 the Duke of Alba accompanied the future Philip II on his journey to marry Mary Tudor and assume the crown matrimonial of England. Alba was still *mayordomo mayor* to the 27-year-old Philip, as he was to remain for the rest of his life. Much to Philip's chagrin, his English subjects had hastily put together a Burgundian-style household for their new king. It was exclusively staffed by Englishmen, including its own English *mayordomo mayor*. Although a concession was made to the Spaniards whereby the son of the Duke of Infantado was permitted to act as cupbearer at the royal table, the Duke of Alba was forbidden to carry his wand of office as rival *mayordomo mayor*; indeed he even had to struggle to be permitted his prestigious, if purely ceremonial, right to pass the napkin to Philip. That this affront to the dignity of the duke, one of Castile's highest noblemen and among Europe's most celebrated soldiers, was acutely resented by his fellow Spaniards is instructive.[24] Far from being a matter of 'demeaning' the nobility, rights to serve at the royal table were badges of rank, jealously guarded and keenly competed for.

An obvious question arises: what prompted this decision to introduce full-blown Burgundian ceremonial into the Castilian court in 1548? One explanation might be that it was yet another innovation whereby 'everything possible…was done by means of both ceremonial and household organization to preserve the sacred character of kingship through the maintenance of distance'. In this interpretation, the monarch, 'as God's representative on earth', was being placed 'at the centre of a universe carefully designed to duplicate the harmonious ordering of the heavens'.[25] But, as we have seen, this description could just as well apply to the rich ceremonial of the Trastámaran court, and probably to many others. Indeed, courtly etiquette *always* serves to enhance the majesty of the sovereign and the numinous quality of kingship; it could hardly be otherwise. For these reasons, it will not do to say that the changes of 1548 simply made the young prince a figure of yet greater authority. We must examine further why the change occurred when it did.

Was there perhaps a vague wish to modernize the royal court, to put in place around the young prince a type of household less 'medieval' in its composition? Certainly the emperor was keen to keep the Spanish nobility at arm's length from political decision-making. The great men of the kingdom would henceforth be appointed to the new household offices as a reward for *personal* service, and no longer simply as a recognition of their pre-eminence in the realm. Charles's desire to put a distance between himself and the grandees of Spain is something he had made abundantly clear in the memorials he had written for his son as recently as 1543, when he warned the prince of the need to maintain his independence from the nobles; moreover, we only have to refer back to Oviedo's list of the six principal officers of the medieval kingdom of Castile to be reminded that some of the chief men in the kingdom owed their position to the very fact that they were officers in the royal household.

In a more 'medieval' conception of the court, court office and the great offices of state tended to go together. Under Ferdinand and Isabella, for instance,

the Constable of Castile was styled *mayordomo mayor*, not just of the household, but of the whole kingdom. The Burgundian system, on the other hand, operated upon quite different premises. Court office was strictly divorced from 'ministerial' office, or at least in theory. Perhaps Charles was indulging in a crude attempt to sponsor an early version of the 'separation of powers', as Christina Hofmann has implied; but if that was his intention, little was achieved.[26]

The multiplication of offices that was also a consequence of 'Burgundianization' could just as easily result in the leading families *increasing* their influence at court. When the Marquess of las Navas, for instance, was appointed one of the four *mayordomos* in Prince Philip's new household, his eldest son found employment as one of the prince's twenty-four *gentilhombres de la boca* (gentlemen servers at the table) and another son served the prince in an only slightly less exalted office.[27] Similarly, Ruy Gómez de Silva, Philip's *sumiller de corps* or groom of the stool, soon became his most trusted political adviser until his death, as Prince of Eboli, in 1573. Even if Philip bridled at the overbearing attitude of his most senior court officer, the Duke of Alba (whom he contemptuously called *tío* – uncle or old man), he made no attempt to oust the duke, and the irascible grandee died in office.[28]

Taking these changes as a whole, it is hard to avoid the conclusion that the changes to the court were the result of a political calculation by the emperor. He saw that there was an advantage to be gained in pandering to the historical and cultural sensibilities of some of his own subjects. The reasons were neither personal nor dynastic, rather they were programmatic. The emperor was trying not so much to impress his subjects in the Netherlands and Germany as to find common ground with them. Looking back at the 1530s, we can see that Castile was already well on the way to becoming the emperor's milch-cow, supplying not only soldiers but increasingly the funds to finance his many wars; at that time the emperor was more than happy to signal his family's identification with his principal Spanish kingdom by permitting his son and heir a Castilian-style household. [29] By the later 1540s, however, the emperor's mind was concentrated on events in and around Germany. His great victory at Mühlberg in 1547 had revived not only his chances of subjugating the Lutheran principalities of Germany,

The Casa Real del Pardo, nine kilometres north-west of Madrid, was one of a series of royal hunting lodges easily accessible from the capital. As with most European courts, the dictates of the chase were the principal determinant of where the prince's household chose to reside during the year.

but also fired him with a desire to thwart his brother Ferdinand's intention of succeeding him as emperor. Charles V concluded that a Burgundian 'image' was what Prince Philip required in order to win over his future subjects in northern Europe; hence it is no coincidence that these momentous decisions about the prince's household were taken before the prince's great tour of Italy, Germany and the Low Countries.

This explanation of the reforms of 1548 has important implications for an understanding of the early modern court. The court can too easily be seen as representing itself to the people, or at least to the 'political nation', that small minority of people that made up the governing classes of early modern Europe; but spectators might also have expectations

that could play an active role in the fashioning of the court. Rightly or wrongly, the emperor seems to have believed that a sizeable number of his subjects within the Holy Roman Empire would discern, in the adoption of a Burgundian-style court in Spain, a signal of reassurance that Charles's numerous lands and territories would not become subordinate to an entirely Castilian-dominated empire.

What reassured the emperor's northern subjects was, by the same token, viewed with resentment by his Castilian ones. Contrary to Professor Helen Nader's avowal that these changes 'aroused no hostility among Spaniards', the introduction of Burgundian etiquette into Spain was in fact bitterly controversial. The emperor had to be prepared to face down considerable opposition from the Castilian nobility in his efforts to make his Spanish-speaking heir, who knew next to nothing of German or Flemish, seem less strange and exotic to the peoples of Charles's northern realms.[30]

The degree to which the introduction of Burgundian household ritual was motivated by the emperor's preoccupations in Germany emerges clearly in Antonio Ossorio's seventeenth-century biography of the Duke of Alba, to whom it fell, as senior officer of the household, to implement the changes.[31] Basing his account partly on papers now lost, Ossorio describes how, when the duke received the emperor's command to reorganize the Castilian court along Burgundian lines, he warned his master of the dangers of an innovation that would be so 'injurious to the Spanish'. Although Charles expressed his regret that his subjects in Spain should take such exception to his plans, the emperor made plain to Alba in his reply that:

this concession [over Burgundian etiquette] is the only bond of affection to me that the German peoples possess, and they are anxious to display their loyalty through these nods in their direction. So, while the [Germans] can puff themselves up with this empty glory, Spaniards may take pride in the fact that they have defeated Germany not only in arms, but through reverence, chivalry and love.[32]

Alba's warnings were appropriate. A political storm blew up in Spain. In the Castilian Cortes, the representative assembly that met in Valladolid in April 1548, the procurators (the representatives of the cities) objected fiercely to the projected absence from the realm of the heir to the throne, as well as that of Charles. In particular, they fastened on to Charles's rejection 'of the majesty and customs of the monarchs of Castile' in favour of the new northern etiquette.[33] Such was the intensity of the controversy that it continued to be raised at meetings of the Cortes throughout the 1550s; and the need to provide Philip's own ten-year-old son, Don Carlos, with a household of his own in 1555 prompted renewed skirmishing over which of the two forms, the distance-creating Burgundian or the more inclusive Castilian, should prevail. Philip was asked 'to command that the Use of these kingdoms of Castile be employed, and not that of the House of Burgundy, so that the sons of the

great lords and the knights could be of service, and *that his highness would get to know them and, coming to like them, show them signs of favour*, as this would be of great benefit to these your kingdoms'.[34] As late as 1593 the Cortes was still calling for the re-introduction of Castilian ceremonies, but despite recurrent requests it was the usage of Burgundy that prevailed.[35]

The rituals prescribed for Philip by his father in 1548 provided, almost without variance, the formal basis for court ceremonial, not only for the remainder of the sixteenth century, but throughout the time the Habsburgs ruled in Spain. The structure of the court also remained fundamentally unaltered. As we have seen, the chief officer was the *mayordomo mayor*, or lord high steward. Second in the hierarchy came the *camarero mayor*, or great chamberlain; and completing the trinity of leading officials was the *caballerizo mayor*, or master of the horse. Among his many duties, the *mayordomo mayor* was responsible for feeding and housing the hundreds of officials in his charge, and both he and the great chamberlain were automatically entitled to rooms in the palace or in nearby houses, whereas the master of the horse could merely hope that he and his own servants would be lodged within the palace or its immediate vicinity. Among the *mayordomo mayor*'s most prestigious ceremonial duties were to hand the monarch his napkin at table and to precede the him, wand of office in hand, whenever he processed to mass as well as to dinner.[36] More mundanely, he was also responsible for administering the oaths of office to other members of the household, dealing with all disciplinary matters at court, and overseeing the accounts.

As we have seen, the chamberlain's duties brought him into more intimate contact with the king. Indeed, under Philip II, the office of *camarero* was superseded by that of the *sumiller de corps*, or groom of the stool (as the English Earl of Clarendon translated the term in the seventeenth century), the officer who attended the monarch on his close-stool.[37] But whether as groom or chamberlain, the duties of the office were to supervise life in the monarch's private chambers and to be present when the monarch rose in the morning, ate and went to bed. It was the duty of the *camarero* or the *sumiller*, for instance, ceremonially to draw back the curtain from the royal bed, just as it

Madrid's Real Alcázar, or royal fortress (top left): the principal seat of government for the Iberian kingdoms under Philip II and his immediate successors. Bullfights are taking place on either side of the Bridge of Segovia (foreground).

had been the *camarero*'s duty in Prince Juan's household to attend his master in the morning.[38] This degree of privileged access to the royal person was what made the office of much greater practical and political significance than that of *mayordomo*; and in the reigns of Philip III and IV (Philip II's son and grandson), as the monarchs of Spain became less directly involved in day-to-day administration than their counterparts in the sixteenth century, the office of *sumiller* became *the* principal office coveted by courtier-politicians. Spain was a personal monarchy

and, within it, it was the groom who enjoyed both access to and, in consequence, influence over the king – even if, as John Elliott has wisely proposed, it is to be assumed that Lerma and Olivares came to some sort of arrangement with their masters whereby they did not have to sleep on a pallet-bed in the royal apartments, as strict etiquette required. Indeed, it is no coincidence that both these ministers combined their roles as *sumiller* with that of master of the horse, thereby gaining the right to regulate the king's life both inside and outside the royal residence.

III. THE COURT-CITY: MADRID AND THE NETWORK OF ROYAL PALACES

When Philip complained to his father about the poor state of the royal palace in Madrid, his father apparently replied that 'kings do not need residences'.[39] But when he finally returned to Spain in 1559, after four years as a 'royal commuter' travelling between England and the Low Countries, King Philip II (1556–98) adopted a radically different point of view. As far as he was concerned, he had already fulfilled one prime kingly duty by having proven himself at war, at St Quentin, in the struggle against the French, in August 1557. He could now retire from the battlefield with honour and return to Castile, the one realm where he felt at home culturally, linguistically and religiously. The original destination of his court was imperial Toledo, Castile's ecclesiastical capital. Within a year or so, however, Philip had decided to move the court to the small but vibrant town of Madrid, some eighty kilometres to the north of Toledo. Whether or not it was what he intended from the outset, the days of an itinerant court in Spain were almost at an end.[40]

Various considerations prompted the move. Traditionally (and plausibly), it has been argued that Philip's French-born consort, Isabel de Valois, inspired the change; she disliked Toledo, and told her mother, Queen Catherine de Médicis (the consort of Henri II of France), that were it not for the company of her husband, the city would be one of the most disagreeable places in the world. It seems likely that Philip also had his own reasons for actively disliking Toledo. It was evident that a modern court could not operate in the narrow, winding and vertiginous streets of Toledo. The carriage was fast replacing horseback as the only decorous means for princes and high officials to travel, but in Toledo 'it was difficult in some streets to ride a horse, and in the majority a carriage was out of the question'.[41] Moreover, sharing the city with the archbishop, who was primate of Spain, was at times uncomfortable for all concerned; there were constant battles over the boundaries between the jurisdiction of the court and that of the Church.[42] Around Madrid, on the other hand, there was far better hunting in the mountains than anything that Toledo had to offer, and

for a king as passionate about the chase as the young Philip II this was of overriding importance.

Above all, the single most important reason behind the move was the need permanently to house a royal household that was far larger than any court that Spain had hitherto known. This was the enduring legacy of the court's Burgundian reorganization in 1548, and it was something that representatives in the Cortes understood full well when they had appealed for the restoration of a Castilian-style court, as 'appropriate, very ancient, and less costly' than that of Burgundy.[43] Under the new regimen, not only did the king's household have to move, but arrangements had also to be made for the staff employed in the households of the queen, the Crown Prince Don Carlos, the king's sister Juana and in the household of their half-brother, Don Juan of Austria. In addition, ambassadors from all the major European courts had to be catered for, as well as members and officials of the Councils of State, Castile, Aragon, the Indies and the various military orders; on the ecclesiastical side, there was the staff of the Chapels Royal to house, and the Inquisition. Such was the pressure even in Madrid that certain ecclesiastics had to be lodged in Alcalá de Henares, the university town to the east of Madrid. Perhaps the most striking indication of the logistical upheaval is to be found in the figures for baptisms in Madrid. In 1560 the surviving registers for Madrid indicate that there were 242 christenings; in 1562, this figure had reached 627, an increase of some 174 per cent over the figure for the year before the move began.[44]

The size of the court seems to have remained roughly constant from the time that the Burgundian etiquette was introduced until well into the seventeenth century. In 1549, for example, it was reported that 1,500 servants accompanied the Prince of Spain on his visit to northern Europe. For the 1620s it has been calculated that there were about 1,700 household officials to be paid and fed.[45] According to Nuñez de Castro, the mid-century court cost at least 670,000 ducados a year to run.[46] His figure seems accurate enough; on 20 May 1658, for instance, the palace treasurers revealed that they had no money at all to pay the monthly costs of the household, which they estimated at some 50,000 ducados.[47]

Just as the king had his own household, so too did the queen and the royal children. The most famous of

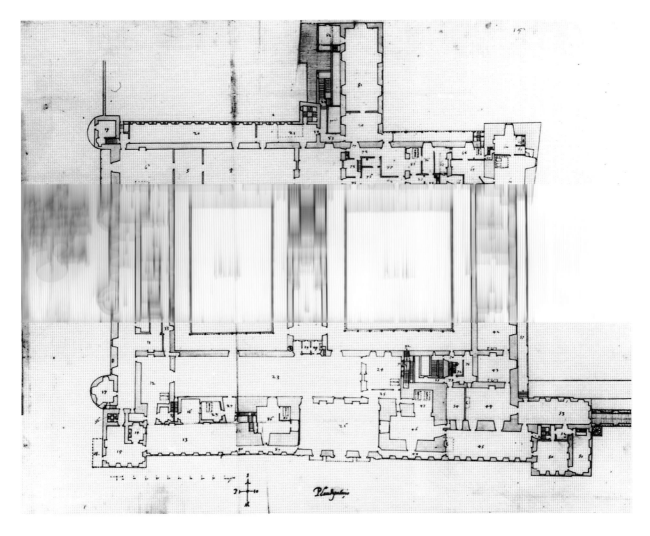

Plan of the principal floor of the Alcázar in Madrid in 1626. Rooms 4–6 are the sequence of first, second and third antechambers, approached by the double flight of stairs (centre). The central range of the palace, containing the court chapel (30), divides the King's Courtyard (left) from the Queen's Courtyard (right). The king's study (15) with its private oratory (14) are in the tower (lower left). The large salón de comedias (23) was the principal setting for court ceremonial and entertainments. The ground floor (not shown) contained the apartments of other members of the royal family and the meeting rooms of the principal royal councils. As with most royal courts, the spheres of the 'administration' and 'household' overlapped and formed complementary parts of a single entity.

these was perhaps that of Philip II's sister and sometime regent of Spain, Princess Juana. She established in Madrid the convent of the Descalzas Reales, where she lived after her semi-retirement from political life in the 1560s. Part palace, part museum for some of the Spanish monarch's most prized paintings and portraits, the convent continued to provide a home for other female members of the royal family throughout the seventeenth century. During the visits of foreign princes, these too were usually provided with their own households at the king's expense. During the visit of Charles, Prince of Wales, in 1623, for instance, it was felt only proper for the prince to be given his own Burgundian-style household: the Count of

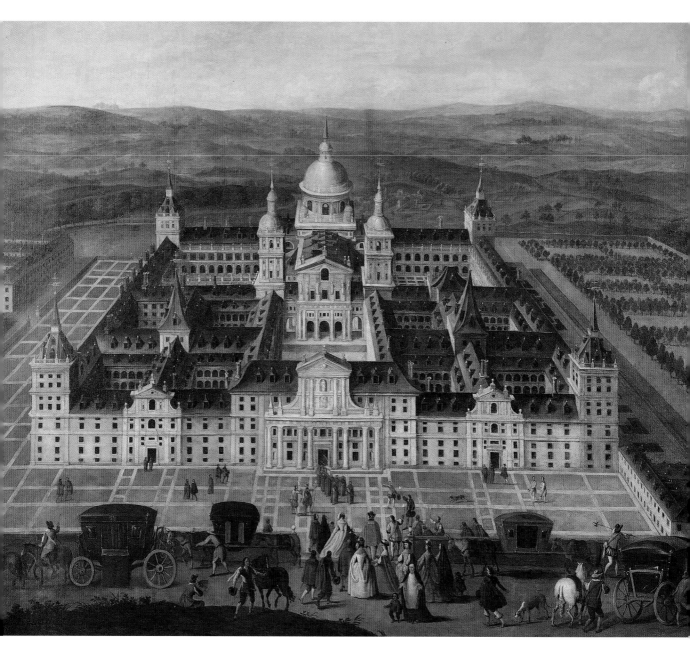

Monterrey was named as his *mayordomo mayor*, along with two assistants, sixteen gentlemen of the table, as well as other lesser officials.[48]

It is testimony to the grandeur of Philip II's conception of what his court should be that his plans involved far more than merely relocating it to Madrid. It included the need for massive rebuilding both within the town and around it. The old royal palace, the Real Alcázar, built on the site of a Moorish castle, had already been enlarged and

redecorated in his father's time. Rooms on the ground floor, immediately below the royal family's apartments, were rebuilt for each of the dozen or so principal royal councils, and here they continued to work when Philip went to the Escorial to keep Christmas and Easter, and when he left the capital during the summer. Indeed, even when, in the early 1580s after the union with Portugal, Philip spent almost two and a half years residing in Lisbon in the hope that his presence might assist the peaceful

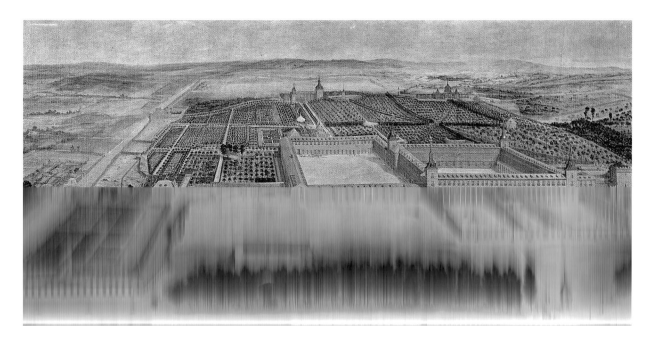

Above: *El Buen Retiro, the largest of Philip IV's palaces (built 1629–40), set in an 'ordered landscape' of formal gardens, fountains and decorative woodland; a painting dating from around 1636 by Jusepe Leonardo.*
Left: *El Escorial, built by Philip II between 1563 and 1584, viewed circa 1610. Dominated by the centrally placed Basilica of St Lawrence, the monastery when completed was the largest in the Spanish kingdoms. While it was the favourite retreat of Philip II, the building was always intended as an ostentatious act of royal piety, not as a seat of the court.*

incorporation of the newly acquired kingdom into his composite monarchy,[49] the great councils of his empire remained resolutely in Madrid.[50]

Although the Alcázar in Madrid was home to a large number of the Spanish monarchy's innumerable councils, it was still but one of the monarch's many residences. From the start of his reign, Philip II planned the construction of a web of palaces with his palace in Madrid as centre – albeit a centre often without the king – of his courtly world. The Alcázar overlooked an obvious area where the king could build: the Casa del Campo was an enormous expanse of wooded land on the far side of the River Manzanares, and it joined up with another royal hunting ground, El Pardo. Here Philip built a whole series of royal residences, including the exquisite royal lodge of Torrelodones. To the south of Madrid, he enlarged the hunting lodge at Aranjuez. With inspiration from the rich gardens he had seen on his visits to

the Netherlands, the king ordered the construction of a series of grand, rectilinear, wooded avenues, each designed to lead the eye towards his new palace.

For Philip II and Philip III, the Real Alcázar in Madrid was the administrative centre of monarchy; in contrast, the smaller palaces and hunting lodges – particularly those at Aranjuez and in the woods of Segovia – were places of recreation. None the less it was San Lorenzo del Escorial that was to become emblematic of Philip II's court. Part monastery, part royal residence, the Escorial was built to honour Philip's victories at St Quentin and in propitiation for the consequent sacking of a church dedicated to St Lawrence. Moreover, the Escorial was intended to house the pantheon of the Spanish Habsburgs, and the remains of Charles V were taken from his monastic restreat at Yuste and solemnly interred there in 1574.

More than any other royal residence, the peculiar layout of the Escorial embodies the most distinctive

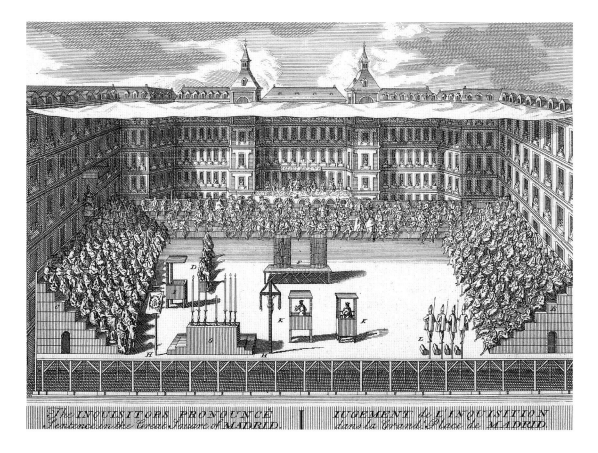

The court's affirmation of orthodoxy: a seventeenth-century auto-da-fé *in the Plaza Mayor of Madrid, watched by the king and queen from their canopied balcony (centre). The condemnation of the accused is accompanied by preaching for the edification of the royal household and the citizens of Madrid. The actual executions took place on the outskirts of the city, out of sight of the court.*

however, an exception largely confined to the last decades of Philip II's reign. For most of the seventeenth century, the Castilian court was once again to be governed by an etiquette that became a byword for solemnity and inflexibility throughout Europe.

To some extent that same solemnity can be discerned in the artistic patronage of the court, at least under Philip II. Although his father was never a great collector (apart from building a Renaissance palace in Granada, his artistic legacy to Spain was extremely limited), Philip more than made up for this. He collected not only objects but also information. He was responsible for commissioning systematic enquiries into the flora and fauna of the recently discovered lands of his empire – to this day the vast library in the Escorial remains one of the great centres

of study for the history of man, beast and plant in the New World. Landscape gardening was also one of the king's passions, but above all he was a collector of paintings. Philip is rightly regarded as the founder of Spain's great national collection of paintings, and its eclecticism, ranging as it does from Italian masterpieces of the quattrocento to the great canvases of Hieronymus Bosch, is a testament to the king's catholicity of taste.

Patronage of the arts had been stepped up in the late 1540s. In a move not unrelated to the introduction of Burgundian etiquette, the late 1540s and early 1550s were a period of dynastic self-fashioning by Charles V. There was a perceptible change in his pictorial image of these years. Titian's portrait of Charles V after the Battle of Mühlberg (1547) brilliantly fused the imagery of imperial Rome – an emperor astride a horse – with all the chivalric aspirations of a knight in armour;[62] in the early 1550s the artist also executed a similar chivalric portrait of Philip. After the deaths of Charles and his sister Maria of Hungary in 1558, many of the great emblematic pictures of the emperor's hopes and aspirations for this troublesome decade were shipped to Spain. However, highly dramatized and symbol-laden portraiture did not accord with the 'hidden monarchy' increasingly espoused by Philip.

these portraits is less an indication of the artists own inclinations and techniques than a calculated reflection of the new distancing of the monarchy. A comparison with the portraits of Philip's former sister-in-law Elizabeth I is instructive. In portraits of the Virgin Queen there is an abundance of classical imagery, ostentatious dress and even the depiction of royal regalia. In Spanish royal portraits of the second half of the sixteenth century there is a studied absence of such outward signs of royalty. This style of restrained portraiture continued during the reigns of Philip III and Philip IV, even in the masterpieces produced by the court painter Diego Velázquez (1599–1660), the royal status of his sitters remains implicit rather than explicit. Among the many meanings that can be given to the great *Las Meninas*, one that is all too often ignored is that of the hidden, yet *all-seeing*, monarchy: the king and queen are merely glimpsed as their reflections are caught in a mirror while they watch the painter at work. A hidden monarchy could still exercise a watching brief, so it is no surprise that the Sala Real of the Palace of El Pardo, to the north-west of Madrid, said to be 'the most ornate and majestic room that his Majesty possesses', contained no fewer than forty-five royal portraits in the 1580s.[63]

Of course, the decoration of royal palaces was not confined to portraiture. The prevailing theme of royal patronage in the sixteenth and seventeenth centuries is that of military victory, often the subject for tapestries. Charles V's adventures in Tunis were the

subject of a celebrated suite of tapestries, and the walls of the Buen Retiro were deliberately conceived as a shrine to Spain's military victories of the 1620s and 1630s. The Hall of Realms alone contained twelve monumental canvases in praise of Philip IV's victories, under the guiding hand, of course, of Olivares.[64] Even so, access to this and other palaces was restricted, and, as John Elliott has warned, in the absence of a native school of engraving, few people could gaze upon even copies of these marvels; the message was clearly

writing for the court. The Sala Grande of the old Alcázar, where the depiction of Philip II's victorious entry into Portugal had once hung, was converted into a room for theatrical performances. But just as the king and queen dined silently and with the minimum of movement, when they attended plays they were again treated as objects: the royal family sat alone, providing the standing courtiers with a spectacle every bit as important as the play or masque that was being performed.[65]

V. THE COURT AND THE CHURCH

In the Royal Chapel the old and the new ceremonial forms co-existed less than peaceably. The chapel had been reorganized along Burgundian lines in the great restructuring of the late 1540s, but points of conflict still remained. The work of the senior *limosnero,* or almoner – a Burgundian office – was persistently interfered with by the chief *capellán*, whose office dated back into Castile's medieval past. To avoid further irritation, Philip was obliged to appoint the same person to both offices in 1584, and two years later the chapel was reorganized yet again, this time 'according to the use of Castile and Burgundy', although it also drew upon the customs of Aragon and Flanders as well as the papal court.[66]

The close association of the Catholic monarch with the work of God was further emphasized in the ceremonies accompanying the monarch's public attendance at mass. When the royal family went to divine service in the Alcázar in Madrid on Sundays and feast days, special seats were put out for the ambassadors accredited to the court and for any high ecclesiastics or grandees who were present. Reserved for the exclusive use of the king and queen was the *cortina* (literally 'the curtain'), a canopied and curtained 'tabernacle' at the side of the altar from which the monarchs heard the liturgy, set apart from other mortals. The *cortina* powerfully symbolized the monarchs' special relationship to God.[67] They were hidden from view by a curtain in precisely the same way that a eucharistic tabernacle was screened from the gaze of those who came to worship.[68] This resulted in an impressive paradox: even on 'public' occasions the king remained for the most part screened and invisible. However, on ordinary days the palace's chapel doubled as the regular place of worship for those who worked in the building. The royal family would hear mass in their own oratories, adjacent to their apartments in the palace, and without formal processions. On 15 March 1555 Charles V had been granted special permission to use a portable altar in his room or anywhere else, and by the end of the reign of Philip III each of the royal children had their own private chapels.

In the Escorial, with its massive collegial church, the pious devotions of the monarch were more private still. The king and queen's minuscule apartments were located to either side of the high altar, where, from a window, they could observe mass while remaining invisible. Access to the basilica was heavily restricted, since it was exclusively conceived of as a royal chapel served by its own religious community. This was at the heart of Spain's 'hidden monarchy', a place where the king was concealed from the gaze of his subjects, as if he alone were in direct contact with the deity.

Under Philip III and Philip IV, however, the public life of the court became more overtly and publicly religious than it had hitherto been. The great processions of Easter Week remained the high-point of the liturgical year; but unlike the practice during the reign of Philip II, when these ceremonies had invariably taken place at the Escorial, witnessed only by a few of the king's subjects, under Philip IV they

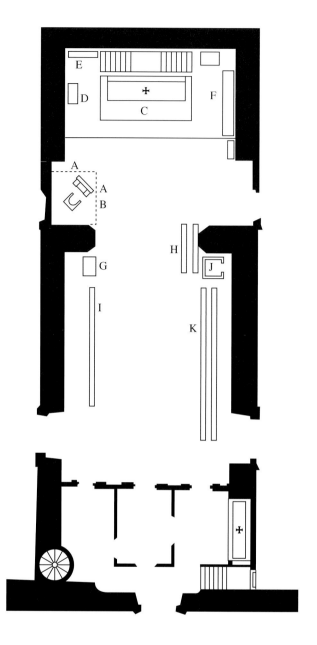

Plan of the royal chapel at the Alcázar in Madrid in the reign of Philip II. A: the royal cortina, *which curtained the king from view for most of the mass. B: the groom of the* cortina *(who drew the curtain for the king). C: the high altar. D: the capellan major. E: prelates. F: the* sedilia *of the officiating clergy. G: the mayordomo mayor. H: ambassadors. I: grandees of Spain. J: the pulpit. K: royal chaplains. As at El Escorial, the church was located on a central axial range, and formed the liturgical core of the palace, flanked by courtyards on either side. The processions to and from the chapel provided rare glimpses of the otherwise 'unseen majesty'.*

took place in Madrid. Here the king, in the courtyard of the Alcázar, participated in the ritualized Maundy Thursday washing and clothing of twelve poor men; the Good Friday veneration of the cross; and the spectacular celebrations of Easter Monday, one of the four principal occasions when he dined publicly in state.

The seventeenth-century emphasis on eucharistic devotion provided still further opportunities for the monarch to be seen in juxtaposition with the 'Body of Christ' held to be present in the consecrated commu-

for his subjects to view their monarch with any frequency, as on most Saturdays he would visit local shrines, especially that of the Virgin of Atocha. Such pilgrimages had an exemplary function, setting a pattern for the Counter-Reformation piety the monarch sought to foster throughout the kingdom. On one characteristic occasion, for instance, when Philip IV was returning from a *Te Deum* in 1634, the monarch noticed a priest carrying the viaticum (the consecrated host) to a dying parishioner. The king and his entourage dismounted and fell to their knees before the sacrament, and then accompanied the priest to witness the administration of the last rites.[69]

Conversely, the court was closely associated with the persecution of heresy and heterodoxy at home and abroad. Little wonder, then, that notwithstanding attendance at bull fights or other ritualized games, held mostly in Madrid's Plaza Mayor, the court was most spectacularly on view to the wider public when the royal family attended *autos-da-fé*, also held in the city's main square. Here relapsed heretics would be forced to recant their errors (or later be burned), while the king and his family, seated under a canopy, would view the proceedings impassively, looking for all the world like a statuesque group of the saints. On one spectacular occasion in June 1680, the king presided over the condemnation of twelve heretics. The king withdrew only after hearing mass, although before those sentenced to die were removed for execution.[70]

VI. THE VALIMIENTO

The political consequences of Spain's fusion of a 'hidden monarchy' with an increasingly hidebound etiquette surrounding the king are perhaps to be found in the emergence, by the end of the sixteenth century, of the *valido* or *privado*: the royal favourite. Trusted intimates of the king, these favourites became the *de facto* 'prime ministers' of the realm, regardless of whether they held actual ministerial office. The devel-

Thenceforth the realm's many councils could only begin discussion on a topic once the *privado*, Lerma, had indicated in writing that this was the king's pleasure. Concerning Lerma, Philip sent a message to his principal councillors in 1612 that not only lauded his *valido*, but also made clear the highly personalized nature of the arrangement between them:

Every day I am more satisfied with how he handles all matters I ask of him, and how well served I feel. Given this and how much he has helped me sustain the weight of state affairs, I order that you obey the duke in all matters. All members of the council are obliged to tell him all he wants to know, and although this system began from the moment I inherited these kingdoms, I have decided explicitly to tell and order you now.[72]

Lerma's hold on power lasted until October 1618, when he retired, or was forced, from office. It had depended on his personal relationship with the king, in particular on the intimacy he enjoyed as *sumiller,* or groom of the stole, an office he had acquired as early as December 1599, and that entitled him to accompany the king almost at all times, even on his visits to the queen.

'If Philip III was the laziest ruler that Spain has had,' one historian has observed, 'Lerma was incomparably the greediest'.[73] Both these statements are somewhat exaggerated, but it is still true that probably the most outrageous example of manipulation

Above: *An* auto-da-fé *in the Plaza Mayor, Madrid, 30 June 1680: one of a series of trials and condemnations of heretics, attended by the king and his entourage in public affirmation of the intimate bonds between the secular and the ecclesiastical powers. The royal presence (upper left) is marked, as usual, by a large canopy. A temporary altar (lower left) has been erected for the celebration of mass.*
Right: *Courtly devotion to the eucharist: Carlos II (1665–1700), the last Habsburg ruler of Spain, kneels with senior courtiers before the monstrance containing the consecrated host, or Corpus Christi. Encouraged by the Council of Trent, public adoration of the eucharist became a central feature of the devotional life of most Catholic princely households in the course of the seventeenth century.*

occurred in 1601–6, when Lerma persuaded his master to relocate his court to the northern city of Valladolid. In the fifteenth century Valladolid had enjoyed, far more than Toledo, the right to consider itself the premier city of Castile. Its monumental buildings, some on the banks of the River Pisuerga, and especially its churches and colleges, all easily outstripped anything provincial Madrid could offer.[74] Even so, the decision to move court and councils to Valladolid, far from being a bold act by a monarch who knew his own mind (as was the case with Philip II's removal from Toledo in 1561), was little more than

an illustration of the hold that Lerma exercised over the indolent Philip III. Valladolid, in the heart of Old Castile, was precisely where Lerma wished to consolidate his landholdings and regional influence. For almost seven years the king's favourite had his monarch exactly where he wanted him, within the confines of his own local power-base.

Since a *valimiento* ('rule by favourite') was so dependent upon the personal will of the sovereign, a change of monarch would normally lead to the rise of a new favourite. With the accession of Philip IV in 1621, it was the Count-Duke of Olivares who dominated

La historia general delas Indias.

Con priuilegio imperial.

Under the Emperor Charles V (King Carlos I of Castile), the Castilian court became the administrative and cultural hub of a world-wide empire. Fernández de Oviedo's General History of the Indies *(1535), one of the many works issued to celebrate the dynasty's newly won possessions, ostentatiously displays the emperor's arms, surrounded by the collar of the Order of the Golden Fleece.*

political life from the moment his master ascended the throne until his own honourable retirement in 1643. Anxious to avoid the opprobrium that had been heaped upon Lerma in his heyday, Olivares at first adopted a low-profile as royal favourite, allowing his uncle Baltasar de Zúñiga to adopt the role of chief minister, while he pretended to desire no more than his place as *sumiller*. Even after his uncle's death in October 1622, Olivares continued to represent himself more as a minister than as a mere favourite, in order to avert

senior councillors. As John Elliott and Jonathan Brown have demonstrated, the building of a new palace for Philip IV, the Buen Retiro on Madrid's eastern edge, was partly an attempt by Olivares to emasculate the king's authority by capturing him within a palace that was in fact a gilded cage, an intention not dissimilar to Lerma's removal of the court to Valladolid.[75] In stark contrast to the Escorial, the new Retiro offered ample space not only for theatrical productions – a personal passion of Philip IV – but also a lake large enough to stage mock sea-battles or *naumachia*.[76] Indeed, the amenities of the Buen Retiro allowed the king to offer entertainments to his courtiers on a scale previously unseen at the Spanish court. Critics dismissed the Buen Retiro as no more than a *gallinero* (a chicken coop) where Olivares could rule the roost through his monopoly of the principal offices. Yet the building of the Buen Retiro set a pattern for the management of the Spanish court that endured with relatively little fundamental change until the end of the seventeenth century. In the reign of Carlos II (1665–1700), the last of the Spanish Habsburgs, the court continued to be the centre of political intrigue. Deformed, melancholy and afflicted with poor health, Carlos was rightly called the *hechizado*, the bewitched; with little interest in the government of his empire, what passed for political life was dominated by his mother, the Queen-Regent Mariana (widow of Philip IV), and a succession of self-interested *validos* whose mark on history is negligible.

VII. CONCLUSION

Ludwig Pfandl, one of the greatest twentieth-century historians of court and society in early modern Spain, remarked that with the introduction of Burgundian etiquette the royal palace in Madrid had already become 'a large and magnificent prison'.[77] While it may now be conceded that Charles V and Philip II were powerful monarchs, who were able to use the court as an instrument of statecraft, Pfandl's remark

were stifled by the stiffness of a court that rotated as if in permanent orbit around their capital city.

Although the costs of the royal household were constantly criticized, both inside and outside the Cortes, there was also a prevailing sense amongst contemporaries that the outward magnificence of the court was an indispensable part of the conduct of Castilian diplomacy. To diminish it was to imperil dynastic, and hence national, prestige.

Perhaps the shrewdest commentary on this need for balance between magnificence and austerity was provided by that perceptive observer of the Spanish court of Philip IV, Nuñez de Castro. He was keenly aware of the need for Spanish monarchs and their courts to be resplendent, but he also knew that there was a fine line between magnificence and ostentation. 'If there is to be respect, we see how necessary it is for there to be some outward show, for that is what distinguishes kings from other men', adding that, 'the deftness lies in knowing how to make this veneration possible without causing offence to vassals, and to bring together all the majesty of the throne, the pomp of the palace, the magnificence of the royal family to achieve the admiration of all but without giving cause for anyone to demur'.[78] This, he said, had been achieved at the court of his master Philip IV. The question remains whether it had been achieved far better at the courts of Charles V and Philip II.

CHAPTER TWO

The Kingdoms of France and Navarre
THE VALOIS
AND BOURBON COURTS

still largely uncharted territory.[1] Long overshadowed by the cata-
clysm of the Revolution that swept them away, French
historiography has traditionally dwelt far more on 'heroic' Jacobins
and Girondins than on the supposedly decadent courtiers of pre-revolutionary
France. More recently, the court has been further obscured by an approach to
the *ancien régime* via the unhelpful terms of social class, and by the rigid demarca-
tion lines between academic disciplines and historical specialisms.[2] The court,
therefore, has too often been overlooked or misunderstood, featuring, at best, as
a distant collective memory.[3] Much of the older writing on the French court has
been little more than a bundle of facile and misleading legends and endlessly
recycled anecdotes. Yet, for all that the court continues to be largely *terra incog-
nita*, it is far from being a foreign country: the court lies at the very centre of
history of early modern France.

For the court cannot be reduced simply to the upper reaches of society glibly
defined as the 'higher nobility'. In fact, it included several social groups. As an
institution whose shape varies with the seasons and with political developments,
capable of taking the form now of a travelling town, now of a military camp, it
calls for a social or, rather, a socio-cultural approach; but, in its diversity, it also
has dimensions relevant to the history of the family, of politics and economics,
and of the Church – to name but a few. We should not confine ourselves to that
supposedly timeless and changeless image that Louis XIV's court created for

*Louis XIV and the Grand Dauphin at Versailles' Grotto of Thetis, dedicated to
the Nereid who, in classical legend, was the mother of Achilles. Completed in 1668, the
grotto was eventually demolished in 1694 to make way for the new court chapel.
The image of the king as the sun whose rays reach all parts of the realm, visible in the
architectural background, belied a more complex and ambiguous series of relations
connecting the court and the provinces of the realm.*

itself, nor should we forget that the king never had a complete monopoly of the court or courtliness: it was long the case that members of the royal family and other great magnates had their own courts, even if the household of *le roi soleil* put the others into the shade.[4]

In his *Dictionnaire* of 1690, Antoine Furetière gave more than one definition of *la cour*. On the one hand, he stated, it is the place where the king lives; but it could also designate the king and his council, the officers and entourage of the prince, or, more generally, the courtly way of life. Despite this variety, the court was fundamentally the group formed by the royal family and its servants; but it was also the heart of the burgeoning monarchical state, a social institution that, in the late seventeenth and early eighteenth centuries, basked in an increasing brilliance purchased at the price of an ever stricter internal discipline.

I. THE ROYAL FAMILY OF FRANCE

At the centre of the court was the immediate family of the king. Indeed, it often tended towards the extended family, since two couples would often live together: the royal couple, and the family of the son and heir who had to await his father's death before acceding to the throne.[5] Among the royal children, the leading figure was inevitably the heir, the dauphin (styled Monseigneur under Louis XIV), while the younger brothers and the grandsons in the direct line were known by the title of their (usually ducal) apanage – Orléans, Anjou, Berry. The daughters and the granddaughters in the direct line were known by their forename with the title Madame.

Accordingly, the life of the court was punctuated by family occasions. There were the royal marriages, although these did not always take place in the capital, especially when the monarch or the dauphin was marrying a foreign princess whom he had to greet at the border. That said, the 'daughters of France' tended towards celibacy: *mesdames filles*, the daughters of Louis XV, almost all remained spinsters, with those that lived long enough becoming *mesdames tantes* (the 'lady aunts') to Louis XVI.[6]

Second only to the dynastic rituals of marriage were the courtly celebrations of births and baptisms.

Childbirth was almost a public ritual: a veritable crowd of onlookers, for example, witnessed the labour of Marie de Médicis, the consort of Henri IV (1589–1610), at Fontainebleau in 1601; their presence as observers served to allay any doubts as to the authenticity of the birth. Children were an intermittent presence at court, and their numbers often sharply fluctuated.

In a dynastic system in which so much depended on the monarch, the illnesses of the king and his heir set the whole court on tenterhooks. Would the monarch's demise mean an end to favour? The prospect of a prompt return to grace? Or the frustration of lengthy manoeuvres with a view to winning the friendship of the future king? The court kept watch, bristled with rumours and held its breath while prayers were offered up in the churches according to courtiers' sense of loyalty or ambition. When the king died the grand master of France broke his staff, the symbol of his office, indicating the dissolution of the old court pending the reconstruction of the new. But the break between regimes became less clear-cut during the sixteenth century as the mystique of the blood royal and the concept of hereditary sovereignty became entrenched. These doctrines, with their emphasis on the lineal transmission of the divine right to rule from father to son, rendered obsolete the fiction of the 'king's two bodies' (the idea that the king had an undying body *qua* king, while he occupied a mortal, corruptible body as a man), and the custom according to which, since 1422, the royal funeral effigy had shown the king as if he were still alive.[7] Henri IV was depicted in such an effigy after his death in 1610, but the reign of his son, the boy-king Louis XIII, opened with a *lit de justice* (a solemn judicial ceremony before the Parlement of Paris) that took everyone by surprise by its prompt affirmation of the continuity of absolute sovereignty. The 'two bodies' were reunited in the person of the new king, who appeared on the throne at the *lit* already crowned, the 'living image of the dead' in the words of the parliamentary president Achille Harlay. From the death of Henri IV onwards, the royal funeral lost the essence of its political content. Heredity, blood and the indivisible sovereignty that accompanied it were now the new order.

Henceforth the royal family enjoyed a quite exceptional status, an elevated quasi-sanctified rank that extended to all those with the blood of St Louis in their veins. The origins of this trend towards elevations of the royal siblings can be traced to the mid sixteenth century when the concept of the 'princes of the blood' gained currency. During the late sixteenth century, the Valois and the Bourbons both found themselves in this emerging category. Once the Bourbons attained the throne in the person of Henri IV, the family's cadet branch of Condé and its own offshoot of Conti stepped into the role of princes of

[several lines illegible/faded]

...enth century the princes of the blood established their precedence over the peers of France.[8]

The princes of the blood also had to reckon with a 'parallel' royal family, the royal bastards: the illegitimate offspring of the reigning king, and the descendants of those of his predecessors. Neither the Valois nor the Bourbons were short of illegitimate brothers and cousins born of various mistresses, but for all the promotion of the royal bastards, most conspicuously by Louis XIV (1643–1715), there was one crucial distinction: these illegitimate offspring never had a formal 'household' of their own; that was a privilege reserved to the 'children of France'.

II. THE ROYAL HOUSEHOLDS

The court was, thus, never a single household. The king and queen, together with the king's brothers and sisters, and the children of the royal couple: each had their own households, with the sole exception of the dauphin, who was attended by the officers of his father. Thus, the number of households varied with the size of the royal family. The king's household was of course always the largest,[9] and the arrangements for the service of the king himself were codified by Henri III (1574–89) in 1578. In fact, the Maison du Roi was a series of distinct households-within-a-household, each presided over by one of the great officers of the court. First, there were those responsible for the

king's 'immortal soul'. The ecclesiastical household was made up of the royal confessor, king's almoners (who distributed the king's charity), chaplains, preachers and other clerics, all under the authority of the grand almoner.

Then came the civil household, under the direction of the *grand maître,* or grand master, of France, which was itself divided into several sub-departments. Pre-eminent were the so-called 'Seven Offices': Gobelet (or Goblet, responsible for serving the king's

[several lines illegible/faded]

...procured other victuals and goods for the royal household). At their head was a butler who supervised their activities and a subordinate, a butler-in-ordinary. Daily service at the royal table was carried out by the butlers and by noble servants.[10] The great crown offices once linked to service at the royal table disappeared in the reforms of 1578, giving way to such offices as first officer of the pantry, first cupbearer and first carver, held by men of much less-exalted birth.

Beyond those serving the king's immediate needs was a third department, the Chambre du Roi, or King's Chamber, under the authority of the grand chamberlain, and the four senior gentlemen of the Chamber, all of senior noble rank, held places of great prestige. These great noblemen in fact enjoyed less intimacy with the king than the four senior valets of the Chamber, who attended on the king's personal needs. Such men acquired considerable influence, witness the famous Alexandre Bontemps so highly regarded by Louis XIV. After these four senior valets came a swarm of lower-ranking officials, including the ordinary valets of the Chamber, the royal pages and a miscellany of specialized officers, including barbers and watchmakers. Completing the principal departments of the household was the Wardrobe, responsible for the furnishing of the king's houses and the apartments of the senior courtiers. From Louis XIV's reforms of 1669, it was managed by a grand master and a second master, each of them holding office for one year and assisted by various pages and valets. To regulate diplomatic etiquette and other aspects of court ritual, a grand master of ceremonies was appointed from 1585 to preside over court ceremonial, with the help of a master of ceremonies and an assistant. That said, ambassadors were usually taken care of by sponsors who were entirely independent of these ceremonial officials.

Controlling most aspects of the court out-of-doors was the Ecurie du Roi, or Royal Stables. From 1582 this was further sub-divided into a Grande Ecurie, responsible for the transport of the court on special ceremonial occasions, and the Petite Ecurie, a largely autonomous body that provided for everyday transport needs. When the court settled at Versailles each branch of the Ecurie was housed in magnificent premises facing the royal residence at the head of the avenues that provided the axial approaches to the palace. The housing of the court during its travels was the responsibility of the grand marshal of the lodgings (*grand mareschal de logis*), also responsible for the billeting of the guards who formed the king's military household.

Separate again, and providing the principal courtly recreation, was the office of the Chasses Royales, the Royal Hunt, sub-divided into Hounds, Falconry and Louveterie (responsible for the hunting of wolves in order to protect other game), each with its own head, but together under the general supervision of the captain general of the hunt (*capitain général des chasses*), himself specifically responsible for the hunting of wild boar.[11]

The king was traditionally protected by a personal guard of Scottish, French and Swiss troops, whose numbers expanded more or less in line with the court, growing into a small army, which, by 1671, was known as the 'military household'. In 1710 this numbered more than 10,000 men.[12] By 1660 the French guards, light horse, gentlemen at arms, Swiss guards and, in due course, the musketeers had come to comprise an élite and highly privileged corps under the authority of the secretary of state of the king's household (*secrétaire d'état de la Maison du roi*). Thanks in part to the venality (or sale for profit) of military offices, these forces readily attracted recruits, who distinguished themselves in action in the seventeenth century and were not spared in even the bitterest military engagements; only in the course of the eighteenth century were they to become less reliable in royal service.

Thus, household service to the king and his family was the basic function of the court long before it became a centrally important political institution in the course of the sixteenth century, one of its central functions thereafter. The court was in its own way a 'perfect' (or complete) society in the sense in which the great Counter-Reformation Cardinal Roberto Bellarmino (1542–1621) used that term of the Church: a society possessed of all the means necessary to attain its particular objective (in this case, the glorification of the king). Far from being merely an assemblage of the higher nobility drawn in from the various provinces of the realm, it was a whole society in miniature, with its own priests, soldiers, officials, tradesmen and domestic servants. It had its own sophisticated social dynamics, and court service famously provided a means for families of the lower or middling nobility to rise in the social hierarchy. The descendants of Louis de Pas of Picardy, butler to François I (1515–47), for example, became Marquis de Feuquières and held high military commands during the following century. For commoners, too, the court offered the chance to slip into what were (at least until the later seventeenth century) the still somewhat vaguely defined ranks of the nobility by the patronage of the king or some great magnate. The merchants who followed the court could likewise find opportunities for advancement – although court employment was never without its risks. Musicians were extensively employed in the royal household, and artists could find there a patron or a protector beyond the restrictive grasp of the trade guilds.[13]

The humanist Antoine Macault reads from his translation of the Greek historian Diodorus Siculus before François I; an anonymous miniature of c. 1530. The entourage includes Cardinal Duprat, on the king's left, and the monarch's three sons. The canopy of state marks out François I, but otherwise the miniature suggests the relative informality of the Valois court, with all of those in attendance being permitted to wear their hats in the presence of the king.

Above all, in a society obsessed with *honneur* and prestige, service at court was honourable, and took many forms. The great officers of the crown – such as the *grand maître*, the *grand chambellan* and the *grand écuyer* (master of the horse) – were a thing apart, not least because the offices were not saleable, and their holders swore oaths to the king in person. Little by little, the concept of the royal domestic official took hold at court. The officers of the Household lodged under the king's roof, had access to his chamber and surrounded him according to their rank. At the head of each household department stood further high officers, not to be confused with the officers of the crown. Next came the proprietorial holders of offices established by edict, time-share officers serving by turns on a half-yearly or quarterly basis, and the holders of commissions that were provided in reversion, like the holders of domestic posts appointed by *brevet* (or patent). If certain offices were reserved for nobles and gentlemen, the king's service was not entirely closed to commoners. The manpower of the royal household expanded visibly when it was imperative to build up a faithful following in troubled times, or to reconcile former rebels to the crown: thus, after the conclusion of the Wars of Religion, the household of Henri IV numbered more than 1,700 souls. Staffing also fluctuated according to circumstances and financial constraints.

Alongside the king's household were others, such as that of the queen and the dauphin, each of which could number several hundred members. The queen consort's household was managed by a lady superintendent (the redoubtable Duchesse de Chevreuse under Anne of Austria in the 1640s) or by a *dame d'honneur* or lady in waiting – invariably of high noble rank.[14] If the queen's ladies in waiting (the *dames de la reine*) and maids of honour (the *demoiselles d'honneur*) came from the higher nobility, then the ladies of the chamber were recruited from the bourgeoisie. Besides these female attendants, the queen also had male servants, prominent among them her chancellor, superintendent of finances, almoners and chaplains, and butler. Service within the palace clergy remained a regular route to major preferment. It was through service in the household of Marie de Médicis, for example, where he was responsible for both the spiritual and the temporal sides, that

Cardinal Richelieu first made his way towards the political heights he was to occupy in the 1620s and 1630s. Beyond the indigenous royal houses, there were the so-called *princes étrangers*, foreign princes (the heads of the Houses of Guise, Gonzaga-Nevers, Rohan and Bouillon) who, although endowed with territories outside the realm, chose to give attendance at the French court.[15]

These subordinate households were always liable to escape from royal control, which, indeed, was by no means invariably secure within the king's household itself. The perennial problem was that the great noblemen who held major office would seek to staff the household with their personal clients, and royal appointments within the household were often made with a view to balancing or checking the aggrandizing ambitions of an over-mighty subject. It was in order to curtail the influence of the then *grand maître* of France, the Duc de Guise, that in 1578 Henri III made Cardinal Richelieu's father his *grand prévôt* (or grand provost), responsible for the maintenance of order at court.[16] Ironically, even when political manoeuvres of this kind were not at stake, the effective delegation of power to court officials, even those of junior rank, often left kings with relatively weak control over an institution, which, in theory, no one could even enter or leave without proper royal authorization.

Given that many court offices could be bought and sold almost as through they were private property – the system of *venalité* – a large number of places in the court tended to escape effective royal control, despite various monarchs' attempts to restrict pluralism, the system by which more than one office was held for profit by a single individual. As the crown's coffers were among the prime beneficiaries of the sale of offices, all the crown could do was to try to regulate a practice that it could not afford to stamp out. It was testimony to the central social and political importance of the royal household that court posts were at a premium in the market for office. Under Louis XIV they could fetch, according to their importance, anything from 30,000 to more than 500,000 livres (although even at this price the most expensive did not match some of the most lucrative posts in the financial administration). These top posts were, under Louis XIV, much the same price as presidencies in the Parlement of Paris, although they appealed to a different market. Court offices seldom carried high salaries, although they could yield a healthy reward in casual fees. In any case, financial yardsticks are an imperfect gauge of the worth of a court appointment, for the profits of an office bore no necessary relation to the honour that it conferred, a commodity itself liable to fluctuate according to the favour of the king.

This commerce in the currency of courtly [text obscured] means exclusively drawn from the ranks of the great families, which had an almost hereditary hold on the most prestigious court offices (as, for example, the Ducs de Bouillon did over the post of *grand chambellan*); indeed, in the period from the 1560s to the reign of Louis XIII (1610–43) in the 1620s and 1630s, they often came from the lesser or provincial nobility, men who occupied an indispensable place as links in the chain of command from crown to locality. For many of the gentry families of Champagne, for example, appointment as a *chambellan* or as a gentleman of the Chamber was a reward that constituted a significant rise in status through royal service.

Recruitment into the orders of chivalry worked in much the same way. By the mid sixteenth century, the Order of St Michael, which Louis XI had founded in 1469, was no longer the exclusive preserve of the greater nobility. Thus, in 1578 Henri III founded the Order of the Holy Spirit in order to reward his noble followers and bind them more closely to his person. The following year he made noble birth a prerequisite for service as a gentleman of the Chamber and for many other Household offices. In the course of the seventeenth century, however, this special political exploitation of Household office lost its importance, and from the time of Louis XIV onwards the king controlled the appointment of officials in other royal households, those of his brother and of his own descendants.

III. DYNASTIC QUARRELS AND POLITICAL CRISIS

In the century or more before the accession of the Sun King, the court regularly served as the arena for the dynastic and familial conflicts of the ruling house. Such conflicts invariably had repercussions in the realm as a whole and, conversely, malcontents sought support and protection, or at least a figurehead, from within the ranks of the royal family. Indeed, between 1559 and [text obscured] the King was at loggerheads with his mother, Marie de Médicis, the queen regent. From the assassination of the regent's first minister, Concino Concini, in 1617, until Marie died in exile at Cologne in 1640, the 'Wars of Mother and Son' dominated early seventeenth-century French politics. Gaston d'Orléans, the king's brother (Monsieur), plotted against the monarch in a series of tedious and ill-fated escapades, but until 1638, when the king's son (the future Louis XIV), was born, Gaston was heir presumptive to the throne, with all the political authority that accompanied the reversionary interest to the current regime. These family quarrels overflowed the bounds of the court whenever Monsieur or some of the princes stormed off in high dudgeon; and the public abandonment of the court was often the prelude to an aristocratic revolt. As the Fronde (1648–53) was to demonstrate, noble magnates and princes of the blood retained the capacity to raise entire regions in rebellion – in large part through the deployment of their client networks – well into the mid seventeenth century.

It was unsurprising, therefore, that the court was the setting, or at least the place of culmination, for most of the major political crises of the age. It was at the court that cabals and conspiracies seethed in troubled times, nourished and complicated by bonds of friendship and, at times, sexual liaisons.[17] In 1626, for example, Madame de Chevreuse informed the Marquis de Chalais of her dislike for Richelieu, in the process unwittingly leading her suitor to the scaffold.

Above: The sixteenth-century religious wars in France reduced court politics to a series of confessionally based factions. The assassination of the Duc de Guise at Blois, a royal château, in December 1588 – depicted in this anonymous contemporary woodcut – removed the leading Catholic candidate for the succession to the throne. His brother, Louis de Lorraine, Cardinal de Guise, was murdered the following day. Right: The château of Fontainebleau, viewed in c.1650. Even after the court's move to Versailles in 1683, the dictates of the hunt continued to ensure that the Bourbon royal household continued to visit the older Valois residences in the Ile-de-France.

Similarly, in her *Mémoires*, Madame de Motteville, one of the ladies in the household of Anne of Austria, gives a vivid pen-portrait of the balance of factions at court in 1643, shortly after the death of Louis XIII. An anti-Mazarin faction, the *Importants*, led by the Duc de Beaufort, was planning to impose its authority on the regent, Anne of Austria, and overthrow the government of her creature, the despised Cardinal Mazarin:

So this fine, grand court was well and truly at odds. Everyone had their own grand design, their own agenda, and their own clique. The cardinal [Mazarin], with his sharp wits and winning ways, went about lobbying all and sundry: Monsieur the Prince [Condé] protected him, and the Duc d'Orléans, despite his love for the Vendômes [Mazarin's enemies], helped raise him to political supremacy; Orléans [supported the cardinal] because his favourite hated the 'Importants' [Beaufort and his friends], and Condé

because he himself was [likewise] flatly opposed to them. Thus it was that the minister [Mazarin] was saved from dire peril, and ruin came upon those who reckoned that they should be in charge – those who, swollen with pride and presumption, scorned him.[18]

It was through action at court, too, that the king could disencumber himself of those courtiers and ministers whose attentions had become an embarrassment or whose services he no longer required. By sudden official coups, carried out by loyal but obscure agents, the king could display for a brief instant the terrifying fullness of his power: arrest could lead to death. Historians continue to argue over the involvement of Charles IX (1560–74) in the Massacre of St Bartholomew, in which thousands of Protestants were murdered at court and throughout the capital in 1572, but there is no doubt about the responsibility of Henri III for the

assassination of the Guise brothers in December 1588, of Henri IV for the execution of Marshal Biron in 1602, and Louis XIII for the assassination of Concini in 1617.[19] Similarly, during the Fronde the queen regent had the rebellious princes of the blood arrested in 1650, and in 1661 Louis XIV had his *surintendant des finances*, Nicolas Fouquet, peremptorily arrested by his agent, d'Artagnan, and used as a political scapegoat for the corruption of the years of Mazarin's ministry. Yet although these extraordinary coups were designed to forestall conflict on a wider scale, they did not always achieve their intended objectives; the destruction of the Guise brothers in 1588, for example, or the attempt on Condé in 1650 each led to years of rebellion and civil war.

Violence was present at the highest levels of the state as a means for resolving, or forcibly neutralizing, conflict. For this reason the king needed men he could trust at court, like the Gascons under Henri III: men who could infiltrate the clientages of his rivals, allies who could help bring down, imprison or exile over-mighty subjects and malcontents, be they a Fouquet or a Condé. Through a series of clearly codified gestures – by the king's silences or by significant absences or withdrawals from court – the court laid open to view the complex evolutions of political and factional strife and the competition for royal favour. Yet the court was far more than a cockpit for aristocratic and intra-familial feuding. In luring to his court the greater nobility and many of the bishops – the lords spiritual who ruled the Church – in ever greater numbers over the course of the seventeenth century, the monarchs of France gradually turned the Maison du Roi into an ever more effective instrument of government.

IV. THE COURT AS AN INSTRUMENT OF GOVERNMENT: ROYAL FAVOUR

It was, above all, the favour of the prince that shaped the political map of the court. Indeed, the intimacy that tended to accompany royal favour sometimes seriously modified the hierarchy of rank and office at court by bestowing unparalleled access to the monarch upon some comrade in arms or hunting partner, a physician or a chief valet of the chamber. Favour took a multiplicity of forms: from a few kind words to selection for high office or command, ennoblement or, the ultimate accolade, recruitment to the Order of the Holy Spirit. After the court settled permanently at Versailles in 1672, the clearest indication of royal favour was to be among those residents who had an apartment in the château, no matter how small. Invitations to hunt with the king were jealously sought after, and under Louis XIV and Louis XV (1715–74), the pinnacle of a courtier's social ambitions was a summons by the king to the Château de Marly, the secluded retreat built for Louis XIV between 1679 and 1686 by Mansart, with its twelve *pavillons* nearby to house the chosen few. 'Sire, Marly?' was, famously, the question posed of the king by courtiers who believed themselves to stand high in royal favour. Winning the favour of the king was the supreme goal of the courtier; this meant being seen and being noticed, keeping an eye on competitors and being well backed by one's friends. Neither a name of illustrious lineage, nor even the exalted rank of *duc et pair* (the highest rank of the nobility), was in itself a guarantee of success.

Complicating the strands of familial and factional rivalry and the whims of royal favour was the presence of yet another potential source of influence over the monarch, the royal mistress. François I, Henri II (1547–59), Charles IX, Henri IV, Louis XIV and Louis XV all had their mistresses: women who occupied an acknowledged and quasi-formal place within the upper ranks of the court hierarchy.[20] Did this constitute a particular feminine variant on the concept of royal service? If nothing else, this demonstrated the king's virility, an essential attribute of kingship. The mistresses (as opposed to the king's casual liaisons) were until the 1750s drawn from the ranks of the provincial nobility, and they never failed to strengthen their family's position at court. The pattern was only broken with Louis XV's later mistresses, first Madame de Pompadour, whose family members were financiers, and later Madame du Barry, who had raised herself from the gutter. At times, the king's mistress enjoyed a role in the social life of the court akin to that of the queen, whom she often served as a lady in waiting (a situation not without its consequent tensions). The mistress's duty was to provide the king with what the queen could not or could no longer provide: wit, warmth, pleasure, self-confidence, even artistic sensibility – but often at the price of adultery on both sides and unwelcome and unhelpful claims on secular and ecclesiastical patronage. That said, few mistresses sought to dabble in matters of state, and however brilliant their careers their fate was rarely enviable.

Outliving Henri II, his mistress Diane de Poitiers had to hand over the Château de Chenonceaux, her favourite residence, to Queen Catherine de Médicis. More than one mistress died in childbirth, as did Mademoiselle de Fontanges, pregnant with the royal bastard of Louis XIV. More often, a lucky rival ousted the *maîtresse en titre* – the officially recognized mistress. Exile was often the end of the liaison, although there were exceptions: Mademoiselle de la Vallière, mistress of Louis XIV in the 1660s, took the veil in a Carmelite convent; and Madame de Maintenon, born a Huguenot and from the *petite noblesse*, made the transition from mistress of Louis XIV to his secret wife when he was an aged but still sprightly royal widower.

For male courtiers with ambitions to influence affairs of state a prominent place at the council table represented the summit of royal favour. Under Henri II the constable, the Duc de Montmorency (the childhood friend of the king's father, François I), became the 'prime councillor' of the realm, the indispensable intermediary between the king and his ministers, ambassadors and military commanders. Personal access to the king, and control over the access of others, were the symbols of such ascendancy. In a period of religious division and civil strife, Henri III surrounded himself with friends of his own age, the so-called *mignons*, whose own client networks he could also rely upon. Drawn from respectable noble stock, though not from the foremost families of the realm, these *mignons* enabled the king to evade the clutches of the magnates who sought to control him. Likewise, under Henri IV, Huguenot solidarity and comradeship in arms with his king brought the Duc de Sully to power, and once peace had been restored he became a figure of critical importance as an influence in royal counsels and as a broker of patronage, even if his authority did not yet reach the heights later scaled by the great cardinals, Richelieu and Mazarin. Richelieu owed his rise during the reign of Louis XIII not so much to royal favour as to the gradual recognition of

king whom he hoped to control and to keep innocent of political ambition. Yet the strategy was not without its pitfalls; it almost went badly wrong for Richelieu in the case of the Marquis de Cinq-Mars, the royal *privado* of Louis XIII, who conspired against the cardinal in 1642. Nor was this the only threat to the chief minister: his ascendancy depended on the king's trust, and this could be undermined by rival courtiers – as Richelieu found to his cost in the first phase of the 'Day of Dupes' (11 November 1630). In the case of Richelieu, his authority was exercised through a network of kinsmen and clients that enabled him to keep control of most of the institutions of the state, and, through those and his network of provincial clients, of the country. In the quest for power, placing dependants at court was a crucial component of his strategy. The minister heaped offices and benefices upon them even as he built up his own personal fortune – in Richelieu's case, amounting to some 22 million livres; during the minority of Louis XIV, Mazarin's wealth totalled some 36 million livres. He who controlled access to the king thus controlled the distribution of patronage, the *sine qua non* of power.

Such predominance on the part of a single man or family inevitably created strong resentments. It was denounced by 'malcontents', for whom it often served as a pretext for ostentatious departures from court, or even for revolt. Those who resented the dominance of the favourite or chief minister could claim to be taking up arms in the name of the king against the 'evil councillors' who falsely imposed their rule against the monarch's goodwill. For the nobility, well into the second half of the seventeenth century, revolt against such 'tyranny' was envisaged in terms of a solemn duty,[21] and early modern French history is littered with examples of aristocratic insurrection, staged in the name of restoring a proper balance to the counsels at court. 'Liberating the king' was the prime objective both of the Conspiracy of Amboise in 1560 and of the

possible: court conspiracy, assassination or revolt – anything that would precipitate his fall; and this strategy was also applied against Mazarin during the Fronde. With the death of Mazarin in 1660, however, the days of the chief minister seemed to be over. Louis XIV's aim in taking over the government in person, without recourse to a chief minister or favourite, seems to have been to stand above ministerial dynasties and court factions, and thus to become both his own chief minister, the undisputed master of his own court. In this, as in so much else, the reign of Louis XIV was an aberration from the general pattern of French court politics. With the accession of Louis XV in 1715, and the beginning of a yet another royal minority, there was a return to ministerial government, which lasted from the start of the Regency (1715–22) to the death of Cardinal Fleury in 1743, when the ageing king finally sought, in his turn, to be his own chief minister.

V. THE COURT AND THE CENTRAL ADMINISTRATION

Amid the competition for place and favour, the feuds between factions and intermittent aristocratic revolts, the everyday business of royal government remained to be conducted; and it was in the court that the king practised his 'trade' – a court that was the heir to the medieval *curia regis* from which various bureaucratic

Above: *The tabernacle of the king: the child, Louis XIV, enthroned under the canopy of sovereignty, with his younger brother, Philippe, the Duc d'Anjou, attended by their governess, the Marquise de Lansac, c.1643.*
Right: *The metropolitan court: the king's coach passing the equestrian statue of Henri IV on the Pont Neuf, by an unknown artist, c.1665. The Palais du Louvre (right) remained the principal seat of the French court under the Bourbons until Louis XIV's move to Versailles in 1683.*

institutions had been progressively hived off. Traditionally the great officers of the crown were the point of connection between the royal household and the 'business of state'. The chancellor, the constable, the grand master, the grand chamberlain, the admiral, the marshals of France and the grand almoner (if he can be counted among them) stood in the closest proximity to the king. All but irremovable from office, possessed of nationwide authority and often heading a large body of servants, their fortunes varied over time. With the exception of the chancellorship, their offices either disappeared or were gradually stripped of their political significance as the king increasingly looked elsewhere for counsel.

The court was the original form of the Conseil (the Council), a body that, in certain exceptional circumstances, could be augmented by means of an Assembly of Notables, or even a meeting of the Estates General. But recourse to such expedients, generally only under severe financial pressure, proved hazardous for the court, which tended to find itself accused of all manner of vice. The king sought to establish his freedom to choose his own counsellors, but it was a long time (if ever) before he could afford to ignore the pretensions of the princes and the magnates who believed they had a right to be consulted. The dangers monarchs faced were not only those of falling into the power of a single noble interest, but also those of the political paralysis that could be caused by the conflict of rival factions in the Council. Like posts in the court, the number of 'counsellors of the king in his councils' (*conseillers du Roi en ses conseils*) varied according to political developments. Louis XIV, for example, reduced the number of members of the Council of State, and his reign also saw the exclusion of the royal family, the princes of the blood, and the *ducs et pairs*. Sessions of the Council that the king attended himself became more frequent and more specialized; but the number of counsellors was much reduced, and their social origins also changed. Only a handful of ministers were called upon by the king to consider domestic or foreign policy in the High Council (*Conseil d'En Haut*) or to discuss economics in the Finance Council. However, the Regency during the minority of Louis XV saw a temporary repudiation of the preceding reign's methods of government, with the return of the

The carrousel, *such as this in Paris's Place Royale in 1615, was to the seventeenth century what the tournament had been to the sixteenth: a spectacular public performance, combining allegorical processions, stage scenery (note the mock castle, centre right), and virtuoso horsemanship. Theatrical display had long since triumphed over any of the tournament's residual martial elements.*

higher nobility to the crowded councils that replaced the former secretaries of state.

At the heart of the court, throughout the seventeenth century, the political role of ministers was rising at the expense of that of the immediate royal household. The monarch chose his own advisers from the ranks of the service nobility, or church hierarchy at home (witness Richelieu) or abroad (the Italian-born Mazarin), and increasingly from the hereditary bureaucracies that tended to control public finances and the judiciary (Colbert, Le Tellier, Phélypeaux and Fleury, are all cases in point). As chief ministers or secretaries of state they constituted, by the king's will, a political hierarchy that was distinct from, and even (according to Saint-Simon) opposed to, the hierarchy of court officers and attendants. Because of the royal favour shown them, their favour in turn became much sought after, and they were often able to make inroads into the territory of their opponents. They forged marriage alliances with the ancient nobility (Colbert married his daughter to the Duc de Saint-Aignan, chief gentleman of the chamber) and, like the scions of the great princely and aristocratic dynasties, placed their younger sons in the episcopate. Not until the middle decades of the eighteenth century, under Louis XV, were affairs of state once again open to the great nobles and the monarch's closest personal attendants; but by this stage the administration of the state, which had once nestled in the heart of the royal *familia*, had long since left its courtly cradle.[22] Ties with the Parlement of Paris, which had been so important in the sixteenth century, gradually loosened in the course of the early seventeenth century. But was not the king in his turn becoming marginalized by the Council, which, in the reign of Louis XV, proved capable of functioning without him? Was 'the state' emancipating itself from the court?

Did the court, then, lose its entire *raison d'être* during the early eighteenth century amidst an institutional evolution that isolated both the king and his council? Must we be satisfied with a picture of the court as pure theatre, a stage-set peopled by noble flunkies – mere extras to the political stage – or even as pure illusion, masking the real structures of power? In the reign of Louis XIV the court undeniably presented the image of an ideal and ordered society, like the great set-piece royal pageants of an earlier age. But it was also more than that: what, then, was its appeal for the traditionally disorderly, or at any rate dedicatedly backwoods, nobility? Education was one element, and

attendance at court was essential in order to benefit from the proliferating apparatus of the regime; henceforth noble revolts aimed less to challenge the court than to seek to control it. Moreover, for those with luck or connections, the court could be immensely profitable. That statement might seem paradoxical, since the court led many to run up heavy debts and even enticed some into financial ruin. Yet the worn-out cliché that the Bourbon kings forced an expensive lifestyle upon their courtiers in order to control them more tightly will no longer do. Financial history shows that, for those who cultivated it, the court was disproportionately a source of rewards, even if some of these were merely the repayment of expenses incurred in the king's service. It was at court that gratuities, pensions and grants from the crown lands were all on offer. Even supplying the material needs of the court provided merchants with an opportunity for healthy trading profits. Above all, most major business dealings were transacted at court.[23] Influential courtiers could propose the name of this financier to that minister, and could invest in their own right in the farming of royal taxation. (It was financial administration that brought Colbert, Louis XIV's great reforming minister, to power in the 1660s.) On the other hand, the crown found a good number of its financial backers among the court nobility and the higher clergy, an underlying community of interest often obscured by the literature of complaint against the self-serving moneylender.

Seen in this perspective, it seems very doubtful that the court should still be accepted as the means by which the crown set about the business of 'taming the nobility'. By the later seventeenth century it is equally valid to see the court as a glittering manifestation of the crown's financial dependence on the French élites.[24] Indeed, by the reign of Louis XIV, one is entitled to ask who had the greater need of the court: the crown or the nobility?

The machinations of court politics affected

brought to bear. Courtiers and even mistresses put forward candidates for the royal nomination, backed, on occasions, by lobbying from the queen and the princes. It was sometimes the king who, recognizing the strength of vested interests in a particular living or diocese, invited nominations, and for a long time the monarch had to concede that his patronage was heavily constrained by long-standing ecclesiastical and family pressures. However, with the Catholic Reformation even courtiers had to adapt themselves to the more exacting moral standards demanded within the post-Tridentine Church. From the early seventeenth century the French monarchy no longer looked upon the episcopate, if it had ever done so, purely as a means of rewarding its clerical servants, and it never entirely forgot that the episcopate was more than a mere marketable and transferable office.

In allocating military commands the monarch had a freer hand, since there was a straightforward series of procedures for the sale of such appointments. The sale of military commissions had never been complicated by allowing them to become hereditary – a development that, from the crown's point of view, had created such problems in the sovereign courts (such as the Parlement of Paris). War and matters military were always a central component of the culture of the court, and as late as the War of the Austrian Succession (1740–48), the court itself could occasionally be transformed into a military camp.

Above: *Tapestry, rather than painting, remained the most prestigious and expensive form of pictorial art throughout the sixteenth and seventeenth centuries. This Gobelins tapestry of c. 1665–80 records the marriage of Louis XIV to the Infanta María Teresa, daughter of Philip IV of Spain, at St Jean de Luz, on 9 June 1660, a dynastic union intended to consolidate the Franco-Spanish Peace of the Pyrenees of November 1659.*

Right: *The intimacy between the monarch and his officer corps: Pierre-Denis Martin the younger's view of the celebrations to mark the inauguration of the Hôtel des Invalides in August 1706, the centrepiece of Louis XIV's project for a vast military hospital and residence for war veterans. Designed by Jules Hardouin Mansart and heavily influenced by the Escorial, the Invalides was originally intended by the king to serve (like the Escorial's monastery church) as the single burial vault of the royal dynasty.*

The cult of the warrior-prince was one of the central themes of palace iconography, and the business of preparing for and waging war was a recurrent, almost normative, aspect of the business of the court. Well into the eighteenth century kings appeared in person on the field of battle, and expected senior courtiers to follow suit. The formalized conventions of siege warfare were particularly suited to the ceremony of the court: Louis XIII, for example, spent some time in person at the siege of La Rochelle in the 1620s, but it was in his son's reign that the court took to making siege-warfare itself a kind of ritual. Yet, for all the ceremony, war remained a bloody business; and the lists of casualties (carefully noted by, among others, Madame de Sévigné) show that the parade of 'noble valour' was no mere charade. Aristocratic casualties were high. Like

the court itself, the conduct of war followed a seasonal cycle. Winter brought back to court those soldier-courtiers whose exploits had been followed in letters and journals. Even when the king did not go to war in person, the pulse of the court beat in time with his military campaigns. Indeed, the 'outward face' of the court could itself form part of the war effort: for foreign diplomats seeking to gauge the relative strengths of the competing sides, the sense of vitality or gloom prevalent at court was an indication of the kingdom's capacity to wage or sustain war.

VI. DISPLAYING THE KING

The court was an institution frequently on the move, even after Louis XIV's permanent relocation of the court to Versailles in 1682–3. During the sixteenth century, it undertook lengthy tours in order to parade the king before his subjects and bolster their loyalty. In 1564–6, the court went as far as the border with Spain,[26] though by the early seventeenth century most of its migrations were confined to the immediate environs of the Ile-de-France. Even so, a royal marriage or a summit meeting between sovereigns could also move the court long distances – as far as the Pyrenees for the peace treaty and the concomitant marriage between Louis XIV and María Teresa in 1659–60. In the course of these voyages the court would make solemn 'entries' into the cities along the way – elaborately choreographed rituals, often featuring temporary triumphal arches and formal obeisances from civic dignitaries – a tradition that dated from the later Middle Ages and flourished as

part of the repertoire of courtly display at least until the ceremonial entry of Louis XIV and María Teresa into Paris in 1662.

In the interim, the 'message' of the royal entry had changed considerably. The character of the occasion as a festive expression of an almost contractual bond between the monarch and his 'good city', during which he confirmed its privileges, was, from the sixteenth century, gradually superseded by a very different emphasis: the ceremonial submission of the city before the glory of the sovereign. With the personal rule of Louis XIV, from the 1660s, other royal ceremonies, such as the *Te Deum* – the religious ritual in which the Latin hymn of praise to the deity came to be appropriated as an expression of the glory of monarchy – took on this quasi-propagandistic function. From the last third of the seventeenth century, anyone who wished to see the king had to travel to one of his residences, where the life of the court itself constituted a sort of permanent ceremonial entry or pageant, no longer encumbered by the irksome presence of provincial civic dignitaries.

In the mid sixteenth century, the natural habitat of the court lay between the game-forests of the Ile-de-France and the Loire Valley. If the Valois lived predominantly at the Louvre, the principal royal palace in Paris, they were also to be found at the Tournelles (until the death of Henri II in 1559), at the Châteaux de Madrid (at Neuilly), Saint-Germain-en-Laye, Villers-Cotterêts, Fontainebleau and occasionally in the Loire Valley itself. This pattern was replicated under the Bourbons, and for the first twenty years of Louis XIV's personal rule (1661–81) the court was once more itinerant, sometimes travelling as far afield as Chambord in the Loire. Even after the move to Versailles in 1682–3, the court was occasionally mobile, albeit far less frequently than hitherto. It was at Fontainebleau, for example, that Louis XIV repealed the Edict of Nantes to end the toleration of Calvinism in 1685. Under Louis XV, who outstripped all French monarchs in his passion for hunting, the court once again returned regularly to Fontainebleau, and was also frequently to be found at Compiègne. The tell-tale signs of an area regularly visited by the court were well-protected forests (to ensure game was preserved for sport), a relatively agreeable environment and a good number of usable roads.

In the last two decades of the seventeenth century, however, all other royal residences took second place to Versailles. The geographical range of the court's mobility was sharply reduced. To ascribe this change in courtly style to the building of Versailles is, however, to put the cart before the horse. The creation of Versailles was the consequence of a change in the style and obligations of royal government, not its cause. By the 1670s the royal bureaucracy and the other sinews of monarchical authority were sufficiently strong for the country effectively to be controlled without the king having to parade himself around it; the increasing professionalization of the diplomatic corps had rendered summit meetings between sovereigns for the most part unnecessary; and, with the single exception of Louis XV at Fontenoy in 1745, changes in attitudes to the conduct of war no longer required that the king lead his troops into battle.

From 1682 the monarch was on permanent and precisely organized display, above all at Versailles. Like most royal residences, this began life as a hunting lodge. The château built by Louis XIII (the Marble Court of the present palace) became an occasional court residence. Its transformation into the major royal palace of the realm was a gradual and lengthy process, not a sudden policy decision. From 1668 Louis XIV commissioned Louis Le Vau (1612–70) to add a new range of buildings with a central terrace that opened on to the gardens created by André Le Nôtre (1613–1700). After the Dutch War (1672–8), the building site once again changed character. Commissioned to enlarge the château, Jules Hardouin Mansart (1648–1708) equipped it with an imposing new façade and two long flanking wings to the east and west. The court took up residence during 1682 in what was still an unfinished building, teeming with an army of craftsmen and labourers. Mansart constructed a magnificent 500-metre frontage facing the gardens, and, after 1687, added the seventy-five metres of the Galerie des Glaces (or Hall of Mirrors) flanked by two *salons*, respectively dedicated to war and peace. The king interested himself in every detail of the architecture, gardens and ornamentation, and under the direction of Le Nôtre, the surrounding marshes were transformed into a network of parterres, grottoes, ornamental lakes and fountains, complete with an orangery and a menagerie of exotic animals. Venetian

sailors were brought to ply the Grand Canal, the great axial waterway that drew the eye from the château towards the distant horizon. By the end of the seventeenth century there were some 20,000 courtiers and servants at Versailles, of whom about 5,000 lived in the château. A whole town, adjacent to the palace, rose from the ground; by 1713 it housed 40,000 people in buildings whose roofs were not allowed to obscure the imposing elevations of the château itself.

If everything was directed towards the glorification of the monarch, this adulation nevertheless continued to evolve. In the 1660s, Louis XIV still drew on classical history and mythology to fashion his image: he was Apollo, as was evident in the palace gardens, where a pair of ornamental pools (bassins), one at each end of the sun's course overhead, were adorned, respectively, with sculptures of the chariot of Apollo (traditionally associated with the sun) rising from the water, and of his mother, Latona. From the beginning of the Dutch War (1672–8), however, the king's glory was literally incomparable, and gods and heroes of myth were now powerless to match it. Mythology and history were set aside in favour of a timeless present, much as the past of his own dynasty was similarly effaced by the image of a king who was the moving principle of all. In the paintings that Le Brun produced for the ceiling of the Galerie des Glaces at Versailles, the king's presence reduces almost all the other figures to an anonymous crowd of interchangeable allegorical faces. Only Monsieur, the Prince de Condé and the Vicomte de Turenne, stand out from this ghostly pageant. The king, it seems, has escaped the trammels of time and space.

While the actual impact of such iconography on courtiers is a matter for debate, it is at least clear that Versailles was deliberately created to promote the illusion – and hence the reality – of power. It was an enchanted world, unique, at once closed and open, designed as it was both to welcome all (of appropriate rank) and to witness the glory of the king. For visitors and even for those unable to make the pilgrimage to the court in person, it was expounded and explained for the further promotion of the renown and reputation of the king in numerous guidebooks. The self-consciously programmatic aspect of the new palace is set out in the first guide to Versailles, written by the king himself between 1689 and 1705, the

Manière de Montrer les Jardins de Versailles, intended to set the pattern for official visits. The king prescribed an exact order so that the palace and its gardens might be seen to its maximum effect.[27] In every aspect of the arts – music, opera, architecture, sculpture, painting – the court occupied an Olympian pre-eminence that set the tone, and was the dominant influence within French culture as a whole.

Yet that courtly culture was simultaneously a highly cosmopolitan one. From Charles VIII's Italian Wars in the 1490s through to the age of Mazarin and the regency of Anne of Austria in the 1640s and 1650s, French court society and culture was open to foreign influences at the highest level. The majority of the queens of France were of foreign birth, two from the *arriviste* ducal house of Medici, the Grand Dukes of Tuscany; and despite the hostility frequently shown to outsiders, many of them played an influential role in determining the direction of court culture. Moreover, from the early sixteenth century there were other foreigners at court: francophile Italian nobles and princelings, financiers, merchants, soldiers, artists, and Flemish, Dutch and Italian engineers who specialized in laying out gardens and the construction of fountains.[28] For all these, the court provided a route whereby they could be integrated into the royal (and other noble) households, acquire offices and benefices, buy lands and houses, rise up the social scale – in some cases even as far as the ranks of the nobility – and become patrons themselves. The Medici queens helped to make the French court largely bilingual. The court was highly receptive to successive translations of the most famous manual of courtly behaviour, Baldassare Castiglione's *Il Cortegiano* (The Book of the Courtier), issued in various editions from 1537, as well as to Giovanni della Casa's *Galateo*, translated in 1609. The Valois court developed a taste for Petrarchan poetry, lute music and the Italian theatre and opera. The warriors and bishops who returned from Italy were not the only ones to dream of palaces in the Italian style; Henri II's queen, Catherine de Médicis (1519–89), decorated the Tuileries Palace in Paris in the Italian manner, and Henri IV's consort, Marie de Médicis, commissioned the rebuilding of the Palais de Luxembourg to plans strongly influenced by the recently completed Palazzo Pitti in Florence. Similarly, it was from Italy that the 'gallery' was copied, first at

Pierre-Denis Martin the younger's view of Marly in 1723. The château was Louis XIV's favourite hunting lodge, with its central residence for the king, and twelve pavilions to house those courtiers who had been favoured with an invitation to join the hunt. Though each of these buildings was dedicated to classical deities, their placement and number clearly suggested the topos of Christ and his twelve apostles.

Fontainebleau (*c.*1527–*c.*1559) and then beside the Seine at the Louvre and at the Luxembourg – long before the Galerie des Glaces at Versailles. Nor was Italy the only source of architectural and cultural innovation. The fascination with Spain was pervasive, despite endemic military conflict, and the southern Habsburg kingdoms regularly exported styles of dress, literature and even its devotional style into France.

The intimate circle of the French queens often included a significant cadre of foreigners, some of whom infiltrated the highest positions of power. Among Marie de Médicis's intimates was Leonora Galigaï, a childhood companion of the queen, whose husband, Concini, rose to power during Marie's regency on the personal influence wielded at court by his wife. The Habsburg princess, Anne of Austria, retained a number of Spanish attendants in her entourage until Louis XIII sent them packing in 1637, and after her appointment as regent on her husband's death in 1643, she chose to retain as chief minister the Roman-trained Cardinal Mazarin, Richelieu's political heir. Mazarin's earlier career at the papal court had taught him an energetic govern-ing style that required close and constant attendance

on the monarch: he actually resided in the royal palace, and made himself a master of the courtly graces.[29] The presence of such foreigners at the highest levels of government nourished a xenophobic literature of complaint against the court, which was allegedly overrun by corrupt and self-serving interlopers. The *Tragiques* of the Huguenot poet, Agrippa d'Aubigné, seethe with fury against the Italian Catherine de Médicis. Throughout the seventeenth and eighteenth centuries, from the *Mazarinades* of the 1640s through to the pamphlets against Marie-Antoinette in the 1780s, the charges remained fairly constant: sexual perversion, Machivellianism and the promotion of the scheming Jesuits (this last the joint product of Spain and Italy); such was the diabolical baggage of the foreigner.

But foreign relations also took more decorous forms. By the early sixteenth century the court of France was the hub of the emerging network of permanent and semi-permanent diplomatic representation. The court accommodated a papal nuncio and ambassadors from Venice and the great monarchies, as well as the representatives of German and Italian duchies and principalities, and the reception and entertainment of ambassadors was one of the principal functions of the court. From the late sixteenth century, the protocol governing ambassadorial receptions became progressively more complicated and rigidly defined, partly in consequence of the general trend towards increased ceremoniousness, partly out of a desire to avoid the disputes over rank and precedence that were the perennial diversions of resident diplomats.[30] At the French courts in general, and at Versailles in particular, an elaborate scenography was developed to enable the king, when greeting the representatives of fellow sovereigns, to articulate a meticulously graded range of rank and esteem. The process arguably reached its culmination in the Escalier des Ambassadeurs, the great ceremonial staircase constructed at Versailles between 1674 and 1680.[31] The presence of two identical flights of stairs obviated the need to determine precedence between two parties claiming equal status, while the point on the staircase at which the king or his household officer chose to receive the visiting diplomat exactly corresponded to the degree of amity or favour the monarch chose to display towards the foreign power.

There was, moreover, a highly competitive element in the manner in which courts represented themselves to one another, through the modes of diplomacy, literature and display. From the second half of the seventeenth century the French court strove to set the tone for the other princely courts of Europe. The Italian model of the court, so influential in the sixteenth and early seventeenth centuries, had been transplanted and reinvented with complete success. It provided a model for the re-export of a distinctively French cultural ascendancy, manifested and articulated through the court. Richelieu, a cardinal of the Church of Rome, adapted the achievements of the Jesuits' Roman College and of the Italian academies to the world of Paris and the promotion of the French language. French was to be for the King of France what Latin was for Pope Urban VIII (1623–44): a magnificent language of celebration. By the time that the Italian architect and sculptor Gian Lorenzo Bernini came to Paris in 1665, it was no longer a matter of cultural importation: a French style had already come into being, distinct from the Roman Baroque. France was no longer in orbit around the Roman sun, but shone in its own right. Buildings, gardens, clothes, table manners – all were parts of a French cultural package diffused in various ways (not without opposition) by the cadet branches of the House of Bourbon installed (after the failure of the Spanish Habsburg line in 1700) by French arms on the thrones of Spain, Naples and Parma. This attempt to obtain cultural hegemony was linked to, and in part the consequence of, the exceptional control that Louis XIV established over his court, and his preoccupation with the ritual and visual manifestations of monarchical power within it.

VI. ETIQUETTE AND THE CONTROL OF THE COURT

The court was an institution on the scale of a city or an army. It needed both provisioning and controlling. Open to nearly all comers, the court was a difficult society to police.[32] For all its glamour, it was surrounded by a sometimes motley crowd of hangers-on, petitioners and goggling tourists. At Versailles smart clothes and a sword at one's side were enough to guarantee access; but within, the staircases stank, and dubious personal cleanliness contrasted sharply with the fine perfumes and splendid clothes. Violence, too, was endemic to life at court, with duels (in theory forbidden by Louis XIII), brawls, the settling of scores and occasional murders, not to mention tense relations with the local population (especially creditors).[33]

How was this world to be controlled? A form of social ritual that came to be called 'etiquette' (a term coined in the eighteenth century at the courts of Madrid and Vienna) appeared during the reign of Henri II, at the latest – further elaborated under Henri III in 1578, 1582 and 1585 – and regulated an increasing proportion of royal activities.[34] During his meals the king set himself apart from his courtiers, behind railings, partly in order to escape the attentions of petitioners. He would receive petitions only after dinner, as he made his way back to his private apartments. Under the new rules, even dukes could not call upon him without prior arrangement. Such ceremonial fulfilled two functions: it protected the king from the press of the crowd and imposed the stamp of his authority on the court. The introduction of these regulations was a blow to courtiers, who resented being kept at a distance, even if the gulf was reduced under Henri IV and Louis XIII, who were less attached to these unpopular and, in their view, burdensome formalities. Court ceremonial was revived, however, after the Fronde and reached its zenith under Louis XIV, with the king himself as master of ceremonies, supreme arbiter of taste and star of the show. He tinkered with it at will, issuing godlike dispensations from the ceremonial order that he had promulgated, but which could not limit his omnipotence. The king's *lever* became the most celebrated of these daily rituals, as courtiers were admitted at varying stages and in varying degrees of proximity, according to their various appointments and degrees of favour, to witness the king rise from bed in the morning.[35]

Festivals, which interrupted the day-to-day rhythm of the court, were also important in its control, not only keeping courtiers occupied and entertained, but in emphasizing the status and majesty of the king.[36] They were often attended by huge numbers: some 10,000 were present at a court tournament in 1612. When Louis XIII was in Paris there was a ballet three times a week, and each year there was a royal ballet at the Hôtel-de-Ville. Other events were for special occasions such as a military victory, an embassy or a marriage.[37] Drama was also highly rated, with many of the major works of the dramatic repertoire by Molière and others being written for performance at court before the king.

But such fêtes were never purely for entertainment. They also had a political and a diplomatic aspect. On 18 August 1674, after a performance of *Racine* at Versailles during the Dutch War, the standards captured in battle by Condé were lowered before the king as he saw a plinth and an obelisk surmounted by a golden sun brought along the Grand Canal, and watched allegorical representations of the victories he had won during the invasion of the Netherlands. From the mid sixteenth century discipline was to an increasing extent instilled into the court through the education of the future courtier – an area in which the Jesuits made perhaps their greatest contributions to French culture.[38]

One of the prime criteria for the success of the court consisted in keeping all eyes focused upon the king. From the reign of Charles IX, in the midst of domestic upheaval, the topos of the monarch as the sun was exploited more and more in royal iconography. While this was not necessarily original, the very concept of 'glory' was undergoing a profound change in France.[39] From the early seventeenth century, the motto SOLI REGI GLORIA (To the king alone be glory) came increasingly to be the watchword of the court: henceforth all glory was owed to the king, and an individual's glory depended upon his degree of association or intimacy with the prince. In 1641 the Oratorian Father Senault likened Richelieu to the foremost of the Seraphim and Louis XIII to God, invoking the mysteries of heaven to explain the relationship between the king and the cardinal. The glory of the king was increasingly expressed in terms of the glory of God in what amounted to a surreptitious apotheosis of the monarch. Around 1680 it was no longer the custom to depict the glory of the king in terms of the primordial glory of God, the source of all glory: for some Jesuit authors it was now the glory of the king that served as the point of reference in expressing the glory of God.[40] Indeed, the suggestion that the heavenly court would be modelled on that of the Most Christian King, adored by his courtiers, was made by Jean de La Bruyère in his *Caractères* of 1688.[41]

The sacralization of the monarch, of course, had a long pedigree. One should never forget that the court was a system that orbited around the Most Christian King, a king anointed and crowned at Reims, the 'son of St Louis' who healed the 'king's evil' (or scrofula) with his sacred touch, and took oaths from his bishops. Ecclesiastically, the court was a sort of little diocese, exempt from the jurisdiction of the local bishop, and governed instead by the grand almoner of France. For the king was no ordinary Christian. His ceremonial rising each morning was framed by prayers, which suggests that the ritual may have owed something to liturgical origins. At mass, the king's status as 'bishop of externals', the protector of the Gallican Church, which reckoned itself 'the salt of the earth', received visible recognition. The aspersion with holy water, the kissing of the gospels and of the corporal, and the administration of communion (which the king received, like a priest, in both species, bread and wine), itself made him an active participant in the liturgy.[42]

This religious dimension of court life has long been lamentably neglected. It is conspicuous by its absence from Norbert Elias's picture of 'court society'.[43] After the many years when his theories have been applauded with somewhat undiscriminating enthusiasm, it is time for a more critical approach, in France as elsewhere.[44] His tendency to conceptualize 'civilization' in psychological terms, as the control of the passions, has led to the neglect of that efflorescence in literature and the arts of which Voltaire, for example, was so aware. One might add that the perspective of the 'civilization of manners', while broad, has nevertheless concealed many aspects of the novelty of the court's impact on contemporaries in the sixteenth and seventeenth centuries.

One principal novelty was that the court became the mainspring of the Catholic Reformation in France. This outcome was far from predictable, since a politically shrewd and dedicated Calvinist minority was entrenched in the kingdom, bent on making France a Protestant nation. The Houses of Châtillon-Coligny, of Navarre and of Condé provided the leading figures in the Huguenot offensive that reached its apogee in 1561, and was eventually destroyed after 1572, with the accession of Henri III. The new king restricted court offices to Catholics, established several religious foundations, participated personally in penitential processions, and supported the new religious orders, even the most rigorous. After Henri IV's conversion to Catholicism, the Bourbon rulers enabled the Jesuits to develop the various aspects of their apostolate in preaching, acting as spiritual directors, hearing confessions and in managing lay confraternities. Their professed house in Paris was established in the rue St Antoine, in the fashionable Marais quarter, and developed close links with the court. Their church was dedicated to St Louis, and its imposing façade displayed, alongside the statues of the Jesuit saints Francis Xavier and Ignatius Loyola, the coats of arms of France and Navarre, as well as those of Cardinal Richelieu, who celebrated the inaugural mass there in 1641. Their famous preachers drew large congregations. Less well known than the Jesuits, but highly influential at the time, were the Capuchin friars (a branch of the Franciscans), who had been active in France since 1574. One of their number, Père Yves de Paris, wrote the *Gentilhomme chrétien*, published in 1666, which laid down a pattern for the Christian courtier.[45]

The atmosphere of the Catholic Reformation was favourable towards the role of women in religion, and the various queens consort and the ladies of their courts actively promoted the new female orders, helping to assimilate what were essentially imports of religious culture from Spain and Italy. Teresa of Avila's order of Discalced Carmelites, for instance, had close links with the royal court, while Anne of Austria, the consort of Louis XIII (Queen regent, 1643–51) was behind the foundation of the churches of Val-de-Grâce and Sainte-Anne-la-Royale, the only French house of the Theatines. Devout courtiers found an outlet for their spiritual energies in the Company of the Blessed Sacrament, founded in 1627, and while some went so far as to renounce the court for the cloister, the majority was convinced by the teaching of St François de Sales that salvation was attainable even amid the worldliness of the court. Equally influential was the Jesuit Father Nicolas Caussin, a confessor to Louis XIII, whose *Cour sainte ou l'institution chrétienne des Grands* (The Holy Court, of the Christian Instruction of the Grandees) was published in 1624. Although he was eventually dismissed by Richelieu because of the doubts he had sown in Louis XIII's mind concerning the basis of French foreign policy, this act in itself

Versailles, before and after. Above: *Pierre Patel's view of Versailles in 1668, before Louis XIV's extensive building projects of 1670s and 1680s. Despite the already ambitious scale of the gardens, the château itself retains its original character as a royal hunting lodge.*
Right: *Versailles transformed: the château in 1722, after Louis XIV had more than quadrupled the size of the original building and turned it into a self-sufficient 'palace-city'. The court chapel, the focal point of much of the court's daily ceremonial life, is the tallest building to the right of the inner court; a painting by Pierre-Denis Martin the younger.*

shows how the internecine conflicts between the Catholic powers in the seventeenth century impinged upon the court, which provided an ideal arena for the arts of casuistry and spiritual direction to become embroiled in politics. Of course, the ideal of a devout court presupposed the sanctity of the king, and Bossuet, preaching before Louis XIV in the 1660s, never hesitated to castigate his failings.

There was also a decidedly Christian aspect to the particular ideal of *honnêteté* (moral decency or honesty) current in the early seventeenth century.[47]

The court itself was often compared with the court celestial, and the 'honest' man – in other words, the noble man – was reckoned to be a perfectible being. Given a proper education, he could flourish in a harmonious society characterized by politeness, conversation, and a gallantry that fostered respect for women. For true gallantry was not so much mere amorousness as a graceful and agreeable mode of speech and action. Courtiers of the seventeenth century retained the notions of service and loyalty embodied in the chivalric romance; they had read

the *Astrée* and were well versed in the conventions of the love letter. In order to please, they relied on appearance, but also on the arts of singing, dancing and mastery of facial expression, vivacity and, above all, on conversation, regarded as the mistress of the social arts. It was thus possible to shine in whatever one's allotted station, and to be humble with style. But the court was not the source of the ideal of *honnêteté*. It was far from being Madame de Rambouillet's model when she was codifying civility and gallantry in her magnificent residence near the Louvre, and when the *précieuses* – the 'affected young ladies' satirized by Molière – were developing a language and casuistry of love in their *ruelles* (demarcated spaces within rooms assigned to elegant social gatherings). Of course, the court benefited from the identification of the 'honest man' with the courtier that came about as Richelieu promoted courtesy as a means of inculcating obedience.[48] But doubts still remained; could one really be 'honest' at court? And was genuine

'conversation' possible only amid the more equable conditions of private life, far from the pursuit of politics and selfish ends?

In the 1650s much of this was called into question, whether by the challenge of the Fronde, the divorce between the ideals of courtliness and honesty or the shattering assault of Pascal's *Provincial Letters* on the moral theology of the Jesuits. The courtier now appeared as one dedicated to dissimulation and flattery. Consecutive redefinitions of 'honesty' made it a virtuous courtly *mediocritas,* or middle-way, comprising easy politeness, refined and gallant elegance, simplicity and readiness to help others. As 'honesty' spread on all sides, at court, in the city and even in parts of the countryside, it lost its religious character. The courtier carried out his duties with propriety in showing himself to be perfectly sociable, a concept that the eighteenth century detached from the context of the court, as Paris regained its paramount role around the first decade of the century. Parisian

Above: *Subsidiary courts: Richelieu's extensive urban residence, the Palais Cardinal – complete with its own theatre – was one of the several focuses of court life and politics that complemented, and sometimes rivalled, its central hub, the household of the king. The cardinal here entertains Louis XIII and the queen to a ballet performance of* The Triumph of French Arms. *Royal heraldry, rather than Richelieu's own as cardinal, is loyally displayed at the centre of the proscenium arch.*
Right: *Engravings such as this, by Israël Silvestre, of the fireworks for a royal fête at Versailles in 1664, brought the splendours of the French court's entertainments to the attention of a Europe-wide audience.*

salons re-appropriated the ideals of conversation and good company from the court, which, under the regency from 1715 to 1722, was itself back in the capital.

The court was never immune from a vein of moral criticism older than itself. From the fourteenth and fifteenth centuries the court had suffered the reproaches of the moralists; wastefulness, rowdiness, luxury, wickedness, hypocrisy and greed were recurrent accusations. Withdrawal was always tempting – the conclusion reached by Alceste, Molière's eponymous *Misanthrope*, brought to the stage as a figure of fun. But the protests did not constitute a united challenge. They might come from exiles who hated and scorned a particular minister or a rival faction, but who were nevertheless hopeful of a return to court. Backwoods gentry and worthy citizens perpetually grumbled about the arrogance of the nobility, the cost of it all and the pretensions and debauchery of courtly young fools.[49] Nor was there any shortage of disappointed noblemen to rail against the courtiers who monopolized military commands, nor of magistrates resentful of the court as the fount of *cassations* (legal acts that overruled the verdicts of lower courts) and mettlesome decrees of the royal councils. Yet such attacks were rarely concerted, and their authors themselves often enjoyed the patronage of some well-placed courtier or officer of the household.

There were more serious challenges. From 1637 to 1638 an alternative account of 'glory' was being promoted from the cloisters of the Port-Royal.[50] The repudiation of what was seen as an un-Christian policy (the crown's support for the Protestant side in the Thirty Years War), and of institutional developments that seemed to make the king an obstacle rather than a mediator between God and his subjects, led to a clash over the concept of *gloire* between the *dévots* – those whom Sainte-Beuve called 'an aristocracy of devotion' – and first Richelieu, and then later Louis XIV. Another challenge to the court was posed by the intermittent stirrings of concepts of limited monarchy, which sought a wider role in government for the Council, the Parlements or the Estates-General. The disciplined hierarchy of the court was contrasted with atavistic myths of free Germanic warriors assembled around a king who was merely *primus inter pares*. Canvassed in the later sixteenth century and again during the Fronde of the 1650s, these ideas, which chimed with those concerning the superiority of the general council over the papacy, became fashionable after 1715, in a century during which the court become synonymous with arbitrary monarchy, intrigue and base servility.

By the early eighteenth century the court was no longer the 'ideal society' around a monarch who kept up traditional appearances even as he emptied them of real meaning. Louis XV retreated to his private apartments to escape the ceremonial burden. He no longer slept in the Chamber, which he visited only in order to make a ritual *lever*. He hid away from his courtiers, upsetting the finely balanced machinery developed by his great-grandfather, who, in his pomp, had sought to locate his peerless royal society outside the trammels of history itself. But no sooner had this ideal been realized than it began to lose its meaning, as the religious basis of royal power was undermined and the élites once more laid claim to a greater say in the affairs of state. Historical and utopian myths were set against the repetitive ritual present of the court. Courtly life was opposed to an ideal of modest frugality, as in the character of Salente in Fénelon's *Télémaque*, or in the 'noble savage' of Polynesia. Against the urbane model of the perfect courtier stood the rustic simplicity and nobility of Rousseau's *Nouvelle Héloise*, in which feelings were measured by virtue and truthfulness. Henceforth, if the court still stood outside history, it was because the monarchy had lost both the cultural and the political initiative as well as confidence in its own perfection.

CHAPTER THREE

The Kingdom of England and Great Britian
THE TUDOR
AND STUART COURTS
1509–1714

JOHN ADAMSON

O F ALL THE COURTS OF ANCIEN-RÉGIME EUROPE, NONE WAS more unequivocally the political centre of the realm than the household of the king of England. The English monarch was supreme over almost all aspects of government: head of the executive, arbiter of justice, the fount of honours and titles, and, from the 1530s, the head of the English Church. And it was pre-eminently at his court that these powers were exercised and patronage and favour were conferred. In the diplomatic sphere, too, England (and, still more, after the union of the Scottish and English crowns in 1603, 'Great Britain'), ranked with France, Spain and the Holy Roman Empire as one of the four wealthiest and most powerful European monarchies. This status was further enhanced, after the Reformation, as the household of the king of England became the premier court of the Protestant world. Accordingly, for most of the period between the accession of the Tudors and the last quarter of the seventeenth century, the English court ranked as a major centre of international diplomacy, and arguably the principal influence on the nation's political, religious and cultural life.[1]

Where the king resided, there, in theory, was the court. But in the sixteenth and seventeenth centuries by far the most important of all the royal houses was Whitehall, the riverside palace on the Thames at Westminster, which Henry VIII had acquired on Cardinal Wolsey's fall in 1529 and extensively rebuilt over the following decade. Recognized by statute in 1536 as the 'King's [New] Palace at Westminster' and his principal residence, Whitehall remained the seat of English government until the palace's destruction by fire in 1698.[2] By then, it had

The relics of the court: Canaletto's view of Whitehall c.1747 reveals the remains of the old palace after the fire of 1698 that razed most of it to the ground. The Tudor 'Holbein Gate', to the left, marked the western end of the former Privy Lodgings range. Inigo Jones's Banqueting House (built 1619–22, right) – which doubled as the principal royal Presence Chamber between 1622 and 1698 – continues to dominate the palace site.

expanded into a gargantuan sprawl of more than 1,000 rooms, a palace so large, one commentator claimed, that it could accommodate the courts 'of two great kings'.[3] It was at Whitehall that the court tended to be based for much of the time between September and June, before escaping from the hot and plague-ridden capital to go on progress during the summer. Yet, while Whitehall was the court's principal seat, it was of course only one of a series of royal residences, varying in size from vast ancient fortresses, such as Windsor Castle,[4] to the great 'standing houses' with their extensive lodgings for courtiers (pre-eminently Greenwich, Richmond and Hampton Court), and small hunting lodges, which could accommodate with comfort only the king and his personal servants – perhaps no more than fifty people.

The court, then, was the seat of the king's household. What gave it its glittering allure in the eyes of contemporaries, however, was that it was also the kingdom's principal seat of power. Because England was a 'personal monarchy', executive authority, with or without Parliaments, rested firmly with the person of the king and his councillors. The personnel of government thus formed part of the monarch's immediate household. By definition, councillors were courtiers, and were usually allocated lodgings in the major royal palaces. Parliaments, which have stolen a disproportionate amount of the historical limelight, came and went, often with years or even decades between them. The court, however, was perennial. It was there that policy was determined, and whence royal bounty – in the form of grants of offices, land, pensions, titles of honour – flowed out to lubricate the lesser patronage-machinery of the localities. Only at court could would-be recipients of this patronage join the competition for the monarch's favour, and if, to many courtiers, the richest plums of royal patronage remained out of reach, there were other opportunities within their grasp, both to receive and help dispense royal bounty. Even a relatively minor courtier – a gentleman pensioner (one of the monarch's largely ceremonial bodyguard), for example – could set himself up as a broker between his gentry neighbours and the great officers of state, thereby enhancing his local standing and prestige.[5]

This jockeying for power and patronage nevertheless needs to be placed in perspective. Only a relatively small minority of courtiers was actively engaged in the heady competition for high office or influence in 'matters of state'. The vast majority of court offices were occupied by men who were of relatively modest means (particularly in comparison to the great courtier nobles); and until the major retrenchments of the early 1660s, the Tudor and Stuart court was a vast caravanserai of upwards of a thousand persons, holding posts in a meticulously graded hierarchy from haughty noblemen down to humble grooms.[6] Roughly three-quarters of this number served as servants in various menial capacities; it was only the last quarter – the élite of some two hundred peers and gentlemen who comprised the 'household above stairs' – who were regularly regarded by contemporaries as 'courtiers': the staff that guarded, attended and waited on the king in various practical and ceremonial capacities – gentlemen pensioners forming the king's ceremonial bodyguard, gentlemen ushers controlling access to the king's apartments, carvers and sewers responsible for serving at the royal table.

Some of these courtiers, no doubt, hoped fondly for the moment when they would catch the monarch's (or the favourite's) eye, and they would be singled out for some prestigious or lucrative preferment. But the majority of the 'above-stairs' household held their posts, not primarily for profit (indeed, many of their offices were either unpaid or entailed expenses far larger than their salaries), but because their positions conferred upon them honour and status, not just at court, but in the wider world. Most of the places in the household-above-stairs were held quarterly, by rota – generally three months service, nine months off – ensuring a regular exchange of personnel between court and the localities. At the end of his regular term of attendance at court, the most junior household officer could look forward to impressing his country neighbours with metropolitan gossip and name-dropping, and savouring the kudos that came from the nearness to power.

The term 'courtier', however, was extended to more than just those who held an office in the above-stairs household. From at least the mid sixteenth century, noblemen and affluent gentlemen regularly arranged to spend part of the year in the capital so that they could 'give attendance' at court, even though they might never acquire a formal post within the

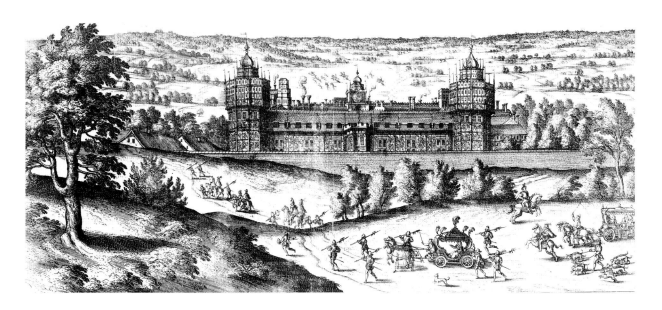

Nonsuch Palace: Henry VIII's attempt to vie with François I of France in the opulence of his palace architecture. As a result of the windfall revenues of the dissolution of the monasteries, the king was able to set a standard in building that none of his successors was able to approach.

household. These 'persons of fashion', as they were termed in the seventeenth-century household ordinances, could usually gain admittance to the ceremonial rooms of the court, depending on the quality of their jewellery, the cut of their clothes or the whim of the gentleman usher keeping the door. For this Tudor and Stuart *beau monde*, the gravitational pull of the court was irresistible. It presented opportunities to lobby privy councillors; to observe the 'show' of state ceremonial; to acquire the latest in manners or clothes; or (no less fashionably) to attend a sermon by a clerical high-flier preaching in the Chapel Royal.

Nor was the king's household the only one at which they could pay court. Whenever there was a royal consort and an heir to the throne, each had their separate households, smaller in size, but organized on similar lines to that of the king.[7] These 'subsidiary courts' were potential rival centres of patronage and political influence. In the case of the heir to the throne, his household served almost invariably as the gathering point for a 'reversionary interest': a court-in-waiting that expected to come into its own on the monarch's demise. Until his death in 1612, the court of Henry, Prince of Wales – the first male heir apparent since the 1530s – briefly showed the

potential to become a focus for opposition to the crown's pro-Spanish foreign policy, as well as for a new cosmopolitanism in the patronage of the arts.[8] A similar reversionary interest gathered around James, Duke of York (the future James II), during the 1670s and 1680s, almost all of whose members were rewarded with court office when their master inherited the crown in 1685. These subsidiary courts also posed a problem of 'rival confessional space'. When the consort was a Catholic (as was the case for most of the seventeenth century), the queen's court frequently came to be seen as a focus for popish conspiracy and plotting (as in the 1610s, 1630s and again from the 1660s to 1688).

I. ORGANIZATION AND ETHOS

To impose order on this vast concourse of the great, the fashionable and the merely curious, the court was divided into four separate major departments, each corresponding to a spatial hierarchy within the palace. The right of access (the entrée) to each department narrowed the closer one approached the palace's inner sanctum, the private apartments of the king. In this,

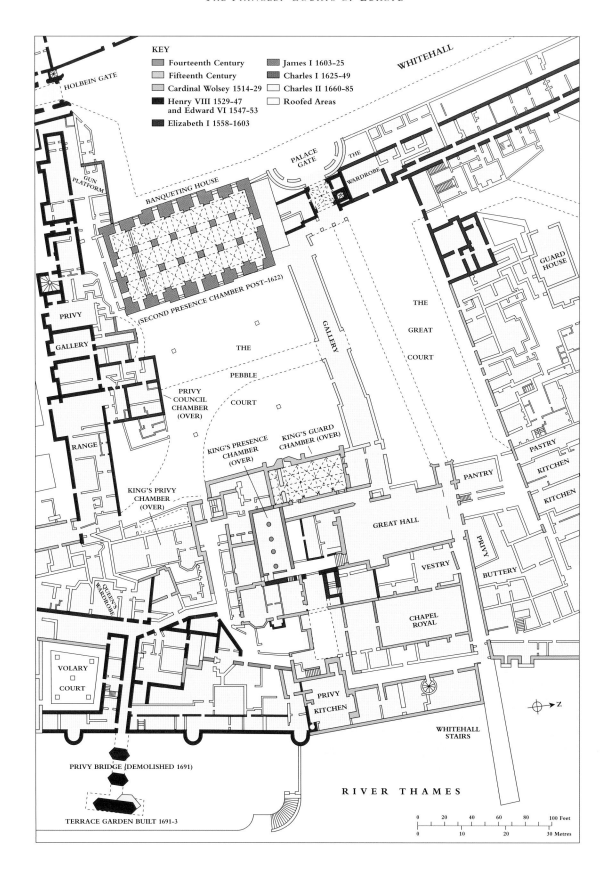

KEY
Fourteenth Century
Fifteenth Century
Cardinal Wolsey 1514-29
Henry VIII 1529-47 and Edward VI 1547-53
Elizabeth I 1558-1603
James I 1603-25
Charles I 1625-49
Charles II 1660-85
Roofed Areas

HOLBEIN GATE

WHITEHALL

GUN PLATFORM

PALACE GATE

THE WARDROBE

BANQUETING HOUSE

GUARD HOUSE

(SECOND PRESENCE CHAMBER POST-1622)

PRIVY

GALLERY

THE

PEBBLE

COURT

GALLERY

THE

GREAT

COURT

PRIVY COUNCIL CHAMBER (OVER)

RANGE

KING'S PRESENCE CHAMBER (OVER)

KING'S GUARD CHAMBER (OVER)

PASTRY

KITCHEN

PANTRY

KITCHEN

KING'S PRIVY CHAMBER (OVER)

GREAT HALL

PRIVY

QUEEN'S WARDROBE

VESTRY

BUTTERY

CHAPEL ROYAL

VOLARY

COURT

PRIVY KITCHEN

WHITEHALL STAIRS

z

PRIVY BRIDGE (DEMOLISHED 1691)

TERRACE GARDEN BUILT 1691-3

RIVER THAMES

0   20   40   60   80   100 Feet
0   10   20   30 Metres

98

Whitehall exemplified a model that had been inherited from the medieval Yorkist court, and the pattern was maintained, with only minor variations, wherever the king's household resided. As in the house of any medieval 'great lord', the largest and most accessible space at Whitehall was the central element of the Household department, under the jurisdiction of the lord steward: the Hall. Its bulk dominated the palace skyline, and, at least until the 1660s, it was here that most of the household dined, and where a large and constantly changing array of guests was daily entertained, according to their status, at the king's expense.[9]

Immediately next to the Hall lay the series of ceremonial rooms known as the Chamber, which constituted the second department, and ritual core, of the palace. Presided over by the lord chamberlain of the household – again, a post normally reserved for a senior noble grandee – the Chamber's sequence of apartments began and ended with a 'sacred space', areas devoted respectively to the deity and to his earthly delegate, the king. The first of these was the Chapel Royal, the principal venue for the court's worship of God; the second was the monarch's Presence Chamber, the main locus of the court's veneration of the prince. Here stood the symbols of the king's sovereignty: a 'chair of estate' (or throne), raised on a dais, canopied under a 'cloth of estate', and richly embroidered with the dynasty's arms. It was here that the monarch received ambassadors, gave audiences and dined in state, attended by the senior members of the household. Connecting the two was a series of ante-rooms and passageways. Immediately before reaching the Presence Chamber was the Watching Chamber, a large, tapestry-hung antechamber, where the security of the king's person was provided by the yeomen of the guard (hence its alternative name as the Guard Chamber). Unless the monarch directed otherwise, all the rooms of the Chamber were accessible, of right, to any nobleman and, at the discretion of the gentlemen ushers, to any 'persons of fashion' they chose to admit.

This sequence of state apartments presented the court's public face. The centre of power, however, lay elsewhere. Beyond the Presence Chamber, entered by a door beside the cloth of estate, lay the third and inmost department of the court: the Privy Lodgings of the king. This was the real hub of courtly politics and influence, and, unlike the semi-public rooms of the Chamber, the right of entrée to these private lodgings was rigorously limited; at any one time it was seldom enjoyed by as many as a hundred persons. Designated the Privy Chamber from around 1495 (and reorganized, after 1603, with a further 'inner' department, the Bedchamber), this inner sanctum was out-of-bounds to all but peers, privy councillors and those to whom the king had specifically granted the entrée, a privilege that might be conferred or removed at the monarch's will. In this relatively private area of the royal house, it was the king's most intimate servant, the groom of the stool (literally, the officer whose duties included attending the monarch on his close-stool) who ruled the department – although not without regular attempts by the lord chamberlain, as head of the Chamber, to extend his authority into the adjoining Privy Chamber at the groom's expense.

After the groom of the stool, only one other officer enjoyed such frequent and intimate access to the monarch, the master of the horse, who, as head of the fourth department of the household, the Stables, was responsible for the two most important aspects of the monarch's life outside the court. He arranged the king's (and the court's) travels and provided the hunters that the king rode in the principal courtly recreation, the chase (usually for bucks or stags). The nearness to the person of the monarch that the office entailed ensured that the mastership of the horse was one of the most prestigious of all court posts, and from the accession of Elizabeth I in 1558 to the death of Charles I in 1649 the list of its holders is almost a catalogue of royal favourites.[10]

Each monarch stamped his personality and preferences on the court: through those he promoted, and in the ordinances he chose to enforce or allowed to lapse. Conversely, however, the court also imposed its

The evolution of Whitehall: after the reign of Henry VIII, the palace's building history was one of almost haphazard accretion, as monarchs with meagre budgets sought, generally unsuccessfully, to adapt its elderly fabric to changing expectations of what a royal residence should be.

own disciplines on the prince. Court life revolved around ritual, and in a political culture that venerated custom at least as much as kingship, inherited traditions and practices commanded an authority that even kings tampered with at their peril. Their longevity is striking. Despite the seismic impact of the Reformation on the ritual life of the Church, most of the major elements of court ceremonial – as laid down in the household ordinances – seem to have survived relatively little changed from the early years of Henry VIII (1509–47) until to the accession of the Hanoverians in 1714. Ordinances could, of course, be broken or just ignored, but the monarch, however pampered and indulged, was always in some measure the prisoner of protocol.

It is time we considered the world in which these courtiers moved, and the functions that the court fulfilled in the political and cultural life of the realm. Four principal aspects emerge. The first is the use of 'magnificence' as a tool of policy – to make manifest the ruler's God-given primacy within the political order; second, the court's place as a setting for a liturgy of monarchy – a yearly cycle of ceremonial that encoded, in a symbolic language of gesture and deportment, a series of precepts about the sacredness of the king's person and the axioms of honour by which he was supposed to rule; and third, the court's role in cultural patronage – in architecture and the visual and performing arts. Finally, we need to examine the court's role as the 'house of policy', the political centre of the realm.

II. MAGNIFICENCE: HOSPITALITY AND DISPLAY

To posterity it is the opulence and quality of the court's material culture that attests most clearly to the magnificence of the royal household: the tapestries, paintings, armour, jewellery, clothing and plate that were created for the king and his immediate entourage. To contemporaries, however, the manifestations of courtly magnificence that registered most deeply were usually transient in form: the extravagant scale of the hospitality afforded within the court, and the ostentatious spectacles and ceremonial displays provided to the world outside it.

In England, perhaps uniquely in Europe, it was hospitality that constituted the prime form of courtly 'magnificence'. It was as 'necessary for the king of England this way to endear the English, who ever delighted in feasting', Edward Chamberlayne noted in the 1660s, 'as for the Italian princes by sights and shows to endear their subjects, who as much delighted therein'.[11] Thus, the first claim on the royal purse, long before the king contemplated spending on architecture, art or public spectacles as manifestations of royal power, was the obligation to feed the voracious horde of councillors, servants, guests and miscellaneous hangers-on who dined daily at court.[12] Until reformed in the 1660s, this daily provision of 'bouche of court' to well over a thousand persons – meals at the king's tables and at the king's charge – remained the largest single item of royal expenditure; the most public expression of the king's 'good lordship'.

This 'magnificent and abundant plenty of the king's tables' also had its political function.[13] Until the major retrenchments of 1662–4, it remained an almost self-consciously archaic symbol of the king's place as the greatest of the feudal lords, with the hierarchy of his subjects, from the greatest nobleman to the beggar at the gate, literally sustained by his royal bounty. When cut-backs were planned in 1663, Charles II's lord steward urged the king to maintain the status quo, arguing that the system had 'acquired so much veneration amongst the people that it is become a considerable part in the government and greatness of the state'.[14] The hospitality of the court – the 'roast beef of Old England' – was an instrument of policy.

The most spectacular public instances of courtly magnificence – the celebration of the dynasty's rites of passage, in coronations, marriages and funerals, and ceremonial entries into the capital – tended to be equally ephemeral. Temporary triumphal arches, bonfires and fireworks, the thousands of metres of cloth consumed as liveries or hangings, as well as the obligatory feasting: all these were deployed to create an impression of the royal household as a place of almost super-human opulence – and at equally prodigious cost. The scale of expenditure offers clues to the importance attached to such ostentation (relative to other areas of royal spending) in sustaining the prestige and authority of the royal house. Thus, in 1511, two years after his accession, Henry VIII spent £4,000 on a tournament at

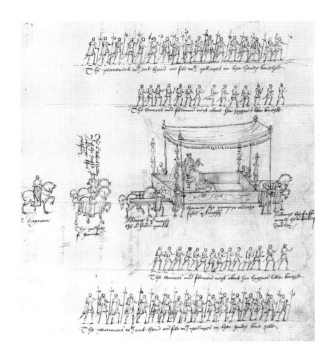

The coronation procession of Elizabeth I in 1559. Like the pre-Reformation eucharist, monarchs were paraded through the streets under a processional canopy. Immediately behind the queen is Lord Robert Dudley (the future Earl of Leicester) in his role as master of the horse (the officer charged with attending the monarch outside the palace). Flanking the queen are rows of footmen and, beyond them, the gentlemen pensioners, with their gilt pole-axes. With the single exception of Dudley, who has been permitted to retain his hat as a mark of favour, all walk bare-headed in the presence of the monarch.

Westminster, a sum that was nearly double the cost (£2,300) of his 900-ton warship, the *Great Elizabeth*.[15] Similarly, the marriage of James I's daughter, Princess Elizabeth, to the Elector Palatine of the Rhine in 1613 cost the Exchequer more than £93,000 – almost an entire year's worth of the crown's landed income.[16]

Staggering though these sums are, they do not take account of the prodigious expenditure by individual courtiers on their jewellery and apparel – sums that, collectively, more than doubled or trebled those paid out of the royal purse. At one end of the scale, a fashionable black suit for court dress might cost around £150 in the early seventeenth century – or the price of building one of the desirable brick houses in the Earl of Bedford's Covent Garden Piazza in the

1630s; at the other end of the scale, the cost of the jewel-encrusted suits worn on state occasions by gentlemen of fashion reached astronomical sums. For the coronation of Charles II, the second Duke of Buckingham allegedly spent £30,000 (the equivalent of an affluent knight's income for a whole decade) on suitably gorgeous clothing for himself and his retinue.[17]

Rulers and their stage-managers (such as John Ogilby and Sir Edward Walker, the planners of Charles II's coronation) were well aware of the theatricality of these flashy ceremonials. That 'princes are set on stages in the sight and view of all the world', as Elizabeth I once famously put it, was one of the clichés of court life.[18] Yet this emphasis on the theatrical element in the court's public ceremonial is in danger of masking as much as it reveals. For, just as with great ecclesiastical pomp – where likewise an element of theatre is rarely absent – this theatrical aspect in court ceremony co-existed with a complementary and at times even more powerful component: liturgy, or the choreography of religious devotion. This is particularly evident when one turns from the great public fêtes – weddings, coronations and the like – to the regular ceremonial life of the court, the rituals observed within the household, week after week, year after year. Here, it is the liturgical and quasi-religious elements that predominate, and, though outward magnificence remains an obvious element, this yearly cycle of Chamber ceremonial employs a wider repertory of symbolism and articulates a far subtler and more nuanced range of meanings.

III. RITUAL AND CEREMONIAL

The starting point of court ritual was the conviction that both political authority and the persons in whom it inhered were sacred commodities. The royal motto *Dieu et mon droit* (God is my right [to rule]), reiterated the divine origins of monarchical power, and was carved, painted and embroidered in a thousand forms throughout the royal palaces. Kings, so medieval doctrine famously held, possessed two bodies: one human and mortal; the other, their 'politic body' as the personification of the realm, enduring and semi-divine. Thus, for all that kings might be rakes and voluptuaries as men, in their 'politic capacity' they were the temporal representatives of divinity. Expressing that divinity of kingship – in architecture, symbolism, gesture and etiquette – was arguably the court's principal *raison d'être*, at least until the Civil Wars of the 1640s. To a degree that had become unimaginable, even by the eighteenth century, court life was governed by an intricately choreographed cycle of ritual and ceremonial, much of it liturgical or quasi-religious in form.

Of all the court's public rituals, that which most overtly demonstrated the numinous, supernatural quality of monarchical power, was the 'touching for the king's evil' – a form of tuberculosis that conveniently enjoyed a high rate of natural recovery, even without monarchically induced divine intervention. The rite, performed by all Tudor monarchs (except perhaps Edward VI) and all Stuart monarchs until 1688, was overtly sacramental, with the king officiating as a priest-like figure, enthroned under a cloth of estate, attended by his chaplains and the senior officers

of the court, mediating the healing power of Christ. Literally thousands flocked to court to receive the 'royal touch'; Charles II, for example, touched almost 1,500 persons in the Whitehall Banqueting House within the space of three months in 1661;[19] and the 'fame' of cures attributed to these therapeutic gifts powerfully enhanced the aura that attached even to the most worldly of kings.[20]

This, however, was only one of many points at which religious ritual was embedded in the ceremonial routines of the court. The entire court calendar was regulated by the Church's 'ritual year'. Both before and after the Reformation, the principal day for regular household ceremonial was Sunday, 'the Lord's day', when the king went in public procession from the Privy Lodgings to the Chapel Royal; often dined in public afterwards; and met with his council. Likewise, other than the king's birthday and accession day (and, after 1605, the commemoration of the Gunpowder Plot), the principal occasions of courtly ceremony corresponded to the twelve major 'solemnities' of the ecclesiastical year. A small number of 'popish' feast-days, such as Corpus Christi,[21] were pruned from the calendar after the Reformation; but otherwise the pre-Reformation calendar remained virtually unchanged, with twelve major court days forming an annual cycle running from Michaelmas (29 September), to All Saints (1 November), Christmas (25 December), New Year's Day (1 January), Twelfth Day (or Epiphany, 6 January), Candlemas (the Purification of the Virgin Mary, 2 February), Lady Day (25 March), Easter, Ascension, Whitsunday, Trinity, and ending with St John the Baptist (or Midsummer, 24 June).[22]

On these 'collar days' – so called because they were days when, by tradition, the officers of the household and the knights of the Garter wore their ceremonial gold-and-enamel chains, or 'collars' – the procession to the chapel took on particular elaboration. Most of the major court office-holders were involved, taking their places according to their rank and precedence, in a procession that extended to perhaps as many as a hundred participants. Immediately before the king came the sword of state (the emblem of sovereignty second only to the crown), usually carried by an earl of 'ancient lineage'; and then, finally, the focal point of the whole procession, the king. On the four greatest

Above: *The collar-day procession to the Chapel Royal (c.1600). Elizabeth I, statue-like in a wheeled chair, makes her way to chapel propelled by a 'groom of the coaches and litters' dressed in the royal livery. Dating from the last years of the queen's reign, the picture is also a celebration of the reciprocity of power and authority between the crown and the 'ancient nobility'. The bearer of the sword of state, occupying the most honorific place nearest the queen, is the 7th Earl of Shrewsbury, whose family had been peers since 1409. The lord chamberlain (the fourth Garter knight from the left) is George Carey, 2nd Lord Hunsdon, a cousin of the queen through the Boleyn line. The picture was probably commissioned by the master of the horse, Edward Somerset, 4th Earl of Worcester (the balding figure in the foreground), whose forebears had been peers since 1397. The gentlemen pensioners with their gilt pole-axes line the processional route. The architectural setting, however, is entirely fictitious: the English court had to wait until 1619 and Inigo Jones's Banqueting House before it acquired anything approaching the classical sophistication of the Italianate building depicted in the background (right).*

Left: *The royal traverse: Henry VIII in his closet, from the* Liber Niger *of the Order of the Garter, compiled c.1534. The colour of the traverse within the royal closet changed with the liturgical seasons: blue in Holy Week, for example, cloth of gold at Easter.*

feasts of the ecclesiastical year (Christmas, Easter, Whitsunday and All Saints), the ceremonial was further dignified by the appearance of the monarch in a purple robe of state, and (at least under the Tudors) the wearing of the closed 'imperial' crown.[23] Yet, perhaps the most symbolically laden of all the collar-day regalia throughout this period was the processional canopy carried over the monarch, a direct appropriation of the canopy borne over the consecrated host (which in Catholic doctrine was believed to be the actual Body of Christ) in pre-Reformation eucharistic processions.[24]

So the king, too, was manifestly sacred; and, once the monarch was inside the Chapel Royal, the deity was forced to share the ceremonial limelight with his earthly representative. The king heard the service from his closet (an elevated gallery at the west end of the chapel), raised above the heads of his courtiers, a figure in every sense 'between heaven and earth'. The sacredness of the king's presence was further emphasized by his seclusion within the closet inside a curtained, tabernacle-like area called the 'traverse'. For the king's reception of the communion (in both pre- and post-Reformation practice), a second, temporary, traverse – 'a little canopy or pavilion' – seems to have been erected to the side of the altar in the Chapel Royal, a practice identical to (and possibly derived from) the Castilian court.[25] For the king's daily and less ceremonious devotions, a second private chapel (also called, confusingly, a closet) was located off the gallery that connected the Presence Chamber and Privy Chamber.[26]

The Reformation obviously altered the pattern of courtly devotions from the eucharist-centred liturgy of the mass to one of preaching and readings – the morning and evening prayer of Cranmer's Prayer Book of 1552 (revised and reissued in 1662). But otherwise, the great Sunday and holy-day processions remained unaltered; the closet continued to be used; even the pre-Reformation custom of the king making an offering of gold at the altar on collar days was retained as a symbol of the intimate link between divine and temporal rule.[27] The use of the altar-side traverse, set up in the sanctuary of the chapel for the monarch's reception of the sacrament, appears to have survived at least until the reign of George III.[28]

By stripping away most of the ceremonial that attended the eucharistic real presence, while leaving the ceremonial attending the king's royal presence almost untouched, the Reformation had the paradoxical effect of enhancing the (mostly pre-Reformation) rituals affirming the sacredness of monarchy. Tabernacles for the host; baldachins for the altar; processions in which the eucharist was carried under a canopy: all these were discarded after 1558 as 'popish superstitions', along with most of the elaborate pre-Reformation choreography of bowings and genuflexions towards the altar. Towards the throne, however, all these objects and practices remained in common usage.

Rituals of royal dining were equally overlaid with quasi-ecclesiastical ceremonial. Their elaborate choreography, largely settled during the reign of Henry VIII, provided the model, with only minor variations, for royal dining in state until the beginning of the eighteenth century. Here, too, practices that, after the Reformation, were forbidden at the altar, nevertheless continued to be de rigueur at the royal dinner table. The frequency with which monarchs dined in state varied from reign to reign: from as often as weekly, on Sundays and collar days, under Henry VIII (and also, it seems, under Charles I), to much less frequent observance under the later Stuarts. For part, or possibly all, of Elizabeth's reign (1558–1603), the practice seems to have fallen into temporary desuetude. On the occasions when the ritual was observed, however, it was held in a setting, and with a liturgical complexity, that self-consciously paralleled the ritualism of the mass. The Presence Chamber was arranged in such a way as to resemble the liturgical east end (the communion-table end) of a church. The king's table, like the communion table, was usually raised on a dais and covered with a fine linen cloth; above it was suspended a canopy and cloth of estate; and, by the 1660s, the king's table was also enclosed by a rail, further emphasizing the altar-like aspect of the setting.

Appropriately, the ceremony began and ended with a ritualized ablution, the washing of the king's hands – just as ritual washing, at the *lavabo* and post-communion, respectively preceded and concluded the consecration in the mass, the archetypal liturgical meal.[29] With the king seated at his table under the cloth of estate, the intricate ritual of the ablution was performed by the two most senior peers present.

From the moment the towel and the water used in the ablution touched the king, they were treated as if they had themselves become sacralized – a point that was strikingly dramatized in the post-ablution procession back to the Ewery, in which the gentleman usher took 'that part of the towel…in which the king hath wiped' and carried it above his head as though displaying a holy relic.[30]

After this stately prelude, the king's dinner began, with the highest ranking prelate present saying the grace.[31] The usual practice was for the king to dine alone, consuming his meal, not, as lesser mortals, for conviviality or even for bodily nourishment, but as an act of secular communion under the canopy before an assembled company standing bare-headed before him.[32] At the conclusion of the meal, when the king withdrew, a series of 'post-communion' rituals proceeded in silence. The fusion of secular and sacred liturgy reached its culmination when the king's almoner – the officer who distributed the king's charity, and almost invariably a bishop – came forward to receive the cloth that had covered the king's table. At the centre of the king's dinner table, he paused and genuflected as if before an altar.[33] Two gentlemen ushers then took the cloth from either end of the table and folded it towards the centre, presenting it to the almoner, 'ready on his knee', who took it 'betwixt his arms' and then carried it solemnly to the Presence-Chamber door where it was received by the yeomen ewer.[34] This sight of a bishop genuflecting before the king's table was perhaps the most vivid acknowledgement of the 'sacramental' aspect of the royal dining ritual: the clear symbolic connection between the king's dinner and the Lord's Supper. In practice, of course, it is likely that these rules varied considerably, according to the general preferences (and daily moods) of individual monarchs;[35] but, at least until the later seventeenth century, the exaltation of the monarch as a sacred object was built into the ordinary routines of court life: in the seasonal observances of the Chapel Royal, and in the regular practices of royal dining in state. As John Donne declared in one of his sermons to James I's court, 'as Princes are Gods, so their well-govern'd courts are copies and representations of heaven'.[36]

These rituals of the Chamber and the Household sent out a more complicated series of semaphores, however, than merely the uncritical adulation of the king. Chamber protocol stipulated that the most honorific elements of the court's rituals were to be undertaken by those 'of greatest estate', that is, those ranking highest in the nobility and holding the greatest offices of state. These rankings were partly a reflection of royal favour, of course, in that the king appointed the great officers of state and could create new peers; and a very small number of great offices (such as the earl marshalcy) were deemed to trump all inherited titles of nobility. But, in general, the prime criterion for precedence at court was degree within the peerage's ascending order of baron, viscount, earl, marquess and duke. Seniority between the members of the same degree was decided by antiquity of title: the older the title, the higher the seniority within each degree.

So the hierarchy that court ceremonial affirmed was one in which the king was, of course, the apex and guarantor; but it was also one of which he personally was only partly the author. In casting the nobles 'of greatest estate' as the immediate participants with the monarch in the public rituals of sovereignty – bearing the sword of state in procession, assisting in the most honourable roles at the king's table – household protocol affirmed a complementary principle: that these same men were entitled to occupy an equally lofty role in the 'counsels of the realm', in the business of defining policy and advising the king. As a treatise dedicated to Charles I's captain of the gentlemen pensioners, the Earl of Salisbury, put it in 1633, the 'principal peers' were the 'watch-towers of the state' upon whom the king should 'bestow…the greatest and highest honours'.[37] Through the language of gesture and deportment, the ceremonies of Chapel and Presence Chamber reiterated weekly this central axiom of the 'ancient constitution'.[38] Ritual spoke more clearly than any treatise.

This complementary, sometimes even competitive, element in aulic ceremonial is in itself a caution against regarding the court in exclusively monarch-centred terms. Beyond the court's status as the king's household, it was also the focal point for a series of aristocratic circles of influence and patronage that both reinforced, and perhaps occasionally rivalled, the supremacy of Whitehall. Nowhere is this competitive interplay more clearly evident than in the patronage of architecture and the arts.

IV. CULTURE AND COURT PATRONAGE

Of all the aspects of early modern culture, the one deemed most 'princely' was architecture, the so-called 'mistress art'. It was the court's buildings that attested most durably and overtly to royal 'majesty' and 'magnificence', and, under the first two Tudors at least, there was no doubt that the monarch himself was unquestionably the kingdom's greatest architectural patron. New palaces were built or acquired at a prodigious rate: Richmond (completed by 1501), Whitehall (acquired and extended from 1529), Hampton Court (1529), St James's (begun in 1531), Nonsuch Palace (begun in 1538), major new building at Windsor, as well as a string of lesser properties, mostly acquired as hunting lodges. Financed in large part out of the windfall spoils from the dissolution of the monasteries, Henry VIII's building projects set a standard for royal magnificence that his successors found difficult, if not impossible, to emulate. There the problems began. After Henry's death in 1547, no major new royal palace was begun until William III began rebuilding Kensington in 1689.[39] In the interim, as builders (or even as remodellers) of the architectural settings of their courts, English monarchs lagged well behind even some of the more moderately prosperous German prince-bishops.

As early as Elizabeth's reign, the exterior of Whitehall had come to seem architecturally *passé*; '[it] has no great appearance for a royal house', the French ambassador, de Maisse, commented in 1597. James I's one major addition, the Banqueting House (erected to Inigo Jones's design from 1619), did provide Whitehall with a ceremonial space – and a new Presence Chamber – to rival the great state rooms of foreign courts; but the juxtaposition of its richly Italianate architecture and monumental scale merely served to point up the obsolete character of the rambling Tudor ranges that surrounded it. Yet, despite Charles I's ambitious plans for the remodelling of Whitehall as an Escorial on the Thames, none of the Stuart kings possessed the financial resources to do more than tinker with the palace's fabric. In 1698 the Duc de Saint-Simon described it as 'the largest and ugliest house in Europe'.[40]

The courtier nobility, meanwhile, built on a prodigious scale in the immediate environs of the court,

profoundly affecting the development of the capital. A single Jacobean courtier, the first Earl of Salisbury, spent more on architectural patronage in the six years 1607–12 than the crown spent on the fabric of Whitehall (including Jones's new Banqueting House) during the entire quarter-century before the Civil War.[41] Like Venice, the river between the City and Whitehall was lined with the palaces of the peerage, most of which were extensively rebuilt between 1550 and 1650. Simultaneously, Covent Garden and Westminster developed as fashionable aristocratic *faubourgs*;[42] and, after the Restoration, there was a further spate of aristocratic palace-building to the immediate north and west of St James's Park – almost all of it for senior office-holders at court.

Yet, while Whitehall itself may have remained externally unprepossessing, its cavernous interiors paraded wealth with Croesus-like ostentation. Modern aesthetic sensibilities have tended to esteem paintings as the most valuable (and certainly the costliest) of the visual arts. In the sixteenth and seventeenth centuries it was generally tapestries, often woven with silver or gold thread, that were the most prestigious and expensive works of art. In the 1640s, when the highest-priced painting by van Dyck could be purchased for £100, the more expensive suites of tapestries in the royal collections were each valued at around £8,000.[43] Although most of the finest pieces continued to come from France and Flanders throughout the sixteenth and seventeenth centuries, domestic tapestry production began in 1619 when James I established a royal manufactory at Mortlake, near London. In the course of Charles I's reign, royal expenditure on Mortlake weaving and other tapestry acquisitions amounted to almost double what the king spent on assembling his celebrated collection of Italian and Flemish paintings.[44]

For many poets and playwrights, too, the court remained their principal source of patronage, either in the employ of the crown, or, through contacts made at court, in the households of the greater nobility. Court culture placed a high premium on literary and rhetorical style, and numerous courtiers – from Henry VIII's privy councillor the Earl of Surrey, to the Earl of Rochester, a gentleman of the bedchamber in Charles II's reign – were themselves accomplished poets and authors. Courtiers vied with each other (and the

Dress as 'conspicuous consumption': Daniel Mytens's portrait of the royal favourite, George Villiers, first Duke of Buckingham, in a pearl-encrusted suit. The value of the pearls worn by the duke exceeded the contemporary price of the picture by at least tenfold.

crown) to have celebrated literary figures attached to their households, and in the sixteenth and early seventeenth centuries London's theatrical companies were normally known by the names of their courtier patrons.

It was the monarch's patronage, however, that carried the greatest cachet. James I's patronage of William Shakespeare represents perhaps the clearest example of the intimate connections between the London theatre and the court. Having worked under the patronage of Elizabeth I's lord chamberlain, Shakespeare's company was singled out for royal patronage by James I within months of his accession. From 1603 it became 'the King's Men', the monarch's own, and the principal company to write for, and perform before, the court. Indeed, Shakespeare and his colleagues formally became members of the royal household as grooms extraordinary of the Chamber. They wore the king's livery (as when they accompanied James I's ceremonial entry into London in 1604);

and their performances formed an integral part of the court's major festivities – with the 'season' concentrated around Christmas at Whitehall (from 26 December to Twelfth Night), and then running intermittently until the beginning of Lent.[45]

Court patronage, then, was a more extensive phenomenon than specifically royal patronage, and the initiative for changes in artistic fashion was as likely to lie as much with the courtier élite as with the preferences of the prince. Nor was court drama, any more than court ritual, purely a matter of sycophantic flattery of the monarch and the ruling élite. The court possessed its own language of criticism, often encoded in historical or mythological allusion, but usually easily decipherable. Literary works produced by or for the court – from the poems of John Skelton (*c*.1460–1529) and the masques of Ben Jonson (*c*.1573–1637) to the Restoration comedies – frequently offered trenchant criticisms of the political and moral corruption of the very audiences to whom they were addressed.[46]

V. POLITICS: COUNCIL AND PRIVY CHAMBER

Once the king left the public gaze and entered the Privy Lodgings the protocol of the Chamber gave way to a far more intimate and less formal world. Here, in the inner sanctum of the palace, the organizing principles were very different. This was a place where the mere fact of access to, and intimacy with, the sovereign could result in political influence potentially far greater than that of any noble grandee; and where courtiers became adept at detecting swings of mood or favour in the slightest change of the monarch's visage. It was this rarefied world that was the political hub of the court, the point where matters of state were decided, and where the fortunes of courtiers were made and unmade.

Of all the influences on the conduct of politics, none impinged more directly than the allocation and control of space within the palace. Unlike France, where the Valois and Bourbon kings lived out almost their whole lives before their courtiers' gaze, public and private spheres in the English palaces were clearly demarcated. The barrier, as we have seen, lay between the sequence of ceremonial 'rooms of state' (the

Chamber) and the monarch's private apartments. By rigorously limiting the right of entrée to the Privy Lodgings, the monarch could distance himself both physically, from his courtiers, and morally, from the importunity of suitors and his ministers' competition for power.[47]

In contrast to the menials who had attended his father, Henry VIII's choice of high-born gentlemen to staff his Privy Chamber provided him with an immediate entourage whose social rank fitted them naturally for the world of diplomacy, counsel and political power. The once lowly place of groom of the stool, the head of the Privy Chamber, was transformed into one of the most influential offices at court, a prominence that he tended to retain, except during the reigns of queens regnant, until the later seventeenth century. So, by around 1520, there had emerged two centres of power at court: the Chamber, the domain of the councillors and great officers of state; and the Privy Chamber, staffed by the king's 'minions' and favourites. Although the formulation of policy still rested for most of the reign with two powerful bureaucrat-ministers, first Cardinal Wolsey (until his fall in 1529), and then Thomas Cromwell (until he, too, was toppled by an aristocratic coup in 1540), they now had to work with, and through, the king's intimate Privy Chamber entourage.

Yet, influence at court, however absolute, could never serve alone as a secure foundation for the exercise of political power. For no monarch – Tudor, Stuart or Hanoverian – could afford to ignore the realities of political authority in the world beyond Whitehall, and in the localities. In the absence of either a standing army or a paid bureaucracy, the efficacy of royal authority depended in large measure on the co-operation of the regional élites – the group that, at court, was represented pre-eminently by the landed aristocratic magnates.

By 1540 the noble-dominated Chamber and the placemen-filled Privy Chamber seemed to stand for almost antithetical political values. In the one, power and status derived from landed wealth and inherited right; in the other, influence stemmed principally (often exclusively) from *ad hominem* royal favour and daily access to the king. The result was an aristocratic coup that toppled Cromwell and drastically weakened the power of the king's inner entourage. To the leaders of this *putsch*, the solution was for the Chamber nobility to colonize the rival centre of power, the Privy Chamber. Thus, on 10 August 1540, a fortnight after Cromwell's execution, a Privy Council – a body that had emerged in 1536 as a small group of aristocratic advisers offering counsel to the king – was finally given a formalized existence. The post-1540 order represented a synthesis of political styles; what might be termed a 'politics of honour and lineage' fused with the 'politics of intimacy'. The new Privy Council was dominated (as councils traditionally were) by the nobility, but its meeting place was now in the heart of the Privy Lodgings, within six metres or so of the king's bedchamber door.[48]

These two early Tudor innovations – the separation of the king's private apartments from the Chamber in the 1490s (which created the Privy Chamber), and the greater nobility's assertion of the right to a formalized place in that private world (which created the Privy Council) – set the pattern for an essentially bi-polar court politics that endured, with surprising resilience, until Parliament became a major influence on court faction in the later seventeenth century.

There was thus never a single 'court politics'. In the business of advising the king, a politics of favour, access and intimacy, played in uneasy tandem with a potentially rival politics of honour, ancient lineage and alleged prescriptive right. Access and intimacy did not always equate with political power; but, where the king chose that it should do so, the existence of a powerful source of back-room counsel invariably created tensions between the staff of the private apartments and members of the Privy Council, the great officers of state who regarded themselves as the 'rightful' hierarchy of the realm. Politics, for king and ministers alike, was the art of balancing the two. Where influence was deemed to have shifted too far towards the entourage, it almost invariably provoked a conciliar reaction – most often couched in the rhetoric of 'evil counsellors' (the idea that basely born parvenus had usurped the influence that should properly be exercised by the *consiliarii nati*).

In the half-century after Henry VIII's death, the general trend was towards the extension of conciliar authority at court. The power vacuum created by the minority of the boy-king Edward VI (1547–53) clearly advanced this process, despite the internecine faction-fighting between rival noble groups within the council. The accession of two female monarchs in succession, Mary I (1553–8) and Elizabeth I (1558–1603), brought to completion the political neutering of the Privy Chamber, for reigning queens required a female Privy Chamber staff; and none of the later-Tudor gentlewomen showed either the inclination or ability to set themselves up, as their male counterparts had done, as major power-brokers at court.[49] Stripped of its political role, the Elizabethan Privy Chamber became a glorified domestic staff.[50]

So power shifted back to the Privy Council, where it remained virtually unchallenged for the next half century. That did not mean that the court was innocent of feuds or factions;[51] and, of course, there were those who were recognized as enjoying the queen's particular favour – Burghley and Leicester, early in the reign; and, later, Sir Walter Raleigh and the second Earl of Essex. For much of the reign, however, a *modus vivendi* prevailed among the leading privy councillors, in which the principal contenders for power 'seem to have decided that while competition was healthy, full-blown factional disputes were a destructive and time-consuming diversion'.[52]

For half a century under Elizabeth, then, the politics of honour and lineage repeatedly trumped the politics of access, a trend that owed much to what the Jacobean courtier, Sir Robert Naunton, called the queen's 'natural propensity to grace and support [the] ancient nobility'.[53] Indeed, it has been estimated that around two-thirds of the Elizabethan nobility were at least 'part-time' courtiers during the early years of her reign, and though this proportion fell later in the reign, it was not by very much – making it one of the most aristocratic courts in English history.[54] Under the early Tudors, the idea that the 'ancient nobility' should enjoy a primacy at court and in counsel had been honoured as often in the breach as in the observance; under Elizabeth, however, it was not only reaffirmed, but came to be regarded as a normative principle of rule. There were some obvious exceptions, such as the promotion of the queen's glamorous favourite and dancing-partner, Sir Christopher Hatton, to the lord chancellorship; or the dangerous narrowing of noble participation on the Privy Council during the queen's last years. In general, however, Elizabethan practice had enshrined three principles that were to have a powerful prescriptive force, particularly when viewed in retrospect from the very different world of the early Stuart court: that the Privy Council was the principal source of advice and the rightful centre of power at court; that the nobility was a sacrosanct political caste; and that the senior places on that council should go to the great men of the realm.[55]

VI. POLITICS: COUNCIL AND BEDCHAMBER

With the accession of James VI of Scotland (the great-great-grandson of Henry VII) as James I of England and Ireland, each of these cosy Elizabethan rules was discarded or rewritten. Whitehall became the seat of government for a triple-monarchy, for the first time ruling the whole of the British Isles. The personnel of the court was transformed root and branch. Because James could no longer be resident in Edinburgh,

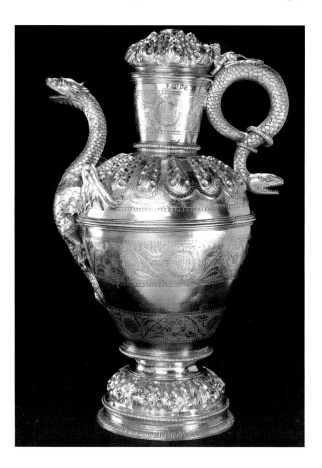

Edinburgh had come to reside in Whitehall. An extensive Scottish entourage arrived with the new king, many of whom had come to stay.[56] Henceforth, James assumed, his would be a British court; a model and epitome of the wider legal union between Scotland and England, which, he hoped, would create a single 'kingdom of Great Britain', with Whitehall at its hub. Royal iconography duly articulated this new ideal. During 1604–5 most of the old Tudor court plate (much of it dating back to the reign of Henry VIII) was painstakingly copied, and the replacements decorated with the king's chosen emblem of union: Scottish thistles interwoven with the Tudor rose.[57]

This decorative scheme found its practical correlative in James's alterations to the organization of the court. There were to be two 'interwoven' centres of power, divided respectively between the two British nations. The public ceremonial side of the court, the Chamber, was to continue to be predominantly English; but the suite of private apartments, which had hitherto constituted the Privy Chamber, was now further subdivided. The inner portions of what had formerly been the Privy Chamber (including the king's bedroom, withdrawing room, study and the smaller rooms that served them) were hived off as a new and separate department: the Bedchamber. The effect of these Jacobean reforms was to create a new barrier within the Privy Lodgings, at the Bedchamber door; and, to the consternation of James's English courtiers, the personnel of this new department was to be almost exclusively Scots.[58]

The real loser was the council. Entry to the inner royal apartment was now forbidden to all but the Bedchamber staff and the princes of the blood, unless specifically invited by the king. All privy councillors and others who enjoyed the entrée to the Privy Chamber, formerly the bar between the 'inner' apartments, now had to wait for an audience with the king – either in the Privy Chamber (now part of the 'outer' court) or, if the king wished to show favour, in the Withdrawing Room or even in the Bedchamber itself, depending on the degree of intimacy that he wished to accord. For the first time since the establishment of a truly Privy Council in 1536–40, the councillors had lost their automatic right of access to the inner apartments of the king. 'Even if the entrée were granted [to privy councillors],' Neil Cuddy has

Above: *The currency of courtly gift-giving: portraits, such as this one of Charles, Prince of Wales, painted c.1620 and given to the prince's uncle, Christian IV of Denmark, formed part of a culture of gift-exchange that encompassed most of the senior members of the court. It is listed in the Frederiksborg Castle inventory in 1650. In this idealized image of the prince's Presence Chamber, a series of visual clues allude to Charles's well-attested ambition to rebuild Whitehall along classical lines. An architect's plan lies ready on the table; imaginary Italianate architecture fills the background; and the throne, with its winged sphinxes, bears a close resemblance to the celebrated Hellenistic marble throne contemporaneously acquired by the earl marshal, the Earl of Arundel.*

Left: *The union of the British crowns: a silver-gilt water jug, part of the set of plate engraved for James VI and I, 1604–5, with interwoven English roses and Scottish thistles. It was sold by Charles I in 1626.*

observed, 'it was enjoyed in much greater measure by the Bedchamber's staff…Council and minister now revolved in a different orbit from the king and Bedchamber.'[59] Indeed, the two most notorious favourites of the reign – Robert Ker, Earl of Somerset, and George Villiers, Duke of Buckingham – both owed their initial rise to power to their positions as members of the inner entourage. By the later years of the reign, the Archbishop of Canterbury, George Abbott, was alleged to have quipped that there were two councils in England, of which 'that of Newmarket [the hunting lodge where the king was attended only by his Bedchamber staff and immediate entourage] was the higher'.[60]

With these major alterations in the political topography of the court, the river of patronage also began to flow through different channels. Under Elizabeth, almost all suits for crown patronage had been directed through members of the Privy Council. They were the kingdom's principal patronage-brokers, and they were also the major recipients of royal largesse. With the shift of power towards the inner apartments, it was the staff of the Bedchamber who became the principal 'promoters' of suits for royal favour; worse still, from an English perspective, it was the Scots who became the principal recipients of royal bounty.[61] As Sir John Holles, himself a courtier and comptroller of the Prince of Wales's household, lamented in Parliament in 1610, the Scots 'not only…possess the royal presence, they be warm within, while the best of ours starve without'.[62]

As a solution to James's immediate political problem in 1603 – how to be an effective absentee king of Scotland – the 'revival of the entourage', and the king's use of it to place distance between himself and his English council, had much to commend it. The creation of the Bedchamber, as both a Scottish enclave at the heart of the Whitehall court and a rival centre of power to the English council, reassured James's Scottish constituency that their king, in going south, had not also gone native. The king was surrounded by men who had their own networks of informants on Scottish affairs, and who acted as vitally important conduits of information. The innovations caused friction with his English courtiers, of course; but James's success in governing Scotland from Whitehall (or Newmarket) probably owed much to the novel

structures he had created within his 'British' household.

If these Jacobean alterations to the court provided an effective solution to the problems of absentee kingship in Scotland, at least in the short term, the presence of a Scottish-staffed Bedchamber and, still more, the actions of the Scottish favourite Ker, were catastrophic for James's relations with the English governing élite. During the mid-1610s, the court's reputation was tainted by allegations of sexual scandal, financial profligacy, corruption and even witchcraft. Rock bottom was reached in 1616 when, amid lurid publicity, Somerset, by now lord chamberlain and reigning favourite, was convicted along with his wife on charges of poisoning and murder.[63]

The accession of the impeccably chaste Charles I in 1625 did much to redress the moral and financial deficiencies of the Whitehall court. Royal expenditure was reined in, and the new king embarked on a reordering of the royal household, treating it as a microcosm of the 'order and decency' that he wished to impose on the macrocosm of the realm.[64] For this reformation of the court, Charles went back to the practices of the Tudors. Henrician usage provided his exemplar in reordering the court's organization and ceremonial; and, as issued in 1630, his household ordinances were closely modelled on Wolsey's Eltham Ordinances of 1526, but with the Jacobean provisions for the Bedchamber unchanged. Similarly, there is an almost Elizabethan quality to the lip-service Charles paid to the 'politics of honour'. He scrupulously reserved most of the great offices of state to members of the 'ancient nobility' (which, by this time, meant those peers of Tudor creation or earlier), even where their views on aspects of policy were known to conflict with his own – witness his appointment of the third Earl of Pembroke, a bitter enemy of the royal favourite, the Duke of Buckingham, as lord steward of the household in 1625. The Order of the Garter was revivified, with its statutes revised (once again, to conform with Henrician practice), and its membership was reserved almost exclusively for peers of ancient lineage.[65]

Yet, this 'altered state of the Caroline court' was more cosmetic than real. The new king did nothing to alter what was widely perceived to be the imbalance of power between the council and Buckingham, the *arriviste* who had succeeded Somerset as James I's favourite and had successfully retained his influence at the accession of the new king. Buckingham 'dishonoured' the old nobility by openly selling peerages, monopolized major offices (including the office of lord admiral and the mastership of the horse), and filled the court and council with his relatives and placemen. The aristocratic reaction was both violent and wholly predictable. During the 1620s court faction spilled over into Parliament with a ferocity that had not been seen since the attack on Cromwell in 1540. The legislature became the forum in which disgruntled councillors chose to pursue their factional vendettas against rival interests at court.[66]

Criticism of the court now centred less on its immorality than on its 'popery'. The charge was encouraged by the presence of a French Catholic consort, the policies of the senior archbishop William Laud and the opening of diplomatic relations with the papal court in Rome. By 1640 the belief that leading members of the court were conspiring to destroy Protestantism in England was so widespread as to weaken profoundly the political standing of the crown.[67] Moreover, in moments of crisis, Charles tended to ignore the aristocratic grandees he had promoted to great office; his ostentatious deference to the 'politics of honour' was exposed as a sham. Instead, he collected around himself a small coterie of yes-men, drawn principally from the Bedchamber, men who could be trusted to give him the advice he wished to hear. Policy still tended to be made in the inner royal apartments and presented to the council as a *fait accompli* (as it had been so often under James).

Beyond the denunciations of the court's 'popery' in religion, however, perhaps the most telling indictment of the king's style of government is provided by his courtiers' choice of allegiance in the crisis of 1642. A strikingly high proportion of Charles I's most senior courtiers – including his lord chamberlain and groom of the stool – supported the war-effort against him in 1642. As the Nineteen Propositions (Parliament's war manifesto of June 1642) declared, one of their key demands was that the control of policy should no longer be formulated by 'unsworn counsellors' (preeminently, the Bedchamber men). It should be restored, instead, so the argument ran, to a council dominated by the aristocratic great officers of state.

Among the many strands that constituted the parliamentarian 'cause' in the 1640s – defence of the subject's liberties, reform of the Church, the dismissal of 'evil counsellors' – there was also a strong emphasis on the rehabilitation of 'honour and ancient lineage' as the proper foundation of political authority at court and in the realm at large.[68]

The outbreak of that Civil War, and the king's removal of what remained of his court to Oxford during the years 1643–6, marked the eclipse of Whitehall as the seat of royal power. Within months of the start of fighting it was reported that the palace's empty state rooms were filled with the 'raw scent' of damp.[69] Debarred from his capital by the rebellious Parliamentarians, the king kept up an improvized court at Oxford until 1646, when its last forlorn remnant was disbanded after the military collapse of the Royalist cause. Yet the idea of a court as a necessary part of government proved far more resilient than its physical reality, and exerted its influence throughout the Civil War and beyond. In 1642 the court's most robust Parliamentarian critics took up arms, not to abolish it, but to reform and redefine it. Throughout the 1640s all but a handful of extremists acted on the presumption that, at the end of the war, the king would be restored to some form of executive authority, however limited, and with his restoration would come, inevitably, the reconstruction of the court. This expectation, in turn, profoundly influenced the conduct of Civil War politics. The factional struggles between 'Presbyterians' and 'Independents' in Parliament during the 1640s were, in effect, a contest between two alternative courts-in-waiting as to which would dominate the post-war government of the realm. So long as the king was regarded as an indispensable element of the political settlement, the Bedchamber men – the 'unsworn counsellors' so deplored in the Nineteen Propositions – continued to be an indispensable part of the conduct of politics. As late as 1646 the Scottish-born groom of the bedchamber, Will Morray, continued to act as a clandestine broker between the victorious Parliament's Presbyterian faction and the captive king.[70]

More striking still is the enduring imaginative influence of the courtly model in the years immediately after Charles I's execution in January 1649 and the creation of an English republic. Even in 1649 many MPs shared the conviction that it was only in a court that the dignity and sovereignty of the state – albeit a republican one – could be properly expressed. Among the first actions of the new republican regime, in February 1649 (a matter of weeks after Charles I's execution), was to restore Whitehall Palace as the seat of executive government for the first time since January 1642. The Council of State (the new republic's executive) was moved into the Privy Lodgings at Whitehall; and the councillors – like their predecessors on the royal Privy Council – were allocated apartments at Whitehall and granted keys to the newly restored Privy Garden (the traditional perk of those who enjoyed the entrée to the Privy Chamber).[71] A surrogate court, with Whitehall once again the seat of executive power, had been established in England within weeks of the abolition of the monarchy. Throughout the 1650s the idea of the court remained almost as potent an element in the definition of a republican political culture as it had been in monarchical culture hitherto. From the inauguration of Cromwell as lord protector in 1653, Whitehall once again became the seat not merely of government, but also of a quasi-monarchy.

From 1653 the personnel and practices of a court came increasingly to define the politics of the Cromwellian regime. The elaboration of the protectoral household, which was measured both in the re-establishment of offices and the reintroduction of etiquette, increased in tandem with the monarchical

pretensions of the regime. By 1655 the lord chamberlainship had been reconstituted, and four gentlemen of the Bedchamber were appointed to attend the lord protector.[72] The increasingly courtly style of protectoral government from 1655 was its own powerful argument for the restoration of the 'kingly title': the mere existence of a court seemed to demand the presence of a king at its head.[73] Thus, it was not so much the establishment of a quasi-monarchy that brought in its train the 'invention' of a protectoral court (as has conventionally been argued); rather, it was the very existence and prominence of the court that acted as a force for the creation of a Cromwellian kingship

VII. THE LATER STUART COURTS: REINVENTION AND REFORM

From this perspective, it is possible to see the restoration of the Stuart court in 1660 not so much as a return to the *status quo ante* of 1640, but as the culmination of a process of returning to the 'known ways' of government, which can be traced back, through the establishment of a quasi-regal Cromwellian household in the mid 1650s, to the restoration of Whitehall as the seat of a *de facto* republican court in February 1649. Like each of his Stuart predecessors, Charles II (king *de jure* from 1649, in fact from 1660–85) used the 'reordering' of his court as a means of proclaiming the priorities of the new regime. Continuity between the antebellum monarchy and Charles's own style of

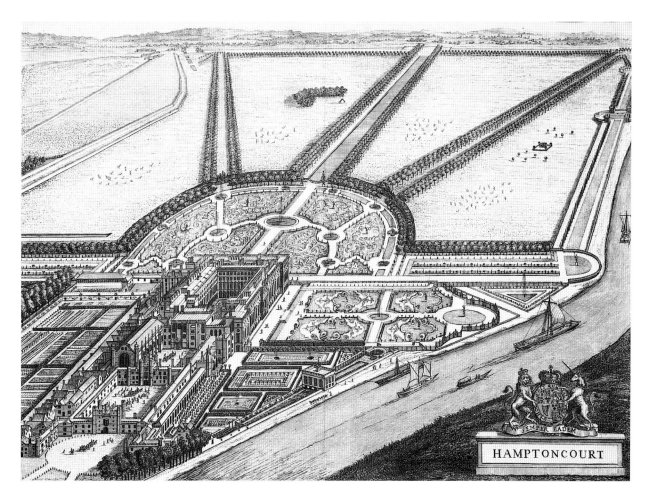

Above: *The poor man's Versailles: Leonard Knyff's view of Hampton Court Palace in the reign of George I (1714–27). The range nearest the semicircular garden, erected in the reign of William III to designs by Sir Christopher Wren, was the closest the English monarchs ever came to turning any of their old Tudor royal residences into the semblance of a 'modern' Baroque palace.*

Left: *The court restored: Dirck Stoop's painting of the coronation procession of Charles II (1661). The ritual emphasized reconciliation and a return to the 'known ways' of government after the disruptions of the Interregnum. The king, wearing the riding-cloak of the Order of the Garter, is followed by the newly created master of the horse, George Monck, Duke of Albemarle, a former parliamentarian general.*

rule was emphasized by an almost slavish re-creation of offices, ordinances and protocol as they had existed in the early years of his father's reign.[74] Even the hospitality of the Hall – perhaps the most antiquated element of regal magnificence – was restored.[74]

There was also an attempt to make the court, once again, the setting for the liturgies of 'divine majesty'. Whatever his private thoughts, in public at least Charles II promoted the cult of sacred monarchy as zealously as any of his predecessors. On his return, he immediately restored its most public ritual, the ceremony of touching for the king's evil, in which, as Pepys noted, the king performed his role 'with great gravity'.[75] In a further effort to underline the legitimacy and 'ancientness' of the Stuart dynasty, Charles II re-established Windsor Castle as one of the principal seats of the court, embarking on the first large-scale remodelling of the royal apartments since the reign of

Henry VIII. The result was a series of Baroque rooms of state (including the frescoed St George's Hall) that outshone anything in the dilapidated and increasingly outmoded Whitehall.[76]

Despite these initiatives, the broader attempt to re-create the structures of the pre-war Stuart court had foundered within two years of the king's return. As Andrew Barclay has shown, the most dramatic break with traditional practice came in 1662, when, unable to meet the crippling cost of maintaining the Household at its pre-1642 size, Charles II suspended (and later abolished) 'bouche of court'. The ancient practice of providing dinner daily for the entire court at the king's charge abruptly ceased, with only the great officers continuing to receive their 'diets' at the king's expense. The size of the household-below-stairs was cut by a third, from 350 to 220 servants (with commensurate savings in cost). The following year, all remaining diets were abolished, enabling further reductions in the Household (the mostly below-stairs staff of the lord steward's department) to 147 – more than halving its pre-1642 number.[77] In 1665 the Hall, now semi-redundant, was refitted as a permanent theatre.[78] Thereafter, the trend was towards further retrenchment, culminating in a series of swingeing cuts instituted by James II at his accession in 1685: the personnel of the Household was reduced by a half; the Chamber by almost as much (from 152 places in 1679 to 88 in 1685); and the Stables by a third.[79]

The changes introduced in the first four years after Charles II's return, and completed by James II, amounted to the dissolution of a system that, in its essentials, had endured largely unchanged since the later Middle Ages – a system founded on the principle that the size of the royal household and entourage attested most clearly to the monarch's authority and power. Retrenchment had its origins, in part, in changes in fashion, as large-scale hospitality came increasingly to be seen as an archaic and redundant form of 'magnificence'. But there is little doubt that the prime motive was financial. Stripped of the prerogative revenues that had helped sustain it until 1640, the gargantuan size of the pre-War court no longer seemed viable. Even defenders of the later-Stuart reforms had to concede that financial stringency had left Charles II unable to maintain the accustomed 'majesty' of the court.[80]

The change of tone is registered in Charles II's household ordinances. Where Charles I's regulations sought to define a setting worthy of a priest-king, his son's read like the management's attempts to impose decorum on the inmates of a disorderly hotel. Servants, it seems, had been profaning the cloth of estate in the Presence Chamber by lolling on the stools near the throne.[81] Worse still, the Privy Gallery – the inner sanctum of Tudor Whitehall, with its strictly enforced rules of entrée – was now in danger of becoming merely a 'common passage' between the semi-public apartments of state on the east side of the palace and St James's Park to the west, used by 'persons who are not qualified to come there'.[82]

Similarly, 'access and intimacy', the twin pillars on which many a pre-Civil War courtier's career had been built, rarely translated into major political influence in the post-1660 world. There are, of course, some obvious exceptions. Royal mistresses, who enjoyed both access and intimacy, did a limited trade in broker-ing royal patronage, and at least one, the Duchess of Portsmouth, was a figure of real importance 'in medi-ating relations' between Charles II and pro-French interests at court in the later years of the king's reign.[83] But many of those who enjoyed privileged access to the king in the bedchamber, or (like the master of the horse) attended him in his coach and the royal barge, remained political nonentities. Of the post-1660 Bedchamber staff, only William III's Dutch-born favourite, Hans Willem Bentinck (later first Earl of Portland), succeeded in using the groomship of the stool as a major political power-base at court.

While the trappings of sacred monarchy were re-instated after 1660, there had been a qualitative change in attitudes. For Charles I the rituals of the court defined the essence of the royal household, its place as the tabernacle of sovereignty. After 1660 there was a subtle shift in perceptions; a new, or at least heightened, awareness that the rituals of the court were part of a public theatre, a choreography to be invented and reinvented at will. At Charles II's coronation even the canopy – that most ancient symbol of the sacredness of power – became the object of an unseemly tussle for ownership between the barons of the Cinque Ports, who had carried it in the coronation procession, and the king's footmen, who wished to claim it as one of their perks.[84] The incident is emblematic of a broader trend, evident as much within the court as outside it, for the icons of majesty to be regarded as theatrical props. As Keith Thomas has argued, 'patriarchal adoration of the sovereign was challenged by a frank republican scepticism, exemplified in the increasingly common assertion that "kings were but men as other men"'.[85]

Diseased rustics continued to throng the Banqueting House in the hope of receiving the 'royal touch' in the 1660s; but the post-1660s world was conspicuously more hard-nosed and sceptical – witness the rapid decline in the belief in astrology after its mid seventeenth-century peak. Among sophisticated courtiers such practices as touching for the king's evil were no more than exercises in public relations designed to impress the credulous. To Pepys, the ceremony 'seemed…an ugly office and a simple [i.e. foolish] one'.[86] Except for a brief, Tory-promoted revival of the practice during Queen Anne's reign, the ceremony was discontinued in England after the accession of the Calvinist-educated William III.[87]

From Henry VIII's reign through to that of Charles I, the court had been '*the* focus of politics, the centre of personal monarchy'.[88] After 1660 its former primacy was strongly challenged by competing centres of political influence and patronage, not least Parliament, which emerged from the 1640s and 1650s as a far more robust institution than it had been before the Civil War. Increasingly, the authority of the royal household had to be buttressed by the creation of a 'court party' in Parliament, a constituency that became, from the 1670s, one of the principal consumers of crown patronage. The council, of course, had long served intermittently as a 'point of contact' between court and Parliament; after 1660 parliamentary management – and, still more, party management – became the preoccupation of the council board.[89]

During the last quarter of the seventeenth century the English court changed more radically and rapidly than at any point since the accession of the Tudors. Feudal hospitality was abandoned; the numerical size of the court was reduced to a mere fraction of its Tudor and early Stuart strength; and the source of finance to sustain the royal household shifted from royal lands and prerogative revenues to parliamentary grant. After its remove under William III, from Whitehall to Hampton Court and Kensington, the court ceased to be the physical centre of metropolitan social life.[90] With an almost operatic sense of timing, Whitehall Palace caught fire in 1698, reducing most of its principal buildings – the great stage-set of Tudor and Stuart monarchy – to a series of charred and smoking ruins.[91]

At first sight, this courtly *Götterdämmerung* seems to fit neatly into a political chronology that sees the revolution of 1688 as marking the beginning of that long 'decline of the crown and court', and the rise of 'modern' parliamentary sovereignty. But the impression of early eighteenth-century decline, either in the powers of the crown or the political influence of the court, is largely an optical illusion. With many of the most contentious areas of conflict between monarch and Parliament settled between 1689 and 1714, the early Hanoverians were able to exercise what remained of the (still extensive) regal powers more freely and arguably more effectively than any of their Stuart predecessors – with obvious implications for the political significance of the royal household. Even after Queen Anne (1702–14), the last and dowdiest of the Stuarts, the court preserved its Tudor and early-Stuart role 'as the prime area of ministerial intrigue and manoeuvre' under George I and George II, with the added complication of the Prince of Wales's court as a recurrent focus for an oppositionist reversionary interest.[92] While the heavy retrenchment of salaried posts between 1662 and 1685 made for a far smaller royal household, the consequent economies and general improvement in royal income during the 1690s and 1700s freed up revenue for expenditure on architecture and artistic patronage on a scale that the earlier Stuarts had only dreamt of.[93]

The first truly large-scale rebuilding of any of the major royal palaces since the death of Henry VIII took place after the revolution of 1688, with William III's rebuilding of Hampton Court as a Baroque palace: a tangible symbol of the renewed power and 'godliness' of monarchy.[94] Ironically, it was the 'constitutional' King William, the darling of the Whigs, not that supposedly despotic aesthete Charles I, who, for the first time since the 1540s, finally succeeded in creating an architectural setting for the English royal household worthy of comparison with the princely courts of continental Europe.

CHAPTER FOUR

The United Provinces of the Netherlands

THE COURTS OF THE HOUSE OF ORANGE
*c.*1580–1795

JONATHAN ISRAEL

THE HOUSEHOLD OF THE PRINCES OF ORANGE OCCUPIED A UNIQUE and unusual position in early modern Europe. In an international system in which monarchy was the norm, theirs was a princely court within a republic. Indeed, the House of Orange-Nassau had gained its special place in Dutch society and culture as a consequence of an act of rebellion: the Dutch Revolt led by Willem I the Silent (1544–84) against the Spanish Habsburgs in the last quarter of the sixteenth century. Even so, the Orange court had already enjoyed an exceptional status and allure in the Low Countries (and beyond) long before 1568, when Willem first took up arms against Philip II of Spain. Since the fifteenth century the house had gradually edged ahead of the other principal aristocratic families of the Netherlands (in terms of lands and revenues). By the early sixteenth century it had already far eclipsed rival lineages, such as those of Croy or Egmont, maintaining an establishment of unprecedented splendour for a non-royal line in and around the Nassau palaces in Brussels, Breda and elsewhere. In the early 1530s, for example, the then head of the dynasty, Hendrik III of Nassau, commissioned a famous series of eight tapestries celebrating the genealogy of his illustrious line. These were not only used to adorn his castle at Breda, he also made a point of taking them with him when travelling in order to impress other great nobles, including during a lengthy stay in Spain when Henry was temporarily resident in Charles V's castle of Simancas in Old Castile.[1]

Theodoor van Thulden, Allegory of the Transfer of the Survivance to Prince Willem, *heir to Frederik Hendrik (c.1641). In a bid to make the provincial stadholder-ates hereditary within the House of Orange, Prince Frederik Hendrik arranged for the right to inherit (or 'survivance') to be formally vested in his young son. Here, the States of Holland (personified by the figure, left) hand over the diploma conferring the right to succeed. The stadholder's military role is suggested by the goddess standing ready with the young prince's shield, and by the orange-cloaked Frederik Hendrik, in full armour, beside her.*

Furthermore, from the time of Willem the Silent's uncle, René de Châlons (1519–44) – who acquired the title and status of Prince of Orange in 1538 – the Nassaus were the only major noble lineage of the Low Countries who were also sovereign rulers in their own right, possessing as they did the tiny, but nevertheless sovereign, territory of Orange neighbouring the papal state of Avignon, in southern France. They were also the richest and most senior branch of a family that included the princely rulers of the German principality of Nassau-Dillenburg.

From the beginning of the revolt against Spain until the assassination of Willem the Silent in 1584, the prince's household – whether in exile, as in the years 1568–72, or based inside the Netherlands – was the nerve-centre of a vast network of political, diplomatic, military and propaganda activity, intrigue and negotiation, which extended not only throughout the seventeen provinces of the Habsburg Netherlands and north-west Germany, but also far beyond. Throughout these years the prince was in close touch with a variety of German Protestant princes, with Huguenot leaders in France, and with the English court and the communities of Protestant Netherlanders in exile in England. He even established contact with the short-lived regime of Dom António (1531–95), Prior of Crato, who was proclaimed King of Portugal in Lisbon by the country's anti-Habsburg faction in June 1580.[2] Until his death in 1595, Dom António stubbornly continued to oppose the Habsburg succession in Portugal with the support of the anti-Spanish party in France, the English Queen Elizabeth I, and the court of Orange-Nassau.[3]

I. THE HOUSE OF ORANGE AND THE CREATION OF A DUTCH REPUBLIC

During the later sixteenth century, the creation of a stable, established Orangist court was hindered by the peripatetic nature of the prince's household. After returning to the Netherlands from Nassau-Dillenburg in 1572, Willem the Silent still had no fixed residence. Until September 1577 he resided chiefly in Holland. From 1577 to 1583 his headquarters were in Brabant – first Brussels and later Antwerp. After abandoning Antwerp,

he spent the months from July to September 1583 in Zeeland. Finally, during the last eighteen months or so of his life, the prince lived in a former nunnery in Delft, placed at his disposal by the city government and renamed the Prinsenhof – or Prince's Court.

This household was a relatively modest affair. Given the tremendous pressures and enormous cost of the conflict with Spain, to which he was so deeply committed, it is hardly surprising that Willem the Silent never had the opportunity to commission many tapestries or paintings, or to initiate a building programme that was concerned with much more than fortifications. Unlike his successors, he collected little. Nevertheless, like many Renaissance princes, he used conspicuous hospitality as an instrument of policy, and to proclaim the 'magnificence' of his house. The prince himself was an ostentatious provider (and consumer) of fine food and wine, often giving lavish banquets; and he took care to maintain a considerable distance between the international, aristocratic and courtly style of his own household, and the mostly rather sober, abstemious circumstances of the civic patricians and officials who formed the bulk of the new rebel state's governing élite during the years of its infancy.[4] The legal position of the House of Orange-Nassau within the emerging Dutch state was ambiguous: clearly more than a primacy of honour and yet far from being that of hereditary sovereign prince. Indeed, during the first decades of the new republic's existence, there was no real possibility for the rebel leadership in the cities of Holland, Zeeland and the other northern provinces to define the constitutional place and role of the stadholder and his family within the state. Yet there was never any doubt from a practical standpoint that the Prince of Orange stood at the head of the new Protestant regime and had a central role within the international network of Calvinist princes.

From time to time, especially in the early 1580s, the regents in the towns and the States of Holland and Zeeland, as well as those of other provinces, contemplated fixing and enhancing the constitutional and international status of the House of Orange-Nassau by bestowing the nominally sovereign title of Count of Holland on the prince. But even had this been agreed by the whole States (or representative assembly) of Holland and Zeeland (the two most powerful provinces of the republic), the prince's power would have been heavily circumscribed. Under the proposed terms of his elevation, which a delegation from the States presented to the prince in his bedchamber on 7 December 1583 (the Prince of Orange frequently negotiated high matters of state lying in bed), forty-nine articles of which he was seemingly ready to accept, he would have lacked even the power to introduce a military garrison into a town without the consent of the city government concerned.

The prince's assassination in 1584 intervened before the matter could be finally resolved and it was decided after his death not to elevate his eldest available son, Maurits of Nassau (1584–1625), to the status of sovereign count – nor, initially, even to the stadholderate.[5] Even so, there was never the slightest doubt, once the revolt against Spain was firmly established, that the prince and his heirs would continue to play a central role in the functioning of the rebel state for as long as anyone could foresee. Maurits had spent the first ten years of his life at Dillenburg, near Giessen and Marburg in west-central Germany, and when his father had him brought to the Netherlands in 1577 he was sent to study at the newly founded Protestant university of Leiden at the expense of the States of Holland which, at that point, recorded their expectation that he would 'serve' the state in an important capacity in succession to his father.[6]

Thus, while the Princes of Orange were in no sense the hereditary rulers of the republic, there was, nevertheless, at least the presumption that they would occupy a major role in the state by virtue of their inherited rank. Maurits of Nassau became the effective head of the House of Orange-Nassau on his father's death in 1584, and was immediately appointed head of the newly established Council of State, although it was only the following year that he was proclaimed stadholder – that is 'governor', or lord-lieutenant, on behalf of the relevant provincial States (the formal sovereign) – of the provinces of Holland and Zeeland. Indeed, following the signing of the Treaty of Nonsuch (20 August 1585) between the States General (the representative assembly of all the Dutch provinces) and the English crown, it seemed quite likely that the House of Orange would be marginalized. For, under the terms of the treaty, the English nobleman and courtier the Earl of Leicester was installed as governor-general of the United

Provinces, and military head of the union. Prince Maurits, with his younger half-brother Frederik Hendrik, Willem the Silent's last wife and widow Louise de Coligny (1555–1620), and the late prince's daughters by his various marriages, were all thrust very much into the background. But confrontation arose between the States of Holland (led by their forceful advocate Johan van Oldenbarnevelt) and the Earl of Leicester, which eventually led, in 1587, to the frustration of the governor-general's aims and his departure from the country. Had it not been for this falling out between Leicester and the States of Holland, the House of Orange might never have secured the central role that it subsequently achieved in the public life of the Dutch Republic.

II. THE CREATION OF AN ORANGIST COURT

The real beginning of the emergence of 'the court' of Orange-Nassau as a fixed centre of influence and patronage, as a complex of buildings and collections, and as a focus of protocol and ceremonial lay in the early 1590s, and perhaps especially in 1591, when Prince Maurits (1618–25), now stadholder of five provinces, first secured an international reputation as a military commander with his spectacularly successful offensive against the Spanish forces in Gelderland and Overijssel. This was also the year in which Princess Louise de Coligny (the prince's step-mother) moved to The Hague, settling in the best available residence, close to the complex of buildings that housed not only the meeting hall of the States General, and that of the States of Holland, but also the still very modest living quarters of the stadholder, a precinct in the centre of the city that was (and is) called the Binnenhof, or Inner Court.

From her nearby household, Louise de Coligny acted as the guardian of her son by Willem the Silent (Frederik Hendrik), now seven years old, and for most of her step-daughters. More importantly, jointly with Prince Maurits, she came to be regarded as the defender and representative of the dynasty in general. The Prinsenhof at Delft remained in the family's hands, however, serving as the residence for Maurits's full sister, Princess Emilia van Nassau, and for his elder half-sister by his father's first marriage, Maria van

Nassau. But it was Louise de Coligny's residence in The Hague – later almost entirely rebuilt by Frederik Hendrik in the 1640s and called the Oude Hof (later the Noordeinde Palace) – that came to be the dynasty's principal seat.

Comparatively modest though it was initially, the court of Orange-Nassau at The Hague grew steadily, both in physical terms and in its international standing. This growth was especially marked after the signing of the Twelve Years Truce (1609–21), a temporary peace in the long armed conflict between Spain and the United Provinces. The truce enabled Maurits to spend far more time at The Hague than had been possible whilst on the frontiers campaigning; and, by conferring a quasi *de jure* legitimacy on the rebel Dutch state, it enhanced the prestige of the fledgling republic as a whole and there was a consequent upgrading of the foreign diplomatic representatives resident in The Hague. Moreover, by allowing reductions in expenditure on the army and navy, it also tended to release funds for building, decoration, art and festivities.

The impact of these changes on the stadholder's court, however, was only slowly felt. During the period from Leicester's departure in 1587 until the overthrow of Oldenbarnevelt in 1618, it was principally the Holland regents (or the ruling élite of the towns), under Oldenbarnevelt's leadership, who directed the Dutch state and decided the main lines of policy. Nevertheless, the States General and provincial assemblies took care to incorporate the court of Orange-Nassau – as well as the courtly culture and aristocratic circles that surrounded it – into the procedures, official rhetoric and publicity of their new republic. This prominence of the princely family in the republic's public protocol is hardly surprising. Since the overthrow of Spanish Habsburg rule in what were now called the United Provinces of the Netherlands, the new state had evinced a purely pragmatic, rather than any specifically ideological, commitment to republican structures and principles. Even during this period, when the House of Orange was not actually controlling policy, the States General nevertheless regarded the stadholder's court at The Hague as an asset in the business of diplomatic negotiation and in keeping up contacts with other powers. Republics were generally regarded with deep suspicion, and the ceremonial prominence of the princely family was a reassuring

sign to a community of European realms that was composed mostly either of monarchies or sovereign principalities. An apt example is the festivities arranged in 1612 for the visit of Friedrich V, Elector of the Palatinate (1610–32), one of the most prominent Protestant princes of the Holy Roman Empire, when he passed through the republic on his way from Heidelberg to London for his marriage to Princess Elizabeth, daughter of James I of Britain. Friedrich (who, through his mother, was both a grandson of Willem the Silent and a nephew of Maurits) was received with elaborate ceremony jointly by the stadholder and the States General. Still more impressive and elaborate formalities were arranged to mark his return from England with his bride, *en route* for the Palatinate. On 27 April 1613 Friedrich and Elizabeth anchored at the port of Flushing in Zeeland and were greeted, amid a magnificent setting, by Maurits, Frederik Hendrik and the 'Prince of Portugal', Dom Manoel, the pretender to the Portuguese throne.[7] (The scene was later commemorated in an imposing painting by Holland's leading marine painter of the time, Hendrik Vroom.) Flushing, like Delft, Haarlem and other Holland and Zeeland towns, had converted one of the best residences in the town into a Prinsenhof where, when visiting, the stadholder, members of his family, visiting royalty and suitable high aristocratic personages could be accommodated at the citizenry's expense. After spending several days in the Prinsenhof at Flushing, the splendid company, including Maurits and a considerable entourage, moved on to Middelburg and spent some time at The Hague before the new electress continued her journey to Heidelberg, whither her husband had preceded her.

Towards the end of the Twelve Years Truce the court at The Hague gained greatly in stature and in political power as a result of Maurits's *coup d'état* of 1618, whereby he gained effective control of the political machinery of the Dutch state. For the time being the States of Holland and the States General were reduced to little more than ciphers. To clinch this shift towards a quasi-monarchy, Maurits insisted on having Oldenbarnevelt executed, despite Louise de Coligny's pleas that the old man be spared. The stadholder, having taken over the direction of the republic's diplomacy, also now began to play an active, indeed crucial, part in the events surrounding the onset and

Adriaen van de Venne, A Hunting Party of the House of Orange *(c. 1620). In the foreground are the three sons of Willem I the Silent: Maurits, Willem and Frederik Hendrik.*

early stages of the Thirty Years War. He encouraged Elector Friedrich of the Palatinate to accept the Bohemian throne, which the Protestant rebels in that country offered him, notwithstanding that this was an obvious provocation to the emperor, who regarded the kingdom of Bohemia as part of the Habsburg patrimonial lands. Moreover, the stadholder encouraged the Bohemian Protestants and the German Protestant Union in their opposition to the Habsburgs with promises of Dutch troops and money, a policy flatly contrary to the irenic diplomacy pursued by James I of Britain.[8] Indeed, from 1618 until the late 1620s (when the French crown, at Richelieu's prompting, again began to oppose Habsburg power in Europe), the court at The Hague could justly be described as the chief focus of anti-Habsburg diplomacy in Europe.

Despite this dramatic upgrading of the status and power of the Prince of Orange's household – a consequence of the coup of 1618 – it nevertheless remains the case that, regarded as a type of court, it continued as before in its unique double role: on the one hand, a public body with defined functions integrated into a formally republican institutional context; on the other, persisting in its private capacity as a dynastic house hovering in international standing somewhere between minor royalty without a crown and the high nobility.[9]

Further enhancement of the international status of the stadholder's court at The Hague accrued from the defeat of the 'Winter King', Friedrich of Bohemia, and his queen, Elizabeth, at the Battle of the White Mountain outside Prague on 8 November 1620, and their subsequent decision to seek refuge in Holland.

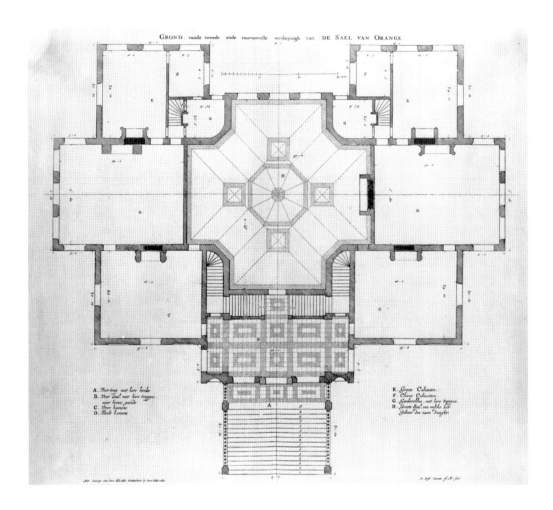

GROND vande tweede ende voornaemste verdiepingh van DE SAEL VAN ORANGE

The Huis ten Bosch: ground floor plan, c. 1655. Begun by Prince Frederik Hendrik, the palace was never intended as a seat for the court but as an exquisite pavillon *glorifying the House of Orange-Nassau. The Oranjezaal (Orange Hall) comprises the core of the building.*

They and their court in exile settled in The Hague where, in effect, their households became an adjunct of the court of Orange. A substantial number of Bohemian and Palatine Calvinist nobles and courtiers accompanied the Winter King and Queen to The Hague, and their combined impact on the cultural and social life of the town, as well as on the stadholder's court, was, at least in the short run, extensive. Although the finances of the exiled court of Bohemia were somewhat precarious, appearances were maintained with the help of a subsidy from London as well as a grant from the States General; in effect, at Maurits's insistence, the Dutch Republic was subsidizing the exiled Bohemian court.

The courtly atmosphere at The Hague during the 1620s was certainly distinctive, even perhaps rather peculiar, in several respects. For one thing, the stadholder's court and its appendage, the household of the Bohemian king and queen, were ostensibly Calvinist, and both were regarded as the seats of illegitimate, upstart dynasties, not only by the Habsburgs, but by most of the Catholic courts of Europe; for another, the two leading figures of the court of Orange, Maurits and Frederik Hendrik, were confirmed bachelors of long standing, and evinced a marked reluctance to marry.[10] (The two were frequently portrayed together by contemporary Dutch artists: riding, hunting or engaged in some military exploit.) For his part, Maurits never married, and was very likely influenced in this decision, as were his brothers, by their father's complicated and sometimes unfortunate marital history. In any event, their status affected the moral tone of their court. Neither Maurits nor Frederik Hendrik was impervious to female charms. Maurits, especially, was a notorious womanizer who was accustomed to receive a stream of girls and women at the stadholder's quarters in the Binnenhof: some ladies of quality, others reportedly mere serving wenches and girls of 'low station'.

From the 1590s until Maurits's death in 1625 the formal etiquette of the court, while elaborately defined, as with all European courts, was confined by the unmarried status of the prince and was outwardly heavily masculine. Reflecting the principal acknowledged public function of the stadholder as captain-general of the army, it was also military in character.[11] The tone of the court's dining arrangements more resembled an officers' mess than the heavily sacralized rituals that attended contemporary princely dining in Tuscany, England, France and Castile-Aragon. One English visitor to Maurits's court in 1618, used to the more ceremonious ways of Whitehall, was unimpressed by the 'state' (or degree of protocol) to be found at the court at The Hague:

At supper, being desirous to see [Prince Maurits's] state, I went into the court, which is open to any, where he sat at supper at the end of the table. On his right [sat] Graf William [Willem Lodewijk, Count of Nassau], on his left the Prince of Portugal, the rest of the table being filled with guests. But their cheer [was] very poor, and ill handled.[12]

A detailed 'Order en Reglement' dating from 1624 survives, which confirms this impression of the dining arrangements at the Prince of Orange's court. It shows that the prince sat at table together with several other prominent persons 'van qualiteite', mostly or exclusively male, who, if they were regulars, held high military positions, among them the captain of the mounted Compagnie des Guardes, the Gelderland noble Herman Otto van Limburg Stirum, and his colleague, the captain of the prince's infantry guards. Nearby, at the second most prominent table, sat the members of the Raedt, or court council of the prince, consisting of a marshal of the court, or *hofmeester*, the prince's treasurer, his two secretaries, the *stalmeester* (stablemaster)

– mostly non-nobles – and also Maurits's two bastard sons by his most favoured mistress, Margaretha van Mechelen, Willem and Lodewijk van Nassau, the first of whom was killed in 1627 at the siege of Grol. The third table in order of seniority was reserved for the prince's 'gentlemen', mostly senior army officers. Fourth came the table of the prince's eight pages, several of whom were French or of a French-speaking background.

This overwhelmingly masculine façade to the court came to an abrupt end with Maurits's death. What continued as before was the tradition of combining a strong noble and military attendance with a significant 'bourgeois' presence in the shape of the prince's secretaries and officials. These tended not to be selected from regent families but rather from families such as the Huygens, who had for generations been in the service of the House of Orange and were often from a Southern-Netherlandish background. On the other hand, the tendency towards the use of French as the court language and towards French patterns of etiquette, already noticeable before Maurits's death, became more marked in subsequent decades. This had little to do with either geographical proximity or the presence of French personnel at court; indeed, the most numerous element among the foreign army officers and prominent figures at court tended to be German relatives of the House of Nassau, especially after 1672, when the republic was frequently at war with France and such French noblemen as there were disappeared from the upper ranks of the Dutch army.

The principal cause for the influence of French culture was the fact that the prince's household, both in its public role as part of the republic's institutional arrangements, and as a great noble house, formed part of the international courtly network and, especially during the second quarter of the seventeenth century, the standing and prestige of the Orange court rose appreciably within that network. It is remarkable, however, that while the strongly dynastic and international flavour of the court inevitably tended to create distance between the court and the regent-dominated assemblies and committees that formed the rest of the republic's political process, on the whole this did not serve to divert or obstruct the stadholders', and the court's, performance of their public functions in state ceremonies, diplomacy, high-level decision-making or the conduct of war.[13]

Despite its public championing of Calvinism, the moral tenor of the prince's household was far from 'godly'. In general, the atmosphere surrounding the court of The Hague would seem to have been more cavalier than Calvinist, with plenty of sexual innuendo and bravado pervading the conversation and humour of both male and female courtiers. The remarkable album of 102 paintings in gouache by Adriaen van de Venne (1589–1662), presented by Frederik Hendrik as a personal gift to the Winter King and Queen in 1626, is riddled with bawdy allusions and witticisms.[14] On a trip made by Elizabeth to the West Frisian towns in 1625, her entourage was much amused by the sight of a preserved elephant penis that they viewed in a private collection in Enkhuizen, and delighted in embarrassing the prudish savant to whom it belonged.[15]

Shortly before his death in 1625 Maurits finally prevailed on his younger half-brother – whom he had named in his will as general heir to all the main possessions of the House of Orange-Nassau in the Netherlands – to marry for the sake of the dynasty and its survival. The 41-year-old Frederik Hendrik (1584–1647) married within the court, choosing as his bride one of Elizabeth of Bohemia's ladies, the forceful and ambitious, as well as attractive, Countess Amalia von Solms-Braunfels (1602–75). Soon after becoming Prince of Orange on his brother's death, Frederik Hendrik was proclaimed Stadholder of Holland and Zeeland, and shortly thereafter also of Utrecht, Overijssel and Gelderland.

Frederik Hendrik inherited from Maurits, besides lands, offices, revenues and emoluments, a greater accumulation of liquid assets than any predecessor had had at his disposal. Maurits's comparatively sparse lifestyle had enabled him to save much of his income, leaving a surplus of some six to seven million guilders. Even so, Frederik Hendrik was by no means the big spender during the early years of his stadholderate (1625–47) that he was later to become. War with Spain, which was once again pressing its claims to overlordship of the Netherlands, had been resumed in 1621; ever since the republic had been in the grip of a deep commercial recession, which lingered on until the early 1630s.[16] As a consequence, funds for the army and navy were desperately short and the atmosphere in the country was one of stringent austerity, which affected almost everything – not least architecture and the art market.[17]

III. STADHOLDER FREDERIK HENDRIK AND THE COURT OF ORANGE-NASSAU AT ITS ZENITH

It was not until the 1630s that Frederik Hendrik and Amalia embarked on their more grandiose projects. The country retreat at Honselaersdijk, begun in the early 1620s and eventually to be the grandest of all Frederik Hendrik's palaces, was extended and furnished. During the mid 1630s the French garden-architect André Mollet laid out the gardens with handsome *parterres-de-broderie* (elaborately shaped beds with symmetrical patterns of flowers), further extended in the 1640s, with a final effect even grander than that originally intended.[18] A new palace was built at Rijswijk (where the European peace congress was to take place in 1697–8), which was impressively decorated and provided with handsome gardens in the mid 1630s. Meanwhile, the stadholder's official residence in The Hague, the so-called 'Stadhouderlijk kwartier aan het Binnenhof', was substantially added to and renovated.[19] The Castle of Buren was provided with handsome gardens to designs by Mollet in the mid 1630s, and its interiors modernized and refurbished during the years 1640–44. At The Hague, Louise de Coligny's former residence, the Oude Hof (or Huis in't Noordeinde), was almost entirely rebuilt during the same period: in 1638, when Marie de Médicis, the widow of Henri IV and former queen regent of France, lodged there with her entourage during a visit to the city, relatively little had altered in the house since the 1590s. During the years 1639–47, by contrast, the palace was thoroughly remodelled and upgraded.[20]

For all these palaces and castles, Stadholder Frederik Hendrik and his consort Amalia needed paintings, tapestries, sculptures, hangings and other *objets d'art* in unprecedented quantities. They spent lavishly to acquire collections of quality, relying especially on the advice of the prince's cultivated secretary Constantijn Huygens (1596–1687), a leading connoisseur and one of the foremost poets of the Dutch Golden Age, and on that of the architect and painter Jacob van Campen (1596–1657). Van Campen's influence on the vast project of renovating and adorning the stadholder's palaces was widely evident

The Binnenhof in The Hague housed not only the stadholder's apartments, but also the meeting place of the States General, the great hall. The premature death of Willem II from smallpox in 1650 without an adult male heir brought about the sudden eclipse of the Orange court, and injected new life into the republic's representative institutions: the 1651 'Great Assembly' of the States General, depicted by Dirck van Delen, meeting in the hall of the Binnenhof, declined to fill the vacant stadholderate.

both in the overall plans and designs as well as in the choice of assistant architects, painters, decorators and sculptors.[21] The basic plans for the Noordeinde Palace, for example, were van Campen's, although the actual direction of the work was entrusted to the architect Pieter Post (1608–69).

These palaces were all rather small compared with the Escorial, the Louvre or even with the Palazzo Pitti in Florence, the principal residence of the Medici grand dukes of Tuscany. The programme of building,

rebuilding and extending embarked on by Frederik Hendrik was not the result of mere whim or a sudden burgeoning of his income, but rather a process of catching up after the very long period of neglect of the House of Orange's palaces and gardens through the decades of war and austerity since the 1560s. It was also a response to the rise in the international diplomatic prestige of the Orange court, and not least the need, for the first time in many decades, for extensive quarters for a princess of Orange, her numerous

The visit of Queen Marie de Médicis, mother of Louis XIII and the former queen regent of France, to Amsterdam in 1638 provided the pretext for the Orangist court to appear at its most monarchical, with Frederik Hendrik portraying himself as a sovereign prince, not merely in Orange, but as de facto *ruler of the Dutch provinces; an engraving by Solomon Savery (c. 1638).*

court ladies, and her several daughters and *their* attendants. Frederik Hendrik's entourage of officers, nobles and pages also tended to be larger than Maurits's had been; the 1630s were a decade of general expansion as well as elaboration of the court. Besides the need for more accommodation, space was felt to be required for more large rooms for receptions, banqueting and ceremonial occasions, and more impressive interior decoration was also needed to reflect the rising status and prosperity, as well as the refined taste, of the court. As for the architectural and garden styles adopted, French classicizing influences were strong, particularly at the Oude Hof; but the overall trend ultimately was towards a quieter classicism, forged especially by van Campen and Post, demonstrating some Palladian influences, but essentially Dutch in character.

This cultivation of courtly magnificence corresponded to a period in which the prince's role as the military defender of the state was gradually being attenuated. As a commander and statesman Frederik Hendrik's prestige stood highest following his great victories over the Spaniards at 's-Hertogenbosch in 1629 and Maastricht in 1632; but by the late 1630s both his vigour as a general and his authority with the provincial assemblies and town governments had waned noticeably. Whilst his real power ebbed, however, the prince's courtly establishment and its status in the eyes of Europe's other courts grew. In 1636, for example, Louis XIII ordered a change in the official French mode of address for the Dutch stadholder from *Excellence* (Excellency) to *Altesse* (Highness), a style generally used to designate lesser royal sovereigns and their relatives. In January 1637 the States General voted to follow the example of the French court and change their mode of addressing the stadholder from *Excellence* to the Dutch term for Highness – *Hoogheid*.

Far more impressive, however, on the international courtly scene, was Frederik Hendrik's success in 1641 in arranging the marriage of his son and heir, Prince Willem II, to the eldest daughter of Charles I of Britain. It was above all to accommodate Willem II and especially his royal Stuart bride, that the Noordeinde Palace was rebuilt during the early 1640s. This was the first of what was to be a series of marriages between the Houses of Orange and Stuart, and indeed the first marriage-alliance between the House of Orange-Nassau and a major European royal dynasty. Despite the largely republican political culture of the United Provinces, this notable enhancement of the House of Orange-Nassau seems, however, not to have aroused any particularly negative feelings among the Holland regents and town governments. On the contrary, the States General and States of Holland seem to have approved warmly of the marriage as driving a useful diplomatic wedge between Spain and an English court, which, for much of the 1630s, had tended to be disquietingly Hispanophile.[22]

As a courtly establishment, the House of Orange-Nassau was at its zenith in the 1630s and 1640s; its status in Europe had never stood higher, and, if the Dutch army under Frederik Hendrik's command no longer achieved great victories during the latter part of his stadholderate, it nevertheless remained the foremost school of war for young noblemen to be found anywhere in Protestant Europe. Not the least imposing aspect of the court was the way it combined influences emanating from Paris, London and the German courts with elements of design and architectural style – as well as art collections – that were essentially Dutch. The court had a thoroughly cosmopolitan character, and yet one that was well integrated into its Dutch context. It also retained its reputation for sexual libertinism, but was now also tinged – in accordance with Frederik Hendrik's own exceptionally tolerant views on religion – with a certain predilection for theological and philosophical libertinage. These tendencies were not to everyone's taste. The young Friedrich Wilhelm, later the Great Elector of Brandenburg-Prussia, who spent the winter of 1637–8 at the court in The Hague after a period of study at Leiden, seems to have been more repelled than attracted by the lax morals he encountered.[23] The moral tone of the court was not improved during the 1640s by the

return from Paris, where he had completed his education, of Frederik Hendrik's bastard son Frederik van Nassau (later styled the Heer van Zuylestein), who filled the court with the latest gossip and risqué jokes from the court at Paris, and quickly won notoriety for his blatant swearing, womanizing and heavy drinking; he is described in the memoirs of a leading courtier as 'd'un esprit fort delié mais libertin outre mesure'.[24] The court at The Hague had more to offer, however, than aristocratic buffoonery and womanizing. Philosophers found powerful patrons in the various royal and princely households resident in the city. The exiled Princess Elizabeth of Bohemia, the learned daughter of the Winter King and Queen, for example, became a close friend and correspondent of Descartes at a time when Cartesian philosophy was beginning to turn the theological and philosophical world of the Calvinist lands upside down. Her brother Karl Ludwig (or Charles-Louis), who was to be restored to the electorate of the Palatinate in 1648 under the terms of the Westphalian peace treaties, was one of the leading connoisseurs and intellectual lights of the court. He, too, was an enthusiast for the new Cartesian philosophy and for religious toleration, and was something of a sensualist. In February 1635 he entertained the entire courtly *monde* of The Hague to a ballet performance at the Oude Hof, entitled *Les plaisirs de la vie*.[25]

During the early seventeenth century, marriage alliances with the major sovereign houses of Protestant Europe were the central plank in a broader strategy to heighten the prestige of the stadholder's court and the international status of the dynasty of Orange-Nassau. As always, marriageable daughters were pawns in such a dynastic strategy. In the mid 1640s there was a proposal to marry the stadholder's eldest daughter, Louise Henriëtte, to Charles, Prince of Wales (the future Charles II of Britain). When that plan unravelled – doubtless because of the disastrous situation of the House of Stuart, then on the losing side of a civil war – attention turned towards the Protestant princes of the Empire. Although Louise Henriëtte herself was found to be in love with her distant cousin Henri-Charles de la Trémoille, Prince de Talmont, one of the stadholder's officers, such a match was out of the question, and – very much against her will and especially at the insistence of her mother – the princess was compelled to marry the young Margrave of Brandenburg,

Friedrich Wilhelm of Hohenzollern.[26] The marriage established an enduring link between the House of Orange and the Hohenzollerns, which, until the end of the eighteenth century, was to rival in importance the connection with the royal house of Great Britain.

The grandeur of the House of Orange-Nassau during these years reached its most consummate expression in the construction and decoration of a new summer villa, called the Huis ten Bosch (House in the Woods), on the outskirts of The Hague. The building of this new palace, intended as a retreat for Amalia von Solms, was largely completed in the years 1645–7 under the direction of Pieter Post, and architecturally marks the zenith of Dutch courtly classicism. After her husband's death in 1647, the princess turned it, in part, into a magnificent mausoleum to commemorate and glorify the achievements of Frederik Hendrik. Work on the paintings and decoration of the famous Orange Hall (or Oranjezaal), a stupendous integration of architecture and painting, began shortly after the stadholder's death and was not completed until 1652. In close consultation with Huygens and van Campen, Amalia selected a set of themes and designs that made possible the successful harmonization of the work of a whole phalanx of Dutch and Flemish painters into an orderly and connected cycle of thirty wall paintings.[27] Van Campen himself painted several of the pictures; others were executed by Gerard van Honthorst, Caesar van Everdingen, Jan Lievens, Pieter Soutman, Salomon de Bray, Christiaan van Couwenbergh, Pieter de Grebber, Jacob Jordaens, Gonzales Coques and Theodoor van Thulden. Frederik Hendrik is heroicized throughout – first as a warrior, then as a bringer of peace, and finally as the founder of a Golden Age. The largest, most complex and most 'Baroque' of the series, *The Triumph of Frederik Hendrik*, was entrusted to the Antwerp Catholic artist Jacob Jordaens. But the Oranjezaal, like the rest of the building, was tucked away out of sight and not part of the Dutch sphere. Such uninhibited glorification of a stadholder who, in terms of the republic's political forms was theoretically a servant of the States, would hardly have been judged seemly had it been intended to function as open political 'propaganda'. Its purpose was more discreet, being intended chiefly to impress intimates and clients of the House of Orange, as well as visiting foreign diplomats.

Yet, despite its acceptance as one of the great princely houses of Europe, the ambiguous status of the increasingly splendid court *vis-à-vis* the institutions of the republic became starkly apparent after the premature death of Willem II after a mere three years as stadholder (1647–50). During the final months of his stadholderate, it seemed that the House of Orange was on the verge of capturing almost complete control of the machinery of the Dutch state. The States of Holland, even the proud city of Amsterdam, appeared to be thoroughly intimidated by the bullying tactics and imperious manner of the new prince. But his sudden death from smallpox late in 1650 plunged the entire court – and the Orangist faction throughout the United Provinces – into the depths of despair. Almost at once, the Holland regents were able to recapture control of the army and navy, the republic's diplomacy, political patronage and its judicial system.[28] The army was drastically reduced in size; suddenly, there was scarcely a place in the military, diplomatic or civil employments of the state that was available to members of the court and its hangers-on – all areas to which courtiers had enjoyed ready access until 1650. The gloom that now descended on the gentlemen and ladies who formed the backcloth to the glory of the House of Orange-Nassau was no doubt as much personal and financial as it was political.

IV. REPUBLICAN REACTION AND THE ECLIPSE OF THE COURT

Throughout the rest of the 1650s the court led an uncertain, somewhat marginal existence, presided over by Princess Amalia (Frederik Hendrik's widow), the 'Princess Royal' Mary (Charles I's daughter and Willem II's widow), and the princely bastard, the Heer van Zuylestein, who acted as the governor of the infant Prince of Orange, later William III of Britain. In a reaction against Willem II's bludgeoning style, the States of Holland, followed by most of the rest of the provinces, resolved against appointing a new stadholder; from 1650 until 1672, when the stadholderate was restored, the office was vacant (hence its designation as the First Stadholderless Period of the Dutch Republic). Under the leadership of Johan de Witt, pensionary of Holland in the years 1653–72, a

Dynastic politics: the rising status of the House of Orange among European princes was attested by the marriage alliances it was able to forge in the 1640s, first with the Anglo-Scottish House of Stuart, and then with the young Margrave of Brandenburg, Elector Friedrich Wilhelm (1640–88), who married the Princess Louise Henriëtte of Orange at the Oude Hof in The Hague in 1646, depicted here by Jan Mijtens.

new, strongly republican sentiment, firmly opposed to allowing the hereditary principle to play any part in the functioning of the republic's political machinery, held sway over the Holland regents.[29]

The fortunes of the House of Orange reached their nadir in 1654 with the passing of the Act of Exclusion, at the end of the First Anglo-Dutch War (1652–4), by which the States of Holland formally barred the House of Orange from ever again holding any major office in the state. It was a measure prompted and supported by Oliver Cromwell, Lord Protector of the English Commonwealth (1653–8), who was as firmly anti-Orange as he was anti-Stuart. Thus, the boyhood of Willem III was passed in an atmosphere that had no

Above: *Dinner in the Mauritshuis on 30 May 1660 to celebrate the restoration of Charles II of England, Scotland and Ireland: although the host is the young Prince Willem III (seated, right, and turning towards the viewer), he yields place to the English king and his aunt, the Queen of Bohemia, who out-rank him as 'sacred persons' and are placed at the head of the table, under the canopy of state.* Right: *Begun during Frederik Hendrik's last years (1645–47), the Oranjezaal of the Huis ten Bosch was decorated with an elaborate cycle of paintings commemorating the prince as founder of a new Golden Age. Here, his grandson Willem III dances with his wife, the English Princess Mary, at a court ball in 1686; an engraving by Daniel Marot the elder (1663–1752).*

real parallel either in the courtly world of the rest of Europe or in the Dutch past. He lived with his English mother at the Oude Hof, which was the hub of what was clearly a princely court that had a certain vague potential (and actual) role in Dutch public life, but one that was for the time being utterly undefined and unclear. While most of the Holland town governments followed de Witt's lead, there were still a few Holland cities (notably Leiden and Haarlem), as well as some towns and individual nobles represented in the other provincial assemblies, that insisted on according greater deference to the House of Orange. They called for the members of the princely family to be restored to high offices in the state, an attitude expressed in the case of Leiden by constantly reminding the States of Holland of Willem II's father, grandfather and

great-grandfather's services to the republic, and by stubbornly opposing all of de Witt's measures to reduce the political role of the House of Orange.

The prospects of the court at The Hague were improved considerably in 1660 with the restoration of the Stuart monarchy in Britain.[30] Given the close dynastic links between the Houses of Stuart and Orange-Nassau, Charles II's resumption of the thrones of England, Scotland and Ireland could be expected to have noticeable consequences in the United Provinces. As the uncle of the young Prince of Orange, the new King of England might well seek to gain influence and leverage in the United Provinces by colluding with his sister to promote the prestige of the court at The Hague, and by calling for his nephew to be restored to his rightful prospects and privileges. Charles himself spent some

two months in the United Provinces in 1660, mostly at Breda and The Hague, before embarking, from Scheveningen, for England in June of that year. (Among the numerous festivities that enlivened his stay at The Hague was a ball at the Oude Hof during which the king danced with his elderly aunt, still styled Queen Elizabeth of Bohemia, a scene recorded by an artist and subsequently published as an engraving.)[31] Although the Orangist cause in the republic did gain ground during the early 1660s, its close identification with the English royal house proved a mixed blessing, for the fortunes of the court tended to recede again during the years of bitter hostility and open war between England and the United Provinces (1664–7), when the Holland regents held the English crown responsible for the conflict and the Stuart connection somewhat compromised the standing of the Orange court.

Willem III's prospects improved again, however, as he neared maturity in the late 1660s, and by 1670 his court and entourage had become the focus of active intrigue against the Holland regents. His hand was strengthened by the obvious support that he enjoyed among wide sections of the Dutch populace. When, in 1672, the republic found itself without allies, with its defences in a poor state and in desperate danger from the formidable anti-Dutch alliance formed by Louis XIV, Charles II, the Elector of Cologne and the Prince-Bishop of Münster, the prestige of the regents plummeted. Even more, when the French overwhelmed the main Dutch defences in June 1672, and rapidly overran three whole provinces of the Union (Gelderland, Overijssel and Utrecht), the people vented their anger and frustration on de Witt and his supporters and turned to the youthful Prince of Orange to rescue them in their hour of need. The prince became stadholder in the same year, rapidly gained complete control of the army, and before long had largely mastered much of the political and diplomatic machinery of the state. Many of the regents who had supported de Witt were purged from the city governments by the prince armed with a commission from the States General, in a procedure reminiscent of Maurits's purging of the Holland town government in 1618.

V. THE STADHOLDER-KING WILLIAM III: THE RISE AND DECLINE OF THE WILLIAMITE COURT

Once Willem III was firmly installed as stadholder – as army commander and effective head of the Dutch government – from the summer of 1672 onwards, the court at The Hague once again became a political nerve-centre of crucial importance, not just for the United Provinces but for the whole of Europe. In the years between 1672 and the 'Glorious Revolution' in Britain of 1688–9, the court at The Hague was Europe's principal hive of intrigue and propaganda directed against the might of Louis XIV. At the same time, albeit more discreetly to begin with, it was also the chief focus of plotting, and eventually also propaganda, aimed against the pro-French and pro-Catholic elements in the Stuart court at Whitehall. A second marriage alliance linking the Houses of Orange and Stuart – between the young stadholder and Mary, daughter of James, Duke of York, the niece of the British king Charles II – began to be discussed as early as 1674 and materialized four years later. But it failed to achieve the kind of alignment between the Dutch Republic and Great Britain for which Willem had hoped.[32] Both Charles and his successor, James II (1685–9), remained fundamentally pro-French in attitude. Inevitably, this rendered the Orange court at The Hague the focus for the hopes and intrigues of the more radical sections of the English Whig opposition.

The Glorious Revolution, triggered by a full-scale Dutch invasion of Britain and the military occupation of London by Prince Willem III, was the culmination of years of clever Orangist scheming and conspiracy. It was the climax of a vast campaign of diplomacy and propaganda, orchestrated by the court in The Hague, which pervaded the whole of Europe and had important ramifications as far afield as Spain, Sweden and the Ottoman Empire.[33] These political and military campaigns were personal triumphs for Willem III – resulting in the dethroning of James II

Prince Willem III of Orange, the future King William of Great Britain, as military commander, painted in 1677 by Caspar Netscher.

and the prince being made King of England (as William III), Scotland and Ireland (albeit jointly with Mary) in his stead. The revolution constituted a vast change in the political and diplomatic constellation of Europe, not the least consequence of which was the partial transfer of the court from The Hague to Whitehall and Hampton Court. Hans Willem Bentinck (1649–1709), the prince's closest friend and adviser and the man who had co-ordinated the Dutch propaganda campaign in Britain, and assisted in drawing up the invasion plans,[34] now became the Earl of Portland and a naturalized English subject. Residing chiefly in England, Bentinck became the senior officer of the English Bedchamber, serving as groom of the stool and keeper of the privy purse to the new king. From 1689 until his death in 1702 William himself lived for much of the year in England and, while he also resided for long periods in the Low Countries, much of this time was spent on campaign in the southern Netherlands or at his hunting retreat, the palace of Het Loo, in Gelderland. After 1689 the prince-king spent comparatively little time at The Hague. The court continued to exist, but it was now split between The Hague and Het Loo and, at any given moment, many of its principal figures were likely to be found in England. Thus, the reduced stature of the courtly establishment at The Hague, which was to be such a marked phenomenon of the first half of the eighteenth century, in effect began with the Glorious Revolution.

Meanwhile, the impressive collections assembled by Frederik Hendrik were kept largely intact by the Princess Dowager Amalia until her death in 1675. Court taste in painting during the seventeenth century seems to have been distinctively different from the preferences of the republic's prosperous bourgeoisie. In contrast to the many admirable 'cabinets' of paintings amassed by regent and merchant art-lovers, the stadholder, his relatives and other connoisseurs at court, tended to eschew, or at least acquired few of, the typically Dutch landscapes, seascapes, still-lifes and genre scenes that were produced in such abundance during these decades.[35] The taste of the court was more inclined to the mythological allegory, heroic scenes, religious paintings and Italianate landscapes. But the stadholders' collections at The Hague also contrasted with those assembled by the English Stuart kings and by the French crown, and did not share the preference for Italian pictures so typical of the great collections in London and Paris. In fact, the stadholders' collections included remarkably few Italian or French pictures.[36] The backbone of the collection of paintings consisted of the more heroic works by Dutch artists such as Honthorst, van Everdingen, Poelenburgh and Rembrandt, supplemented with a number of Flemish works by such artists as Rubens, van Dyck, Jordaens, van Thulden, Gonzales Coques and Jan Breughel.

William III collected on a smaller scale than Frederik Hendrik, and, in any case, during the opening years of his stadholderate, he was much too preoccupied with the exigencies of the war with France (1672–7) to pay a great deal of attention to building up his collections or renovating his palaces. Nevertheless, we know that he was interested in art, and already in the 1670s knew a number of important artists personally. In 1672 the prince sat for several hours to Gerard ter Borch, both in Deventer and at The Hague. In different circumstances he might well have evolved into one of Europe's greatest collectors. A worse setback occurred as a consequence of Princess Amalia's death, for her will divided the paintings between her three surviving daughters and her Hohenzollern grandsons – the children of the daughter who had predeceased her, Louise Henriëtte, Electress of Brandenburg. As a result, most of the choice works in the collections – including pictures by Rembrandt, Rubens, Lievens and Honthorst – were dispersed between the electoral household at Berlin and other court cities in the Empire.[37] By 1676–7, however, the prince had begun collecting seriously in his own right, and came into contact with various art dealers and artists in Antwerp. Among the latter, he is known to have paid a personal visit to the now 86-year-old Jacob Jordaens. Behind this artistic patronage seems to have been, once again, the figure of Hans Willem Bentinck, who advised the prince in artistic matters, as in so much else, and was a noted connoisseur of the visual arts, gardens and furniture. Bentinck doubtless encouraged his master to collect in many fields, as well as to spend substantial sums on his palaces and gardens at Het Loo, Rijswijk and elsewhere. William's political ambitions and dynastic preoccupations probably also help explain the fact that he had his portrait taken so many times, frequently striking heroic poses. Altogether he was portrayed during his lifetime by more than thirty painters, sculptors

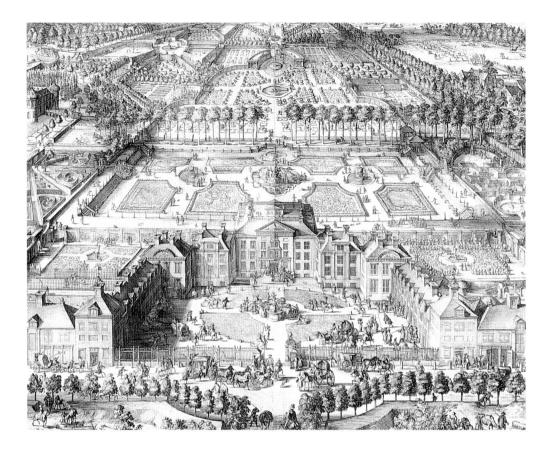

Orange splendour: after Het Loo (above), William III was unimpressed by London's dowdy Whitehall.

and engravers.[38] Engravings were the most widely circulated of all visual representations, and were relatively cheaply reproduced. The skills of expert engravers – among them Romeyn de Hooghe, the most famous engraver and book illustrator of the period – were put to use in adding a visual dimension to William's extensive propaganda, glorifying the Dutch state, and its stadholder, while simultaneously deriding Louis XIV. By the 1680s and 1690s William III had assembled a not unimpressive collection of books and works of art. A large proportion of his pictures was displayed at Het Loo; others were kept at The Hague and elsewhere; moreover, after becoming King of England, Scotland and Ireland, William used the resources of the English royal collections to enrich the furnishings of the palaces in the Dutch republic. A number of works, including several Holbeins, were transferred to Holland – to be reclaimed, after his death, by his successor in England, Queen Anne (1702–14).

William's death in 1702, without a male heir, marked a major reversal in the position of the stadholderate and in its artistic fortunes, as picture collections were dispersed and palaces fell into disrepair. William's legacy – his titles, lands, revenues, works of art and buildings – was claimed on the one side by the Frisian branch of the House of Orange-Nassau, and on the other by the Hohenzollern Margrave of Brandenburg (now King in Prussia) who, as heir to Louise Henriëtte, claimed to be the rightful Prince of Orange.[39] But this was only one cause of the dispersal of the collections and the rapid deterioration of some of the palaces at this time. It seems, however, that even more was alienated in the 1710s, after the death of William's successor as Prince of Orange, Johan Willem Friso (1702–11); financial problems forced his widow, Marie Louise of Hesse-Cassel (who was acting as joint guardian of the infant Willem IV of Orange with her father, the Count of Hesse-Cassel) to sell large portions

of the former court collection.[40] In 1713 the new King in Prussia, Friedrich Wilhelm I (1713–40), visited The Hague, inspected the buildings that had fallen to his share, and took a large number of paintings back with him to Berlin. Over the next years Marie Louise sold a good many more. Nevertheless, some remained, and these were later to form the nucleus of the Dutch royal cabinet of paintings housed from 1822 until today in the Mauritshuis at The Hague. William III's superb library was sold off in 1749.

During the so-called Second Stadholderless Period (1702–47), the States of Holland and assemblies of most of the other provinces again decided to dispense with the office of stadholder. As a consequence, the court at The Hague was, once more, of only marginal significance in the public life of the United Provinces. Because of the dispute over the legacy of William III, as well as the straitened circumstances of the princely family, the palaces of the court in and around The Hague fell into a state of neglect and disrepair. The new Prince of Orange, Johan Willem Friso, established his court at Leeuwarden where he resided as Stadholder of Friesland, as did his successor Willem IV, until 1747. The House of Orange-Nassau returned to the status of minor princelings. However, in 1747, after disturbances in many parts of the country amounting almost to a revolution, the stadholderate was restored in Holland and in the other provinces that had dispensed with the office. Riding a wave of popular enthusiasm, the Prince of Orange was brought back from Friesland to The Hague. For a moment, republicanism was once again discredited and the charisma of the House of Orange, and the strong support for it among the common people in all the provinces of the Union, was confirmed.

From this point on, until the Batavian Revolution of 1795 – which overthrew the Orangist regime and caused the last stadholder, Willem V (1751–1806), to flee the country and seek refuge in England – the court at the Hague functioned once again as the nerve-centre of the republic and as the country's main source of power, influence and patronage. For the United Provinces as a whole, the period from the 1740s to the 1790s was one of steep decline in almost every sphere: political, economic, maritime, colonial and cultural; for the court of Orange-Nassau, however, it was one of revival, renewed influence and greatly increased affluence and wealth.

During the stadholderate of Willem IV (1747–51) in Holland, the United Provinces had undergone fundamental changes in the structure of power and influence; but his stadholdership was too short to enable the prince to revive the outward manifestations of near sovereign status, among them the dynasty's palaces and collections. Most of the work of renovation, the task of reassembling collections and adding new glitter to the court, was carried out from the 1750s; in particular, by the prince's widow, Princess Anne of Hanover (1709–59), a daughter of George II of Great Britain. In the 1750s, with the stadholderate restored to the dynasty, it was she who presided over the court of Orange-Nassau at The Hague – which meant, in effect, that she and her favourites presided over the whole of the United Provinces and its colonial empire. The princess was able to buy back those palaces that had been assigned to the Prussian crown after the death of William III. These included the Oude Hof in The Hague and Honselaersdijk, both of which were refurbished by Anne of Hanover at great expense; by 1756 much of the work of renovation was completed, and a famous ball was held at the Oude Hof that year to mark the eighth birthday of the infant stadholder Willem V, and the revived glory and reputation of the House of Orange-Nassau.

On reaching his majority in 1766, Willem V (Stadholder of the United Provinces 1751–95) soon showed himself to be weak and vacillating, as well as a not very knowledgeable head of the Dutch state; but there was one field in which he excelled – and that was as an art connoisseur. At the age of only twenty, in 1768, he paid 50,000 guilders for the famous cabinet of paintings built up by the recently deceased Govaert van Slingelandt (1694–1767), including some forty paintings of high quality, including works by Rembrandt, Rubens, van Dyck, Holbein, ter Borch and others.[41] In 1774 Willem V opened a large part of his collection to the public, thereby creating one of the first great modern art museums.[42]

In the age of the Dutch Republic's decadence, from the 1740s onwards, the court at The Hague was the country's main source of political patronage and its dominant institution. While many of the outward forms and constitutional procedures of the past remained intact, power and influence throughout the United Provinces were now chiefly wielded by an assortment

Prince Willem arriving at Dordrecht (c. 1680) to the sounds of trumpets (lower left): the yachts of the prince and his entourage (centre) are marked out respectively by the heraldic figure of the lion of Orange adorning the bow of the one and the achievement of the prince's arms on the stern of the other.

of courtiers and court-connected army officers with aristocratic pretensions (often quite recent), most of whom sported the title of 'baron'. Not surprisingly, this was also a period in which a powerful aversion to the court welled up at times in a society increasingly susceptible to republican and democratic tendencies. During the so-called Patriot Movement of the 1780s and the pro-French Batavian revolution of 1795, major elements of Dutch society (especially in the towns) entered into active opposition to the Orangist court. Yet, the court's continued popularity, perhaps especially among the Calvinist orthodox and the less well educated, both in town and country, remained formidable.

Thus, while republican ideas and pressures were reactivated within the Dutch Republic in the 1780s and 1790s, and there was plenty of support for the French-backed Batavian Republic (1795–1806), at least initially, both the charisma and appeal of the House of Orange among large sections of the public remained considerable. Eventually, in the second half of the nineteenth century, a balanced compromise between monarchy and democracy emerged, although for several decades after 1813 the House of Orange – newly promoted as kings of the Netherlands after the defeat of Napoleon – became a real monarchy with a fully developed court and utterly preponderant within the Dutch political process. Yet much of the strength of the nineteenth-century Dutch monarchy lay in a sense of continuity with the past that was by no means entirely imaginary.[43] For the monarchy was that of the House of Orange-Nassau, a royal house both national and international, aristocratic and bourgeois, and the extent of its success was in no small degree the consequence of the long-standing traditions of its court, and its widespread influence on Dutch life built up ever since the sixteenth-century revolt against Spain.

S.^{mus} D.N. celebrante missa, oes Card.^{les} et Epi ri̇̃l parati
pluuialibus, et mitris.
Quando celebratur p̃nte S.D.N. Papa, Card.^{les} cappas
hent rubeas, uel uiolaceas iuxta temporis consuetudine
et Epi et Prelati hent cappas uiolaceas.
Familia S.D.N. semper rubeo uestitur.

The Patrimony of St Peter
THE PAPAL COURT AT ROME
*c.*1450–1700

HENRY DIETRICH FERNÁNDEZ

THROUGHOUT ITS LONG HISTORY, THE PAPACY HAS FUNCTIONED both as a religious and as a political institution.[1] It has survived and maintained this dual status by constantly changing, reshaping and re-forming its dual ecclesiastical and monarchical identities. During the period from the mid fifteenth century to the end of the seventeenth, the papacy demonstrated an ability to absorb political shocks, such as the sack of Rome by imperial troops in 1527, that could have resulted in the complete collapse of less resilient institutions. It also underwent a dramatic change in its identity. The Roman pontiff had been a secular as well as a spiritual ruler since the early Middle Ages. But it was only during the later fifteenth and early sixteenth centuries that his rule within the 'papal states' was consolidated, and his court at Rome was transformed into one of the great monarchical courts of Europe. The period also witnessed a decisive alteration in the style of papal monarchy. From the reigns of Eugenius IV (1431–47) and his successor, Nicholas V (1447–55), there was a perceptible change in the balance between the priestly and regal aspects of papal power, a shift away from the pastoral towards a new emphasis on the monarchical character of the papal office. Under Nicholas V, the pope greatly reduced the occasions on which he performed his priestly offices before a congregation, limiting his public appearances as celebrant of the mass to around three occasions in the course of the year.[2]

The central ritual of the Roman court: the papal household assembled for mass before the pope in the Sistine Chapel – the court chapel. God on the altar and his earthly lieutenant on the papal throne are designated by canopies of equal height. Each member of the court had his appointed place in the chapel, according to status; the conservatores of Rome, for example, had the right to sit on the steps of the papal throne; the pope's physician on the first row of benches to the left. In the foreground (centre), the Swiss guard, with pole-axes, line the processional route that leads from the Sala Regia to the adjacent chapel.

From the late fifteenth century the papal realm became what has been termed a *Tempelstaat*, a religious state ruled over by a monarch who is simultaneously spiritual pastor and secular king.[3] By the death of Urban VIII (1623–44), the balance between the two seemed to have shifted decisively towards the latter role. As one contemporary noted, 'he wished to be seen as a prince rather than as a pope, a ruler rather than as a pastor'.[4] The image of the pope-king was embodied, not only in the apostolic figure of Peter, but in the prophetic figure of Moses, who acquired a new prominence in papal iconography. Given expression most famously in Michelangelo's monumental sculptural figure for the tomb of Julius II (1503–13),[5] the Mosaic theme formed a recurrent motif in papal iconography from the Sistine Chapel frescoes of Sixtus IV's reign (1471–84) through to the decoration of the *casino* of Pius IV (1559–65) and the Moses Fountain of the Aqua Felice for Sixtus V (1585–90) almost a century later. Over the intervening period, the ceremonial spaces of the Vatican Palace were expanded and extensively rebuilt, and with this expansion came a corresponding increase in the size of the papal entourage. Ritual and household protocol were also elaborated to highlight the pope's role as a secular prince.[6]

Between the fifteenth and seventeenth centuries, the court of the papal monarchy became one of the most influential models – in terms of ceremony, music, art and architecture – for the royal households of early modern Europe. As a major centre for politics and diplomacy in the Italian peninsula and beyond, for manners and etiquette, and for literary and artistic tastes, it ranked as one of the pre-eminent courts of the *ancien régime*. At least until the Reformation, its primacy in the field of diplomacy was unrivalled. Between 1490 and 1500 it has been estimated that there were some 243 diplomats in Rome as against 161 at the court of Emperor Maximilian, 135 at the French court and around 100 in Milan.[7] While Venice is usually given pioneering status in setting up foreign embassies, Rome urged the republic, well into the seventeenth century, to send its most able ambassadorial candidates to Rome to learn the art of diplomacy at the papal court. Conversely, Rome sent out far fewer papal nuncios and envoys than it received ambassadors

from foreign princes, something that is itself indicative of the Roman court's awareness of its own centrality. Even after the Reformation, the cultural influence of the Roman court continued to be felt in Protestant courts as disparate as Charles I's Whitehall of the 1630s or Friedrich I's Berlin of the 1700s.

Yet, in many respects, the papal court remained a highly idiosyncratic institution. It ranked with Poland, the Empire, and ducal Venice as one of the few elective monarchies in Europe; and the juridical relations between the papal monarch and the body of his electors, the Sacred College of Cardinals – the 'princes of the Church' who formed the higher nobility of the papal court – were always problematic. Renaissance popes asserted their juridical 'plenitude of power' (*plenitudo potestatis*), and their absolute sovereignty over the Sacred College, and even over General Councils of the Church. Compared with their secular brother-monarchs, however, when it came to making good their claims to sovereign power, they started with certain disadvantages. They tended to be elected relatively late in life, and thus to reign for far shorter periods than secular monarchs. The possibilities for the consolidation of power through the exercise of patronage, the aggrandizement of their families and the creation of connections were accordingly more limited – not least through the absence of any right of dynastic succession. As has been pointed out, at the Roman court, 'rulers' changed with extreme frequency and thus, unlike the courts of secular kings, so did the ruling house: there was a change of 'dynasty' whenever a new pope was elected.[8] Before considering how this highly atypical court functioned, we must first examine the composition of its core: the household and immediate entourage of the pope.

I. THE PAPAL HOUSEHOLD

As with any princely household, the papal court at Rome was maintained by a small army of ecclesiastical attendants and servants, many of whom acted out dual, if not triple, roles at court. The functions of papal 'government' and the pontiff's private 'household' were intimately intermixed. Officers of the *famiglia pontificia* (the pontifical household) inevitably overlapped with those entrusted with guardianship of

The interior of the Sala Regia in 1620, by Pietro da Cortona (1597–1669), during a public consistory – the most prestigious form of audience. Pope Paul V receives the emperor's ambassador, Prince Paulo Savelli (lower left, in the white ruff, with the gold collar of the Order of the Golden Fleece), who announces the imperial alliance against the Protestants in Bohemia in the opening phase of the Thirty Years War (1618–48).

the *cappella pontificia* (the pontifical chapel). At the summit of the hierarchy was the figure of the pope himself. His triple crown, or tiara, introduced in the reign of Benedict XI (1303–4), symbolized the pope's triune jurisdiction as prince, judge and priest.[9] While the composition of the papal household may have varied over the centuries according to the politics and tastes of the reigning pontiff, the structure of the private inner circle tended to remain constant. Within the papal *famiglia*, it was the so-called palatine (i.e. palace) cardinals who occupied the topmost rank of the hierarchy: members of the 'ecclesiastical aristocracy' who held offices within the household or the ecclesiastical administration. Pre-eminent among these were the vice-chancellor, the principal officer responsible for the administration of the Church, and the cardinal-nephew (*cardinale nipote*), who, from the 1530s to the 1690s, effectively served as the pope's patronage and diplomatic manager in the day-to-day administration of the regime.[10]

The next group in the court hierarchy was formed by the senior officers of his household, known collectively as the Noble Privy Antechamber. At its head was the *maestro di casa*, the master of the house-hold (known from 1626 as the *maggiordomo,* or high steward), responsible for the administration of the household. Tenure was at the pope's pleasure, and could be brief. (Paul III had no less than eight or nine *maestri di casa*, beginning with Ascanio Parisani of Tolentino, the Bishop of Rimini, and also including Alessandro Guicciardini and ending with a Neapoli-tan relative of the Sienese Piccolomini family, Bernardino Silveri de Piccolomini in 1546.)

Beneath the *maggiordomo* came the master of the sacred palace (*magister sacri palatii*), by tradition, always a Dominican, who served as the pope's personal theologian. His wide-ranging brief including advising the pope on the iconography and symbolism associ-ated with any work of art executed within the papal palaces. Between 1508 and 1512, for example, Julius II's master of the sacred palace advised both the pope and Michelangelo on the theological themes expressed in the Sistine Chapel ceiling decorations.

Still within the Noble Privy Antechamber came the administration of the papal state, a body presided over by the master of the chamber (*maestro di camera*). Three cardinals headed the Chamber.[11] Under the cardinal chamberlain (*camerlingo*), the Chamber super-vised the collection of taxes and the other revenues of the papacy. During Martin V's papacy (1417–31), the role of treasurer was divided between 'public' and 'private' accounts. Henceforth, there was a general treasurer of the Holy See, usually chosen from among the clerics of the Chamber, and responsible for the revenues of the papal state. A secret treasurer adminis-tered the pope's 'privy purse' income and expenditure; and the opportunities for access to the pontiff that went with this office were frequently used by incum-bents to further their careers. Paul III's privy treasurer, Bernardino della Croce, for instance, gradually won a series of promotions, ending as a Canon of St Peter's in 1540, and Bishop of Asti in 1547.[12]

In the third rank of the household came the so-called participating privy chamberlains, usually between six and eight in number. These were responsible for the secretarial side of the papal admin-istration, and for providing for the pope's personal requirements. Among the busiest was the master of the wardrobe, charged with supervising the pope's cloth-ing and furnishing. Under Paul III (1534–49), the post was held by Pier Giovanni Aleotti, described as one of the busiest members of the papal *famiglia*. Among his 'one thousand tasks' were duties ranging from the pur-chase of vestments, vessels for the papal chapel, shirts for the pope (the best ones were from Mantua), main-taining the pontiff's birds, medicines and perfumes, conserving his antique medals and, not least, providing the papal spectacles. In June 1536 Paul III's master of the wardrobe, Aleotti, supervised the making of a prayer book for Charles V, which was painted by Vincent Raymond and engraved by Benvenuto Cellini.[13]

Other participating privy chamberlains provided the pope's immediate secretariat. The privy almoner dealt not only with the dispensing of charity, but also with the allocation of benefices within the Church; he was, accordingly, a major conduit of papal patronage. Beside him ranked the secretaries – the secretary of letters to princes, responsible for diplomatic corre-spondence; the secretaries for code, Latin letters and embassies; the under-datary; and the sacristan, who was not only responsible for the jewel-encrusted papal vestments and church plate, but also served as the pope's chaplain.[14] The papal secretariat attracted some of the finest scholars of the age, lured by the prestige

of the court and the lucrative opportunities for promotion that it provided. The Medici pope, Leo X (1513–21), with his penchant for classical scholars and literary men, promoted the humanists Pietro Bembo and Jacopo Sadoleto as 'domestic prelates'. Bembo, over the course of more than thirty years, received no less than thirty-one ecclesiastical offices, many of which he held in plurality; indeed, a large part of his energies would seem to have been devoted to scheming to obtain these awards. Sadoleto received some thirteen during roughly the same period, and was particularly successful as a broker of patronage for his family.[15] Similarly under Paul III, the secretary of codes, through whom the pope communicated with foreign princes, was held by Trifone Benci, a man described with some justification by a contemporary as 'a philosopher of ancient faith and virtue, the master of perfect handwriting, a writer of prose and of the sweetest and most elegant Tuscan [vernacular] and Latin verse'.[16] Their intimacy with the pope was also reflected in court ceremonial. The privy chamberlains wore purple, and at divine service attended immediately on the pontiff. One carried his cross, another his train; the papal chaplain (clericus cappellae privatae) carried the triple crown and the papal mitres on the major feasts of the Church when the pope attended a cappella before the court.[17] By the seventeenth century all of these offices, with the exception of the master of the sacred hospice (magister sacri hospitii), responsible for the reception of high-ranking visitors to the court and one of the participating privy chamberlains, were held by ecclesiastics.[18]

Forming the ecclesiastical administration (the curia), but housed near the papal palace, were the departments of the Chancery (cancelleria), responsible for the letters and bulls (so called from their metal seals or bullae) issued by the Holy See; and the Sacred Rota (the college of papal lawyers), so named from their round table (or rota), which was the main papal judicial tribunal.[19] The papal Mint was not only responsible for the minting of coins with a negotiable cash value, but also for the issuing of commemorative medals to mark the foundation of major architectural projects.

Laymen were confined largely to equestrian and military roles. The participating privy chamberlains of sword and cape were composed largely of members of the Roman nobility, many of whom held office by hereditary right. Among the military posts, many of which were virtual sinecures commanding large salaries, were the offices of captain-general of the Holy Church (the commander-in-chief of the papal army), general of the papal galleys, castellan of the Sant'Angelo (the ancient fortress dominating the city), commander of the Swiss guard, the bearer of the Golden Rose (the traditional papal gift to fellow monarchs), as well as the various posts of colonel and lieutenant in the papal guard.

Within the ranks of the participating privy chamberlains of sword and cape, perhaps the most important lay office was the role of master of the horse (or maestro di stalle), who presided over the court stables and made arrangements for the court's travels. Cardinal Alessandro Farnese, the future Paul III, for example, had some ninety 'mounts for [his] gentlemen' alone, without counting carriage horses or mules, and during the Farnese pontificate in the 1530s and 1540s the number of stable personnel grew. By the mid-sixteenth century, the staff included a sub-master, twenty stable-hands, a water carrier, a master of the oats, a master of the mules, nine mule hands and a carriage master.

For, despite the papal court's ecclesiastical character, the hunt and equestrian pursuits formed a central feature of courtly recreation, as they did in secular courts. Presided over by a principal huntsman (principe cacciatore) and the custodian of the papal kennels, the hunt provided a privileged inner circle with intimate and relatively informal access to the papal monarch. In the process, the presiding officers of the hunt were frequently, or came to be, trusted confidants of the pope. Under Leo X, for example, the master of the kennels, one Giovanni Lazzaro de Magistris, originally a parish priest from Aquila, rose to become one of the pontiff's most trusted advisers.[20]

The provision of hospitality and dining at the Vatican Palace required a large administrative hierarchy. The various dining chambers (tinelli) of the palace were graded into three ranks – greater, lesser and privy dining rooms – served by a staff of carvers (calchi). The catering staff formed an army of functionaries, clerks and retainers: from the private purveyor (spenditore segreto), charged with purchasing food for the popes, to the two 'papal dispensers' (dispensieri), responsible for distributing and keeping

track of tableware and plate for various dining rooms. To guard against poisoning, there was a food taster, who often accompanied the pope on his travels.[21]

With a household largely composed of unmarried and (in theory) celibate clergy, the part played by women at the papal court was inevitably somewhat limited. While courtesans were not an official part of the papal household, Johann Burchard, master of ceremonies to the Borgia pope Alexander VI (1492–1503), describes celebrations at which prostitutes were present. Filippo Beroaldo the younger, another of Leo X's domestic prelates (along with Bembo and Sadoleto) acquired a reputation as something of a connoisseur of the courtesans of Rome; those who attended to his needs included Settima, Albina, Faustina, Giulia, Cesarilla and the famous Imperia, a favourite of future Clement VII (1523–34).[22] At the other extreme, almost the only other women employed by the papal household were the 'papal laundresses'. Given their sex, they were housed outside the palace proper, but still within the Vatican walls on the Belvedere. Paul III had two 'secret laundresses' and another one for the secret dining room.

Like almost every other princely household, the papal court had a staff of clowns, although the court was perhaps unusual in that many of its freaks and fools had also taken holy orders of some description, and occasionally succeeded in moving on to major office in the household. In the early sixteenth century, the Dominican Mariano Fetti, the arch-jester known as 'il Buffone Cucullato' (the cowled fool), became renowned for his coarse and witty sayings, and eventually succeeded Bramante as the keeper of the papal seal.[23] Others seem to have been purely figures of ridicule.[24] There was Camillo Querno, sarcastically given the title of 'arch-poet,' whose drunken verses greatly amused Leo X; and one Barballo, whose attempt to ride Leo's elephant Hanno from the Vatican to the Capitoline Hill, had to be aborted after the beast refused to go any further than the Ponte Sant' Angelo.[25] Paul III was accompanied by his fool, Cagnetto the Clown, on a visit to Nice to meet François I and Charles V, the Holy Roman Emperor.[26]

Beyond those who held formal office in the *famiglia* or in the chapel, the papal court played host to a large concourse of temporary or occasional visitors:

ambassadors and other diplomatic representatives; travellers on the Grand Tour; pilgrims ranging in rank from emperors and kings to mendicant friars. The lay and the ecclesiastical members of the household formed a single integrated hierarchy of status and precedence. After the cardinals and patriarchs, for instance, ranked the Roman grandees, the Duca di Paliano (head of the Colonna family) and the Duca di Bracciano (head of the Orsini), who in theory took their place in papal processions accordingly.[27] The Orsini and the Colonna used the matter of their place in the papal procession as a battleground to carry on their centuries-old feuds. They fought bitterly and acrimoniously over the question of *super praecendentia* – which of them had the right to process to the right of the pope – with the consequence that both families were banned from attending papal ceremonies between 1590 and 1656. A compromise was eventually agreed whereby the Orsini and Colonna undertook to attend ceremonies alternately.[28] At a *cappella pontificia* (a religious ceremony attended by the pope in formal state within the palace chapel), for example, visiting princes and their eldest sons had the right to be censed immediately after the cardinals.

Before turning to the question of how this highly complex court functioned in its threefold administration of papal household, territorial state and universal church, we need first to consider the physical setting of the papal monarchy: the Apostolic Palace, its adjoining Basilica of St Peter, and the city of Rome. What were the influences that enabled the papal court to emerge, by the mid seventeenth century, 'as the most spectacular Baroque court in Europe'?[29]

II. THE ARCHITECTURAL SETTING

The re-invention of Rome as a city in which architectural magnificence and integrated urban planning gave expression to the authority of a monarch and his court dated from the early fifteenth century. It took its rise from the re-establishment of papal government in the city after the Great Schism (1378–1417) and the reassertion of papal monarchy after the challenges of the conciliar movement. The resulting buildings of the Vatican palace and its adjacent basilica are a palimpsest

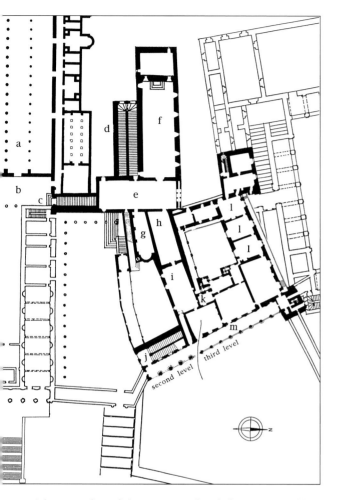

Schematic plan of the Vatican Palace before 1521. Old St Peter's Basilica (a) and its narthex (b) were linked by Bramante's Via Giulia Nova (c), via the old Scala Regia (d) to the papal apartments of state on the floor above (this ceremonial staircase was later rebuilt by Bernini, 1663–6). The Sala Regia (e) was flanked by the Sistine Chapel (f), and the Capella Parva (g), later rebuilt as the Pauline Chapel (1534–49) by Antonio da Sangallo. The second and third Audience Halls (h) and (i), were later combined by Bernini to form a single Sala Ducale on the second level. Bramante also designed another cordonata *(j), ramp stair, that led up to Julius II's apartments next to the Chapel of Nicholas V (k), Raphael's Stanze (l) and the Loggia (m) on the third level.*

of architectural styles and forms, regularly re-negotiated in response to the ever-changing political and religious needs of succeeding pontificates. The palace's elaborately decorated façades, halls, chapels,

staircases and corridors were primarily created to provide a setting for pageantry and ceremonial, and, not least, to glorify the fame and memory of their builders. Although the spectacular architecture of the Vatican complex today seems endowed with a certain inevitability, its present state is, in fact, the result of centuries of architectural additions, demolitions, compromises and changes. The buildings that comprise the core of the palace date back to the Middle Ages and, in the case of the basilica, to the time of Constantine. But it is the additions and embellishments dating from around the 1450s, the time of Nicholas V, through to the 1660s, the papacy of Alexander VII – the 'golden age' of the papal court – that give the Vatican the legible identity visible today.[30]

Ever since the re-establishment of the pontifical household at Rome in the 1420s, the papal court had been in the vanguard of the cultural movement dedicated to the revival of classical principles in art, architecture and scholarship.[31] Nicholas V (1447–55) employed as his secretary the distinguished Florentine humanist Leon Battista Alberti,[32] and commissioned Bernardo Rosselino (1409–1464) to design a new 'choir' (the part of the basilica where the clergy would later celebrate the mass) to extend the apse at the west end of the Constantinian basilica. Structural problems with the old basilica were regarded with concern by Nicholas V, and it was Alberti, acting as his architectural adviser, who may have suggested the solution that for the time being saved the basilica from demolition. In his treatise *De re aedificatoria* (On the Business of Building), presented to Nicholas V in 1452, Alberti prescribed that, wherever possible, important ancient monuments, such as the basilica, should be preserved – a sentiment that Julius II would later comprehensively ignore.[33]

Another pressing need, however, was for a suitably dignified setting for the daily liturgy *within* the palace. The Chapel of Nicholas V, decorated by Fra Angelico (c.1387–c.1455) and located immediately adjacent to the pope's apartments, recalled the splendour of the palatine chapels of the Avignonese court and fulfilled this need.[34] The most important setting for the papal court's daily liturgy, however, was the Sistine Chapel, built by Sixtus IV between 1477 and 1484 to designs possibly by either Giovanni dei Dolci or Baccio Pontelli.[35] First used on 9 August 1483, the anniversary

The ceremonial hub of the palace: the Sala Regia, used here for the crowning of Cosimo de' Medici (kneeling, centre, before the papal throne) as Grand Duke of Tuscany, on 18 February 1570. The elevation from ducal to grand-ducal rank positioned the Medici rulers immediately below anointed kings. A large tapestry of the grand-ducal Medici arms, surrounded by the collar of the Order of the Golden Fleece, has been hung in honour of the occasion (left).

of Sixtus IV's election as pope,[36] its original decoration included a frescoed ceiling, an ultramarine field punctuated by gold stars, by Pier Matteo d'Amelia, and a mural cycle depicting the lives of Moses and Christ, by some of the most celebrated painters of the day, including Pietro Perugino, Sandro Botticelli, Domenico Ghirlandaio, Luca Signorelli, Bartolomeo della Gatta, Piero di Cosimo, Pinturichio and Cosimo Rosselli.

This concern with creating a suitably magnificent setting for the papal court was 'inherited' by Sixtus IV's nephew, Giuliano della Rovere, who assumed the papal office as Julius II in 1503. Familiar with the amenities of the papal court at Avignon, where he had served as papal legate between 1476 and 1482,[37] with its opulent papal chapel, stately consistory (or Audience Hall) and splendid gardens, the Avignonese

model seems to have exercised a powerful influence on Julius II's ideas for the renovation of his own palace at the Vatican. With the papacy's Roman palace appearing a poor second, Julius seized the opportunity to surpass the example at Avignon through the artistic expertise of his architects, such as Giuliano da Sangallo (1445–1516) and Donato Bramante (c.1444–1514), the brilliance of Michelangelo Buonarotti (1475–1564) as architect and painter, and Raphael (Raffaello Santi, 1483–1520) and other decorative designers, who included Giovanni da Udine and Perino del Vaga.[38] This artistic collective was to create a setting for courtly pomp and splendour, and to endow Julius's Vatican with an easily legible political imagery.

The need to integrate the various ceremonial foci of the palace complex (particularly the papal apartments, the court chapel, the Audience Hall and the

basilica) prompted a series of major architectural initiatives. Just before November 1505 Julius relocated the papal living quarters, moving them from the apartments occupied by his Borgia predecessor, Alexander VI, on the second level of the Vatican Palace, to apartments on the third level of the palace (occupied by Nicholas V and subsequently by Julius's uncle, Sixtus IV).[39] This move, in turn, seems to have inspired Julius to consider a way of linking these third-floor papal apartments by way of a ceremonial route, which, as we will see, ultimately connected the basilica and the great ceremonial areas of the palace: the Sistine Chapel and the principal audience chambers, the Sala Ducale (the Ducal Hall) and what was in effect the papal 'throne room', the Sala Regia (the Royal Hall).

The Sala Regia was the ritual centre of the pope's life as monarch, just as the Sistine Chapel and the basilica defined the two principal foci of the court's religious liturgies within the Vatican. Here stood the grandest of the chairs of state to be found within the palace, elevated on a dais, approached by a short flight of three stairs, and surmounted by a curtained canopy, the traditional emblem of sacred sovereignty, hung with cloth of gold.[40] This room was likewise heavily remodelled at Julius II's command. Also from Julius's reign is Bramante's innovative tripartite window, positioned on the upper part of the north wall of the Sala Regia, immediately above the papal throne. Its distinctive form, with its central light capped by an arch between two rectangular flanking openings, was later extensively emulated.[41] It recurs in Philip II's memorial to the Habsburg kings at the Escorial (dating from the 1590s), and in Inigo Jones's design for the Queen's Chapel (erected 1623–7) at St James's Palace, Westminster, which was originally designed for Catholic use by the Spanish infanta (though the intended marriage, to the future Charles I, never took place).[42] At the Banqueting House at Whitehall, commissioned by James I of Britain (erected between 1619 and 1622), in what appears to have been a self-conscious act of referencing, Jones also employed a very broad interpretation of a *Bramantesca* window in the composition of the upper wall immediately above the royal 'state' (or throne), as in the pontifical Sala Regia. The influence of 'Caesaro-papism' could have had no clearer architectural expression.

The third and most ambitious element of the Julian programme was the demolition of the old Constantinian basilica, the prime church of Christendom since the fourth century, and its replacement by a new and still greater basilica, to designs by Bramante. Begun in April 1506, the new St Peter's was not only important in realizing the pope's vision of a new and far grander setting for papal ceremonies, but also as a public symbol of his renovation of the faith. The enterprise set new architectural standards, in part through Bramante's innovative interpretation of the 'antique', but not least through the sheer physical scale of the new St Peter's. The new setting for the papal court could be seen as competing directly with the magnitude of republican and imperial Roman antiquity.

The final element in Julius II's grand design was the creation of a suitably stately processional way that would link the entrance to the basilica with the principal ceremonial rooms of the palace – and, above all, the Sala Regia. A few months after the pope had moved to his apartment on the third level, in May 1506, he began his renovation of the Vatican Palace by having Bramante demolish the old ceremonial staircase that had connected the portico of the old basilica, via the old Scala Regia, to the Sala Regia. This older staircase was replaced by a *cordonata*, a ramp stair, negotiable by horses, that became known as the Via Giulia Nova.[43]

The Via Giulia provided a processional way from the main ceremonial hub of the palace (the Sistine Chapel, the adjacent Sala Regia, the *aula secunda* and the *aula tertia*), to the portico of the basilica, and thence to the piazza and the city. Bramante's further plans for unifying the Vatican Palace allowed the pope to move with dignity and decorum from his papal apartments (on the third level of the palace) on the *sedia gestatoria*. His procession from his apartments on the third level moved through a door on the west side of Raphael's Loggia, leading down another new *cordonata* and through a narrow corridor on the second level of the palace that opened into the *aula tertia*, then via the *aula secunda* (the two lesser audience halls later combined by Gian Lorenzo Bernini to create the Sala Ducale), to the Sala Regia and on to his final destination, the Sistine Chapel.[44] (Sangallo the younger's architectural adjustments during the 1510s to the same route aligned the enfilade of doors between the *aula secunda* and the Sistine Chapel so that, from 1517, the papal

throne in the Sistine Chapel was visible immediately the procession entered the *aula tertia*.)[45] Once in the chapel, the pope was assisted to his canopied chair of state, located immediately to the left of the altar. From this privileged vantage point the pontiff could contemplate Michelangelo's frescoed ceiling decorations, unveiled on 31 October 1512, shortly before Julius II's death. From this same position, Paul III and future popes would view Michelangelo's vision of the *Last Judgement*, executed between 1534 and 1541, painted on the liturgical east-end wall of the chapel, above the high altar.

Elsewhere, a team of artists and architects was at work on the subsidiary rooms of the palace. During Julius II's papacy, Raphael, the superbly talented twenty-five-year-old artist from Urbino, was decorating the pope's private library (later known as the Stanza della Segnatura), and, after Bramante's death at the age of seventy in 1514, succeeded to the management of his various architectural projects.[46] Raphael thus assumed responsibility for the completion of the *cordonata*, the east façade of the Vatican Palace, and Bramante's weightiest architectural enterprise, the construction of the new St Peter's. In order to keep up with the increasing volume of work, Raphael's workshop took full advantage of the architects inherited from Bramante's workshop, a group that included Baldasarre Peruzzi (1481–1536) and Antonio da Sangallo (1485–1546).

From this period also dates Sangallo's Pauline Chapel, commissioned by Paul III (1534–49), as a second liturgical space, supplementing the Sistine Chapel and the Sala Regia.[47] Here, Michelangelo executed his frescoes *The Crucifixion of St Peter* and *The Conversion of Saul* (painted 1542–50). From the 1550s the Pauline Chapel acquired a fixed series of functions in the life of the palace, as the venue where ballots were cast in the election of a new pope, as the setting for the Advent ceremonies that began the ecclesiastical year, and as the site of the altar of repose for the sacrament between Maundy Thursday and Easter eve.

Most of the major ritual centres of the Vatican complex were subject to repeated adaptation and changes of plan, partly in response to changes in architectural fashion, but also in response to alterations in ceremonial use. The great task of completing the new basilica went through a series of architectural

administrations lasting more than a hundred years. After the death of Raphael and Sangallo, it was Michelangelo who, in the autumn of 1547, at the age of seventy-two, took on the task of completing the great church. By the time of his death on 18 February 1564, Michelangelo's design, with all but the façade and the dome finished, had given St Peter's its defining identity. Liturgical demands, however, necessitated further changes to Michelangelo's symmetrical, Greek-cross plan. Under Paul V (1605–21), Carlo Maderno (1556–1629) was commissioned in 1607 to extend the nave of the church, thereby creating an extended processional approach to the high altar and to the papal throne immediately to its left. The colossal façade was finally completed in 1612.

The last and grandest of the Roman court's 'ceremonial spaces' was created during the flamboyant papacy of Alexander VII (1655–67), Fabio Chigi of Siena. Among the very first actions of his pontificate was the commissioning, in 1656, of Bernini to create the two curved colonnades flanking St Peter's Square – *Il Teatro* (or The Theatre) as it was sometimes called.[48] Spatially, the colonnades gave the square a well-defined sense of enclosure while allowing crowds of pilgrims to filter through its huge, stoically disposed Doric columns. Henceforth, the new piazza became the setting for a series of major events in the court year, from the annual papal benediction at Easter, the Corpus Christi Day procession, and the starting point of the *possesso* procession, which inaugurated each new pontificate.

The final stage in the development of the palace's principal elements was the creation of a new 'royal staircase', or Scala Regia, connecting the new colonnades and replacing the existing staircase (Bramante's so-called Via Giulia) between the various levels of the papal palace. To designs by Bernini, a corridor was created (1661–4) axially connecting the north colonnade with the base landing of the new Scala Regia (1663–6).[49] Exploiting illusionistic effects in order to create an exaggerated sense of size and distance, the Scala Regia was designed to provide an impressive ceremonial approach to the papal palace and its most magnificent hall of state, the Sala Regia, where, during consistories (or audiences), the pope himself sat enthroned. Its creation was intimately connected to the practices of court ceremonial and

Il Teatro: *Bernini's colonnades flanking the basilica, commissioned by Pope Alexander VII (1655–67), and the open piazza they surrounded were intended as a spectacular setting for the liturgical processions and diplomatic protocol of the court. Here, the French ambassador, the Duc de Choiseul, drives out of the square having taken his formal leave of the pope at the end of his embassy of 1753–7 to the Roman court.*

diplomacy. Visiting dignitaries could now alight at the end of the north colonnade and then proceed up the Scala Regia, past the first landing, connecting with the entrance to the basilica, onwards to the Sala Regia, and its adjacent ceremonial spaces, the Sistine Chapel and the Sala Ducale.

Beyond this 'inner' court space, there was a series of other sites within and near the city that provided extensions of the court. As elsewhere in Europe, the papal *famiglia* possessed a series of residences, most of them within easy reach of the principal palatine 'seat'. In addition to the Vatican Palace, the principal papal seat, there were two major palaces within the walls of Rome itself: the ancient Lateran Palace and the Quirinal Palace, begun by Gregory XIII (1572–85) and much extended by Paul V in the 1610s. Both provided lodgings for members of the court and alternative settings for ceremonies of state, and, in the case of the Lateran, also for church ritual. The pope was crowned Bishop of Rome in the cathedral of San Giovanni in Laterano and thus there were liturgies that took place there specific to the Lateran, as opposed to St Peter's.[50] Beyond the city, in the immediate environs of Rome, lay Castel Gandolfo in the Alban Hills, the country residence purchased by Urban VIII in 1626, and subsequently extensively rebuilt.[51]

In addition to these residences acquired *ex officio* there were the private palaces of the reigning papal family. Each major dynasty to occupy the papal throne either possessed, or usually acquired, a palace in or near to Rome. In the 1510s, under Leo X, for example, the Villa Medici (later known as the Villa Madama) served both as a pleasure retreat for Leo X's court and as a way station where visiting dignitaries could be accommodated on their approach to Rome from the north. In this manner, the Villa Madama can be understood as an integral part of a sequence of court spaces, an extension of the primary Vatican Palace itself.[52]

As the great heraldic displays and monumental inscriptions adorning these various projects announced, the patronage of art and architecture was as much concerned with individual renown and dynastic 'fame' as it was with the glorification of the Universal Church. Yet, whether as acts of vanity or piety, each of these great structures fulfilled a larger purpose. They defined the ceremonial setting of the court, and they can only be fully understood in relation to the ritual life and liturgical needs of the household that called them into being.

III. COURT CEREMONIAL

More than any other royal household, the papal court existed to give exemplary public expression to the religious calendar of Catholic Christendom. The rhythms of the ceremonial year were dictated by the ancient cycle of feasts and solemnities that marked out great events in the life of Christ and the saints. It

The survival of the Renaissance court: the papal coronation ritual, viewed here at the coronation of Pius XII in 1939, remained virtually unchanged from the late fifteenth century to the 1960s. The pontiff is carried under a processional canopy on the sedia gestatoria. *The twin fans, symbolizing universal lordship, probably derive from the Byzantine imperial court.*

began in the late autumn with the first Sunday of Advent, the start of the ecclesiastical year, and continued through the sequence of Christmas, Epiphany, the Annunciation of the Virgin (25 March), Holy Week and Easter, Ascension, Pentecost and Trinity Sunday. It culminated in mid summer with the feasts of Corpus Christi (the Thursday after Trinity) and of SS. Peter and Paul, the traditional founders of papal Rome (29 June), finishing with All Saints (1 November). Scattered between these celebratory peaks were over a hundred lesser feasts and commemorations. The calendar of these observances was heavily pruned and reordered after the Council of Trent (1545–63), and the introduction of the new Roman Breviary (setting out the daily prayer of the Church) in 1568 and the Missal (providing the liturgy for the celebration of mass) in 1570 promulgated the new arrangements, imposing a uniform pattern throughout Catholic Christendom,[53] and leaving roughly 150 days free of feasts.[54]

Catalano, the eighteenth-century antiquarian of papal ceremonial, found that between the late fifteenth and early eighteenth centuries there were nearly forty occasions in the liturgical calendar that required the holding of a *cappella pontificia* (a 'papal chapel'), when the pope and all the cardinals present in Rome attended divine service together. As one English observer noted in the 1580s, only on the greatest feasts – which he listed as Christmas, Epiphany, Easter, Ascension, Pentecost and St Peter's Day – was the *cappella* held in the newly completed basilica. On the other 'solemn days in the year', including Lent and Holy Week, the 'solemnity is for the most part kept within the palace, in the Pope's [Sistine] Chapel'.[55] During the holding of a *cappella pontificia*, courtiers and members of the nobility would attempt to find a place in the chapel. The number of cardinals attending depended on the status of the feast, with each cardinal being attended by a retinue numbering from a minimum of two to as many as twenty.[56] So great had the pressure for places become by the mid seventeenth century that Alexander VII instituted a series of reforms, banning all non-participatory observers from the chapel, and strictly enforcing the criteria for attendance.[57]

Overlaying this cycle of religious devotions were the rituals specific to the pontiff as spiritual and secular ruler. From about the time of Pope Nicholas V (1447–55) these ceremonies acquired an increasingly elaborate form, stressing not only the pope's quasi-divine attributes as 'Christ's vicar on earth', but also his role as the successor of Constantine: the heir to imperial Rome. One leading expert on Roman ceremonial has described Nicholas V's reign as the 'end' of the papacy's pastoral liturgy. Although it is sometimes difficult to reconstruct the exact nature of papal ceremonial before the fifteenth century, it is clear that Nicholas, well known for his love of pomp and ceremony, celebrated saints' days with public processions in a way previously almost unknown in Rome.[58] More importantly, there seems to have been a conscious decision to minimize the priestly aspects of the pontiff's role. Until the mid fifteenth century, popes had continued to celebrate the mass in public and to preach as the Bishop of Rome. Gradually, however, these 'pastoral' practices were discontinued. By the beginning of the sixteenth century, the Pope celebrated mass in public only three times a year; even then, he did not preach but was present, enthroned in the sanctuary immediately to the left of the high altar.[59] The trend towards ever greater emphasis on the pope's role as secular monarch seems to have received particular impetus from Leo X (1513–21) and his master of ceremonies, Cristoforo Marcello.[60]

Yet, it was not only the sacred and the numinous that were evoked by the ceremonies of the papal court. Renaissance and Baroque popes had a keen sense of their role as the restorers of a Roman 'golden age'.[61] The imagery of classical, imperial Rome figures prominently in court iconography from the reign of Nicholas V in the 1450s through to Innocent X in the 1650s. From the time of Julius II's victorious entry into the city after his recovery of Bologna in 1507, staged as the return of a Roman *imperator*, the emblems of imperial triumph mingle easily with those of traditional ecclesiastical pomp.[62] As ruler of Rome, the pope was easily represented as the successor of the deified Roman emperors, though the nature of his divinity was cast in traditional Christian terms. Inevitably, there were those who were uncomfortable with this syncretism of Christian priesthood with sacralized medieval kingship and 'deified' Roman imperial rule. In 1575, a jubilee year when the Counter-Reformation was in full spate, those in Cardinal Carlo Borromeo's circle seem to have suggested (largely ineffectually) a return to the older 'pastoral liturgy' gradually lost after the changes of Nicholas V.[63]

Even earlier than other European courts, the public rituals of the papal court tended to elide the sacralized person of the papal monarch with the rites and symbols attending the *Corpus Christi*, the 'body of Christ' present in the communion wafer. The most obvious point at which the identification was made was on the feast of Corpus Christi itself (on the Thursday after Trinity Sunday), when the pope and his court processed through the streets bearing a monstrance containing the consecrated host. As early as the reign of Pius II (1458–64), during the Corpus Christi procession of 1462, actors staged a dramatic tableau along the route, paraphrasing the text describing the arrival of the messiah (Psalm 23, verse 7). 'Who is this

King Pius?' they demanded, while other actors dressed as angels replied, 'The lord of the world,' leaving it ambiguous whether the answer referred to Christ present in the eucharist or to the pope himself, who bore the monstrance containing the host.[64]

From the mid sixteenth century, in part in response to the Council of Trent's encouragement of eucharistic devotion, the veneration of the host took on a heightened significance within the court calendar. From the 1550s the beginning of the ecclesiastical year, the first Sunday of Advent (in late November or early December), was marked in the Pauline Chapel by the ceremony of Forty Hours' Devotion, in which the host was displayed in a monstrance for the veneration of the court. First held in 1550, the practice was institutionalized by Clement VIII (1592–1605) in the year of his election, and was thereafter celebrated with increasingly elaborate pomp. For painters and architects, the *apparati* – in effect, the stage scenery – built to display the host for these devotions were major commissions and utilized the full repertory of Baroque theatrical contrivance. Bernini's *apparato* for Advent 1628 was considered as much a masterpiece as any painting or sculpture, employing the light of 2,000 concealed candles to illuminate a representation of the 'Glory of Paradise' surrounding the consecrated host.[65]

Similarly, the festival of Corpus Christi, already an important feast in the fifteenth century, became from around the 1550s one of the most lavishly celebrated in the court calendar. As in other European monarchies, the feast-day was used to emphasize publicly the intimate connection between eucharistic 'power' and monarchical authority. Beginning with a mass celebrated by the pope in the Sistine Chapel, the procession moved through the Vatican Palace, out into the Borgo (the quarter between the River Tiber and St Peter's that was not part of the commune of Rome), and finally returned to the basilica. The ostensible purpose of the procession, of course, was to encourage adoration of the host. In practice, however, the 'meaning' of the ritual was far more ambiguous. With the pope carrying the monstrance, pontiff and eucharist shared the same processional canopy, attended on either side by great peacock-feather fans, symbols of imperial rule believed to have derived from the Byzantine court.[66] They formed a single

focus of reverence for the 'audience' observing the procession, who were required by court etiquette to kneel before the pontiff (with or without a monstrance), just as liturgical practice demanded they kneel before the host. The ceremonial arrangements thus blurred the distinction between the honour due to the Corpus Christi and that due to the *Vicarius Christi*. As Tod Marder has recently demonstrated, this connection between eucharistic and monarchical power was further emphasized by the juxtaposition of works of art along the processional route. In the eighteenth century, for instance, a tapestry of Leonardo's *Last Supper* (at which the eucharist was instituted) was hung on the landing of the Scala Regia beside the statue of the Emperor Constantine. Later, a copy of the tapestry was hung next to the statue of Charlemagne on the south side of the portico. 'These juxtapositions emphasized the role of rulership in the dispensation of the host and its efficacious effects… Adoring the host, [the pope] would have given living form to the symbolic connection between eucharist and papal authority.'[67]

Even during Holy Week, the major religious rites were celebrated within the chapels of the palace, with the pope only emerging on Easter Day to celebrate mass in St Peter's. Burchard's account of the rituals observed by Alexander VI's court during Holy Week 1497 describes a series of ceremonies that remained virtually unchanged well into the eighteenth century. After mass in the Sistine Chapel on Holy Thursday, the host was carried in procession through the papal Audience Hall, the Sala Regia, to the nearby chapel (later the Pauline Chapel), where it was reserved until the Vigil Mass on Easter Eve. On Good Friday, Alexander led the procession into the chapel, where the veneration of the cross was led by one of the papal household, Cardinal Domenico della Rovere. On Easter Sunday, the central feast of the Christian year, the pope was carried on the portable throne, the *sedia gestatoria*, in procession to St Peter's, where he celebrated High Mass before the hundreds of pilgrims who converged on the city to receive the papal blessing.[68] It was at Easter, moreover, that some of the greatest relics in Christendom were displayed for the veneration of the faithful: the veil with which St Veronica had wiped the face of Christ on the way to his crucifixion, and the lance that had pierced his

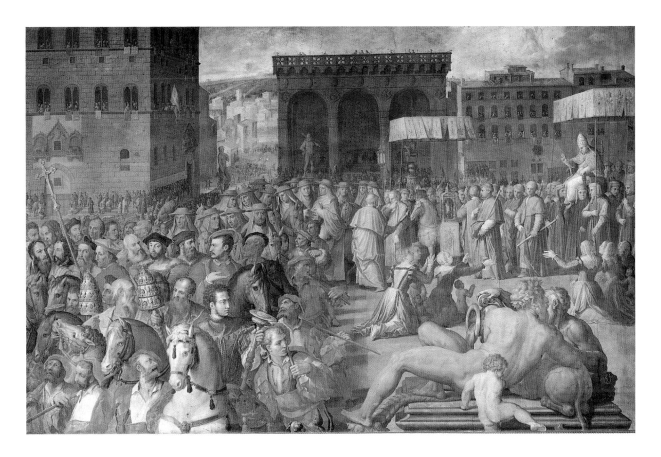

*The triumphal entry of the first Medici pope, Leo X (Giovanni de' Medici), into his native Florence in
1515 – a fusion of the classical* pompa *of a victorious Roman general with the emblems of spiritual
monarchy. The election of this son of Lorenzo, il Magnifico, marked a decisive stage in the transformation
of the Medici from Florentine bankers into a princely dynasty.*

side, were displayed at St Peter's. At the basilica of St
John Lateran, the pope's cathedral church as Bishop of
Rome, the heads of St Peter and St Paul were exposed
for veneration. These relics were more than ghoulish
reminders of the time of the apostles. They were
numinous and talismanic objects in their own right,
possessed of miraculous qualities, which conferred
both prestige and power upon their possessors.

The most public of the court ceremonies were,
inevitably, those that took the papal household in procession through the Roman streets. The start of any
new reign began with the so-called *possesso* (or rite of
taking possession), in which the new pope, dressed in
his papal vestments for the first time, travelled from
the Vatican Palace to the Lateran Basilica to take
possession of his episcopal see.[69] Each newly elected

Pope selected and designed the precise route on
which his *possesso* would proceed, thereby honouring
friends and snubbing enemies at court.[70]

The reception of visiting monarchs similarly
entailed elaborate out-of-doors processions. In a rite
that seems to have remained unchanged at least from
the mid fifteenth to the early eighteenth centuries,
emperors and kings were greeted outside the city
walls by curial dignitaries, before entering Rome in
procession by the Porta del Popolo.[71] A double-
reception took place once the royal visitor reached the
Vatican. He was received by the pope at the steps of
the basilica (if he was to be crowned), or within its
doors if there was to be no coronation. After homage
at the tomb of St Peter, a second formal reception
then took place in the Sala Regia (the first Audience

Hall, or *aula prima*), where the monarch performed his homage, kneeling three times before the pontiff. As the early sixteenth-century chronicler of papal ceremonies, Cristoforo Marcello, observed, all mortals of whatsoever dignity were required to genuflect when they came in sight of the pope, and 'in honour of Our Saviour, Jesus Christ, whose Vicegerent on earth he is, [they] kiss his feet'.[72] The only papal concessions to royal rank was that he received his visitor standing, rather than seated, under the canopy; and that kings, 'great princes' and their ambassadors were admitted *ad osculum manuum et oris*: to kiss not only the pontiff's feet, in submission to Christ, but also the pope's hands and cheek, in recognition of their status as brother monarchs.[73] This ceremony was followed by a more intimate meeting in the *aula secunda* or *aula tertia* (the two smaller Audience Halls later converted by Bernini into a single Sala Ducale). The degree of privacy allowed to the final meeting acted as a measure of the esteem and favour in which the pontiff held his guest.

Within the palace, the focus for the rituals of the papal court was the Sala Regia, a room that doubled as royal throne room and an antechamber for processions passing into the adjacent Sistine Chapel. Here, the pope appeared before his court, enthroned under the canopy, to hear petitions, receive ambassadors and receive the homage of visiting 'pilgrims' whose rank entitled them to admission. The regularity of these audiences varied according the preferences and energies of individual pontiffs: from as little as once a week under Urban VIII in the 1620s, to daily audiences under Alexander VII in the 1660s, when the pope often sat in consistory for as long as six or seven hours.[74]

Those seeking to attend an audience made an application to the *maggiordomo*. As Baron von Pöllnitz observed, 'the form of demanding audiences is the same here as at other courts, and…the difficulty of obtaining it every whit as great'. Once obtained, the visitor entered the upper palace via the Scala Regia, his approach culminating at the top of the stairs in the presence of the pope, enthroned at the opposite end of the Sala Regia. Then, in a ritual that seems to have remained unaltered between the late fifteenth and early eighteenth centuries, the visitor knelt three times – on entering the hall, in the middle and then again immediately before the papal throne – as the pope gave his blessing in the name of the three persons of

the Trinity. On reaching the throne, the visitor was permitted to kiss the pope's slippered foot in an unambiguous gesture of fealty, submission and humility. At the conclusion of the audience, the visitor retraced his route, walking backwards lest he turn his back on 'Christ's Vicar on earth', and kneeling three times once again to receive the papal benediction.[75] No court ceremonial in Europe elided so completely the person of the prince and the divine powers with which he was endowed.

Visual evidence of an early seventeenth-century court ceremony in progress in the Sala Regia is provided in a painting by Pietro da Cortona (1596–1669), commemorating one of the defining moments in the Thirty Years War. Also recorded in documentary form in a papal *avviso* of 9 May 1620, it depicts the audience given by Paul V to Prince Paolo Savelli, the ambassador of Emperor Ferdinand II. Savelli bore the formal announcement by the emperor of his campaign against the Bohemian Protestants that was to culminate with the Battle of White Mountain, outside Prague, in November that year. Savelli, as the emperor's emissary, had been permitted to make a formal entrance into Rome through the Porta del Popolo – the traditional mode of approach for royal and imperial visitors – accompanied by bishops and senior prelates. He had then been accorded the highest honour available to a visiting diplomat, and had 'been received in the public consistory [in the Sala Regia] by His Holiness [Pope Paul V] and by the Sacred College of Cardinals…and by all the court'. Dressed in the black court dress of the imperial household and wearing the chain of the Order of the Golden Fleece, Savelli presented his letter of credence from the emperor, and after speeches and a reply from the papal secretary *dei brevi*, the consistory ended. The pope then permitted the ambassador to dine with him, a favour accorded to Savelli not in his own right, but as he was deemed to 'represent', and hence merit the privileges of, the emperor.[76]

Music also played a major part in both court ceremonial and in the liturgy of the papal chapels. It was in this sphere that the influence of the court of Burgundy, and of Burgundian musical culture in general, was most marked. Until the early sixteenth century, the majority of the Sistine Chapel's singers were Flemish; one Gaspar van Weerbecke held a place in the choir from the foundation of the chapel by

Sixtus IV (1471–84) to the pontificate of Leo X (1513–21). Choral music, often without accompaniment, formed a central element of papal ceremonial. As in most great ecclesiastical foundations, the daily office (particularly matins and vespers) and mass were set to music, in either plainchant or polyphonic settings. The choir consisted exclusively of male singers, with boys or castrati providing the treble lines of the music.

The Burgundian dominance of the court chapel's musical establishment was a long one. In the 1530s, at the beginning of the long reign of the Farnese pope, Paul III (1534–49), the choir was composed of seven Italians and eleven French or Flemish voices, but under the direction of an Italian, Bartolommeo Crotti. It was during Paul III's pontificate that the national balance within the choir changed from a Franco-Flemish majority to an Italian one, a character that it then retained into the eighteenth century and beyond. To Paul III, in particular, the status of the choir and the quality of music in the chapel were important sources of the court's prestige and international renown. Indeed, to ensure that there was no bar to recruiting the most accomplished singers of the age, the pope issued a bull in 1545, revoking the rule prohibiting members of the chapel choir from marrying.

In the period after the Council of Trent (1545–63), Paul III's innovatory attitudes to music in the Vatican were replaced by a more austere spirit. There was a new insistence that 'sacred music' should be qualitatively different from secular forms, and during the second half of the sixteenth century, the greatest exponent of the 'reformed' style was Giovanni Pierluigi da Palestrina (*c*.1525–94), who composed extensively for the Sistine Chapel liturgies, particularly during the reign of Pope Gregory XIII (1572–85). Among his contemporaries, Palestrina's polyphonic music came to be regarded as perfectly exemplifying the reformed spirituality of the post-Tridentine period. Accordingly, his music for the papal court exercised an extensive influence across the Catholic world, being regarded in many quarters as providing the 'ideal' musical setting for the celebration of the mass.

Nor was the musical culture of the court confined to sacred and liturgical settings. Court dining was regularly accompanied by singing and instrumental music, and, as elsewhere in Europe, some form of musical education and ability to play an instrument were as important for an ecclesiastical courtier as for any young man hoping to make his way in the princely courts of Europe. The private performance of music, either on lute or clavichord (later the harpsichord) formed an essential element of courtly recreation. During the 1530s and 1540s, for example, Pope Paul III insisted that his granddaughter, Vittoria Farnese, should be taught the clavichord. His grandson, Ottavio, was instructed by one of the best musicians in Italy, Francesco da Milano.[77] Despite the celebrity of Palestrina's sacred music, the papal court also provided commissions for secular works; and during the seventeenth century, opera became a major art form at the papal court.[78]

IV. COURT POLITICS

The life of the papal court was intimately connected to the city that provided its architectural setting. Rome's urban fabric, with its historical associations as the seat of empire and its numerous subsidiary palaces of the great noble and cardinalitial families, contributed heavily to the prestige and renown of the court. There was a close relation between the papacy's urban policies and 'construction' of the papal monarchy from the mid fifteenth century. Initiatives such as the fortification of the Vatican palace in the 1450s and the encouragement of the building of new palaces for the nobility and higher clergy can be seen as tangible expressions of the papacy's success in suppressing the power of the old Roman baronial families, or at least in negotiating a peaceful *modus vivendi* with them. The secular authority of the papacy within the peninsula was further consolidated in the half-century before the Reformation, as a series of military ventures, culminating in the campaigns of Julius II, brought the troublesome fiefdoms within the patrimony of St Peter under the direct rule of Rome. By the early sixteenth century, 'the transformation of the provincial seigneurial aristocracy and the Roman baronage into a courtly society, as a class relieved of true political power', had removed external threats to the stability of the papal court.[79] Yet, while the old Roman clans may well have been brought to heel, the relationship between pope and the nobility (both secular and ecclesiastical) was always a highly complex one. For all the rhetoric of the pope's 'absolute' *pleni-tudo potestatis*, in reality, papal authority was hedged around by a series of conventions that imposed practical limitations on its supposedly untrammelled power.

For the successful papal families, the opportunities for advancement were legion. The incumbency of the Chair of Peter was decisive to the rise of many a noble house. It was with the help of their most successful son, Alexander VI (1492–1503), that the Borgia rose from the status of frontier knights from Valencia to the ranks of the high nobility. The Farnese already enjoyed noble rank when Paul III (1534–49) was elected pope, but with his assistance 'they climbed [into] a prince's throne'.[80] Internally, however, the politics of the papal court was profoundly destabilized by the electoral politics of the College of Cardinals.[81] The fifteenth century seems to have witnessed a relative decline in the authority of the college at the expense of the papal office. Where once they had acted as a form of ecclesiastical senate, whose approval and advice was practically necessary on matters of major policy, by the end of the sixteenth century the cardinals had substantially lost their senatorial character. They remained the electoral body for the papal office, but political responsibility increasingly lay in the hands of the pope and his immediate entourage, who were usually drawn from a faction within the college or who soon 'received the red hat'. Numbers were limited to seventy under Sixtus V's Bull of 1586. Moreover, during the course of the sixteenth century, the membership of the college became increasingly Italian,[82] with Italians constituting more than eighty per cent of the cardinals in the Roman curia by 1600.[83] Innocent X (1644–55) did promote three foreigners to the cardinalate, Cardinals Camus, Barbarigo and Denhoff; but it was believed that he did so to spite their rulers, with whom these prelates were out of favour.[84] Even among the Italians, membership tended to be dominated by a small number of 'papal' families, notably the Borgia (originally of Spanish origin), the

della Rovere, the Medici and the Farnese. Despite occasional attempts to promote men of saintly piety and theological learning to the cardinalate, the internal politics of the college was notoriously governed by considerations of nepotism and faction. As one English commentator remarked cynically, 'Most of the prelates in Italy are better skilled in the knowledge of law and politics than in divinity, and where there is one advanced to the cardinalship for his learning and divinity, there are ten promoted for being eminent lawyers and politicians'.[85]

The election in March 1513 of Cardinal Giovanni de' Medici as Pope Leo X, for example, produced an influx of the Medici clientele to Rome and a consolidation of the family's political alliances, both local and foreign. Among the principal beneficiaries of the new pontificate was the new pope's secretary and boyhood tutor, Bernardo Dovizi da Bibbiena.[86] Seven months after Leo X's election, Bibbiena was raised to the cardinalate, despite his lack of any formal theological training, and served as treasurer, chief adviser and confidant to the Medici pope. Bibbiena's power was reflected in, and in part founded on, his physical proximity to the pontiff. His suite of rooms (partly designed by Raphael) was located directly above Leo X's apartment and connected by a 'secret' (or private) staircase, permitting direct access to the pope unobserved by other members of the papal household.

The new pope's desires to reward members of his own entourage nevertheless had to be fulfilled within certain limits laid down by convention. Enough booty had to be left to his successors;[87] and where one pope was deemed to have overstepped the mark, there was usually a heavy price to be paid by his placemen on the election of his successor. When, for instance, Giambattista Pamphili became pope as Innocent X in September 1644 (1644–55), one of his first tasks was to forge alliances with the enemies of his predecessor, Urban VIII (Maffeo Barberini, 1623–44), who had notoriously used his long reign to advance the interests

The centenary celebrations of the Jesuit order in the Gesù, in 1639–40, were organized and financed by the Cardinal-Nephew Antonio Barberini, chamberlain of the Church (in scarlet, centre, with his biretta visible in his right hand). He processes in the place of honour, at the right hand of his uncle, Pope Urban VIII. The cardinals' carriages and sedan-chairs are drawn by mules (foreground), emulating Christ's choice of conveyance at his Palm Sunday entry into Jerusalem. The retinue includes a court dwarf (foreground, left).

of his dynasty. On the principle that 'my enemy's enemy is my friend', Innocent X looked to ally with the long-time opponents of the Barberini, notably the Borghese, Aldobrandini and Ludovisi – all families that had held the papacy within the previous forty years. As Giacinto Gigli recorded in his diary, the cause that united them was that 'they have no greater desire than to see the Barberini brought down'.[88] Indeed, with so many quondam ruling families and former cardinal-nephews present at the papal court, precedence disputes were endemic. So disruptive had the squabbling over rank become that in 1600 Clement VIII ordered that when it came to cardinal-nephews and the relatives of dead popes, no rule of precedence should apply but the individual's age.[89]

Regional clienteles came and went in Rome according to the local origins of the reigning pontiff. It was a momentous day for Bologna when its leading cleric, Ugo Buoncompagni, was elected Pope Gregory XIII (1572–85). Buoncompagni was the first Bolognese pope for 400 years, and his election held out the prospect that at least for the duration of his pontificate his fellow townsmen would run Rome and dominate its court. Even artistic patronage was influenced by regional rivalries. The machinations of the Bolognese faction at the papal court deprived the distinguished painter Federico Zuccaro (c.1542–1609) of commissions. When the disgruntled artist exhibited a cartoon mocking the Bolognese, Gregory XIII (1572–85) was constrained to expel him from Rome. Intervention by outsiders on Zuccaro's behalf was useless, the ambassador from the court at Urbino noted sadly, for 'at court they are all Bolognese and they pass the *palle* [ball] from one to the other'.[90] The major recipients of papal patronage tended, however, to be the members of the family of the pontiff himself. The elevation of nephews and other male relations to the cardinalate, in turn, was aimed not only at garnering the status and revenues that high ecclesiastical office could confer, but also at creating a 'dynastic interest' that could outlive the family's relatively brief incumbency in the Chair of Peter. For lay relatives, there was the prospect of elevation to ducal or princely rank. The rise of the Borghese as a major aristocratic family, for instance, followed a familiar pattern. In return for appointing the Spanish Infante Fernando, then aged ten, a cardinal and administrator of the archbishopric of

Toledo, the richest see in Christendom, Paul V (Camillo Borghese, 1605–21) was able to obtain for the Borghese Prince of Sulmona the status of grandee of Spain, the highest rank in the Spanish nobility. Of papal courtier dynasties, only the Colonna and Caetani had risen so high.[91] Likewise, the Florentine-born Maffeo Barberini, once elected pope as Urban VIII, set up his nephew, Taddeo Barberini, as founder of a princely dynasty. He was loaded with lucrative court offices, found a bride among the 'old nobility', the Colonna, and finally purchased the title of Prince of Palestrina in 1629. As the Barberini case exemplifies, marriage alliances with other great noble or, ideally, royal houses, were a regular means whereby papal families of relatively modest lineage could move up in the world.[92]

Nor was the papal household the only 'foyer' of patronage. The palaces of prominent courtier cardinals, and, above all, of the great papal families (Chigi, Farnese, Medici, Borghese, Barberini, among others) also provided alternative and rival routes to court influence and favour. Where a cardinal was in residence, these formed courts in their own right, complete with a hierarchy of office-holders and the observance of often elaborate household ceremonial.[93] Cardinals, like princes, had the right to hang a *baldacchino,* or canopy, over the dais in their audience chamber and to have another in their antechamber. Like the pope, they were entitled to have a small bell standing on a table in their audience chamber, a traditional badge of princely ecclesiastical rank, with which to 'summon' their court.[94] In the case of cardinals exercising one of the great offices within the papal government, their 'courts' often became important centres of political and diplomatic activity in their own right. During the 1620s a succession of Venetian ambassadors came to the conclusion that the real source of policy at Urban VIII's Rome was the 'court' at the Quirinal Palace of Cardinal Lorenzo Magalotti, the secretary for correspondence with princes.[95] Professor Gigliola Fragnito suggests that the papacy encouraged the proliferation of cardinals' separate courts, on the grounds that they would promote the idea of papal magnificence throughout the city, while allowing its weaknesses to escape scrutiny.[96]

The effects of these highly competitive dynastic strategies were not universally helpful to the good government of the Church or the papal state. During the sixteenth and early seventeenth centuries, this nepotism and favouritism progressively weakened the College of Cardinals, sapping its power of autonomous political action and gradually transforming it into a 'courtly aristocracy', one in which the ascendant faction was dependent upon the pope as a monarch. In consequence, two types of cardinal tended to emerge. The first is the 'cardinal protector', one who, regardless of his own nationality, would take upon himself the defence of the interests of his 'nation' within the Church. He would attempt to ensure that local rights and privileges were respected in Rome, and act as a patronage broker between his constituency and the Roman curia.[97] Almost invariably acting in alliance with their 'nation's' diplomatic representative in Rome, the cardinal protectors exercised an influence that contributed heavily to the deterioration of the pope's overall control of decision-making and to the slow attrition of papal powers of patronage (particularly in relation to bishoprics). With the college dominated by factions that reflected the dynastic interests of his immediate predecessors, one of the first priorities of new popes was the creation of their own familial 'interest' within the cardinalate. There was, thus, little continuity in the higher echelons of the papal court. New popes tended to employ only those who were already intimately linked to them by ties of kinship, friendship or patronage.

It is these 'ties of kinship' that, from the late fifteenth century, brought about the rise of the second principal 'type' of cardinal, the *cardinale nipote,* or cardinal-nephew. The list is an extensive one, and the 'office' occasionally provided the springboard for the favoured cardinal's own ambitions to wear the tiara. Instances had already emerged in the fifteenth century; Cardinal Giuliano della Rovere, for example, the future Pope Julius II (1503–13), rose to power on his familial ties as the nephew of Sixtus IV (1471–84).[98] However, from the appointment of Cardinal Alessandro Farnese, the grandson of Paul III (1534–49), through to Pietro Ottoboni, the nephew of Alexander VIII (1689–91), nepotism became an institutionalized system of rule. Throughout the intervening period there was always a male relative, usually but not always a nephew, who could be appointed *superintendens status ecclesiastici* (or overseer of the ecclesiastical state).[99] He enjoyed a place, recognized

in court protocol, second only to the pope himself, as the principal broker of political and ecclesiastical patronage, both in Roman society and throughout the Italian peninsula. Where there was no suitable family member, an outsider could be 'co-opted' into the pope's *famiglia* and assume the title of cardinal-nephew. Writing in the 1660s, Giovanni de Luca described the development of the role in terms of the tendency for other secular rulers to remove power from traditional office-holders and to vest it instead in one who was outside the formal hierarchies of power and entirely dependent on the ruler for his position: the role of the *privado,* or court favourite. This was 'today's fashion, and what the practice of [secular] rulers teaches'. The cardinal-nephew was an 'overseer general of the whole ecclesiastical state, hence for this reason he signs letters and other warrants that are issued in the pope's name for the government and administration of what is termed the temporal principality'. On the other hand he rarely involved himself in the spiritual administration of the Holy See, or what he termed 'the power of the keys' (the authority 'to bind and loose' given by Christ to Peter and enjoyed by the pope as his successor).[100]

This development, in turn, profoundly affected the whole *modus operandi* of the papal court, and has been seen as a traditional example of the 'rise of the state'. After the sack of Rome by imperial forces in 1527 and the 'mid sixteenth-century crisis' precipitated by the Lutheran revolt, Paulo Prodi has argued, the trajectory of papal policy became explicitly 'directed externally against imperial and Spanish domination in Italy, and internally towards strengthening the state structure, leaving little room for autonomous family politics'. Henceforth, the dynastic interests of the papal families took second place to a larger task, the maintenance and consolidation of the 'state' on which their fortunes depended. 'It was…the pope's nephews or purchasers of the curia's venal offices who decided and controlled every initiative,' he writes, 'as partners in an undertaking whose stake was no longer autonomous [familial] political power but enrichment and the remuneration of invested capital'.[101]

Yet it is doubtful whether this transformation of an 'honour politics' of dynastic power and prestige into a tame 'court culture', in which the great papal families were merely shareholders in *Ecclesia* Incorporated, ever

The papal court as tourist attraction: the Girandola, or 'grand fireworks', depicted here in the 1770s, was staged annually at the Castello Sant' Angelo to mark the feasts of Easter and SS. Peter and Paul on 29 June, and, less frequently, to celebrate the coronation of a new pope. Although the prestige and political influence of the papacy had slipped drastically by the 1750s, Rome and the papal court continued to be a major centre of artistic patronage, and a favoured destination of eighteenth-century Grand Tourists.

really took place. At least until the end of the seventeenth century, whenever a new pope acquired the throne, there was the habitual reallocation of major offices to members of the new 'reigning family'. Thus, on the election of Paul V (1605–21), his brother became captain-general of the Church and commander of the papal galleys, while his younger brother became commander of the papal guards, castellan of Sant' Angelo and of the fortress of Ancona, and governor of the Borgo (the area immediately between the Vatican and the Tiber). At a time when an affluent cardinal's stipend was around 405 scudi per month, Paul III's gifts to members of his family in the course of his reign totalled in excess of one million scudi.[102]

The cardinal-nephew acted as the pope's patronage-broker, creating an appearance of a dignified distance between the pope's formal role as a *commune padre*, above mere faction, and the day-to-day conduct of diplomacy and court politics. As Reinhard has noted, within the papal clientele, as late as the early eighteenth century, it was 'personal quasi-feudal fidelity of a servant' to his patron that counted, 'not any abstract and neutral fidelity of service'. For the ambitious curialist on the make, the routes to preferment had changed little in centuries. Blood relations, even very remote ones, remained the 'most important basis of social relations in Roman society'.[103] Patronage networks, however, were rarely mutually exclusive affairs. Alliances could be formed with other networks, and, given the international scope of Rome's jurisdiction, it was inevitable that factions at the Roman court developed links with corresponding networks at courts elsewhere in Italy and Europe.[104] As Renata Ago has shown, Cardinal Bernardino Spada, recognized as head of his family, consistently manoeuvred to place members of his family at courts throughout Italy.[105] The time spent in Paris as papal legate by Cardinal Maffeo Barberini, the future Urban VIII (1623–44), ensured close links between his clientele and the Bourbon court. The diplomatic alignment of the papal court could thus change quickly on the election of a new pontiff, depending on the new ruling house's international patronage connections and its dynastic ties.[106]

Dynastic rivalries remained an endemic and debilitating feature of the papal court throughout the sixteenth and seventeenth centuries. If this competitiveness yielded a magnificent legacy in terms of artistic and architectural patronage within Rome, it nevertheless had a generally enervating effect on the structures of the papacy's temporal 'realm'. While the office of captain-general of the Holy Church was exploited to provide a lucrative income to an endless series of short-term papal relatives, by the seventeenth century it had become a virtual sinecure. The devising of long-term strategies for the defence of the papal realm was an impossibility. The demise of the papal army, the largest in the Italian peninsula in the mid fifteenth century, left the states of the Church largely dependent on foreign protectors, and hence perilously vulnerable. This had more than merely military implications. By the later seventeenth century, the lack of an army, not only as a fighting force but also as 'an institution of social integration' for the small nobility and civic élites of the papal territories, became, in Prodi's phrase, 'one of the most important causes of an institutional crisis that slowly became inevitable'.[107] The taming of the Roman baronage may have helped secure papal authority in the short term. But the long-term consequence of the papal monarchy's ceaseless changes of 'ruling house' was that it never developed a strong enough ruling class capable of sustaining the weight of the papal government. By the early eighteenth century, the Papal States had acquired a reputation as being among the most lawless and capriciously governed in Europe.

Territorial weakness in turn affected the juridical status of the papal monarch and the relative importance of his court. In the course of the early eighteenth century, the slow seepage of clerical patronage away from the papacy's control became a flood. The Holy See made ever greater concessions in order to avoid confrontation with secular monarchs keen to advance still further their rights of ecclesiastical patronage within their realms. Under the terms of the 1753 concordat (or treaty) concluded by Benedict XIV (1740–58) with Spain, for instance, Rome conceded the right of presentation to 12,000 benefices to the Spanish crown; the pope was left with exactly fifty-two. Some 4,000 Spaniards, in Rome to lobby for preferment at the papal courts, were reported to have left the city on publication of the news. Even the Duchy of Parma, the diminutive sovereign state that had once been under papal rule, contributed its mite to the humiliation of the Holy See. In 1768 it erected a formal 'royal supremacy' of its own, forbidding all appeals to the court of Rome and banning all papal bulls except with the duke's permission.[108]

By the early eighteenth century, there was a palpable sense of stagnation in the unchanging rituals of the Roman court. When Pöllnitz attended the coronation of Clement XII (1730–40), he observed that even this, traditionally the most splendid of all papal ceremonies, lacked 'magnificence'. According to custom, the basilica was hung with red damask laced with gold fringe; but the cloth was looking tired, he noticed, and was no more than would have been put out 'upon every grand festival'. Nor was 'St Peter's Throne [the papal chair and canopy], richer than ordinary'.[109] This change, a general declension from earlier standards of courtly splendour, was also registered in the daily routines of the court. Consistories in the Sala Regia, once the focal point of the court's veneration of the papal monarch, were held far less frequently. As at other European courts, by the 1720s the pope tended to withdraw from the capital and the ritualized life of the Vatican and Quirinal, preferring instead the residences outside the city, Monte Cavallo and Castel Gandolfo.[110]

Rome, which had always been a city of pilgrims, became a city of tourists.[111] Yet, if the eighteenth-century papal court lacked the vigour and assurance of its Renaissance and Baroque predecessors, the cultural impact of its former achievements remained immense. From Christopher Wren's London to Carlo Rastrelli's St Petersburg, in domes and cupolas, churches and palaces, even in the rituals of some Protestant royal households, the influence of the papal court and its architectural setting continued to be discerned, long after its builders had been laid to rest, dressed in full pontificals, in their expensive marble tombs.[112]

CHAPTER SIX

*The Archduchy of Austria and the
Kingdoms of Bohemia and Hungary*

THE COURTS OF THE AUSTRIAN HABSBURGS
c.1500–1750

JEROEN DUINDAM

'VIENNA IS THE CAPITAL OF GERMANY, OR RATHER OF THE WEST; there one sees the majesty of the Empire, as in the past in Rome', noted Charles Patin in his description of Vienna around 1670. Almost sixty years later, in 1729, Freiherr von Pöllnitz began his more captious account in similar terms: 'One cannot deny that the court at Vienna is the largest and most magnificent in Europe because of the great number of princes and lords there'.[1] While Patin continued in the same vein, Pöllnitz quickly pointed out that in some respects the court of Charles VI (1711–40) seemed to lag behind European standards. Rigid ceremonial, he argued, gave the imperial court 'an air of constraint'. Moreover, of all monarchs, the emperor was 'un des plus mal logés', and the interior of the palace hardly fitted his elevated rank.

Indeed, most visitors to the imperial court noted a contradiction between the emperor's hierarchical supremacy among European rulers, and his relatively less brilliant *repraesentatio maiestatis*.[2] They explained the apparent disparity in different ways: some argued that it was a deliberate policy intended to stress the emperor's 'inherent' pre-eminence; others that it merely reflected a lack of style. Pöllnitz preferred the latter interpretation, but could not fully explain the austerity of the imperial household at a time when courtly opulence had reached its apogee in most contemporary European courts. Why, he asked, did

The Ratstube – *the principal public audience chamber – of Emperor Ferdinand III in the 1650s. The emperor's throne is surmounted by a canopy resembling a tabernacle, or tented pavilion, with its curtains drawn to reveal the royal presence inside. The* Hofmarschall, *carrying the sword of state, stands on the emperor's right. The emperor's son and heir, Ferdinand IV, King of the Romans (1653–4), sits enthroned under his own smaller canopy (left). Except for the cardinal (left), a Prince of the Church, all below princely rank stand bareheaded before the emperor.*

THE PRINCELY COURTS OF EUROPE

the emperor choose to live in these sparsely decorated apartments? 'I don't know why, because the storerooms must be full of lavish tapestries, superb paintings and other beautiful furnishings; apparently it is not done to use these.'[3]

The questions remain: did the emperors in fact create their own reserved style of courtly *grandezza*? Could their court attract and captivate the élites from the patchwork of otherwise unconnected Habsburg dominions? These questions are best answered by studying the period extending roughly from the beginning of the division of Charles V's heritage in the 1520s until the succession crisis following the death of Charles VI in 1740.

I. DOMINIONS AND DYNASTY

The composite nature of the Austrian Habsburgs' realms remained evident longer than in most other dynastic possessions.[4] 'Austria' primarily indicated the archduchy that was the core of the Habsburg *Erblande*, or hereditary lands, a group of possessions that also included Styria, Carinthia, Carniola, Tyrol and the *Vorlande* (or western provinces). After the death of the Jagiello king of both Bohemia and Hungary in the Battle of Mohács (1526), the Habsburgs also held these elective crowns. Only in the decade following the Battle of the White Mountain (1620), however, was Bohemia absorbed into the Habsburg hereditary lands. Hungary followed a century later, but retained a stronger sense of autonomy. Neither Bohemia nor Hungary easily fitted the label 'Austrian'.

The Holy Roman Empire, moreover, can hardly be described as Austrian, or even Habsburg territory. Some of the Habsburg dominions lay outside the Empire, while Habsburg rule in the Empire was severely restricted by the near-sovereignty of the territories, a situation formally endorsed by the Peace of Westphalia in 1648. Thus, at one extreme, we find the Habsburg dynast as prince in his own archduchy, while at the other extreme the same dynast was elected imperial suzerain; in between, we find the two initially elective crowns of Bohemia and Hungary. Emperor, king, archduke: the Habsburgs ruled each of their territories with a different title, and with a different set of rights and duties.

The Austrian Habsburgs' interests were closely linked to the senior Spanish branch of the dynasty. In the two centuries preceding 1700 Habsburgs were on the throne in both Madrid and Vienna. The Spanish and Austrian branches entertained close – if not always cordial – relations, while Habsburg spouses extended the family network even further. During the sixteenth century an upbringing in Spain was customary for the Austrian Habsburgs, and while this habit declined in the seventeenth century, a strong commitment to the Counter-Reformation maintained Habsburg union.

Dynastic fortune became less certain in the second half of the seventeenth century. Carlos II of Spain (1665–1700) died without heirs, leaving the Spanish empire to Louis XIV's grandson Philippe d'Anjou. This sparked off the War of Spanish Succession (1702–14), which finally brought the Bourbon dynasty to the Spanish throne. At the same time, the Austrian succession was far from secure; Leopold I (1657–1705) came to the throne unexpectedly, after the death of his elder brother, and he had trouble securing his imperial election in 1657–8. Moreover, only his third marriage produced the much hoped for male offspring, Joseph in 1678 and Charles in 1685. But Charles, succeeding to his brother Joseph in 1711, died in 1740 without male heirs, and this caused a crisis that cost the Habsburgs Silesia, and for a short time brought the Bavarian elector to the imperial throne.

With their diverse territories, the Austrian Habsburgs also inherited a multiplicity of residences. Frederick III (1448–93) resided mainly in Wiener Neustadt; Maximilian I (1493–1519) preferred Augsburg and Innsbruck. Charles V (1519–56) maintained a peripatetic court; in 1521–2 he assigned the government of the *Erblande* to his brother Ferdinand, who became emperor only after Charles's abdication in 1556. In Ferdinand's reign Vienna became the customary residence, but the capital of the newly acquired Bohemian lands offered another attractive option, and in 1583 Rudolf II (1576–1612) transferred the court to Prague.

With the accession of Ferdinand II (1619–37), and the advent of the new Styrian branch of the dynasty, Vienna regained its position. This relocation implied both a growing distance from the Empire's heartlands and the hazardous propinquity of the Turkish threat. It might not be a coincidence that during the reigns of

Ferdinand II and Ferdinand III (1637–57) the Turks were at peace with the Habsburgs, whereas the Empire was ravaged by the Thirty Years War (1618–48).

Although the court became far more sedentary during the seventeenth century, it still travelled regularly, and Vienna was never its sole residence – the Bohemian and Hungarian capitals Prague and Pressburg (and later Budapest); archducal capitals such as Linz, Graz and Innsbruck; imperial free cities such as Frankfurt or Regensburg; and Brussels in the Southern Netherlands – all retained their own importance.

Setting priorities for ruling this assemblage of territories was inevitably a highly complex task. Most choices would have different consequences for any of the constituent parts, and it was clearly impossible to find a course acceptable to all. Institutions in Vienna and elsewhere reflected their heterogeneous heritage: some were focused on the Reich (Empire), others on the hereditary lands, Bohemia or Hungary. Emperors stuck to their role as the leading secular ruler of Europe; but their imperial dignity was a liability as well as an asset. It justified their ambitious policies in the German territories or in northern Italy, but it also involved them in an interminable round of legal, diplomatic and military conflicts. The traditional view, however, that in the course of the seventeenth and eighteenth centuries the Habsburgs steadily focused on consolidating their Austrian domains, and thus increasingly left the Reich to itself, is open to question. The close link between imperial dignity and the Roman Catholic Church secured the emperor the culturally and politically crucial role of patron of the *Reichskirche* (the Imperial Church). Moreover, the imperial court always offered the Empire's élites an attractive alternative to their own prince's court. Indeed, the readiness of local élites to attend on the emperor potentially strengthened both the pivotal role of Vienna as a political and cultural centre, and the influence of the emperor on the princes of the Empire. Finally, although the treaties of Utrecht (1713) and Rastatt (1714) put a Bourbon on the Spanish throne, they also gave the Southern Netherlands and important territories in Italy to the Habsburgs. While the Netherlands remained a somewhat isolated outpost, Italy became the focus of a new 'imperial' Habsburg policy, echoing the Italian policies of medieval emperors.

II. The Household

What is a court? At its simplest, it was the *familia,* or *Hofgesinde* (household), of a ruler. This would include his kin, a retinue of fellow-noblemen, servants and guards. The highest ranking in the retinue of the ruler were expected literally to serve him, often on a regular basis, but at least in more ceremonial settings. The medieval emperor theoretically was served by princes of the empire, who occupied the main court offices: *Marschall, Kämmerer* (chamberlain)*, Schenk* (cup-bearer) and *Truchsess* (high steward).[5] In reality, however, the princes exerted their office by deputy. The marshal initially was the most important court officer in the German lands, but in the later Middle Ages the *Hofmeister* (master of the court) surpassed both the marshal and the *Truchsess.* The court ordinances introduced by Ferdinand I in 1527 and 1537 gave the offices of the court the form they retained during the next two centuries.[6] There were four main court offices, each overseeing its own department: *Obersthofmeister* (high steward, or major domo), *Obersthofmarschall* (marshal), *Oberstkämmerer* (chamberlain) and finally the *Oberststallmeister* (master of the horse). All other officers and servants fell under the authority of these senior officers.

The major domo's responsibilities included management of the court household: the kitchens, cellars, court dining and the provision of linen and plate. He supervised not only provisioning and personnel, but, with his deputy, the *Oberststabelmeister* (master of the table), also oversaw the ceremonial of dining. The major domo was often the most important confidant of the emperor, and he could formally represent his sovereign on many state occasions.

While the major domo may formally have had control over all other courtiers, the marshal had jurisdiction over all courtiers and servants, who enjoyed immunity from normal legal procedures. As the maintainer of discipline and mores within the court, he functioned as the 'eyes and ears' of the emperor. Diplomats and foreign visitors also came within his jurisdiction, and he had an important role in establishing and maintaining contact with them. At first, the marshal's office had had responsibility for all matters concerning the stables, a critically important department in a court that was so frequently on the move; but gradually, however, the tasks immediately concerned with the stables were delegated to the master of the horse, while the marshal retained the responsibility for the court travel arrangements, and therefore for assigning accommodation to members of the court while on progress. In Vienna, the cramped situation of the Hofburg made quartering a permanent necessity.[7]

The chamberlain was responsible for the chamber and wardrobe, and thus for the audiences, *Ankleiden* and *Abziehen* (approximating to the *lever* and *coucher* of the French court). He carried the symbolic key to the emperor's apartment. He, or one of his deputies – *Kämmerer* (chamberlain), *Türhüter* (doorkeeper) and *Kammerdiener* (valet) – introduced foreign representatives and other visitors. The chamberlain's right to determine the sequence of audiences gave him considerable influence. He was also responsible for the monarch's personal movable property, and for the court collections – a major responsibility in a household in which art was highly prized. Finally, there was the master of the horse, the officer responsible for control of the emperor's stables, horses and carriages, and for supervising the *Edelknaben*, or noble pages, in attendance at court. He had a ceremonial role whenever the emperor left the palace on horseback or in a carriage, either riding beside the monarch or travelling with him in his coach; and such close access to the emperor brought both prestige and influence.

Next to these four most senior court officers came the *Obersthoffjägermeister* (master of the hunt) and the *Obersthoffalkenmeister* (master of the falcons), responsible for organizing the various forms of hunting that formed a central part of courtly recreation. Finally, there were the departments responsible for the security of the emperor's person: the *Hartschierenhauptmann* (captain of the archers) and the *Trabantenhauptmann* (captain of the footguard).

The major domo and the marshal were obviously the two most important court dignitaries. The balance between them remained fluid; any emperor could change it, while the personality of the incumbents was also a determining factor. Court offices were closely linked to the ruling emperor; when he died, the whole establishment formally lost its positions. The new emperor could create a new court, and would often choose his own confidants for the highest offices. The heir apparent, once elected King of the Romans, formed his own court establishment (or Hofstaat), members of which hoped to rise with their patron.

The highest court offices were invariably held by the upper nobility, *Grafen* (counts) or *Fürsten* (princes). To these can be added a multitude of court places, held mostly by lesser nobles. There is a clear distinction between the court offices conferring honour and prestige, and restricted to the nobility, and the humbler tasks of the court's clerks and domestics. The hierarchy of the different departments neatly mirrored the social hierarchy: nobles, non-noble clerks and servants, corresponding to government and ceremony, administration and menial tasks.[8] Integrated into this hierarchy was the Hofkapelle (Chapel Royal), including the court's clergy and the chapel's choristers. A swarm of councillors, artisans, artists and various specialists was also included in the *Hofgesinde*, most members of which received some remuneration and could expect to be fed and lodged at the court's expense. Pay was often late, and generally meagre.[9] The highest court officers and the chapel's *virtuosi*, however, received substantial salaries. Being part of the household could bring many advantages; not only freedom from taxes, but also gratuities; visitors were annoyed by the general habit of courtiers demanding a fee to introduce them into the emperor's rooms.[10]

What, then, was the size of the Habsburg court? The Hofstaat (literally the list of the household establishment, but also a general term for the household), when it is preserved, gives a fairly accurate idea of the extent of the household. At the end of the reign of Maximilan I the court was composed of some 500 persons.[11] In the 1520s Ferdinand's court started more modestly, and became the imperial court only after 1556. His successor Maximilian II's establishment again amounted to 500 persons (1564–76), and under subsequent rulers this number gradually increased, probably not exceeding 600 persons until the second half of the seventeenth century.[12] Only during the reigns of Leopold I, Joseph I (1705–1711) and Charles VI, did figures rise dramatically, finally reaching some 2,000–2,500 persons in the second quarter of the eighteenth century. E. G. Rinck listed the personnel of the different departments of the Hofstaat in the last year of Leopold's reign: he estimated that there were 258 for the major domo (excluding the chapel staff and the musicians, who accounted for a further 150); 487 for

The Austrian and Spanish Branches of the House of Habsburg

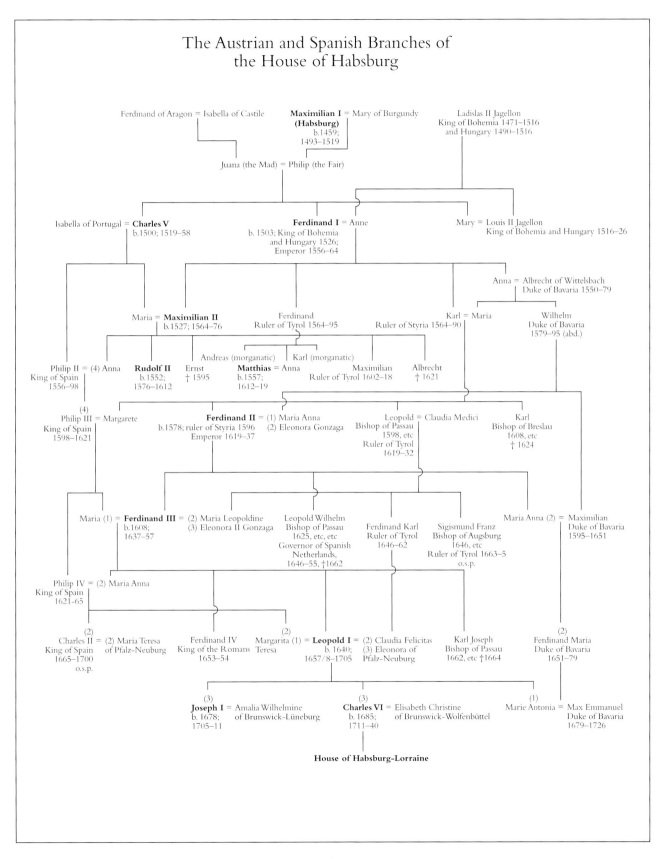

Courtly recreation: the Emperor Rudolf II (wearing red breeches, centre) takes the waters at a spa near Prague, depicted by the Flemish painter Lucas van Valkenborch (c. 1590). With Flanders and Bohemia both under Habsburg rule, many of the most talented Flemish painters were drawn to the court at Prague.

the chamberlain (an inflated figure, containing 423 *Kämmerer*, or honorary chamberlains); 27 for the marshal; and 216 for the master of the horse. Rinck listed a further 113 for the archers, 110 for the footguard, 57 for the master of the hunt, and 28 for the master of the falcons. Adding the empress's court and

the administrative staff, he came to a grand total of 1,840,[13] a figure that accords with the estimate by Johann Basilius Küchelbecker, who thought the Vienna Hofstaat stood at some 2,000 persons in 1729.[14]

While Rinck's and Küchelbecker's aggregates were more or less similar, their computations and categories differ. Different choices could be made when counting the Hofstaat. Dowager-empresses, empresses, Kings of the Romans and archdukes or archduchesses maintained their own households. These could be very limited, but could also reach substantial levels. Guard regiments could inflate the numbers – did they belong to the court? Moreover, do we add those holding sinecures but not actually appearing at court? Finally, office at court would often be held on a rotational basis. Evidently, the Hofstaat can sometimes lead us to over-estimate the number of those actually residing at court.

The growth of the court's personnel was matched by a corresponding increase in expenditure, exacerbated by the growing demands of magnificence. Again, the reign of Leopold seems to have been a turning point. Expenditure increased fivefold between 1660 and 1705, and continued to rise during the reigns of Joseph and Charles; by the 1730s spending had again almost doubled. The reign of Maria-Theresa (1740–80) reversed this trend, and Joseph II (1765–90) further reduced court spending.[15]

iii. The Orbits of the Household

The court, however, was a much larger phenomenon than the sum of those who appeared on the Hofstaat. While it is more or less clear who belonged to the court, it is evident that the group depending on the court in other and different ways was much greater. Petitioners, those *piliers de l'antichambre* (pillars of the antichambers), were not listed in the Hofstaat but permanently added to the numbers surrounding the ruler. The same holds true for many artists and fortune-seekers offering their services and vying for the ruler's patronage. The court was a meeting place and a crossroads for the most diverse groups and interests – the Hofstaat was only the nucleus of a larger and varied entourage surrounding the court.

At court, the two categories of 'household' and 'government' were inevitably mixed. Officers of the household were initially responsible for the government of the realm in the broadest sense, but gradually many administrative tasks pertaining to the monarch's territories, rather than his person, were taken over by clerks.

The Hofgesinde included both the officers of the household and the administrators of the Habsburg realms. Both were duly listed in the Hofstaat, and were active in the main agencies of government at the emperor's court. The Geheime Rat (Privy Council) was apt to become too large and unwieldy, and therefore was regularly trimmed to conform to its original composition: a small circle of knowledgeable advisers supporting the ruler. Here, the emperor's noble companions remained the strongest group.

The Reichshofrat was the supreme court of justice for the Empire and for the Habsburg lands, but it also dealt with administrative and political matters, especially those pertaining to the Empire. The Reichshofkanzlei handled all government correspondence: its head, the Reichsvizekanzler, therefore had a pivotal position in the Reichshofrat. In 1620 Ferdinand II created the Österreichische Hofkanzlei, which slowly took over much work from the Reichshofkanzlei. The Hofkanzler, accordingly, could often be more important than the Reichsvizekanzler, and his position was further strengthened in 1749 when the Österreichische Hofkanzlei was united with the Bohemian chancery. The Hofkammer, or court treasury, administered the revenue coming from the Habsburg domains, and collected indirect taxes. Finally, the Hofkriegsrat was responsible for matters relating to war, and administered the grants coming from the Estates in the *Erblande*.[16]

In general, noble participation became rarer in the face of the need for financial or legal competence and when the element of personal service to the ruler diminished. Ferdinand I's court ordinances of 1527 and 1537 can be read as a first attempt to clarify the distinction between the honorific and the administrative (or the personal versus the territorial) responsibilities at court. In the succeeding centuries, the administrative apparatus expanded, gaining more autonomy in the process. For all practical purposes, however, the separation of household and government remained a dead letter until the reforms of Maria-Theresa after the Austrian Succession War of 1740–48, and it can be argued that this situation persisted far into the nineteenth century. In the early modern age, 'administration' was not the assertive young cuckoo slowly pushing the older courtly apparatus out of the nest. If anything, the court forced the newer cadres of state servants into its own ways, and it remained the heart of government.

The court as a stage for dynastic theatre: The Battle of the Elements, *an equestrian ballet staged to celebrate the marriage of the Emperor Leopold I (1658–1705) to the Infanta Margarita Teresa, the sister of Carlos II of Spain, in 1667. The range in the background is the recently completed wing of the Hofburg, the Leopoldine Tract (erected 1660–66) by Filiberto Lucchese, the new emperor's attempt to create in Vienna a monumental palace that could compete with the architectural splendour of the great Spanish, French and Italian courts.*

IV. THE EMPERORS' RESIDENCES

The Vienna Hofburg was the principal domicile of the emperors in the early modern age.[17] A warren of interconnected buildings, the earliest dating from the thirteenth century, it was progressively extended or adapted to conform to new exigencies. After the siege of Vienna in 1529 Ferdinand I repaired and extended the damaged Hofburg, while retaining its crucial defensive function. Soon, however, Ferdinand had to enlarge and redecorate the complex to accommodate his children, and towards the end of his reign he had a new building constructed for the Hofstaat of the King of the Romans, Maximilian. When the latter succeeded, he moved into the Hofburg proper, turning the newly erected building into the court's stables – hence its current name, Stallburg. Maximilian II, too, had to provide room for the Hofstaat of his sons Rudolf and Ernst, and in 1575–7 he constructed the wing that later became known as the Amalienburg to accommodate them. In the course of the seventeenth century the palace complex acquired a bath-house, a hall for court balls, and a Komödienhaus, or court theatre. Yet, for all these amenities, it still did not strike visitors as a particularly majestic domicile. Matthaeus Merian noted in his *Topographia Germaniae* that the Hofburg was 'not particularly splendidly constructed, and was rather small for such a mighty and supreme potentate, and such a large court establishment'.[18]

These shortcomings were partially remedied by Leopold I, who planned and built a grand new wing in the 1660s, the so-called Leopoldine Tract, which was destroyed by fire shortly after the emperor took up occupancy. Although rebuilt by 1681, the wing was only in use for two years before the Turkish siege of Vienna in 1683, when it was once more heavily damaged, the Hofburg being one of the prime targets of the Turks' artillery bombardment. Only after the emperor's successes in the war with the Turks had rendered the defensive structures of the Hofburg obsolete could the palace be adapted truly to conform to the standards of *repraesentatio maiestatis*. Even so, budgetary difficulties continued to limit the emperors' building activities. Montesquieu, visiting Vienna in 1729, could still with some justification contrast the motley Hofburg with the splendid domiciles of the greatest court nobles. Between 1683 and 1749 some forty-six palaces were constructed in Vienna, with Prince Eugen's Belvedere being among the finest of these.[19] During the 1720s and 1730s Charles VI provided the Hofburg with the more befitting Michaelertrakt, and added the majestic court library to the complex. Charles also cherished another project: the austere residence at Klosterneuburg, inspired by the example of the Escorial, although only a small part of this was ever constructed.

In the seventeenth century Schönbrunn was a modest hunting lodge.[20] In the 1690s, however, when it was to become the residence of Joseph, King of the Romans, the great architect Johann Bernhard Fischer von Erlach presented the court with proposals to turn Schönbrunn into a palace surpassing the ambitions even of Versailles. In the event, Fischer's far less grandiose second project was constructed. For most of the first half of the eighteenth century, use of Schönbrunn by the imperial court was largely confined to hunting expeditions and occasional celebrations. Charles VI lived there intermittently from 1728; but only after the accession of Maria-Theresa (1740–80) did it become an important seat of the court.

The Hofburg thus remained the habitual residence of the emperor, while variety was provided by sojourns in the hunting lodges at Laxenburg, Favorita, Ebersdorf, Schönbrunn and the Neugebäude. The Prague castle, or Hradčany, however, was more than comparable to the Hofburg: the great Luxembourg emperor Charles IV (1347–78) had turned the castle into a centre of patronage. Vladislas II Jagiello, who combined the Hungarian and Bohemian crowns from 1490, tried to emulate Charles; and Ferdinand I built a palace for his queen nearby. Rudolf II, taking the court to Prague in the 1580s, could fall back on a rich heritage, and during his reign Prague regained its former pre-eminence. The castle was further expanded and embellished, but Rudolf's reign ended in débâcle, and Prague lost much of its attraction for the Habsburgs after the Thirty Years War. Emperors visited Prague, but they were never again to turn the Hradčany to their seat, although Maria-Theresa initiated important reconstructions.

V. THE CALENDAR OF COURT LIFE

The most important factor structuring the court calendar was the Roman Catholic liturgical year: the Christmas and Easter cycles, and the feasts of saints.[21] Every year there was the same sequence of religious celebrations and *Andachten* (devotions). The emperor often worshipped publicly, walking with part of the Hofstaat from palace to church. Ambassadors were expected to accompany the emperor in his public religious observances. During Lent the regime seems to have been particularly demanding – Justus Eberhard Passer, envoy from Hessen-Darmstadt in the early 1680s, noted the round of processions, pilgrimages, masses, matins and vespers in his diary. Little had changed half a century later, when Küchelbecker recorded a detailed account of the court's activities in 1729; again religious observances dominated. In 1726 the worldly Duc de Richelieu complained that only the sturdiest of monks could endure the court's religious observances. He calculated having spent more than a hundred hours with the emperor in church, from Palm Sunday until the day after Easter.[22]

Court ceremonial and court festivities were intimately tied to the liturgical year. The emperor dined publicly in the Ritterstube (or Knights' Chamber) of the Hofburg on at least four occasions: St Andrew's Day (30 November, when he dined with the knights of the Golden Fleece), Christmas, Easter and Pentecost. The *Wirtschaften*, a mixture of comedy, masquerade and ballet in a pastoral setting, performed by courtiers, were invariably organized during Shrovetide. Passer noted the cast in 1680: high court nobles dominated, the Spanish ambassador participated in the role of a Bohemian farmer and the emperor and empress danced in the ballet.[23] During Holy Week, like other rulers, the emperor would wash the feet of twelve poor men on Maundy Thursday. Passer reported this repeatedly, at one time stressing that the poor were thoroughly cleansed beforehand. An elaborate meal was part of the ceremony, and the guests could take their tableware home; those unused to such affairs had to be carried home by the footguards.[24]

The knights of the Order of the Golden Fleece had their own sequence of celebrations in Vienna. In addition to the order's major celebration on St Andrew's Day, Küchelbecker listed fifty 'Fleece Days' in his calendar, most again connected with religious activities.[25] Also included in the court calendar, but not strictly determined by the liturgical year, were the birthdays and namedays of the members of the dynasty. During these galas, compliments could be offered to the celebrant, and *divertissements*, operas and concerts would be organized.[26]

There was also a seasonal aspect to court life. In Vienna, the Hofburg functioned principally as the winter residence. In spring, however, the court moved to the hunting lodge at Laxenburg; in summer it moved to the Favorita; and in autumn to Ebersdorf. In the eighteenth century Schönbrunn gradually took its place in the schedule; and here, as at Versailles, what began as a hunting lodge was finally transformed into a summer residence fully capable of serving as a seat for the court. Life in the 'outdoor' dwellings was less ceremonious, with the ruler accompanied by a relatively intimate circle, administrative work continuing at a lower pitch, and hunting, always a favourite pastime at court, dominating the schedule.

While seasons and the liturgical year structured the court's calendar over the months, the domestic ceremonies of *Ankleiden*, dinner, supper, and *Abziehen* structured the daily rhythm at court – a sequence common to almost every major noble household.[27] The day began with the *Ankleiden*, in the company of the chamberlain and his deputies. In Leopold's time it was enlivened by court jesters and dwarfs. As was to be expected, religious observance figured prominently in the morning hours, either in the Hofburg chapel, in the Augustiner or Hofkirche (physically connected to the Hofburg), or in one of the other churches in Vienna. Then came the demands of government:

reading dispatches, conferring with councillors, or presiding over council meetings.[28] After dinner, which took place shortly after midday, the court, women included, could go hunting near Vienna, or shoot at targets.[29] The Swedish resident Esaias Pufendorf noted in his description of a *Fuchsprellen* in March 1672 that it was truly 'remarkable that the emperor himself beat the foxes with a club, and threw it at them when they had been struck, and that he was joined in this by the fools and little boys – which seemed to me to be somewhat out of keeping with the imperial dignity'.[30] Leopold's fervour was nothing exceptional among monarchs: each of his predecessors and successors was an equally passionate hunter. In the afternoon, after hunting or as an alternative to it, the imperial family could indulge in recreational games. Unlike hunting, however, card games were far from an addiction, as they were at many other courts. On the other hand, music was an important pastime. Most Habsburgs had some musical talent; they composed, performed and directed. Leopold's correspondence with his librarian Lambeck suggests that he must also have devoted some time to reading.[31] In the late afternoon or in the early evening both the emperor and the empress would be available for audiences. After supper there could be further audiences, musical performances or comedies. The emperors were early risers, and the *Abziehen* can hardly have taken place very late.

Can this tentative sketch of the emperor's days be extended to encompass the day of a courtier? Probably not – all courtiers did not take part in every one of these occasions. What strikes the eye is the large amount of the ruler's time that was spent without spectators.

VI. COURT CEREMONY

The tasks, position, appearance and deportment of those present at court were to a large extent predetermined.[32] Some ceremonies were limited to the ruler and his immediate circle; others were much more public. In Vienna, the *Ankleiden* and *Abziehen* remained secluded domestic ceremonies, very different from the French *lever* and *coucher*. Meals and audiences could be either 'public' or 'private'. Religious ceremonies could take place in the Hofburg chapel, but often had a

Dining as liturgy: at the coronation of Joseph II in 1765, emperor and empress dine under a canopy (its cloth of estate is visible behind their chairs), on a raised dais at the end of the hall. The cope and dalmatic worn by the emperor are ecclesiastical vestments, symbolizing his role as both rex et sacerdos, *monarch and quasi-priest, mediating between divine and earthly authority.*

public character, as the processions from the Hofburg to the church, and vice versa, show. High points of the dynasty – births, funerals, marriages, elections, coronations – always had their train of public ceremonies, in Vienna, Prague and Pressburg, and in the cities of the empire connected to these events, mainly Frankfurt and Regensburg.[33]

Dress, too, was prescribed to a certain extent. The livery of the emperors' court was dominated by black

and yellow (or 'gold'); valets and chamberlains had their own, somewhat similar but richer, apparel. The emperors themselves wore the Spanish court dress, a black costume enlivened by golden embroidery, red hose and shoes, and a hat decorated with red, yellow or white feathers.[34] While other court officers were freer in the choice of their costume, they seem also to have adhered to a sober style. During the frequent galas, however, costume would be more sumptuous, and jewellery played a particularly important role in demonstrating rank.[35] The knights of the Order of the Golden Fleece departed from the habitual preference for black: their costume was red with golden embroidery and worn with the order's gold chain.[36] The French court style, still frowned upon by Charles VI, was finally introduced by Francis I. Joseph II favoured a military court costume.

Both public and private meals were served according to fixed rules. If the emperor and empress dined in public, generally in the Ritterstube, they were accompanied by the senior court dignitaries, with the archers and footguards standing near. They were served, on bended knee, by an array of other court officers: Vehse, a nineteenth-century scholar, calculated that every dish went through twenty-four pairs of hands before it actually reached the emperor.[37] All those in attendance had to remain standing, and could only withdraw 'as soon as his imperial majesty had taken the first draught'.[38] Visitors reported many details of public dining. Edward Brown noted 'three remarkably low dwarfs' during the public dinner at Christmas.[39] Pöllnitz counted forty-eight dishes, observing that the emperor and empress dined together, but were served by their own Hofstaat, and from their own kitchen. Within the limits of available space, the '[persons] attired in keeping with the place and the occasion' were admitted to the ceremony.[40] The emperor's table stood on a dais, and his chair was marked by a canopy of state. He would remain covered throughout the meal, only taking off his hat during prayers, or when the empress drank to his health. On Sundays, and during galas, public dining was enlivened by the court's musicians. In the Hofburg, 'the side of the empress' and 'the side of the emperor' alluded to the habit of dining in the afternoon *en famille* in the emperor's apartments, and in the evening with guests in the empress's apartments. Dining on the emperor's side generally took place in the Ratstube (council chamber), but public dining would take place in the larger Ritterstube. A range of intermediate stages stood between the ceremony of public dining and the truly private and less ceremonial dinner of the emperor in his own rooms.[41]

Emperor and empress had their own sequence of antechambers, meeting at the centre in their contiguous apartment. Only persons of a certain rank could progress from the Ritterstube towards the centre,

passing through the first antechamber, second antechamber, Ratstube or audience room, and finally reaching the imperial apartment itself. Each 'threshold' demanded an extra step in the courtly hierarchy. The Ritterstube was open for all members of the Hofstaat; entrance to the first antechamber was limited to *Kavalieren* (knights), pages and choirmaster; only *Freiherren* (barons), counts, *Hofkriegsoffizieren* (court military officers) and prelates could enter the second antechamber. Finally, only ambassadors, electors, princes of the empire, senior court officers, privy councillors, chamberlains, archbishops and bishops were allowed in the Ratstube. The contiguous apartments of the emperor and the empress, the inner rooms to which the sequence of antechambers on both sides finally led, were only accessible to court dignitaries, domestics and, of course, the imperial family.[42] Thus, they did not have a conspicuous role in the more public ceremonies. On the emperor's side, the Ratstube functioned as audience room, but depending on the rank of the visitor, either the second antechamber or the emperor's *Retirade* could also be used. On the empress's side, matters proceeded similarly, with the audience room taking the place of the Ratstube. In the Ratstube stood the symbols of rulership: an elevated platform, a carpet and a canopy – insignia that were also set up in the other places where the emperor resided.[43]

Those wanting to address the emperor had to ask the chamberlain for a place on the list for the private audiences. An audience with the empress had to be requested through her major domo. Diplomats and prelates took precedence over most others, and there are reports about petitioners waiting for months.[44] The chamberlain took the visitor through the antechambers to the audience room. Entering the audience room or Ratstube, the visitor had to make the *Tieffe Reverentz* or *Spanische Compliment* three times, a deep bow on bended knee. Withdrawing, he or she had to keep looking towards the emperor and repeat the three 'Spanish compliments'. During these private audiences, the emperor would receive his guest standing under a canopy and leaning against a table. There were no spectators: even the chamberlain or doorkeeper left the room, or waited behind a screen near the entrance. Audiences with the empress were similar, but a *Hofdame* (lady in waiting) would visibly remain in the room. Differences in court conventions could lead to awkward moments. Saint-Simon reports that the French envoy Cheverny, introduced into Leopold's audience room, mistook it for yet another antechamber.[45] He haughtily paced the room, ignoring what he took to be the servant leaning against the table in the middle of the room, until this figure made himself known as the emperor, and Cheverny desperately sought to find excuses for his *faux pas*.[46] While the story seems somewhat unlikely, it exaggerates and ridicules a difference noted in many other accounts.[47]

During pilgrimages and processions, or in church, the Hofstaat took part in its own hierarchical order. The court's progress from the Hofburg to the church, convent or shrine was strictly choreographed, again by rank. In church, too, the emperor was conspicuously present. On Palm Sunday in 1682 Passer saw the emperor 'with the entire court establishment and ambassadors proceed three times around the church at the Augustinians and finally halt before the altar, all of them with palm branches in their hands'.[48] Brown witnessed a St Stephen's Day procession to the Stephanskirche, where the emperor 'went up to the altar, kneeled, and kissed the plate [the paten] wheron the Hostia had lain'.[49] The emperor, however, seems to have attended religious celebrations in his own *oratorium*, a canopied booth open towards the altar, but closed towards the congregation.[50]

The development of permanent diplomacy added substantially to the ceremonial and ostentation of court life. As the hierarchy among the rulers of Europe had to be replicated in the contacts between their representatives, complications over precedence abounded. Permanent diplomacy certainly was an important factor in urging the different courts to create an all-encompassing 'table of ranks' governing mutual exchanges. The diplomatic encounters at court had a distinctly worldly element: the competition between rulers. By the same token, competition between equals in the upper layers of courtly society found expression in their competition for ceremonial precedence.

Visitors to the emperor's court stressed both the unchanging rhythm of life, and the antiquity of its severe ceremonial, yet both are open to question. The clockwork precision of the emperors' schedule seems to have been regarded, *a priori*, as concomitant with their elevated status, whereas the descriptions actually show many variations. Similarly, the ceremonies were once thought to have been copied from sixteenth-century Spain, and thereafter to have been carefully maintained. While it is clear that court life in the sixteenth century had its ceremonial components – particularly those connected to the liturgical year and the major dynastic events – it is not easy to ascertain either the extent of Spanish influence or the degree of ceremonial continuity from the sixteenth to the eighteenth centuries. The Spanish example did not truly shape the court of the Austrian Habsburgs. The court ordinances of Ferdinand I hardly constituted a break with earlier tradition; they offered a structured extension of prevailing practice. Only the Chapel Royal and the *Hartschieren Leibgarde* (archers) seem to have been directly adapted from the Burgundian-Spanish example.[51] The Spanish character of the Viennese court may have been limited to the 'Spanish compliment' and a general resemblance in deportment and dress.

Did the court become more ceremonious? From the mid seventeenth century there was a new emphasis on the precise codification of court ceremony. During 1651 and 1652 a commission of councillors discussed a handbook for ceremonies, deliberations that coincided with the creation of a *Zeremonienamt* (or office of ceremonial) in the major domo's department.[52] From the same period the Hofstaat and the court's cultural activities started to expand. These developments continued during the reigns of Leopold I, Joseph I and Charles VI, but the trend was arrested with the advent of Maria-Theresa, and still more during the reign of her son, Joseph II. While the period ranging from the Peace of Westphalia (1648) to the death of Charles VI (1740) was one of both the growth of the Hofstaat and the dominance of ceremony, it would be unwise to regard ceremonial convention as having governed each and every exchange at court. Most visitors seem to have exaggerated the court's rigidity. More perspicacious witnesses, such as Pufendorf or Passer, mention occasions where the straightjacket of ceremony seems to have been absent.

The relatively secluded existence of the emperors may be the most important contrast with their Bourbon rivals. Louis XIV, particularly, sought to present his rule as an open monarchy, with the king accessible and visible to his subjects: the French court certainly harboured far more 'spectators' than the Habsburg court in Vienna. The spatial distance created by the sequence of rooms in the 'German' style became largely a matter of timing in the French case, the various *entrées* taking over the role of the antechambers' hierarchical thresholds. Moreover, the ruler's own apartment played a major role in French ceremonial, while in Vienna it remained a truly private apartment. The 'closed' style of court life had an important consequence: social contact among élites most frequently occurred outside the court. While the court must have been the nexus of élite life in Vienna and throughout the Habsburg lands, it did not provide for everyday entertainment, as the French court did with the sequence of *appartements*, theatre and opera. Emperors could organize opera and comedy in the Hofburg complex, as Leopold often did, although outshone by the dowager-empress Eleonora II Gonzaga, whose court was also reported to have a more open and worldly style.[53] Did the disparaging remarks by visitors about the Hofburg, contrasting it with the more splendid palaces in Vienna, have their parallel in social life? Did the magnates' palaces in Vienna and elsewhere offer the sort of entertainment and sociability the emperor's court seemed to lack? If so, we should relate these activities to their political role in the *Monarchia Austriaca*.

The 'function' and 'meaning' of court ceremonial have recently received rather more attention than its actual forms. Ceremony, it has been argued, by making rank clearly visible, functioned as an instrument of power in the monarch's hands: it enabled him to manipulate courtiers by stimulating and exploiting their competition for status. In part, this is obviously true; rulers and nobles alike were obsessed with rank and ceremonial dignity. Yet it is far from clear that court ceremonial enabled kings to keep their nobles in check.[54] Such a functionalist approach tends to underrate the religious element inherent in court ceremonial, and the self-evident authority that the hierarchical conception of society exerted over all those within the court. Ceremony was a collective performance of devout adherence to hierarchies terrestrial and celestial. It instituted and reinforced the compact between the ruler and the highest officers of the household and the state. Ceremony structured court life through rank, and thus not only made rank visible, but also assured those enjoying high rank of access to the ruler. Moreover, in many respects, the *gravitas* of ceremony constrained and burdened rulers.

It proclaimed and legitimized dynastic superiority, but it so doing restricted the incumbents' personal and political freedom of movement. To be seen to be trying to 'manipulate' the court through the use of ceremony would be to forfeit, or at least damage, the aloofness and superiority that was in theory the very essence of their position, and most rulers refrained from manifest meddling.

VII. EMPERORS AND ELITES: THE FORMATION OF A RULING CASTE

The élite around 1700 was an intricate mixture. Nobles from the *Erblande*, Bohemia, Hungary and the German principalities formed the core of a group that also included *émigrés* from other parts of Europe. The social origins of this group were as varied as their geographical provenance, although many of the names that dominated the Habsburg court by the early eighteenth century maintained their position well into the nineteenth century.

The character of this ruling caste had evolved relatively recently: in the course of the seventeenth century, and particularly through the religious and political upheaval that lasted from the later years of Rudolf II to the 1630s.[55] Lutheranism and Calvinism had been highly successful in all the dominions of the Austrian Habsburgs. The majority of the nobility had converted to one of the Protestant creeds, and they dominated most Estates. Around 1600 the religious question had severely strained the connection between emperor and nobles, and indeed the whole body politic. The Turkish wars and the fiscal power of the Estates seemed to augur a further expansion of Protestantism. Rudolf's eager successor Emperor Matthias (1612–19) and his senior adviser Bishop Melchior Khlesl tried to advance the cause of Catholicism, but this only exacerbated the situation. Finally, the Bohemian crisis of 1618–20 and the parallel revolt of the Upper and Lower Austrian Estates led to full-scale warfare. The turmoil enabled the new emperor, Ferdinand II, to implement his Counter-Reformation policies.[56] Through his generals' military successes, Ferdinand could impel many nobles to follow him, at the same time enticing them by

*Rites of passage: the arrival of the Bourbon princess, Isabella of Parma, for her marriage to the future
Emperor Joseph II (1765–90) in 1760. Temporary triumphal arches, such as those depicted here, formed
a regular feature of major dynastic celebrations, coronations and formal entries into cities.*

promises of titles and wealth. Protestant nobles had to
disavow their faith, or have their territories confiscated
and redistributed among loyal Catholic nobles. In
Bohemia and Moravia between half and three-quarters
of all noble property changed hands, and half the noble
families were ruined.[57] Often families were torn apart,
one half supporting the dynasty, the other continuing
its opposition. The nobility declined in absolute numbers and in proportion to the population as a whole.
In Austria Protestants among the *Ritter* (or knights),
the lower nobility, already weakened by the continuing

subdivision of their holdings, almost disappeared: they
either converted and rose to the *Herrenstand* (which
might roughly be equated with the peerage) or lost
their position. High nobles, too, suffered losses: prominent magnate families, such as the Zierotin in Moravia
or the Jörger in Austria, lost their wealth and status.

In Moravia the Dietrichstein and Liechtenstein
families profited hugely. The Liechtensteins acquired
princely rank and a duchy, while during the Thirty
Years War they more than tripled the numbers of
subjects in their possessions. Finally, in 1719, they even

Opera as the vehicle for dynastic imagery: the performance of Marc' Antonio Cesti's Il Pomo d'Oro *in 1668 as part of the celebrations for the marriage of Leopold I and the Empress Margaretha-Theresa, who sit at the front of the audience, on a raised and carpeted dais.*

acquired their own semi-sovereign territory. Similarly, one of the main proponents of the Habsburg dynasty and of Catholicism in Bohemia, Zdenek Lobkowitz, secured princely rank for his family and extended his domains.[58] Loyal families in the *Erblande*, such as the Auersperg, Trautson, Lamberg[59] or Trauttmansdorf, established their pre-eminence. Descendants from the Protestant rebels of the 1620s, however, could revive their status if they proved loyal, as did the Starhembergs and the Jörger in Austria, or the Czernin in Bohemia.[60] Similar processes occurred in Hungary after the magnates' conspiracy of the late 1660s. The Esterházy profited from the discomfiture of the

extremely wealthy Nádasdy: they, too, were promoted to the *Reichsfürstenstand* (princes of the Empire). Other loyal Hungarian magnates, such as the Batthyány and Pálffy, followed the same course.

From the Empire, particarly its western and south-western territories, a steady flow joined the ranks of the new élite – Schwarzenberg (a family of Bohemian origins who had served in Brandenburg and Bavaria), Fürstenberg, Oettingen, Königsegg and Salm. In the Thirty Years War and afterwards, *émigré* generals, such as Bucquoy, Leslie, Piccolomini, Montecuccoli and Eugen, paved their way to fortune through military success. But it was not only high nobles who improved their position. Ferdinand II's major domo and favourite councillor, Johann Ulrich von Eggenberg, the son of a burgermaster of Graz, became *Reichsfürst* and acquired the Duchy of Krumau, turning him overnight into the greatest landholder in Bohemia, on a par with the Lobkowitz and Liechtenstein families. Loyal administrators of more humble origins, such as the chancellors Prickelmayr, Hocher, Stratmann and Seilern, were ennobled; like the many who followed, they did not fully integrate into the closing circle of the ruling caste. More aloof from the worldly grandees, but nevertheless an essential element of the Habsburg environment, were the Jesuits, Capuchins and Augustinians offering spiritual guidance to the rulers.

Thus, a new caste of Roman Catholic ruling families emerged to forge a lasting compact with the Habsburgs. While the dynasty was indeed the main agent in the formation of this ruling caste, we should not depict the latter as a *Dienstadel* (or service nobility) intimidated into obedience by the ruler. The magnates dominated the Privy Council, army and diplomacy, and held the major court offices; they acquired huge domains and could also exert power through the local Estates. The Estates, in turn, could approve or reject the crown's financial requests, and the perennial warfare strengthened their leverage in many fields.[61] The magnates' lands were often consolidated by a *Fideicommissum*, a settlement securing their dynastic ambitions by protecting their domain from the financial excesses of individual members of the family. Through their position in the Estates and as landholders, the magnates dominated the entire network of local and provincial government; in the absence of direct administrative links between the emperor and his subjects they were the essential intermediaries of power. The princes had rights that gave them the semblance, if not the reality, of sovereignty.

The classification 'courtier' fitted the members of this caste only imperfectly; the group of nobles actually residing at court remained small, partly because accommodation could not be found for all those holding and exercising court office. Magnates established their own palaces in Vienna, as well as in the surrounding countryside, and on their estates. They belonged to the emperor's court, but simultaneously maintained their own courts. While the metaphor of sun and planets certainly fitted the hierarchical relationship between emperor and high nobles as it was mutually understood, in other respects it cannot be said that the planets merely reflected the sun's radiance. To contemporaries, both the political realities and the ostentation of the noble households in Vienna, Prague and elsewhere could suggest the opposite: a somewhat pale centre, illuminated and upheld by an orbit of brilliant satellites. Together, the dynasty and the cosmopolitan élites succeeded in governing the array of territories; their compact has rightly been described as dual governance, or dyarchy, which continued well into the nineteenth century.

VIII. FACTIONS AT COURT

The relationship between emperor and élites, however, was never as unchanging and unruffled an alliance as their unity in court ceremonial suggested. Competition for the emperor's patronage and factional strife between groups and individuals were commonplace at court.

Access to the monarch was much coveted. It brought honour, material advantage and political leverage. Although the distribution of honours was not exclusive to the emperor, nevertheless finding his ear was one of the surest means of procuring offices and privileges. Successful restriction of this access, or even the expectation of it, antagonized supplicants, who invariably tried to redress the balance. Rulers sought to avert such problems by having a variety of confidants – a solution that could backfire if it fomented competition among their advisers.

Foreign favourites often provoked resentment. Ferdinand I's retinue of Spanish and Dutch confidants proved unacceptable to the Austrian Estates,[62] and when in 1666 Margaretha-Theresa brought her Spanish retinue to Vienna, this immediately caused grumbling about a 'Spanish court camarilla'; moreover, it upset the delicate equilibrium of allocating quarters at court.[63] The Spanish favourites huddling around Charles VI after his accession to the imperial throne aroused equal displeasure; the Dutch envoy reported that nobles were openly complaining, and cabals were forming to reverse the situation.[64]

Mistresses and favourites, however, rarely achieved the prominence that led to such bitter complaints elsewhere. Most Habsburgs seem to have been impervious to the charms and dangers of mistresses, and only Charles VI's favourite, Michael Johann Althan, attained some notoriety as a favourite. The emperors, however, tended to cling to their trusted advisers: childhood friends and tutors all too frequently came to be regarded as gatekeepers between the ruler and his court.

Junior branches ruling their own territories (Styria until the accession of Ferdinand II in 1619, and Tyrol until the extinction of the Tyrolean branch in 1665) could further complicate matters: their autonomous courts were not necessarily subservient to that of the ruling emperor. Younger brothers, potential heirs to the throne, could form the nucleus of serious opposition, particularly if there was thought to be little likelihood of male offspring. Matthias's undermining of the already crumbling situation in the last years of Rudolf can be seen as an example of such a predicament. These sources of strife dwindled during the seventeenth century, but 'the court' still generally consisted of more than one court. The dowager-empress's court was a consistent feature of Vienna from the death of Ferdinand II (1637) to the advent of Maria-Theresa (1740). From 1657 to 1686, for example, Eleonora II Gonzaga's court was a centre of cultural and political patronage, and she was mentioned as 'leading' one of the court's factions. Charles VI's mother also occasionally meddled in the affairs of the court, and Joseph I's widow Amalia-Wilhelmina remained a force to be reckoned with, although she generally kept aloof.[65] The court of the reigning empress and that of the King of the Romans were permanent features of aulic life, but tended to remain more subservient to the emperor. They could, however, offer an alternative source of patronage, or a route for indirect influence over the monarch. The Hofstaat of the King of the Romans could also become the centre of opposition to an ageing emperor: the *junge Hof* surrounding the restive Joseph in the last years of Leopold's reign clearly prepared for a change of direction.

While favourites could provoke faction, the multiple courts of the ruling dynasty could serve as rival foci of influence. Foreign representatives would scrupulously attend these courts, too, and examples of their interference in the court's factions abound.[66] Diplomats sought to advance their interests by adroitly utilizing the divisions of court life,

sometimes exacerbating them with bribes or threats.

Social origins, often suggested as an explanation for courtly strife, do not seem to offer a key to the understanding of competition at the Habsburg court. On the contrary, ennobled chancellors, princes or counts, and non-noble clerics did not primarily seek support among their peers, but rather against such possible rivals. Only incidentally did social or functional differences surface as a clear cause for faction, as in the early years of Charles VI when the ministers from the *Geheime Konferenz* (Privy Conference) were opposed by a faction of courtiers.[67]

IX. THE COURT AS A CULTURAL CENTRE

After seeing the Schatzkammer (treasure chamber), and listening to fine music in the chapel, Matthaeus Merian revised his earlier, somewhat negative, appraisal of the Hofburg, and granted the court truly imperial rank.[68] Indeed, Habsburgs excelled in both fields.

Their collections of paintings, naturalia, scientific instruments, regalia and dynastic curiosities were the wonder of visitors. Like court ceremony, the *Kunst- und Wunderkammer* was part and parcel of the dynastic pursuit of harmony and hierarchy. The microcosm of the collection mirrored the harmony of the macrocosm, establishing and demonstrating the dynasty's position in the larger whole. Thus, the alleged unicorn horn (actually the ivory tusk of a narwal), the *Achatschale,* and other remarkable objects in the collection had their role in promulgating Habsburg rule. The unicorn traditionally had strong associations with purity and Christianity, and had often been used for the insignia of rulers, particularly for the sceptre. The *Achatschale* had an inscription that was thought to have 'grown' in the stone, and was falsely read as a monogram of Christ. It was thought to be somehow connected with the Holy Grail. These objects were relics both of Christianity and rulership, they underpinned Habsburg pedigree and *Gottesgnadentum* (divine right).[69]

As a patron, Rudolf II, often judged to have been a lackadaisical character at best, was a conspicuous success.[70] The court in Prague became a truly European centre for arts and sciences.[71] Aegidius Sadeler, Bartholomeus Spranger, Hans Vredeman de

Vienna and the Lower Belvedere seen from the Upper Belvedere, built in 1721–2 for Prince Eugen of Savoy, to designs by Johann Lucas von Hildebrandt. Prince Eugen's palace (lower right) was one of the series of princely and aristocratic palaces around Vienna that operated as alternative 'foyers of power' – and as rivals in architectural magnificence – to the imperial court at the Hofburg.

Vries and many other artists propagated the Prague Mannerist style. Sadeler effectively did so through the medium of print as well. Rudolf may have indulged in the bizarre, erotic, esoteric and the occult, but his environment proved highly fertile. Tycho Brahe and Johannes Kepler served the enigmatic emperor, whose famous picture collection contained works by Dürer, Brueghel, Leonardo, Titian, Correggio, Parmigianino, Veronese and Tintoretto. It was only in the scale of his collections, however, that Rudolf was exceptional, and the famous imperial collections long remained a magnet for any visitor to Vienna.

Most Habsburgs took their collecting seriously. Ferdinand of the Tyrol, brother of Maximilian II, rebuilt Ambras castle near Innsbruck to house his famous *Wunderkammer*. The *Wunderkammer* reached its zenith in the late sixteenth and early seventeenth centuries – it embodied the ideals of harmony while religious turbulence in Europe was at its peak. Later Habsburgs continued the tradition, although Counter-Reformatory zeal and and budgetary limitations reduced its proportions. Cardinal-Archduke Leopold-Wilhelm, younger son of Ferdinand II, for example, accumulated an impressive collection of pictures.[72]

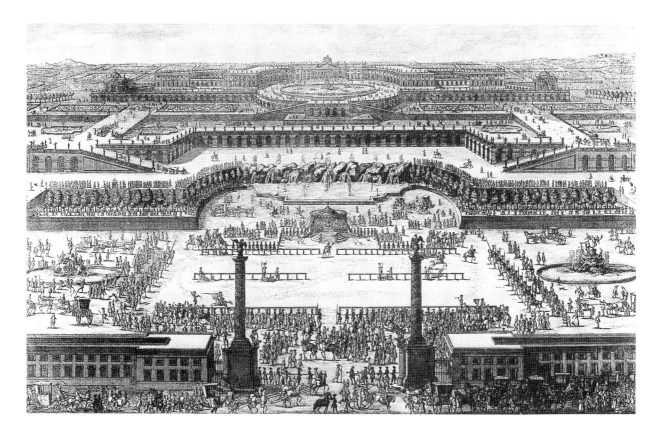

Plans for a truly imperial court: Johann Bernhard Fischer von Erlach's proposal, c.1690, for the remodelling of the hunting lodge at Schönbrunn to create a seat for the court that would outshine all other European princely residences in magnificence. In this imaginary view, a carrousel – the Baroque inheritor of the Renaissance chivalric tournament – is being staged in the foreground before the emperor, who watches from the tented pavilion (centre).

Leopold took over this collection, and certainly cherished the dynastic regalia and rarities.

Collecting, however, was later replaced by other interests, music figuring prominently among them. Habsburgs shared a passion for music. In the sixteenth century Flemish musicians held the major positions in the Hofkapelle: Philip de Monte served Maximilian II and Rudolf. After the marriage of Ferdinand II and Eleonora I Gonzaga in 1622, however, Italian influence became stronger, and the musical forms changed. Eleonora encouraged opera at court, founding a tradition that would outlive the dynasty. The third marriage of Ferdinand III, in 1651, brought another Mantuan princess to Vienna, Eleonora II Gonzaga, who dominated musical life in Vienna until her death in 1686.[73] In 1665 Lodovico Burnacini constructed a large theatre adjacent to the Hofburg, which was used for the festivities celebrating Leopold's marriage with Margaretha-Theresa. Despite the influence of Italian composers and musicians in court opera, the Germans were more important for instrumental and sacral music. Johann Heinrich Schmelzer, Heinrich Ignaz Biber, Johann Jakob Froberger, Johann Pachelbel, Georg Muffat and Johann Joseph Fux all worked for Habsburg courts, in Vienna and elsewhere.

Music was also used to project the image of the dynasty, and while court nobles performed for a small circle of their peers, professional musicians were employed for public performances. Public concerts and operas were more generally accessible. Similarly, Baroque opera had an enormous potential for conveying dynastic imagery, offering the public the art of emotion and illusion in a highly developed form.

In the outdoor festivals accompanying dynastic celebrations, huge temporary structures were erected, not only triumphal arches, but also whole landscapes, serving as backdrops for performances in which the court actively participated. These festivals could include entries, tournaments, carrousels, fireworks, performances by huge brass and woodwind ensembles, even battles with ships.[74] The festivities for Leopold's marriage to Margaretha-Theresa encompassed the whole range, and lasted from early December 1666 to the end of January 1667, only really ending with the performance of court composer Marc' Antonio Cesti's opera, *Il Pomo d'Oro* (The Golden Apple) more than a year later. Such manifestations often contained implicit, sometimes explicit, references to the rivalry between the Habsburgs and Bourbons, and were widely disseminated by the publication of illustrated descriptions. A rather surprised Passer noted that during the festivities to celebrate the coronation of Leopold's third wife, Eleonora of Pfalz Neuburg, as Queen of Hungary: 'no money is given out, no wine poured or spilled, no oxen roasted', suggesting that this was usually a common occurrence.[75]

These outdoor *Gesamtkunstwerke* were closely paralleled in religious processions and pilgrimages, and religious and dynastic imagery intertwined in the great dynastic festivals, particularly burials. Processions, however, were the most effective medium of Habsburg dynasticism. They often centered on the 'plague columns', such as those of 1679 on the Graben in Vienna, which depicted the emperor praying as intercessor for his peoples and realms, and thus by his devotion vanquishing the threat of the plague – and that other plague, the Ottomans.[76]

Thus, a certain pre-eminence in collecting and music may be granted; the strong connection with the Church, one of the main institutions 'moulding' cuture, is evident. Did the court's cultural example extend beyond this? Did it offer as conspicuous an example as the Italian courts? Italians long dominated the arts in the Habsburg lands, as they did in France. Both in France and in the Habsburg lands, the Italian hegemony slowly disappeared, and artists developed their own styles. The Italian language, however, was far stronger in Vienna than in Paris: Italian diplomats, or the chapel's *virtuosi,* had no need to learn German, for they could converse in Italian.[77] Could the Habsburg court set the standard either for court life in Germany, or for élite mores and behaviour in the Habsburg dominions?

In the seventeenth century the political and military conflicts between Austrian Habsburgs and Bourbon France were accompanied by a battle of images. The Empire had been the main battlefield, and the adoption either of a more 'Bourbon' or of a more 'Habsburg' courtly style could indicate where the princely household stood in relation to the contest. The success of Versailles may have been exaggerated, but it is difficult to find specific imitations of the Habsburg court. Many German households shared a medieval heritage with the Habsburg court, so similarities were not necessarily imitations. Nor can the High Baroque in South Germany be regarded as mere copying, even when the architects or artists had also worked in Vienna, as in the case of Johann Lucas von Hildebrandt. Bavaria, for example, closely linked to the emperor in the Thirty Years War, began to look towards France in the later seventeenth century, a time when several marriages with French princesses were contracted. Court culture and political alignment underwent a parallel development, and the mixture of Habsburg and Bourbon influences remained characteristic of the Wittelsbach court. In northern Germany, the rulers' Protestantism made the adoption of either model more complicated. The ambivalent outcome of the Habsburg–Bourbon contest confirmed that each dynasty was supreme in its own style. While Leopold I may not have been suited to the heroic imagery cultivated by Louis XIV, he surpassed the Sun King as an image of profound devotion. The influence of the imperial and French courts on German court life in the late seventeenth and early eighteenth centuries needs more research before the victor can be decided, and indeed the influence of a Protestant German model of court life must also be taken into account.

Could the solemn regiment of court ceremony offer a matrix for *politesse mondaine*? Deference can be part of both, and certain habits at court might be emulated elsewhere; but nothing suggests that court ceremony anywhere actually 'moulded' élite behaviour. Only if the court were the principal *salon* of the realm might it truly have acted as such an example; but the Habsburg court never aspired to such a role in this period. It was no breeding ground for fashionable *nouveautés*; it neither 'dictated' the style of its cosmopolitan élites, nor did it systematically strive to reorganize the cultural and scientific communities to further dynastic interests. We should be careful, moreover, not to confound general cultural influences and the more limited role of the different courts. As a rule, courts dominated only certain segments of culture, and then only for limited periods. Both the strong link with the Church, and the equally solid compact with the magnate caste suggested that the Habsburg court would remain aloof from suave brilliance. Above all, the Habsburgs were effective in turning their dominions into a bulwark of Roman Catholic piety, a role that sat uneasily with any attempt to appear the source of the *politesse mondaine* often associated with a libertine style. Moreover, in Vienna, patronage of the arts was not limited to the ruler, and the combined patronage of the magnates must easily have surpassed that of the emperor. Perhaps only in the scale and quality of their patronage of music did the emperors – particularly Leopold and Charles – retain supremacy. The splendour of the palaces of magnates such as the Liechtenstein, Schwarzenberg, Althan and Schönborn was no coincidence: they dominated Vienna as much as its Baroque churches dominated its skyline; and the Belvedere of Prince Eugen surpassed all, the emperor's residences included.

X. THE COURT AS LOCUS OF A COMPOSITE HERITAGE

The Habsburg dominions were ruled neither by a centralized bureaucracy nor by a centralized military establishment. Without a doubt, the most efficacious 'centralizing' agency was the court. It left the regional fabric intact while attracting the élites to a central forum. The court was the point of convergence for the dominions, but it shared this role with the magnates' palaces and the Church.

Notwithstanding tentative Prussian challenges and French successes in the Empire, the emperor remained the realm's foremost patron: nobles and talented *roturiers* alike flocked to his court to further their careers. Elites from Bohemia and the *Erblande* had long since found their way to Vienna, and their Hungarian peers soon followed. The cosmopolitan milieu powerfully stimulated the integrative role of the court, and while careers were not open to every talent, the amount of both geographical and social mobility fostered by the court from the last years of Rudolf II's reign through to the end of the seventeenth century is remarkable. Many of the outstanding names of Habsburg history in the eighteenth and nineteenth centuries rose to princely rank in this unsettled period. These families dominated court offices and the highest echelons of the administrative machinery. Their loyalty to the overarching idea of Habsburg rule, embodied in the court of Vienna, kept the assortment of otherwise unconnected territories together, partly because the nobles' prestige made the outlying regions more amenable to Vienna's authority. Finally, they added a lustre and conviviality to Viennese social life that the imperial court itself could not always offer.

While the court and its constellation of magnates acted as a magnet for those seeking opportunities for advancement, the intimate link between the Habsburgs and the Roman Catholic Church offered betterment in a more celestial category. During the seventeenth century service to the dynasty became closely equated with service to the Church. Habsburg rulers from Ferdinand II onwards actively fostered the Counter-Reformation, and this policy not only provided the restored Church with a powerful patron, but also endowed the ruler with a potent medium for the dynastic message. The lasting quest for a grand vision of Habsburg imperial rule, evident in the much censured efforts of Rudolf II, had reached a less heterodox and highly effective finale. The Habsburg dominions were permeated with a satiating fusion of dynastic and religious imagery.

The court in Vienna was smaller than its Spanish or French counterparts. Until the second half of the seventeenth century, it was often looked upon as the less eminent of the two Habsburg courts. After the Peace of Westphalia and the decline of the Spanish Habsburgs, the imperial court was often (and inappropriately) adversely compared to the norms and ideals of the triumphant French court of Louis XIV. The Habsburgs were at their worst when they tried to fight the French on French terms; they were strong when they remained true to the basic tenets of their rule.

The model of Versailles not only dominated courts from the late seventeenth century, it has also dominated

Belated magnificence: only by the 1750s had Schönbrunn – viewed here around 1760 – become the principal seat of the imperial court.

aulic history until today. Louis's propaganda, further embellished in memoirs and novels, imbued historians with a lopsided view of court life, at Versailles and elsewhere. We have thus not only to fill the gaps in recent research, but also to redress the bias inherent in its approach: religion was undoubtedly a stronger force than the older historiography has suggested, and not simply in Vienna; the ruler rarely meddled as actively in factional struggles at court as has been claimed. Finally, the cultural dominance of the court has been overrated – courts always had both accomplices and competitors for influence in many spheres. The example of the Austrian Habsburg court, always the counterpoint to the French model, can be instructive in reassessing the Ludovician heritage, and thus in conveying a more balanced approach to aulic history.

FLORVS ANGLO·BAVARICVS

LEODII APUD GUILIELMUM HENRICUM STREEL ANNO 1689

i. del Cour. del.

Hu. Spiesz fe.

CHAPTER SEVEN

The Duchy of Bavaria
THE COURTS OF THE WITTELSBACHS
*c.*1500-1750

RAINER BABEL

THE HISTORIAN WHO SETS OUT TO SKETCH THE COURT OF THE Dukes and (from 1621) Electors of Bavaria is faced with a body of research that remains patchy in many areas: despite important monographic studies of organizational and cultural issues,[1] and despite the impact of impressive recent exhibitions on the Wittelsbach dynasty and on some of its most outstanding representatives,[2] there is still no systematic treatment of the subject that takes into account the research perspectives of modern court studies.[3] There are very few studies that focus on an extended time period: Eberhard Straub's valuable study of the festival culture of the Munich court[4] has only recently been supplemented by the important work of an American historian on the social and ceremonial functions of court architecture.[5] We still do not know enough, however, about the internal social structures of the Bavarian court; relationships of patronage and clientage networks are still far too indistinct to permit us to construct a clear picture of the court's role as a political instrument and centre of power. This state of affairs imposes certain constraints upon a systematic survey of the history of the Bavarian court from the sixteenth to the eighteenth centuries – in view of the still incomplete state of the research on structural interconnections, brief indications of problem areas will often have to suffice. On the other hand, of course, courts always reflect the influence of sovereign personalities who seek to shape their material, ideological and social environments in accordance with their own conceptions.

Counter-Reformation piety: the frontispiece to a work published in 1685 commemorating the action of the Elector Maximilian II Emanuel (1679–1726) and his wife, Maria Antonia, daughter of the Emperor Leopold I, in founding an English College in Liège (one of the numerous prince-bishoprics controlled by the Wittelsbachs) to assist in the reconversion of Protestant England. The eagle symbolizes God favouring the project, while twin figures of Fame trumpet the virtue of the electoral couple. The achievement of arms impales Wittelsbach (left) and Habsburg (right).

A brief survey, focused on the reigns of the dukes and electors, will therefore sketch, at least in broad strokes, the background against which the development of the Bavarian court took place; it will also provide the framework for deeper reflection on the organization and society of the court.

I. THE DUKES AND ELECTORS OF BAVARIA AND THEIR COURT

'Among cities, even ducal seats of princes, which, like kings, are outstanding for their size and extent, she excels and out-dazzles [all] in her elegant cleanliness':[6] so Braun and Hogenberg characterized Munich in the 1576 edition of their *Civitates Orbis Terrarum* (Cities of the World). Their judgement reflects Munich's rise to become the pre-eminent city of all Bavaria in the half century that followed the ending of the territorial partition of the Wittelsbach lands in 1506. The process was in no way hindered by the fact that members of the ducal house maintained court establishments of their own elsewhere, as, for example, Duke (Herzog) Wilhelm V (1579–97) did in Landshut during his last decade as crown prince.[7] In 1576, however, Bavaria was under the rule of Duke Albrecht V (1550–79), an artistically minded prince and an important patron who had been largely responsible for the creation of the splendid court establishment that so impressed Braun and Hogenberg. Albrecht's interest in painting and sculpture and his collector's passion for all kinds of *objets d'art* prompted him to establish a separate Kunstkammer (or cabinet of art) and an Antiquarium (or gallery of classical art) to accommodate his acquisitions, measures that placed him – at least in the context of the Holy Roman Empire – at the forefront of contemporary developments.[8] Albrecht's interests also extended to the cultivation of court music: Orlando di Lasso was a resident at the Munich court from 1557, first as a singer, and later (from 1562) as director of the court chapel, an office that he retained until his death in 1594. Lasso, in turn, attracted a substantial number of Italian masters to the Bavarian court, among them musicians of the calibre of Andrea and Giovanni Gabrieli. The duke gave Lasso a relatively free hand in the selection of his musicians. While this helped to establish the court chapel, with its sixty-odd singers and instrumentalists and its additional complement of boy choristers, as a musical centre of European rank, it also devoured enormous sums of money, much to the exasperation of the Bavarian councillors entrusted with managing the ducal finances.[9]

In Wilhelm V (1579–97), the aesthetic and artistic preferences of the father lived on. After his marriage with Renata von Lothringen in 1568 he maintained a separate court establishment in the castle of Trausnitz, near Landshut, which had been renovated by the Munich court architect Friedrich Sustris. From here Wilhelm purchased courtly luxury goods, works of art and curiosities through the mediation of agents throughout Europe, and supported musical activity, theatre and social entertainments of all kinds.[10] But Wilhelm's personality was also marked by a strongly religious orientation: as early as the reign of Albrecht V, Bavaria had become one of the foremost powers of the Counter-Reformation within the Holy Roman Empire. As duke, his successor Wilhelm enthusiastically continued the measures for internal reform of the Catholic Church introduced by his father, and supported, above all, the further consolidation of the recently founded Jesuit Order, which acquired a college in Munich in 1559. The city's church of St Michael, with its attached Jesuit college, is striking evidence of Duke Wilhelm's esteem for the order. This religious policy in turn affected his attitude towards external relations, in which he consistently pursued a policy of seeking the appointment of members of his house to the great imperial bishoprics, thus considerably extending Bavaria's influence within the Empire. The most important consequence of these efforts was the acquisition of the archbishopric of Cologne for his younger brother, Duke Ernst, in 1583: thereafter the see came to constitute a kind of ecclesiastical 'right of the younger son', and was to remain in Wittelsbach hands until 1761. Yet, despite these undeniable successes, Wilhelm's government foundered on the

Princely piety: Elector Ferdinand Maria (1651–79) and his family, from the altarpiece by Antonio Zanchi (1631–1722) of St Cajetan's, Munich's court church, which was commissioned by the elector in 1662.

financial problems brought on by the enormous expenditure on the court and the civil administration (including, of course, the costs of foreign policy). After conceding a kind of co-regency to his son Maximilian in 1594, he withdrew from affairs of state in 1597, opting instead for a life of pious contemplation.

With the accession of Duke Maximilian I (1597–1651), educated and formed by the Jesuits, the most vigorous and long-lived of the Wittelsbach sovereigns took the stage.[11] By means of a thorough-going reform of the royal administration, Maximilian placed the instrumentalities of the royal government on a new footing, eventually even bringing the regime's financial crisis under control.[12] He took a major role in the Thirty Years War (1618–48), and, as the head of the Catholic League – the association of anti-Protestant princes of the Empire – he succeeded in playing an independent role *vis-à-vis* the emperor, with whom the specific territorial and dynastic interests of Bavaria tended to bring him into conflict.

The war also enabled Maximilian to achieve one of his central political goals, achieved provisionally in 1621 and permanently after the 1648 Peace of Westphalia: the acquisition for his own house of the electoral title that had formerly been held by the Palatine branch of the Wittelsbachs, the Protestant Electors Palatine of the Rhine. Maximilian ordered that weighty works of antiquarian research be compiled to enhance the reputation of his dynasty in general (whose imperial rank had to be emphasized, for example, by the reha-bilitation of his ancestor the Emperor Ludwig the Bavarian [1328–47]), and to support his bid for the electoral title in particular. Predictably, the scholarly authors came for the most part from the ranks of the Jesuits, men such as Jakob Keller and Johann Vervaux.[13]

Counter-Reformation religious culture suffused most aspects of court life. Like Maximilian I's scholarly champions, the poets Jakob Balde and Jakob Biedermann were also Jesuits and helped to shape the spiritual culture of the court.[14] Indeed, Maximilian's most pronounced character trait was a strict and genuinely felt religiosity, which expressed itself in, among other things, an ardent Marian piety. Among the visible signs of this veneration of the 'Patrona Boiariae' (or Patroness of Bavaria) were the placing of a statue of the Virgin on the western façade of the ducal *Residenz*, and the erection of a Marian devotional column on the

Schrannenplatz in central Munich.[15] The elector urged the city authorities to observe exemplary conduct in their religious observances. The magistracy of Munich, the city where the court was primarily based (the *Residenzstadt*), for example, was enjoined to participate in weekly Thursday religious processions; failure to comply resulted in substantial fines.[16] In the light of the present state of the research, the role of the court in shaping the forms and manifestations of religious life in the city can hardly be determined with any precision, but the strict regulation of life at the Munich court can certainly be detected in the notices of many contemporaries. In 1606, for example, a visitor from Holland described the members of the court as 'all temperate, strict in morals and upright; every vice is banned at this court; the prince hates drunkards, rascals and idlers; everything is directed to virtue, temperance and piety'.[17] A French envoy, the Abbé de Coulanges, expressed himself in similar terms only a few years later: 'there is no monastery where one lives with greater discipline and severity than at this court.'[18]

Notwithstanding the thrifty streak in his personality, Maximilian was always aware of the value of courtly representation and its implications for princely reputation. He systematically, indeed almost obsessively, pursued works by Albrecht Dürer, whom he held in extraordinarily high esteem, and in addition to paintings acquired valuable tapestries, jewels and carvings – as is clearly recorded in the reports of a favourite agent in the acquisition of works of art, the Augsburger Philipp Hainhofer.[19] On the other hand, it was characteristic of Maximilian's concept of his role as sovereign that he should withhold his artistic posses-sions from the eyes of the court, storing them in rooms to which he alone had access. He thereby 'distanced' himself from his entourage and further emphasized the remote and almost untouchable majesty of the prince. The duke dealt in a similar fashion with the precious reliquaries (the caskets containing relics of the saints) that he acquired: appropriate sanctuaries within the res-idence were found for these in the form of the Reiche Kapelle (the Rich Chapel, so called for the sumptuous-ness of its decoration, completed in 1607), and the Kammergalerie (completed in 1608).

Under Maximilian's son, Ferdinand Maria (1651–79), there was a loosening of the pious strictures that had hitherto determined the character of the court, a change for which Ferdinand's consort, the Electoral Princess Henriette Adelaide of the House of Savoy (1636–76), was also in part responsible.[20] The rather constrained entertainments that had taken place at court during the lifetime of Maximilian's widow, the Habsburg Dowager Princess Maria Anna (1610–65) – even during Carnival, the period immediately preceding the start of Lent, festivities were seldom permitted to last beyond midnight – were less regimented once Henriette Adelaide had begun to set the tone for the ducal household. The Carnival now became the occasion for a cycle of festivities extending over several weeks. Similarly, in the second half of the seventeenth century there was a markedly increased interest in the Italian opera, first introduced to Munich under Maximilian. In 1671 a troop of actors was established at the court to perform French comedy, an arrangement that was done away with after the death of the electoral princess in 1676, but renewed under her son, Maximilian II Emanuel (1679–1726).

The focus of the court's social life began to shift visibly beyond the margins of the city into the countryside: on the Starnberg Lake the *bucintoro*, designed on the model of the Venetian ship of state, served as a backdrop for festivities and social occasions.[21] In political terms, Ferdinand Maria sought a closer involvement with France with a view to safeguarding the political opportunities that had arisen from the treaty he had signed with the Habsburgs in 1646, under the terms of which the Wittelsbachs were conceded the right of accession to the imperial throne in the event that there should be no male heir to the House of Habsburg. The first son of Emperor Leopold (1657–1705), Joseph, was not born until 1688, and in the interim the Wittelsbachs held out hopes of supplanting the Habsburgs as the premier dynasty of the Empire.

The relation between these two great Catholic Houses of the Empire, the Wittelsbachs and the Habsburgs, oscillated between amity and rivalry. Elector Maximilian II Emanuel (1679–1726) moved back at first to the emperor's side, serving him as a genuinely able commander in the Turkish Wars from 1683. His marriage in 1685 to the emperor's eldest daughter, Maria Antonia, regarded by many as the heiress of the childless King Charles II of Spain, opened up the further prospect of inheriting the Spanish Netherlands, or possibly even the entire

Spanish patrimony – notwithstanding that Maria Antonia was required to renounce this upon her marriage. With this in prospect, the electorate developed close links with the Spanish branch of the Habsburgs. From 1692 to 1701 Max Emanuel acted as Carlos II of Spain's viceroy in Brussels (the seat of government in the Spanish Netherlands), and when Carlos II appointed the elector's son, Ferdinand Joseph, as his own universal heir in 1698, the prospects of the House of Wittelsbach seemed even more splendid. These dynastic hopes were dashed, however, by the sudden death of Ferdinand Joseph, and the disappointed elector switched back from a pro-Spanish diplomatic stance to the side of France, which now promised him, among other things, the retention of the Spanish Netherlands.

In the short term, however, this change of allegiance was a disaster for the dynasty. Driven out of Bavaria by Austrian troops during the War of the Spanish Succession that followed Carlos II's death in 1700, Max Emanuel was only able to return to Bavaria from French exile at the end of the war in 1714; he had never relinquished his hope of acquiring a royal crown, even if this had to be achieved through the exchange of his hereditary lands.

His plans for territorial aggrandizement having failed, the elector's dynastic ambitions found expression in building; and he achieved more in this sphere, most notably through the construction of Schleissheim Palace, than as an art collector or patron, although he was certainly no stranger to these aspects of courtly aesthetics.[22] Generally speaking, Max Emanuel's conception of his own role was permeated with that 'charismatic sense of divine legitimacy' within which the representative function of the court was regarded as essential to the self-presentation of the monarch; it was thus these aspects of the court's role that he tended most actively to reinforce.[23]

It is doubtless true that the impact of the French influences introduced under Ferdinand Maria and Henriette Adelaide on the life of the Munich court during the mid seventeenth century increased under Max Emanuel in the decades before 1700: French comedy and courtly ballet on the French model became permanent features, and there was a rise in the volume of luxury goods consumed at court that had been purchased in Paris.[24] The elector was familiar with the châteaux of Louis XIV and drew inspiration from them for his own building projects. As he remarked in a letter sent to Paris after his final return to Munich in 1715: 'I spend all my time in my summer residences, and I am able to imitate French taste in châteaux and gardens, but the people remain the same.'[25]

Max Emanuel's successor, Karl Albrecht (1726–45), inherited the dynastic ambitions of his father, who in 1714 had secured French support for a Wittelsbach succession to the imperial throne in the event that the Habsburgs should die out in the male line;[26] and after the death of the Emperor Charles VI in 1740 this contingency eventually materialized. The Elector Karl Albrecht duly refused to recognize the succession of the young Maria Theresa, the Habsburg claimant; instead, backed by French and Prussian help, he marched into the Habsburg lands, where he had himself recognized as Archduke of Austria and crowned as King of Bohemia – in other words, the lawful heir to the Habsburg patrimony. But by January 1742, when Karl Albrecht was elected Emperor Charles VII in Frankfurt, the tide of support for the Wittelsbach claim had already begun to turn within the Empire. In retaliation, as early as February 1742 Maria Theresa occupied the Duchy of Bavaria, preventing Karl Albrecht's return until the end of 1744, within a few months of his death in January 1745.

The Wittelsbach attempt to claim the imperial throne had proved to be a fiasco. By the treaty of Füssen, Karl Albrecht's son, Maximilian III Joseph (1745–77) formally recognized Maria Theresa's right of succession to the Habsburg patrimonial lands, and promised to use his electoral vote to support the election of her spouse, Franz Stephan of Lorraine, as the new emperor. The dynastic illusions nurtured by Max Emanuel and Karl Albrecht were thus irrevocably lost: within the Empire, Bavaria returned for the rest of the century to the role of a distinctly middling, though by no means insignificant, power.

II. THE COURT ESTABLISHMENT: ORGANIZATION AND CEREMONIAL

At every point in its development, from the sixteenth to the eighteenth centuries, the institutional and social character of the court faithfully reflected the political standing of the Bavarian princes and the strength of their personal patronage. With a court establishment (or Hofstaat) that already encompassed some 866 persons in 1571,[27] the household of the Bavarian dukes was among the most substantial in the Holy Roman Empire, and even bore comparison with the imperial court in Vienna.[28] Its expansion had been rapid: some sixty years earlier, in 1508, the Munich court had comprised only 162 members, and the crucial phases of development can be clearly identified as having taken place in the second half of the century. By 1552 the number of court members had risen to 384; only four years later, however, in 1556, it had grown to 485, a number that was almost to double again over the following fifteen years.

This growth of the court establishment and the high costs it incurred had always prompted reservations and protests from the ducal councillors and the territorial Estates (or representative assemblies), and these were sometimes seconded by attempts at regulation. For the historian concerned with reconstructing the court's history, these protests constitute a singular stroke of luck, for the sources generated thereby shed extensive light on the costs and structure of the court: the memoranda, for example, of councillors entrusted with assessing the financial condition of the territory; or court decrees that sought, on the insistence of the Estates, to stem the flood of expenditure. Sources of this kind reflect distinct stages in the court's evolution and offer far more insight than official court lists could ever provide into its internal diversification and the dynamics of its growth.[29]

In view of the fact that the court and the 'administration' were not yet separate, the figure from 1571 also reflects the development of a Bavarian 'machinery of the state' and the expansion of the central government. Under Albrecht V (1550–79), the administrative bodies based at the court were reorganized. The traditional Court Council (Hofrat), which assisted the duke in administrative and, above all, in legislative matters, was now joined by the Chamber (Hofkammer) as the body specifically responsible for the administration of finances, and by an ecclesiastical council (Geistlicher Rat) responsible for the exercise of the duke's territorial rights over the Church. For the first time, the Court Council, headed by the highest-ranking court official, the major domo (Obersthofmeister), began to

Fame and architectural splendour: a bird's-eye view of the Munich Residenz, *looking east, by Michael Wening, c.1700. The figure of Fame (upper right), with her twin trumpets, announces the 'renown' that has been won for the dynasty through its architectural 'magnificence'.*

take on a more sharply defined role. It now brought together selected members of the other councils, who sat with the leading figures in the household establishment.[30] This interweaving of household and administration can also be seen in the fact that the Hofrat also included, in addition to the trained jurists of the 'scholars' bench', a number of noble holders of high court offices from the 'knightly bench'. Their household responsibilities generally claimed more of their time and commitment than did their participation in the Hofrat, and for this reason Duke Maximilian I (1598–1651) saw fit to free the members of the Court Council from most of their household duties; in the reign of Maximilian a clearer division between the court, on the one hand, and the state, on the other, certainly began, although there was, as

elsewhere, never an absolutely neat distinction between the two spheres.[31] Household and bureaucracy were at least nominally distinct.

The surviving figures for the sample years 1511, 1550 and 1595 indicate that the members of the ducal 'bureaucracy' constituted the smaller contingent within the personnel of the court. Thus, the number of council members given for these respective dates rose from sixteen to twenty-two to forty-five; the number of secretaries rose from four to eight to twelve; and the number of clerks rose from twenty in 1552 to a total of forty at the end of the century.[32] It is, thus, clear that the explosive growth in court personnel during the sixteenth century took place, above all, in the domain of household service proper: the immediate domestic entourage of the prince.

The chivalric cult: a tournament, with running at the ring, in the Brunnenhof of the Munich Residenz, in the 1610s.

The figures show that the period of Albrecht V – the third quarter of the sixteenth century – was by far the greatest period of expansion of the court establishment. In addition to increases in hunt, stable, kitchen and cellar staff, the second half of the century was characterized by the creation of new household departments. Thus, a new ducal bodyguard was established; and the fact that chamberlains of noble birth, valets, doormen, messengers and so on swelled the ranks of the court personnel in such great numbers points clearly to an increasing differentiation and regulation of the everyday life of the court in this period. The increasingly frequent mentions of painters, sculptors and craftsmen of various kinds in the court accounts provide additional evidence for the intensification of the court's artistic sponsorship and patronage.[33]

Naturally, the costs of the court rose in proportion to increases in the size of its membership. Wage payments to members of the household were by no means the largest item, although they rose during the second half of the sixteenth century from around 13,000 florins in 1550 to approximately 60,000 florins in 1590. The administrative side proved to be especially costly: one third of all money spent as ducal expenditure on the court went to members of the central administrative bodies. Another significant element in these costs was the court's choral establishment (*Kantorei*), which

alone accounted for some twenty per cent of all wage payments. The largest costs, however, were generated by the household itself: by the ducal stables and through the provision, free of charge, to members of the court of various benefits in kind: board and clothing to court servants, and expenditure on the court kitchens, cellars and for the workshops of the court tailors. This element of expenditure shot up from 50,000 florins in 1550 to some 120,000 in 1590.[34]

Critical voices repeatedly warned of the malign consequences that resulted from this explosion in court costs. As early as 1557 a delegation of ducal councillors had openly criticized the prince's handling of the courtly finances. In the face of repeated claims by the profligate Duke Albrecht that courtly expenditure was essential to the maintenance of his princely 'reputation', they denounced the excess of 'superfluous clothing, jewels, ornaments and eating, drinking and other sensual pleasures', and reminded the duke of his sovereign obligation to see to the welfare of his subjects.[35] At the same time they demanded that ducal subjects be given preferential treatment in appointments to court offices, right down to the rank of valet – an important indication, given the absence of any systematic studies of the social composition of the Munich household, that the court was already very attractive to foreigners at this time.[36]

But the self-confident Duke Albrecht V was not the man to yield to such demands, and in the following years the cost of the court continued to attract criticism from councillors and from the Estates. In addition to demanding reductions in the court establishment, critics repeatedly recommended that the provision of meals for courtiers be replaced by a system of allowances. Above all, it was urged that expenditure on antiquities, art and building works, as well as that on the musical, wardrobe and hunting establishments, should all be reduced. A memorandum of 1571 went even further, demanding a reduction in the apparently frequent sojourns of the court outside Munich, since these greatly increased the costs of the ducal entourage's upkeep and transportation. When Duke Albrecht died in 1579, having continued to hold out against any serious reduction in the costs of his representational activities, the territorial Estates immediately presented his son, Wilhelm V, with their long-standing complaints, and demanded cuts to

expenditure in all the areas complained of in 1571. In response, Wilhelm instituted economies, and by 1586 had succeeded in cutting costs by twenty per cent, particularly by reducing the much-criticized choral establishment and the ducal bodyguard.

These measures notwithstanding, the total number of court personnel did not sink below 700 at any time before the end of the sixteenth century. There was, in other words, no substantial diminution of the size of the court as it stood in 1571.[37] This suggests that even the sincerest intentions on the sovereign's part to reduce expenditure were not in themselves sufficient to reverse the growth of the court. Its role as an employer and a means of social advancement, and its significance for trade and manufacture in the residential city (both of which depended to a considerable extent on commissions from the court), all stood in the way of effective reductions. In any case, a curtailment of the representational aspect of the 'court' was no longer reconcilable with the prince's conception of his own role. This was true not only of Albrecht V, but also of a statesman as thriftily inclined as Maximilian I (1597–1651). Maximilian may have sought to achieve savings in court expenditure, but he made no far-reaching changes to the size of the court: in the year 1615 it is reported to have comprised no fewer than 770 persons.[38]

In contrast to this pattern of steady growth, the evidence for the increase in the overall size of the Bavarian court is far less consistent for the seventeenth century, but it is beyond doubt that its significance remained undiminished. Indeed it kept pace with the growing political importance of the territory as a whole, whose sovereign acquired the electoral title in 1621, despite the reduction in court size that appears to have occurred during the Thirty Years War.[39] When Elector Maximilian Emanuel returned to Bavaria in 1701 after his governorship in the Spanish Netherlands, he is said to have been followed by a court establishment of around 2,000 persons.[40] This was a scale of entourage that exceeded purely Bavarian resources and requirements. In 1705, however, there were still no fewer than 1,030 court members; for 1738 as many as 1,340; and for 1781 some 2,140. These figures document a renewed expansion of the court establishment during the eighteenth century, an expansion whose exact contours can be clearly

discerned in a newly emerging primary source – the court calendar.[41] Naturally, caution is advised when making comparisons with figures reported for other court establishments, since such statistics are not necessarily calculated according to the same criteria. However, if one considers developments in Bavaria from the 1500s to the 1780s against the general

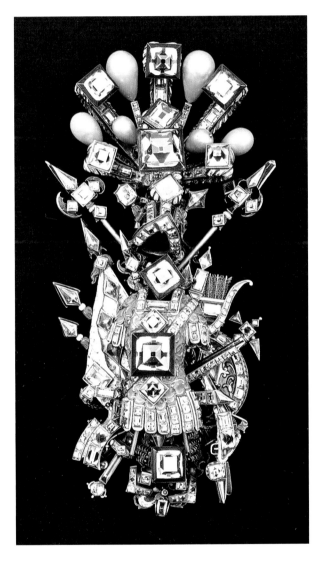

The glorification of war: Roman weapons, cuirass and helmet, set as an agraffe (or hat jewel) for Duke Maximilian I; pearls, diamonds and rubies in enamelled gold. Dated 1603, it was probably made by the Augsburg goldsmith Georg Beuerl for the susbstantial fee of 1,300 florins. It was one of the items added by Maximilian to Albrecht V's list of inalienable heirlooms of the ducal house.

background of its potential competitors, then the general trend would seem towards the establishment of a court that, in the size and the magnificence of its household, could compete with all the greater princely and electoral courts of the Reich.[42]

Like most other princely households, the Bavarian household had been organized since medieval times according to a strict hierarchy at whose apex stood the bearers of the highest court offices. The highest titular officer was the major domo (*Obersthofmeister*), who generally also held the institutionally separate office of territorial steward (*Landeshofmeister*). It was he who presided over the Hofrat, or Court Council, and he was followed in rank by the high chamberlain (*Oberstkämmerer*, or head of the electoral household), then by the senior chancellor (*Oberstkanzler*) and by the master of the horse (*Oberststallmeister*) – the latter an office that was only created under Albrecht V in conscious imitation of the example set by 'other high-ranking princes'.[43] The separate households of the electoral princess and of the princes were headed by a major domo and a separate steward respectively.[44]

The highest court offices were continuously in the hands of a few influential native noble families; and with a few exceptions this is also true for the official functions of the master of the kitchens (*Oberstküchenmeister*), the chamberlain of the plate (*Oberstsilberkämmerer*) and the director of the court opera (a post established in 1655). The functions of the post of gentleman of the Chamber and chamberlain (*Kammerherr* and *Kämmerer*), whose task was originally to wait personally upon the prince and to fulfil various ceremonial functions in the course of the day, gradually became an honorary title reserved for members of the nobility and liberally bestowed; it eventually involved very little in the way of real court service. While there were hardly more than a dozen persons who bore the title of chamberlain at the beginning of the seventeenth century, that number had risen to around 130 within a few decades; and by the end of the eighteenth century it stood at more than 400.[45]

Apart from supplying the highest court officers, the interest of the indigenous nobility in life at court tended to be limited, at least in the sixteenth and early seventeenth centuries. At the beginning of the sixteenth century, the Bavarian chronicler Aventin had remarked in his *Description of the Customs of the*

Country: 'the nobility lives on the countryside outside the city, passes its time with hounds, and hunting; and does not ride to court except to do service and receive payment there.'[46] Economic motives played a certain role here: after a brief spell of service on the Court Council, most of its aristocratic members returned to the management of their estates, or switched from the central government to more lucrative administrative positions in the hinterland.[47] At the territorial Diet of 1612, the poor remuneration of court service was still a cause of explicit complaint. For legally trained non-noble subjects, on the other hand, service in court councils was a channel of upward social mobility that could lead, in the best case, to ennoblement, and a number of Munich bourgeois families succeeded in entering the nobility in this way.[48]

Noble interest in court service increased after the 1620s when estate incomes plummeted as a result of the Thirty Years War; but urban patricians, nobles of recent title or foreign origin, as well as a few members of the bourgeoisie, remained the predominant group within the bureaucratic structure. From the second half of the seventeenth century and into the eighteenth century, however, the Bavarian court became a central focal point, even for those noble families who were not dependent upon princely service. In this respect the Bavarian experience reflected more general developments.[49] One indicator of this transformation is the growing presence of noble palaces in the environs of the residential city. If the nobility had been relatively poorly represented among property owners in the city during the sixteenth century,[50] this had changed fundamentally by the end of the seventeenth century: of the 235 houses of the Kreuzviertel surrounding the electoral residence, a large proportion were in noble hands by around 1700.[51]

The organization of Munich court life was, of course, open to a variety of influences. In so far as the state of research permits us to judge, it would seem that the gravitational pull of the imperial courts in Vienna and Prague was greater than that of any other. But at Munich there was also interest in the other lesser European princely courts, to many of which the Bavarian ducal house was tied by blood or by marriage, among them the courts of Lorraine, Turin (Savoy), Mantua, Ferrara and the Saxon electoral court in Dresden. These establishments often supplied the

A display goblet of enamelled gold by Hans Reimer, made in Munich in 1562 for the Schatzkammer *of Duke Albrecht V (whose arms appear in the central cartouche). Pieces such as this were displayed before members of the court on the buffet when the duke dined in state in the Ritterstube. At other times, however, access to the finest* Schatzkammer *treasures could be a privilege conferred by the ruler as a mark of favour to an inner-court élite.*

standards by which contemporaries judged court life in Munich.[52] Moreover, the exchange of personnel between these courts guaranteed a certain degree of interconnection. It was not unusual for court servants to come to Munich from service posts at other courts.[53]

In its ceremonial organization the rituals of Bavarian court life, like those of most German princely courts from the sixteenth century onwards, were modelled closely on imperial court etiquette. These, in turn, drew extensively on what became known as the 'Spanish court ceremonial' (*Spanisches Hofzeremoniell*), which, in its turn, seems to have been largely derived from the Use prevailing in the Habsburg Duchy of Burgundy at the beginning of the sixteenth century. With regard to the person of the prince, the most striking feature of the Spanish Use was the clear distinction it drew between the sphere of the prince's public performance and the sphere of his private living, which remained hidden from view.[54] This separation of functions was of major importance to the monarchical self-image of a man such as Maximilian I (1597–1651); hence the construction of specific refuges within the *Residenz*, such as the Reiche Kapelle (with its precious reliquaries) in 1607, to which, as we have seen, only the duke himself had access.

While it is true that there was a growth in Italian and particularly in French influences on Bavaria from the middle of the seventeenth century, this did not result in any thorough-going changes to the Bavarian courtly style. At no point was the person of the sovereign or his immediate surroundings opened to public view in the virtually unlimited sense exemplified by the French model. Whereas the palace of Versailles could be entered by practically anyone who wished, admission to the Munich *Residenz* was strictly regulated. Unlike at the Bourbon court, where the private chambers of the monarch were opened in his absence to the gaze of the curious, the private apartments of the electoral family were sanctuaries to which even select circles had only partial access. In the reign of Maximilian, the rituals of *Ankleiden* and *Abziehen* – the terms employed in the Munich (as in the imperial) court ordinances of the sixteenth and seventeenth centuries for the French *lever* and the *coucher* – took place in the presence of only a very small number of courtiers, who assisted the prince according to a strict etiquette. The circle of persons involved in these ceremonies expanded considerably in the middle decades of the eighteenth century, as a result of the court ordinances issued by Maximilian III Joseph (1745–77) in 1766 and 1769; but the process never showed any sign of taking on the public character of the Versailles *lever* and *coucher*.[55] Public dining by the prince or the princely family was confined to particular occasions and took place in the Rittersube or Hall of Knights, and thus had the character of a high act of state.[56] In general, however, the prince's dining was a private affair, with meals taken in the inner areas of the ducal apartments, most often in the bedchamber.[57]

III. COURT ARCHITECTURE AND ITS SOCIAL FUNCTIONS: THE RESIDENZ

From the early sixteenth century, the usual seat of the Bavarian court and the context for its social life was the *Residenz*, or Residential Palace, in Munich, which had gradually emerged as the amalgamation of several distinct building complexes.[58] The dukes had initially resided in the Alte Hof, or Old Court, built on the north-eastern wall of the town in the second half of the thirteenth century, but this structure was soon enveloped by the rapidly expanding city. The dukes, whose relations with the citizenry were often strained, constructed a further castle in the 1380s known as the Neue Veste or Neuveste on the new city wall, which provided them with an unimpeded point of entry to and exit from the town. An agreement secured by the citizenry stipulated none the less that the court was forbidden to settle there; the duke, moreover, was permitted to enter the new complex with only a limited number of companions.

Only under Duke Wilhelm IV (1508–50) was the Neuveste finally established as the seat of the ducal court and the core of the *Residenz*, the exterior of which was completed more than a century later under Maximilian I. Among the building initiatives launched by Wilhelm IV was the construction of the so-called Rundstubenbau on the foundations of a bastion of the former fortified wall in the south-eastern corner of the Neuveste, as well as the Georgskapelle (St George's

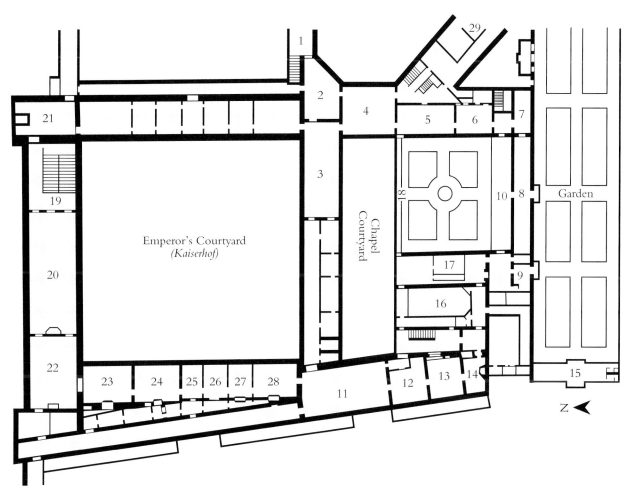

The piano nobile, *or principal floor, of the Munich* Residenz, *c.1630–58. 1. Staircase; 2. Anteroom; 3. Herkules-Saal.* ELECTOR'S APARTMENTS: *4. Ritterstube; 5. Antechamber; 6. Audience Chamber; 7. Zimmer; 8. Chamber Gallery (Kammergalerie); 9. Bedchamber; 10. Terrace.* ELECTRESS'S APARTMENTS: *11. Tafelstube; 12. First Anteroom; 13. Second Anteroom; 14. Bedchamber; 15. Gallery.* OTHER STATE ROOMS: *16. The Court Chapel; 17. Reiche Kapelle; 18. Gläsernes Gängl; 19. Emperor's Staircase; 20. Emperor's Presence Chamber (Kaisersaal); 21. Hall; 29. Antiquarium wing.* EMPEROR'S APARTMENTS: *22. Ritterstube; 23. Antechamber; 24. Audience Chamber; 25. Bedchamber; 26. Zimmer der Ewigkeit; 27. Zimmer der Religion; 28. Zimmer der Kirche.*

Chapel), separated from the Neuveste by the pleasure garden to the east of the complex.

The alterations made to the construction of the palace during the reign of Duke Albrecht V kept pace with the general expansion of the role of court life in Munich. New storeys were added to the Rundstubenbau under the supervision of the court architect, Wilhelm Egkl, and between 1558 and 1562 it was connected with the Georgskapelle by way of the

St George's Hall (*Georgssaal*) with its rich decorations and coffered ceiling. The result was the first space constructed specifically for court festivities; it was here that the celebrations marking the marriage of Wilhelm, heir to the Bavarian throne, and Renata (1544–1602), daughter of the Duke of Lorraine, took place in 1568.

Of all the German princes, Albrecht was the first to erect buildings specifically for the purpose of housing his art treasures. Between 1563 and 1567 a building was completed to the north of the Alte Hof whose second storey served as a *Kunstkammer* where paintings and other *objets d'art* were housed. In close proximity to the Neuveste, construction work began in 1568 on the Antiquarium, a free-standing, two-storey building that was intended to accommodate Albrecht's library together with his collection of classical statues. Albrecht's son Wilhelm V (1579–97), made his contribution to the expansion of the *Residenz* by adding new building complexes to meet the requirements of the ducal family. He moved his own living quarters out of the Neuveste and settled provisionally in the upper storey of the Antiquarium – with the result that a new building had to be built to house the library. In 1581 he commissioned his court architect Friedrich Sustris to construct a residential complex adjoining the western side of the Antiquarium, which consisted of three wings enclosing the Grottenhof (or Grotto courtyard) to the north. To the south of the main wing, the so-called Gartenbau, the palace garden (also known as the Hofgarten), was laid out, bordered on the western side by further buildings for Wilhelm's mother Anna (the Witwenbau), and for the heir to the throne, Maximilian, who returned from his studies in Ingolstadt in 1593. Construction of the Hofdamenstock (Ladies in Waiting Wing) opposite the residential complex and the Grottenhof was probably also begun during the reign of Wilhelm V. And on the old walls of the Neuveste at the south-eastern end of the entire complex, a covered tennis court was built to house the ball games that had become so popular with the Bavarian court.

However, the Munich *Residenz* really took on its definitive outward appearance only in the early seventeenth century under Wilhelm's son Maximilian.[59] In the first decade of his rule the strained condition of the ducal finances obliged the young duke to confine himself to elaborating the interior of the existing buildings. In order to extend his wife's apartments in the west wing of the residential complex, he had the Erbprinzenbau demolished. Maximilian's own apartments were situated in the southern wing of the residential complex, between the palace garden and the Grottenhof; and in 1608, as we have seen, the duke built the Kammergalerie, a free-standing building in which selected paintings and objects were displayed for the delectation of the prince and his especially favoured guests.[60]

Entering Maximilian's apartments, the visitor was led through two reception rooms: an entrance hall was followed by the Herkules-Saal, which had probably been completed by the end of Wilhelm's reign (1597), but was later substantially altered by Maximilian, who raised the ceiling by one storey and furnished the room with a decorative scheme eulogizing the dynasty. The history of the House of Wittelsbach and the deeds of its dukes provided the theme for the decoration in the upper portion of the walls; below were hung tapestries illustrating the legend of Hercules. The Herkules-Saal was used for the staging of public ceremonies and also doubled as a guardroom. All guests who gained entry to the palace on the grounds of their status or for the purpose of a visit could proceed this far. In order to gain entry to the adjoining Ritterstube, which in effect functioned as a first antechamber, one had to belong to a more exclusive circle. In other respects, however, the Ritterstube still doubled as a space that had 'public' functions: as the setting for the elector's 'dining in state', and as the place where the bodies of deceased members of the ducal family lay in state.[61]

The erection of the Kaiserhofbau (Emperor's Wing) in 1612 inaugurated the last significant extension of the *Residenz* before the nineteenth century. This consisted of three further wings added to the already existing Hofdamenstock. The western range housed a suite of rooms that were to be kept for the exclusive use of the emperor on the occasion of his visits to Munich, and were thus known as the Kaiserzimmer. Further rooms in the eastern wing provided accommodation for other princes passing through Munich (these came to be known as the Trierzimmer after a long sojourn at the Munich court by the Archbishop of Trier). The north wing was dominated by the two-storey Kaisersaal (or Emperor's Chamber) decorated with allegorical paintings, to which was attached a smaller festive hall – known on account of its iconography as the Vierschimmelsaal (the Four Horses' Hall).

The outward appearance of the *Residenz* complex that had evolved over several centuries was now harmonized through extensive alterations. The demolition of the Pallas and Silver Tower of the old Neuveste removed the last traces of medieval defensive

The Enlightenment domestication of majesty: the electoral families of Bavaria and Saxony enjoying the amusements of the haute bourgeoisie, *by Peter Jakob Horemans, 1761. The Elector Maximilian III Joseph of Bavaria (1745–77) plays cards at the red-draped table; his wife, Electress Maria Anna Sophia, pours coffee into a saucer (at the table, right); while his Wittelsbach uncle, Archbishop-Elector Clemens August of Cologne, plays the cello. The older iconography of 'sacred' authority has all but disappeared.*

architecture still attaching to the *Residenz*; and the interlinking of the individual building complexes produced an organized series of enclosed courts and gardens. Contemporaries now saw the residence as an architectural ensemble of impressive diversity, and even the hostile Swedish king, Gustavus Adolphus, who reached Munich with his troops during the Thirty Years War, could not conceal his admiration. In an unpublished manuscript dating from 1644, Baldassare Pistorini described the *Residenz* as an imperial, rather

than a ducal, palace – a city in miniature – and in its architectural scale the palace gave expression to the Wittelsbachs' ambitions of exercising a leading, and possibly imperial, role within the Empire.[62]

Maximilian's successors did not make any far-reaching changes to the architectural structure of the *Residenz*, but confined themselves largely to modifications of the interior. In 1664, for example, when Henriette Adelaide of Savoy, the spouse of Elector Ferdinand Maria, ordered the extension and redecoration of the apartments of the electoral princess, they were modelled in part on the ducal palace in her home city of Turin. Further innovations included the addition, in around 1667, of a suite of 'antechambers' (incorporating the former apartments of the recently deceased dowager princess) whose central point was the newly created Golden Hall, which henceforth served as an audience chamber.[63]

Electors Max Emanuel (1679–1726) and Karl Albrecht (1726–45) turned their attention above all to the private apartments of the prince. Between 1680 and 1685 Max Emanuel had the living quarters of his predecessors redecorated with motifs from the life of Alexander the Great and thus created the suite of the so-called Alexanderzimmer. The Antiquarium and the residential complex were joined by a short connecting wing that housed audience chambers as well as rooms for work and private use. Towards the end of his life, Max Emanuel even conceived a plan to convert the electoral apartments into comfortable winter quarters. After his death, his son Karl Albrecht commissioned Joseph Effner to continue this work, but the rooms were destroyed by a devastating fire shortly before their completion in 1729. François Cuvilliés the elder lost no time in resuming this work; the result was the so-called Reichen or Schönen Zimmer (sumptuous or beautiful rooms), which Jakob Burckhardt, that exacting critic, described as 'the most splendid Rococo on earth'.[64]

With the construction of Karl Albrecht's Grand Apartments in 1726–33, the expansion of the electoral quarters had reached its fullest extent. A further differentiation could be observed with regard to the social function of the individual rooms. While the antechambers and the audience chambers were accessible to appropriately qualified members of the court, the electoral apartments – in particular, the cabinets and bedchambers – could only be entered by family members, close confidants and the personal servants and chamberlains of the elector, or by special invitation.

Only at the beginning of the seventeenth century, under Maximilian I, did the subdivision of the electoral apartments become more clearly defined: the Ritterstube opened onto an antechamber, an audience chamber, a withdrawing room, and the bedchamber, with the door from the Ritterstube marking the boundary between the public and the private. When the elector wished to dress, he moved from his bedchamber into the neighbouring room and rang for the servants waiting in the adjacent antechamber. This custom of positioning a sequence of three rooms in front of the bedchamber was also observed when the electoral apartments were extended through the construction of the Alexander Rooms under Max Emanuel. The room that been called a withdrawing room under Maximilian I was now termed an 'inner' audience chamber or Great Cabinet, in which private audiences, conferences involving small circles of the most trusted associates, or even family gatherings could be held. It was here that Max Emanuel received Eugen of Savoy; and the banquet that followed also took place in this room. When the 'sumptuous rooms' were built under Karl Albrecht between the late 1720s and 1739, the Great Cabinet was retained as a generic space, but was shifted to the south wing of the residential complex to make way for a new Green Gallery, which also functioned as an audience chamber. The number of other audience chambers was also increased. The first, or outer, audience chamber was now followed by a Great Audience Chamber, an arrangement that permitted finer grading in the attribution of social rank. Reception in these inner audience chambers could be used to bestow distinction upon senior-ranking envoys.

Max III Joseph, who famously returned Bavarian policy in the second half of the eighteenth century to a more realistic path than those pursued by his grandfather and father, nevertheless continued to use the Grand Apartments in accordance with their traditional public and social functions, but drew an even sharper line between the public and the private spheres by retaining the private quarters that he had occupied as crown prince above the Antiquarium. His reign saw the erection of the opera house (later known as the Old *Residenz* Theatre), built by François Cuvilliés in 1750–55, to the south-east of the Antiquarium and the Brunnenhof. This building was needed after fire – the third and last great fire in the *Residenz* – broke out in the Neuveste and spread to the *Residenz* in 1750, destroying St George's Hall, which had housed a court theatre since 1740. The first Munich opera house had been built on the Salvatorplatz as early as 1655, but Cuvilliés's opera house was the first theatre building to be incorporated within the *Residenz*.

It was under Elector Max Emanuel, too, that French-derived forms of courtly sociability, which had already established themselves in the electoral private chambers, began to take root in the conduct of the Munich court as a whole. In Versailles, Louis XIV had begun to invite the court to the so-called *appartements* on two or three evenings a week; these were occasions for the informal enjoyment of card games, music and dance where, according to the Duc de Saint-Simon, courtiers were free to do, or not to do, whatever they wished.[65] The first evidence of such *appartements* in Munich dates from the 1680s;[66] and although the sources yield only scanty information, one can be certain that the *appartements* generally took place in the quarters of the elector, or occasionally in the those of the electoral princess – and thus, in both cases, within the 'private' zone of the palace. During Max Emanuel's reign part of the Alexander Rooms, which looked out on to the Grottenhof, were presumably used for this purpose; and, after these were demolished by Karl Albrecht to make way for the new Grand Apartments, the Green Gallery at the threshold to the Antiquarium became the venue for the *appartements*.

The change in venue did not, however, mark a change in their exclusivity. According to a court ordinance of 1769, access to the *appartements* was restricted to those members of the court who were *kammermessig*: in other words, those who were permitted to enter the antechambers of the elector and the electoral princess. No one below the rank of chamberlain or gentleman of the Chamber was permitted to take part in the card games or to place themselves in the immediate proximity of the electoral family.[67]

In other respects, the early decades of the eighteenth century marked a relaxation of the rigid rules of the Spanish etiquette. At the beginning of the century the court adopted the practice of holding *Akademien,* or 'academies', which were open to a far wider circle of court members than hitherto.[68] On such occasions musical performances – including performances by members of the electoral family – were staged within the context of a relatively relaxed and leisurely sociability, not unlike that of the *appartements*. But the exclusivity of the elector's private apartments was retained; for the *Akademien* were not permitted within the prince's private lodgings: they were initially held outside the *Residenz* in the Redoutenhaus (Redoubt Building), but later within the palace's rooms of parade, particularly the Kaisersaal.

IV. THE SEATS OF THE COURT: THE COUNTRY RESIDENCES

In the course of three centuries, the Munich *Residenz* was supplemented by a number of country palaces and hunting lodges that became increasingly important as scenes of courtly sociability. Of these, the palaces of Schleissheim (built 1597–1600 and 1701–26) and Nymphenburg (built 1664–1730) are probably the best known.[69] But even in the sixteenth century, there had existed a number of lesser country seats – Wasserburg am Inn, Haag, Schwaben, Lichtenberg am Lech, Starnberg and Berg – that served as accommodation for the duke on progress through the country, or travelling with hunting parties. The most important lesser residence was initially Dachau, where an already existing country house had been converted by Albrecht V into a four-winged palace with 108 residential rooms and a splendidly decorated Ballhaus, or Reception Hall (it is worth recalling in this connection the complaints cited earlier by councillors and Estates at the costly sojourns of the court away from Munich). After his abdication in 1597, Wilhelm V began building a *Schweige* in Schleissheim, originally intended to serve both as a country seat and as a model farm, which later provided the core of the palace built on the same site; three wings housing servants' quarters and utilities were joined to a central residential structure. As Philipp Hainhofer, who visited Schleissheim in 1611, observed of Wilhelm's country retreat, 'there is extensive accommodation on this estate and all rooms are fully equipped…His Highness now has over 100 oxen, 100 cows and calves, 1,100 sheep, 20 goats, 18 buffalo, 50 pigs, 50 horses in the stud'.[70] When Wilhelm handed Schleissheim over to his son in return for a yearly pension in 1616, the outhouses were kept in use but the residential building with its forty rooms was torn down and replaced by a new complex of 200 rooms, later known as the Old Palace.

In the 1630s and 1640s, the later years of Maximilian's reign, this enlarged country residence at Schleissheim seems to have become the elector's favourite haunt outside Munich. In 1651 more than half the 104 days on which the court is reported to have been absent from the Munich *Residenz* were spent there.[71] These sojourns seem in the main to have served as brief retreats into the private sphere, and above all as opportunities for private religious observance; by contrast with his successor, the elector reduced his official activities and public duties to a minimum during these retreats to the countryside. When the experienced Hainhofer, bearing a letter from the Duke of Brunswick, sought an audience at Schleissheim in 1636, he was told that, 'although [the elector] may be at Schleissheim, he did not usually grant audiences to any envoys, for he had no councillors or secretaries with him, and therefore he did not generally negotiate, and instead sought peace and quiet'.[72]

The transformation of Bavarian court style that occurred during the reign of the Francophile Elector Ferdinand Maria (1651–79) – brought about in part by his consort, Henriette Adelaide of Savoy – was also marked by the increased use of rural locations for courtly entertainments. In Schleissheim, for example, the Reception Hall was erected at her prompting. Henriette Adelaide's influence even extended to the laying of the foundation stone for the second major country residence after Schleissheim, the palace of Nymphenburg. On land that had been presented to her by the elector on the birth of the heir to the throne, Max Emanuel, Henriette Adelaide commissioned Agostino Barelli and Enrico Zuccalli to erect a five-storey cube-shaped building inspired by the royal hunting lodge, the Veneria Reale, near Turin, which had been completed for her brother only a few years earlier. When the electress died in 1676, the construction work was still incomplete, not least because of the costs incurred in the refurbishment of her apartments in the Munich *Residenz*.

This trend towards the disengagement of the court from its urban base was intensified in the last quarter of the seventeenth century. As contemporary observers soon noticed, Ferdinand Maria and Henriette Adelaide's son, Maximilian Emanuel, had little taste for the urban environment and preferred, whenever possible, to spend his time at the country residences.[73]

In consequence, substantial additions were made to both Schleissheim and Nymphenburg during his reign. In 1685, for instance, the elector ordered the construction of a summer house, intended to function as a *maison de plaisance*, to the east of the Old Palace of Schleissheim; it consisted of a central hall, two symmetrical apartments, each of four rooms for the electoral couple, with eight 'Cavaliers' Rooms' on the upper floor, and was flanked on each side by a free-standing pavilion. The elector's further plans for a new palace were so financially ambitious that it is tempting to set this construction project against the background of the grandiose dynastic strategy pursued by Max Emanuel after his marriage to the emperor's daughter, Maria Antonia, a strategy that culminated in his son's claim, endorsed in the Testament of King Carlos II, to the Spanish throne.[74]

The elector pursued this building project with unfailing vigilance: even during the years when, as governor-general of the Spanish Netherlands (1693–1701), he was no longer residing in Bavaria, Enrico Zuccalli regularly forwarded his architectural drawings to Brussels. When the premature death of the Bavarian crown prince in 1699 shattered Max Emanuel's hopes of placing a Wittelsbach on the Spanish throne, he did not relinquish his plans for a spectacular refurbishment of Schleissheim. When the elector began in 1700 to press ahead with the work, the original plans for a four-winged structure with an enclosed courtyard were scrapped in favour of a more modern three-sided palace. Construction work on the east wing, the only one to be built, began in 1701, but was impeded, first by the collapse of the garden façade in 1702, and later by the occupation of Bavaria by imperial troops after 1704, following the elector's involvement on the anti-Habsburg side in the War of the Spanish Succession. Work was only resumed under the French-trained court architect, Joseph Effner, after the Peace of Rastatt in 1714, and Max Emanuel's

Talismans of sacred power: the Reliquary of St George *(c.1586–97), from the* Schatzkammer *(or treasure house) of the Munich* Residenz. *One of the masterpieces of late sixteenth-century goldsmiths' work, it houses a relic of St George, the patron of the Wittelsbach dynasty, given to Duke Wilhelm V by his brother Ernst, the Archbishop of Cologne. Fifty centimetres high, and set with diamonds, rubies, emeralds, pearls and other precious stones, it easily surpassed in monetary value and contemporary importance even Dürer's works in the Wittelsbach collection.*

return to his country after his years in exile.[75] The palace interiors, designed throughout in the Rococo style, had largely been completed by 1726, along with Zuccalli's Dutch-inspired gardens, the summer house with its flanking canals and central 'Mailbahn' (court for playing the game of *Mail*).[76] Contemporaneous with the construction of the new palace at Schleissheim was the extension of the palace of Nymphenburg, which had remained unchanged since the death of Henriette Adelaide. By 1716 the central building had been connected by four galleries with four newly constructed residential ranges. A summer apartment was installed for the elector in the pavilion to the north of the main building; the southern pavilion was equipped with rooms for the children of the elector and his spouse.

The Nymphenburg's surrounding park was one of the most deliberate adaptations of the French model in the history of Bavarian court architecture: Max Emanuel specifically ordered that it be laid out in emulation of the French originals he had become acquainted with during his exile in the Ile-de-France in the early 1700s. The westerly orientation of the park, the relationship between designed garden and neighbouring woodland, the inclusion of a dominant central canal from which lateral channels and basins were supplied: all this was clearly inspired by the style developed by André Le Nôtre at Louis XIV's Versailles. With the construction of the Pagodenburg (the Pagoda Pavilion) and the Badenburg (the Bathing Pavilion) in 1717–19 and 1718–21, respectively, the elector added two further *maisons de plaisance* in the Nymphenburg park. The first, decorated with exotic chinoiserie, contained a salon and, in the upper storey, a small apartment with an antechamber, a Cabinet and a bedroom, and was used mainly for smaller entertainments and soirées. The second, the Badenburg, contained a spacious bathing area and restricted quarters for courtiers and staff, as well as the elector's apartment. Such a free-standing bathhouse on this scale was a rarity, and may well have been inspired by the Turkish bathhouses that the elector must have encountered during the Turkish wars of the 1680s.[77]

The reigns of Karl Albrecht (1726–45) and Max III Joseph (1745–77) brought no further additions to the existing buildings, apart from the erection of the Amalienburg (the Amalia Pavilion) in the grounds of the Nymphenburg for Karl Albrecht's consort, Maria Amalie of Austria in 1734–9. From the later years of Max Emanuel's reign, in the early 1720s, and throughout the entire eighteenth century, it was the Nymphenburg Palace that remained the preferred summer residence of the electoral family; Schleissheim was visited for only some two weeks in any year.

This annual *campagne*, or retreat to the country, generally began towards the end of April or the beginning of May and lasted until the end of October, punctuated by regular intermissions when the elector returned to Munich for council meetings and diplomatic receptions. For fully half the year the immediate electoral entourage was absent from the principal seat of the court. The electoral couple were followed by a considerable part of the court establishment, especially the holders of senior court offices and the members of their households. Around 1770, for instance, this meant that some 160 people had to be accommodated in the summer residence – a considerable number bearing in mind that at other times of the year most members of the electoral court resided in the city rather than in the Munich *Residenz*.

The custom of holding *appartements* several times each week was kept up during the summer sojourns in the country, either in Munich, in which case the electoral entourage temporarily returned to the city, at Schleissheim, or (more often) at the Nymphenburg. When the weather permitted, this form of sociability took place in the open, either in the courtyard of the Munich *Residenz* or in the parks of the country seats, where the greater space permitted more elaborate festivities to be held.[78] Of all these locations, none was better suited for the staging of the open-air *appartements* (soon known as *Hofgärten*), than the gardens of the Nymphenburg, which provided an ideal setting not only for the usual card games, but also for promenades, chaise rides and rowing parties on the canals.

V. CONCLUSION

Two centuries lie between these late eighteenth-century festivities in the palace gardens of the Nymphenburg and the first phase of the Bavarian court's development under Duke Albrecht V, in the 1550s and 1560s. The question as to which cultural forces influenced, or had a decisive impact upon, the

The Grottenhof, or Grotto courtyard, of the Munich Residenz, erected by Wilhelm V in the 1580s.

Munich court has met with a far from unanimous response from scholars. In his study of the festival culture of the Bavarian court, for instance, Eberhard Straub stressed the strong and continuous influence of imperial court practice, and thus, indirectly, of the Spanish-Burgundian model. From this perspective, French influence was only of very limited significance; even the 'French' characteristics of the court that had become so conspicuous by Karl Albrecht's reign in the late 1720s and 1730s 'did not bring anything fundamentally new to Munich: there could be no question of an imitation of Versailles'.[79]

Recent research (principally by Samuel Klingensmith) furnishes arguments for a fusion of French *and* imperial influences as early as the reign of Maximilian II Emanuel (1679–1726).[80] But even granted the predominant cultural and ceremonial influence of the imperial Habsburg court, there remained a significant difference in tone between Munich and Vienna. During the second quarter of the eighteenth century, under Elector Karl Albrecht, contemporary observers stressed that while the Bavarian court followed the Viennese model very closely in matters of ceremonial, life there was otherwise much freer and easier.[81] Many questions remain to be answered. To what extent was the Bavarian court influenced by the lesser and middling princely courts of the empire and beyond, with which it had dynastic connections and exchanged personnel? What was the influence of the Wittelsbach court beyond the confines of the Duchy of Bavaria? And can one speak of Munich, with respect to its role in shaping the forms of courtly culture, as one of the 'leading courts' of the Empire?[82] Definitive answers to these questions await far more research; but in the meantime an observation dating from 1762 by the Italian traveller Count Ludovico Bianconi suggests that the answer, at least to the last one, may well ultimately turn out to be in the affirmative: 'The Bavarian court has long been a school of fine gallantry among the Catholic courts of Germany; just as in Versailles and Dresden, unfailing courtesy, amorous affairs and the resulting love of life have always reigned within its circle'.[83]

CHAPTER EIGHT

The Margravate of Brandenburg and the Kingdom of Prussia
THE HOHENZOLLERN COURT 1535–1740

MARKUS VÖLKEL

Nowadays, most of the states of Europe have ceased to have the monarchical form of government with which they grew up or ended their days. In the case of Prussia the situation is exacerbated further. The state itself does not exist either. Brandenburg and Berlin, which have once more come into existence today as states of the Federal Republic of Germany, have good reason for avoiding being linked with the name of Prussia, as they used to be. Perhaps they could still be termed Prussia's 'head', but it is a head entirely without limbs. Prussia, the old duchy beyond the Vistula that gave the kingdom its sovereignty, is today divided up between the Russian 'rayon' and the Polish voivodeships. Silesia, which gave the kingdom its European standing, is now called Slask, and like Pomerania – Pomorze, the state's prime military canton – now belongs to the Republic of Poland. The Rhineland provinces, once Prussia's window on to Holland, are now part of the German state of North Rhine–Westphalia and are located far away from Berlin.

Prussia today is less than a torso; it is a memory whose trophies are administered by the Stiftung Preussischer Kulturbesitz (the Prussian Cultural Foundation). The rest of Europe does not even miss the memory of Prussia, and that is astonishing, for it owes Prussia a great deal: England its standing as a major power after the Seven Years War; France valuable provinces on the Rhine; Russia Eastern Poland; and Austria major conquests in the East. By contrast, the rest of Christian Europe has Prussia to thank for admirable lessons in religious tolerance, together with its much-disdained emergence as a powerful militarist state, which, without exception, it imitated more or less openly.

Given this absence of Prussia today, the question of the Hohenzollern court has a strange ring about it. Did a 'courtly society' ever exist in Prussia? What rank may 'Prussian courtly culture' lay claim to in the European context? Was

Elector Joachim II Hektor of Brandenburg (1535–71), painted by Lucas Cranach the younger (1515–86), c. 1570.

there a Prussian 'courtly style'? True, these are possible questions, but as soon as one takes a closer look, they become slanted, almost embarrassing ones. They do not really do justice to this phenomenon and, inspired as they are by the south- and west-European model, merely demonstrate ignorance of the 'circumstances in the Brandenburg March'.[1] Prussia is different, as evidenced by the fact there is no real 'research on the Brandenburg court' even today. Present-day Berlin regards the court solely as a phenomenon of art history.

Anyone wishing to study the court of Prussia as a socio-historical entity must do so nowadays in the shadow of the era of Emperor Wilhelm II and the *Hohenzollern-Jahrbuch* (Hohenzollern Yearbook). By presenting himself as an absolute monarch, this ruler combated the monarchy's loss of power in German society as it aspired to democracy.[2] Once researchers have shaken off the largely Prusso-nationalist tendencies, which depict the Hohenzollerns in retrospect as *the* politico-cultural centre of Germany, they are faced with a very limited store of both monuments and archive material, most of which cannot be categorized. Paradoxically, a kind of pre-Wilhelmine 'Old Prussian perspective' would serve best here. But how is this to be gained, since the intermediate link between it and the present is missing? The contemporary researcher can do little more than describe fragments, but must avoid fashioning them into a unified whole for, from the very outset, this could only be ideological in content. The Prussian court can only attract archaeologists, not conservationists, because there is no written discourse that would give it structure. Neither is one likely ever to emerge because it would only be a postscript to a preface, which the phenomenon itself did not furnish us with.

I. Court and Principality
1640–1713

If, like the hero of a Baroque novel, a Prussian Icarus had taken a bird's-eye view of the Brandenburg March in 1700, he would have espied an idyllic landscape: hundreds of lakes skirted by charming woods and meadows, small settlements linked by canals and winding lanes, a great deal of nature and little commercial activity. A closer look would have revealed more to the high-flying observer: dozens of summer residences and hunting lodges strung out along dead-straight avenues, cutting star-shaped into the landscape and giving it a geometric aspect; large palaces being built at strategic points, canals purposefully linking the waterways between the Elbe and the Oder to form a network; and new urban areas in the royal capital, Berlin.

Admittedly, Icarus would have gained only a diffuse impression of the 'Electoral State of Prussia' on his flight over Brandenburg: so-called 'Royal Prussia', the former territory of the Teutonic Order, which gave the realm its name, stretched some 500 kilometres eastwards, and some 400 kilometres to the west were the small but commercially important outlying possessions in the Rhineland – the March, Cleves and Ravensberg. Extending west to east for 1,100 kilo-metres, 'Prussia' could rival the largest European monarchies; in the central Brandenburg section, however, it was at most 250 kilometres deep from north to south; more often than not, rather less. With 112,000 square kilometres and 1,650,000 inhabitants, Prussia in 1712 was only a medium-sized territory in the venerable Holy Roman Empire of the German Nation, albeit by far the largest in terms of area after Austria. Following the conversion of Augustus the Strong (Duke of Saxony from 1694, and King of Poland 1697–1733) to Catholicism, Prussia was also the uncontested leader of the Corpus Evangelicorum. Nowhere did this state form a geographical and economic unit, and it had only a single, and moreover remote, port on the Baltic. However, since 1660 the Elector of Brandenburg had possessed full sovereignty over his possessions in East Prussia, and from 1701 he also bore the royal title 'King *in* Prussia' – not yet '*of* Prussia', because West Prussia remained part of the Polish crown until 1772.

Major parts of Prussia were thus a territory of the Empire and its ruler was an imperial elector. What, then, was the status in the Empire and among the European monarchs of a 'king-like elector', who later bore the title of king of a duchy territorially remote from the Empire?[3] Compared with other German domains, Prussia was powerful, but *vis-à-vis* the European monarchies it was a *quantité négligeable*. Politically, Prussia did not mount the European stage

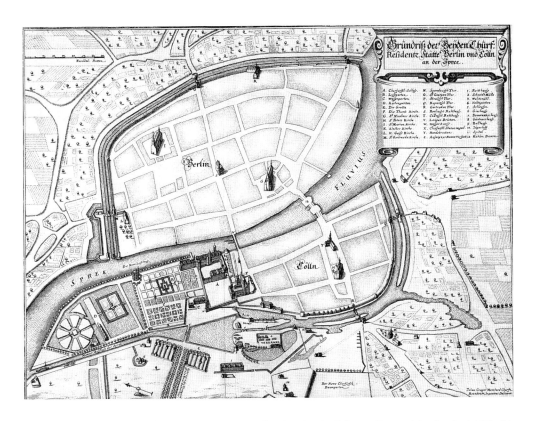

Berlin in the mid seventeenth century: engraving, after drawing by Johann Gregor Memhardt, 1650–51.
The royal palace, with its formal garden, occupies the island (lower left).

until the reign of the Elector Friedrich Wilhelm II (1640–88), albeit initially as a lever of French or Austrian politics in northern and eastern Europe. At this time, the Prussian rulers could only tentatively think of formulating expansionist goals of their own and using the court as a vehicle for 'self-representation' throughout Europe. In those days even practical politicians could at most conceive of a court as an expression and public form of power, never as a source of power itself in a way that the possession of territory, or the army and economic resources were. Consequently, the actual courtly era in which representative needs and legal-fiscal means were in relative equilibrium lasted a short time only – from 1660 to 1713. Before that, one can speak of a court only in the sense of one relating to a patriarchal, territorial state (*Teritorialstaat*). If a state were partitioned, the Hohenzollern prince ruling his new territory autonomously, such as the Neumark with Küstrin in about 1535, would receive a princely seat of his own.

II. THE HOUSEHOLD

Brandenburg, where the Hohenzollerns assumed power in 1411, was slow to develop into a permanent seat of the dynasty, given its important possessions in East Prussia and Franconia. Admittedly, the Ascanians already had an *aula*, the Great House in Berlin, in the late thirteenth century; but it was only in 1442 that the Hohenzollerns had subjugated the twin city of Berlin-Cölln and began to build a magnificent palace in Cölln (1448–51). The *Itineraries* of the period show that the traditionally peripatetic rule of the electors was superseded by rule from a royal seat.[4] This first new palace of the Elector Friedrich II (1440–70) bordered on the River Spree in the east, was partly surrounded with a wall, and was incorporated into the fortifications of the city. After 1537, Elector Joachim II Hektor (1535–71) converted it into a German Renaissance palace that still bore architectural features of a defensive nature, but was no longer a 'fortified castle'.[5] Rather, it gave expression to the fact that the sovereign was now complete master of his capital as though in possession as a private individual: that is, economically and, above all, by owning the land, Spandau, which, when developed into a square citadel after 1560, served as a substitute fortress. As a princely residence, Berlin gained visibly in prestige, but as a municipal entity it suffered from total powerlessness, a state of affairs that still pertained at the time of unification of the German Empire in 1870–71.[6]

The 'old court' of the first Hohenzollerns resident in Berlin consisted of between 300 and 500 people and, as was customary in the Empire at the time, combined princely 'representation' with the business of administration. Opposite the palace was the Mühlenhof, one of the Hohenzollerns' large estates, in which agricultural produce, mill revenues and customs duties were accumulated to support the court. Well into the seventeenth century the court, although located in the centre of Cölln, was economically self-sufficient.[7] In military and representational terms, however, the court was only partially autonomous. The prince's counsellors still had to provide the sovereign with horses and armed horsemen. In the fifteenth century it was knights from Franconia and, in the sixteenth century, landed gentry from the Brandenburg margravate who escorted the prince in large numbers, being in attendance during state visits and ceremonial funerals. Indeed, it was the very presence of office-holders and wealthy members of the nobility that enabled the various electors to vie with each other in displaying their status.[8]

Only the most tentative statements can be made about the structure, size and financing of the Brandenburg court in the sixteenth and seventeenth centuries.[9] As a rule, it rarely comprised more than 500 to 800 people, and its court ordinances were modelled on those of Saxony and Mecklenburg.[10] There appear to have been four principal court offices. That of high chamberlain (*Oberkämmerer*) was the principal one for, after all, the elector was himself arch-chamberlain of the Empire. Then came the marshal (*Obermarschall*), under whom served the castellan, chief cupbearer and the marshal of the household (*Schlosshauptmann, Oberschenk* and *Hofmarschall*). The third office was that of master of the horse and the fourth that of master of the hunt;

and given the passion of the electors for hunting, these offices were extremely arduous and entailed heavy expenditure.[11] By contrast, the prince's personal entourage was usually modest by the standards of the day. In 1683 the Great Elector had only two gentlemen of the Chamber (*Kammerherren*) in his service, together with eighteen grooms of the Chamber (*Kammerjunkern*), six grooms, twenty-one pages and four equerries.[12] Under King Friedrich I (Elector 1688, King in Prussia 1701–13) these numbers swelled enormously, only to fall far below the European average under his two successors. Throughout the period examined here, the Prussian court was among the medium-sized, even small, courts of Europe. The structure of the court offices scarcely changed, and although there were ceremonial reasons for the growth in number under the first king (1701–13), this merely resulted in an increase among senior court offices, their number rising to twelve in about 1712. Friedrich Wilhelm I reduced the number of positions to about five or six, while in 1786 his successor nominally maintained nine senior court positions but only filled four of them. Structurally, the Prussian court was always of the north-east German Protestant variety, in which the organizational structures, doggedly adhered to, as a rule conceal any fluctuations of expenditure of note.

The rule of Elector Joachim II Hektor (1535–71) was extremely lavish, and with the conversion of the Berlin castle into a Renaissance palace and the building of hunting-lodges in Potsdam, Grunewald, Bötzow and Köpenick, the foundations of what was to become Brandenburg's 'palace landscape' were laid. With the destruction during the war of the so-called Erasmuskapelle (Erasmus Chapel) in the wing overlooking the River Spree, one of the few parts of the second Berlin palace to have survived when the later Baroque building was lost. This was also where part of the electors' famous collection of Cranach paintings was housed. Joachim II was an enthusiastic organizer of knightly tournaments and, joined by his friends among the Guelph, Hessian and Wettin princes, brought about a last flowering in Prussia of this courtly sport.[13] Under his successor, Johann Georg (1571–98), work was continued on the Berlin palace, but there was no grand design, say, of a compact four-winged structure. In the 1610s, on the eve of the

Cultural rivals: the contemporary tendency to see court collections as a microcosm of the marvels of the world found its clearest expression in Kunstschränke, or cabinets of virtù, which opened to reveal hidden paintings, symbolic carvings, inlaid work, and precious objects that reputedly constituted an epitome of the universe. The most famous was that created for Duke Philip II of Pomerania-Stettin (1606–18), depicted seated with his consort (left), examining rare shells contained in one of the cabinet's drawers. The work of over twenty artists (each of whom is depicted in the foreground, right), the Pomeranian Kunstschrank was executed at Augsburg in 1605–7, and housed in the ducal palace at Stettin (now Szczecin in Poland). Until its extinction in the male line in the mid-century, the family were among the Hohenzollerns' principal rivals as collectors and patrons of the arts.

Thirty Years War, the Hohenzollerns had nothing to rival the architectural expressions of princely power within the Empire, such as the Aschaffenburg Palace (1605–14) of the Archbishop of Mainz and Arch-Chancellor of the Empire, Johann Schweikart von Kronberg, or the ducal *Residenz* in Munich (begun 1568). Admittedly, the House of Hohenzollern gradually grew in status at this time due to the consistent use of marriage alliances, but it also owed territorial gains (as we shall see) to a change in its religious denomination. While both factors together gave life at the elector's court a specific direction, neither could fully come to fruition until after the disaster of the Thirty Years War (1618–48).

III. THE REINVENTION OF THE COURT

In 1605 Elector Joachim Friedrich (1598–1608) went to the Duchy of East Prussia as regent for the last duke, Albrecht Friedrich, who was incapacitated; and in 1614 his successor as elector, Johann Sigismund (1608–19), was able to come into half – at least – of the long-sought-after inheritance on the Rhine: Cleves, the Mark and Ravensberg. In order to achieve this foreign policy objective, the Lutheran elector had converted to Calvinism on Christmas Day 1613. The hoped-for Dutch assistance was eventually forthcoming, but henceforth the Brandenburg court was divided into a minute core of Calvinists and a large, reluctant group of Lutherans. The Elector of Brandenburg was now free to reside anywhere between the Rhine and the Pregel, but everywhere he was something of a stranger. Thus, in addition to the fact that these major successes brought with them foreign policy involvements far exceeding the electorate's means, they also produced great uncertainties for the court. Basically, the court once more became a peripatetic one and had only one firm cultural and political orientation, the Dutch alliance, which was to mould the character of the court well into the second half of the seventeenth century.[14]

Elector Friedrich Wilhelm II, the Great Elector (1640–88), inherited a realm that was greatly weakened by the ravages of war and by a declining population, and with only modest resources for the

state to assert its meagre power and to 'represent' itself. In all fields he is deemed to have founded the Prussian state a second time, indeed to have invented modern Prussia and its court. He limited the influence of the Estates on taxes, officialdom, and over the army; that is, he enforced princely autonomy in the government of the provinces, new excise duties and a standing army. This army won its first victory of major significance against the Swedes in 1672, and in the process made Prussia a force to be reckoned with in the politics of the major European powers. Moreover, in 1646 the Elector married Louise Henriëtte of Orange (1627–67), the daughter of the Frederik Hendrik, Stadholder of the Dutch States General and Prince of Orange-Nassau. Everywhere in Brandenburg, the Netherlands became an envied model, even to the extent of aspiring to a colonial policy that led to Brandenburg briefly establishing trading posts on the Gold Coast (1683–1717).

For the first time, increased tax revenues, combined with French subsidies, generated sufficient funds to finance a European princely lifestyle and a court based on a distinctively 'Prussian' cultural model. Nominally the court was situated in Berlin, at Cölln; *de facto*, however, the elector, like all the Hohenzollerns up to King Friedrich II (1740–86, 'Frederick the Great'), was an itinerant prince. Friedrich Wilhelm II's sojourns in his 'peripheral palaces', particularly in the early years of his reign, add up to a substantial period: seven years in Königsberg alone, six in Cleves, numerous stays in Oranienburg, and ultimately his death in his favourite new palace in Potsdam. This leaves just twelve years of residence in Berlin.[15] Although the elector was present in Berlin so seldom, the city nevertheless played a central role in his self-representation. Berlin was to become a major stronghold of the realm and, following the Dutch approach, the residents of Berlin were expected to undertake much of the court-related building themselves. By the time the costly construction work was completed, it was already outdated stylistically; but to the outside world Berlin appeared an ideal city. And for the first time, it had also become a garrison town, because of the prolonged billeting of troops.

In addition to the soldiers, large numbers of court officials resided in the vicinity of the elector's palace.

Breite Strasse (Broad Street) in particular, which led down to the River Spree, was considered a fashionable address for court dignitaries. The Great Elector increased their wealth out of calculated self-interest, so as to expand the city, by giving them tax-free gifts of land on condition that they erected grand residences. All three of the elector's 'private cities' in the environs of Berlin – Friedrichswerder, Dorotheenstadt and Friedrichstadt – were colonized by courtiers in similar manner. The palace itself, already a principal seat of the administration, owed much of its development to the stimulus of the elector, which was not to be forthcoming in the same way from his successor.[16] A large banquet hall, the Alabastersaal (the Alabaster Hall), was built in 1680, and a magnificent gallery (135 metres long) overlooking the Hofgarten (the court garden) was planned, with which the elector sought to acquire international fame.

In order to gain an idea of the actual standing and image of the Brandenburg court in the time of the Great Elector, however, one would have to imagine the Dutch style transposed to the lakes and woods of the March. As a boy, the elector-designate had already been strongly influenced by things Dutch during his first visit to the Netherlands (1634–37). Moreover, the Electress Louise Henriëtte of Orange brought with her, along with her dowry, Dutch architects, painters, engineers and craftsmen to her new homeland. Orange became the favourite colour at the Brandenburg court. Her consort took many members of the House of Orange-Nassau into his service, and drew on their literally world-wide experience for his own administration, no sphere of courtly life being left untouched.

Prince Johann Moritz of Nassau-Siegen (1604–79) may be considered the prime intermediary in this complex of courtly and cultural influences. From 1636 to 1644 he had been the governor of the Dutch West Indies Company in Brazil. His achievements in the colony included planning the city of Dutch Recife, and conducting an extensive geographical exploration of the country and its flora and fauna. He also brought with him works of art featuring the natives of Brazil and their landscape that were particularly enthusiastically received in Europe. Johann Moritz was a good organizer as well as an accomplished architect and enthusiastic collector. His particular forte lay in being able to harmonize spatial plans with each other, whether for the construction of a palace or the design of entire landscapes – qualities that enabled him to make a great impact in Prussia. As Governor of Cleves, he first upgraded the elector's residence there, and laid out a new garden linking up the Prinzenhof (Prince's Court) via a complex of avenues to new outer grounds. At Potsdam, work began in 1664 on building a palace in the Dutch manner, this main palace being surrounded, on the model of Cleves, with summer residences (Bornim, Glienicke and Caputh) linked by spacious avenues. The conversion of the pleasance at Bötzow into the palace of Oranienburg as the private residence of the Electress Louise Henriëtte, again including a model Dutch estate, began in 1651 and proved to be an important addition to this building project. At the same time, new court ordinances were issued. This palace had the same peripheral position in relation to Berlin (north-west) as did Potsdam (south-west), and it was linked to it by the Havel. If one includes the hunting lodge at Köpenick on the Spree in the south-east, which had just been magnificently overhauled for his heir, Electoral Prince Friedrich (the future Elector Friedrich III), it will be seen that Friedrich Wilhelm had established a system of water residences between which he could travel by canal, as on a Dutch *gracht*, and whose focal point was clearly the Havel basin lying before the capital. As part of the organization of the realm, these palaces had the effect of being 'colonies'; established to meet the court's accommodation and transportation needs in the Brandenburg March after the Thirty Years War, they effectively created an infrastructure.[17] Similar services were performed by the courtiers in Berlin when they built palaces, roads and gardens as 'settlers' in the elector's new cities of Friedrichstadt and Dorotheenstadt.

After 1662 Oranienburg received a Porcelain Cabinet, the first Prussian palace to do so. Here, as in the rest of the artistic decoration of the palace's state rooms, the elector on the one hand emphasized his affiliations to the House of Orange, as when he had the Marmorsaal (Marble Hall) of the palace of Potsdam furnished with statues of Willem I and Willem II of Orange; on the other hand he isolated

Louis XIV's revocation of the Edict of Nantes in 1685, ending toleration for Protestants, forced the dispersal of Huguenots (French Calvinists) throughout Europe. The response of Elector Friedrich Wilhelm (1640–88), himself a Calvinist, offering Huguenot refugees his protection, resulted in a massive influx of French personnel and cultural talent into Berlin. In this allegorical engraving commemorating the event, the elector appears crowned with a victor's laurel wreath, welcoming the suffering Huguenots.

the Hohenzollerns from the Holy Roman Empire of the day, identifying the dynasty, instead, with the emperors of Roman antiquity. This trend was most clearly apparent in the new Alabastersaal of the Berlin palace, where twelve full-length statues of Hohenzollern electors stood facing four Roman emperors.[18] This was suggestive of the fact that the electors in the Empire enjoyed royal standing; so the view, often expressed after the coronation of Friedrich I, that the Great Elector himself already had had royal aspirations, cannot be dismissed out of hand.

In the lifestyle of the Brandenburg ruler, older patriarchal forms were permeated by Franco-Dutch practices and, later, by increasingly military ones. Apart from ambassadorial protocol, the elector seems not to have attached too great an importance to ceremonial matters.[19] The visits of princely relatives to Berlin were numerous, and the court's visits to spas were prolonged, as in Bad Pyrmont (24 June to 28 July 1681), where there was hunting and banquets in elaborate marquees. But there is no overlooking a propensity for pompous display. After his successful campaign in western Pomerania, the Great Elector was welcomed into the capital on 12 December 1678 by no less than eight triumphal arches and magnificent displays of homage.[20] Of the approximately 20,000 soldiers that Friedrich Wilhelm maintained under arms, considerable numbers were stationed in the citadels of Spandau and Berlin and could, therefore, be used for ceremonial purposes. When there were military victories to be celebrated, triumphal entries would be arranged, as on 13 December 1686 when 6,000 men returned from the conquest of Ofen in Hungary. The officers wore Hungarian dress and had Turkish prisoners and booty with them. For a short time, things Turkish were all the vogue in Berlin.[21]

Friedrich Wilhelm would not tolerate any favourites as protégés. However, he did have confidants, such as his first lord chamberlain, Kurt von Burgsdorf, whom he often accorded considerable influence. Noble lineage did not play a decisive role in this. On the contrary, the elector favoured the advancement of counsellors from the bourgeoisie, and these proved to be indispensable to his successor as well. The assertion that Prussia was essentially founded by the bourgeoisie sounded as though motivated by liberal principles when it was first made by Eduard

Vehse in 1851, but the long list of names that he was able to cite – Distelmeyer, Meinders, Fuchs, Derfflinger, Danckelmann, Kraut, Bartoldi, Ilgen, Thulemeyer and Cocceji – proves him right. Many of these had begun their careers under the Great Elector, acquired large fortunes and intermarried; but, while they could certainly be described as an élite power group, they controlled neither the state nor the monarch.

At the end of Friedrich Wilhelm's reign, Prussia was already an invigorated realm with a considerable army and growing revenues.[22] The peripatetic nature of the court and courtly society played an important role in integrating the scattered provinces. The elector wanted to attract a larger number of Protestant princes to his court, but both he and later his son failed to build up a system of client princes comparable to that at the Viennese court. At the same time the court, competing as it did with the European monarchies, performed functions that were uncommon enough, as, for example, in its work of 'colonizing' Berlin and the Brandenburg March.[23] In the first half of the elector's reign, the historical matrix for the Hohenzollerns and the formal model for the court was predictably the Netherlands, which was also the source of most of the imported luxury goods. Later, and paradoxically during the period after 1683 in particular, when diplomacy focused on the emperor and the Empire, French influences began to dominate. While Friedrich Wilhelm freed himself diplomatically from the French system with the Edict of Potsdam in 1685 and the admission of many Huguenots, he opened up his country as never before to the French cultural model. After 1700, French refugees made up one-fifth of the population of Berlin and the ever-more magnificent court was a centre of power as never before or since in Prussia. At the same time, of course, the refugees were far outnumbered by Protestant immigrants from the Palatinate, Franconia, Thuringia and Austria. In retrospect, the form and functioning of the court under the Great Elector have the appearance of a homogeneous whole that split into two parts under his successors: civil and military. His court was a military, administrative and representational machine and, at the same time, a place where political power was exercised, albeit without ever having been the actual source of this power.[24]

IV. THE CREATION OF A ROYAL COURT

His successor, the Elector Friedrich Wilhelm III (1688–1713, King in Prussia from 1701), is regarded by historians of Prussia as a lamentable exception among its rulers. His demeanour was not impressive; he was no warrior; he hired out his troops without a qualm and he left behind debts and a territory that had scarcely expanded. His grandson, King Friedrich II – Frederick the Great – nevertheless spoke of him with a measure of grudging respect:

All the new settlements that the Great Elector had established only really began to flourish by the time of Friedrich I. This prince profited from his father's labours. We were then manufacturers of tapestries equal to those of Brussels; our lacework rivalled that of France; the clarity of our mirrors from Neustadt surpassed those of Venice; the army was clad in our own cloth.[25]

This was the time, in Frederick the Great's view, when it was largely through monarchical 'representation' that Prussia was placed among the great powers of Europe. Friedrich Wilhelm III had gained experience in self-representation on a grand architectural scale as electoral prince when, together with his father, he had extended the old hunting lodge at Köpenick. A room such as the Wappensaal (Heraldic Hall) on the upper floor of the palace (c.1695) is not only one of the few Brandenburg state rooms from the seventeenth century to have survived, it also bears witness to the ruler's desire to raise the standing of his realm as a legal and dynastic unit, and to present it as such.[26]

On his accession as the new elector in 1688, Friedrich III had no dearer wish than to assume the title of king as quickly as possible, and with the international consent, moreover, of his fellow sovereigns. However, it was only when the question of the succession to the Spanish throne briefly made Prussia indispensable on the international stage that he saw his chance. In the *Krontraktat* (Crown Treaty) of 16 November 1700, Friedrich declared his willingness to provide military support for the Habsburg claim to Spain on condition that the emperor consented to his elevation in rank. On 18 January 1701 his coronation took place in the royal palace of Königsberg, as a self-coronation modelled on that of the Swedish king

Karl XII.[27] The speed with which the coronation was performed in the middle of winter made two things clear: first, that the Prussian ruler was determined at all costs to seize the favourable opportunity; second, that the entire machinery of the court and state had been in readiness for this great event for years. Indeed, remarks made by the elector before 1700 on the question of his status suggest that Prussia was already a kingdom in all but name: 'If I have all the attributes of kingliness and in greater measure than other kings, why should I not seek to bear the title of king?'[28]

Clearly, Friedrich had considered himself king from the moment he had come to power and had conducted his court and cultural policies accordingly. He was the only Hohenzollern to do so with complete consistency. He could well be nicknamed 'Friedrich the ceremonial', although we do not know which ceremonial exactly was in use at the Berlin court. Friedrich Carl von Moser, who was probably best acquainted with it, does not comment on this matter in his *Teutsches Hof-Recht* (German Courtly Law). The rules and regulations of many medium-sized courts are found in Moser's Appendix, but not those of Berlin and Vienna, although Moser frequently quotes Friedrich's grandson as *Maître de Sanssouci* and an authority on matters of the court, albeit always in anti-courtly tones. If contemporary accounts are to be believed, Friedrich's *lever* followed the French model.

The coronation, according to Pöllnitz, drew in part on ritual used in England for the anointing of kings, with the newly appointed court bishops wearing cassocks similar to those of the Anglican Church.[29] Towards his peers in the Empire, Friedrich now felt obliged to use the royal 'Danish' ambassadorial ceremonial.[30] Otherwise his ceremonial zeal can only be deduced from the numerous ordinances concerning court hierarchy, the last version of which dates from 1712 (after versions in 1688, 1705, 1706 and 1708) and lists 141 orders of rank and twelve senior court offices. Typically, this obsession with regulation was confined to his own court at first for, at European level, his new royal rank was accepted only slowly and with painful limitations. Brandenburg was immediately at odds with the German princely houses with whom it was close, as Kassel, for example, where Friedrich's daughter Louise, who was married to the Hereditary Prince, was now to be addressed as 'Royal Highness' and at her father's insistence had to claim precedence over her own mother-in-law. Landgrave Karl, however, felt unable to accept this imposition, if only so as not to allow the distance between the old aristocracy and the electoral houses to widen still further.[31]

Although King Friedrich I planned all the great monarchical ceremonies of state himself – from his coronation in Königsberg to his funeral in Berlin – he was assisted in this by the most famous specialist of the day, the *Ober Ceremonienmeister* (chief master of ceremonies) Johann von Besser (1654–1729). Besser, who was not of noble extraction, was respected for his reliability, his ease with the pen when librettos or panegyrics needed composing, and above all for his great erudition. He owned one of the largest libraries on ceremonial of the day, and with him etiquette in Berlin must have taken on a strikingly historical aspect.[32]

This was also the case with the king's coronation in the winter of 1700–1701. Here, Friedrich was in his element. The day before, he had founded the Order of the Black Eagle, naturally with an orange ribbon, and held its magnificent first chapter.[33] The coronation ritual, in particular the inclusion of 'the people' in the festivities, in many ways resembled the coronation of the emperor in Frankfurt-am-Main. Friedrich personally placed the crown on his queen's head.

As the court had come to Königsberg as that of a simple elector, it seemed all the more important to stage the departure from the coronation city with distinctively royal grandeur. The people of Königsberg thus enjoyed the rare pleasure of a triumphal procession of the royal entourage 'that was entirely in keeping with its new status'.[34] The new king headed the procession magnificently attired, followed by the queen in the state coach. Triumphal arches and royal salutes attended the passage from the city of the royal party, which stopped 500 metres outside the walls at a royal marquee. From there it returned once more to Königsberg and only then made its way to Berlin.

When his consort Queen Sophie Charlotte died in Hanover at the age of thirty-seven, a wave of monarchist expressions of mourning swept the land. Once again Friedrich himself arranged the funeral ceremonial, and a vast cavalcade accompanied the coffin from place to place until it reached Berlin, where the most elaborate state funeral that Prussia had ever seen was held. Pöllnitz claimed that the obsequies had been modelled on those of Queen Mary of England in

1695. At a cost of 80,000 Reichstaler, the catafalque was of truly royal pretensions. As if to reconcile himself retrospectively with his long-since estranged queen, Friedrich left her entire household intact and even completed the buildings that she had begun.

With the death of Sophie Charlotte, a long period of marital competition thus came to an end, for, to Friedrich's regret, the queen, whose mother had brought the Hanoverian House of Guelph the succession to the English throne, tended to act independently of her husband. When, after several attempts, the king had finished extending the ancestral palace in Cölln, the queen had long since chosen the hunting lodge at Lietzenburg, before the gates of Berlin, as a setting for a household in keeping with her nature-loving lifestyle. The king loved fifes and drums, while the queen was an excellent cellist and chose her Italian musicians herself. Sophie Charlotte was also the driving force behind the founding of the Berlin Academy in 1700.

The royal couple completed the circle of residences around Berlin as a kind of amicable contest. Whereas in the days of the Great Elector the focus had clearly been on the west of Berlin, on the Havel, Friedrich I preferred to reside in the east of the city, as it was facing the eastern roots of his monarchy. In 1691 he acquired Schönhausen, in 1693 Tegel, in 1697–8 Rosenfelde (thereafter Friedrichsfelde), followed by Blankenfelde, Rosenthal and Malchow. Publicly circulated images of this complex series of palaces and *maisons de plaisance* were published only long after the king's death in a set of engravings that presented a scarcely intelligible mixture of actual and fictitious buildings.[35]

All these endeavours were eclipsed, however, by the attempt to have the now royal residence in Berlin rival those of the French, Saxon and even Roman models. The fact that Prussia came to hold its own in the battle for artistic prestige was largely the work of the court architect, Andreas Schlüter (1659–1714), who, along with Johann Bernhard Fischer von Erlach, was probably the most prominent Baroque architect in the German-speaking world. Between 1695 and 1707 Schlüter was responsible for many important sculptural and architectural projects for the court. He was actually a sculptor by training, but, as a self-taught architect, he had the makings of genius, though he ultimately foundered on the excessive and technically unrealizable demands of his royal master.

Schlüter supervised the design and execution of the bronze equestrian statue of the Great Elector (cast in 1700, mounted in 1703) that was to be placed on the new Schlossbrücke (Palace Bridge), now the Lange Brücke (Long Bridge), together with a programme of twelve statues. This was Berlin's attempt to rival the Engelsbrücke and the Pont Neuf in Paris with its equestrian statue of Henri IV. Schlüter continued work on the Zeughaus (Arsenal), begun in 1695, and embellished with his own unique sculptural decoration, and in 1698 presented his model for reconstruction of the palace. He could now proceed to transform the old Renaissance palace into a four-winged building having a uniform façade.[36] At the time of the coronation, the palace wings facing on to the Lustgarten and the Schlossplatz (Palace Square) were executed simultaneously and at great speed so as to have a large triumphal arch as the endpoint of the grand entry, staged when the newly crowned king returned from Königsberg on 6 May 1701. In the spring of 1700 work had begun under Schlüter's direction on the interior decoration of the palace, in which the members of the recently created Academy of Arts were commanded to participate. In 1702 Schlüter built the grand new double-flighted staircase that led up to the large Schweizersaal (Hall of the Swiss Guard), the latter being one of the most obvious symbols of royal rank. Banquet halls and state apartments were soon to follow. In 1703 the new Rittersaal (Knights' Hall) was inaugurated with a banquet of the Order of the Black Eagle, whose ritual Friedrich had devised with the utmost meticulousness. At this banquet the famous silver buffet of the Hohenzollerns was on display along the eastern wall, a crown treasure transformed into Augsburg silversmiths' work, as it were, a part of which is nowadays located in the palace of Köpenick. Moreover, the monarch was soon able to move into his new state apartments. Here Schlüter had created a suite of rooms (including the pretentious court chapel) that, leading off from the Schweizersaal, occupied half the Lustgarten wing and met the highest ceremonial demands.

Schlüter fell from favour when two buildings personally inspired by the king miscarried technically. A giant, 91-metre-high tower, begun in 1702 not far from the Lindenallee, which would have made the palace stand out far to the west as a kind of royal steeple, was too much for its foundations and had to be dismantled. Similarly, the courageous design of an open hall in the palace of Freienwalde, which was to be borne by Corinthian columns, also collapsed. Thereafter Schlüter fell into disgrace with the king, was dismissed as court building director and received no more royal commissions. What Schlüter might have accomplished for the king is also apparent from the buildings that he constructed for prominent courtiers, such as the Palais Wartenberg at the Lange Brücke, or the suburban summer residence for Minister of State Bogislav von Kamecke in Dorotheenstadt. Where palace construction is concerned, Schlüter could have made Berlin almost a match for Vienna. His conception of the environs of the main palace also differed from what was actually built. A design signed by Jean-Baptiste Broebes, a professor at the Academy of Arts, depicts the palace as seen from the River Spree, its mass repeated in a symmetrical building for the royal stables, with a complete reconstruction of the old Dom (cathedral) linking the two. The Lange Brücke, with its equestrian statue of the Great Elector, forms the central visual axis, for, unlike that which was actually executed, this was planned to lie in the centre. The imposing campanile and the Zeughaus complete the grandiose design. If implemented, it would have rivalled Paris, London or St Petersburg. After Friedrich I, however, no other Prussian king took such an interest in representational urban planning.

The second highlight of the construction work of the day was the Charlottenburg Palace (1702–6, gardens 1696–1714), the later summer residence of the Hohenzollerns.[37] Friedrich I not only resided here as a rule from April to October, but actively supervised work on the magnificent additions, which included the celebrated domed hall, a free-standing flight of stairs for large ambassadorial receptions and a *cour d'honneur*. In 1712 work on the exterior and parts of the interior decoration were largely complete, and so important events, such as the wedding of the crown prince in 1706, or the Triple Alliance of 1709 – with Augustus II of Poland (1697–1733, 'Augustus the Strong') and Frederick IV of Denmark (1699–1730) – could be celebrated there. Even before becoming king, Friedrich had attached importance to large

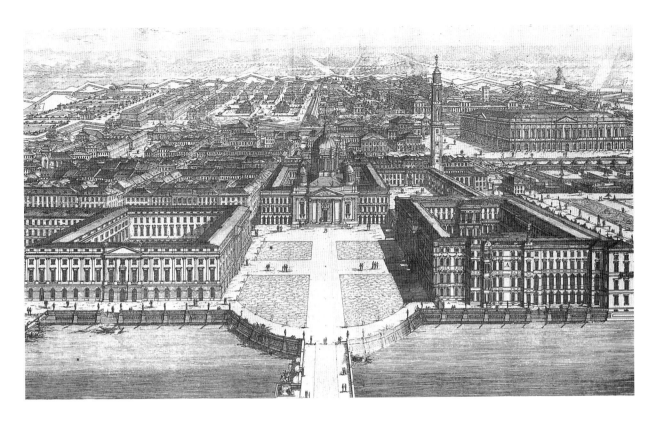

Royal Berlin, c.1702–3: an idealized view of how Andreas Schlüter might have transformed the architectural setting of the Hohenzollern court. The royal palace, extensively remodelled by Schlüter in the 1690s, is to the right of the central square, with its Lustgarten beyond (right). The Arsenal (built 1695–1706), embellished with sculptures by Schlüter, is in the middle distance (right). The failure of the great tower designed by Schlüter and shown here shortly before its demolition, contributed to the architect's fall from royal favour. The domed cathedral, on axis with the bridge and also planned by Schlüter, was never built.

dynastic celebrations. The wedding celebrations of his only daughter Louise to the Hereditary Prince of Kassel in the spring of 1700 lasted almost fourteen days. Rivalries of status played no small part in this, for the Prussian pomp was so extravagant that it caused the heavily indebted Landgrave of Kassel serious concern. He himself said that the nuptials cost him more than 140,000 Reichstaler: a large amount of money for a not very attractive bride, but nevertheless a good investment, as the Danish queen, the landgrave's sister, wrote in a letter to Kassel.[38] The crown prince's wedding to his Guelph cousin in 1706 was celebrated in a similarly extravagant manner. On that occasion, still more elevated connections played a role in the ceremonial, for the bride's attire

was chosen personally in Paris by her great-aunt, Lieselotte of the Palatinate.[39]

Friedrich I was unrivalled in the manner in which his royal apartments were appointed. Only in the standard and quality of her music and the sciences was Queen Sophie Charlotte his superior by far. Although the king did not permit her to have a permanent ensemble, she was nevertheless able to assemble a troupe of 'borrowed musicians', mainly Italians, and to stage a few operas, the first in Berlin. Sophie Charlotte not only owned Berlin's only large theatre, in the Breite Strasse, but also owned a private theatre near her own palace. It was she too who, together with the ill-appreciated first minister Eberhard von Danckelmann, encouraged Leibniz to pursue his plans to establish an

Academy of Sciences; the queen's untimely death in 1705 contributed to this institution's laboured beginnings. The Academy of Arts of 1696 fared somewhat better, it having two clearly defined functions: to have an appreciation of classical art take firm root in Berlin and to train local (and, thus, less expensive) court artists.

If one attempts to interpret the scant information about the state budget under the first Prussian king, it soon becomes clear that, of the revenue of 4 million Reichstaler, a good half was spent on the army, while of the other half, allegedly some 50,000–150,000 Taler per annum only were spent on his royal building projects.[40] What happened to the rest, about which there are next to no records? It was probably swallowed up by the day-to-day expenses of the vast royal household, the king's penchant for large receptions and processions, his gifts to favoured courtiers, his fleet of pleasure boats on the River Spree and his extravagant purchases of jewels. His successor, King Friedrich Wilhelm I (1713–40), must have felt exceedingly uneasy when trying, in the spring of 1713, to gain an idea of his father's expenditure and debts. The debts were indeed considerable; but the existing assets exceeded all expectations. Like many of his ancestors from the House of Orange, the first king also left behind a veritable Nibelung horde of silver, jewels and *objets d'art*. Certainly, from the moment of his succession, Friedrich Wilhelm I was consumed by the idea of turning this 'unreal' treasure into real political power.

V. THE COURT OF KING FRIEDRICH I

'A large court models itself on the standing of the sovereign, no matter what the state may be like; a small court does likewise', wrote Moser. Likewise, during the reign of Friedrich I Berlin was a typical German *Residenzstadt*, or town with a princely court, and took its character from its king. In 1709 four of its constituencies had been given a uniform administration under a royal governor. The court dominated the town economically and culturally in every way.[41] The citizens had to resign themselves to their political insignificance, and all they could do was try to profit economically from the presence of the royal household. In terms of numbers, by 1700 this must have

been the largest German court after that of Vienna. On his accession to the throne, Friedrich Wilhelm I found himself attended by three troops of palace guards, a Swiss Guard, a royal stables of 600 horses and eighteen royal carriages, and ministers who were required to follow the king from one amusement spot to another with a cavalcade of thirty horses. A costly royal bodyguard ensured the king's personal safety, while within the monarch's entourage an elaborately liveried body of Chamber staff saw that court ceremonial was properly observed: the highmarshal of the household (*Oberhofmarshall*), the marshal of the household (*Hofmarshall*), the castellan (*Schlosshauptmann*), grand master of the wardrobe (*Grandmaître de la Garderobe*), fifteen gentlemen of the Chamber (*Kammerherren*), thirty-two grooms of the Chamber (*Kammerjunker*), and seven grooms of the household (*Hofjunker*).[42] The late king had furnished his third wife, Sophie Luise of Mecklenburg Schwerin (1685–1735), with numerous servants and countesses as ladies-in-waiting, all of whom resided in the palace. There were thirty-seven chamber musicians employed in the court orchestra, not counting the twenty-six court trumpeters and drummers. A corps of twenty-four pages was on hand to serve the food that was prepared in the palace kitchens by a hundred chefs, cellarers and bakers. Friedrich's personal attendants – one was responsible solely for shaving the king, another for preparing his chocolate – in turn had servants of their own, and some of them rode to the court in a coach to perform their duties.

As late as 1712, expenditure on the staff of the court totalled 157,647 Reichstaler.[43] This sum was sufficient to meet the king's new representational requirements. There is no denying, however, that the form and content of this self-representation were largely imported. Like the city in which it had taken up residence, the Prussian court in 1700 was a 'colonial court'. The ceremonial was imported, as were the ministers, the artists and the French menu. The first king even shared his eccentric passions, such as the amassing of jewels and the accumulation of silver furniture, with peers such as Louis XIV and Augustus the Strong, even if the latter indulged in such pursuits with more business acumen. Berlin at the time was a *tabula rasa* on which Dutchmen, Frenchmen, Italians and many Germans from various corners of the Empire played a game called 'Prussia'. The fact that this court had no economic and social basis, that it was a completely artificial product, is evidenced in retrospect, too, by the artificial and synthetic nature of the realm that it symbolized. At the same time, the court at the time of Friedrich I did indeed reflect Prussia's political and economic resources. If, of course, the court had continued in this fashion, in the long run it would have cost it the greatness that it strove to represent. Prussia was not the only state in the German Empire to be confronted by this problem – witness the example of Saxony – but Prussia was the only one to resolve it with complete consistency.

This is an appropriate point to examine the nature of the first Prussian ruler's patronage of the arts and whether there was a 'Prussian style'. The situation in Berlin is unequivocal only in its ambiguity. By 1700 Berlin, together with Potsdam, Charlottenburg and Oranienburg, was the undisputed *Residenz*, albeit one without any local art tradition of note and with a single potent patron – the king. Consequently, the artists continually had to be imported by the court and oriented towards the king and his officials, who were not necessarily art-lovers themselves. The situation regarding commissions, which was often precarious, the mysterious process by which they were placed and the as yet very limited urban character of Berlin discouraged celebrated artists from settling there permanently. The foundation of the Academy of Arts in 1696 did little to change matters.[44] Neither the court itself nor the circles close to it developed any particular direction in 'taste'. Quite the opposite: it tended to accept without demur the suggestions of artists coming from all over Europe, only to abandon their works half-finished from one moment to the next, or to content itself with mere planning exercises. In those days, *Baumeister* (or master builders) had no formal training (they could not yet be designated 'architect'), and therefore all manner of engineers and decorators offered their services to the Prussian court. Planning and execution of all the major projects in the capital were marked by a roller-coaster movement that has been a source of great consternation to art historians in search of a 'national style'. The Prussian court developed neither a 'Protestant' nor a 'Prussian' iconography; the only tangible trait here is a pronounced leaning towards classical antiquity.[45]

VII. RETRENCHMENT AND REFORM, 1713–40

Anyone familiar with Crown Prince Friedrich Wilhelm in his youth, his aversion to Latin and French, gentlemanly virtues and pomp, his early turning to Pietism, his pronounced response to his two educational trips to Holland, his hatred for his father's favourites, his assiduous work in the Privy Council from 1703 to 1713, his two stays in the Duke of Marlborough's camp in 1706 and 1709: anyone familiar with all this could not but have expected an anti-court policy on his succession, but few could have foreseen its radicalism.

After the new King Friedrich Wilhelm I had resolutely transformed the old administration into a cabinet government entirely dependent on himself, while retaining the former regime's best members, he turned his attention to his father's court. No other Baroque court underwent such extensive changes. Few courtiers were spared dismissal and total loss of salary; those who were permitted to remain served for a paltry salary, performing entirely different duties.

Before these measures came into effect, however, the old king was buried with traditional pomp and interred in a magnificent sarcophagus designed by Andreas Schlüter. The lying-in-state in the old Berlin cathedral took place in a style that referred to the heroes of antiquity. The choir of the church was completely transformed into a necropolis. Classical incense burners stood in front of the sarcophagi of the twelve electors, while statues of Friedrich I's two consorts, who had predeceased him, flanked the royal catafalque. The vault over the catafalque was supported by four heavy pillars that bore testimony in words and images to the ruler's chief works, and panels in the vault recalled the story of the king's coronation, but after this last gesture of extravagance, the new king implemented his austerity programme with great severity. The new royal style can also be seen as a departure from the classical imagery that had predominated hitherto in the Hohenzollerns' self-representation: soldiers assumed prominence instead of Bellori's classical statues.[46] Friedrich Wilhelm's plan was twofold. First, the existing standing army of 30,000 men, which could be maintained only with the aid of Dutch and English subsidies, was to be brought up to a peacetime strength of 40,000, manned solely by Prussians and maintained from the kingdom's own resources. Second, the financial and in some cases personnel resources of the 'old court' were to be redirected to maintain the 'new army'. This new army was to assume the former functions of the court in the spheres of social discipline, administration, the economy and even royal ceremonial. It followed that the prevailing urban court economy also had to be transformed into a military form of the local economy.

The king abolished almost all the high offices of court, including that of the master of ceremonies, and retained just four gentlemen of the Chamber. Henceforth, any courtier who had a military function lived off his income from it. The dowager queen's household, and above all its famous 'countesses' table', were abolished, as were the court orchestra and most of the stables and the court kitchens. To everyone's amazement, the king now dined 'German-fashion', simply, and enjoying 'home cooking'. Most court artists were dismissed, among them Eosander von Göthe, the architect of both the Charlottenburg Palace and the Berlin Schloss, and the Academy of Arts barely survived, while the newly founded Academy of Science went into decline. The king was unimpressed by Leibniz.

The troops of palace guards were turned into field regiments. In their stead, the king expanded his existing royal bodyguard to regimental strength, with the famous *Lange Kerls* (Tall Lads) forming the army's First Battalion. At the old king's court the tone had been set by the lower nobility, such as the infamous favourites Wartenberg, Wittgenstein and Wartensleben – some of them from other parts of the Empire – as well as by counsellors drawn from the bourgeoisie. Under Friedrich Wilhelm I, the native *Junker* (country gentry), in the form of an officer, was placed in the forefront. The new rank conventions privileged the military and accorded the same status to civilian servants of the court only where their rank was readily comparable with that of an officer.

The new king again lived 'in the Dutch manner', even building his hunting lodges in Dutch style, but it was no longer the princely House of Orange-Nassau that served as the shining example, but the Dutch burgher himself. At the Berlin Palace, the king retained only the small apartment that he had

occupied as crown prince. Except for the Fahnensaal (Banner Room), antechambers, audience chambers and a study, the king used none of the staterooms for himself. The recently completed rooms in the new wing of the palace were left mainly unfurnished and whitewashed. The treasures of state were now consigned to the basement, protected by heavy palisades. The new residence that was to find favour with the king was Potsdam, which he energetically expanded into a city of arms manufacturing, barracks and parade grounds. Wherever the monarch lived, he did so as simply as possible: he would attend to his own toilette, there naturally being no *lever*; he always wore officer's dress and also kept his family on a tight rein. Moreover, Friedrich Wilhelm I was constantly travelling; yet unlike his predecessor, his travels were not for ceremonial or recreational purposes, but were down-to-earth inspection trips. He might be said to have been driven by a boundless restlessness, for hardly a year went by without a lengthy journey. [47]

It would be misleading to claim, however, that the soldier-king abstained from all forms of courtly representation or that he left behind nothing in that sphere. The fact is that, after his father's death, he had work on the Berlin Palace completed (1716), albeit on a minimal scale. The so-called Weisser Saal (White Chamber) in the new wing of the building was magnificently furnished to mark the visit of King Augustus of Poland in 1728. Their majesties 'inspected the tall Grenadier guards' on the former Lustgarten (pleasance), which had been turned into a parade ground, and in the evening the entire city was illuminated. Family festivities were also celebrated with due ceremony. The splendour of the furniture in the Berlin palace amazed visitors, who had expected something more austere, and in the Rittersaal the king could point to his trumpeters' gallery made of two tons of solid silver. Undaunted by the king's retrenchments, Sophie Dorothea (1687–1757), the royal consort, tried to maintain a court of her own in her palace of Monbijou, which she furnished with magnificent collections.

The monarch himself, however, was far more interested in military displays and hunting than in any festivity; the spring revue in the cordoned-off Tiergarten was a spectacle for the entire city. By contrast, Friedrich Wilhelm's hunting expeditions were

The electoral Residenz *at Cölln on the Spree, viewed c.1690, showing the old Renaissance palace of Joachim II before its rebuilding by Schlüter.*

conducted with a comparatively small entourage.[48] The king's model in hunting lore is said to have been his father's cousin, Prince Leopold of Anhalt-Dessau (1676–1747), the 'Alter Dessauer', or Old Dessau. The Dessau battues were modelled on the French, required large enclosures and hunting lanes converging on a single point, and were conducted according to strict rules. The king went hunting in uniform and was accompanied by a smaller entourage than, say, the Saxon ruler at Hubertusburg. The season began in August and did not end until November. Then the king would generally return to Berlin; but he would often be back in Wusterhausen for Christmas, when the wild boar season began. (The king's personal best was 3,602 wild boars in a season.) Naturally, there was hunting on a grand scale during state visits.

Whenever he wanted to, therefore, Friedrich Wilhelm I could fall back on the standard forms of courtly representation. He also enabled the heir to the throne to lead a life in keeping with his status at the palace of Rheinsberg after he had submitted to his father's wishes. But the king seldom turned to the older forms of representation, and deliberately chose another way of presenting the House of Hohenzollern. To his patriarchal way of thinking, Prussia was to present itself as powerful and the dynasty as the repository of that power. To this end, it was necessary for the country, populace and ruling house to blend into a single military machine.[49] The *Lange Kerls* replaced the rows of court attendants, and were even given a picture gallery of their own in the palace in Potsdam; the vast troop formations could be moved to and fro on the parade grounds like ballet dancers. The conventions of military rank replaced the courtly; the building of barracks, manufactories, fortresses, garrison churches and military orphanages, which the king pursued on a grand scale, replaced that of summer residences and pleasances; the quartering of thousands of soldiers in the homes of the bourgeoisie did more than any court protocol to ensure a hierarchically ordered and subservient society. The element of demonstrative display apart, the replacement of a courtly by a military 'culture' had an undeniable advantage. Every court must primarily represent power on a symbolic level; it acts as a secondary system to the spheres of business, society and religion. The Prussian innovation was as simple as it was ingenious and dangerous: no power is more convincing than the power that displays itself.

Friedrich Wilhelm I's style of representation found imitators even during his lifetime. Tsar Peter I undoubtedly shared a kindred spirit, but even

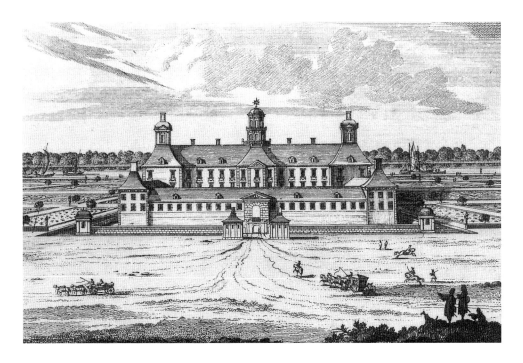

The residence at Potsdam in the reign of King Friedrich I (1701–13), depicted in 1702, before its major rebuilding in the early eighteenth century

courts in western and southern Germany, such as Hessen-Kassel and Hessen-Darmstadt, soon followed suit. The more 'enlightened' German princes became, such as Emperor Joseph II, the more frequently they would appear in uniform and banish ostentation and archaic ceremonial from their private apartments.

VII. THE MILITARY COURT
1740–88

All that had to be done by Friedrich II (1740–88) was to perfect his father's system. The *Lange Kerls* were not really fit for war service, so he created a 'new personal regiment made up of the most handsome members of the crown prince's regiment'.[50] He made only a modest increase to the size of the royal household after the absolute low under the soldier-king. Under Friedrich II there were once more nine principal court offices, of which only four were actually filled at the time of his death in 1786. In 1741, on marching into Silesia, he bestowed three of these at a single stroke on prominent families of the region (Beess,

Schaffgotsch, Henckel-Donnersmarck). However, the modest blossoming of the new court lasted only until the Third Silesian War in 1756. On the other hand, after his accession to the throne in 1740, the king's young male entourage increased considerably, altogether totalling about one hundred (pages, personal pages, personal huntsmen, court huntsmen, messengers, gentlemen of the Chamber and grooms). They were put into new uniforms, which retained the same fetching cut until the end of the reign.[51]

All in all, the new court remained small in terms of numbers. Christine Amalie, Friedrich's consort, was banished to Schönhausen and Monbijou and had to be content with forty to fifty attendants. After 1763 the king required only about five per cent of the total budget, some 1,200,000 Taler, for his personal purposes. Of that amount only 220,000 Taler were directly needed for the king's household; the queen received a mere 41,000 Taler. The king made savings everywhere, in particular on ambassadorial salaries. It would have been unthinkable for him to have spent 105,000 Taler on a single embassy, as his grand-father had done in Utrecht. In Bavaria, Saxony and

Württemberg, the gentlemen of the Chamber numbered hundreds; Prussia in 1786 had sixty.

Great festivities were a rarity, but coincided with the moments that were opportune in publicity terms, such as during the stay of Voltaire in Berlin. Although Friedrich II had a new apartment furnished for himself in Berlin during the mid 1740s and one of his five identical libraries was located there, he did not really appreciate the city palaces.[52] The king seems to have used the palace of Charlottenburg for the last time in 1773. This *de facto* restraint in Berlin does not mean, however, that the king abstained altogether from grand building projects – especially those of a courtly, representative nature. But it is difficult to imagine a ceremonial court life in the grand buildings he planned, given the actual modest size of the royal household.

From 1744 the king began building the terraced palace of Sanssouci, being involved in its design and execution down to the very last detail. Friedrich lived here on a modest, if comfortable, scale: bedroom, study, music room, library and dining room. From the very outset there had been no thought of court ceremonial, but rather of a private picture gallery, and this was actually built during the Third Silesian War. The fact that the monarch spent so much time here after 1763 does not mean that he had intended his lifestyle to be so restricted from the very outset. Quite the reverse is the case. In 1744–52 work on the conversion of the palace at Potsdam into a state winter residence was completed, and this work was hardly finished before still more ambitious planning began.[53] The pleasance in front of Sanssouci was to be provided with elaborate fountains and rounded off by a representative new building with a gigantic colonnade directly opposite the palace. Had this design been executed, the present visual impact made by Sanssouci would have been completely altered, making it merely a *point de vue* for a new principal palace.

The plans were altered, however, probably after the king's visit to Westphalia and Holland in 1755. The new residence was moved about one-and-a-half kilometres to the west and set at right angles to the royal vineyard. A new building technique using brick with chippings of hewn stone enabled the palace to be constructed in barely six years, despite the marshy ground that was reminiscent of Versailles. An interpretation of the so-called Neues Palais (New Palace), along with its splendid ancillary ranges (the Communs) as outer utility buildings, could give an indication of possible plans regarding the future court life, if the functions of the rooms were subjected to a thorough analysis. There is, however, no overlooking the fact that the entire building was designed to house a large number of royal guests and was equipped with magnificent staterooms. Here, the House of Hohenzollern could receive the dynastic rulers of Europe on an equal footing. How this gigantic stage could have been filled by the small-scale royal household as it existed in, say, 1780, is something that cannot be speculated upon.

What we do know is that the king's brothers and his sister assumed more and more representational duties, and undertook these from subsidiary courts based in urban and country residences: Prince August Wilhelm in Oranienburg and the Kronprinzenpalais, Prince Heinrich in Rheinsberg and the present-day Forum Fridericianum, Prince Ferdinand in Ruppin and the Johanniterpalast at Wilhelmsplatz, and Princess Amalie as Abbess of Quedlinburg in the former Palais Vernezobre on Wilhelmstrasse.[54]

Friedrich II came to spend more and more time in Sanssouci, however, and it was here that he assembled his Round Table, an all-male company. It was not made up exclusively of Prussian soldiers and officials, as in the *Potsdamer Tabakskollegium* (Potsdam Smoking Club), but included French-speaking intellectuals. The Berlin Academy, which in his father's day had been of no significance whatsoever, flourished again under Friedrich II. Swiss and French scholars poured into Prussia and enjoyed generous financial support from the crown. If the king took a liking to them they were made knights of his Round Table. It was only here that the king found truly agreeable company.

At Sanssouci, the ageing king withdrew increasingly from courtly life. Anecdotes celebrating his frugal yet bucolic lifestyle abound, with greyhounds tearing curtains and upholstery to shreds, and tobacco trickling on to unwashed shirts. We are no longer at court, but have arrived instead at the mythical Marquis de Brandebourg, as Friedrich II himself took some pleasure in seeing himself. His last wish, appropriately, was to be buried alongside his favourite hounds on the terrace of Sanssouci.

CHAPTER NINE

The Duchy of Savoy and the Kingdom of Sardinia
THE SABAUDIAN COURT
1563–c.1750

ROBERT ORESKO

TURIN, THE OFFICIAL SEAT OF THE DUKES OF SAVOY, later kings of Sardinia, was one of the most visited courts in early modern Europe.[1] During the seventeenth century, when the Piedmontese-Lombard plain was frequently a theatre of war, the court received, and was observed by, significant numbers of (mainly, but not exclusively, Catholic) foreign princes and military commanders. As confessional strife loosened after 1648, the court of Turin became an obvious stopping-point for those northerners (including Protestants) visiting the Italian peninsula via the western Alpine route, while the emergence of the Sabaudian court as a major European centre for élite education gave it a central role in the evolution of the Grand Tour. This cosmopolitanism was reinforced by the truly bilingual nature of the Savoy court, for the composite state of the dynasty embraced both the French-speaking duchy of Savoy, with its capital at Chambéry, and the Italian-speaking principality of Piedmont, the centre of which was Turin; fluency in both languages for the duke's courtiers was taken for granted and was essential for political advancement and for the protection of landed and family interests in a sovereignty that straddled the Alps. This is a different phenomenon from the emergence of French as the preferred court language in eighteenth-century Europe; at Turin both French and Italian were, of necessity, interchangeable. The court of Turin was a polyglot nodal point on a critically important north–south European axis, related to such concepts as Lothar's kingdom, 'le pays entre les deux', the Burgundian system and the Spanish road.

The exaggerated perspective of this painting emphasizes the key role of the two-storey-high central hall as the assembly point for the court when at the hunting palace of Stupinigi. From it radiated four diagonally positioned wings, all of a single storey, each allocated to a principal member of the royal family.

1. FROM ENTOURAGE TO COURT

Such cosmopolitanism would have been unthinkable for the first half of the sixteenth century, when Turin was simply a provincial town and the seat of the court was located at Chambéry. Turin became a capital only early in 1563, when Duke Emanuele Filiberto (1528–1580), restored to his states following the Treaty of Câteau-Cambrésis (1559), took the relatively early decision to transfer his court from Chambéry, constantly exposed to French military occupation, to the alpine-protected Turin. From this point, the history of the court of Savoy and that of the city of Turin become, at times, indistinguishable,[2] for successive dukes were confronted with the double problem of re-establishing a court: its administrative structure and its distinct visual expression. They also needed to create a capital city to function not only as a purveyor to the practical needs required to service an increasingly sophisticated and cosmopolitan court, but also as an urban emblem. The city of Turin had to be transformed into a larger and more obviously prestigious framework and setting for the court. All such decisions affecting both court and city were made at a time when the debate surrounding the 'ideal city' occupied an important place in the writings of architectural and political theorists. There are some striking similarities between the court-enforced expansion of Turin and the creation of St Petersburg. Like St Petersburg, Turin remained the seat of a court for only a few centuries, for in 1863 the King of Sardinia abandoned his capital to settle his court, temporarily, at Florence, as part of the House of Savoy's unificatory strategy for an Italian kingdom. Also, as with St Petersburg, the presence of a court in the early modern period left an indelible impression on the city and its culture long after the court itself had departed. Yet St Petersburg, as with, on a less significant level, Valletta, Sabbionetta and Charleville, was specifically created from nothing to be the seat of a court. The ancient city of Turin, instead, had a court imposed upon it, and here the closest models are Madrid, where the court had a vacillating presence until the second decade of the seventeenth century, and, especially, Modena, which found itself the adopted home of the Este court only after the dynasty's principal duchy of Ferrara had escheated to the papacy in 1597.[3]

The definitive installation of a court in a city long-accustomed to regulating its own internal affairs was a very mixed blessing. Inevitably the presence of the court swelled the size and importance of the city, and, indeed, Turin was one of the few Italian cities to register demographic growth during the early modern period. But balancing the concomitant and inevitable economic growth were the political problems implicit in the permanent presence of the court in a city where the patterns of power-holding were structured by long-entrenched vested local interests. The sovereign was now a constant factor in urban life and could intervene in and regulate much more directly its affairs than when the court had been settled elsewhere.

The court of Turin was, throughout the early modern period, in regular conflict with both the city and the Church, and it would be possible to see the tensions within this triangle of power-holding – court, communal council and archbishop – as the dominant historical element had not the court itself been so profoundly factionalized and heterogeneous. Homogenized courts, even those of sovereignties much smaller than that of Savoy, were very rare and belong more to the absolutist fantasies of nineteenth- and twentieth-century scholarship than they do to the realities of power in early modern Europe, but the court of Turin provides an extreme example of a court divided against itself. The collapse of the Savoyard sovereignty in the mid 1530s – the invasion of the Pays de Vaud by the Canton of Bern, the double politico-confessional revolution in Geneva, the Valois and Habsburg military occupation of the composite state of the Dukes of Savoy – simply eliminated a recognizable court. Duke Charles II retreated into an internal exile at Vercelli; his only surviving child, Emanuele Filiberto, with few expectations of restoration until a general European peace settlement had been agreed, entered the service of his maternal uncle, Emperor Charles V. Both father and son had, during the period from roughly 1535 to 1560, entourages, a cluster of loyal followers; they did not have courts, with their hierarchically arranged system of office-holding. In effect, throughout these twenty-five years of political crisis, the court of Savoy had ceased to exist.

Risorgimento historiography has emphasized the role of Emanuele Filiberto as a 'state-builder', the re-creator of *'lo stato sabaudo'*, the precursor of unified

Borgognio's bird's-eye perspective of Turin belongs to a set of engravings recording the cities and provinces ruled by the Duke of Savoy. Although idealized, this print captures the dominating position (upper left) of the citadel and the rigid urban grid plan that was followed in all future enlargements of the capital.

Italy. Such an approach has neglected the fundamental point that, after a long period of exile, the sovereign duke had to re-establish a court. The return of the duke in 1559 to his patrimonial lands was one of the earliest examples of 'restoration'. This historical phenomenon was later repeated by the restorations of the House of Bragança in Lisbon (1640), the Palatine branch of the House of Wittelsbach in Heidelberg (1648), the House of Stuart in London (1660), the House of Lorraine in Nancy (1698), and the Bavarian branch of the House of Wittelsbach in Munich (1713). The absence of the sovereign dynasty and its court over a protracted period dictated a retrieval of tradition in order to re-establish and to validate the customary co-operation between the sovereign dynasty and the socio-political élites, the natural meeting place of which was the court. The obvious point of difference between the restored Sabaudian court of 1559 and subsequent examples during the seventeenth and early eighteenth centuries was that of geographical identity. All the other restored courts returned to and built upon the archaeological and architectural remains of their predecessors; reclamation of space identifiable with the court, however long it had been vacated,

equated with political validation. The 1563 transfer of the Savoy court from Chambéry to Turin meant that Emanuele Filiberto was, very boldly, attempting to re-create a Sabaudian court tradition in an entirely different geographical and linguistic terrain to that which had nurtured its original version.[4]

The functional chaos surrounding the transfer to Turin reflected the profound problems of re-creating a court after a generational lacuna. Turin, a claustral, grid-planned Roman town, simply had no space to accommodate permanently an increasingly elaborate court structure. The duke and his duchess, Marguérite of France, daughter of François I and aunt to three consecutive French kings, installed themselves in the old Palazzo di San Giovanni, the official residence of the Archbishop of Turin, an early indication of the tensions between court and Church, or, more precisely between court and archiepiscopacy, specifically over juridical definitions of space within the capital. Their entourage, then evolving into a recognizable court establishment, was housed disparately in sets of private accommodation as close to the ducal couple as was possible. There simply was no direct architectural state-ment of the presence of a court, and even after the

The ephemeral form of entertainment known as 'court ballet' combined sung and declaimed text with dance and scenographic display, providing a vehicle for transmitting coded political messages. The concept of the 'King of the Alps' refers directly to the royal aspirations of the court and its claims on parts of Switzerland: Il dono del Re dell'Alpi a Madama Reale, *performed on 10 February 1645.*

construction of a new palace in the mid seventeenth century the architectonic envelope of the court of Turin would preserve the nature and character of a precinct, a sprawl of buildings, rather than the presentation of a central edifice to house the sovereign, surrounded by supporting household and ministerial buildings: the classic 'Versailles model'.

Topographical drawings and engravings dating from the 1570s and 1580s, preserved at both the Archivio di Stato and the Biblioteca Reale in Turin, demonstrate clearly how exiguous and incoherent the residence of the court was, crammed into a triangular wedge between the cathedral and the medieval castle, and marginalized to the extreme frontier of the bastions. Traditionally, Emanuele Filiberto's seeming indifference to palace building has been attributed to the duke's near obsession with the construction of his celebrated defensive citadel, the building of which was so costly and time-consuming as to preclude expenditure on a ducal palace. The decision to select as an architectual 'status symbol' a major citadel rather than a major palace reflected the duke's previous career in Habsburg service, specifically as governor-general of the Netherlands, where the citadel of Antwerp had deeply impressed him. Emanuele Filiberto's conviction that the citadel was of such essential practicality for the defence of his sovereignty may have led to his neglect of organized accommodation for his court, but it did introduce one visual element that would have a long-lasting influence upon the appearance of the palace precinct, the centre of court life: brick. By engaging Francesco Paciotti, one of the most celebrated military architects of his time, to design and construct the citadel, the duke established the figure of the official court architect as an engineer, a tradition that would not be broken until the entry in 1714 of Filippo Juvarra into Savoy service as the central administrator of all court artistic patronage, an appointment for which the dominance of Charles Le Brun at the court of Louis XIV was an obvious precedent. Paciotti was born in Urbino, frequently described as *'la città di mattone'* – the city of brick – and the widespread use of brick in Turinese building probably dates from this period. Building in brick was relatively more efficient and certainly less expensive than constructing stone-clad buildings, and for a court eager both to expand its 'surface space' and to create a capital city as a suitable setting for its site on the basis of a provincial town, brick provided an obvious answer. The severe external appearance of the palace area would ultimately clash with the richness of the interior decoration; but the reliance upon brick facilitated the rapid expansion of both the court precinct and the city in the early seventeenth century, at the cost of severe legislation governing the felling of forests in order to assure that the ducal kilns were regularly supplied with necessary quantities of fuel.

II. The Consolidation of the Sabaudian Court

By the time of his death, in 1580, Emanuele Filiberto had made a significant number of contributions to the definition of Sabaudian court life, most of which survived throughout the early modern period. Some of these reached back, as an exercise in validatory retrospection, to the 'golden age' of the fifteenth century, while others were novelties. Into the first category falls the renewal of chivalric orders. In 1572 Emanuele Filiberto restored the long-defunct Order of St

Maurice (S. Maurizio), named after the patron saint of Savoy and founded by the first Duke (as distinct from Count) of Savoy, Amadeus VIII (later the anti-Pope Felix V), the progenitor of so much of Sabaudian court ritual and tradition. In the same year he also obtained papal permission to merge this order with that of S. Lazzaro to form the military Order of SS. Maurizio and Lazzaro, comparable to those of the Knights of Malta and of S. Stefano, the religio-naval arm of the Medici court of Tuscany, the primary rival to Turin in the political centre of the Italian peninsula. The stated purpose of the restored and re-created order, based in the county of Nice, the third of the major component elements of the Sabaudian sovereignty, was control over the western Mediterranean, blocking Ottoman and piratical intrusions.

Although senior members of the sovereign dynasty and the high aristocracy were nominated to the Order of SS. Maurizio and Lazzaro, it remained the secondary court order. The highest order was that of the Annunciation (the Annunziata), founded in the fourteenth century – the precise date and circumstances are uncertain – during the reign of Amadeus VI. Limited to forty members, by the time of Emanuele Filiberto's restoration its numbers had dwindled to five, the last promotion having been made in 1529, thirty years earlier; even the duke himself had not been created a knight of the order. In 1568 Emanuele Filiberto moved to 'restore' the order, promoting nine new knights, followed by an additional five in the next year. The revival of the Annunziata, prefiguring the creation of the Saint-Esprit by Henri III of France and the so-called 'restoration' of the Garter by Charles I of England, provides an early example of 'retrieval politics' in early modern court society. Emanuele Filiberto, after some twenty-five years of exile, used both the Annunziata and SS. Maurizio and Lazzaro as symbolic devices to bridge the gap opened up by the military and political collapse of the House of Savoy in the 1530s and, by extension, the absence of a court.

As the statutes of the Annunziata insisted upon exclusivity of membership – as did those of the Garter (and much later the Scottish Thistle) and, until 1700, the Saint-Esprit and what became the Spanish (as distinct from Austrian) branch of the Burgundian Golden Fleece – no knight, apart from the master of the order, could belong to any other order – the court of Savoy gave an early indication of its drive towards recognition of hierarchical parity with those of Vienna, Madrid, Paris and later Versailles.[5]

The restoration of chivalric orders had a potent visual and iconographic force; it also possessed significant potential importance for the fundamental practicalities of re-creating a court. Emanuele Filiberto was born in Chambéry in 1528. He was, therefore, seven years old when the foreign invasions of the Savoy sovereignties began, and only seventeen when he left his father's establishment at Vercelli, eventually to enter Habsburg service. During the period between these dates and the restoration of 1559, much of the Savoyard and Piedmontese nobility had collaborated with the occupying military forces, either Valois or Habsburg. The re-knitting of loyalties between the restored duke, by this point a mature prince with a European-wide reputation for military prowess, and a nobility whose devotion to the dynasty had loosened during the quarter-century of troubles and exile, occupied a prime position on Emanuele Filiberto's political agenda.

Linked to this broader question of the widely based Sabaudian aristocracy as a whole was the more immediate problem of the re-creation of a specifically 'court' nobility, and this issue was complicated by the decision to transfer the seat of the court to Turin in 1563. Although some families did follow the court from Chambéry to Turin, many of the noble clans whose lands were, exclusively, in the duchy of Savoy, decided against migration over the Alps. The family of Saint François de Sales provides a telling example of aristocrats prepared to renounce their administrative and ceremonial roles at the court of Turin in order to preserve their local baronial interests on the western side of the mountains, while, at the same time, attempting to find a means of direct access to the ducal power base now located on their eastern side. The move to Turin, therefore, drove Emanuele Filiberto and his successors into an ever-increasing reliance upon the Piedmontese, as distinct from Savoyard, nobility, a nobility of which he had very little direct knowledge. In ordinary circumstances throughout Europe, the heir, upon his succession, had acquired straightforward and personal experience of the grandees who structured the court. Emanuele Filiberto had not had this experience of being raised amongst his future

courtier-servants, and, therefore, to create a court in Turin it was necessary to forge a system of relationships between the newly established duke and the Piedmontese élite who would henceforth direct and manage his court. Emanuele Filiberto, therefore, consciously used his revival of the august House orders as one of many means to establish a working relationship between the sovereign and the major aristocratic families upon whom he was dependent for staffing and populating his newly established court at Turin.

The duke also reached back to the validatory past with the somewhat delayed transfer of the Holy Shroud (the SS. Sindone) from the Sainte-Chapelle at the Château of Chambéry to Turin. While all princes south of a geo-politically defined line in Europe were Catholic, some, to paraphrase George Orwell, were more Catholic than others. The profoundly rooted reputation of the House of Savoy's devotion to Catholicism found its visual expression in the posssession and regular display ('ostension') of the Shroud, deemed to be one of the most important relics of Christendom. In abandoning Chambéry, a move that disrupted the renascent court and which threatened to alienate the Savoyard élites, Emanuele Filiberto had been careful to leave the Holy Shroud behind; its removal from the duchy of Savoy at this early stage would have sharpened the sense of injury caused by the transfer of the seat of the court. Yet, the iconographic importance of the Holy Shroud and its self-conscious utilization by the House of Savoy to underscore the dynasty's elevated hierarchical position dictated its eventual installation in Turin.

A suitable pretext presented itself in 1578 when the Archbishop of Milan, Cardinal Carlo Borromeo, expressed his intention to make a pilgrimage on foot to Chambéry to venerate the Shroud, enabling Emanuele Filiberto to transfer the Shroud to Turin in order to ease Borromeo's votive journey from Lombardy. From this point on, the Holy Shroud became the central element in religious ceremony at the court of Turin, displayed in public on important feast days or in celebration of significant dynastic events such as baptisms and weddings. It also acted as a lure for foreign princes and grandees, who were customarily granted private access to the relic. The transfer of the Shroud helped to make the court a place of pilgrimage throughout Catholic Christendom, but at the same

Twentieth-century controversies over the authenticity and the preservation of the Holy Shroud have obscured the key role it played in court ceremony and the frequency with which it was displayed. Other Italian courts possessed rival holy relics; for instance, the Holy Blood preserved in Mantua by the Gonzaga dukes.

time its housing posed problems. Juridically, the Shroud was the private property of the dynasty; it was a court object not a Church object. The necessity to express clearly and visually the attachment of the relic to the court rather than to the Church demanded a direct architectural statement, but this proved impossible until the palace itself could be organized. Both problems were resolved only during the second part of the seventeenth century.[6]

While the installation of the Shroud in Turin in 1578 indicated straightforwardly Emanuele Filiberto's intentions to use older traditions in order to confirm the credentials of his restored court, he also deployed religion in ways that were entirely novel. From the very beginning of the restoration the duke had shown

himself sympathetic to the Society of Jesus, and by 1567 the Jesuits had established their presence in Turin. The weight of the Jesuit presence in early modern court culture in general can be overestimated, and, as with most other Catholic courts, that of Turin eventually spread its patronage and favour among a number of orders. While by no means exercising a monopoly over spiritual patronage at the court of Turin, by the middle of the seventeenth century the Society of Jesus had established a central position for itself in a variety of court activities: not only erudition and education, but also theatre and festivals.

Another durable innovation in court life, one also linked to religious identity, was initiated by Emanuele Filiberto following the renewal, in 1576, of the alliance between the House of Savoy and the Catholic cantons of the Helvetic Confederation. As a result of this accord, the duke undertook to employ a company of Swiss soldiers as his official bodyguard, thereby placing his court within a broader European tradition, one that survived until the end of the *ancien régime*, where the maintenance of an Helvetic guards corps at the seat of the court indicated sovereign rank. The permanent presence at the Sabaudian court of the Swiss guards would ultimately influence the ground-plan of the state rooms of the new palace.

The court that Emanuele Filiberto bequeathed to his only legitimate child Carlo Emanuele on his death (1580), a mere seventeen years after its establishment in Turin, possessed a number of elements recognizable in other European courts of the period, while lacking a key feature of general court culture – a coherently organized system of residences both within and outside the capital city. Duke Carlo Emanuele I succeeded his father at the age of eighteen, a prince who had reached his juridical majority, but one who had scarcely had the time to acquire the experience of government that Emanuele Filiberto had been able to call upon at his restoration. During an exceptionally long reign of fifty years (1580–1630) he built upon the achievements of his father in re-establishing a court and initiated the transformation of his capital into a major European city. Much of the credit for forging the court of Turin into one of nearly royal status can be attributed to the young duke's consort, the Infanta Catalina Michaela, the younger daughter of Philip II of Spain, whom he married in 1585. Although Catalina Michaela's presence in Turin was relatively brief – she died in 1597 after twelve years of marriage and nine pregnancies – her influence in shaping the structure of her husband's court was longer lasting. Her experience of life at the court of her father propelled her to sharpen definitions of etiquette and precedence at Turin, and by the time of Carlo Emanuele I's death, the court of the Duke of Savoy possessed clear structures of both hierarchy and administration.[7]

III. THE STRUCTURE OF THE COURT

At the pinnacle of the hierarchical system stood the duke and his immediate family, that is, his duchess and their children, the nuclear ducal, soon to be royal, family. Immediately beneath them were the princes of the blood (*principi del sangue*), those members of the House of Savoy with a right to the succession to the throne should the main line die out or 'daughter out', the Sabaudian crown not being susceptible to female succession. During the seventeenth century, this category was represented by the Ducs de Nemours and by the Principi di Carignano. The Ducs de Nemours, descended from a younger brother of Duke Charles II of Savoy, settled at the French court of François I, who had pursued an active policy of attracting cadet princes of foreign sovereign houses into his service. The French dukedom of Nemours was among the rewards accorded to Philippe of Savoy for establishing himself at the French court, while his son Jacques obtained from Emanuele Filiberto the elevation of his Savoyard *apanage*, the county of the Genevois, to the level of a dukedom in 1564. This alpine power base of the Nemours branch of the dynasty, with its capital at Annecy, posed continual worries for the court of Turin, from which it was geographically distant and, thanks to the mountain range, topographically protected. As possessors of a substantial and coherent block of territory located at the furthest northern extent of the Sabaudian lands, the Ducs de Nemours consistently harboured ambitions to detach themselves from Turin, creating their own sovereignty, and, during the sixteenth-century French Wars of Religion, expanding their territory into the Dauphiné. During the early seventeenth century Henri de Nemours, who nurtured hopes of marrying one of Duke Carlo Emanuele I's daughters, had spent substantial time at the court of Turin, where he played a fundamental role in organizing court festivities. Nevertheless, for most of the sixteenth and seventeenth centuries the attention of

Dating from 1853, Bossoli's gouache illustrates the use by the Savoy court of one of the most technically advanced palace staircases of eighteenth-century Europe. The open windows, the presence of the hunting dog on the half-landing and the horse at the entry underscore the role of the staircase as the zone of transition between the interior space of Palazzo Madama and the outside world.

the Ducs de Nemours was focused on Paris, the dukedom of Nemours and Annecy, where, if there was not a definable court, there certainly existed an entourage and an administrative system that could serve as a magnet for the francophone nobility of Chambéry, which was distanced from service at the court of Turin. The last Duc de Nemours died in 1657, and the marriage in 1674 of the elder of his nieces to the head of the house, Duke Carlo Emanuele II, facilitated the incorporation of the private landholdings of this always menacing branch of the dynasty.[8]

In establishing the Carignano *apanage* for his youngest son, Francesco Tommaso, as a scattered collection of territories, Duke Carlo Emanuele I demonstrated that he had learned from the mistakes of geographically consolidating Nemours power, but he also guaranteed the nearly permanent presence of the Princes of Carignano, not only at the court, but also within the capital of their cousins in the senior line. The fixed installation of the Carignano princes in Turin brought its own hazards, for the cadet branch established its own court, which in effect became an alternative court to that of the Dukes of Savoy. The architectural expressions of the Carignano court were the imposing Palazzo Carignano (begun 1681), virtually within sight of the ducal palace, and the extra-urban Castle of Racconigi (begun 1679), within easy communication of the capital where the Carignano princes built up their own precinct of influence.[9] The Carignano court was similar to the ducal court both in hierarchy and administration, with titles of offices replicating the senior posts of the ducal household. The Carignano court had its clientele and patronage systems, both political and cultural, and, indeed, the Theatine priest Guarino Guarini, the great mathematical and architectural theoretician who designed both Palazzo Carignano and Racconigi, was officially a member of the Carignano household – even if he did work 'out on loan' on some highly significant commissions for the duke. The Carignano princes frequently pursued their own separate foreign policy, pro-Habsburg during the seventeenth century, pro-Bourbon during the eighteenth, while a sequence of marriages, some meeting with royal disapproval, established a specifically Carignano kinship network with access to the courts of Versailles, Rome and Vienna. The Carignano cousins have been called the

'Orléans of Savoy' because of their perceived 'liberal' opposition to the ruling branch of the family during the *ancien régime*, and it was with this reputation that they finally succeeded to the crown itself in 1831, after the extinction of the main branch of the dynasty.

If, for much of the early modern period, there were two courts in Turin, during the years from roughly 1685 to 1720 there were in effect three. When finally compelled in 1684 to relinquish the regency for her son Duke Vittorio Amedeo II, the formidable Maria Giovanna Battista, known as 'Madama Reale', moved out of the ducal palace. She installed her household in the adjacent medieval castle and organized a hierarchy of offices similar to those of the ducal and Carignano courts. From here she engaged in cultural rivalry with her son, eventually commissioning Filippo Juvarra to design one of the great European baroque façades and staircases (begun 1720, and clad, significantly, in stone), for her residence, called Palazzo Madama and sited on a line perpendicular to the understated and more modest façade of the ducal palace.[10] Maria Giovanna Battista also pursued her own foreign policy, and the Palazzo Madama became the centre of the French faction at the court of Turin, in contrast to the Carignano court, which initially looked to Madrid, and eventually, as Prince Eugen emerged as a power at the imperial court, to Vienna. The existence of three courts, the power bases of which, Palazzo Reale, Palazzo Madama and Palazzo Carignano, were located within several hundred metres of each other, inevitably acted as competing magnets for the loyalties of the factionalized Piedmontese nobility, whose fissures, so obvious in the decades leading up to the 1559 restoration, had been sharply defined again during the civil wars of 1638–42. The model of Turin as three courts within one challenges the notion of the early modern court as a homogenized unit, and the concept of the court as a collection of courts, of competing foyers of patronage, can be applied with profit to courts as diverse in size and external splendour as those of Versailles and Modena, indeed to any court where cadet branches structured their own households along the lines of the central court and pursued their own strategies of patronage and political policy.[11]

In terms of court precedence, immediately beneath the princes of the blood ranked the *signori del sangue* or lords of the blood. Between them, Dukes Emanuele

Filiberto and Carlo Emanuele I sired roughly nineteen illegitimate offspring; the precise number will never be known. As all but one of these were born when the duke was either a bachelor or a widower, this brood of bastards did not suffer the stigma of adultery, facilitating their legitimization and their incorporation into court service and, indeed, the administration of government. The *signori del sangue* consisted of the recognized male bastards, the recognized female bastards and, significantly, those men who married the latter and the offspring produced from these unions. As only two of the legitimized sons married and neither had children, there was no attempt to establish bastard lines, as at Versailles, and as only one received the Annunziata, the 'genealogical purity' of the supreme House order was preserved. Yet they played a central role at court, acting as intimate advisers to successive dukes and regents, and, in the administration, holding such key posts as the governorships of the duchy of Savoy and the County of Nice. The same can be said of the men who married the legitimized daughters, for, unlike their brothers, most of the bastard girls married – and married extremely well – into such families as the Simiane and the Masserano, clans with some claim to sovereign status, and their husbands frequently did receive the Annunziata.[12] Thus, these three strata, the nuclear ducal family, the princes of the blood and the *signori del sangue*, constituted the extended dynasty and, accordingly, stood at the centre of court life and at the pinnacle of the court's hierarchy and etiquette; but it was precisely this external court etiquette that was used to express the distinctions maintained between the three levels. Precedence in such public rituals as court processions on the most important religious feast days was an obvious means; so were the regulations governing court dining in public, when the form of chair, the position at the ducal table, the type of service – for instance, whether or not the cup was 'tasted' (the *assaggio*) – and the identity and status of the servant, all indicated rank within the extended dynasty.[13] In 1713 Vittorio Amedeo II, elevated by the Treaties of Utrecht as King of Sicily (forcibly exchanged in 1720 for the crown of Sardinia), instituted a reform in court ceremonial that was careful to specify the different colours of the cushions on which members of the extended House of Savoy were to kneel, according to rank, when the entire dynasty attended mass together in public.

At the next level came the great noble court clans, but here too there were internal distinctions. The Knights of the Annunziata took precedence over all nobles, however ancient their lineage, however elevated their title (the highest title of nobility was that of *marchese,* or marquess; the title of duke or prince was reserved for members of the dynasty, and could only be obtained by subjects from outside the Sabaudian realm), thus reinforcing the prestige of the House order. Some form of special status seems to have been accorded to the very understudied *signori forestieri,* or 'foreign lords', those nobles (such as the Lascaris family of Nice) who held some claim, however unrealizable, upon a (usually defunct) sovereignty. This style still carried considerable prestige at both court and in government well into the second half of the eighteenth century, and it seems likely that the families who bore it constituted the upper echelon of the roughly one hundred clans who could trace their nobility back to the medieval period, the core of the court nobility. By 1700 the nobility as a whole has been estimated as encompassing at least 5,000 families, reflecting the rapid expansion of the second estate; but it has been argued that while the much older families were remarkably successful in maintaining their hold on power and influence at court, they were equally remarkably resilient, at least in the seventeenth century, in absorbing, sometimes after only a generation or two, the newly ennobled families, drawn largely from financial and juridical backgrounds, by means of intermarriage. The older feudal clans still dominated the court nobility at Turin, but they moved rapidly to ally themselves with the wealthier and, in terms of governmental administration, powerfully positioned newcomers.[14]

The factionalism within the élite group of courtiers, so clear in the sixteenth and early seventeenth centuries, erupted once again into full view during the regency (1675–84) of the Duchess Maria Giovanna Battista, and the extent to which the high court nobility could operate against crown policy is a necessary corrective to the carefully nurtured historiographical view of these clans as a service corps united by devotion to the duke. While the level of intermarriage was certainly very high among this élite, as at most European courts, some families, profiting from the very cosmopolitanism of the court itself, entered employment or negotiated marriages outside the Sabaudian realm. The dal Pozzo family owed its title of Principi della Cisterna to favour at both the Spanish and papal courts, while a member of the Turinetti family entered imperial service and worked closely with Prince Eugen in the Southern Netherlands. In the second half of the seventeenth century, Munich and Vienna became poles of attraction at least as forceful as Paris, Madrid and Rome. The Marchese di Parella's sister married into the upper echelons of the Viennese court and provided a direct means of contact between the emperor and the Duke of Savoy when open diplomatic negotiations were impossible, while the heir to the Scaglia di Verrua family married, with disastrous results, into the highest reaches of the French ducal peerage. Indeed, this match demonstrates yet again how the cosmopolitanism of certain elements of the high court aristocracy of Turin enabled its members to act with varying degrees of flexibility and even independence. In the late 1680s the Contessa di Verrua, the daughter of the Duc de Luynes and a Rohan princess, abandoned her husband in order to become the acknowledged mistress of Duke Vittorio Amedeo II; as the duke turned increasingly away from an enforced alliance with Louis XIV, thus marginalizing the pro-French (and already humiliated) Scaglia clan, which had provided four knights of the Annunziata, the cuckolded count abandoned Turin and moved his family to Paris, where he entered French service.[15]

The dynasty was dependent upon the greater court nobility for a number of functions and services. They were essential for administration in the provinces, the close identification of the Alfieri family with the important city of Asti providing a good example. If newer nobles increasingly staffed the governmental administration, the older families and, indeed, the upper layers of the aristocratic élite as a whole, held a virtual monopoly upon the senior and most prestigious military commands in the cavalry and the infantry, while their grip on the diplomatic corps was, if anything, even tighter. The court grandees played a central and indispensable role in one of the House of Savoy's most cherished projects, the expansion of the claustral urban cube into a capital suitable as the setting for their court, a policy requiring, by means of investment and building, the co-operation of the second estate, particularly its wealthier members with the means to indulge in conspicuous consumption.[16] It was, however, by its dominating presence in the hierarchy of courtly – as distinct from governmental – office that the paramount importance of the upper Sabaudian nobility was at its most apparent.

At his death in 1630, Carlo Emanuele I bequeathed to his heir, Vittorio Amedeo I (1630–37), a fully developed court structure, one that is clear from a list of court office-holders drawn up in 1631.[17] The court of Turin was, as were many European courts, divided into three broad departments: the Casa (the Household), the Camera (the Chamber) and the Scuderie (the Stables). A fourth major department was established in the eighteenth century as part of the successful attempt to remove confessional life at court from the jurisdiction of the Archbishop of Turin. At the apex of the hierarchy of the Casa stood the grand master, seconded by the first *maggiordomo* (high steward or major domo), and to them fell the responsibility of the maintenance and the victualling of the court as a whole, as the very title *gentiluomini di bocca*, awkwardly rendered into English as 'gentlemen of the mouth', indicates. Service by quarters, with the gentlemen rotating duty every three months, was customary. This was the highly public and official face of court life in Turin. The Camera was governed by the grand chamberlain, beneath whom were the first esquires of the Chamber followed by the gentlemen of the Chamber. Throughout the seventeenth century the gentlemen of the Chamber numbered between twenty and twenty-five, and these were selected from the cream of the court nobility, for it was the Camera and not the Casa – although the higher offices there were also filled by aristocrats – that was the real seat of power. One element of court life, eating, will help to explain the source of such power, and here a distinction must be made between the preparation of food and its serving. The kitchens where the food was prepared were the preserve of the Casa, and when the duke dined or supped in public he was served by the *gentiluomini di bocca*, who belonged to the Casa. When, however, the duke dined privately in his Camera – which was, in fact a private appartment rather than a single room – the grand chamberlain and his staff assumed the responsibilities of serving the food. In these circumstances, the Casa had control of the food until it reached the door separating Casa from Camera, but when, arriving at this door, the servants of the Casa handed the food over the threshold – not stepping over it – to the servants of the Camera, from this point the esquires and gentlemen of the Chamber served the duke. The frontier between Casa and Camera was palpable and jealously guarded, for, apart from his consort, his children or his mistress, it was the officers of the Camera, not the Casa, who had the most direct access to the sovereign when he was in private and when he was *indoors*, from which privilege derived the importance accorded to nomination to the Camera.

'Indoors' is the operative word, for the Dukes of Savoy, like most of their brother sovereigns, spent a great deal of time outdoors, normally mounted on a horse, and this was the realm of the third great court department, the Scuderie, or Stables. The importance of the role of the *grande scudiere*, the equivalent of the English master of the horse or the French *grand écuyer*, has frequently been undervalued by students of European courts. The Sabaudian master of the horse was in charge not simply of the stables, horses, dogs and apparatus needed for the hunt, but also of the entire service of the duke as soon as he set foot out of the palace. All displacements of the duke and his court, either by land or by water – and the nearby presence of the River Po was an important factor in court life – were under the control of the master of the horse, as, obviously, was the hunt, one of the more compelling reasons for the duke to leave his capital and one of the key conditioning factors in the evolution of ducal and, later, royal building policy outside Turin. During the 1660s and 1670s the cult of the ducal hunt of Carlo Emanuele II was emphasized iconographically by artists in Sabaudian service; but, if access to the Camera was rigorously restricted, inclusion in the hunt, with all the attendant possibilities of assassination, was even more tightly controlled, limited to those enjoying distinct ducal favour and to the officers serving with the master of horse – hence the occasional doubling of posts between the Casa and the Scuderie. Both departments were nodal points of court power, when intimacy with the duke facilitated requests for advancement, the proferring of advice and the gathering of information.[18]

Amongst the many duties of the master of the horse was the supervision of the education of the court pages, the future courtiers, and here he played a role, albeit a limited one, in the emergence of the court of Turin as one of the centres of European élite education. The main factor in this development was the Academy, built as virtually an extension of the palace. By the late 1680s the Academy had established a strong reputation, based upon a curriculum in the courtly arts, from horsemanship and fencing to dancing and languages, and it attracted – indeed, consciously recruited – students from the upper ranges of the northern European (including Protestant) aristocracies and princely families. The students frequently stayed for more than one year, and those belonging to sovereign dynasties were absorbed into life at court, dining in public with the duke and his family; adding during their stay to the general cosmopolitanism of the capital and, on their return, spreading knowledge of the court.

IV. THE MATERIAL CULTURE OF THE COURT

If, by 1630, an articulated court hierarchy and a codified administrative system had been set in place in Turin, neither differing radically from most of the other court structures in early modern Europe, Duke Carlo Emanuele I had also initiated projects involving 'material culture' – in his case the collecting of objects and the erecting of buildings – that increasingly came to support claims to sovereignty and acted as 'significators' of status and power throughout Christendom. It has recently been suggested that the order in which the Infanta Isabel Clara Eugenia, the governor of the Spanish Netherlands (1621–33), entailed her collections at the Brussels court is applicable to other courts for the hierarchy of importance, prestige and value accorded to different fields of collecting. The first part of her collection to be placed in entail was the armour, followed by the tapestries and later by paintings; the intrinsic, realizable worth of gold- and silverwork on the armour, and woven as thread into the tapestries, being one of the reasons that these two elements of the collection were valued above framed and painted pieces of wood or canvas.[19]

Carlo Emanuele I did, indeed, invest much time and organization in his collections of arms and armour: the most valuable and highly crafted pieces were arranged in terms of a collection not of an arsenal. Annotations in the duke's own hand, and entire documents drafted by the duke himself, testify to his central involvement in planning the elaboration of the gallery linking the palace to the medieval castle as a home for this growing collection. Both the objects within this gallery – referred to as the Grand Gallery of Carlo Emanuele I – and the decoration of its walls called attention to the warlike grandeur of the dynasty.[20] The walls functioned as a form of ancestor gallery, painted with portraits of the duke's predecessors that depicted visually his direct descent from the Saxon dukes, a favourite theme in Sabaudian court iconography. The duke also bought heavily in the tapestry market, especially during the second half of his reign, although largely to decorate the walls of his residences, a practical, rather than museological, function.[21] He did, however, attempt to introduce some discernible order into the growing mass of pictures, which, by a variety of means, the dynasty had acquired since 1559. As with the gallery for arms and armour, Carlo Emanuele's direct engagement in this process can be documented from archival sources, for an autograph list, again dating from 1605, records those paintings that the prince deemed the most valuable. The development of a court post of curator of pictures suggests a growing concern to organize the collection, while Carlo Emanuele's son Duke Vittorio Amedeo I took the process of systematization one stage further in 1635, by engaging a Roman painter, Antonio della Corgna, to undertake a comprehensive inventory of the ducal pictures.

Such rationalization of the interior of the palace was reflected in Carlo Emanuele I's determination to extend the surface area of his capital with the first of three amplifications in the early modern period, each of which repeated the grid pattern inherited from the claustral block of antique Turin. Grandeur of expression certainly played its role here, and it has been argued that the duke and his court became adept at exploiting the potential for public display and procession in the expanded city, which became an external theatre of the dynasty. But so did the more practical pressures of easing the discomfort of a growing court that had never been happily settled in the confined space of the old city. The first major extension dates from the end of the second decade of the seventeenth century, pushing the city's boundaries to the west towards the citadel; the second 'amplification' was

initiated in 1669, opening up a southern quarter, but stopping just short of the militarily indefensible River Po; and the third phase, in the early eighteenth century, thrust to the north along an axis fixed squarely on the old castle, now clad in Juvarra's classicizing and imposing façade. The line along which the first extension ran was placed at a strict right angle to the palace precinct, and thus it is clear that the lay-out of all the 'amplifications' was designed to draw maximum visual attention to the court. All three extensions were the result of the determination of the duke to expand his capital and, accordingly, he bullied and threatened, lured and bribed the high court nobility to purchase, sometimes under very favourable terms, empty lots in the new quarters and to build their own imposing private, family palaces upon them.[22]

V. FROM DUCHY TO KINGDOM: THE CREATION OF A REGAL COURT

Carlo Emanuele I's pretext for forging ahead with the early seventeenth-century extension was the arrival in 1619 of his son's bride, Marie-Christine of France, sister of Louis XIII, who made her official entry through the new gateway ('la porta nuova') and proceeded along a straight line through the new quarter directly towards the palace. She and, initially, her husband became the key figures in the evolution of the Sabaudian court during the three middle decades of the century. Although the reign of Vittorio Amedeo I (1630–37) was brief and largely concerned with armed conflict in the Italian theatre of the Thirty Years War, the new duke made one decision that transformed the nature of his court. In 1632, building upon a number of his father's unrealized political ambitions and buoyed by the birth of his own son and heir, Vittorio Amedeo publicly proclaimed the royal status of the House of Savoy on the basis of the dynasty's claims upon the kingdom of Cyprus. His court was no longer a 'ducal' or a 'serene' court, but, specifically, a 'royal' court. From this point on, until at least 1713, with the acquisition of Sicily, but most likely well beyond this date, all activity at court, all the ceremonies, all the festivities, all the hierarchies, indeed all the expenditure was gauged at Turin against those of the courts of Paris (later

Versailles), Madrid and Vienna, with which the Dukes of Savoy sought to gain parity of status. The elaboration and sophistication of the court, which, it was posited, only a royal monarch could sustain, was used consciously and explicitly as an argument in the gradual but ultimately successful struggle to extract recognition of the royal status of the Sabaudian realm and its sovereign ruler.[23]

Although Vittorio Amedeo I's reign made this central contribution, it was his consort Marie-Christine who emerged as the real heiress to her father-in-law. After the turbulence of the civil wars of 1638–42, the duchess governed the states of her young son, Duke Carlo Emanuele II, in the juridical quality of regent until the duke's technical majority in 1648; but even after the formal end of her regency she succeeded in maintaining her hold on governing power until her death in 1663. For the central twenty years of the century Marie-Christine was the dominant force at the court of Turin and she used her considerable knowledge of other European courts both to build upon Carlo Emanuele I's achievement and to solve some of the problems he bequeathed his heirs. Marie-Christine, with her formidable knowledge of the workings of the French court, also had access to those of her Medici and Gonzaga cousins and, as her two sisters were the Queens of Spain and of Great Britain, Turin could now draw closer to Madrid and Whitehall as well.[24]

Perhaps the major challenge at court inherited from Carlo Emanuele I stemmed from his failure, despite some ambitious projects, to build a coherent and architecturally 'regular' building immediately recognizable from its exterior as a ducal, and later a royal, palace. As late as 1622 the visiting Prince de Condé commented on the palace compound that it had become 'very extensive but without rule of construction or architecture'. Initial building plans in the new reign, which must have been related to the royal declaration of 1632, had been frustrated first by the drain on resources of the Thirty Years War, and then by the chaos of the civil wars. It was only in 1646 that very tentative initiatives were undertaken, and the completion of the new royal palace waited until the late 1650s, towards the end of Marie-Christine's life. The design of the austere and understated façade is due to Amedeo di Castellamonte, another representative of the characteristic Turin court 'type', the official

architect with a strong background in military fortification planning. However undemonstrative the architectonic envelope was – particularly when compared half a century later to the sophistication and vibrancy of the façade of the adjacent Palazzo Madama – the luxury of the interior space set a pattern for conspicuous consumption to be followed by successive rulers.[25] Castellamonte also succeeded in imposing a coherent order on the sequence of state apartments. A massive official staircase led to the Hall of the Swiss Guards, the most accessible space in the palace and, therefore, one decorated with images destined for public consumption: the heroic deeds of the Saxon sovereigns from whom the Dukes of Savoy claimed descent. This was the only room in the sequence that was two storeys high and embraced the entire depth of the main central wing. From it, two doors opened on to parallel enfilades of state rooms, re-worked almost beyond recognition in the late 1830s by the great neo-classicising architect and decorator Pelagio Palagi. The duke's sequence (from 1713 the king's) faced the inner courtyard and the garden; that of the duchess (subsequently queen) gave directly on to the formal entry courtyard defined by Castellamonte's façade; the consort's – and not the sovereign's – suite being the focal point for all approach, in ceremonial and urban terms, to the palace itself. Thus, while endorsing the broader European courtly tradition of distinct 'male' space and 'female' space, as enshrined in the later example of Versailles, Turin placed these sectors back-to-back along the central spine of the palace. At Turin, one massive staircase led to one central 'reception space' from which the rooms of the sovereign and those of his consort bifurcated. The workings of this system are thrown into sharper relief during the 1680s by the ceremony of the Washing of the Feet on Maundy Thursday. The duke washed the feet of, and with his senior courtiers served midday dinner to, thirteen poor boys, while his duchess and his mother with their principal ladies, including *signore del sangue*, did the same for thirteen poor girls in the female sector. The duke and the two duchesses were waited upon with food provided by the Casa in the common space of the Hall of the Swiss Guards; the food was set down in one joint space, the ceremony then divided along lines of sex in separate rooms cut off from one another by a single wall. Unlike Versailles, where there were several

Above: *Miel depicts the extent of courtly display in the countryside, paralleling that within the palace precinct. The Flemish-born painter was one of many northern artists to find employment at the court of Turin, and his celebrated series of equestrian portraits of courtiers underscores the role of the master of the horse.*

Right: *The* curea *was the high point of the royal hunt, the moment the stag was killed. This crowded canvas indicates the impressive size of the hunt at the court of Turin and belongs to a sequence of paintings by the Cignaroli family, which recorded court activity and which, through landscape paintings used as palace decoration, depicted the seigneurial holdings of the dynasty – a statement of ownership.*

'foyers of reception' – the king's staircase and the queen's staircase – the official spaces of the sovereign and that of his consort were more tightly bound together by the distribution of rooms within the heart of the palace. Also, unlike the Versailles model (where the male and female wings determined the outward appearance of the entry façade, the chapel and theatre being twinned, right of centre, next to one another in the eighteenth century), at Turin it was precisely the chapel and the theatre that defined the boundaries of the central block of the palace. Their symmetrical role, placed at the extremities around the central conjugal core, stands in stark contrast to the separation of the male and female sides of the French system.

Organizing the royal palace was only part of Marie-Christine's achievements in regularizing the entire system of the Sabaudian 'residences', still referred to as *le residenze sabaudiane*. To understand this part of the building programme, so central to court life, it is necessary, yet again, to look back to the problems posed by the transfer of the seat of the court to Turin in 1563. While the absence of a functioning palace in the capital posed its own set of difficulties, Duke Emanuele Filiberto and his immediate successors were also

deprived of the network of subsidiary palaces on the Italian side of the Alps, the increasingly elaborate villas and hunting lodges, which had come to characterize, throughout Europe, the seasonal displacements of the court from its urban seat to the countryside. This concept is entirely different from that of the so-called 'itinerant' court, travelling from castle to castle over a wide geographical extent. Instead, a tight band of secondary residences evolved around the capital. Their use depended exclusively upon climate – outdoor festivities, of which, for Turin, regattas and fireworks on the Po provide a good example – and the hunt, the identity of the animal who was the object of the chase at specific points in the calendar year – the basic pattern that also determined Bavarian court life. Emanuele Filiberto repossessed castles such as Rivoli, in the shadow of the mountains on the subalpine plain, and Moncaliere, sited on a sharp bend over the Po, but it was not until the final decades of Carlo Emanuele I's reign that his daughter-in-law Marie-Christine and his son Cardinal Maurizio developed the idea of the fluvial castle-villa, using the Po as an extension of the expanding city. In 1617 Maurizio acquired the building that ultimately became known as the Villa della Regina (the queen's villa), which served as a temporary retreat from formal court life, but it was Marie-Christine who established a new pattern with her major building work at Valentino, sited directly on the Po but also just outside the new (first) extension of the city. English equivalents are inadequate for terms such as *delizie* (literally 'delights') or *maisons de plaisance* (houses of pleasure, another awkward and misleading rendering), but all these residences became, in effect, suburban outposts, albeit very large and imposing ones.[26]

During the reigns of Carlo Emanuele II (1638–75), Vittorio Amedeo II (1675–1730) and Carlo Emanuele III (1730–75), this system of subsidiary fluvial residences was complemented by the erection of substantial hunting palaces, such as Venaria Reale and Stupinigi. Venaria Reale developed into another experiment in town planning, as the ducal palace extended beyond the inner fabric to embrace a sequence of squares and churches to house and to service the staff that itself serviced the court.[27] As at Venaria Reale, the principal court church at Stupinigi was dedicated to St Hubert, the patron saint of the hunt, and such iconography advertised the purpose of the building.

The hunt, in all its different forms, varieties and targets, played a critical role in court life throughout Europe, dominating afternoons, determining the displacements of the court, facilitating access to the sovereign, signalling shifts in favour by inclusion in or exclusion from the hunting party, and strengthening the role of the master of the horse in protecting the prince when outdoors. The hunt was also a prime moment for the display of courtly magnificence, when the size of the train, the social composition of the party and the display of the garments of hunters and huntresses and the caparisons of the horses and the collars of the dogs were deemed to be important enough to be commemorated in a sequence of large-scale oil paintings. The hunt at the court of Savoy, therefore, inhabited an oxymoronic world, at once the space for intimate requests for favour and for 'networking', but also providing the occasion for the visual and very obvious 'representational' validation of the court itself through ostentation, thus touching the slippery concept of 'magnificence'. Carlo Emanuele II was actually called '*il magnifico*' – which, as Gregorio Leti pointed out in 1675, justified the rank of his establishment as a specifically 'royal' court.[28]

Both Venaria Reale and Stupinigi were large palaces, endowed with sufficient space to house the entire court, certainly those whom the princes chose to invite. This situation points to further contradictions, for while the Dukes of Savoy and the subsequent Kings of Sardinia were profoundly concerned with expanding their capital, the royal palace played a diminished role in their lives. The court was installed in Turin during winter, yet for the rest of the year a different pattern of residence emerged; Rivoli, Moncaliere, Venaria and Stupinigi all 'housed' the court for weeks or even months at a time, while the official seat of the court remained fixed at Turin.

The case of Stupinigi provides a useful example.[29] Large enough to provide impressive apartments for the principal members of the dynasty, the court could accommodate itself within this hunting palace without difficulty; yet, set out on a direct axis to the city of Turin, only sixteen kilometres away, the capital and the court were in easy reach of one another. This was true of the entire 'corona' or 'coronet' of residences; all were large enough to house the court, but all were close enough to Turin to permit ministers, ambassadors and foreign visitors to present themselves at the non-resident court and still return to Turin within the same day.

This tight system of 'movement' and 'control' was complemented by the princes' attitude to their non-Italian-speaking territories. Composite states inevitably required the presence of the prince and his court from time to time in those regions that were not the home of the capital; this presence soldered loyalties and guaranteed that the clientele system was maintained. The duchy of Savoy was visited regularly, for six weeks or two months at a time, and this dictated that the Château of Chambéry be maintained in appropriate state to receive and house the court. During the eighteenth century the development of spas at Évian and Aix-les-Bains provided further reasons for the king and his court to spend time in the Francophone part of the realm, and Nice similarly commanded attention. Such frequent displacement dictated that the system of court administration extended beyond the corona of Piedmontese residences in order to embrace the palaces and châteaux on the other side of the Alps.[30]

If Marie-Christine played an essential role in organizing palace space, she also did much to establish a distinctly Sabaudian theatrical and visual court culture. The highly erudite wall decorations, with historical, emblematic and allegorical allusions, owed a profound debt to the presence of court scholars, either members of or closely associated with the Society of Jesus: for instance, Emanuele Tesauro or François-Claude Menestrier. Jesuit erudition also informed the court spectacles, the jousts, tourneys and carousels, but also the distinct form of entertainment called the *ballet de cour*, a combination of dance, sung music and chivalric display that always carried a political charge – here, persistent allusions to the royal pretentions or to claims on the kingdom of Cyprus. The dominance of the *ballet de cour* at the court of Turin retarded the emergence of a court opera,[31] with 'sung-through' texts performed by professional *virtuosi*, the form of entertainment that was slowly establishing itself as the dominant mode at other Italian, and, indeed, European courts. Marie-Christine and her youngest daughter, the Bavarian electress, were also devoted supporters of the Theatines, and the duchess also enthusiastically encouraged Carmelite foundations in the capital, including her own 'name church', S. Cristina. While the Savoy court was amongst the most demonstrably

Catholic of Europe – along with Vienna, Innsbruck, Munich, Mantua and Nancy – it was also very careful to prevent any one order from exercising a monopoly on its confessional affinities. The Jesuits played a critical role in court life and in court culture, but they were not permitted at Turin to exclude other orders from access to the centres of power and influence.

Marie-Christine had been alarmed by the sexual attraction of her son Carlo Emanuele II to his Nemours kinswoman Maria Giovanna Battista, and arranged instead for his marriage to one of her Orléans nieces. Her death in January 1664, only weeks after that of Marie-Christine herself (December 1663), meant that the duke was free to wed, in May 1665, his distant cousin. If Marie-Christine was the effective heir to Carlo Emanuele I in forging the structure and culture of the court of Turin, then Maria Giovanna Battista, however much the two women disliked each other, assumed the mantle of her mother-in-law. In addition to the academies of education and learning that she founded, and her important architectural enterprises – the façade of S. Cristina that she commissioned, her restoration of S. Lorenzo, the official court chapel, and her spectacular re-working of Palazzo Madama – Maria Giovanna Battista resolved one of the outstanding problems of the court of Turin: the housing of the Holy Shroud, which by the death of Carlo Emanuele II (1675) still had no permanent home. Guarino Guarini received in 1667 the commission to realize the Shroud Chapel, a task completed during Maria Giovanna Battista's regency.

The chapel is sited between the palace and the cathedral. Although juridically attached to the palace, it is indeed the architectural zone of transition between the two buildings. The Holy Shroud could thus be venerated by the sovereign, his court and his guests privately, thanks to access from the palace, but it could also be seen in its altar from the nave by anyone in the cathedral.[32] Moreover, the prince and his court could enter the cathedral through the Shroud Chapel, without leaving the palace precinct, although on the most formal occasions the court progressed from the palace in public and entered the cathedral through its main doors. Guarini's Shroud Chapel captures architecturally the tensions between court and Church, as does the construction of the basilica of Soperga on a hill overlooking and dominating the city of Turin.

Conceived as the result of a vow made by Vittorio Amedeo II just before the battle that lifted the 1706 siege of Turin by the French, the basilica of Soperga became the responsibility of the Messina-born architect Filippo Juvarra.[33] Clearly inspired by Philip II's Escorial in its combination of basilica and monastery, Juvarra and Vittorio Amedeo II followed the Castilian model in one further respect: the inclusion of a royal necropolis. The burial arrangements of the House of Savoy had previously been unsatisfactory, with members of the dynasty being entombed in the cathedral. With the elaboration of Soperga, the Turin archbishop's control loosened over an important court activity: court mourning.

Above: *Medieval Rivoli was one of the buildings in Piedmont that the court of Savoy absorbed into its system of residences after its transfer to Turin. Unlike Valentino or Stupinigi, it was not built anew but had its existing structure transformed into a royal castle. Pannini's painting depicts the ideal, not the realized, reworking.*

Left: *The dominance of court ballet at Turin delayed the adoption of opera as the presiding mode of court music-theatre, unlike the situation at other Italian-speaking courts. The technical and mechanical resources required for opera were met only in 1740 with Benedetto Alfieri's Teatro Regio, a model for the design of other court opera houses.*

The engagement of Juvarra as court architect was a direct result of Vittorio Amedeo II's coronation in Sicily in 1713, and of the new king's determination that his court in Turin should reflect his elevated status in competition with the other royal courts of Catholic Europe.[34] Juvarra dominated visual culture at the court of Turin between 1714 and 1735 and his classicizing architectural vocabulary, based to a large extent upon his knowledge of Roman palace and ecclesiastical design, endowed the court and the city of Turin with a new sophistication and cosmopolitanism. His appointment terminated the long tradition of official court architects with a strong background in military engineering, and his extensive brief, including control of festivities and providing designs for, and

commissioning from other artists, furniture, paintings and silver, led to the expansion and the effective organization of court arts around a team of artists, artisans and craftsmen, a system that had the appearance of a governmental department with Juvarra as its director.[35] This 'bureaucratization' of the court arts at Turin continued into the subsequent reign, but with the difference that the single controlling hand of Juvarra was replaced by a collective leadership. It seems probable that Carlo Emanuele III put up no great resistance to Juvarra's request in 1735 for a three-year leave of absence in order to design the new royal palace in Madrid, and that the king preferred to work with younger and different artists than the architect he had inherited from his father. A troika emerged in the

1730s of the architect Count Benedetto Alfieri, scion of one of the leading families in Albi, the painter Claudio Francesco Beaumont and the furniture-maker Pietro Piffetti,[36] and this remained in place until Beaumont's death in 1766 and Alfieri's in 1767.

VI. THE 'COMPLETION' OF THE COURT 1730–73

The long and strangely understudied reign of Carlo Emanuele III is traditionally divided, both in political and cultural terms, into two halves, from the king's accession in 1730 on his father's abdication to roughly the 1750s, and the second from the 1750s to the king's death in 1773. The earlier half is characterized by an ambitious foreign policy and a cultural explosion at court in the post-Juvarrian period; the second by political caution and artistic stasis, if not torpor. While such a model is clearly an oversimplification, a case can be made for suggesting that during the first two or three decades of his reign Carlo Emanuele III 'finished' the court founded two centuries earlier by Emanuele Filiberto through a sequence of decisions that resolved the outstanding problems and filled the remaining gaps in the structure of court life in Turin.[37] One key alteration was the creation of a fourth major court office, that of the grand almoner (*grand elemosiniere*), which finally resolved the jurisdictional tangle between court and Church by removing the court from the direct authority of the Archbishop of Turin. The first recipient of this new post was Vittorio Amedeo delle Lanze, who as the (legitimate) son of one of Carlo Emanuele II's unacknowledged bastards, was virtually a member of the family. Initially endowed with benefices traditionally and emblematically associated with the dynasty, his promotion to the post of grand almoner in 1745 made him the head of all religious activity at court; as at so many other Catholic courts, Turin now had its own 'court bishop'. In that role, Amedeo delle Lanze collaborated closely with the king to regulate religious life at court and to distribute benefices and nominate bishops, thus making an impact on the realm as a whole. His elevation to the cardinalate in 1747 also had important implications. The King of Sardinia, in his quest for equality with other Catholic royal sovereigns, here obtained the longed-for right of naming a 'crown cardinal'. Thus, during the eighteenth century the court of Turin, again in common with the major Catholic courts, had the prestige but also the obligation of housing and accommodating a prince of the Church.

The reorganization of religious life at court points to a fundamental characteristic of Carlo Emanuele III's reign, an overriding concern with administration. Another example is provided by his archives. The inner courtyard of the royal palace had never been closed on all four sides and remained open to the royal gardens. As early as 1730, the year of his accession, Carlo Emanuele had set in motion the construction of the missing fourth wing designated specifically to house the dynasty's private archives and, thus, blocking off the view on to the gardens from the main entrance to the palace. In 1731 Juvarra drew up designs for a second archival building, the so-called Royal Archives, now the State Archives, housing those documents relating more to government than to the family. This wing of the palace complex closed off yet another open courtyard, one between the palace itself and the Academy. The king's concern to house his papers and documents in artistically distinguished surroundings signals the court's concern with its own organization, one that altered the fabric of both the palace and the palace complex.[38]

These early commissions pre-dated by only a few years another – one that resolved the outstanding problem of court theatre. The architectural revolution engineered by the Galli Bibiena family concretized the need for every court to create a lavish structure exclusively and permanently consecrated to theatre and opera. The public appearance of a prince at the theatre became as important as his public appearance at mass. Although most theatrical representations at the court of Turin had been staged in the official appartments or in the gardens, no real theatre complete with the necessary stage machinery existed, despite projects by Juvarra. As part of his policy to ensure that the court of Turin possessed all the necessary 'equipment', in 1738 Carlo Emanuele III commissioned Benedetto Alfieri to design and build the Teatro Regio (Royal Theatre) on the right-hand wing of the royal palace, which symmetrically balanced, but was also opposed to, the religious sector on the left-hand side. The tensions between religion and theatre, those two prime areas where princes traditionally 'exposed' themselves to public view, frequently appeared in the architectural and spatial arrangements at court. The creation of a permanent court theatre and its technical achievements were advertised abroad in 1741 by the publication of Alfieri's book of engravings documenting the architect's technical skill and validating the regal status of the court to which he was attached.[39]

Such validation was also sought in the elaboration of a full-scale picture gallery, an essential element of court culture. During the seventeenth century the dynasty's collecting had been haphazard, restricted to family portraits and devotional works. Vittorio Amedeo II had commissioned paintings from Sebastiano Ricci and Francesco Solimena, but their function was mainly 'decorative', part of the fabric of the wall rather than touching the concepts of a 'collection' organized into a 'gallery'.

The death of Prince Eugen of Savoy in 1736 provided the ideal opportunity to plug this particular gap. Eugen had died intestate, and the sale of his highly prestigious collection of paintings, with their immediately identifiable frames, was negotiated in 1736–7. With their acquisition, the court of Turin took posession of both a collective emblem of attachment to one of the great military heroes of Christendom – hence the iconic importance of the frames – but also, at a stroke, a picture gallery deemed worthy, indeed necessary, for a royal court.[40] What it is now fashionable to call cultural artefacts, those objects contained in armouries, libraries and picture galleries, played an important role in establishing the image and the status of the court. They became – as did an architecturally coherent palace, a capital city of sufficient extent and splendour, a court bishop and a complete and 'magnificent' system for the hunt – suppliers of the practical needs of court life, but they also functioned more symbolically as indicators of the ability of one specific court to participate in a more general, European-wide system of court life and culture.

So did the royal tapestry works, elaborated in 1737, and the ceramics works at Vinovo, in which Pierre-Antoine Hannong, a member of the celebrated Alsatian family of faïence-makers, played a key role. Similarly, the position of the Boucheron family as court silversmiths drives the argument back to function, both practical and symbolic.[41] The court required objects to cover the walls of the palaces and to furnish its tables; but the foundation of tapestry, glass and ceramics works, supported and funded by the court – Sèvres and Gobelins in France, Meissen in Saxony, Nymphenburg in Bavaria, even Mortlake in England – became essential to the definition of a court. All courts needed such manufactories in order to assert the range of their activities within a broader cultural framework. The establishment of tapestry or ceramics works equated itself with notions of sovereignty – no mere subject could undertake to support and to promote such manufactories – and competition between courts merely increased the number and variety of producers and their products. The Turin court's attempt to encourage such manufactories is part of a larger European pattern of emulation and competition.

In the second half of the eighteenth century reactions to the court of Turin varied dramatically. Gibbon found it one of the best ordered and regulated courts of Europe, while Casanova thought it boring and suffocating. The importance of the court of Turin lies in its gradual metamorphosis, in the transformation of a small city, effectively 'invaded' by its sovereign and his entourage in 1563, into a major European capital. The gradual construction of a court from nothing provides a key to understanding and to defining the essential elements of court life, from the organization of the household and the patronage of artists to the care of horses and dogs. Older, established courts took such inherited procedures for granted; courts that had been restored (such as Turin and Lisbon) or recently founded (such as Parma, Florence and St Petersburg) had to create or to re-create their own court systems. This frequently painful process elucidates what were then viewed as the essential constituent elements of a court, of court life and court culture; since there had been no seamless transition from the late-medieval court ethos, the structure and organization of the restored or new courts were clearly articulated in a way that older courts would not have found necessary. The two-hundred-year evolution of the court of Turin gave the House of Savoy an important training in creating and elaborating a court. This experience proved remarkably valuable in 1870 when, in Rome, the dynasty was faced, despite implacable papal opposition, with the task of forging a court at the Quirinal Palace, a court that reflected the political realities but also the misguided aspirations of a unified Kingdom of Italy.

CHAPTER TEN

The Grand Duchy of Tuscany
THE COURTS OF THE MEDICI
1532–1737

MARCELLO FANTONI

T HE CREATION OF THE MEDICI COURT WAS A CONSEQUENCE OF the Florentine state's transformation from a republic to a dynastic principality in the first decades of the sixteenth century. With the establishment of the Duchy of Florence in 1532, the former city-state's leading family metamorphosed from the status of merchant princes to that of quasi-kings. Yet a recognizable court came into being in Florence only with the accession of Duke Cosimo I (1537–64), not before: not in the short-lived reign of his predecessor Alessandro (1532–7), and still less in the previous republican period, notwithstanding the remarkable cultural patronage of Lorenzo the Magnificent (1449–92). For a court is a precise spatial, social, political and cultural entity, and it is only with Cosimo I that it is possible to speak of a true court in Florence. In this sense, the period of Medicean courtly rule with which we are concerned lasted precisely two centuries, from the 1530s to the extinction of the Medici dynasty on the death of Gian Gastone de' Medici in 1737,[1] although there would continue to be a court in Florence well into the nineteenth century: during the period of Lorraine rule (1765–99); in the Napoleonic period (1801–14); during the Lorraine restoration (1815–60); and finally under the House of Savoy (1865–71).

Thus, by Italian standards, the Medici court was one that came into being relatively late (its only points of comparison in this respect being the courts founded by the Farnese and Savoy dynasties), and one whose disappearance occurred when it was still at the apogee of its expansion. For despite Tuscany's political and economic decline from the end of the seventeenth century, the grand-ducal court still enjoyed a reputation in the early years of the eighteenth century as one of the most magnificent in Italy; and Florence, with its palaces and collections, its 150 churches and 20 theatres, its 90 monasteries and

The marriage in 1608 of Grand Duke Cosimo II (1609–21), right, to the Habsburg princess Maria Maddalena of Austria, sister of the Emperor Ferdinand II, consolidated the status of the Medici as equals of the most illustrious European ruling dynasties. They are depicted with their son, Grand Duke Ferdinando II.

convents, and its paved streets,[2] held a continuing fascination for ambassadors and dignitaries from all over Europe. In the years in which the dynastic crisis was reaching a head, Medici patronage and the splendours of the court even appeared reinvigorated, partly as a result of Cosimo III's acquisition of the title of Royal Highness in 1699.

This was not a court that experienced phases of profound structural change (as, for example, was the case with the courts of the Po Valley); rather, the Medici court organized itself from the outset along what were once termed 'absolutist' lines, and assumed a bureaucratic and ritualistic character. Where art is concerned, the picture is more complex, in that the arc of time that interests us spans the age of the Mannerism of Giorgio Vasari (1511–74), through to the Baroque of Pietro da Cortona (1596–1669). The Medici court was, moreover, extremely diverse in its cultural interests, making important contributions in many different fields of knowledge.

In the 200 years of its existence the Medici court oscillated between widely diverse political and cultural poles, gravitating from the oppressively Spanish-dominated ethos of Cosimo I's court in the 1530s and 1540s, to the French cultural influences of Ferdinando II's reign (1621–70), and later passing into the orbit of the states of the Habsburg Holy Roman Empire (a development increasingly marked from 1691, when Anna Maria Luisa, Cosimo III's daughter, married the Elector Palatine). These influences were the result of dynastic connection through marriage into some of the most illustrious royal houses of Europe, and they reveal the breadth and prestige of the network of relationships that the House of Medici succeeded in weaving around itself. Here, too, virtually no signs of decline are apparent in the course of the seventeenth century: the Medici court was anything but the 'incorrigibly provincial' household described by Sir John Hale.[3] The marriages of Catherine (1533), Cosimo I (1539), Francesco I (1565) and Ferdinando I (1589), with, respectively, Henri II of France, Eleonora of Toledo, Joanna of Austria and Christine of Lorraine, were followed by those of Marie de Médicis to Henri IV of France, of Cosimo II with Maria Maddalena of Austria, sister of the Emperor Ferdinand II, in 1608, and of Cosimo III with Marguerite d'Orléans, cousin of Louis XIV, in 1661.

Nor is this simply a case of a minor power attaching itself to the coat-tails of a series of major ones. The Florentine court, for its part, had a substantial and durable influence on court culture elsewhere in Europe:[4] one only has to examine its impact on French culture during the successive regencies of, first, Catherine de Médicis (1560–73), and, half a century later, Marie de Médicis (1610–17).[5] The same might be said of the Medicean court's relations with the Hispanic world, which drew no small number of themes, artefacts and artists from the great court workshop of Florence. A similar influence may be registered in the case of the Habsburg-Lorraine courts, this time in their role as later inheritor and custodian of the Medici treasures following their succession to the Tuscan throne in 1737. Likewise, the European dimension of Florentine court culture, and its role in originating and propagating styles, tastes and cultural formulae goes beyond a strictly artistic context, extending to the fields of science, historiography, music and linguistic study (as with the Accademia della Crusca, founded in 1582) – not to mention its massive influence on theatre and the staging of public spectacle.

I. THE PALACE AND THE CITY

Where civic space is concerned, the moment that marked the birth of the court in Florence was Cosimo I's decision to abandon the family's old urban palace in the Via Larga – and, with it, all the earlier Renaissance projects to make this building the centre of gravity for the Medici clan and its power.[6] Cosimo's move to Palazzo della Signoria in 1540, formerly the seat of the city's republican government, signalled a novel approach to the problem of town planning and the re-invention of the family's public identity, in that it was the first step in a process that would eventually lead to the establishment of a fully fledged princely residence created by the physical remodelling and ideological recharging of the old republican palace of the commune. Vasari worked for years on this project in his various roles as architect, painter and courtier, and was responsible for the courtyard inaugurated for the wedding of Francesco I in 1565, the monumental entrance staircase, the Salone dei Cinquecento, and many other interventions that radically changed the

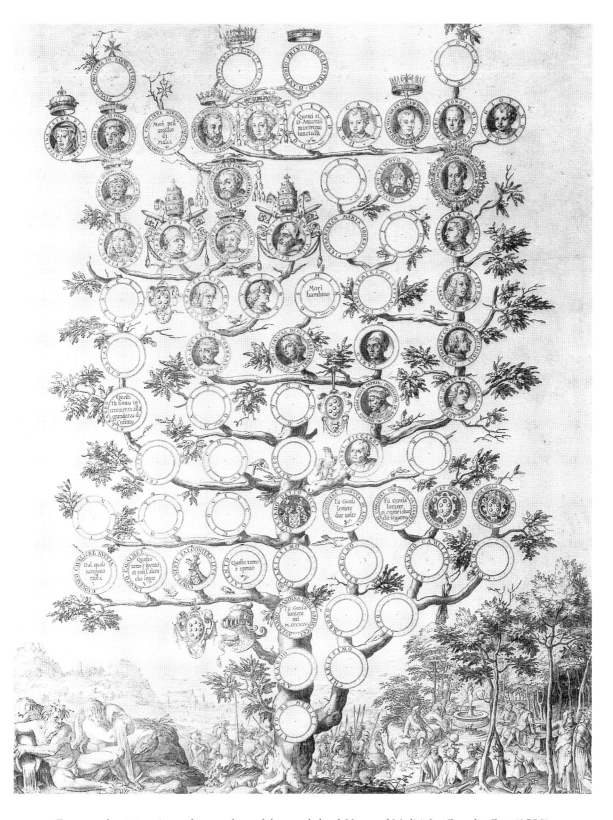

From merchants to princes: the genealogy of the grand-ducal House of Medici, by Cornelis Cort (1589).

disposition of space within, and the external appearance of, the building.[7] Vasari worked in close consultation with the grand duke, and in collaboration with Francesco Salviati, Vincenzo Borghini, Cosimo Bartoli and a substantial team of artists, craftsmen and designers of figurative schemes, who worked on the *studiolo* of Francesco I and the apartments of Eleonora of Toledo and of the Medici Pope Leo X, all decorated with elaborate mythological, historical and astrological allegories in a sophisticated Mannerist style.

During the final decades of the sixteenth century there was a further relocation of the court, this time to the opposite bank of the Arno, where the work began on realizing what was to become a genuine palace, fit for a sovereign: the Pitti Palace. The transfer to the Pitti marks a second watershed both in the structural development of the Medicean court and in the evolution of its figurative language, as well as in the monarchical ideology of the regime – even though with the Pitti, as with the Palazzo della Signoria, we are still talking about the conversion of an existing Renaissance building into a ducal residence, rather than building *de novo*. With the move to the Pitti Palace, the Medici court began its process of expansion into a vast and articulated corpus of constructions, with a distinctive physiognomy conferred on it by the famous 'elevated corridor'. This umbilical cord, connecting the elements of what was basically a bipartite court (with one pole in Piazza della Signoria and another in the Pitti and the Santo Spirito district), took in directly along its way, the Uffizi and the church of Santa Felicità. This palace complex was completed by the Boboli Gardens (laid out in 1549) and the fort of the Belvedere (erected 1590–95).

Cosimo's plan to convert the Pitti Palace into his official residence had begun almost with the establishment of a quasi-regal Medicean household in 1537. He entrusted the task to the architect Bartolomeo Ammannati, but the plans took effect only after the peace of Câteau-Cambrésis in 1559 and the death of Eleonora of Toledo in 1561. During Eleonora's lifetime, when the Medici had acquired the former residence of Luca Pitti (1549), the initial intention had been to create a suburban villa, as is clear from the famous lunette painted by Justus Utens in 1599. Work on the palace proceeded slowly, and both Cosimo and his son Francesco I spent much of their time residing elsewhere. Indeed, before the ascent to the throne of

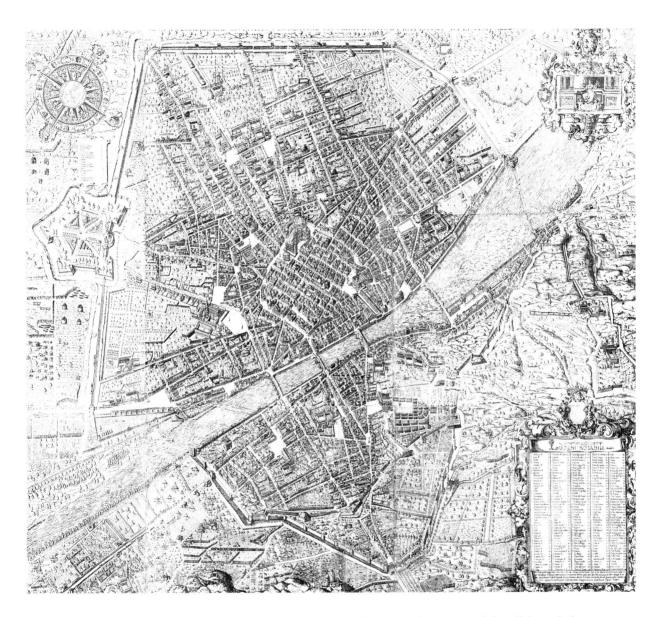

Above: 'Aulic space' within sixteenth- and seventeenth-century Florence extended well beyond the Medici palaces: the ceremonial ambit of the court extended from the Palazzo della Signoria and the Church of the Annunziata on the north bank of the Arno to the Pitti Palace on the south, a map of 1584.

Left: From republican to hereditary rule: until the creation of the Medici duchy of Florence in 1532, the Palazzo della Signoria, depicted here in inlaid stone by the goldsmiths Bernardino Gaffurri and Jacques Bylivelt, had served as the seat of Florence's republican government. Cosimo I took up residence in the palace in 1540, and it remained the seat of the Medici ducal court until the court's move to the Pitti at the end of the century. The equestrian statue of Cosimo I in the guise of a Roman emperor further attests to the grand duke's monarchical aspirations. It was one of a series of mid sixteenth-century sculptural commissions by the Medici for the city's major civic spaces that deployed Roman imperial iconography to recast the image of the family in explicitly princely terms. Inlaid pietra dura work of the type depicted here became one of the celebrated specialisms of the Florentine ducal workshops.

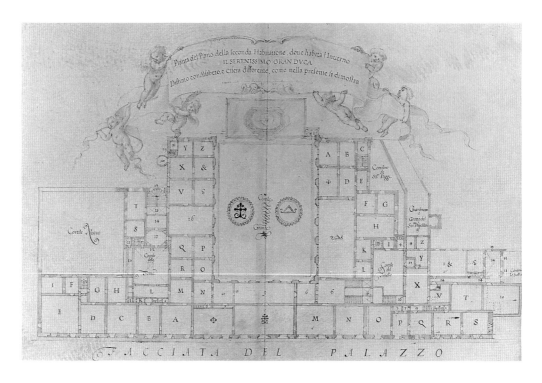

Plan of the principal floor of the Pitti Palace in 1662, by the architect Diacinto Maria Marmi.

Ferdinando I (1587), the Pitti Palace has been described as a kind of 'sumptuous hotel' for the Medici's most important guests.[8] Only in 1588, it appears, did the works reach completion; simultaneously, the Vasarian 'elevated corridor', which, until 1565, had terminated at the Grotta Grande in the Boboli Gardens, was extended so that it reached its culmination in the new palace. Even so, it was only under Diacinto Maria Marmi, employed in the domestic administration (*Guardaroba*) of the court between 1648 and 1702, that the Pitti Palace took on its definitive shape, both from a spatial and a ceremonial point of view. The task of conversion of the palace was almost continuous, and was assigned successively to the leading Florentine architects of the day. Ammannati's work on the palace (1561–70), which produced the great courtyard and various extensions, was followed by Bernardo Buontalenti's work in the Boboli Gardens (1576); by the modifications to the body of the palace by Giulio Parigi (1571–1635); and, finally, by the interventions of Giovanni Battista Foggini (1652–1725).[9]

From an urban perspective, too, Florence can be said to have acquired a princely aspect only in the early seventeenth century – despite the impact of Cosimo I's building projects in the 1540s and 1550s. The process of metamorphosis was gradual. Politically, the most crucial project was undoubtedly the Uffizi: the functional heart of the 'modern' and efficient bureaucracy centred in the hands of the prince. The demolition that took place to clear a space for this new building (which cost the exorbitant sum of 400,000 scudi) began in 1545, coinciding with Cosimo's first substantial modifications to the institutions, the administration and the bureaucracy of the realm.[10] The formal rigour of its façade, the solemnity and symbolism of its foundation ceremony and the allegories expressed in its ornamentation all declare the ideological, as well as functional, impulses behind the construction of Vasari's great building, which is linked to the ducal apartments by a bridge spanning the Via della Ninna.

If the architectural setting of the Medici court took shape with the Pitti Palace and the Uffizi, then the regime's interventions in the urban fabric were directed towards creating a civic space that would be semantically and ceremonially appropriate to Florence's new courtly identity, as this gradually supplanted and sought to obscure the traces of the city's bourgeois and mercantile past. The nature and scale of these interventions varied; the imposing Fortezza da Basso was designed by Antonio da Sangallo the younger in 1534 in the wake of the investiture by the emperor of Alessandro de' Medici as first Duke of Florence in 1532, and the establishment of princely rule.[11] But they include the splendid sequence of Medici villas and residences, and the buildings, spaces and routes created to accommodate the rituals of the Medicean court, such as the two processional axes of the Via de' Servi and the Via Maggio, which cumulatively had the effect of redrawing the political map of the city. The first axis created a link between the cathedral and the sanctuary at the Santissima Annunziata; the second served as a ceremonial approach to the Pitti Palace. One might also consider in this connection the adaptation of the great city churches to accommodate the new theatricality of liturgical practices as they were introduced after the Council of Trent.[12] Besides the great churches of Santa Maria Novella and Santa Croce (remodelled, respectively, in 1565–72 and 1564–5), this work of transformation and appropriation also embraced the principal sacred sites associated with the Medici court, which served as focal points for court ritual. Outstanding among these was the Cappella dei Principi in San Lorenzo, begun in 1604, and destined to become the mausoleum of the dynasty.[13]

Simultaneously, symbols of the new regime proliferated, both in Florence and throughout its subject territories – articulated in heraldry, statues and on public buildings. One might point, for example, to the 'pantheon' of statues in the Piazza della Signoria (renamed Piazza del Granduca), exalting the virtues of the grand duke and the legitimacy of the new regime: Baccio Bandinelli's *Hercules and Cacus* (1534); Ammannati's Neptune fountain (1575); Giambologna's equestrian statue of Cosimo I (1595); the marble group by Danti (1563–72) on the façade of the Uffizi, with Cosimo I as Augustus flanked by political allegories; and Giambologna's *Rape of the Sabine Women* (1579–83). Of similar ideological import are the two monumental columns erected in the Piazza Santa Trinità (1569) and the Piazza San Felice (1570) to commemorate the grand duchy's victories at Montemurlo and at Marciano over the Florentine political exiles who had aimed at the restoration of the republic. The same theme emerges in the equestrian statue of Ferdinando I, erected in 1608, dramatically placed at the centre of Piazza Santissima Annunziata.

At times of festivals and dynastic celebrations, the face of the city was transformed by vast ephemeral architectural structures – triumphal arches, *faux* façades and the like – that provided theatrical props for courtly display. The princely regime was also celebrated in the countless Medici busts and heraldic devices disseminated throughout Florence and her subject cities.[14]

Of course it was not only Florence that was affected by the creation of a court. The lesser Tuscan cities and summer resorts underwent a similar process of adaptation in this period to meet the demands of a household that was still itinerant for much of the time, as well as to express the new reality of Medici political domination. Evidence of this process is clearly visible in Arezzo, the site of numerous interventions by the Medici court architect Vasari after 1540; in Siena after its conquest in 1555; and in Pisa in its role as summer residence for the court and as the seat of the chivalric order of Santo Stefano (founded by Cosimo I in 1562). The impact of grand-ducal power is also apparent in the frontier fortress of Terra del Sole and the mining centre of Portoferraio-Cosmopoli – indeed, throughout the entire territory, in the form of irrigation works, fortifications, aqueducts and other modifications to the infrastructure.[15] Each individual piece within this vast architectonic scheme was closely correlated with the new regime's own process of legitimization and self-definition; in manner, it was consistent with the practice of the other courtly regimes of the Italian cinquecento, both great and small. With painting and sculpture, historiography and language, the architecture and urban planning of the Medici court in this period testify to a gradual process of assimilation of earlier institutions and customs within the ideological canons and priorities of the new regime.

In urban planning, Medici court patronage appears to have adhered to theories codified in contemporary writings on the ideal city, which, since the time of Leon Battista Alberti, had proposed a precise spatial typology and ornamental order for seats of princely power. In Florence, in particular, if we wish to grasp the logic underlying the many and heterogeneous interventions of the Medici, it is necessary to turn to the projects –

which might almost be said to amount to draft treatises on urban design – of Bartolomeo Ammannati (1584) and Giorgio Vasari the younger (1598).[16] These writings, incomplete and unsystematic as they are, hint at the existence, beyond what can look like a casual sequence of building projects, of a master-plan for the construction of a city corresponding to the canons of functionality, decorum and 'magnificence' imposed by the presence of a court.[17]

II. THE COURTIERS

In the 1540s, when the Medici transferred their residence to Palazzo della Signoria, the household of the first grand duke, Cosimo I, was still composed of a distinctly limited number of servants: by the time of his abdication in 1564, the number of servants had increased to 168, while under Francesco I (1564–87), they numbered 233. The decisive leap, however, was to occur with Ferdinando I and Cosimo II during the years 1587–1609 and 1609–21, when these figures more than doubled. In 1695 the number of members of the household reached a peak of 792, and the Pitti establishment was maintained at this level until the death of Gian Gastone in 1737.[18] To this figure must be added what were known as the 'mouths' (non-residents who nevertheless received some provision of foodstuffs from the court), as well as those serving in the satellite courts of Medici relatives, the incumbents of high military offices, government functionaries and palace guards. It has been estimated that around the mid seventeenth century the Medici court comprised more than 1,500 people, if we are to include with those employed on a regular basis those whose association with the court was more casual. From a demographic perspective, the impact of the court on the city was immense. If one estimates that the households of these court-associated individuals contained an average of four people, it emerges that something like eight or ten per cent of the inhabitants of Florence were in some way tied to the court.

Questions of numbers aside, it is important to note that the 'household' (*familia*), the palace personnel taken as a whole, and the mass of mere 'employees' (*salariati*, whose relationship with the court was a purely financial one), made up distinct cadres within the population of the palace. These sections were further sub-divided into various different departmental and professional groupings (kitchen staff, secretaries, pages, the staff of the gallery, linen-room, bedchamber and chapel, for example). A further distinction is necessary between this resident staff, considered as a whole, and the heterogeneous mass of those whose relations with the court were conducted on a casual or a strictly commercial basis: artisans, merchants and

Above: *Anna Maria Luisa de' Medici, dancing with her husband the Elector Palatine of the Rhine in 1695.* Right: *The court as centre of production: the Medici court employed hundreds of metalworkers, semi-precious stoneworkers, jewellers, engravers and medallists, organized from 1588 as the Opificio delle Pietre Dure. This imaginary view by Alessandro Fei (c. 1540–92) gives an impression of the diversity of the luxury goods produced not only for the court, but also to supply international connoisseurs.*

suppliers of manufactured goods and raw materials, members of the regular clergy, casual labourers, innkeepers, landlords of buildings rented by the prince, gamekeepers, the rural nobility, members of the order of Santo Stefano – even exorcists, as we find in 1620.

A further well-defined group is that employed in the production of art within the framework of the department known as the Reale Cappella e Galleria (the Royal Chapel and Gallery), founded by Ferdinando I in 1588: an institution that, along with the famous semi-precious stone workshop of the Opificio delle Pietre Dure, also incorporated jewellers and goldsmiths, miniaturists and silversmiths, engravers and weavers, and workshops for the manufacture of porcelain and medals. In the reign of Cosimo III (1670–1723), more than a hundred artists and artisans were employed in this sector, organized into various workshops under different masters. The offices of the Reale Cappella were flanked by the Mint, similarly based in the Uffizi (in the rooms previously occupied by the foundry), and by other court manufactories: the tailoring operation of the Guardaroba del Taglio, and by a hybrid range of workshops producing furniture and other domestic items, livery for horses and carriages, arms, and liturgical objects.

The court, then, is revealed as not just a centre of consumption, but also a massive centre of production, certainly the largest and the most diversified and centralized of the city. The artisans labouring to meet the needs of the court amounted to several hundred – far more if one includes the related fields of architecture and the construction of theatrical and ceremonial apparatus. From the archives of the Fabbriche Medicee (the Medicean Building Work), in which all this varied activity is recorded, there emerges a colourful galaxy of employees: regular and casual labourers, humble workmen and sophisticated professionals, Florentines and immigrants from the *contado*, men and women, industrious businessmen and petty parasites. In the early modern era, in a city of the size and character of Florence, the court played a key role in the redistribution and mobilization of human and economic resources.

At the same time, these administrative documents reveal how the work of skilled artisans employed by the Medici was ever-more closely regulated by contractual clauses and fixed wages and working hours. From the 1580s, the production of goods became increasingly enmeshed within a meticulous accounting regime, while within the individual workshops professional roles became more rigidly defined, and the relationships between employees tended to crystallize into a hierarchy graded according to pre-defined duties and ranks. This mass of individuals, dependent on the court in differing ways and to different extents, none the less cumulatively weighed heavily on the financial resources of the ducal household. Court expenditure, moreover, was a cost that expanded and diversified with the growth in the number of dependants and the increase during the seventeenth century in standards of luxury thought appropriate to the court. After 1580, Medici expenses never again dropped below double what they had been for the dynasty's first half-century in power. Between 1630 and 1660 the cost of maintaining this establishment (including wages, clothes, food, carriages, horses and gardens) stabilized at around 130,000 scudi a year, or somewhere between twelve and seventeen per cent of the annual budget of the realm.

More than sheer numbers, however, it was the rank of the courtiers and the 'magnificence' of their surroundings that conferred dignity on the court. To the keen eyes of Venetian ambassadors, the relatively low social status of the members of the Medici court, at least until the end of the sixteenth century, lent it the air of a private aristocratic household. The grand dukes appeared more in the role of *pater familiae* than as truly sovereign princes. This lack of a genuine native aristocracy was gradually remedied by the Medici, who, from the time of Cosimo I onwards, showed themselves eager to ennoble the old mercantile patriciate of Florence. Such integration took place by various means, although admittance to the court remained an important indication of social 'arrival'. None the less, some time was needed before a genuine Medicean courtly ruling élite could emerge – time and, occasionally, quite complex mechanisms of social advancement, among which the conferring of grand-ducal letters patent creating titles of nobility; appointment to state offices and to the chivalric Order of Santo Stefano, with its system of ranks and commendations; and the co-option of numerous branches of the pre-Medicean nobility drawn from the Tuscan subject territories and beyond.[19] In 1685 the diplomat

and memorialist of court practice, Gregorio Leti, was in a position to list – not without a heavy dose of flattery – the 'great number' and 'nobility' of those who 'honoured' Cosimo III with attendance at his court. Besides his 'thirty pages, all noble', Leti records that the grand duke's major domo, gentleman of the Bedchamber, master of the horse and other high-ranking courtiers were also of aristocratic extraction, while numerous marquesses, counts and other 'noble lords', could all be found within the broader compass of the court.[20]

The new ruling élite centred on the Medicean court was thus heterogeneous in composition, comprising individuals of different geographical provenance and status; and those who had risen to the rank of nobility by a number of different routes, each of which implied diverse and complex processes of territorial or political subjection and subsequent social co-option. The creation of this élite depended closely on the network of personal relationships between the prince and his courtiers and functionaries, relationships based on the practice of 'favours' and on the value of loyalty. It was also bound up with a larger process, whereby closer ties were established between the centre and the periphery of the realm. In particular, many members of the provincial ruling class were lured to the capital, where, through their relations of clientage with the grand duke, they became integrated into the Florentine aristocracy and came to occupy positions in government or in the household.

The social dynamics introduced by the creation of a court in turn gave rise to a further (and parallel) process of cultural co-option on the part of the new élite. Most obviously, we see an attempt on the part of Medici parvenus to attain Florentine 'citizenship' and create marriage ties with Florentine patrician families. Alongside this, however, we may also observe a broader process of acculturation on the part of the élite as a whole, the essential stages of which include the building or purchase of a *palazzo* and a private chapel in Florence, as well as the acquisition of courtly manners and habits of consumption. The old republican values were, nonetheless, never entirely eradicated, and the Medici court remained one in which traces of the old 'communal' mentality and culture persisted in ways that are difficult to quantify, but that remained tangible and significant into the eighteenth century.

III. Hierarchies, Etiquette and Ceremonial

Where – and how – did those who had the privilege of residing at court actually live? What were their duties? What were the norms and codes that governed the social dynamics between them? At least some of the answers to these questions may be found in the so-called *Diari di Etichetta*, which allow us to follow public life at the Pitti Palace on a day-to-day basis over the entire duration of the grand-ducal regime.[21] From the many surviving volumes of these journals in the Medici archives, we learn of the rules governing the distribution of gifts, and the socio-political significance of this system; are told of the hierarchy of personal access to the prince; of the various phases of the daily ceremony of the court; as well as the technicalities of diplomatic etiquette and the extreme volatility of rank and favour within the ducal household. If the information provided by these journals is supplemented by an analysis of the Medici notarial archives, a clear picture emerges of the typology of, and the criteria for allocation of, lodgings and clothes; of the preparation and symbolism of food at court; of the complex machinery governing the court's seasonal movements and the rhythms of work in the palace and its workshops.

Just as every ceremonial gesture and domestic operation had to respect precise norms of conduct, so each individual in the entourage of the prince occupied a clearly defined place in the court hierarchy, determined by factors such as inherited rank, or the degree of personal favour shown by the sovereign. The clearest outward indicator of status was dress. The manufacture, maintenance and care of garments, and their seasonal distribution, fell under the jurisdiction of the palace tailors of the Guardaroba del Taglio. The department's records reveal that each courtier had at least four outfits, one for winter and one for summer, both for the city and the country. An analysis of this vast documentation affords insight into the multifarious symbolic significance of court dress. Most immediately and obviously, the quality of this livery, along with the number of persons wearing it, were signifiers of the power of the sovereign, following the well-known dynamic of 'conspicuous consumption'. At the same time, to wear court dress was to appear in the guise of a subordinate, one of the 'prince's men'.

Not fortuitously, the occasions of an individual's acceptance into the court or expulsion from it were marked, respectively, by symbolic acts of vesting or disrobing. Moreover, the fabric, colour and style of the court livery, and the circumstances and manner of its donation, constituted a symbolic language sanctioning each individual's presence at court. Dress, and the rituals connected with it, thus had a precise function in the social semantics of the court. In consequence, matters of apparel were the subject of strict regulation, and could give access to privileges, guarantee forms of immunity, and impose forms of conduct consonant with the dignity of the prince to whom the livery, and the person wearing it, belonged.[22]

Accommodation, too, acquires a heightened significance when read in the light of its socio-political symbolism. In the second half of the seventeenth century, the Pitti Palace contained twenty-two 'principal apartments', comprising in all 399 rooms, including 'great and small halls and salons to the number of seventeen; chapels to the number of eleven; twelve linen-rooms; three privy offices; two foundries; four pantries; eight cellars; and eighteen fountains, distributed in divers places throughout the Great Palace.'[23] This labyrinth of rooms, with its mezzanines, its public and secret stairways, its decoration and furnishings, was a world that lay under the jurisdiction of the Guardaroba Generale; and it is to this entity and its archives that we must turn if we wish to decipher the uses and meanings of space in the palace.

The palace was divided into various zones on functional grounds. With its noble quarters and servants' quarters, its kitchens and guest rooms, its functional spaces and ceremonial spaces, its pharmacy, chapels, wine-stores, and workshops, it made up a city in miniature, closed to the outside world, self-sufficient and rationally structured. The fact that the palace was divided into different apartments for different members of the Medici family testifies, in turn, to the presence of more than one court in the building; to be precise, there was a 'court' for each member of the grand duke's family. These residential units had a life of their own, often following distinctive rhythms dependent on the particular public role of the princely relative at their head.

The character of the court was in any case subject to various types and rhythms of change. An obvious cause of this change was the succession of individuals and generations. As some spaces within the palace were freed for redistribution on the death of their occupants, by temporary absences or the departure of spouses, others came to be required as new members of the dynasty were born or arrived from other parts; and this would entail, each time, an overall redistribution of space, provoking in turn costly works of adaptation and acting as a spur to ambitious plans for redecoration. Then there were the seasonal cycles during which the various courts migrated from one floor of the Pitti Palace to another, or from Florence to Pisa or to one of the surrounding country villas. Related to the upheaval involved in adapting space to new uses was the dislocation entailed by large-scale, laborious removals of persons and household objects, in which areas of the palace – or sometimes entire buildings – would be left temporarily empty. Finally, reallocations of space within the palace were provoked by the arrival and departure of visitors, from the everyday comings and goings of guests and diplomats to the prolonged sojourns of vast numbers of visitors on the occasion of great ceremonial events. One has the impression of a palace in continual and frenetic transformation, with no fixed arrangement of furnishings, and with rooms that periodically changed their physiognomy (often quite radically), transformed at the hands of the extensive staff of the Guardaroba Maggiore and according to an established etiquette that imposed a strict correspondence between the type of space allocated and the rank and identity of those to whom the space was assigned.

The first codification of this system of etiquette dates from 1648, when, for the first time, systematic written rules came to replace the less formal tradition of memoranda by which court protocol had up to that time been transmitted. As in other Italian courts, then, it was only from the mid seventeenth century that ceremonial practices became fully standardized (in that precise equivalencies between social hierarchies and etiquette on different occasions could be far more easily and reliably established by means of a rule book than by consulting a series of voluminous 'diaries').[24]

The close relationship between physical space, ceremonial order, and social hierarchy manifested itself at different levels and in different ways, depending on whether the space being allocated was for the consumption of food, for sleeping or the reception of

Siena was brought under Medici rule only after its conquest in 1555. Courtly celebrations, such as this tournament in honour of Grand Duke Ferdinando I (1587–1609), staged in Siena's Piazza del Campo, served as a means of integrating the formerly independent local élites into the structures of Medici rule.

visitors. In the case both of courtiers and of outsiders visiting the court, the size of their rooms, their location and furnishings, and the identity and number of those with whom they were shared, were reliable indicators of the inhabitant's status. A fundamental criterion of differentiation was whether one was assigned a place within the palace itself. Courtiers' families and the lower ranks of court servants were allocated rented lodgings in the town, while less important guests were given lodgings in the secondary residences of the prince or in the palaces of court dignitaries (in particular, such families as the Strozzi, Corsini, Bardi, Niccolini). At a still lower level came the inns of the city, where the lesser ranking members of the entourages of visiting princes, ambassadors and cardinals would be lodged at the grand duke's expense.

Perhaps the most important indicator of status for courtiers, however, was the degree of intimacy they enjoyed with the prince, and, for those from outside seeking an audience, the facility with which they procured access to his presence. The higher one's rank and one's place in the prince's favour, the more easily one might be admitted to the prince's private sphere. Only a few courtiers (the high ranks of his *familia*) had the privilege of access to the prince, and it was considered a signal honour to be admitted to his 'Chamber'. Still more reserved was his bedchamber: only his secretary, chamberlain, close advisers, and – exceptionally – cardinals travelling on private business were received by the grand duke 'in the chamber in which he sleeps'.[25] This gradation of access reflects the role played by the individuals in question in the circulation of information, as well as illuminating the daily process of decision-making at court.

Similarly, the more elevated the status of a visitor to the court, the further the prince was prepared to emerge from his Chamber to greet him: Florentine court etiquette dictated precisely the point at which such 'encounters' and 'accompaniments' were to take place, gauged according to the rank of the ambassadors

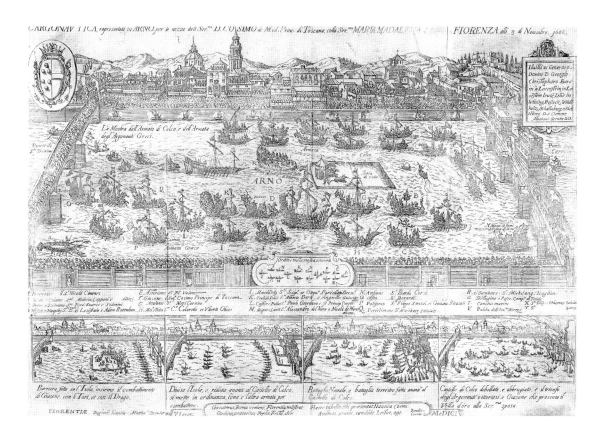

The water fête of Jason and the Argonauts *on the River Arno to celebrate the marriage of Prince Cosimo de' Medici – the future Cosimo II (1609–21) – to Maria Maddelena of Austria in 1608. Cosimo took the role of Jason, the mythological hero who won the Golden Fleece, a topical reference to the highest Habsburg chivalric order, the Order of the Golden Fleece.*

in question and of the state they represented. Space was mapped out by a series of ceremonial boundaries, like so many concentric circles, starting at the confines of the realm, and closing in through the city walls and the palace gates to centre on the throne-room. Here, art reinforced the symbolic language of protocol. To penetrate the heart of the court, the visitor had to pass through the long sequence of rooms on the left side of the first floor of the Pitti Palace, where the allegories in the frescoes (1637–47) by Pietro da Cortona complemented the complex protocol governing the opening and closing of curtains and doors as the visitors passed on their way to their audience. Each individual step on the great staircase had its part in measuring out the hierarchies of the court: the etiquette of the Pitti Palace was sufficiently pervasive to define exactly at which point visitors might be received and by whom.

IV. RITUAL AND SACRALITY

Apart from the pope, Italian princes, unanointed as they were, did not have the status of *personae sacrae* or anointed 'sacred beings'. None the less, they did come to be invested with particular forms of sacrality, revealed in the symbolism and ritual surrounding them. In the case of the Medici, the precise form assumed by this sacrality varied over time, altering with the changing cultural climate. Thus at the beginning of ducal rule in Florence, Cosimo I's attempts to construct a divine identity for himself were modelled on imperial mythology. From the time of Ferdinando I, however, partly as a result of his experience as a cardinal in the papal court, the religious matrix of court ceremonial was accentuated; much energy was devoted to creating a network of courtly places of worship, establishing a

pantheon of dynastic saints, and acquiring relics and sacred images that were (or came to be) associated with the grand-ducal household. Thus, the first period of ducal rule, roughly the half-century from the establishment of the duchy in the 1530s to the 1580s, was dominated by a classicizing iconography and language; what followed was an age in which the practices and categories of religious piety came prominently to the fore. The division is not an absolute one, but the difference in atmosphere between these two periods is tangible, and their respective political implications demand to be read in quite different ways. An example of this was the ritual of the prince's dining in state, which took place in a special room and, with its ablutions, its preparations, its rites for the transportation, serving and consumption of food, presented striking analogies with the liturgies of the mass. In the course of this banquet, the grand duke would be surrounded by a crowd of servants at the orders of his major domo, and, more significantly, he would be observed by an audience of gentlemen, Tuscans and foreigners. The banquet was a political performance with sacral overtones, whose aim was to exhibit the grand duke's sovereignty and to reaffirm the social hierarchies of the court.

A further illustration of the enhanced religious emphasis that is to be discerned from the later sixteenth century is the attempt on the part of the Medici court to appropriate to itself the famous sacred frescoed image of the Madonna in the church of the Santissima Annunziata, whose cult had deep roots within Florentine religious and political culture. This attempt to associate the miraculous powers of the image with the court took various forms. It is apparent in the devotional literature of the period, and in the published works associated with the Servite Order (patrons of the basilica that contained the fresco, painted – it was claimed – by angelic hands in 1252). It also found expression in the coining of tokens and medals, and, most significantly, in court architecture and court liturgy.[26] The journal of Cesare di Bastiano Tinghi, an *aiutante di camera* (gentleman of the Chamber) to Ferdinando II from July 1600 to November 1623, regularly notes 'mass at the 'Nunziata' as a sacrosanct Sunday morning ritual, accompanied by a solemn procession of the grand duke and his courtiers through the streets of Florence. The sacred image of the Madonna, usually covered with a silver veil, was

shown only to honoured guests and high-ranking courtiers. It became the private monopoly of the prince, a talisman protecting, sanctioning and preserving his power and his dynasty. From the end of the sixteenth century the church of the Annunziata came to serve as the second most important court space after the Pitti Palace – in effect, an annex to the palace.

The ritual horizon within which the prince moved thus extended well beyond the palace walls. Baptisms, coronations and weddings were conducted in the Duomo,[27] as was (except during the reigns of Cosimo I and Ferdinando I) the robing ceremony for new grand masters of the chivalric Order of Santo Stefano. Here, too, the prince would come in a 'procession of carriages' on the main civic feast-days. It was in the family church of San Lorenzo, by contrast, that Medici funerals were conducted, as were the memorial requiems held on the deaths of leading Catholic sovereigns. Both forms of ceremony meticulously reproduced the sacred symbolism of kingly and imperial ritual north of the Alps.[28] Similarly, for the entire Medici regime, so-called 'grand-ducal chapels' were held in San Lorenzo, conducted according to an ancient and immutable rite: the Bishop of Florence would welcome the prince and his entourage at the doors of the basilica, and then step aside, leaving the prince to sit *in cornu evangeli* – on the 'gospel side' or liturgical south side of the sanctuary – as orchestrator and focal point of the ceremony. Those present were ranked according to a rigid hierarchy. These events were choreographed so precisely, and with such a complex array of symbolic and gestural rituals, that all who attended were able to participate actively, both in the sanctioning of grand-ducal power, and in the public parade of the social spectrum that surrounded and sustained that power. Courtiers, knights of Santo Stefano, government bureaucrats, clerics and simple feudatories of the grand dukes came together in a great concert of social entities, rigorously marshalled into a hierarchical order. In the final years of the dynasty the royal status granted to Cosimo III by Pope Innocent XII in 1699 still further enhanced the significance of this regal rite, which had its roots in late Christian antiquity.

Further contributions to the religious culture of the Medici court came with the successive canonizations of Tuscan saints, notably of SS. Andrea Corsini (1629),

Gian Gastone de' Medici – the last of the Medici grand dukes. Dissipated, valetudinarian and childless, he was forced to pass the grand ducal throne to François II of Lorraine in 1735.

Maria Maddalena de' Pazzi (1669) and Filippo Benizi (1671). The increasingly sacralized stamp of life at the Medici court in the era of the Counter-Reformation is also attested to by phenomena such as the presence within it of so-called 'living saints' (the holy women who acted as counsellors of the grand duke, documented in 1714), as well as by the numerous pilgrimages of members of the court to sanctuaries in Tuscany and elsewhere, their assiduous attendance at monasteries and convents and their devotion to Florentine sacred places (such as the Madonna dell'Impruneta as well as the Annunziata).[29] By assuming responsibility for these vehicles of divine intercession and taking on the role of the magnanimous dispenser of the privilege of access to them, the

grand duke was able to present himself in the guise of mediator between the celestial and terrestrial spheres.

As at other courts in Italy and indeed throughout Europe, the palace chapel was the focal point of the expression of princely majesty. It was this institution that impressed the Venetian ambassadors in 1579, when they asserted that Francesco I's ducal dignity as reflected in his chapel was such as to rank him 'on a par with kings'.[30] The 'holy of holies', or sanctuary, of the Pitti Palace chapel was indeed richly furnished with relics; in an inventory of 1616 these items are already listed in their hundreds, but in successive documents they amount to something like a thousand, not including liturgical apparatus, sacred images and *agnus dei*. These objects had numerous functions,

serving most immediately to protect the palace and its inhabitants, but also as holy 'fixatives',[31] conferring an aura of divinity on their possessors. The grand duke would make use of these relics as instruments of intercession on a daily – sometimes more than daily – basis, integrating his devotional practices with his conduct of the affairs of state.

The ducal collection of relics was not a fixed one, but changed over the years, as items were received or given away as gifts (to mark the sealing of diplomatic alliances or as restoratives in cases of illness). This collection constituted a 'treasury', which could also become, at the grand duke's discretion, an object of display. Eucharistic adoration seems also to have figured prominently in the courtly religious cult. In one of the funeral orations delivered on the death of Cosimo II, for example, mention is made of the populace visiting the palace chapel, described as 'resembling a Temple of the Lord in that the Holy Sacrament is displayed there'.[32] In contemporary accounts, these visits are represented as by special dispensation, due to the kindly condescension of the grand duke, the high priest of the eucharistic mystery in a palace now transformed into a kind of Solomonic temple.

V. ART, SCIENCE AND COURT CULTURE

With Cosimo I's ascent to the throne in 1537 and the stabilization of the hitherto precarious Medicean princely regime, there followed a major revival of cultural patronage in Florence.[33] In architecture, the great protagonists of Florentine Mannerism were Giorgio Vasari (1511–74) and Bernardo Buontalenti (c.1536–1608); in painting, Pontormo (1494–1556), Agnolo Bronzino (1503–72), and again Vasari; and in sculpture, Baccio Bandinelli (c.1493–1560), Bartolommeo Ammannati (1511–92) and the Fleming, Giambologna (1529–1608). When it came to planning the great public fêtes and court festivals of the late sixteenth century, Vincenzo Borghini (1515–80) and again, Buontalenti, were the chief masterminds. Similarly, it was during this period that the palace art workshops and the Fabbriche Medicee were founded, and a team of artists and scholars was permanently employed in the service of the grand duke. The Medici court became a leading centre for the elaboration and propagation of the new figurative styles and themes, and a specifically Medicean artistic rhetoric was developed by means of the Accademia del Disegno, founded by Cosimo I in 1562.

Florence's transformation into a principality likewise demanded the elaboration of a new iconography of power, whose symbolism was heavily dependent on the imperial myth as reconstructed by the Holy Roman Emperor Charles V (1519–56). Medicean art under Cosimo I adopted an idiom centring not only on Augustus as the archetype of the transition from republican to princely rule, but also on the Augustan literary paradigm of the return of the Golden Age.[34] The repertoires of classical mythology furnished a series of stock images for the torrent of statues, busts, medals, engravings and paintings portraying Cosimo I: he appeared regularly in the guise of either Neptune, the god of the sea, or as Hercules, an identification that celebrated his achievement in re-establishing Florentine pre-eminence within Italy.

This rehabilitation of classical mythological motifs, and of the heroes, artistic forms (medals, equestrian statues) and figurative language of antiquity, testifies to the central role played by classicism – and in particular the Roman imperial past – in the process of the legitimization of princely power in the sixteenth century. The palace in this period showed a tendency to transform itself very self-consciously into a 'cabinet of wonders': tapestries, gems, bronzes, maps, paintings, precious hangings, ceramics, cameos, ancient coins, books, reliquaries, clocks, objects worked in ivory, silver, lacquer, wax, or semi-precious stones; collections of natural curiosities from the entire known world, from ostrich eggs to the seeds of exotic plants: all these contributed to the cumulative effect of the court as the locus of the 'marvellous', a vast treasure-house of incomparable wealth.[35]

The later sixteenth and early seventeenth centuries were also a period when foundation myths concerning Tuscany's Etruscan origins were revived and elaborated, reinforced, among other things, by the compilation of a fantastic genealogy tracing an Etruscan descent for the Medici family itself. The linguistic heritage of Etruria was also relaunched in this period. In compliance with grand-ducal directives, court intellectuals and the Accademia Fiorentina (founded by Cosimo in 1541) engaged in the

ambitious project of asserting the supremacy of the Tuscan language as an expression of the politico-cultural hegemony of the new princely state.[36] Associated with this aim of imposing an ethnic and linguistic unity on the grand duchy, and reinforcing its distinctiveness within Italy, was a new grammar of the Tuscan language, commissioned by Cosimo I in 1550. These various academies, which served as instruments of Cosimo's cultural politics, played a key role in fashioning the Medici imagery of power.[37] Along with the University of Pisa (reopened in 1543), these institutions reflect the emergence of a circle of intellectuals and artists under the direct control of the prince. They are also indicative of the way in which, in parallel with the birth of the court, ancillary institutions were founded with the aim of forming a local ruling élite and of subjecting it to a process of cultural indoctrination.

The period of Cosimo's successor, Francesco I, was strongly characterized by more esoteric tendencies,[38] and was followed by the far more markedly religious emphasis in court culture, which began with Ferdinando I (1587–1609) and reached its zenith with Cosimo III (1670–1723). From the beginning of the seventeenth century, the tendency to draw the grand duke and his court into the sacred sphere became more and more insistent: Cosimo II was portrayed as St Michael in the first half of the seventeenth century; Cosimo III, first as St Joseph and then, more curiously, as the Christ child in a *Holy Family* by Justus Sustermans, painted in 1645. Successive grand duchesses were likewise depicted either as saints or as other holy figures, while images of the prince in the guise of a penitent or experiencing monastic life were circulated widely. Each sovereign evolved his own distinctive figurative programme, translated into visual terms by the artists and craftsmen in his employ, within the overall framework of a dynastic cult. Far from declining into decadence, this grew in vigour over the two centuries of Medicean rule.

From a stylistic perspective, the Baroque reached the Florentine court only with the arrival of Pietro da Cortona, the painter, architect and polymath who worked at the Pitti Palace between 1637 and 1647.[39] Subsequently, a native Baroque school developed and flourished throughout the second half of the seventeenth century.[40] Leading exponents of this in Florence included Giulio Parigi (1571–1635),

Giovanni Battista Foggini (1652–1725), Pietro Tacca (1577–1640) and the artists associated with the Accademia Fiorentina in Rome. The dominant figure, however, active in Florence over a sixty-year period, was undoubtedly the Flemish painter Justus Sustermans (1597–1681).[41] New artistic genres developed in this period, such as Jacopo Ligozzi's botanical studies,[42] or the tradition of work in semi-precious stones centred on the Opificio delle Pietre Dure, which found expression in the vast enterprise of the decoration of the Cappella dei Principi in San Lorenzo. Sacred art, too, prospered and developed, as is shown by the hundreds of precious reliquaries produced in this period, and the numerous works stimulated by the introduction into Tuscany of new religious orders, such as the Alcantarines in 1678 and the Trappists in 1705.

Yet perhaps the Medici court's most striking and important contributions to European culture was the style of its great public fêtes and spectacles. The celebration of marriages, coronations, baptisms, visits from foreign monarchs, even funerals; all these entailed the construction of complex and lavish ephemeral *apparati* (or decorations), and the staging of full-scale theatrical events. Out of the *intermezzi* of these performances, new and ultimately autonomous forms of artistic expression developed, such as opera and ballet.[43] Although the Florentine court was not the only sources of these influences, it remains the case that artists throughout Europe frequently drew on the patterns set by Florentine archetypes: Inigo Jones recycled Buontalenti's and Giulio Parigi's scenographic ideas in the court masques of early Stuart England; Joseph Furttenbach imported them into Germany; while Cosimo Lotti and Baccio del Bianco transported the conventions of the Medicean theatre to Madrid in the 1750s.[44]

Among the initial aims of this patronage of spectacle was to foster that sense of 'wonderment' and cultural pre-eminence through which the Medici hoped to legitimize their new-found sovereignty in the eyes of the reigning houses of northern Europe, and to erase the memory of their bourgeois origins. 'Magnificence' thus represented, for the grand dukes, a concrete instrument for asserting their sovereignty. Besides the obvious fact that all such events entailed the display of wealth, each individual occasion was charged with a more precise meaning, in that they

The Uffizi theatre: Giulio Parigi's sets for the first intermezzo *from* La Liberatione di Tirreno *(1617).*

were intimately linked to one or other of the dynasty's rites of passage. In 1589, for example, the theme was the marriage of Christine of Lorraine and Ferdinando I, while the 1661 performance of the mounted ballet, *Il mondo festante* (The World at Play) was staged to celebrate the wedding of Cosimo III to the Bourbon princess Marguerite Louise d'Orléans.

Where science is concerned, even after the death of the great Galileo Galilei in 1642[45] and the closure of the Accademia del Cimento in 1667, the Florentine court still played host to such distinguished scientific figures as the physician Francesco Redi (1626–98), the mathematician Vincenzo Viviani (1622–1703), and

the Medici continued to sponsor work in a wide diversity of fields, from engineering and mechanics, to anatomy and astronomy, botany and cartography.[46]

During the late seventeenth and early eighteenth centuries, the Medici court seemed to be reaching ever greater levels of splendour. It was extinguished in 1737, not by political insurrection, *coup d'état* or financial crisis, but by the simple fact of the biological failure of the male line. During the previous 200 years, however, the talents it attracted, its organization, the opulence of its setting, the elaboration of its ceremony and its artistic and cultural vitality had made it one of the epicentres of court culture in *ancien-régime* Europe.

CHAPTER ELEVEN

The Kingdom of Sweden
THE COURTS OF THE VASAS AND PALATINES
c. 1523–1751

FABIAN PERSSON

I N 1521 THE NOBLEMAN GUSTAV VASA OVERTHREW THE DANISH KING Christian II's rule in Sweden, bringing the union of Sweden and Denmark, dating from 1397, to an end once and for all. Gustav set about the creation of a new Swedish monarchy to replace the Union monarchy, which had been dominated by Denmark since its inception. First as lord protector (1521–3) and then as king (1523–60), Gustav founded not only a dynasty and a new Swedish bureaucracy, but also a new royal court. Although earlier lords protector (*riksföreståndare*) certainly had households of their own, the new royal household was of greater scale and magnificence than anything hitherto known. What emerged was a court that was actually resident in the country, although its distinctively Swedish character should not be overstated. Many of its courtiers were in fact from the German states of the Holy Roman Empire; court ordinances were drawn up after German models, and some financial accounts and court regulations were actually written in the German language.

The residences available to Gustav were suitable neither for the new, enlarged court, nor for the national bureaucracy that travelled with it. He therefore rebuilt on a grand scale, constructing a network of royal residences, the most important of which were at Kalmar, Vadstena, Gripsholm, Örebro and Uppsala. Having started out as combined households and military fortresses, some of these castles later became the residences of the king's sons, and the seats of their courts, from where they ruled their own semi-independent duchies. After Gustav's death in

The founder of the dynasty, King Gustav Vasa (1523–60), painted c.1550 by Willem Boy. The leader of the successful aristocratic rebellion against Christian II of Denmark's 'Unionist' rule over Sweden, Vasa was elected king by his fellow nobles on 6 June 1523. During a reign of almost forty years, he not only established his family as a hereditary monarchical dynasty, but also created a royal court that looked to the German-speaking princely households of the Holy Roman Empire for its models – not least in the richly embroidered clothes depicted in Boy's portrait.

1560 these ducal courts became alternative centres of power, in competition with the royal court. Yet the king's court at Stockholm was unlike any other focus of power, and to understand its character and workings we must first examine its composition, and chart the changes it underwent in the two centuries after its creation in the 1520s.

I. THE CREATION OF THE SWEDISH COURT

The reinvention of Swedish monarchy begun by Gustav was continued by three of his sons, Erik, Johan and Karl, each of whom was to succeed to the throne. The eldest, Erik XIV (1560–68), introduced a more elaborate court ceremonial and new court offices, such as the great master or major domo (*överhovmästare*: literally, over court master), the officer who governed the court, assisted by several court masters (*hovmästareas*) as deputies. During the 1560s Erik also began to use the title of 'majesty' (which had been adopted by most major European monarchies during the early sixteenth century), and his coronation in 1561, inspired by examples from England, marked a new pinnacle of royal splendour. New and more magnificent regalia were acquired, and later monarchs added further to the number and diversity of objects in the royal collections.[1] Some of these innovations in protocol and household organization were short-lived, but most managed to survive Erik's successors, Johan III (1568–92) and Sigismund (1592–9), and in the first decades of the seventeenth century the Swedish court finally achieved the form that it would retain for most of the next two centuries.

In the sixteenth century the court was usually headed by a court marshal (*hovmarskalk*), and divided into different departments called *kammare* (chambers), each with different areas of responsibility.[2] Thus, there were departments for silver (*silverkammaren*), clothing (*klädkammaren*), furs (*skinnkammaren*), silk (*sidenkammaren*), spices (*kryddkammaren*), furniture and furnishings (*husgerådskammaren*) and armour (*livrustkammaren*), as well as such obvious departments as the kitchen (*köket*) and cellar (*hovkällaren*).[3] Each chamber was headed by a master (*mästare*) or a clerk (*skrivare*). This pattern of organization changed slightly during the first decades of

the seventeenth century for reasons that are not entirely clear. Thus, from 1634 the titles of household offices were upgraded: the court marshal was renamed marshal of the realm (*riksmarskalk*) and took on extensive responsibilities for all court ceremonies, finances and security (the colonel of the guard, the senior officer of the king's bodyguard, was answerable to him). In keeping with this enhanced status, the post was thereafter always held by a councillor of the realm. The marshal of the realm (formerly the court master) was usually expected to be present at court at all times, although the court marshal, who from 1634 ranked second in the hierarchy of the royal household, could act as his deputy if necessary. Under the court marshal served a noble élite who attended the king in his private apartments: the gentlemen of the Chamber (*kammarjunkare*, also styled, from the 1640s, Chamber esquires, or *kammarherrare*), court gentlemen (*hovjunkare*), and pages (*pager*). The *kammarjunkare* was the equivalent to the French *gentilhomme de la chambre* and the English gentleman of the Privy Chamber under the Tudors: the intimate attendant and companion of the monarch. Erik XIV's court ordinances of the 1560s state that 'their duty is always to be present in his Majesty's Presence Chamber, especially in the morning, when his Majesty is rising, and they should always follow his Majesty wherever he goes'.[4] During the seventeenth and eighteenth centuries, the Chamber gentlemen served in daily shifts on a monthly basis,[5] while the oldest also acted as deputy to the court marshal. The court gentlemen and pages carried the food from the kitchen to the dining room, where the court gentlemen served the meat while the pages were in attendance behind the chairs.[6]

No less important were the officers who supervised the court's second major department, the stables, a department of critical importance to a court regularly on the move. Here there were four principal figures. The stable master of the realm (*riksstallmästare*) had general responsibility for the stables and studs in all the royal residences, while the court stable master (*hovstallmästare*) had specific charge of the royal stables at court, wherever the court happened to be. Hunting, which was the principal royal recreation in Sweden, as elsewhere in western Europe, came under the jurisdiction of the court master of the hunt (*hovjägmästare*), who attended to the king's personal hunting arrangements; while the royal parks, chases and forests

The metropolitan seat of the court: the inner courtyard of the Tre Kronor Castle, Stockholm, c.1670, looking west. Medieval in origin, and extensively added to during the sixteenth century, the castle was widely regarded as being outmoded by the 1670s. It lacked the architectural order and coherence deemed necessary by the later seventeenth century for a truly 'magnificent' court.

were run by yet another officer, the master of the hunt of the realm (*riksjägmästare*).

Complementing the court's male staff was a smaller number of 'gentlewomen of the court' (*hovfruntimret*), who served the queen consort and the princesses. This department was headed by a mistress of the court (*hovmästarinna*), and consisted of several maids of the court who were invariably of noble birth (*hovjungfrur*), as well as several Chamber serving women (*kammarpigor*), who were usually of non-noble origin.

The difference between court and 'government', or the central administration, became much clearer in the seventeenth century, principally because the administration became increasingly bureaucratic, and was permanently based in Stockholm from the 1620s. The death of Gustavus Adolphus in 1632 and the accession of a minor prompted further major change. The higher aristocracy advanced its powers under the constitution of 1634. Henceforth the court was defined as being governed by the marshal of the realm, and the central administration was specifically excluded from his control, thereby resolving the question of where court ended and bureaucracy began. Contemporaries referred to the court by using two terms, *hov* and *hovstat*: the first simply meant the court in general, a loose term that could include the central administration; the second was used in official records to denote the household establishment, the immediate domestic royal staff, including both aristocrats and commoners. It should be noted that the Swedish court was never clearly divided, as was, for example, the English, between Chamber and Household; the word *hovstat* covered both.

Outside the *hovstat*, the central administration consisted of the council, the five 'high officers of the realm' (the chancellor, the treasurer, the admiral, the commander in chief of the army and the chancellor of the judiciary), and the *kollegium*, or main administrative institutions, such as the College of Accounts (*kammarkollegium*), the College of Mining (*bergskollegium*) and the Admiralty (*amiralitetskollegium*). These institutions, dominated by the aristocracy, wielded formal power, unlike the informal power of the royal household, although the great officers of state continued to be part of the social world of the court.

Central to understanding the institutional structure of the court and its ramifications is the question of where the court convened. In the sixteenth century the Swedish kings regularly moved about the country with their entourages and the court was truly peripatetic. Of course, Stockholm was clearly the most important seat of the court, and the Tre Kronor (or Three Crowns) Castle was by far the most important royal residence.[7] Yet this was only one of a network of royal seats, and at various times during the year the court took up residence at one or other of the numerous royal houses, including Vadstena, Svartsjö, Örebro, Västerås and Nyköping. This high degree of mobility lasted only until the early years of Queen Christina's reign (1632–54); thereafter, there was a marked alteration in the pattern of the court's residence. It not only became more sedentary, but also more closely tied to the capital, since all the other royal residences that remained regularly in use were close to Stockholm: Uppsala, Karlberg, Drottningholm, Ulriksdal, Strömsholm, Svartsjö and Gripsholm, as well as the hunting lodge of Kungsör. Architecturally these

residences varied enormously. Some, like Drottningholm (begun in the 1660s), exhibited the latest in the Baroque style; yet, ironically, perhaps the least impressive of all the royal residences was in fact the court's principal seat, the old Tre Kronor Castle in Stockholm. It had some admirers; one Italian visitor, in 1674, noted that the royal palace was 'very beautiful…[and] mostly built by King Johan [III] following Italian proportions rather than the barbarous taste of the country'.[8] But by the later seventeenth century it was beginning to look distinctly outmoded, and foreign visitors were rarely impressed. 'The palace hath nothing in it very remarkable', noted Guy Miège, a servant of the English ambassador, in 1664. A French observer described it a few years later as 'nothing less than an architectural monstrosity, a residence without form, without coherence or balance, a complete mess, a jumble of levels, wings, towers, chambers and stairs'.[9] The Swedish court was equally aware of the palace's shortcomings, and of the problems inherent in its essentially medieval plan. Extensive proposals for rebuilding were put forth in the 1650s and 1690s, but it was not until 1692 that a radical rebuilding programme was begun. All these efforts were brought to naught by the total destruction of the Tre Kronor Castle by fire in 1697; the new royal palace, designed by Nicodemus Tessin the younger (1654–1728), was not completed until the 1750s.

The Swedish court was small in comparison with its European counterparts. Even though Sweden was an important power in the seventeenth century, and the major power in the Baltic, it had a court no larger than that of a small German principality. At the start of the seventeenth century, perhaps the simplest way to gauge the size of the court is from the palace kitchen tally, but even this is problematic, since numbers varied from about 400 when the court was outside the capital to as many as 700 when the court was in Stockholm, where the central administrative staff was included in the tally. By the 1640s, however, the kitchen tally is less useful for a headcount, partly because the chancery and accounting staff went out of court and partly because many court servants began to receive boardwages in lieu of meals. Fortunately, however, at this point the *hovstat* accounts become more reliable, and it appears that approximately 400 people served at court during the rest of the century, of whom some hundred were from aristocratic families. In 1700 this total had grown to about 450 people serving at the combined courts of the king and the queen dowager, of whom roughly seventy were of aristocratic birth. To this figure can be added the guard, which usually numbered a couple of hundred men.

In many ways the small scale of the Swedish court is unsurprising. The population of Sweden in 1600 was only about 1.2 million, and it was a vast country, sparsely inhabited, with a handful of towns and a very small 'nobility' numbering only about 450 adult men, ranging from well-to-do farmers to the great noblemen of the realm.[10] The structure of the nobility was stratified by the introduction of the titles of count and baron by Erik XIV in 1563, but the titular nobility continued to be a very small group until the beginning of the seventeenth century.[11] From the 1640s the aristocratic class grew rapidly, through the creation of numerous new noble families and the influx of foreign nobles into the realm; yet it would continue to remain small by comparison with other European states well into the eighteenth century. In 1700 the Swedish nobility still numbered only around 2,500 adult men.[12] The proportion of the aristocracy attending at court at any one time was, therefore, relatively high, and at least until the later seventeenth century there was a close identification between the aristocratic caste and the monarch's court.

Most of the court's administrative structures survived into the nineteenth century, although there were some minor reforms. Some of the changes in the organization of the court clearly seem to have been related to the ruler's personal preferences. The 1653 household ordinances of Queen Christina, for example, reflected her current interest in all things French: through the introduction of certain French titles for existing court officers, such as the marshal of the realm who became the *grand maître* (or great master of the household), and through the creation of a handful of new officers, such as the *grand chambellan* (or lord chamberlain), copied from the French court hierarchy.[13] The queen also sought to make the court more visually impressive by improving the appearance of her attendants; so much so that, the vast sum of 2,412 daler silvermynt apiece spent on the liveries of the twelve Chamber pages aroused the jealousy of other courtiers.[14] The personal aspect of Christina's

involvement in these changes is clearly demonstrated by the fact that following her abdication in 1654 many of the innovations were reversed, including all of the French-inspired innovations in court nomenclature and organization.

The impact of the royal personality, although of a very different kind, is again revealed during Karl XI's reign (1660–97), which ushered in a period of obsessive concern with domestic administrative minutiae. During the 1680s and 1690s detailed instructions were issued to servants at all levels in many household departments, stipulating procedures for the daily countersigning of minor court records, and precise instructions on subjects as diverse as drains, window latches, the plucking of fowl and even how the legs of the royal horses were to be cleaned. In other reforms the senior officer of the court, the marshal of the realm, was renamed chief marshal (*överstemarskalk*) from 1682, and at about the same time the arrangements for the royal hunt were simplified by the abolition of the offices of stable master of the realm and master of the hunt of the realm.

Yet the idiosyncrasies of royal preferences were not the only cause of change. Some were necessitated by financial exigencies. Starting in the 1710s, for example, the number of unsalaried positions at court increased rapidly, apparently in response to the problem created by the need to take on younger household staff at a time when an ageing court limited the number of paid positions available, and tight parliamentary control of expenditure prevented the creation of further salaried posts. Otherwise, the overall pattern was one of stability, with the structure of the court established during the early Vasa period remaining intact until the early nineteenth century.

II. COURT CULTURE, CEREMONY AND RECREATION

Of course, much of the court's 'magnificence' was ephemeral in form, in the fireworks that frequently accompanied major public celebrations, or in such festivities as the *carrousel*, a kind of tournament, such as that held in 1672 to celebrate the coming of age of Karl XI.[15] The most conspicuous ceremonies in the cycle of court life were the instances of public celebration and mourning: coronations, weddings and funerals,[16] but these of their nature were infrequent events, and, in evaluating the role of the court in political and social life in Sweden, perhaps less important than other more commonplace aspects of the royal household. What is far more revealing is the everyday pattern of court life, a daily round that framed the lives of both the monarch and the politically influential. From the effort that went into these day-to-day events one can infer that great importance was attached to the impression they created, although it is unclear just how much of that effort was directed towards impressing an external audience, as opposed to one that was internal to the court.

Ordinarily, the focal point of the day was the monarch's dinner, and a description by a visiting German aristocrat in 1648 provides a detailed account of the ceremonies that accompanied royal dining at the Swedish court in the time of Queen Christina.[17] One hour before the meal the kettledrums sounded; then the court marshal and the court gentlemen went in procession through the courtyard down to the kitchen. As they carried the food back to the dining hall, they were once again accompanied by the sound of kettledrums and trumpet fanfares. A French diplomat noted that the kitchen doorway through which the food was carried was flanked by two enormous Russian cannons, war trophies of Gustavus Adolphus (1611–32), 'as if the bravest of kings wished to have his food spiced and perfumed with the reek of gunpowder from the cannons of the vanquished; this agreed well with the din of drums and trumpets, which throughout the north accompanies royal meals'.[18] In the dining hall, the pages served the food, which was made up of two courses, each of twenty separate dishes, while the Chamber gentlemen presented and served the wine. The 1648 account also noted that a German court gentleman, Conrad Pless, carved the meat and presented the finger-bowls, while four Chamber pages stood behind the queen's chair; immediately behind her stood her French physician Durietz, who conversed with the queen throughout the meal. Yet, unlike many other royal houses, the Swedish monarch did not dine alone. Also eating at the queen's own table were the Palatine family, the queen's cousins, the *hovmästarinnorna*, and the daughters of the councillors Per Brahe and Jacob de la Gardie. The

female members of her household ate at another table in the dining hall, together with Conrad Pless (the carver), and the Chamber gentleman Fleming. The rest of the court gentlemen and the officers of the guard ate at a third table. The leftovers from the queen's table were carried to the other two tables or into another room where dinner was served to the pages. Ceremony was rarely absent; and foreign visitors sometimes tired of meals that were 'too tediously ceremonious'.[19] Even when Karl XII (1697–1718) was campaigning in Turkey in the first decades of the eighteenth century, the presentation of food at his table continued to be announced with a trumpet fanfare.[20] Ceremony was equally important in the formal reception of foreign diplomats, and in 1673 Karl XI had asked the Swedish residents abroad for information about diplomatic ceremonies at the courts of Paris, Vienna, Copenhagen and London with a view to maintaining the ceremoniousness of his own court on a par with his foreign rivals.[21]

Everyday life at court was imbued with religious practice. The court year revolved largely around the feasts of Christmas, Easter and Pentecost, and inevitably there were strongly religious elements in many court ceremonies such as coronations, funerals, weddings and christenings. In common with the rest of the country, a number of *stora bönedagar* (literally 'great prayer days') were observed each year, when special services were held on themes (and days) decided upon a year in advance by the king and his council. Sermons were also regularly used as a vehicle for the exaltation of the monarchy. Characteristically, when the cleric Bodinus attended the Swedish Parliament of 1686 he heard several sermons in the royal chapel, in which a recurrent theme was the praise of Karl XI, and the good fortune of Sweden to have been blessed with such a monarch, now absolute ruler of the kingdom.[22] Unsurprisingly, court chaplains usually did well in the clerical hierarchy, tending to become bishops, and thus forming the clergy's élite.

Perhaps the most striking feature was that the liturgy employed at court was wholly unlike that of the rest of the Swedish Church. Ever since Karl IX had seized power in the late 1590s, the court liturgy had strongly Genevan Calvinistic overtones, with no vestments, no element of exorcism in the baptism ceremony, no celebration of the Annunciation and much less music.[23]

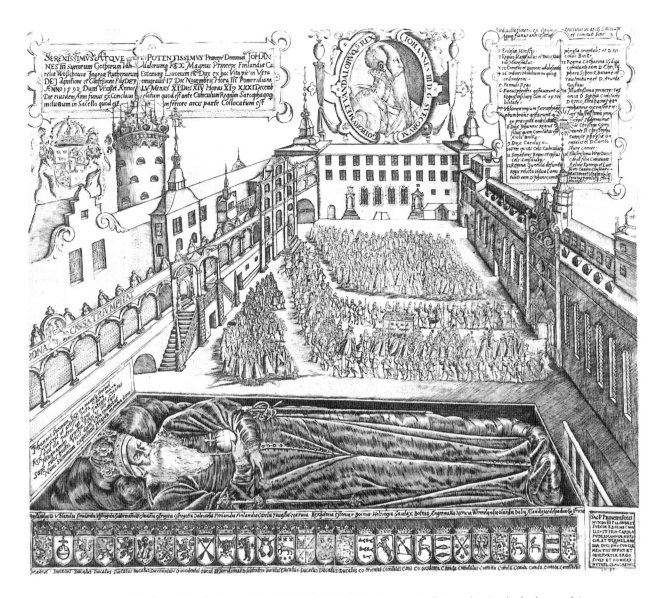

The rituals of royal death: King Johan III (1568–92) lying in state in his regalia. In the background is the king's funeral procession leaving from the inner courtyard of the Tre Kronor Castle.

Even in the later seventeenth century, the court liturgy resembled a 'calvinistiske cultu' or Calvinistic rite, according to Per Brahe, one of Karl XI's councillors, although at the time he made this observation steps had already been taken to make court usage conform with the far less austere practices of the Lutheran Swedish liturgy. In the 1660s the court's order of service for christenings was changed; in the 1670s vestments were introduced; and by the 1690s most of its peculiarities were gone, although some minor differences remained.

Many of the religious observances of the court – especially the monarch's communion – were performed outside the Stockholm palace chapel. Communion was often taken privately, 'in nooks and crannies':[24] in the late seventeenth century, for instance, Karl XI as a rule travelled to one of his nearby palaces in the environs of Stockholm to receive the sacrament, as did his mother and his daughters.[25] While some were clearly relaxed, even indifferent, in their attitudes towards religion, some, both monarch and courtiers, were devout; and in the late sixteenth century Karl IX (regent 1599–1604; reigned 1604–11), and in the late seventeenth, Karl XI and his daughter Queen Ulrika Eleonora (1718–20), were all noted for their personal piety.

That standards of behaviour at court were in theory expected to be exemplary is reflected in the court laws (*hovartiklarna*), promulgated by royal proclamation, and generally issued once during each monarch's reign. It was customary for the list of court laws to begin with a number of clauses dealing with religion and moral conduct. In the very first paragraph of the court law of 1560, for example, court servants were instructed to live according to God's commandments. Swearing was forbidden on pain of imprisonment in the palace gaol, and offenders caught more than four times were to be banished from court. All serving in the royal household were required to attend prayers, with the court chaplains being charged to ensure attendance. Those who missed a Sunday sermon lost a day's meals and were ordered to pay a fine in the form of alms to the poor.[26] Each of these regulations was repeated in later court laws, but by the court law of 1687 – where once again the first chapter deals with religion, prohibiting blasphemy, heresy, swearing, sorcery and prophesying – the penalties had become more exacting. The third time a servant of the royal household was caught swearing or not attending communion he was to be banished from court for a month or more, and part of his salary was to be docked and given to the poor. Conviction a fourth time meant permanent banishment.[27]

The reiteration of these pious injunctions makes it apparent that they were often blatantly disregarded. When it came to prayers, courtiers were frequently absent, and in 1693 it was said that there were not enough attending services to 'sing the hymns properly'. This problem extended to the main chapel services, and in 1698 a court chaplain complained that 'only a small minority of the court was present, and some of those strolling in the courtyard would put their noses round the door and then quickly vanish again'.[28] Even those who did attend services did not always behave themselves, and in 1680 the clergyman Olaus Ekman railed against 'those who occupy themselves with various frivolities when at prayers, something that happens much at court'.[29]

Although the devotional life of the court was ever-present, it was compromised by the worldliness of courtiers' drinking, gambling and duelling, their sexual indiscretions and arguments over precedence. Negative views of the court and courtiers abounded in the early modern period, for the court was a byword for ungodliness: 'whoever wants to be pious', it was said, 'must leave the court.'[30] In the Swedish version of *Reynard the Fox*, published in 1621 and probably translated by the former court chaplain Sigfrid Aronus Forsius, it is stated that 'courtiers, physicians and lawyers keep idolatry in their baggage'.[31]

The same holds true for court ceremonial, where theory and practice did not always coincide. The impression left by the official records and court

Above: *The horse trappings commissioned for the coronation of Karl IX in 1607. Executed by the Hamburg goldsmith, Ruprecht Miller (fl. 1606–23), who worked in Sweden for much of his career, the two aigrettes (above right) would have been placed, respectively, at the horse's forehead and at the crupper of the tail, and once held ostrich-feather plumes. The crescent-shaped cantle (below centre) and the pommel (above left) decorated the king's saddle. Worked in silver-gilt, gold, enamel and precious stones, objects such as these commanded a prestige and monetary value among contemporaries that far exceeded even the costliest of paintings.* Left: *King Gustavus Adolphus (1611–32), the greatest of Sweden's warrior kings, wearing the laurel wreath of a Roman victor. Worked in gold and coloured enamels, such high-value portrait medals were regularly presented to visiting ambassadors, and were part of a currency of gift-exchange that was an essential element of* ancien-régime *diplomacy.*

regulations suggests that the dignity and glamour for which the regime strove was by no means always achieved. The machinery of pomp and circumstance often creaked badly, and some parts of court life were more likely to repel than to impress. At times, court staff shirked their duties, became drunk and fought

with each other. Nor was there anything particularly edifying in the occasions of all-too-conspicuous consumption by court servants who, it was reported, gorged themselves on food and drink and then reeled off to 'vomit or commit indecencies in the beds of good men, soiling and spoiling their bedclothes'.[32]

Yet, for all its shortcomings, the Swedish court remained a focus for cultural life, if not within a European dimension, then at least within the immediate context of the realm. Throughout the sixteenth and seventeenth centuries contemporaries saw it as a centre from which fashions and tastes spread out across society at large. Members of the royal family were the country's pre-eminent patrons of the arts, not least because they commanded the largest resources when it came to acquiring paintings, buildings and *objets d'art*. Keeping up 'magnificence' was obviously important to the prestige of the court; yet the 'political' rationale for cultural patronage should not be overstated. The potential audience for many of these efforts was of course limited, nor should it be forgotten that the purchase of objects might not be ideologically motivated: members of the royal family were perfectly capable of surrounding themselves with beautiful and expensive objects for pleasure's sake alone.

All members of the Vasa dynasty attempted to raise artistic standards by turning to foreign craftsmen, both for commissions from abroad and by cultivating foreign craftsmen already active in Stockholm. Thus, when Erik XIV commissioned the regalia for his coronation in 1561, the new closed 'imperial' crown and orb were made by Flemish goldsmiths in the capital, and the sceptre and the key by Germans. Subsequent monarchs added to this permanent collection of regalia, and Karl IX's coronation in 1607 was remarkable for an increase in the regalia to ten items. Similarly, there were continuous royal purchases of silver tableware and plate, with the likes of Petter Henning (1688–1714) and Johan Nützel (fl. c.1700), working extensively for the royal household.[33]

The court was similarly the principal source of patronage in the other visual arts. Medals with the monarch's image and gold chains were standard presents to foreign diplomats, and plate was also commissioned on a lavish scale for presentation by Swedish diplomats in foreign courts. The first Swedish portraits, which date only from the 1540s, were commissioned by the royal family.[34] Since there were no Swedish artists sufficiently competent, in 1542 Gustav Vasa had to borrow the Danish court painter Jacob Binck to paint his portrait, and foreigners continued to dominate the artistic life of the Swedish court well into the late sixteenth century. During Queen Christina's reign of the late 1640s and 1650s there was a renewed attempt to raise the court's artistic profile, and her patronage was given to the painters David Beck from Delft (*fl.* 1647–51), who had previously instructed the sons of Charles I of England in drawing; the French painter Sébastien Bourdon (employed 1652–3); and the miniaturists Pierre Signac (employed 1647–84) and Alexander Cooper (hired in 1647), respectively, from France and England. Other accomplished artists worked in Stockholm for brief periods in the 1650s and 1660s, among them the German painter Jurian Ovens (active in Sweden in the 1650s) and the Antwerp portrait painter Abraham Wuchters (active in Sweden 1660–62). The Swedish painter Johan Sylvius and the French sculptor Jacques Foucquet concentrated on architectural decoration. Bourdon's equestrian portrait of Queen Christina is perhaps one of the finest products of this influx of foreign craftsmen and artists. During the late seventeenth century the distinguished medalist Arvid Karlsteen was active at the court of Karl XI. In general, however, seventeenth-century court art in Sweden was pedestrian and provincial, exemplified by the efforts of the diminutive miniaturist Anders Behn, who worked for the Queen Dowager Hedvig Eleonora, the long-lived widow of Karl X Gustav, the first king of Sweden from the new dynasty, the House of the Palatinate (1654–60).[35]

Most of the major commissions continued to go to foreign artists. Karl XI's court painter was the German David Klöcker Ehrenstrahl, while the dominant court artist of the first decades of the eighteenth century was his nephew, another German, David von Krafft. Sculpture was similarly monopolized by foreigners.[36]

The decorative arts in Sweden were also dominated by royal commissions and royal taste. Plate and other *objets d'art* were purchased from Augsburg goldsmiths throughout the seventeenth and eighteenth centuries. Tapestry production in Sweden was begun in 1552, when the Flemish maker Paul de Bucher set up a royal manufactory at Gustav Vasa's invitation.[37] It

flourished during the 1550s and 1560s, but slowed thereafter, and the last workshop was closed in 1614.[38] Domestic glass manufacture was also begun by Gustav Vasa in the 1550s, and depended heavily on the court for its survival.[39] Likewise, until the mid seventeenth century practically all Swedish stucco work was commissioned by the royal family.[40] For coronations, coaches were purchased by the court at great cost.[41]

Until the mid seventeenth century, garden design was practised at court on a modest scale.[42] Gustav Vasa imported a German gardener in 1545, while his son Erik XIV employed a Frenchman, Jean Allard (who was later involved in plots to reinstate Erik XIV, who had been deposed in 1568). In 1648 Queen Christina, with her Francophile tastes, brought in the French garden expert André Mollet, who had already received court commissions throughout Europe. Architecture at court dealt mostly, naturally enough, with the several royal palaces;[43] and of the various royal architects, Nicodemus Tessin the younger (who worked during the years 1681–1728) was an architect of international standing.

The scholarly life of the court was usually restricted to a limited circle.[44] During Queen Christina's brief 'French period' a few European luminaries were to be found at the otherwise intellectually lacklustre Swedish court. The presence of René Descartes, who visited Sweden in 1649–50; of Gabriel Naudé, Cardinal Mazarin's librarian who fled to Sweden during the Fronde; and such scholars as Isaac Vossius, resident in Sweden from 1648–54, all gave Sweden a short-lived international distinction. Usually, however, the intellectual life of the court was low key, centring on a professional 'historiographer' (or official historian), the royal tutors and the tutor of the court pages. A new infusion of intellectual life had to wait until the patronage of Queen Louisa Ulrika in the mid eighteenth century.

Although the royal musical establishment varied in scale and quality, no nobleman or private citizen could match the scale of court patronage.[45] In an attempt to add lustre to the Swedish monarchy, foreign composers were attracted to the court from the early seventeenth century. The German Andreas Düben served from 1620 until 1662; and the Italian Vincenzo Albrici worked at the court of Queen Christina from 1652 to 1654.[46] Music for the royal court was usually performed by a band of strings with trumpets and drums, and was employed extensively at court ceremonies, used daily to accompany the king's dining. Under Christina, the court's musical culture reached a certain degree of cosmopolitan sophistication, with the importing of Italian and French instrumentalists and singers. While it is unclear whether fully staged opera performances formed part of the court's musical culture, it is evident that from the 1680s onwards sections of operas by composers working in the style of Jean-Baptiste Lully were performed before the royal household in Stockholm. Court theatre usually took the form of shows by travelling actors, or of masques and ballets performed by courtiers.[47] Georg Stiernhielm, the 'father of Swedish poetry', wrote the texts for several court ballets in the 1640s. These so-called *ballets d'entrées* were introduced at the Swedish court from France in 1638, and were staged frequently from the 1640s to the 1670s; from 1650 a number of *värdskap*, a form of German masquerade imitating life at an inn, also formed part of the repertory of court entertainment. In the late 1690s and early 1700s a number of large masquerades inspired by French models, especially those of Jean Berain, were arranged by Nicodemus Tessin, the court marshal from 1700. Yet, for all the cultural diversions on offer, there was always the danger of tedium. In the early 1650s a court gentleman, Johan Ekeblad, at first rejoiced at taking part in these court ballets, but later came to tire of them, being more concerned with his aching feet than with the glamour of the scene before him.[48]

Out of doors, as elsewhere, it was the hunt that was the principal royal recreation, and it provided the court with an opportunity to combine a favourite pastime with royal display. However, hunts were not exclusively the business of the department designated the Royal Hunt; the actual planning of hunting expeditions and arrangements connected with hunting parties involved other departments of the court, and courtiers would join the king as his comrades in the hunting field. Like riding, hunting remained an important part of royal life in early modern Sweden. The late seventeenth-century monarch, Karl XI, was an addict, delighting in 'no other recreations', according to one contemporary, 'besides riding, fencing and hunting'.[49] He made careful diary entries throughout his life setting down the number of wolves, bears and other quarry he had killed in the course of his various hunts, even to the point of recording the number of shots he had taken.

Viewing the cultural life of the early modern Swedish court in general, it is all too easy to overstate the brilliance of craftsmanship and artistry to be found in the royal household. But even if the Swedish court was not in the forefront of artistic patronage within Europe, the combined effect of the jewellery, clothes, palaces, gold and silver plate, coaches and processions could still create the impression of opulence and magnificence, not only on Swedes but also on sophisticated foreign observers. In describing the formal entry of Queen Hedvig Eleonora into Stockholm in November 1654, the French nobleman the Comte de Brienne noted that 'the pomp of it was superb, and everything was done magnificently; never have I seen such beautiful carriages'.[50]

III. THE COURT AND THE ROYAL FINANCES

One area where the theory of a stately and well-ordered royal household clashed violently with reality was the court's finances. Economic crisis was commonplace during the first century of Vasa rule, with household servants frequently going unpaid for lengthy periods, although this state of affairs was partly rectified in the later seventeenth century, when, with improved royal revenues, there was an attempt to pay the court servants' salaries in full. Expenditure on the court was substantial by Swedish standards, and from at least the 1630s contemporaries saw it as an institution with a financial administration that was clearly separate from that of other government departments. Although the Swedish court may not have been expensive by international standards, it swallowed a large part of the state's expenditure; usually ten to twenty per cent of the realm's budget was spent on the court each year, expenditure that covered salaries, food, clothing, transport and liveries, although predictably this shrank during the two twelve-year periods when the monarch was a minor (in 1632-44 and 1660-72), when the court was much reduced in size.

In the course of the seventeenth century there was a dramatic change in the manner in which members of the household were paid. Under the early Vasas, members of the household had received a combination of cash and such payments-in-kind as cloth (for liveries), food, drink, firewood and stabling for staff and their servants. Only a select few, such as the marshal of the realm (from the inception of the office in 1634), the court marshal and the noblewomen attending the queen consort, were given lodgings at court. During the first half of the seventeenth century, however, payments became increasingly cash based, and, as elsewhere in Europe, the provision of meals in court was sharply curtailed. From 1648 most servants received cash in lieu of meals, and within a few years most of the payments in livery cloth had also ceased. Cash payments seem to have been deemed more efficient and less wasteful than free meals, and payments in livery cloth (another traditional mode of payment in kind) were not always popular with courtiers, who frequently complained that they had 'nothing *à la mode*' to choose from in the royal stores.[51]

In addition to these ordinary expenses, there were fireworks, masques and receptions of foreign ambassadors to be paid for, as well as the costs of such one-off events as coronations, royal weddings and funerals. The cost of 'satellite courts' should also be stressed. Often there were queens dowager to be accommodated, each of whom had extensive establishments of her own, and these represented a heavy charge, especially when the longevity of a number of the queens dowager is borne in mind: Katarina Stenbock lived as queen dowager from 1560 to 1621, Hedvig Eleonora from 1660 to 1715.[52]

In some ways the Swedish court was unusual in comparison with other early modern European

Above: *Queen Christina among the men of letters: the seventeenth century saw the foundation of a series of academies for the promotion of the arts and sciences, usually under the sovereign's patronage and closely associated with the court, that gave formal institutional structure to the earlier* ad hominem *patterns of courtly sponsorship of learning. During the 1640s and early 1650s Queen Christina's court attracted scholars of international fame and celebrity, including Descartes, Vossius and Cardinal Mazarin's former librarian, Gabriel Naudé.*

Left: *The court as witness: Jurian Ovaens's* The Bedding Ceremony of King Karl X Gustav and Queen Hedvig Eleonora in 1654. *In a culture where lineal succession was usually the principal determinant of the right to rule, the ruler's wedding night was often a quasi-public event, witnessed by senior courtiers.*

courts. Some differences were simply a matter of geography; as Europe's most northerly court, for instance, the expense of lighting the court occupied a disproportionately large element of the household budget.[53] Similarly, the Swedish court was unusually militarized, especially during the reigns of Gustavus Adolphus, Karl XI and Karl XII, a characteristic perhaps most clearly reflected by the proportion of the court's budget allocated to military personnel. Even in peacetime, between twenty-five to thirty per cent of court expenditure was earmarked for the royal guard; during the Great Nordic War with Peter the Great's Russia (1700–1721), however, this rose to about fifty per cent.

The court of the queen dowager: Drottningholm Palace, the seat of Karl X's widow, Hedvig Eleonora, in 1692. Acquired by the queen dowager in 1661, the second year of her widowhood, and completely rebuilt over the next twenty years to designs by the Tessins, father and son, Drottningholm exemplifies the capacity for the royal widow's court to act as a major independent focus of cultural and political patronage.

Yet, if the financial underpinnings of the court were often precarious, the experience of seventeenth-century Swedish monarchy suggests that sound finances were perhaps less important to the success of a court than maintaining the outward appearance of 'magnificence'. During the 1650s Queen Christina's finances were clearly over-stretched, and her indebtedness made her a byword for extravagance; yet her court had a reputation for splendour that was generally regarded by foreign diplomats and the native élite alike as bestowing prestige upon Sweden. Contemporaries did not distinguish between magnificence purchased with hard cash and that obtained on credit.

The one clear exception to the general picture of chaotic royal finances was the meticulously regulated court of Karl XI in the second half of the seventeenth century – although his experience suggests that a balanced budget created as many problems as it solved. The king, noted for his financial rigour in other areas, successfully held down court expenditure without recourse to the drastic cuts imposed by other contemporary monarchs (such as Charles II of Great Britain). Yet the king's economies were not viewed favourably: 'In Sweden the king is commonly accused of parsimony, because he keeps such a mean household', noted the Prussian diplomat Christoph von Brandt.[54] But it was not only the Swedes who were unimpressed. An English diplomat noted that 'the frugality of his Majesty's temper is everywhere visible in his court, in which there is little regard had to splendour and magnificence, either in furniture, tables, or attendants, or other things of that nature'.[55] In fact, royal expenditure had changed little since Queen Christina's day; what had altered were current expectations. Around 1690 it had become obvious that Sweden's image had been damaged by not keeping up in this competition for 'magnificence', and efforts were made to reverse the trend. The most important manifestation of the change of direction was the complete reconstruction of the royal palace in Stockholm, the Tre Kronor Castle, work on which began in 1692.

IV. COURT AND POLITICS

The importance of the Swedish court cannot, however, be measured only in terms of its artistic or architectural patronage, areas in which it was clearly eclipsed by many other European royal courts. The centrality of the court in the life of the Swedish Empire derived from the fact that it was the centre of politics and principal locus of power. When the English ambassador Bulstrode Whitelocke came to Stockholm in the 1650s, he did so in order to forge an alliance with the major Baltic power that would buttress the fledgling English Republic, not to admire the local art.[56]

In the early modern Swedish government, the monarch was the single most powerful figure in the realm, and the scale of patronage at his disposal was enormous. As a result, being close to the king, in any sense of that term, provided if not immediate power then at least the *possibility* of power. Thus, the Swedish court was the absolute centre of the realm, the frame for contacts between the monarch and the political élite. A large percentage of the nobility was employed at court, and the offices of Chamber gentlemen, court gentlemen, pages, maids of the court, court stable master and court hunt master were all strictly preserved for those of aristocratic birth.

Courtiers' patronage was exercised in a variety of ways. Court connections were probably at their most indispensable in the scramble for offices; but they had other uses, whether in overturning judicial decisions, getting leave from the army or obtaining a royal presence at a family funeral. The importance of court contacts was not only social, but also financial, as demonstrated by the group of court servants who controlled the tobacco monopoly from the 1660s to the 1680s. Courtiers were often instrumental in gaining grants of royal lands, both for themselves and for their clients,[57] and while most courtiers did not manage to amass huge fortunes by these means, many were more than comfortably well-off.

A few, however, reached the pinnacle of power by acquiring the status of royal favourites, men singled out for exceptional grants of royal largesse, and who exercised disproportionate influence in affairs of state solely by virtue of their relations with the monarch. The most notable examples appear in Queen Christina's reign, when the young courtiers Claes Tott, Magnus Gabriel de la Gardie and Christopher Delphicus von Dohna were granted large estates, titles and places on the royal council.

The long-serving court marshal Bengt Rosenhane (who held the office from 1669 to 1700), is perhaps characteristic of the way in which, as in most European royal courts, intimacy with those in power enabled courtiers to act as brokers. Rosenhane's influence derived from his close daily contact first with Karl XI and later with his successor Karl XII (1697–1718), and he was regularly bombarded with suits from friends, relatives and clients requesting assistance in securing offices, advice on how to press suits or even asking that he should say a word on their behalf to the king. The flow of supplicants to Rosenhane began with a vengeance in 1672, when Karl XI was declared of age, and friends turned to him begging help because, as one supplicant put it, 'I know you have great influence with the king'.[58] Sometimes he needed to co-operate with other courtiers to achieve the desired end; in 1672, for example, a friend begged him to remind the mistress of the court, Countess Riperda, to speak with the queen dowager, adding the request that Rosenhane himself should 'help me along with a good word to his Majesty'.[59]

As this letter suggests, the royal household was a place where the noblewomen of the female court establishment (or *hovfruntimret*) could also exert influence. At times the requests were overwhelming. Asked for a recommendation by a prospective client in the 1670s, the maid of the court, Anna Maria Clodt, noted wearily 'there are so many who have asked for that [same thing] from me'.[60] An important way in which women at court could wield influence, and make money in the process, was as matchmakers in royal dynastic marriages. Foreign diplomats hoping to find a Swedish royal bride for their masters would contact the household ladies close to the princesses in question in order to sound them out, often parting with cash for their assistance; thus, diplomats hoping to secure the hand of Princess Ulrika Eleonora (later Queen of Sweden, 1718–20) had to reckon with her powerful maid of the Chamber, who 'wholly possessed her'. Those who lacked court connections, from ambassadors to clergymen, felt the disadvantage acutely. As the cleric Jesper Swedberg preached indignantly in 1689, 'he who marries a maid from court, gains such an advantage, that no one, be he ever so learned, may be promoted before him'.[61] For the ladies themselves, there was also the prospect of an advantageous match with noblemen of the court.[62] Marriage, however, usually spelt the end of their court careers, since there were few positions in the households of the queen or the princesses that were open to married women.

What, then, of the role of the nobility at the Swedish court? Taking the early modern period as a whole, several thousand Swedish aristocrats served at court for at least a couple of years, generally before moving on to careers in the royal administration or the army. Service at court was, thus, to a great extent associated with youth, and with the acquisition of the manners requisite for a life amongst persons of gentility. Not until a young man knew how to speak and comport himself well, observed Per Brahe in the late seventeenth century, and had mastered the military skills of a knight, did he have 'the right to be known as an *aulicus* or "courtier"'.[63] The court was, in the words of the court marshal, Carl Adlerfelt, 'the best school in the world for a young man of quality'.[64] As a rule the pages, young noblemen between the ages of ten and twenty-five years, were the youngest court servants. For them, court service was part of their education, and they were taught by their own *preceptor*. Over and above mere book learning, the pages were expected to master the military skills of swordsmanship and riding, as well as the social skills expected of a gentleman. Thus the court was equipped with a fencing master and a dancing master. The young courtiers' accomplishments were displayed in ballets and *vårdskap*, masquerades and balls.[65]

But the Swedish court's influence on the nobility should not be overstated. It has been suggested (following the thesis advanced by Norbert Elias in relation to French Bourbon monarchy) that courts were used by the crown to 'tame' the *noblesse d'épée*, and to remove the military threat that they might otherwise pose to the supremacy of the king.[66] The court during Swedish 'absolutism' (1680–1718), a period that corresponds to that studied by Elias, does

not, however, conform to his model, and indeed during the seventeenth century as a whole the Swedish court was actually far too small to absorb more than a fraction of the nobility. In 1600, when there were in all some 450 Swedish male aristocrats over the age of twenty, there were about 110 noblemen at court (of whom a number were foreigners). Thus, at the beginning of the seventeenth century, somewhere between ten and twenty per cent of the Swedish nobility served at court. This proportion decreased steadily during the course of the century, so that by 1700, when the number of adult Swedish noblemen stood at around 2,500, only about fifty served at court, or no more than one to two per cent of the total number of the nobility.[67]

Moreover, the Swedish court élite did not tend to come from the old military noble families. Apart from the very top officers, such as marshal of the realm and court marshal, the principal court families came predominantly from the new nobility.[68] This was especially true of the court gentlemen and the pages. Although the more prestigious office of Chamber gentleman was usually reserved for the 'ancient nobility', it was primarily amongst the female attendants at court that the old noble families were represented. The success of the newly created nobility in gaining offices at court accelerated sharply under Karl XII in the first decades of the eighteenth century; indeed, it is no exaggeration to say that the changes effected during his reign amount to a social revolution at court. Men from families in the non-aristocratic court departments rose to occupy offices hitherto reserved for the nobility – such as court marshal, Chamber gentleman, court gentleman and page. During the last years of the king's reign, some of the most senior offices at court came be occupied by parvenus. Karl XII's court was governed at one time or another by the chief marshal Carl Piper, who was the son of a recently ennobled clerk; the court marshal Nicodemus Tessin, the son of the ennobled court architect; and the court marshal Gustaf von Düben, the recently ennobled son of the master of the royal music (*hovkapellmästare*).

The military ethos of the Swedish court was perhaps its most dominant characteristic. For most male courtiers, the royal household was akin to a military finishing school: after they had served at court for a couple of years, almost every page and most court gentlemen went on to a career in the army. The great

The Tre Kronor Castle, Stockholm, from the south-west, c.1650.

Swedish generals in the Thirty Years War had all served at court when young: Johan Banér (Chamber gentleman, 1617–21), Gustaf Horn (Chamber gentleman, 1618–21), Lennart Torstensson (page, 1619–22; court gentleman, 1623) and Carl Gustaf Wrangel (Chamber gentleman, 1632–3). The prominence of the military ethos at the court was, in turn, heavily influenced by the fact that, during the early modern period, Sweden was almost continuously at war: it was a Prussia before the rise of Prussia. With a few brief exceptions, Sweden was constantly at war between 1560 and 1720, a period that saw the triumph of a policy of forceful and vigorous Swedish expansion. New provinces were conquered on the eastern side of the Baltic and on the Scandinavian peninsula, and to meet the need for manpower and a socially élite officer corps most Swedish noblemen served in the army at some point.

Sweden's spectacular military successes in the seventeenth century affected the culture of the court in numerous ways. Swedish monarchs of the period continued to lead their armies in battle until the

eighteenth century and several (including, most famously, Gustavus Adolphus in 1632) were actually killed on the battlefield. Military courtiers on active service also risked being killed or wounded, or being dragged away into captivity (for possible ransom later). At times when manpower shortages were acute even the stable boys and the court's menial servants were called upon to fight; in the war against Denmark of 1611–13, even the court dwarf, 'Little Grey', was armed. A part of the royal household always followed the king on his campaigns, and hence at various times the king kept his court abroad: in the Holy Roman Empire in the 1630s, in Denmark in the 1650s, in Russia and Poland in the 1700s, and as far afield as the Ottoman Empire in the 1710s. This peripatetic existence resulted in a highly cosmopolitan royal household, with various Germans, Turks and Jews finding employment in the court-on-campaign.

Conversely, the court acted as a unifying force in the Swedish conglomerate empire, decisively influencing the character of what has been called Sweden's 'imperial experience'. Of the foreigners at court who came from outside the Swedish empire, Germans always dominated, although there were numbers of Scots, Englishmen, Frenchmen and central-European Calvinist émigrés. German influence was probably at its height in the mid sixteenth century under Gustav Vasa, when courtiers from the principalities of the Holy Roman Empire held some of the highest offices at the Swedish court; but Germans continued to be well represented at the Swedish court throughout the remainder of the sixteenth century. The gentlewomen of the court, too, numbered many German members – so many at the beginning of the early seventeenth century that the queen was obliged to take action before her coronation in 1607 to redress the imbalance, writing letters to the old Swedish nobility to recruit 'some fair Swedish maids of good and noble stock and family'.[69] Even during the 1650s, when Queen Christina promoted French personnel to places at court, German courtiers always outnumbered their Gallic colleagues. In the eighteenth century, however, the number of foreign courtiers decreased rapidly as the Swedish empire steadily contracted.

As we have seen, the nobility used the court as a place where they could exert influence and cultivate contacts; but for the average nobleman court service was only a temporary episode in their ascent up the *cursus honorum*. This may in part have been because of the highly competitive environment in which courtiers vied with each other for royal favour and for the fruits of office; inevitably there were many who fell by the wayside. Indeed, there was a Swedish saying in the seventeenth century that 'at court ten strive for the success of one'.[70] Whatever the reason, few stayed on at court for more than a few years, though many worked hard to retain their contacts there.

Of course, attendance at court was more than a matter of the making or breaking of individual fortunes; it had a broader political significance. It set the tone for each regime, and defined who was in, and who out, of power. In the 1590s, after Karl IX had won the Civil War and deposed his nephew King Sigismund, he naturally filled his court with aristocrats drawn from families who had been loyal to him; wartime opponents were ostracized. At his death in 1611, however, his son and successor, Gustavus Adolphus, effected a radical reversal of this policy. Instead of maintaining the political isolation of the

families of his father's enemies, Gustavus used his court to reintegrate them into the political mainstream. As a gesture of reconciliation, he filled his court with the sons of men who had been executed by his father, among them Lars Sparre, who became court marshal, Axel Banér, who became stable master, and the Chamber gentleman Anders Grip (whose father's head had been put on a spike above the town gate of Kalmar).

During the power vacuum that accompanied royal minorities, on the other hand, there was almost invariably an attempt by powerful courtiers to achieve a monopoly over appointments to major offices in the household. It has long been recognized, for example, that during the twelve years of Queen Christina's minority (1632–44), the Chancellor Axel Oxenstierna, Sweden's Richelieu, filled the council and the chancery with his relatives and clients.[71] It has never been fully realized, however, that Oxenstierna was no less systematic and diligent in gaining control of the royal household as well. Close relatives and clients were installed in almost every department. The chancellor's cousin Elisabet Gyllenstierna was appointed mistress of the court, and her daughters maids of court. Gyllenstierna was succeeded by Beata Oxenstierna (another cousin of the chancellor) who also brought with her a daughter as maid of court; the chancellor's niece Kerstin Kurck became a maid of court; and his nephew Axel Åkesson Natt och Dag became a Chamber gentleman. The new marshal of the realm was the chancellor's brother-in-law Åke Axelsson Natt och Dag; the court marshal Ture Sparre was another connection by marriage (the brother-in-law of the marshal of the realm); and one of the chancellor's sons was the first to receive the newly created and highly prestigious court office of senior gentleman of the Chamber.

During the next royal minority, that of Karl XI (1660–72), Magnus Gabriel de la Gardie, chancellor and uncle by marriage to the young king, failed to repeat Oxenstierna's successful colonization of the household with his placemen. In the absence of a single clearly dominant figure, a series of acrimonious struggles ensued in both the council and in the Swedish Parliament over who should be allowed to serve in the court during the king's minority. The Swedish Parliament consisted of four estates (nobles, clergy, burghers and peasants), of which the nobility was politically by far the most important. The nobility was divided into three classes according to title and birth, and the result of any vote was always based on the majority achieved in voting by class, because two classes (even if numerically in the minority) could always outvote a third (even if it was the most numerous of the three). Except during a minority, Parliament generally did not dare to dabble in court affairs; but during the minority of Karl XI, the lower nobility sought to preserve some court offices for nobles outside the royal council and they also wanted to keep foreign nobles away. The attitude of the council, dominated by the high nobility, was quite different; there, councillors worried about courtiers from the lower nobility.

V. THE COURT TRANSFORMED

In the century after the creation of a Swedish royal household under Gustav Vasa, thousands of young Swedes passed through the court, *en route* to careers in the military or in royal service. The court of Karl XI, however, marks a watershed in the development of the Swedish court, and stands in sharp contrast to the practices that had prevailed under the Vasas. Royal revenues improved. The crown's income – which had long depended on taxes, tolls and the revenues of crown lands – was further expanded in the 1680s, when Karl XI began the so-called 'reduction', the redemption of vast areas of crown land that had formerly been given away to the nobility. The long period of peace between 1680 and 1700, unequalled during Sweden's time as a great power, also relieved the crown of the horrendous cost of war during the latter part of Karl XI's reign. Courtiers tended to serve for ever longer periods, and, in consequence, their average age climbed steadily. Even newly appointed Chamber gentlemen and court gentlemen were generally older than before; whereas courtiers during the first half of the seventeenth century had mostly been unmarried and in their twenties, their Caroline counterparts were often middle-aged men with families. To take a post in the court was no longer a first step on a much more varied ladder of preferment; it had turned into a lifetime career.

This trend towards an increasingly static body of court personnel can also be measured by the number of 'veteran' courtiers in service in the household. If one examines the numbers of aristocrats who served at court for ten years or more throughout the period 1521–1718, some striking differences emerge. During the 1620s and 1630s, of the noblemen who began careers at court, only two subsequently served for longer than a decade. Similarly, at Queen Christina's abdication in 1654 there were only four noblemen at the court who had served for ten years or more. Taking the period 1615–75 as a whole, there were usually no more than about five noblemen at court who had served for ten years or more, and during the turbulent 1640s there were occasions when there was not a single one. From the 1670s onwards, however, the group of 'veterans' – those who had served for a decade or more – increased rapidly to between fifteen and twenty courtiers at any one time. During the so-called 'Age of Liberty' (1719–72), when royal powers were severely curtailed, the number of long-term courtiers increased yet further. By the mid eighteenth century, the geriatric quality of the Swedish court had become almost proverbial; as one courtier quipped, 'the master of the horse was handless, the court painter was blind, the master of the royal music was deaf and the dancing master lame'.[72] Thus the Caroline court closed in on itself, and instead of attracting new blood it tended to recruit from families already well established at court. It was exclusive in the sense that those outside this charmed and elderly circle could almost never get a toehold. Offices seldom fell vacant, and when they did it was the entrenched court families who stood the best chance of filling them.

The court, observed Johan Adler Salvius in 1649, 'is like a fire: too close and you burn yourself, too far away and you grow cold'.[73] To people living in the sixteenth, seventeenth and eighteenth centuries, the Swedish court was quite clearly the focal point of the realm, the nucleus of political, cultural and social life. Even the apparent decline in royal power and in the importance of the court in the eighteenth century carried with it the seeds of something new. In the 1740s and the 1750s renewed aspirations were reflected in the creation of a court party formed around Adolphus Frederic (1751–71) and his wife Louisa Ulrika. The royal *coup d'état* of 1772 finally succeeded where an earlier attempt in 1756 had failed miserably, and marked the beginning of a new period of strong monarchical power and the renewed ascendancy of the court.

CHAPTER TWELVE

Russia
THE COURTS OF MOSCOW AND ST PETERSBURG
*c.*1547–1725

LINDSEY HUGHES

O N 16 JANUARY 1547 GRAND PRINCE IVAN VASIL'EVICH of Moscow was crowned tsar in the first ceremony of its kind in Russia. To Western eyes his was a 'barbarous' kingdom on the fringes of Christendom, which as recently as 1480 had claimed independence from the Mongol khans, whose ancestors had conquered most of the Russian lands in the thirteenth century. In the fourteenth and fifteenth centuries the principality of Moscow had assumed political and ecclesiastical leadership of Russia. The complex process of 'gathering the Russian lands' was, in reality, achieved by a combination of force of arms, collaboration, intrigue and good luck; but the fifteenth and early sixteenth centuries saw the elaboration of an ideology that underlined the ancestral *right* of the House of Moscow to rule. They were heirs to the early princes of Kiev and Vladimir; to the semi-legendary Viking chief Riurik, who had been allegedly invited to rule Rus' in about 862 AD, and provided the dynasty with its name. The House of Moscow, it was claimed, was the successor to the eastern steppe empire of the Mongol khans and to the fallen Christian realm of Byzantium, the eastern Roman Empire.

Texts devised by bookmen to endorse these claims incorporated the legend that the royal regalia – the crown of Monomakh and a pectoral cross containing a fragment of the True Cross – had been sent to Kiev in the eleventh century by the Byzantine Emperor Constantine IX Monomachus. Spurious genealogies proved kinship with the rulers of imperial Rome, while the adoption of the Byzantine emblem of the double-headed eagle in the fifteenth century under-scored not only Moscow's Byzantine inheritance, but also its claims of equality with the Holy Roman Emperors, the successors of the erstwhile western Roman Empire. Accordingly, Moscow was variously hailed as the New Rome, the New Jerusalem and the New Constantinople, the epicentre of Christian civilization.[1]

The ceremonial transference of the regalia of Tsar Mikhail Fedorovich at his coronation in 1625, in front of the Kremlin Cathedral of the Dormition.

I. Autocrats and Servitors

Students of early modern Russia do not need to concern themselves with the pecking order of rival courts; by the second half of the sixteenth century all power was formally vested in the person of the tsar. Muscovy had serfdom, fixed in statute as late as 1649, but had never known feudalism in the Western sense, nor had it ever developed a knightly cult of chivalry. Many magnates bore the title prince (*kniaz'*), the only Russian hereditary title, but they were bound to the crown by service on the same basis as non-titled nobles. Local allegiances were weak, and while the nobles' scattered estates provided income and servants, they did not serve as power bases. Power and prestige were measured in degrees of physical proximity to the sovereign. Closest to the throne were the tsar's councillors (often referred to as the 'boyar duma' or, in recent literature, as the 'boyar élite'), men with the rank (in descending order) of boyar (*boiarin*), lord in waiting (*okol'nichii*), and a smaller group of so-called gentlemen of the council and professional conciliar secretaries. Nobles immediately below the men of the council (often younger aspirants to membership) bore the titles *stol'nik* (table attendant), *striapchii* (escort), *dvorianin moskovskii* (Moscow noble) and *zhilets* (attendant). In the sixteenth century the Duma rarely exceeded two dozen men; in the seventeenth, numbers varied from 28 to 153.[2] None of these ranks could be inherited or purchased, and although they once had specific duties assigned to them, these had lapsed by the seventeenth century. The boyar élite commanded regiments in wartime and ran chanceries in peacetime, as did non-Duma nobles, but the latter served in lesser grades. All of them – boyar and non-boyar – were charged with performing ceremonial duties at court. A larger body of nobles resided in the provinces – *gorodovye dvoriane* (provincial gentry) and *deti boiarskie* (literally, boyars' sons, the most junior servitors); but these had no access to the court.

There was no regular system of court office-holding, but courtly titles such as carver (*kravchii*) and armsbearer (*oruzheinichii*) were conferred sporadically as marks of personal favour. The posts of chamberlain (*postel'nichii*) and gentleman of the Bedchamber (*spal'nik*) were generally reserved for a handful of younger members of distinguished boyar families, who thereby gained access to the royal presence in anticipation of being admitted eventually to the boyar council, while more experienced men were appointed as personal attendants (*d'iadki*) to the tsar's sons.

Courtly etiquette prescribed ritual forms of abasement for even the grandest members of the tsar's entourage. At first sight, the rhetoric employed even by boyars in their addresses to the sovereign suggested servile powerlessness: they referred to themselves as the tsars' 'slaves' and prostrated themselves in the royal presence. Yet, as recent studies have argued, Muscovite autocracy was in some respects a 'façade'.[3] By and large, men from powerful clans became boyars or *okol'nichie* in a regular pattern according to their seniority within their family, rather than as a direct result of the sovereign's favour. Likewise, a code of precedence or place system (*mestnichestvo*) determined the allocation of military commissions and other appointments on the basis of a clan's service record and seniority within it. The tsar generally did not disrupt the traditional promotion structure, although royal marriages and favouritism could adjust the balance between clans by introducing fresh blood. In the sixteenth and seventeenth centuries a number of clans, such as the Shuiskiis, regularly enjoyed positions of prominence at court and access to the royal presence. The Golitsyn and Dolgorukii clans had men in the Duma throughout the seventeenth century and remained prominent in the eighteenth. On the other hand, the power of the Miloslavskii and Naryshkin families, whose fortunes rose as a result of Tsar Alexis's first marriage to Maria Miloslavskaia in 1648 and his second to Natal'ia Naryshkina in 1671, was short-lived. Personal favour and access to the monarch did not on their own guarantee the establishment of a successful aristocratic dynasty.

The independent cultural life of the Muscovite élite outside the royal household was extremely restricted. There were no schools or universities, no public entertainments, no secular press. Travel abroad required the permission of the tsar and the patriarch. Balls and masques were out of the question, since royal women lived in seclusion in the *terem* quarters, an arrangement that was replicated in boyar households, although not in the population at large.[4] The Muscovite court knew no cult of beauty, still less

Red Square and the Kremlin: the Palm Sunday procession, 1636.

did it publicly celebrate or indulge in amorous conquests. Curtained recesses in church and closed carriages for outings shielded royal women from prying eyes as they went about their round of female devotions.

II. THE KREMLIN

During the formative period of the Muscovite state in the fourteenth and fifteenth centuries, the court's imperial pretensions were far more impressive than its physical surroundings. The Kremlin, the seat of both government and Church, was at first just one of the many wooden and earthwork forts that occupied the centre of many Russian towns. This changed in the reign of Tsar Ivan III (1462–1505), who built or embellished a complex of religious and secular buildings adjacent to his palace.[5] The Cathedral of the Dormition (1475–79, by the Italian architect Aristotele Fioravanti), the scene of coronations and the installation of metropolitans and patriarchs, fused Renaissance engineering and proportions with traditional Orthodox architectural conventions. To the south stood the royal necropolis, the Cathedral of the Archangel Michael (1505–9, by a Venetian architect known as Alevisio Novii), the exterior of which displays Italianate sculptural features. The interior walls and columns were decorated with stylized images of princes of the House of Moscow, whose remains were assembled in a symbolic recreation of the 'gathering' of the Russian lands.[6] The Cathedral of the Annunciation (1484–9, by builders from Pskov) served as the chapel royal. It was linked to the royal residence, as was the Palace of Facets (1487–91, by Marco Friazin and Pietro Antonio Solari), a hall used for ambassadorial receptions, banquets, the presentation of heirs and other major state occasions.

The residence, reconstructed in the 1490s, was a warren of chambers, chapels and passages. Its upper storeys (1630s) were known as the *terem* and provided both the tsar's private apartments and accommodation for the royal women and children. If the Kremlin was a city within a city, the residence was its inner sanctum, often referred to in documents simply as *verkh* (up above). Non-courtiers were not admitted even to the palace courtyard, still less to the inside of the building, which contained no public rooms. Even higher officials had to dismount at a specified distance from the entrance and approach it on foot.[7] Inside the palace, access was further limited by status. The closest that non-Duma nobles could

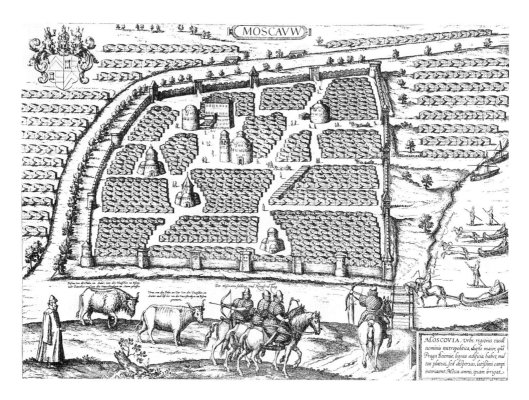

Above: *The seat of empire: Moscow in the fifteenth century – the first known plan.*
Right: *The convergence of holy place and sacred power: a stylized representation of the Cathedral of the Dormition, the holiest of the Kremlin's churches, and the setting for the coronation ritual. To the left stand the two joint-tsars, Ivan V and Peter I with Peter's infant son, Alexis; to the right, represented on terms of virtual equality, stand the two highest clerics, the Patriarch Adrian and the Metropolitan of Kiev. The Mother of God, in the central arch, confers her benediction equally on secular and ecclesiastical authority. This parity between tsar and patriarch ended during the reign of Peter I.*

get to the tsar's chambers was to a point outside, on the so-called Bedchamber Terrace (*postel'noe kryl'tso*). Higher clergy and boyars attended the tsar in the Antechamber (*peredniaia*), to which favoured foreign ambassadors were also admitted. It adjoined the Golden Throne Room (*Zolotaia palata*), which was adorned with frescoes depicting the kings of Israel as victors, builders, lawgivers and judges alongside analogous scenes from the life of the princes of Kiev.[8] Beyond was the royal study, which only boyars designated as 'close' (*blizhnie*) could enter, and beyond it the tsar's bedchamber. The women's quarters were out of bounds to all except designated noblewomen (*boiarini*), with the Golden Hall of the Tsaritsas (rebuilt in the 1580s) providing a slightly more public space for female receptions.

Processions sometimes spilled out into the territory adjoining the Kremlin, passing through the Gate of the Saviour on to Red Square and towards the Cathedral of the Protecting Veil of the Mother of God (erected 1555–61, and better known as St Basil's Cathedral). The River Moskva, to the south of the Kremlin wall, was commandeered for the blessing of the water (at a spot designated 'the Jordan') on 6 January (Epiphany), and on 1 August for the feast of the Bringing Forth of the Cross, derived from the Constantinopolitan ritual of parading the relics of the True Cross (allegedly found outside Jerusalem by Constantine's mother, St Helena) on the first day of the fast of the Dormition. The blessing of the waters with Moscow's own fragments of the True Cross associated this festival with the baptism of Rus' in 988.[9]

The court visited more distant churches and monasteries for particular festivals, but rarely ventured far beyond the Moscow region. Courtly display was intended not so much to impress the tsar's subjects as to reinforce both the bonds and the distance between autocrat and servitors, who 'presented a common ceremonial front'.[10] For parades and receptions, the boyar élite (men only, needless to say) donned appropriate ceremonial robes (often issued from the royal treasury because of the great expense involved) and stood or walked in a sequence determined by their rankings in the Code of Precedence. To the 'middle-service class' in the provinces, those members of the lesser gentry known as 'boyars' sons', who formed cavalry regiments in wartime, the decorousness of the court must have seemed impossibly remote. Indeed, it has been argued that Russian provincial nobles lacked the manorial tradition and 'gentility' usually associated with noble status elsewhere in Europe; the general picture of noble life in the provinces is one of 'almost unrelieved rudeness and coarseness, with a frequently repeated motif of drunkenness and violence'.[11] The culture of the court was self-consciously distanced from this boorish provincial world, although there is ample evidence of brawling and disputes over ranking and precedence among the nobility in Moscow.

III. MUSCOVITE COURT CEREMONIAL

Court ritual reached new heights in the reign of Ivan III's grandson, Ivan IV (1533–84), whose coronation in 1547, devised and stage-managed by Metropolitan Makarii, was closely based on late Byzantine models. This was 'legitimizing ritual' *par excellence*: the tsar

wore the Monomakh regalia and the ceremony was described as an 'ancient rite', although, in fact, its rituals were new to Russia. To mark the conquest of Kazan' in 1552, Ivan again donned the regalia to enter Moscow in a great victory parade. Several of the chapels in St Basil's Cathedral were dedicated to feast days associated with Muscovite victories of the campaign, while the dedication of the cathedral's westernmost chapel to the Entry into Jerusalem made explicit the link between Moscow and the Holy Land, as well as evoking Christ's triumphal Palm Sunday entry into Jerusalem. In Moscow and elsewhere, churches, icons and fables celebrated the role of the Mother of God, Protectress of Constantinople, as Moscow's special patron.[12] Similarly, Ivan and his successors made use of pilgrimages to 'mark out' their territory beyond Moscow, as, for example, in the annual expedition to the Trinity Monastery, forty miles to the north, for the feast of St Sergius on 25 September.[13] Each royal 'outing' was meticulously recorded for posterity in rosters (*razriady*), which were consulted for questions of precedence and protocol.

This typical seventeenth-century example demonstrates the strictly observed hierarchies:

In 7186 [1678 in the Western calendar], on the tenth day of July, on the feast of the Deposition of the Robe of our Lord God and Saviour Jesus Christ, the great sovereign Tsar and great Prince Fedor Alekseevich, autocrat of all Great and Little and White Russia, deigned to attend divine liturgy in the cathedral and apostolic church of the Dormition of the most Holy Mother of God. Behind the great sovereign went the boyars and *okol'nichie* and gentlemen of the council and privy councillors and *stol'niki* and *striapchie* [escorts] and Moscow nobles and secretaries and *zhil'tsy* [attendants] and military and chancellery servitors of all ranks wearing fresh robes with gold and silver embroidery.[14]

The court calendar was dominated by the liturgical year (numbered from the Creation), which began on 1 September and reached its climax in Holy Week: from the Palm Sunday parade to Red Square, when the tsar, on foot, led the patriarch seated on a donkey or a colt, in an enactment of the Byzantine 'symphony' of tsardom and priesthood, to the celebration of the Resurrection.[15] The other twelve major feasts of the Orthodox calendar, and countless lesser ones (dozens of new saints were created during

Ivan IV's reign), all required the royal presence, as did rites of passage and dynastic anniversaries, all marked not only by church services but also by lavish banquets. This exhausting programme constantly reinforced the belief that the Muscovite tsardom was rooted in the idea of the involvement of the great Russian realm in universal Christian history, a role that was greatly enhanced, in symbolic if not in practical terms, after the fall of Constantinople in the fifteenth century, and significantly modified in the sixteenth, when the tsar's rule was extended to non-Christians in conquered territories. The tsar's role as God's representative was foremost; he was both mortal and yet higher than ordinary mortals. The courtiers played a supporting role to the tsar, but ceremonial order and protocol – placings at banquets, escorting the coffin at royal funerals, or guarding the tomb in the forty-day vigil observed thereafter – reinforced their hierarchical relationship to one another within the royal entourage.[16]

IV. THE AGE OF TRANSITION

After the extinction of the Riurikid dynasty with the death of Ivan IV's son Fedor (1584–98), his successor, the elected tsar Boris Godunov, struggled hard to maintain ceremonial continuity within the court in an effort to compensate for his lack of legitimacy in the eyes of his fellow boyars. After Boris's death in 1605 a bizarre collection of pretenders and boyar tsars failed to stem the collapse of central authority, or to prevent invasions by Poland and Sweden, both of which sought to exploit Russia's internal chaos to their own territorial advantage. Yet Muscovite ceremonial customs survived this 'Time of Troubles'; indeed, amid the political chaos of early seventeenth-century Russia, ritual certitudes were more necessary than ever as a buttress of royal authority. Thus, the sixteen-year-old Mikhail Romanov was crowned in 1613 according to the Byzantine-influenced rite of 1547, and with his monarchical prerogatives intact; but his youth and inexperience (like that of his immediate successors in the tsardom) meant that initially royal power was expressed in ceremony and symbol rather than in concrete achievement.

Courtly pomp was particularly dazzling during the reign of Mikhail's son Alexis (1645–76), dubbed the 'most pious' (although, in maturity, an assertive and active ruler), and continued unabated under Alexis's immediate successors. Along with the major religious festivals, which Alexis observed meticulously, familial commemorations were also treated with particular solemnity during his reign. For example, the namedays of Alexis's numerous children, as well as his own and his wife's, were celebrated annually by liturgies for the feast of the nameday saint and by the distribution of special pastries to courtiers and churchmen. In 1667 the thirteenth birthday of his eldest son, also Alexis, was marked by ceremonies at which courtiers paid homage to the young prince as heir; and after the youth's premature death in 1670, the new heir, Fedor, was presented 'to all ranks of people of the entire Muscovite state' in a series of religious ceremonies conducted in the Kremlin cathedrals.[17]

The disaster of the 'Troubles' contained within it the seeds of change. Acknowledgement of the need for military reform brought numerous foreign military and technical personnel to Moscow; and new cultural influences also penetrated from Catholic Poland through the Ukraine (annexed by Moscow in 1654), and the Grand Duchy of Lithuania. In the 1650s Orthodox clerics from these regions were invited to Moscow to participate in church reforms, and these in turn precipitated a schism within Russian Orthodoxy that shook the power of the Church. Not only did tens of thousands of dissenters, known as Old Believers, reject the changes and break away from the official Church, but Patriarch Nikon, who masterminded the reforms in order to bring the Muscovite liturgy and ordinals closer to Greek models, clashed with Tsar Alexis over patriarchal interference in secular politics. For this challenge to monarchical authority he found himself deposed from the patriarchate. This period saw a general reduction in the jurisdiction of ecclesiastical courts and the imposition of limitations on the Church's land holdings. By the mid seventeenth century, the tsar's authority over the spiritual realm had been powerfully enhanced at the expense of the clergy.

The changing relationship between Church and monarchy, together with Western influences brought in by foreign craftsmen and military personnel, may well have facilitated modest 'closet' reforms at court, mainly hidden from the eyes of the populace. These included the belated introduction into Russian art of the practice of portraiture from life. Alexis is the first Russian ruler of whom we have something approaching an accurate likeness, although his portraits are still heavy with Orthodox imagery. Similarly, he initiated a short-lived experiment in court theatre and instrumental music (1672–6), both of which posed problems for traditional Orthodox sensibilities. The theatrical performances, staged within the confines of royal palaces before strictly vetted audiences, were an extension of courtly spectacle – albeit wholly designed to impress the court élite.[18]

There was innovation in architecture as well, though here constraints were also imposed by the strength of indigenous tradition. Around Moscow, several palaces were embellished for summer recreation, notably at Kolomenskoe, where the tsar's new wooden palace combined traditional carpentry construction and carving with Western interior design and furnishings, and at Izmailovo, which boasted Western formal gardens, complete with hothouses. Alexis maintained lodges for hunting and falconry, even devising a book of rules for this 'glorious sport',[19] and employed Russia's first court poet, the Belarusian monk Simeon Polotskii. Yet the fact that Polotskii's verses mainly languished in the palace in unpublished single copies, specially bound as presentation manuscripts, underlines the limits of seventeenth-century Russian 'Westernization'. Muscovite courtiers did not read poetry nor, indeed, very much at all beyond the Psalter and the lives of the saints. Their mansions may have displayed decorative elements of the classical orders, which their Russian builders gleaned from foreign engravings, but neither the patrons nor the employees could decipher the Latin script of the texts.

Changes were also being brought to the structures of power. Alexis often suspended *mestnichestvo* (the hereditary code of precedence), and in 1682 his son, Fedor (1676–82), abolished it altogether, thus marking the beginning of the decline of boyar influence within the regime. During the 1680s, when factions around the joint-tsars Ivan V (1682–96) and his younger half-brother Peter I ('the Great', 1682–1725) vied for power, the increased membership of the Duma reduced that body's exclusiveness and confined many boyars to purely ceremonial roles. Despite Ivan's mental and physical handicaps, he proved a pliant participant in the stately and heavily robed business of court ritual. From 1682 to 1689, however, real power was in the hands of his sister (and Peter's half-sister) Sophia and her circle, notably the leading boyar Prince Vasilii Golitsyn. In the meantime, Peter shirked his ceremonial duties at every opportunity in order to train his personal troops and to indulge his other passion, the building and sailing of ships. It was with some difficulty that his supporters eventually forced him to overthrow Sophia's regency in 1689, and for several years thereafter a handful of nobles, headed by Peter's maternal uncle Lev Naryshkin, ran both domestic and foreign affairs while Ivan performed the monarch's ceremonial duties.

From the mid 1690s, however – and especially after Tsar Ivan's death in 1696 – reform of the court's ossified culture and ceremonial became overt under the impact of Peter's efforts to modernize Russia. One of the first public displays of change was the military parade held in Moscow in 1696 to celebrate the capture of the port of Azov from the Ottomans, the earliest example of the advent of Roman classicism in Russia: triumphal arches bore the legend 'I came: I saw: I conquered'; images of Mars and Hercules abounded. Although some texts continued to compare Peter to Constantine the Great, the shift away from the tsar's role in universal Christian history to his worldly achievements was signalled as religious symbols ceded the limelight to classical and mythological images in a belated version of Renaissance festival culture.[20] Thereafter all victory parades followed this pattern, most magnificently after the Battle of Poltava in 1709. Yet the 1696 parade also illustrated Peter's tendency to subvert his own triumphs: the tsar did not ride on a steed as a conquering hero or even in a carriage, but instead he marched in the guise of bombardier behind the official heroes of the hour, Admiral Franz Lefort and General Aleksei Shein. Courtiers steeped in the traditions of the old Muscovite court were forced to make major adjustments.

These reforms were clearly inspired, in part, by the tsar's first-hand experience of other European royal households. During his so-called Grand Embassy of 1697–8, Peter had visited courts in Prussia, the Dutch Republic, England (where he toured Kensington Palace, Hampton Court and Windsor Castle), Austria and Poland. Among the lessons he learned was that,

from dress codes to dancing, the habits of Muscovite 'courtiers' fell far short of the models that informed the etiquette of most Western and Central European courts, even the least sophisticated. While in England, residing in John Evelyn's house at Deptford, the Russian delegation had taken pot shots at pictures and almost totally destroyed the fine garden. Sophie Charlotte, the Electress of Brandenburg, who met Peter in 1697, was unimpressed with his behaviour: 'It is evident that he has not been taught how to eat properly', she complained, although she liked his 'natural manner and informality'.[21] Peter's early measures to Westernize his 'crude' courtiers included the introduction of Western fashions, the banning of beards for the urban population, and the desegregation of the sexes, as élite women were forced to bare their heads and bosoms and to 'socialize'.[22] Soon he was also to provide the court with a new setting.

V. THE 'PARADISE' OF TSAR PETER THE GREAT

The Great Northern War against Sweden (1700–21) had a crucial impact on the life of the Russian court, not least in bringing about its physical and psychological relocation. In 1703 Peter founded an island fortress on captured territory on the Neva river and named it St Petersburg; in the early 1710s he moved the court and major government departments there.[23] The Muscovite closed model of the court – a walled citadel containing the main church and state edifices in a restricted space with an inner sanctum at its heart, 'oriental' looking to Western eyes – was replaced by an open, polycentric plan, a set of buildings and public spaces located on the banks of the River Neva and adjoining waterways, all designed by foreign architects in a modern classical idiom. Outdoor space played a major role, partly as a result of Peter's dislike of being cooped up or sitting still for extended periods. The main sites of activity included the original fortress, with the Cathedral of SS. Peter and Paul (by the architect Domenico Trezzini, erected during 1712–33); the Summer Palace (again by Trezzini, built during 1710–12, and decorated by Andreas Schlüter, who had built part of Friedrich I's palace and gardens in Berlin); the first and second

The murder of the Tsarevich Dimitri Ivanovich at Uglich in 1591 robbed the tsar, Fedor III, of an heir
to the throne, and brought the Riurikid dynasty to an end on Fedor's death in 1598.

Winter Palaces (by Georg Johann Mattarnovi, a product of the 1710s); the Cathedral and Senate building on Trinity Square (neither of which survives); and the Alexander Nevskii Monastery (another of Trezzini's commissions from the 1710s). Other major building projects included the palaces of Peter's favourites, Fedor Apraksin (to plans by Jean-Baptiste Le Blond, dating from the 1710s) and Alexander Menshikov (by the German architect, Gottfried Johann Schädel, built during 1713–27). In November 1718, in an attempt to extend polite society beyond the royal residences and the palaces of the more powerful magnates, Peter issued a decree on assemblies, which, as the document itself explained, was 'a

French word (*assemblés*), that cannot be expressed in Russian in one word, but means a free meeting or gathering in someone's house not only for amusement but also for business'. Sixty-five such gatherings took place between the issuing of the edict and Peter's death in 1725.[24]

The city's major sites, all situated on the river bank, were linked by water transport in summer and by sledges travelling on the ice in winter. (Peter declined to order the building of bridges in order to encourage his subjects to master seamanship.) In summer the water circuit was extended out of town to the shores of the Gulf of Finland, where Peter had built the Peterhof Palace and gardens (begun in 1714 to designs by Johann Friedrich Braunstein, Le Blond and others). The influence of Versailles and of the French court in general is clearly in evidence, with fountains, formal gardens in the French Baroque manner, and garden pavilions named Mon Plaisir, Marly and l'Hermitage. A flotilla of pleasure craft, sometimes escorted by warships, might sail from the Peter-Paul Fortress, stop at Peterhof and continue westwards to the favourite Menshikov's summer residence at Oranienbaum (another of Schädel's works, constructed between 1713–25), or cross to the island naval base at Kronstadt.

For all these worldly delights, it would nevertheless be false to draw a distinction between Holy Moscow and Secular St Petersburg. The tsar's new priorities required, instead, a new brand of 'holiness'; despite the court's Westernization, the emphasis on the sacredness of the monarchy remained as strong as ever. One example was the revival of the cult of St Andrew, one of the apostles who, according to legend, had visited the land of Novgorod to the south of St Petersburg.[25] It is said that, while in Windsor in 1698, Peter had witnessed the ceremony of the knights of the Garter on St George's Day and had even been invited to accept the Garter by William III, but had declined on the grounds that he was about to found his own chivalric order. In 1698 or 1699 Peter indeed instituted his own knightly order, dedicated to St Andrew, perhaps as a result of the influence of his Scottish friends, General Patrick Gordon and James Bruce. Just as English ships flew the cross of St George, red on a white ground, so Peter began to use the St Andrew's cross, blue on a white ground, on

the flags of his new navy from the early 1700s. The Order of St Andrew was reserved to a handful of leading magnates for 'faith and loyalty', and henceforth St Andrew's Day, 30 November, became an important date in the court calendar.[26]

In a similar way, Peter also promoted the cult of the canonized medieval prince, St Alexander Iaroslavich 'Nevskii' of Novgorod (1220–63). In 1710 the tsar dedicated a monastery to him near the alleged site of Alexander's victory over the Swedes in 1240. Alexander Nevskii was thus enlisted as one of the tutelary saints of the new Russian monarchy, and the parallel between Tsar Peter and his princely antetype was made explicit in the regime's public pronouncements. Alexander, it was declared, had 'held firm the rudder of his fatherland in those difficult times' when Russia was 'enfeebled and poor, very like a ship in distress'; Peter was his 'living mirror'.[27] In 1724, amid lavish ceremonies, the saint's relics were transferred from their ancient resting place in Vladimir to the new capital, St Petersburg. In addition to the whole court, led by the tsar himself, and a thousand priests and monks (who accompanied the relics), an estimated 6,000 spectators turned out to witness the procession to Trezzini's recently completed monastery, dedicated to the saint, and to view the firework displays that accompanied the festivities. The association between Alexander Nevskii's legendary victory over Sweden and Peter's own achievements was further emphasized by moving the saint's feast day from 23 November, the date on which it had been observed for centuries, to the new date of 30 August, the anniversary of the 1721 Treaty of Nystadt with which Peter had recently ended his own war with Sweden.[28]

Similarly, invented traditions served to eulogize the scale of Peter's achievement in such areas as the creation of the Russian fleet. The most highly personalized of these were the ingenious ceremonies devised for Peter's little sailing dinghy, the boat in which he had first learned to sail, and which had come to be known as the 'grandfather' of the Russian fleet.[29] This vessel was moved from Moscow to St Petersburg in time to celebrate the tsar's birthday on 30 May 1723, when the dinghy was taken out on the Neva to the sound of artillery salutes from the Peter-Paul Fortress; the boat was assigned an equally important symbolic role in a grand regatta for the entire imperial navy

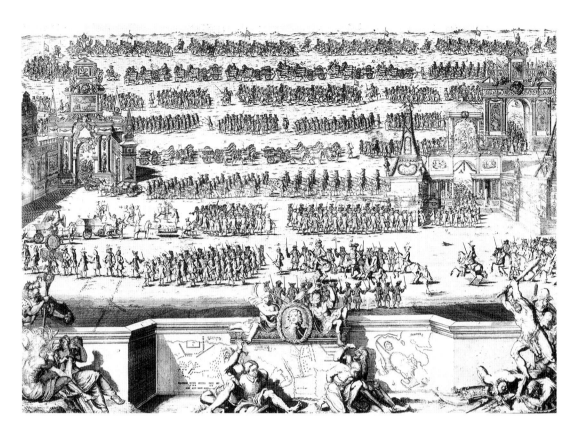

The delayed realization of Renaissance festival culture: Peter I's entry into Moscow as a classical triumphator in 1710, to celebrate his victory over the Swedes at the battle of Poltava the previous year. Despite the move of the capital to St Petersburg, Moscow nevertheless retained its ancient role as the setting for victory parades and coronations.

organized outside Kronstadt on 30 August that year.[30] The small craft, steered by the tsar himself, was rowed between the warships of the Russian navy, 'in order that the good grandfather of the fleet could receive due honour from all his splendid grandsons'.[31] The festivities concluded with a service in the Alexander Nevskii Monastery, where Peter ordered that henceforth the boat be taken every year on 30 August.[32] Its journey on that anniversary the following year formed an important part of the celebrations to mark the transfer of Alexander Nevskii's relics from Vladimir.[33]

Images of these saintly protectors, Andrew and Alexander, converged in public ceremonial to invest the tsar with the charisma of sanctity and his projects with a divine, providential purpose. It is not too fanciful to associate these events with the notion of a lost 'paradise' located on water, even though Peter himself, who was neither a classical nor a biblical scholar, did not attempt to define a precise antetype. However, appropriate references were supplied in abundance by leading churchmen. St Petersburg, for example, was identified with the New Jerusalem described in Revelation, 'the holy city, New Jerusalem, coming down out of heaven from God' [21:2], and the Neva with the 'river of [the] water of life' [22:1]. Peter himself often referred to the city, in which he planted trees and laid out gardens, as his 'paradise', 'this holy land', or his 'Eden'.[34]

In the creation of this identity, St Andrew, Alexander and the little boat were all 'mobilizing' myths, used to legitimize the move from one holy location to another. The land around St Petersburg was sacred, not to be relinquished lightly, and the fact that

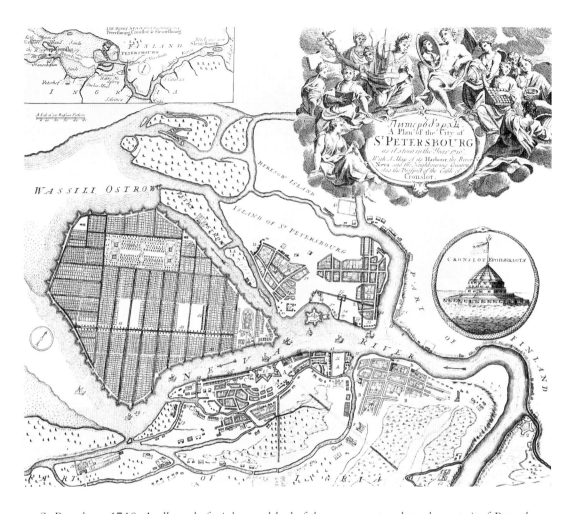

St Petersburg, 1710: Apollo, god of wisdom and lord of the muses, contemplates the portrait of Peter the Great (top right), while the goddess beside him cradles a model ship, the emblem of the tsar's campaign to turn Russia into a major naval power.

some conservative critics of Peter's regime associated St Petersburg with the reign of the Antichrist gave even more reason for bolstering the city's sacral credentials.[35] Peter's associates were constrained to follow the tsar's lead, even if they did not share his enthusiasm for the new courtly city. The nobility was uprooted from Moscow and forced to settle in the new capital, where at one moment they might be expected to take to the water in their own boats to swell the number of vessels in one of the tsar's regattas, and at the next to appear with their wives at a court ball. In fact, their function as supporting cast to the ruler had hardly changed, but the new ceremonial forms and amended hierarchies of the relocated court must have made St Petersburg seem like another, and distinctly foreign, country.

VI. THE HOUSEHOLD OF THE TSAR: PETER THE GREAT AND THE REFORM OF THE COURT

Peter's polycentric court accommodated several overlapping groups of personnel. The old boyar Duma and chanceries were phased out and replaced by new institutions, such as the Senate (composed of ten men appointed by the tsar) and the collegiate boards of the civil service. All nobles were required to undergo basic

schooling and to work their way up through the ranks in either the army, the navy or the civil service in order to serve the 'common good'. In 1722 Peter formalized the new court and social hierarchy by issuing the Table of Ranks. Commoners who attained the lowest officer's rank in the armed services (rank fourteen), or rank eight in the civil service, became hereditary nobles, although in reality it was the members of older noble families who continued to dominate the top military commissions and offices of state. Clause VIII of the Table of Ranks granted free access to those places where the court assembled to sons of princes, counts, barons and other members of the aristocracy (*znatneishago dvorianstva*), but, the tsar declared, 'we wish to see them distinguish themselves from others in all cases according to their merit'; they would not be awarded any commission or office in the military or civil service until they had performed services to the tsar and fatherland. Once the old designations such as boyar and *stol'nik* had disappeared, there was no formal or ordered ranking of the nobility outside of the Table of Ranks. This led to tensions between, on the one hand, those who perceived themselves as distinguished by virtue of their princely title or pedigree, and, on the other, well-qualified new-comers who lacked a distinguished ancestral history.[36]

Moreover, there was a further factor to consider, one that was not governed by statute. When it came to enjoying Peter's favour, opportunity and personal chemistry often proved more significant than rank or hereditary qualification. The tsar's intimate circle was a flexible and peripatetic group: Peter was forever on the move. This inner entourage was small in number, no more than a few dozen men, sometimes fewer (not for Peter the thousands of retainers at Versailles). It possessed no readily discernible hierarchy, and although a number of its members held high rank in the army, navy or administration, none of Peter's inner circle held formal court office. Several of the men close to Peter reached their positions by clan connections. Admiral Fedor Matveevich Apraksin (1661–1728), for example, was the brother of Tsaritsa Martha, widow of Peter's brother Tsar Fedor. The ancestors of Chancellor Gavrila Ivanovich Golovkin (1660–1734), former gentleman of the Bedchamber, had been boyars since the early sixteenth century. Peter's favourite, Alexander Menshikov (1673–1729),

on the other hand, was an illiterate commoner, raised above boyars and princes of ancient lineage to become the most titled man in the realm after the tsar himself. At the height of his power, after Peter's death in 1725, the favourite was grandiloquently styled as an

illustrious prince of the Holy Roman Empire and [the] Russian realm and Duke of Izhora, *reichsmarshal* [marshal of the Empire] of Her Imperial Majesty of all Russia and commanding general field-marshal of the armies, actual privy councillor, president of the state War College, governor-general of the province of St Petersburg, vice-admiral of the white flag of the fleet of all Russia, knight of the Orders of St Andrew, the Elephant, the White and Black Eagles and St Alexander Nevskii, and lieutenant-colonel of the Preobrazhenskii lifeguard, and colonel over three regiments, captain of the company of bombardiers.[37]

As a young man, the much-titled Menshikov had served in Peter's own Preobrazhenskii regiment of guards, which, founded by the tsar in the 1680s, afforded a route of advancement for many men of humble origin. As so often with a court favourite, his meteoric rise created widespread resentments. Notoriously corrupt and rumoured to enjoy a homosexual relationship with the tsar, none aroused such hostility among the traditional élite as Menshikov. He owed his survival to Peter's support and the friendship of Peter's second wife Catherine, herself an illiterate peasant of Livonian origin.

Catherine's rise to fame and fortune caused perhaps even greater consternation among the old nobility. Yet such elevations were not particularly exceptional in the context of the Petrine court, for the tsar also enjoyed the company of a group of men who were without either government posts or military commands, and of a status that would have made social relations between them and their ruler unthinkable in most contemporary courts. Among Peter's companions were his lowly born private secretary Aleksei Makarov, his cook Jan Felten and an assortment of dwarfs, jesters and foreign shipwrights. There were no household ordinances to govern the relations between the members of this motley retinue.

The expenditure for this reformed household was handled by the tsar's private office, the Cabinet (*kabinet*), which also had extensive responsibilities for overseeing such matters as Russians studying abroad

and foreign specialists working in Russia; the St Petersburg Chancellery of Building; certain state enterprises, such as the mines at Olonets and Petrovskii Zavod; the tsar's Chamber of Curiosities (the *Kunstkamera*); and his Gardening Office, which included the royal aviaries and menagerie. The Cabinet also dispensed items of 'petty expenditure', such as wages and clothes for palace servants, goods purchased by agents abroad for Peter and his family, the costs of Peter's turnery and personal boats, tips and gifts dispensed on namedays, and payments to carol singers and couriers. It also paid the tsar his salaries in his various ranks as captain, colonel and ship's carpenter. Its personnel kept the tsar's appointments, diaries and journals, and supervised the writing of the official history of the Swedish war. The total number of staff under the Cabinet's jurisdiction thus ran into many hundreds, but only a relatively small number constituted the tsar's inner retinue. In 1721, for example, the annual payroll for the immediate members of the tsar's household totalled 13,662 roubles 60 kopecks for approximately 115 persons, including court architects and painters, librarians, cooks, tutors, bird-keepers, orderlies, dwarfs, stable lads and lackeys. The largest single category (fifty-five) was the oarsmen who manned the royal river transports. The highest salary (5,000 roubles) was paid to the Italian architect Niccolò Michetti; the lowest (20 roubles) to an unidentified 'old woman'. The list also included one Stefan 'Medved' (the Bear), with whom Peter often played chess.[38] Figures for court expenditure as a whole fluctuated over time and are notoriously difficult to calculate, given the wide range of activities covered by the Cabinet office. Pavel Miliukov's estimates for the allocation of a state budget totalling 6,243,197 roubles in 1724 includes 186,227 roubles for the court, as compared, for example, with 3,140,888 for the army, 781,312 for the fleet and 495,654 for diplomacy. The figure for expenditure on the court is thus relatively low by contemporary standards, and may be even lower if, as is possible, the total also includes the 69,432 roubles spent on Catherine's coronation, a figure that included special celebratory salary payments and ransom money for prisoners of war.[39]

In contrast to the relative informality of his own household, Peter established a more formal court in imitation of Western models for his consort Catherine. This household was organized under a series of court officers (*pridvornye chiny*) with names borrowed from German usage. At the head of the tsaritsa's court was the *obermarshal* (which conferred status as rank two in the Table of Ranks; there was no rank one for court personnel, only for the army, navy and civil service). Next were the master of the horse (*oberstthalmeister*, rank three) and the major domo and head chamberlain (*oberhofmeister* and *oberkammerger*, both rank four). At the other end of the scale, rank fourteen included the court librarian, the head chef (*kukhenmeister*), and the court barber. Women were also graded, from the steward or major domo of the empress's household (*oberhofmisterina*) to the *kamer-freiliny* (ladies in waiting).[40] In practice, however, many of these ranks existed only on paper, and a more or less regularized and stratified royal household was established only in the reigns of Tsar Peter's successors.

More striking still are the reforms that Peter introduced to the annual programme of court festivals and liturgical observances. After the move of the capital to St Petersburg, the number of religious festivals officially celebrated at court was drastically reduced in comparison to former Muscovite standards, with a host of saints relegated to purely local significance. Associated pilgrimages and expeditions to monasteries likewise disappeared. By the 1720s a regular court calendar had evolved that marked both national anniversaries (notably 'victory days' for the battles of Narva, Poltava, Hangut, Lesnaia and others) and royal days.[41] The Palm Sunday ceremony, in which the tsar, walking on foot, used to hold the reins of the patriarch's mount, was particularly distasteful to Peter; but he avoided the need to abolish the custom, since the last patriarch died in 1700 and in 1721 the tsar replaced the patriarchate with the Holy Synod. Peter also relegated the cult of the royal ancestors, even though he often paid written tribute to the work of his father Tsar Alexis. Similarly, out of the court calendar went requiem masses for his predecessors as tsar and the commemoration of their name days. This change in court custom seems to have been part of a conscious policy of distancing the monarchy from the hereditary principle, and representing himself as the founder of an entirely new form of imperial rule. Peter's abandonment of the cult of the royal ancestors is at one with his disinheriting and condemnation to death of his eldest son, the Tsarevich

Tsaritsa Natalia, second wife of Tsar Alexis (1645–76), driving out in state in a carriage-sled drawn by six horses. Her husband's reign saw the first phase of the westernization of the Muscovite court, and the creation of a short-lived court theatre.

Alexis, in 1718, and the introduction in 1722 of a new law of succession that allowed the ruling monarch to select his own successor.

Peter's immediate reasons for both the condemnation of his son and the new law were personal and pragmatic. Alexis had failed in his duties and fled from Russia; and the death of his younger son in 1719 had left Peter without a male heir. A more sophisticated rationale, the treatise *The Justice of the Monarch's Right to Choose the Successor to his Throne*, attributed to Archbishop Feofan Prokopovich, drew on biblical and classical models of parental disinheriting and monarchical freedom of choice in the matter of successors. All this accorded with a strand in contemporary discourse that Peter had 'created' Russia, a theme that was enthusiastically taken up in court-sponsored literary and visual culture. After the liturgy held on 22 October 1721 to celebrate the Peace of Nystadt, Chancellor Gavrila Golovkin delivered a speech declaring that Peter had taken Russia 'from the darkness of ignorance on to the stage of glory before the whole world, so to speak, out of nothingness into being, and has brought us into the society of political nations'.[42] A panel on the base of a bronze bust of

Peter by Carlo Rastrelli, dating from 1723, depicts the tsar as Pygmalion fashioning a statue of the new Russia, represented as the sea-nymph Galatea.[43] This theme was further reflected in the new imperial titles that the tsar adopted in the final years of his reign: Emperor, Father of the Fatherland, and Great, all of which had classical antecedents. Even the adoption of the Western custom of using a regnal number to designate the emperor as Peter *the First* suggested a new beginning: previous Russian rulers had been referred to not by number, but merely by name and patronymic.[44]

In other areas, ancient usage was fused with the innovations of 'Western' practice. A case in point is the coronation in Moscow of Peter's wife Catherine as empress-consort in May 1724, ostensibly as a belated reward for her bravery during a campaign against the Turks some thirteen years earlier.[45] Muscovite tsars did not crown their wives, with the sole exception of Marina Mniszek, the Polish wife of the first False Dmitrii, crowned in 1605. So, in an attempt to add authority to the questionable coronation of a foreign commoner, whom many nobles privately despised and some churchmen openly denounced, the event was staged in the Kremlin's most sacred sites: beginning with the crowning in the Cathedral of the Dormition (which continued to be used as the place for royal coronations), and concluding with a visit to the tombs of the royal ancestors in the Archangel Cathedral and the Convent of the Ascension. Both rituals were traditional elements of the ancient Orthodox coronation rite. Yet the new culture was also much in evidence, not only in the mixed company and Western dress of the congregation, but also in the use of Western military music and gun salutes, both innovations of the Petrine era, in conjunction with Orthodox choral chants and the traditional pealing of church bells.

In the end, however, it is the element of newness, of the regime's self-conscious distancing of itself from the practices of the past, that is the dominant theme. Nowhere was ceremonial innovation so clearly marked as at Peter's funeral in March 1725, which broke with Muscovite traditions by including a Catholic-style lying-in state (around the open coffin stood four bronze statues depicting mourning figures of Russia and Europe, Mars and Hercules); a funeral parade with massed troops and artillery salutes; and interment not in Moscow, the traditional burial place of the tsars, but in St Petersburg's new Peter-Paul Cathedral. There, Archbishop Feofan Prokopovich delivered an oration after the manner of Lutheran funeral sermons. Both the absence of an officiating patriarch and the reading of a sermon at a royal funeral were departures from Orthodox tradition, as was the fact that Peter was buried, not on the day following his death, but more than a month later, to allow time for the organization of the elaborate public mourning. Leading magnates, including Menshikov, played prominent roles as marshals, escorts and bearers of the tsar's regalia and orders.[46]

For all its copying of contemporary court usage elsewhere in Europe, the Russian imperial court nevertheless retained a number of distinctive idiosyncrasies. From the 1690s until his death, Peter maintained a mock court, ruled by 'prince-Caesar' (*Kniaz'-kezar'*), a post held until his death in 1717 by Fedor Iur'evich Romodanovskii, who was succeeded, in turn, by his son. Peter's letters to Romodanovskii were addressed to 'Min Her Konich' or 'Sire', and formulated in the manner of correspondence between an underling and his superior.[47] In October 1698, for example, Romodanovskii received the credentials of the returning ambassadors, Lefort and Golovin, while Peter mingled with the rank and file.[48] The mock court originally had its residence in the royal village of Preobrazhenskoe just outside Moscow, where Peter spent much of his time training and drilling his new guards regiments in the 1680s and 1690s. Both in its early days and later, when it was at the tsar's beck and call, convening at his convenience, this court generally comprised no more than the 'prince-Caesar' himself and a handful of 'courtiers' chosen from whichever personnel happened to be available at the time. Romodanovskii was distinguished by his steadfast loyalty to Peter, and evidently enjoyed lording it over his own immediate subordinates. It was the prince-Caesar who authorized the wages that Piter Michailof (or Peter Mikhailov, the tsar's pseudonym) drew from the Admiralty for his work as shipwright. Likewise, the prince-Caesar was always among the first to receive notification from his 'humble subject', the tsar, of Russia's military and naval victories.[49] Romodanovskii also headed the *Preobrazhenskii prikaz*, Peter's 'secret chancellery', which handled allegations of *lèse-majesté* and treason.

This mock court overlapped with the tsar's 'All-Mad, All-Jesting, All-Drunken Assembly' – as Peter designated it.[50] Space does not permit a thorough investigation of this intriguing phenomenon, which parodied the ecclesiastical establishment through an inconsistent mix of Orthodox and Catholic ritual and bawdy invention. There was even a female wing of the Assembly presided over by an all-drunken 'abbess'. The wedding (a real not a mock one) of the 'prince-pope' Peter Buturlin, a member of a distinguished noble family, in September 1721 illustrates this 'world turned upside down', when Roman soldiers mingled with Turks, Indians, abbots, monks and nuns, shepherdesses, nymphs and satyrs, artisans and peasants, a Bacchus in a tiger skin, and giants dressed as babies; the tsar himself attended as a ship's drummer. After the feast, the bride and groom were led to an improvized bedchamber inside a wooden pyramid on Trinity Square, with holes drilled in the walls for spectators. Day two featured a crossing of the river by the prince-pope and his 'cardinals' on a pontoon of linked barrels drawn by Neptune on a sea monster. The prince-pope floated in a wooden bowl in a great vat of beer into

Peter I 'the Great', painted by Jean-Marc Nattier in 1717. The tsar wears the blue riband of the Order of St Andrew, the chivalric order of knighthood he had created by 1699, probably in imitation of the English Order of the Garter.

which he was tipped when he reached the other side.[51] The full political and religious significance of this and other aspects of the All-Drunken Assembly, not to mention its origins, awaits a thorough investigation. If there were an anti-Catholic element in its activities, it was neither consistent nor was it reflected elsewhere in Peter's programme; his pragmatic need to hire and communicate with foreigners of all religious persuasions dictated what was, in practice, a relatively tolerant religious policy. Nor did the Assembly have a clearly 'didactic' function, as Soviet historians often used to claim; it seems, rather, to have owed its *raison d'être* principally to the tsar's personal whims and his own rather perverse sense of humour.

'Real' court life and its parody were thus never wholly separate entities. The wedding of the royal dwarf Iakim Volkov, for example, on 14 November 1710, shortly after the wedding of Peter's niece Anna

Ioannovna to the Duke of Courland, reveals not only how far the two overlapped, but also how the tsar promoted the dwarfs' wedding as a burlesque commentary on the duke's nuptials of state. Indeed, Peter himself planned the two weddings simultaneously. Thus, the Duke and Duchess of Courland were themselves guests at the dwarfs' wedding feast, which was held in the same room in Menshikov's palace as their own wedding reception had been just two weeks earlier, and with more or less the same guests.[52] Dwarfs in Moscow were rounded up and sent to St Petersburg to attend Volkov's wedding, where about seventy of them filled the fortress church of SS. Peter and Paul. The ceremony followed the usual religious rites, accompanied by the stifled giggles of the congregation and the priest, and with the tsar himself holding the wedding crown over the head of the dwarf bride. At the subsequent nuptial feast, the dwarfs sat at miniature tables in the centre of the room, while full-sized guests observed from tables placed at the sides. A similar process attended Iakim's funeral in 1724. All the dwarfs of St Petersburg were ordered to follow his coffin, walking in pairs, the smallest at the front, the tallest bringing up the rear; six miniature ponies pulled the catafalque, and the smallest priest in the city officiated.[53] Again, dwarfish rituals parodied the solemnities of state ceremonial, with the monarch himself acting as stage-manager of the burlesque.

Although such antics may appear highly eccentric, there was nothing unusual in either Western or Russian experience about Peter's taste for dwarfs. He rarely travelled without a pair of dwarfs in his entourage, and they had a prominent comic role in a number of state festivities.[54] Several instances are recorded of dwarfs leaping from cakes, as, for example, during the celebration of the birth of Tsarevich Peter Petrovich in 1715, when a naked female dwarf was served up at the male courtiers' table and a naked man at that of the female courtiers.[55] At the other extreme, the tsar sought to breed a race of 'giants' by mating men and women of exceptional height. In 1720 the huge Frenchman Nicolas Bourgeois was married to a Finnish 'giantess', apparently in the hope of breeding additional tall recruits for Peter's guards regiments.[56] After Bourgeois's death in 1724, his internal organs and a stuffed effigy made of his skin went on show in Peter's cabinet of curiosities.

VII. CONCLUSION

The claim that Peter was too indifferent to the niceties of etiquette and the customs of grand palaces to maintain a court in the sense then current in the West is clearly erroneous, even though his court was quite unlike any other in Europe.[57] Ironically, this misunderstanding was actively encouraged by Petrine mythology, which played up his reputation as 'a great contemner of all pomp and ostentation about his own person', who 'set no store by rich garments, fine furniture, carriages and residences'.[58] Campredon, the French minister in St Petersburg in the 1720s, noted the 'informality' of the Russian court in comparison with others of his acquaintance. There were, for example, no regular formal receptions of the diplomatic corps to mark royal birthdays and other state occasions, which meant that diplomats had to take their chance when attending at the royal palaces, waiting for the tsar to appear. Peter was so often on the move that it could be difficult to make a formal appointment for an audience. At the same time, Campredon noted the huge expense of diplomatic life in St Petersburg: the legation had to maintain its own river transport; the prices of foodstuffs were high; attendance at one masquerade given by the tsar cost half his monthly salary.

Yet, for all the sophistication of architectural and visual culture at the imperial court, other aspects of court life had more in common with the customs of the steppes than with those of the *salon*. Louis XV's minister was horrified by the heavy drinking indulged in at court. A party held at the Senate building in May 1723 to celebrate Peter's birthday lasted from twelve noon to three o'clock the following morning, during which time no one was allowed to leave and rough grain vodka was served from wooden scoops dipped into barrels by officers of the guard. Never in his life, Campredon later confessed, had he so feared anything as much as the approach of these 'cups of sorrow'.[59]

Campredon's observations confirm that Peter's court life, notwithstanding its 'informality', was complex rather than simple. It is true that many staple features of other European courts – theatre, opera and ballet for example – were lacking. Perhaps the most striking omission was hunting, which Peter disliked. On the other hand, the tsar's court displayed a high degree of theatricality. Novel twists were added by the mock court, the All-Drunken Assembly and by naval motifs, with ships and regattas replacing the horses, carousels and jousts so beloved elsewhere in early modern Europe. Peter staged masquerades at least twice a year. Even at his wedding to Catherine in 1712, Peter was married not in his coronation robes, as had always been the tradition at tsars' weddings, but in naval uniform, with Admiralty personnel in positions of honour: in other words, he appeared to marry, not as tsar, but in one of his many 'roles', in this case that of naval captain. This wedding to a peasant woman may have seemed to many observers like another example of Petrine burlesque.[60]

Paradoxically, the idea of the elevation of the monarch was evident even in Peter's 'simplicity', which made him extraordinary among rulers. Peter's first wooden cabin in St Petersburg, wrote the author of an early guidebook, was 'more exalted than the splendid palace of Emperor Cyrus, the many-chambered mansion of Solomon and as worthy of honour as splendid Versailles', in an elaborate formulation of a notion that had become commonplace even before Peter's death.[61] Even so, Versailles remained a model, especially after Peter's visit to Paris in 1717. He attempted to incorporate some of Versailles's external features into his own new palace at Peterhof, about which he was alternately proud and self-deprecating. Campredon recorded a telling incident during a visit to Peterhof in summer 1723, when 'the tsar did me the honour of saying that as I had seen so many beautiful things in France he doubted whether I would find anything of much interest at Peterhof, adding that he hoped that [the French king] had such a beautiful view at Versailles as here at Peterhof, from where one has a view of the sea and of Kronstadt on one side and St Petersburg on the other'.[62]

Peter set the tone for a new courtly ritual that had an enduring influence on the Russian imperial court. Attempts by some members of the old nobility to reassert themselves, and even to return the court to Moscow, repeatedly failed. But his immediate successors as monarch – his wife Catherine I (1725–7), his young grandson Peter II (1727–30), his niece Anna (1730–40), his infant great-nephew Ivan VI (1740–41) and his daughter Elizabeth (1741–61) – each had to make adjustments to the routines of the court and

their style of rule in keeping with their sex, age and accomplishments. They revived the cult of ancestral lineage – not for them the luxury of disregarding dynasty or pretending to be shipwrights – in some cases compensating for unheroic personal attributes by stressing their 'Petrine' qualities through descent or association with their forebear. Archbishop Feofan Prokopovich had provided a lead in his funeral oration for the tsar in 1725, when he had addressed his words to the empress, assuring her that 'the female sex is no hindrance to your being like Peter the Great…like gold refined in a crucible, he has formed an heir to his crown, power and throne'.[63] Myths, such as that of the return of the virgin goddess Astraea, were propagated by the post-Petrine monarchy in order to cope with the unprecedented series of female rulers who succeeded to the Russian throne.[64]

The post-Petrine court also acquired a greater degree of order and ceremonial. Eccentricities, such as the All-Drunken Assembly and the mock court of the prince-Caesar, disappeared, although heavy drinking and the taste for crude practical jokes did not. The court establishment, which Peter had formally promulgated (but in practice had failed to implement within his own household), was regularized. In 1730–31 the Empress Anna issued new instructions regarding the major domo, who was to be a man 'of such high Christian morals and behaviour that he sets the tone for his subordinates and other court servitors more by his own example than by punishments'. She issued revised lists of salaries and court ranks setting out the duties required of each courtier.[65] As a foreign observer remarked, Anna loved magnificence in her court and household and encouraged luxury and outward display until they 'rivalled that of the court of France'.[66] The Empress Elizabeth (1741–61) was famed for her sumptuous wardrobe and for the grand architectural creations of Bartholomeo Rastrelli, which included the Catherine Palace at Tsarskoe Selo and the fourth Winter Palace. She cultivated the opera, ballet and theatre, founded the Academy of Arts and encouraged French as the court language. But she did not forget that she was her father's daughter: for the wedding of the future Peter III and Catherine II in 1745 she escorted Peter's little dinghy, the 'grandfather of the Russian navy', in a regatta on the River Neva, dressed in the uniform of a naval officer.[67]

NOTES

INTRODUCTION

1 A note on terminology: throughout this book, the terms 'prince' and 'princely' are used inclusively, as they were by contemporaries, to encompass the various ranks of European sovereign ruler, of either sex, whether secular or ecclesiastical. 'Monarchy' is used synonymously, in its original Aristotelian (and early modern) meaning of rule by single prince. Within this group of sovereign rulers, contemporaries nevertheless distinguished between the rank of kings (and emperors), who were *personae sacrae*, and inferior ranks of ruler. The adjective 'royal', accordingly, is confined exclusively to matters relating to kings or their courts. I am deeply grateful to Dr Jeroen Duindam, Professor Marcello Fantoni, Dr Jarl Kremeier, Dr Roger Mettam, Dr Glyn Redworth, Mr Edward Smith, Mr Dougal Shaw, Professor Malcolm Smuts and Dr David Watkin for reading and commenting on earlier drafts of this chapter.

2 For general studies of the European courts, see A. G. Dickens (ed.), *The Courts of Europe: Politics, Patronage, and Royalty, 1400–1800* (London, 1977); Ronald G. Asch and Adolf M. Birke (eds.), *Princes, Patronage, and the Nobility: The Court at the Beginning of the Modern Age, c. 1450–1650* (Oxford, 1991); August Buck, Georg Kauffmann, et al. (eds.), *Europäische Hofkultur im 16. und 17. Jahrhundert*, 3 vols. (Hamburg, 1981). On the historiography of the court, see Cesare Mozzarelli and Giuseppe Olmi (eds.), *La corte nella cultura e nella storiografia. Immagini e posizioni tra Otto e Novecento* (Rome, 1983); and the important critique by Jeroen Duindam, *Myths of Power: Norbert Elias and the Early Modern European Court* (Amsterdam, 1995). For its economic role, see Maurice Aymard and Marzio A. Romani (eds.), *La Cour comme institution économique* (Paris, 1998).

3 Malcolm Smuts, Commentary on 'Renaissance Monarchy', delivered at the Anglo-American Conference of Historians, Institute of Historical Research, London, July 1998. I am grateful to Professor Smuts for sending me the typescript of his remarks.

4 By way of example, see Roland Mousnier, *La Venalité des offices sous Henri IV et Louis XIII* (2nd edn., Paris, 1971); William Doyle, *Venality: The Sale of Offices in Eighteenth-Century France* (Oxford, 1996), pp. 65-6; E. G. Léonard, *L'Armée et ses problèmes au XVIIIe siècle* (Paris, 1958); for a case study, see D. A. Parrott, 'The Administration of the French Army during the Ministry of Cardinal Richelieu' (unpub. D.Phil. diss., Oxford, 1985).

5 Friedrich Polleross, 'From the *Exemplum Virtutis* to the Apotheosis: Hercules as an Identification Figure in Portraiture', in Allan Ellenius (ed.), *Iconography, Propaganda, and Legitimation* (Oxford, 1998), pp. 37–62.

6 See the vast survey by Wolfgang Braunfels, *Die Kunst im Heiligen Römischen Reich Deutscher Nation*, 6 vols. (Munich, 1979–89); for the financial implications of court patronage, Michael Stürmer, 'An Economy of Delight: Court Artisans of the Eighteenth Century', *Business History Review*, 53 (1979), 496–528; M. Pade, L. W. Petersen and D. Quarta (eds.), *La corte di Ferrara e il suo mecenatismo, 1441–1598* (Copenhagen, 1990).

7 Emmanuel Le Roy Ladurie, *Saint-Simon, ou le système de la cour* (Paris, 1997), pp. 269–72.

8 J. A. Guy, *The Public Career of Sir Thomas More* (Brighton, 1980); Alfredo Perifano, *L'Alchimie à la cour de Côme Ier de Médicis: savoirs, culture et politique* (Paris, 1997), pp. 42–77; Mario Biagioli, *Galileo, Courtier: The Practice of Science in the Culture of Absolutism* (Chicago, 1993).

9 Joseph Bergin, *The Making of the French Episcopate, 1589–1661* (New Haven and London, 1996).

10 Flavio Rurale, *I Gesuiti a Milano. Religione e politica nel cinquecento* (Rome, 1992), p. 95 (for quotation); J. H. Elliott, *Imperial Spain,*

1469–1716 (London, 1963), p. 91; Henry Kamen, *Philip of Spain* (New Haven and London, 1997), p. 105.

11 Joseph Bergin, *Cardinal Richelieu: Power and the Pursuit of Wealth* (New Haven and London, 1985), p. 199; and see his *The Making of the French Episcopate*. It is hardly surprising that what one writer has termed the 'high water mark of royal Gallicanism', the Four Articles of 1682, coincided with the apogee of the Sun King's court: Robin Briggs, *Communities of Belief: Cultural and Social Tension in Early Modern France* (Oxford, 1989), p. 197.

12 For the decline of the papacy, Eamon Duffy, *Saints and Sinners: A History of the Popes* (New Haven and London, 1997), pp. 181–94, 215.

13 For court preaching, Thérèse Goyet and Jean-Pierre Collinet (eds.), *Journées Bossuet. La predication au XVIIe siècle* (Paris, 1980); Peter E. McCullough, *Sermons at Court: Politics and Religion in Elizabethan and Jacobean Preaching* (Cambridge, 1998).

14 Gustavo Corni, 'Il mito prussiano ed il concetto di corte nella storiografia "borussica" del XIX–XX secolo', in Mozzarrelli and Olmi, *La corte nella cultura*, pp. 123–34; and see John C. Röhl, *Kaiser, Hof und Staat: Wilhelm II. und die Deutsche Politik* (Munich, 1988); Eng. trans., *The Kaiser and his Court: Wilhelm II and the Government of Germany* (Cambridge, 1995).

15 Peter W. Thomas, 'Charles I of England: The Tragedy of Absolutism', in Dickens, *The Courts of Europe*, pp. 191–211; Jürgen Freiherr von Krüdener, *Der Rolle des Hofes im Absolutismus* (Stuttgart, 1973). For a critique, see Nicholas Henshall, *The Myth of Absolutism: Change and Continuity in Early Modern European Monarchy* (London, 1992); and Duindam, *Myths of Power*.

16 Nobert Elias, *Die höfische Gesellschaft* (Darmstadt and Neuwied, 1969); Eng. edn. as *The Court Society*, trans. Edmund Jephcott (Oxford, 1983).

17 Rudolph zur Lippe, 'Hof und Schloss: Bühne des Absolutismus', in Ernst Hinrichs (ed.), *Absolutismus* (Frankfurt-am-Main, 1986), pp. 138–61; Peter Burke, *The Fabrication of Louis XIV* (New Haven and London, 1992), p. 89, drawing on Elias; Roland Mousnier, *Les Institutions de la France sous la monarchie absolue, 1598–1789*, 2 vols. (Paris, 1974–80); Hubert C. Ehalt, *Ausdrucksformen absolutistischer Herrschaft: Der Wiener Hof im 17. und 18. Jahrhundert* (Munich, 1980); Wlad Godzich and Nicholas Spadaccini, 'Foreword: The Changing Face of History', in José Antonio Maravall, *Culture of the Baroque: Analysis of a Historical Structure* (Manchester, 1986), pp. vii–xx.

18 Carol Gibson-Wood, *Studies in the Theory of Connoisseurship from Vasari to Morelli* (New York and London, 1988), and her 'Jonathan Richardson and the Rationalization of Connoisseurship', *Art History*, 7 (1984), 38–56; Francis Haskell, *Rediscoveries in Art: Some Aspects of Taste, Fashion and Collecting in England and France* (Ithaca, 1974). For important exceptions see, for example, Michael Baxandall, *Painting and Experience in Fifteenth-Century Italy* (Oxford, 1972); Jonathan Brown and J. H. Elliott, *A Palace for a King: The Buen Retiro and the Court of Philip IV* (New Haven and London, 1980); and Jarl Kremeier, *Die Hofkirke der Würzburger Residenz* (Worms, 1999).

19 For an important corrective, Reinhold Baumstark and Helmut Seiling, *Silber und Gold. Augsburger Goldschmiedekunst für die Höfe Europas* (exh. cat., Munich, 1994), a reference I owe to Dr Jarl Kremeier; and Peter Krenn and Walter J. Karcheski, *Imperial Austria: Treasures of Art, Arms, and Armour from the State of Styria* (exh. cat., Melbourne, 1998).

20 See Peter Burke's warning of the dangers inherent in the propagandist approach, in his *Fabrication of Louis XIV*, pp. 4–5, 65 (fig. 21).

21 For example, for art and architecture, Ulrich Keller, *Reitermonumente absolutistischer Fürsten Staatstheoretische Voraussetzungen und politische Funktionen* (Munich, 1971); Burke, *Fabrication of Louis XIV*, p. 89; Ellenius, *Iconography*; for courtesy and etiquette, Orest Ranum, 'Courtesy, Absolutism, and the Rise of the French State, 1630–1660', *Journal of Modern History*, 52 (1980), 426–51; Elias, *The Court Society*, pp. 244–5.

22 Ronald G. Asch, 'Introduction: Court and Household from the Fifteenth to the Seventeenth Centuries', in Asch and Birke, *Princes, Patronage, and the Nobility*, p. 19 (my emphasis).

23 Friedrich Carl von Moser, *Teutsches Hof-Recht*, 2 vols. (Frankfurt and Leipzig, 1754–5), quoted in Wilfried Hansmann, *Baukunst des Barock: Form, Funktion, Sinngehalt* (Cologne, 1978), p. 88.

24 This is not to suggest that royal households were fixed and immobile after they acquired resident 'seats', generally in the course of the sixteenth century. They continued to move, usually seasonally, between a series of royal residences. But from the early sixteenth century the pattern of movement (in, for example, England, France, Spain and the Empire) tended to be within a far more narrowly defined geographical area than had been the case hitherto. 'Residential' courts in this sense had, of course, existed before (the papal courts at Rome and Avignon being the most obvious examples). It is the consistency with which most early modern courts adopted the residential model that is their striking feature.

25 Where the presence of the *Residenz* was perceived as threatening traditional urban liberties, there are instances of the urban élites rallying to drive out the court and to force it relocate to a more pliant town: thus the court at Cologne was forced to transfer to Bonn; that at Lüneberg to Celle; and the court of the Dukes of Braunschweig (Brunswick) to Wolfenbüttel. I am grateful to Dr Jarl Kremeier for a discussion of this point.

26 For the papal court, see Geoffrey Parker (ed.), *At the Court of the Borgia: Being an Account of the Reign of Pope Alexander VI written by… Johann Burchard* (London, 1963); Peter Partner, *The Pope's Men: The Papal Civil Service in the Renaissance* (Oxford, 1990), pp. 20–46; and M. A. Visceglia and C. Brice (eds.), *Cérémonial et rituel à Rome (XVIe–XIXe siècle)* (Rome, 1997); Gianvittorio Signorotto and M. A. Visceglia (eds.), *La Corte di Roma tra cinque e seicento* (Rome, 1998).

27 The Tudor Kings of England obtained a new residential base at Whitehall, at Westminster, in 1529; Munich had established its primacy as the seat of the Wittelsbach Dukes of Bavaria by the 1520s (if not sooner); the newly elevated Medici, later Grand Dukes of Tuscany, settled at Florence in the 1530s; the Austrian Habsburgs at Vienna from the 1540s, and later at Prague between 1583 and 1615. Similarly, the 1560s saw the move of the Spanish Habsburgs to Madrid, and the transference of the Savoyard court from the alpine fastness of Chambéry to Turin in 1563; and the Kings of Poland, under Sigismund III Vasa, transferred the capital to Warsaw in 1597. Even in the Dutch Republic, the Princes of Orange acquired a resident court at Delft in 1583 and later at The Hague.

28 The Valois court tended to be equally peripatetic; 'never, during the whole of my embassy', complained one ambassador to François I of France (1515–47), 'was the court in the same place for fifteen consecutive days'; N. Tommaseo (ed.), *Relations des ambassadeurs vénitiens sur les affaires de France*, 2 vols. (Paris, 1838), I, pp. 107–11; quoted in R. J. Knecht, *Francis I* (Cambridge, 1982), p. 92.

29 Jean-François Solnon, *La Cour de France* (Paris, 1987), pp. 281–4.

30 M. J. Rodríguez-Salgado, 'The Court of Philip II of Spain', in Asch and Birke, *Princes, Patronage, and the Nobility*, pp. 206–7.

31 For a case study of Rome, see Gigliola Fragnito, 'Cardinals' courts in sixteenth-century Rome', in *Journal of Modern History*, 65 (1993), 26–56; Stefano Tabacchi, 'Cardinali zelanti e fazioni cardinalizie tra fine Seicento e inizio Settecento', in Signorotto and Visceglia, *La corte di Roma*, pp. 139–65.

32 Figures given in Maximilian Lanzinner, *Fürst, Räte und Landstände. Die Entstehung der Zentralbehörden in Bayern, 1511–1598* (Göttingen, 1980), p. 22.

33 I am grateful to Dr Philip Mansel for a discussion of this point. For retrenchment under Louis XIV, see Solnon, *La Cour de France*, pp. 307–10; for the statistics for England, where precise tallies are available for the three constituent departments of the royal household

(the lord chamberlain's, lord steward's and that of the master of the horse), see J. C. Sainty and R. O. Bucholz, *Officials of the Royal Household 1660–1837. Part I: Department of the Lord Chamberlain and Associated Offices* (London, 1997), p. 92 (fig 1A).

34 David Starkey, 'Court, Council, and Nobility in Tudor England', in Asch and Birke, *Princes, Patronage, and the Nobility*, p. 200n.

35 Mia J. Rodríguez-Salgado, 'Honour and Profit in the Court of Philip II of Spain', in Aymard and Romani, *La Cour comme institution économique*, p. 77.

36 The phrase is Dr Starkey's; see his 'Introduction: Court History in Perspective', in David Starkey (ed.), *The English Court from the Wars of the Roses to the Civil War* (London, 1987), p. 13.

37 In Castile-Aragon, for example, the two great ministers who dominated the first half of the seventeenth century, the Duque de Lerma and the Conde-Duque de Olivares, each combined conciliar office with the key household office that entitled them to attend the king in private apartments, the *sumiller de corps*, or head of the king's Bedchamber staff. J. H. Elliott, 'The Court of the Spanish Habsburgs: A Peculiar Institution?', in idem, *Spain and Its World, 1500–1700* (London, 1989), pp. 142–61.

38 Hugh Murray Baillie, 'Etiquette and the Planning of State Apartments in Baroque Palaces', *Archaeologia*, 101 (1967), pp. 169–99.

39 Elias's contention that the concept of 'privacy' was a late and essentially bourgeois invention is belied by the spatial arrangements in most early modern courts from the early sixteenth century onwards; cf. R. J. W. Evans, 'The Court: A Protean Institution and an Elusive Subject', in Asch and Birke, *Princes, Patronage, and the Nobility*, pp. 481–91.

40 For important case studies, see Peter Holman, *Four and Twenty Fiddlers: The Violin and the English Court, 1540–1690* (Oxford, 1993), and Frederick Hammond, *Music and Spectacle in Baroque Rome: Barberini Patronage under Urban VIII* (New Haven and London, 1994); and see Fiona Kisby, 'Music and Musicians in Royal, Ducal, Imperial, and Papal Courts to c.1700: An Introductory Bibliography', *The Court Historian: Newsletter of the Society for Court Studies*, 3 (1998), no. 1, pp. 37–48.

41 Norbert Elias, *The Civilizing Process* (Oxford, 1982), p. 236.

42 Geoffrey Parker, *The Military Revolution: Military Innovation and the Rise of the West, 1500–1800* (Cambridge, 1988); Jeremy Black, *A Military Revolution? Military Change and European Society, 1550–1800* (Basingstoke, 1991).

43 Jean Bérenger, 'Noblesse et absolutisme en Europe à l'époque de la Contre-reforme', *Il Pensiero Politico*, 11 (1978), 145–68, esp. p. 156; for ceremonial, see Christina Hofmann, *Das Spanische Hofzeremoniell von 1500–1700* (Erlanger Historische Studien VIII, Frankfurt and Bern, 1985), p. 63. Such was the 'vast and bureaucratic despotism' erected in seventeenth-century France, Professor Salmon has claimed, that by the reign of Louis XIV the 'high nobility had been reduced to the role of subservient courtiers': J. H. M. Salmon, *Cardinal de Retz: The Anatomy of a Conspirator* (London, 1969), p. 2; cf. Krüdener, *Der Rolle des Hofes*.

44 This can be roughly defined as *ducs et pairs* in France, the grandees of Spain, the dukes and princes of the Empire, earls and their seniors in England and Scotland.

45 For the Empire, where the possession of household offices gave access to the council (the *Rat*), see Georg Heilingsetzer, 'The Austrian Nobility, 1600–50: Between Court and Estates', in R. J. W. Evans and T. V. Thomas (eds.), *Crown, Church and Estates: Central European Politics in the Sixteenth and Seventeenth Centuries* (London, 1991), pp. 245–60.

46 R. J. W. Evans, *The Making of the Habsburg Monarchy, 1550–1700* (Oxford, 1979), pp. 146–51; H. F. Schwarz, *The Imperial Privy Council in the Seventeenth Century* (Cambridge, Mass., 1943), pp. 33–6.

47 The Duc de Beauvillier, for example, a member of the highest rank of the French nobility, the *ducs et pairs* (dukes-and-peers), straddled both. He combined high office in the household (as *premier gentilhomme de la chambre du roi* from 1666 and tutor to the Duc de Bourgogne from 1689) with a critically important 'administrative' appointment, *chef du conseil des finances*, from 1679. Duindam, *Myths of Power*, p. 64.

48 James van Horn Melton, 'The Nobility in the Bohemian and Austrian Lands, 1620–1780', in H. M. Scott (ed.), *The European*

Nobilities in the Seventeenth and Eighteenth Centuries, 2 vols. (London, 1995), II, pp. 110–43; Brenda Meehan-Waters, *Autocracy and Aristocracy: The Russian Service Elite of 1730* (New Brunswick, NJ, 1982); Jay M. Smith, *The Culture of Merit: Nobility, Royal Service, and the Making of Absolute Monarchy in France, 1600–1789* (Ann Arbor, 1996); for a statement of the older view, see R. O. Crummey, *Aristocrats and Servitors: The Boyar Elite in Russia, 1613–89* (Princeton, 1983), pp. 170–73.

49 For a different view, see Asch, 'Introduction: Court and Household', p. 24: at court, the nobles had 'to subject themselves to the discipline of the *monarchic state*' (my emphasis).

50 Cf. Duindam, *Myths of Power*, pp. 40–41; Volker Press, 'The Habsburg Court as a Center of the Imperial Government', *Journal of Modern History*, 58 Supplement (1986), 23–45.

51 By the reign of Louis XIV, the number of offices for sale in the household, stable, and hunt available for purchase approached 1,500; J. Boucher, 'L'évolution de la maison du roi: des deniers Valois aux premier Bourbons', *XVII siècle*, 34 (1982), 359–79. In all major departments of the French royal household, at least until Necker's attempted reforms in the 1780s, 'every post…was at the disposal of the great officer in charge. Normally he would sell them for his own profit'. Doyle, *Venality*, p. 65; for the Necker reforms, see Solnon, *Cour de France*, pp. 514–17.

52 James S. Pritchard, *Louis XV's Navy, 1748–62: A Study of Organization and Administration* (Kingston and Montreal, 1987), p. 3.

53 Roger Mettam, 'The French Nobility, 1610–1715', in Scott, *The European Nobilities*, I, p. 122.

54 Evans, *The Making of the Habsburg Monarchy*, p. 177; Hannes Stekl, *Österreichs Aristokratie im Vormärz: Herrschaftsstil und Lebensformen der Fürstenhäuser Liechtenstein und Schwartzenberg* (Munich, 1973).

55 On the Lobkovices, see Evans, *The Making of the Habsburg Monarchy*, pp. 172, 205.

56 Evans, *The Making of the Habsburg Monarchy*, p. 178; for the political significance of the family, see Cesare Mozzarelli (ed.), *'Familia' del principe e famiglia aristocratica*, 2 vols. (Rome, 1988); and Christine Lebeau, *Aristocrates et grands commis à la cour de Vienne, 1748–91: le modèle français* (Paris, 1996), a case study of the Zinzendorf.

57 For the development of stratification within the 'second estate', see H. M. Scott and Christopher Storrs, 'Introduction: The Consolidation of Noble Power in Europe, c.1600–1800', in Scott, *The European Nobilities*, I, pp. 49–50.

58 For Montesquieu, Duindam, *Myths of Power*, p. 50. For three important recent case studies, see Tommaso Astarita, *The Continuity of Feudal Power: The Caracciolo de Brienza in Spanish Naples* (Cambridge, 1992), pp. 202–32; Ignacio Atienza Hernández, *Aristocracia, poder y riqueza en la España moderna. La Casa de Osuna, siglos XV–XIX* (Madrid, 1987); M. A. Visceglia, *Identità sociali: la nobiltà napoletana nella prima età moderna* (Milan, 1998).

59 For a case study, see William Beik, *Absolutism and Society in Seventeenth-Century France: State Power and Provincial Aristocracy in Languedoc* (Cambridge, 1985), pp. 316–39; for a still more sceptical assessment of 'absolutism', see also Roger Mettam, *Power and Faction in Louis XIV's France* (Oxford, 1988), Ch. 2, and his 'Power, Status, and Precedence: Rivalries among the Provincial Elites of Louis XIV's France', *Transactions of the Royal Historical Society*, 38 (1988), 43–62.

60 Pierre Lefebvre, 'Aspects de la "fidélité" en France au XVIIe siècle: le cas des agents des princes de Condé', *Revue Historique*, 250 (1973), 59–105; Pritchard, *Louis XV's Navy*.

61 For a case study, Felicity Heal, 'Reputation and Honour in Court and Country: Lady Elizabeth Russell and Sir Thomas Hoby', *Transactions of the Royal Historical Society*, 6th series, 6 (1996), 161–78.

62 Mervyn James, 'English Politics and the Concept of Honour, 1485–1642', in his *Society, Politics, and Culture: Studies in Early Modern England* (Cambridge, 1986), pp. 308–415.

63 Joanna Woods-Marsden, *The Gonzaga of Mantua and Pisanello's Arthurian Frescoes* (Princeton, 1988); John Adamson, 'Chivalry and Political Culture in Caroline England', in Kevin Sharpe and Peter Lake (eds.), *Culture and Politics in Early Stuart England* (London, 1994),

pp. 161–97; Arthur B. Ferguson, *The Chivalric Tradition in Renaissance England* (Washington, 1986).

64 Mazarin's arch-enemy, the Cardinal de Retz, was sufficiently sensitive to the accusation that he was a parvenu that he employed the scholar Pierre d'Hozier to rebut the politically dangerous charge. The resulting treatise 'proved' that de Retz was entitled to 128 quarterings of nobility in his coat of arms, and that his family had belonged to at least the Florentine patriciate since 1176. Salmon, *Cardinal de Retz*, p. 11 and n.

65 Henry Howard, Earl of Northampton, *A Publication of his Majesty's Edict and Severe Censure against Private Combats* (London, 1614), p. 8 (I owe my knowledge of this text to Professor Caroline Hibbard).

66 Kristen B. Neuschel, *Word of Honor: Interpreting Noble Culture in Sixteenth-Century France* (Ithaca and London, 1989), p. 16; Hernández, *Aristocracia*, pp. 55–7; Smith, *The Culture of Merit*, pp. 93–123.

67 C[alybute] D[owninge], *A Discourse of the State Ecclesiasticall of this Kingdome* (Oxford, 1633), p. 46. Downing was chaplain to the second Earl of Salisbury, the captain of the band of gentlemen pensioners at the court of Charles I.

68 An important new survey appeared too late to be considered in this book: J. H. Elliott and L. W. B. Brockliss (eds.), *The World of the Favourite* (New Haven and London, 1999). For the 'minister-favourite', see A. Lloyd Moote, 'Richelieu as Chief Minister: A Comparative Study of the Favourite in Early Seventeenth-Century Politics', in Joseph Bergin and Laurence Brockliss (eds.), *Richelieu and his Age* (Oxford, 1992), pp. 13–43, esp. p. 16.

69 Blair Worden, 'Favourites on the English Stage', forthcoming in Elliott and Brockliss, *The World of the Favourite*. It was probably at its strongest during the century between 1560 and 1660, what Robert Evans has termed 'that great age of the European *valido*': R. J. W. Evans, 'The Austrian Habsburgs', in Dickens, *The Courts of Europe*, p. 133.

70 [Refuge, Monsieur de Eustache], *Arcana Aulica: or Walsingham's Manual of Prudential Maxims* (Eng. trans., London, 1652), p. 3.

71 Just as there had been numerous examples of 'miserable eunuchs' at the Byzantine court promoted to head councils and armies, wrote the Seigneur de Balzac, so 'other more recent histories produce such as were barbers, tailors, grooms of the chamber the evening before, [who] the next morning [were] chang'd into chamberlains…'. [Jean-Louis Guez, Seigneur de] Balzac, *Aristippus, or Monsr. de Balsac's Masterpiece. Being a Discourse concerning the Court*, trans. by R.W. (London, 1659), pp. 25–6.

72 Evans, 'The Court: A Protean Institution and an Elusive Subject', p. 487.

73 Doyle, *Venality*, p. 72 (for quotation); Rodríguez-Salgado, 'Honour and Profit in the Court of Philip II', p. 77. For a case study, see R. A. W. Browne, 'Court and Crown: Rivalry in the Court of Louis XVI and its Importance in the Formation of a Pre-Revolutionary Aristocratic Opposition' (unpub. D.Phil. diss., Oxford, 1991).

74 For a contemporary statement of the principle, see [Refuge, Monsieur de Eustache], *Arcana*, p. 3.

75 Arlette Jouanna, *Le Devoir de revolte: la noblesse française et la gestation de l'état moderne, 1559–1661* (Paris, 1989), pp. 8–12; Caroline Hibbard, 'The theatre of dynasty', in R. Malcolm Smuts, *The Stuart Court and Europe: Essays in Politics and Political Culture* (Cambridge, 1996), pp. 156–76.

76 José Antonio Maravall, *Poder, honor, y élites en el siglo XVII* (Madrid, 1979), pp. 32–41; James, 'English Politics and the Concept of Honour'; John Adamson, 'The Baronial Context of the English Civil War', *Transactions of the Royal Historical Society*, 5th series, 40 (1990), 93–120; Harold A. Ellis, 'Genealogy, History, and Aristocratic Reaction in Early Eighteenth-Century France: the Case of Henri de Boulainvilliers', *Journal of Modern History*, 58 (1986), 414–51; and idem, *Boulainvilliers and the French Monarchy: Aristocratic Politics in Early Eighteenth-Century France* (Ithaca and London, 1988); Julian Swann, 'The French Nobility, 1715–1789', in Scott, *The European Nobilities*, I, p. 148.

77 Duindam, *Myths of Power*, Ch. 6.

78 A distinction ought to be made, however, between etiquette as, in one meaning, the quasi-liturgical rituals of state, and etiquette as *politesse*: a series of mannerly gestures defining daily personal comportment at court. See, above, p. 27.

79 For the influence of Castiglione, see Carlo Ossola and A. Prosperi (eds.), *La Corte e 'Il Cortegiano'*, 2 vols. (Rome, 1980); Carlo Ossola, *Dal 'Cortegiano' all' 'Uomo di Mondo': storia di un libro e di un modello sociale* (Turin, 1987), esp. pp. 131–51.

80 The phrase is Keith Brown's, 'Gentlemen and Thugs in Seventeenth-Century Britain', *History Today*, 40 (1990), 28. On the duel, Micheline Cuénin, *Le Duel sous l'ancien régime* (Paris, 1982); François Billacois, *Le Duel dans la société française des XVIe–XVIIe siècles. Essai de psychosociologie historique* (Paris, 1986), esp. pp. 193–219. An abridged English translation of Billacois's work was published in 1990; page references here are to the French edition.

81 Billacois, *Le Duel*, pp. 218–9, 322–6; for its later history, see V. G. Kiernan, *The Duel in European History: Honour and the Reign of Aristocracy* (Oxford, 1988), pp. 92–115; Ute Frevert, *Ehrenmänner: Das Duell in der bürgerlichen Gesellschaft* (Munich, 1991; Eng. trans. Cambridge, 1995), esp. Ch. 1.

82 Other examples include, in Savoy, the revival of the Orders of the Annunziata in 1568, and of San Maurizio in 1572; in France, the inauguration of the Order of the Saint-Esprit in 1578; in Russia, Peter the Great's foundation of the Order of St Andrew, apparently modelled on the English Garter, in 1699; and in Brandenburg-Prussia, the institution of the Order of the Black Eagle, founded to mark the elector's elevation to kingly rank in 1701. For the Order of the Saint-Esprit, see Pierre Boitel, *La Relation des…ceremonies observées à la reception des Chevaliers de l'Ordre du Sainct Sprit* (Paris, 1620) [BL, 9930. B. 7]; for Henry VIII and the Caroline revival of the Garter, Elias Ashmole, *The Institution, Laws and Ceremonies of the Most Noble Order of the Garter* (London, 1672), Ch. 6; for the Santo Stefano, see the series of essays by Franco Angiolini, *Cavalieri e il principe. L'Ordine di Santo Stefano e la società toscana nell' età moderna* (Florence, 1996).

83 For its survival into the twentieth century as a basis for political action, see Peter Hoffmann, *Claus Schenk Graf von Stauffenberg und seiner Brüder* (Stuttgart, 1992); Eng. trans., *Stauffenberg: A Family History, 1905–1944* (Cambridge, 1995).

84 See, for example, Pauline M. Smith, *The Anti-Courtier Trend in Sixteenth-Century French Literature* (Geneva, 1966); Linda Levy Peck, *Court Patronage and Corruption in Early Stuart England* (London, 1990), pp. 161–207; David Howarth, *Images of Rule: Art and Politics in the English Renaissance, 1485–1649* (London, 1997), Ch. 8; Burke, *Fabrication of Louis XIV*, Ch. 10.

85 For the court of Maximilian II, Howard Louthan, 'Johannis Crato and the Austrian Habsburgs: Reforming a Counter-Reform Court', *Studies in Reformed Theology and History*, 2, no. 3 (1994), esp. 1–11.

86 Biblioteca Nacional, Madrid, MS 18434 (unfoliated): Olivares's 'Consulta de Su Magestad' [1632]; quoted in R. A. Stradling, *Philip IV and the Government of Spain, 1621–1665* (Cambridge, 1988), p. 143.

87 E. W. Zeeden, *Konfessionsbildung: Studien zur Reformation, Gegenreformation und katolischen Reform* (Stuttgart, 1985); Heinz Schilling, 'Die Konfessionalisierung im Reich: Religiöser und gesellschaftlicher Wandel in Deutschland zwischen 1555 und 1620', *Historische Zeitschrift*, 246 (1988), 1–45.

88 Chapter 6, below; Franz Matsche, *Die Kunst im Dienst der Staatsidee Kaisar Karls VI. Ikonographie, Ikonologie und Programmatik des 'Kaisarstils'*, 2 vols. (Berlin, 1981); for the trials of diplomats obliged to attend these religious rituals, see M. F. Barrière (ed.), *Mémoires du Maréchal Duc de Richelieu*, 2 vols. (Paris, 1868–9), i, p. 209.

89 Peter Brown, 'Relics and Social Status in the Age of Gregory of Tours', in his *Society and the Holy in Late Antiquity* (London, 1982), p. 249.

90 Similarly, in Munich the Bavarian court all but took over the city's principal lay confraternity, the Major Congregation, in the century after 1584; by 1673, some 71 of its 171 members were 'dignitaries from the court' or members of the provincial administration with close ties to the electoral household. Jean Delumeau, *Catholicism between Luther and Voltaire: A New View of the Counter-Reformation* (London, 1977),

pp. 89–92. The French edition is published as *Le Catholicisme entre Luther et Voltaire* (Paris, 1971).

91 T. A. Marder, *Bernini's Scala Regia at the Vatican Palace: Architecture, Sculpture, and Ritual* (Cambridge, 1997), p. 247; for the *festa* in Naples, see A. Wilton and I. Bignamini (eds.), *Grand Tour: The Lure of Italy in the Eighteenth Century* (London, 1996), p. 198; and M. A. Visceglia, *Identità sociali: la nobiltà napoletana nella prima età moderna* (Milan, 1998), pp. 195–204.

92 Richard Ingersoll, 'The Ritual Use of Public Space in Renaissance Rome' (Ph.D. diss., University of California, Berkeley, 1985), pp. 162–3; quoted in Marder, *Bernini's Scala Regia*, p. 247.

93 For a survey of the clergy at the Italian and Iberian courts, see Flavio Rurale (ed.), *I religiosi a corte: teologia, politica, e diplomazia antico regime* (Rome, 1998).

94 Gabriella Zarri, 'Pietà e profezia alle corti padane: le pie consigliere dei principi', in Paolo Rossi et al. (eds.), *Il Rinascimento nelle corti padane: società e cultura* (Bari, 1977), pp. 201–37; Bernhard Duhr, *Die Jesuiten an den deutschen Fürstenhöfen* (Freiburg, 1901); Caroline Hibbard, *Charles I and the Popish Plot* (Chapel Hill, 1983), p. 56; Cuthbert [Hess], *The Capuchins*, 2 vols. (London, 1928).

95 For Lamormaini, see Evans, *The Making of the Habsburg Monarchy*, pp. 72–3; Carlo Carafa, 'Relatione dello stato dell'Imperio e della Germania', ed. J. G. Müller, *Archiv für Österreichische Geschichte*, 23 (1860), 101–449, at 259–64. See also Ernst-Albert Seils, *Die Staatslehre des Jesuiten Adam Contzen, Beichtvater Kurfürst Maximilian I. von Bayern* (Lübeck and Hamburg, 1968), pp. 7–19; Henar Pizarro Llorente, 'El control de la conciencia regia: el confessor real Fray Bernardo de Fresneda', in José Martínez Millán (ed.), *La corte de Felipe II* (Madrid, 1994), pp. 149–88; Carlos Javier de Carlos Morales, 'La participacion en el gobierno a traves de la conciencia regia. Fray Diego de Chaves, O. P., confesor de Felipe II', in Rurale, *I religiosi a corte*, pp. 131–57.

96 Catherine Wilkinson-Zerner, *Juan de Herrera, Architect to Philip II of Spain* (New Haven, 1993); Fernando Checa, *Felipe II: mecenas de las artes* (Madrid, 1992), pp. 201–39.

97 For Tuscan examples, Marcello Fantoni, 'Il bigottismo di Cosimo III: da leggenda storiografica ad oggetto storico', in M. Verga, V. Bergagli and F. Angiolini (eds.), *La Toscana nell'età di Cosimo III* (Florence, 1993), pp. 389–402; and idem, 'Il "principe santo". Clero regolare e modelli di sovranità nella Toscana tardo medicea', in Rurale, *I religiosi a corte*, pp. 229–48.

98 Thomas DaCosta Kaufmann, *Court, Cloister, and City: The Art and Culture of Central Europe, 1450–1800* (London, 1995), pp. 302–5; for these buildings, see also Günther Brucher, *Barockarchitektur in Österreich* (Cologne, 1983).

99 Antonio Filipe Pimental, *Arquitectura e poder: o Real Edificio de Mafra* (Coimbra, 1992); Timothy Mowl, *William Beckford: Composing for Mozart* (London, 1998), p. 169 (for quotation).

100 For Lutheran Sweden, see Chapter 11, below.

101 McCullough, *Sermons at Court*, pp. 42–4; Howarth, *Images of Rule*, pp. 24–5. Even Friedrich II of Prussia's Sanssouci was originally 'conceived as a [mock] "monastery" with Frederick as the abbot': Giles MacDonogh, *Frederick the Great* (London, 1999), p. 199.

102 Nicolas Caussin, *Cour Sainte*, 2 vols. (Rouen, 1655 edn.), i, p. 32; quoted in Delumeau, *Catholicism between Luther and Voltaire*, p. 107; Eng. trans. by T[homas] H[awkins], *The Holy Court, or The Christian Institution of Men of Quality* (Paris, 1626), with a dedication to Queen Henrietta Maria, sig. **★★**.

103 Evans, *The Making of the Habsburg Monarchy*, p. 152; for England, see R. Malcolm Smuts, *Court Culture and the Origins of a Royalist Tradition in Early Stuart England* (Philadelphia, 1987), pp. 183–213.

104 See also Duindam's remarks on the 'charisma' of the imperial office, even after 1648: *Myths of Power*, p. 67.

105 Tony Claydon, *William III and the Godly Revolution* (Cambridge, 1996), Ch. 3, 'The propagation of courtly reformation'.

106 Kevin Sharpe, *Criticism and Compliment: The Politics of Literature in the England of Charles I* (Cambridge, 1987).

107 Alain Boureau, 'Les Cérémonies royales françaises entre performance juridique et compétence liturgique', *Annales* (1991), no. 6, pp. 1253–64.

108 Elias, *The Court Society*, pp. 88–102, esp. at p. 89; Karin Plodeck, *Hofstruktur und Hofzeremoniell in Brandenburg-Ansbach vom 16. bis zum 18. Jahrhundert. Zur Rolle des Herrschaftskultes im absolutistischen Gesellschafts- und Herrschaftssystem* (Ansbach, 1972).

109 Dirk Schümer, 'Der Höfling. Eine semiotische Existenz', *Journal Geschichte* (1990), no. 1, pp. 15–23.

110 For an introduction to the literature, see Roelof van Straten, *Iconography, Indexing, Iconclass: A Handbook* (Leiden, 1994).

111 Clifford Geertz, *Negara: The Theater State in Nineteenth-Century Bali* (Princeton, 1980), esp. pp. 103–36. For important exceptions among the historians, David Cannadine and Simon Price (eds.), *Rituals of Royalty: Power and Ceremonial in Traditional Societies* (Cambridge, 1987); Ingersoll, 'The Ritual Use of Public Space in Renaissance Rome'.

112 H. C. Ehalt, 'Zur Funktion des Zeremoniells im Absolutismus', in Buck, Kauffmann, et al., *Europäische Hofkultur*, II, pp. 411–19.

113 As summarized by Michel Mollat, *Genèse médiévale de la France moderne, XIVe–XVe siècles* (Paris, 1977), p. 173 (a reference I owe to Professor Paravicini).

114 Werner Paravicini, 'The Court of the Dukes of Burgundy: A Model for Europe?', in Asch and Birke, *Princes, Patronage, and the Nobility*, pp. 90–102; see also Holger Kruse and Werner Paravicini (eds.), *Höfe und Hofordnungen* (Sigmaringen, forthcoming); G. Kipling, *The Triumph of Honour: Burgundian Origins of the Elizabethan Renaissance* (Leiden, 1977).

115 Paravicini, 'The Court of the Dukes of Burgundy', p. 99; Hofmann, *Hofzeremoniell*, pp. 40–50; O. Shena, *Le Leggi palatini di Pietro IV d'Aragona* (Calgiari, 1983).

116 Aloys Winterling, *Der Hof der Kurfürsten von Köln, 1688–1794. Eine Fallstudie zur Bedeutung 'absolutistischer' Hofhaltung* (Bonn, 1986), p. 156.

117 Volker Bauer, *Die höfische Gesellschaft in Deutschland von der Mitte des 17. bis zum Ausgang des 18. Jahrhunderts* (Tübingen, 1993), pp. 90–91; S. J. Klingensmith, *The Utility of Splendor: Ceremony, Social Life, and Architecture at the Court of Bavaria, 1600–1800* (Chicago, 1993), pp. 118–44.

118 Paravicini, 'The Court of the Dukes of Burgundy', p. 89.

119 Sergio Bertelli, '*Rex et sacerdos:* the Holiness of the King in European Civilization', in Ellenius, *Iconography*, pp. 123–145, esp. pp. 141–4.

120 I am grateful to Miss Juliet Glass of Johns Hopkins University for information on this point. Cf. Gérard Sabatier, 'Le Roi caché et le roi soleil: de la monarchie en Espagne et en France au milieu de XVIIe siècle', in Charles Mazouer (ed.), *L'Âge d'or de l'influence espagnole: la France et l'Espagne à l'époque d'Anne d'Autriche, 1615–66* (Mont-de-Marsan, 1991), pp. 113–24, esp. p. 122.

121 Sergio Bertelli, *Il corpo del re: sacralità del potere nell'Europa medievale e moderna* (2nd edn, Florence, 1995), p. 135 (fig. 38).

122 The word is derived from the Italian *traversa*, meaning a 'curtain that could be pulled across': Samuel Pegge, *Curalia: or an Historical Account of Some Branches of the Royal Household*, 3 parts (London, 1791), I, p. 21n; B[ritish] L[ibrary], Additional MS 71009 (John Norris's Duties of a Gentleman Usher), fo. 13.

123 Juliet Glass, 'The Sixteenth-Century Spanish Chapel Royal: the Alcázar at Madrid', unpublished paper delivered to Society for Court Studies Conference on 'Chapels Royal: Politics, Doctrine and the Arts at the Early Modern Court, 1400–1720', London, 14 February 1997. I am grateful to Ms Glass and to Professor Luc Duerloo (of the Catholic University of Leuven) for a discussion of these points.

124 Glass, 'The Sixteenth-Century Spanish Chapel Royal'.

125 Paulo Prodi, *Il sovrano pontefice. Un corpo e due anime: la monarchia papale nella prima età moderna* (Bologna, 1982); Eng. trans., *The Papal Prince* (Cambridge, 1987); and Chapter 5, below.

126 For the *scabellum*, see [Cristoforo Marcello], *Sacrarum Cerimoniarum sive Rituum Ecclesiasticorum Sanctae Romanae Ecclesiae* (Rome, 1560), fo. 99v; *Memoirs of Charles-Lewis, Baron de Pollnitz*, 2 vols. (London, 1737), II, p. 99 (for quotation).

127 Likewise, in Tudor England, at least until the Reformation, Good Friday was the one great ecclesiastical day when the king went in public procession to the Chapel Royal *without* the sword of state being carried before him. While Christ was dead and entombed, so too, symbolically, was the potency of worldly sovereigns. BL, MS 71009, fo. 15; Sloane MS 1494 (Court usage, *temp.* Henry VIII), fo. 32.

128 For the Corpus Christi canopy, see Eamon Duffy, *The Stripping of the Altars* (London, 1996), plate 6.

129 For a contemporary illustration, see Jonathan Brown, *Kings and Connoisseurs: Collecting Art in Seventeenth-Century Europe* (New Haven and London, 1995), p. 34.

130 BL, Add. MS 71009, fo. 8v (a eucharistic canopy); Ashmole, *The Institution of the Garter*, pp. 571–2; BL, Add. MS 37998 (Sir Edward Walker papers), fos. 50, 51v.

131 *Memoirs of Baron de Pollnitz*, II, p. 55. He describes an audience of Clement XII in 1731; but the protocol had not changed materially in two centuries; cf. Marder, *Bernini's Scala Regia*, pp. 224–6.

132 Ehalt, *Ausdrucksformen absolutistischer Herrschaft*, p. 125; Hofmann, *Das Spanische Hofzeremoniell*; see Chapter 6, below.

133 McCullough, *Sermons at Court*, Ch. 1. The Roundhead sensibilities of Samuel Pepys were obviously shocked when, attending the Whitehall Chapel in August 1660, he observed that even a former parliamentarian divine, invited to preach before the court, was 'very officious with his three reverences to the king, as others do': Robert Latham and William Matthews (eds.), *The Diary of Samuel Pepys*, 11 vols. (London, 1972–83), I, p. 220.

134 For Elias's very different reading, see *The Court Society*, pp. 101–2.

135 For princely dining, see Bertelli, *Il corpo del re*, pp. 167–88; and idem, '*Rex et sacerdos*', pp. 141–4; Marcello Fantoni, *La corte del Granduca. Forme e simboli del potere mediceo fra cinque e seicento* (Rome, 1994), p. 15; Plodeck, *Hofstruktur und Hofzeremoniell in Brandenburg-Ansbach*, pp. 152–4; Klingensmith, *Utility of Splendor*, pp. 162–3; Catherine Arminjon (ed.), *Tables et festins de cour en Europe* (Paris, forthcoming); for English practice see BL, Stowe MS 562 (Household ordinances, *c.*1660–70), fos. 3v, 5v; and Chapter 3, below.

136 Briggs, *Communities of Belief*, p. 229 (for quotation); see also, R. J. Knecht, 'Francis I: Prince and Patron of the Northern Renaissance', in Dickens, *Courts of Europe*, p. 102.

137 Fantoni, *La corte del Granduca*, p. 15: 'un sistema semantico profondamente radicato nella struttura e nei valori della collettività'.

138 Miri Rubin, *Corpus Christi: The Eucharist in Late Medieval Culture* (Cambridge, 1991); Jacques Chiffoleau, Lauro Martines and A. P. Bagliani (eds.), *Riti e rituali nelle società medievali* (Spoleto, 1994).

139 John Bossy, *Christianity in the West, 1400–1700* (Oxford, 1985), pp. 153–61, at p. 154. (I am grateful to Mr Dougal Shaw for drawing my attention to this passage.)

140 The precise chronology of the introduction of the triple reverence awaits further research. For the practice at the Habsburg court, Chapter 6, below; for France, see John Rogister, *Louis XV and the Parlement of Paris, 1737–55* (Cambridge, 1995), p. 74.

141 Sergio Bertelli and Giuliano Crifò (eds.), *Rituale, ceremoniale, etichetta* (Milan, 1985); Bertelli, *Il corpo del re* and his '*Rex et Sacerdos*'; Fantoni, *La corte del granduca*; Visceglia and Brice, *Cérémonial et rituel à Rome*; see also Gotthardt Frühsorge, 'Der Hof, der Raum, die Bewegung. Gedanken zur Neubewertung des europäischen Hofzeremoniells', *Euphorion: Zeitschrift für Literaturgeschichte*, 82 (1988), 424–9.

142 Jean-Marie Apostolidès, *Le Roi-machine: spectacle et politique au temps de Louis XIV* (Paris, 1981). See also Michael de Ferdinandy, 'Die theatralische Bedeutung des spanischen Hofzeremoniells Kaiser Karl V.', *Archiv für Kulturgeschichte*, 47 (1965), 306–20; Ralph E. Giesey, *Cérémonial et puissance: France, XVe–XVIIe siècles* (Paris, 1987).

143 Geertz, *Negara*, p. 103.

144 For Königsberg, see Chapter 8, below; for Palermo, Robert Oresko, 'The House of Savoy in Search for a Royal Crown in the Seventeenth Century', in idem, G. C. Gibbs and H. M. Scott (eds.), *Royal and Republican Sovereignty in Early Modern Europe: Essays in Memory of Ragnhild Hatton* (Cambridge, 1997), p. 348; *Bruxellensium Triumphus Serenissimo Principi, Hispaniarum Infanti, Ferdinandi* (Brussels, 1635), pp. 1–56 (CUL, Cc. 12.47.2).

145 *Pompa Intoitus Honori Serenissimi Principis Ferdinandi* (Antwerp,

1641); Baudouin, *Rubens*, pp. 264–70; J. R. Martin, *The Decorations for the Pompa Introitus Ferdinandi* (Corpus Rubenianum Ludwig Burchard, XVI, London and New York, 1971); for Le Pautre, see Barbara Coeyman, 'Social Dance in the 1668 *Feste de Versailles*: Architecture and Performance Context', *Early Music*, 26 (1998), 264–82.

146 Gérard Sabatier, 'Beneath the Ceilings of Versailles: Towards an Archaeology and Anthropology of the Use of the King's "Signs" during the Absolute Monarchy', in Ellenius, *Iconography*, p. 238.

147 For papal usage, [Marcellus], *Sacrarum Ceremoniarum*, fo. 19r–v; for Spain and England, see Chapters 1 and 3, below.

148 The increasingly precise codification of court rank from around the turn of the seventeenth century (the French *règlement* of 1689, the English 'Establishment' of 1692, the Swedish regulations of 1696, the Danish of 1699, and the Prussian of 1705) further refined, but did not fundamentally alter, this system. The major exceptions are the Prussian court regulations of 1713, and the Russian table of ranks, introduced by Peter the Great in 1722, each of which accorded precedence to the military hierarchy over that of the court.

149 For Castile, Chapter 1, below, and Rodríguez-Salgado, 'Honour and Profit in the Court of Philip II', p. 69: 'Had Charles V destroyed the *Casa y Corte de Castilla* he would effectively have destroyed Castile as a sovereign unit'. For Queen Christina, see Ulrich Hermanns (ed.), *Christina, Königin von Schweden* (Osnabrück, 1997), a reference I owe to Dr Jarl Kremeier.

150 J. H. Elliott, 'Philip IV of Spain: Prisoner of Ceremony', in Dickens, *The Courts of Europe*, esp. p. 175.

151 Brown and Elliott, *A Palace for a King*, p. 68; cf. Elliott, 'The Court of the Spanish Habsburgs: a Peculiar Institution?', pp. 150–51.

152 Roy Strong, *Art and Power: Renaissance Festivals, 1450–1650* (Woodbridge, 1984). See also, B. Mitchell, *Italian Civic Pageantry in the High Renaissance: A Descriptive Bibliography* (Florence, 1979).

153 Peter Burke, *Culture and Society in Renaissance Italy, 1420–1540* (London, 1972), p. 165 (for quotation); but note his second thoughts in his revised edition, issued as *The Italian Renaissance* (Cambridge, 1987), p. 128; for other examples, see Sabatier, 'Le roi caché et le roi soleil', p. 118; Ellenius, *Iconography*, passim.

154 Friedrich Zunkel, 'Ehre, Reputation', in Otto Brunner, Werner Conze and Reinhart Koselleck (eds.), *Geschichtliche Grundbegriffe. Historisches Lexicon der politisch-sozialen Sprache in Deutschland*, 8 vols. (Stuttgart, 1975–97), II, pp. 1–63, esp. 17–23.

155 J. B. Bossuet, *Politique tirée des propres paroles de l'écriture sainte*, ed. J. Le Brun (Geneva, 1709), Livre X; quoted in Burke, *Fabrication of Louis XIV*, p. 5.

156 Elliott, 'The Court of the Spanish Habsburgs: A Peculiar Institution?', p. 23.

157 At the Russian court, for example, in the half century between 1647 and 1699, gifts from the Swedish monarchs alone totalled some 342 separate objects weighing a staggering 610 kilos of silver; Guy Watson, 'Royal Gifts', *Apollo* (September 1997), pp. 54–5.

158 R. Malcolm Smuts, 'Art and the Material Culture of Majesty in Early Stuart England', in Smuts, *The Stuart Court and Europe*, pp. 90, 106; Albert J. Loomie (ed.), *Ceremonies of Charles I: The Note Books of John Finet, 1628–41* (New York, 1987), p. 320.

159 For a case study, *Von Sanssouci nach Europa. Geschenke Friedrich des Grossen an europäische Höfe* (exh. cat., Potsdam, 1994), a reference I owe to Dr Kremeier.

160 For diplomacy and the court, see William Roosen, 'Early Modern Diplomatic Ceremonial: A Systems Approach', *Journal of Modern History*, 52 (1980), 452–76.

161 Sabatier, 'Le roi caché et le roi soleil', p. 118.

162 Elliott, 'Power and Propaganda in the Spain of Philip IV', in idem, *Spain and Its World*, esp. pp. 183–7; for Munich, see Klingensmith, *Utility of Splendor*, pp. 126–7; for Florence, Janet Cox-Rearick, *Bronzino's Chapel of Eleonora in the Palazzo Vecchio* (Berkeley and Los Angeles, 1993), pp. 250–51, 260.

163 For the *studiolo*, see Luciano Berti, *Il principe dello studiolo. Francesco I dei Medici e la fine del Rinascimento fiorentino* (Florence, 1967); Scott

J. Schaefer, 'The *studiolo* of Francesco I de' Medici in the Palazzo Vecchio in Florence' (Ph.D. diss. Bryn Mawr College, 1980), pp. 8, 126. For its location within the palace, see Wolfgang Liebenwein, *Studiolo: die Entstehung eines Raumtyps und seine Entwicklung bis um 1600* (Berlin, 1977), pp. 146–7.

164 For a general introduction to the art of the *Kunstkammer*, Géza von Habsburg, *Princely Treasures* (London and New York, 1997); see also Elisabeth Scheicher, *Die Kunst- und Wunderkammern der Habsburger* (Vienna, Munich, and Zurich, 1979); Paula Findlen, 'Cabinets, Collecting, and Natural Philosophy', in Eliška Fučíková et al. (eds.), *Rudolf II and Prague: The Court and the City* (Prague and London, 1997), pp. 209–19; Jill Bepler (ed.), *Barocke Sammellust. Die Bibliothek und Kunstkammer des Herzogs Ferdinand Albrecht zu Braunschweig-Lüneberg* (Weinheim, 1988).

165 At the court of Saxony, for example, the so-called Grüne Gewölbe consisted of a series of vaulted, semi-public rooms for the display of the elector's *Kunstkammer*, and was readily accessible. See Ulli Arnold and Werner Schmidt (ed.), *Barock in Dresden. Kunst und Kunstsammlungen unter der Regierung des Kurfürsten Friedrich August I. von Sachsen* (exh. cat., [Leipzig], 1986); Dirk Syndram, *Das Grüne Gewölbe zu Dresden. Führer durch Geschichte und seine Sammlungen* (Munich, 1997).

166 Findlen, 'Cabinets, Collecting, and Natural Philosophy', pp. 211–12; Schaefer, 'The *studiolo* of Francesco I', Ch. 2.

167 For the role of the 'secret' in early modern culture, see Carlo Ginzburg, 'High and Low: The Theme of Forbidden Knowledge in the Sixteenth and Seventeenth Centuries', *Past and Present*, 73 (1976), 28–41; William Eamon, *Science and the Secrets of Nature: Books of Secrets in Medieval and Early Modern Culture* (Princeton, 1994). For the secretiveness of Rudolf II in relation to his *Kunstkammer*, see R. J. W. Evans, *Rudolf II and his World: A Study in Intellectual History, 1576–1612* (Oxford, 1973), p. 178.

168 Sabatier, 'Beneath the Ceilings of Versailles', pp. 226–7.

169 I am grateful to Professor Malcolm Smuts, of the University of Massachusetts at Boston, for a discussion of this point.

170 Similar arrangements prevailed in the Munich *Residenz* of the Wittelsbach Dukes (and from 1623 Electors) of Bavaria, where one of the greatest concentrations of treasure was to be found in the Kammerkapelle, dedicated in 1607 and located immediately beside the duke's private apartments (Chapter 7, below). For Florence, see Fantoni, *La corte del granduca*; for Halle, Friedhelm Jürgensmeier, *Erzbischof Albrecht von Brandenburg, 1490–1545* (Freiburg, 1991).

171 Theodore Rabb, 'Play, Not Politics: Who Really Understood the Symbolism of Renaissance Art?', *Times Literary Supplement*, 10 November 1995.

172 Brown, *Kings and Connoisseurs*, pp. 227–8.

173 Ex inf. Dr Thomas Campbell, of the Metropolitan Museum of Art, New York. For the Mantuan sale, see Alessandro Luzio, *La Galleria dei Gonzaga venduta all'Inghilterra nel 1627–28. Documenti degli archivi di Mantova e Londra* (Milan, 1913).

174 Honor Levi, 'Richelieu collectionneur', in Roland Mousnier (ed.), *Richelieu et la culture* (Paris, 1987), pp. 175–84, esp. p. 180; Honor Levi, 'L'inventaire après décès du Cardinal Richelieu', *Archives de l'Art Français*, 27 (1985), 9–83.

175 Charles I, for example, sold most of his court plate in 1626; Louis XIV dispatched his gold service to the Mint to remedy a cash-flow crisis in 1689–90. For Charles I, Samuel Pegge, *Illustrations of the Manners and Expences of Antient Times* (London, 1797), 'A Particular of the Plate…1626'; 20,021 ounces of plate were sold. For Louis XIV, see Gabriel-Jules comte de Cosnac and Arthur comte Bertrand (eds.), *Mémoires du marquis de Sourches sur le règne de Louis XIV*, 13 vols. (Paris, 1882–93), III, p. 181 (I owe this second reference to Dr Duindam). For Brandenburg-Prussia, see Christiane Keisch, *Das grosse Silberbuffet aus dem Rittersaal des Berliner Schlosses* (Berlin, 1997).

176 Oskar Raschauer, *Schönbrunn. Eine denkmalkundliche Darstellung seiner Baugeschichte* (Vienna, 1960); Hellmut Lorenz, *Liechtenstein Palaces in Vienna from the Age of the Baroque* (New York, 1985). In England, the disparity was even more sharply marked. The architectural incoherence of Whitehall Palace was a subject of criticism at least from the 1590s until its destruction by fire in 1698. St James's, which became the metropolitan seat of the court thereafter, was notoriously worse, prompting Baron von Pöllnitz to remark in the 1720s that one of the most powerful of monarchs in Europe was also the worst housed.

177 Karl Czok, *Am Hofe Augusts des Starken* (Stuttgart, 1990); Arnold and Schmidt, *Barock in Dresden*.

178 Duindam, *Myths of Power*, p. 193.

179 See, esp., the observations in Astarita, *The Continuity of Feudal Power*, pp. 202–3; and Volker Press, 'La corte principesca in Germania nel XVI e XVII secolo', in Mozzarelli, *'Familia'*, p. 159.

180 Thomas Ertman, *Birth of the Leviathan: Building States and Regimes in Medieval and Early Modern Europe* (New York and Cambridge, 1997); see also Stephen Krasner, 'Approaches to the State: Alternative Conceptions and Historical Dynamics', *Comparative Politics*, 16 (1984), 223–46.

181 Evans, 'The Court: A Protean Institution and an Elusive Subject', p. 483. In England, no one was permitted to press 'too near…the state, or to sit down upon the stools or foot stools under our state': BL, Stowe MS 562 (Household ordinances, Charles II), fo. 5. See also Thomas M. Greene, 'Shakespeare's *Richard II*: The Sign in Bullingbrook's Window', in Lucy Gent (ed.), *Albion's Classicism: The Visual Arts in Britain, 1550–1660* (New Haven and London, 1995), pp. 313–23.

182 Even in the Netherlands, where political allegiance rested on very different foundations, the 'charisma' of the House of Orange served as a 'binding force' within the Dutch commonwealth that retained an enduring potency for much of the period between the revolt against Spain and the Napoleonic wars: Chapter 4, below; and Marika Keblusek and Jori Zijlmans (eds.), *Princely Display: The Court of Frederik Hendrik and Amalia van Solms* (Washington, 1998). For a more sceptical view, see Heinz Schilling, 'The Orange Court: The Configuration of the Court in an Old European Republic', in Asch and Birke, *Princes, Patronage, and the Nobility*, pp. 453–4.

183 Briggs, *Communities of Belief*, p. 229.

184 Pegge, *Curalia*, II, p. vi.

185 Briggs, *Communities of Belief*, pp. 229–30. I am grateful to Dr Duindam for pointing out to me the cultural importance of the War of the Spanish Succession in this context.

186 Drouin Regnault, 'Dissertation historique touchant le pouvoir accordé aux rois de France de guérir les écrouelles', in idem, *Historie des sacres et couronnements des nos rois* (Reims, 1722), appendix; Jeffrey W. Merrick, *The Desacralization of the French Monarchy in the Eighteenth Century* (Baton Rouge, La., and London, 1990), p. 20. There were still those, however, who maintained the king's touch was a 'miraculous power [and] a gift from heaven'; Merrick, *Desacralization*, pp. 18–20.

187 For Schönbrunn, see Raschauer, *Schönbrunn*; for Caserta, George L. Hersey, *Architecture, Poetry and Number in the Royal Palace at Caserta* (Cambridge, Mass., and London, 1983); Claudio Marinelli (ed.), *L'esercizio del disegno: i Vanvitelli. Catalogo generale del fondo dei disegni della Reggia di Caserta* (exh. cat., Rome, 1991).

188 'The pleasures of the court, [or] of what is called good taste [*bon ton*]', wrote the Marquise de Bombelle while serving at the court of Louis XVI, 'have no attraction for me, and I have too bourgeois a way of thinking for that place'. The court, she concluded, 'was a dog of a place'; quoted in C. Fairchilds, *Domestic Enemies: Servants and their Masters in Old Regime France* (Baltimore and London, 1984), p. 47.

189 Volker Bauer, *Hofökonomie: Der Diskurs über den Fürstenhof in Zeremonialwissenschaft, Hausväterliteratur und Kameralismus* (Vienna, 1997), pp. 239–90.

CHAPTER ONE

The authors wish to thank John Adamson for his kindness and patience in producing this essay.

1 Alfonso X, *Las siete partidas del Rey Alfonso el Sabio: cotejadas con varios códices antiguos* (Madrid, 1807), I, p. 56–86.

2 Alonso Nuñez de Castro, *Libro histórico político, sólo Madrid es corte y el cortesano en Madrid* (3rd ed., Madrid, 1675), I, esp. p. 5.

3 Cited in José Deleito y Piñuela, *El Rey se diviete* (Madrid, 1988).

4 Here we paraphrase the definition offered by John Adamson in Chapter 3, above.

5 Jeroen Duindam, *Myths of Power: Norbert Elias and the Early Modern European Court* (Amsterdam, 1995), p. 194.

6 Christina Hofmann, *Das Spanische Hofzeremoniell von 1500–1700* (Erlanger Historische Studien, VIII, 1985), pp. 31–2.

7 Gonçalo Fernández de Ouiedo, *Libro de la Cámara Real del Prínçipe Don Juan e officios de su casa e seruicio ordinario* (Madrid, 1870), pp. 8–10. This edition is based largely on a MS in the Escorial, though the most authoritative copy is Biblioteca Nacional, Madrid, MS 1027, a version once in the library of Philip V.

8 For this translation and others, we follow Sir John Elliott; see his seminal article, 'The Court of the Spanish Habsburgs: a Peculiar Institution?', in his *Spain and its World, 1500–1700* (London, 1989). His 'Philip IV of Spain: Prisoner of Ceremony', in A. G. Dickens (ed.), *The Courts of Europe: Politics, Patronage, and Royalty, 1400–1800* (London, 1977) offers a detailed and vivid account of the court of that reign. The only work to match his contributions is the article by Mía Rodríguez-Salgado, 'The Court of Philip II of Spain', in R. G. Asch and A. M. Birke (eds.), *Princes, Patronage, and the Nobility: The Court at the Beginning of the Modern Age, c. 1450–1650* (Oxford, 1991), pp. 205–44; and now see the essays in José Martínez Millan (ed.), *La corte de Felipe II* (Madrid, 1994). Since this essay was written, Mia J. Rodríguez-Salgado has published an important essay analysing the continuing existence of the Casa de Castilla in the later sixteenth and seventeenth centuries: 'Honour and Profit in the Court of Philip II of Spain', in Maurice Aymard and Marzio A. Romani (eds.), *La Cour comme institution économique* (Paris, 1998), pp. 67–86.

9 *Libro de la Cámara Real*, p. 5.

10 *Libro de la Cámara Real*, pp. 14–17.

11 *Libro de la Cámara Real*, pp. 25–6.

12 Teófilo Ruíz, 'Une royauté sans sacre: la monarchie castillane du bas moyen âge', *Annales*, 39 (1984), 429–53.

13 *Libro de la Cámara Real*, p. 87.

14 Informality was never precluded from court life. Queen Isabella habitually referred to her son as her angel and chastised him for filling his chests with old clothes. She advised him to share out his unwanted garments among his servants on his birthday: *Libro de la Cámara Real*, p. 61.

15 *Libro de la Cámara Real*, p. 7.

16 'Report on the manner of service in the Emperor's household': Biblioteca Nacional, Madrid, MS 1080.

17 Elliott, 'Court of the Spanish Habsburgs', p. 143.

18 Sigonney tells us (fo. 4) that his point of reference was the fifteenth-century 'Use' drawn up by the Chancellor of Burgundy, Olivier de la March, of which there are several early modern copies in the Biblioteca Nacional.

19 Biblioteca Nacional, Madrid, MS 1080, fo. 4.

20 Ibid.; Hofmann (*Das Spanische Hofzeremoniell*) concurs with Sigonney's assertion.

21 Iuan Christoual Caluete de Estrella, *El Felicissimo Viaje del muy alto y muy Poderoso Principe Don Phelippe* (Antwerp, 1552), p. 2.

22 H. Kamen, *Philip of Spain* (New Haven and London, 1997), p. 35.

23 A. Rodríguez Villa (ed.), *Etiquetas de la Casa de Austria* (Madrid, 1913), p. 13.

24 *Calendar of State Papers Spanish*, ed. G. A. Bergenroth et al. (London, 1862–1954), XIII, 9, 11.

25 Elliott, 'Court of the Spanish Habsburgs', p. 143.

26 Hofmann, *Das Spanische Hofzeremoniell*, p. 63.

27 Alfredo Alvar Ezquerra, *Felipe II, la corte y Madrid en 1561* (Madrid, 1985), p. 17, esp. n. 34.

28 James M. Boyden, *The Courtier and the King: Ruy Gómez de Silva, Philip II, and the Court of Spain* (London, 1995), pp. 15–17.

29 After all, this was precisely why he had called for a memorial to be drawn up of Prince Juan's household before all knowledge of it passed out of living memory. See Oviedo, *Libro de la Cámara Real*, p. 1.

30 In her 'Habsburg Ceremony in Spain: The Reality of the Myth', *Historical Reflections*, 15 (1988), 293–309, Professor Nader argues that no objections to Burgundian etiquette are to be found in the outward-looking Spanish society of the sixteenth century, and that they date only from the seventeenth century, when Spain's internationalism had been soured by military defeat. In support of this, she avers that 'petitions of the cortes do not record complaints about a Habsburg ceremony at the court, nor about any other aspect of courtly life except its expense' (p. 296). Professor Nader appears unaware of the extensive complaint made in 1555 (for which see below, n. 34). It is also suggested that 'the first hint of rejection' of Burgundian ritual appeared in the biography of Charles V by Prudencio de Sandoval (1605). It is claimed that although Sandoval based his account on Calvete de Estrella he inserted 'a patriotic claim that the displaced Castilian household organization should have been retained "because of its antiquity if nothing else"'. It is important to note that Sandoval's addition is but a paraphrase of the Cortes' own comments about the antiquity of Castilian royal etiquette. In the final footnote of her article, Professor Nader suggests that supporters of the reinvigorated Cortes of the nineteenth century 'invented the idea that it was the Cortes that had first complained about the introduction of the Habsburg ceremony in the sixteenth century'; the note's subsequent referral to the printed proceedings of the early modern Cortes is to passages that refer neither to nineteenth-century myth-making nor to editorial insertions.
31 Antonio Ossorio, *Vida y Hazañas de Don Fernando Álvarez de Toledo, duque de Alba*, trans. by José López de Toro (Madrid, 1945).
32 See Ossorio, *Vida*.
33 'La magestad y disciplina de los Reyes de Castilla', Ossorio, *Vida*, p. 164.
34 Ossorio, *Vida*, pp. 163–4 (emphasis added); and *Cortes de los antiguos reinos de León y de Castilla*, v (Madrid, 1903), p. 627, p. 355 (for 1548), p. 731 (for 1558).
35 Kamen, *Philip of Spain*, p. 194.
36 Biblioteca Nacional, Madrid, MS 1080, fo. 13.
37 As noted in Elliott, 'Court of the Spanish Habsburgs', p. 144.
38 Cf. *Libro de la Cámara Real*, p. 25, and the report of the Venetian Ambassador to Philip IV, *Relazioni degli ambasciatori veneti al senato*, x (Turin, 1979), 136.
39 Kamen, *Philip of Spain*, p. 31.
40 The work of Alfredo Alvar Ezquerra is definitive regarding the removal of the court to Madrid, and he clearly established that the move took place in 1561. Alvar Ezquerra, *Felipe II, la corte y Madrid*, esp. Ch. 3. Previously, the dating ranged from 1560 to 1565.
41 Ibid., p. 4.
42 Ibid., p. 5.
43 *Cortes de los antiguos reinos de León y de Castilla*, v, 731.
44 Alvar Ezquerra, *Felipe II, la corte y Madrid*, pp. 18–22.
45 Elliott, 'Court of the Spanish Habsburgs', pp. 144–5. See also C. Lisón Tolosana, 'El cronotopo ritual de Felipe II', in *Torre de los Lujanes*, 33 (1987), 71–80, at p. 74.
46 Nuñez de Castro, *Sólo Madrid es corte*, p. 217.
47 Deleito y Piñuela, *El Rey se divierte*, p. 142.
48 Gascón de Torquemada, *Gaçeta*, pp. 148–9; and José Martínez Millán, 'Familia real y grupos políticos: la princesa doña Juana de Austria (1535–73)', in his *La corte de Felipe II*, pp. 73–105.
49 He wrote to his daughters that 'they want me to dress in brocade, much against my wishes'; Kamen, *Philip of Spain*, p. 245.
50 Alvar Ezquerra, *Felipe II, la corte y Madrid*, p. 16.
51 Entry into Madrid came to have a special significance for Habsburg consorts: a new wife could not undertake royal duties before her formal *entrada* into the court as queen, so her marriage had to be solemnized in a city other than Madrid; see Hofmann, *Das Spanische Hofzeremoniell*, p. 159.
52 J. H. Elliott, 'Power and Propaganda in the Spain of Philip IV', in his *Spain and its World*, pp. 165–7.
53 Rodríguez-Salgado, 'Court of Philip II', p. 213.

54 B. Perreño, *Dichos y hechos del Rey D. Felipe II* (Madrid, 1941), pp. 295–6.
55 We are grateful to Professor Jeremy Lawrance for this information.
56 On 5 January that year, the Count-Duke of Olivares wrote to say that the count would be welcome to dine with the king the following day. What is interesting is that the count did not view this so much as granting him privileged access to the king as giving him the opportunity of penetrating the inner recesses of the court, and there bending the ear of the favourite; Trevor Dadson, 'Diego de Silva y Mendoza, Conde de Salinas (1564–1630), y el arte de la supervivencia política', *Studia Aurea: Actas del III Congreso de la AISO*, I (Toulouse and Pamplona 1996), pp. 309–17, esp. 314–5.
57 Deleito y Piñuela, *El Rey se divierte*, p. 104.
58 Gascón de Torquemada, *Gaçeta*, pp. 148–9.
59 Rodríguez-Salgado, 'Court of Philip II', p. 241; see also Alvar Ezquerra, *Felipe II, la corte y Madrid*, pp. 72–3.
60 Kamen, *Philip of Spain*, p. 231.
61 We owe this reference to the generosity of Professor Geoffrey Parker.
62 Fernando Checa, *Tiziano y la Monarquía Hispánica. Usos y funciones de la pintura veneciana en España* (Madrid, 1994), and idem, *Felipe II: mecenas de las artes* (Madrid, 1992).
63 See M. Kusche, 'La antigua galeria de retratos del Pardo: su reconstrucción arquitectónica y el orden de colocación', *Archivo Español de Arte*, 64 (1991), 253, 1–28; idem, 'La antigua galeria de retratos de El Pardo: su reconstrucción pictórica', *Archivo Español de Arte*, 65 (1992), 261–92.
64 Elliott, 'Power and Propaganda in the Spain of Philip IV', pp. 162–88.
65 According to José Simón Diaz; see Elliott, 'Court of the Spanish Habsburgs', p. 156.
66 Gérard, 'Los sitios de devoción del Alcázar de Madrid', p. 278.
67 R. A. Stradling, *Philip IV and the Government of Spain* (Cambridge, 1988), p. 343.
68 Gérard, 'Los sitios de devoción del Alcázar de Madrid', pp. 275–284. Ms. Juliet Glass is working on Habsburg ceremonial and I am indebted to her for discussions of the role of the *cortina*. It is unclear to me whether this was a Burgundian import, possibly dating from 1506, when Philip the Fair tried to introduce a Burgundian-style chapel, because there is an earlier mention of a screen in Prince Juan's household, *Libro de la Cámara Real*, p. 72. The *cortina* was operated by the groom of the curtain; see Hofmann, *Spanische Hofzeremoniell*, p. 64.
69 Quoted in Stradling, *Philip IV*, p. 343.
70 Henry Kamen, *The Spanish Inquisition* (London, 1965), pp. 191–2.
71 Our view of Lerma, and the office of *valido* in general, has been revolutionized by Antonio Feros; in particular, see his 'Twin Souls: Monarchs and Favourites in Early Seventeenth-Century Spain, in Richard L. Kagan and Geoffrey Parker (eds.), *Spain, Europe and the Atlantic World* (Cambridge, 1995).
72 Quoted in Feros, 'Twin Souls', p. 38.
73 John Lynch, *The Hispanic World in Crisis and Change, 1598–1700* (Oxford, 1992), p. 19.
74 It has been estimated the city council spent more on royal visits than on any other item, apart from recurrent purchases of wheat and the expenditure which followed the great fire of 1561. A. Cabeza Rodríguez, M. Torremocha, R. Martín de la Guardia, 'Fiesta y política en Valladolid. La entrada de Felipe III en el año 1600', *Investigaciones Históricas: época moderna y contemporánea*, 16 (1996), 77–87.
75 Jonathan Brown and J. H. Elliott, *A Palace for a King: The Buen Retiro and the Court of Philip IV* (New Haven and London, 1986).
76 Elliott, 'Power and Propaganda in the Spain of Philip IV', pp. 167–9; Brown and Elliott, *A Palace for a King*, p. 217.
77 'Ein grosses und prunkvolles Gefängnis': see Ludwig Pfandl, *Philipp II* (Munich, 1938), pp. 138ff.
78 Nuñez de Castro, *Libro histórico político*, p. 194.

CHAPTER TWO

1 The only general survey is the pioneering study by J. F. Solnon, *La Cour de France* (Paris, 1987); apart from the *Dictionnaire du grand siècle*, ed. F. Bluche (Paris, 1990), there is now much to be learned from the articles in the recent *Dictionnaire de l'ancien régime*, ed. L. Bély (Paris, 1996), especially those by L. Bély, Y.-M. Bercé, J. Chagniot, J.-F. Labourdette, O. Poncet, R. Oresko and J. F. Solnon. See also J. Boucher, *La Cour d'Henri III* (Rennes, 1986); R. Hatton, 'Louis XIV: at the Court of the Sun King', in A. G. Dickens (ed.), *The Courts of Europe: Politics, Patronage and Royalty, 1400–1800* (New York, 1977), pp. 233–61; and M. Antoine, *Louis XV* (Paris, 1989), pp. 211–26. More readily available is J. Levron, *La Vie quotidienne à la cour de Versailles aux XVIIe et XVIII siècles* (Paris, 1984).

2 O. Chaline, 'Combien de royaumes nous ignorent? La Cour dans l'historiographie française', in *Annali di Storia Moderna e Contemporanea*, 2 (1996), 384–92.

3 The idea advanced by Jacques Revel in 'La Cour', in P. Nora (ed.), *Les Lieux de mémoire: III, Les France. 2, Traditions* (Paris, 1992), p. 135.

4 The brilliance of Louis's reign poses two challenges: to remember that the court existed both before and after him, and to speak of Louis himself in a balanced fashion. Louis and the artists with whom he surrounded himself largely succeeded in removing the court from the realm of historical time, although the history of the court cannot in reality be confined to the years 1660–1715, nor to the palace of Versailles. French historians have had great difficulty in doing justice to Louis. Like the writers of memoirs before them, they have opted either for bitter criticism or for absurd encomium. Among the memoirs from Louis's court one must mention first the Duc de Saint-Simon's *Mémoires*, ed. A. de Boislisle, 44 vols. (Paris, 1879–1930), profoundly hostile to the king, and based in part on the *Journal* of the Marquis de Dangeau, 9 vols. (Paris, 1854–60). More moderate views are found in the *Mémoires du marquis de Sourches sur le règne de Louis XIV*, ed. G. de Cosnac and E. Pontal, 13 vols. (Paris, 1882–93). Nor should we overlook the king's own *Mémoires*, ed. J. Longnon (Paris, 1978). An outsider's view can be found in E. Spanheim, *Relation de la cour de France en 1690*, ed. C. Schefer (Paris, 1882).

5 For the first decade of the eighteenth century see E. Le Roy Ladurie, 'Rangs et hiérarchie dans la vie de cour', in K. M. Baker (ed.), *The French Revolution and the Creation of Modern Political Culture: I. The Political Culture of the Old Regime* (Oxford, 1987), pp. 61–75. See also H. Brocher, *A La Cour de Louis XIV: le rang et l'étiquette sous l'ancien régime* (Paris, 1934).

6 Unlike the House of Habsburg, the Bourbons rarely furnished recruits to the Church. Between the Cardinal de Bourbon at the end of the sixteenth century and Madame Louise, daughter of Louis XV, a Carmelite nun in the later eighteenth, there were no royal recruits to the Church.

7 R. E. Giesey, *The Royal Funeral Ceremony in Renaissance France* (Geneva, 1960); French trans., *Le Roi ne meurt jamais: les obsèques royales dans la France de la renaissance* (Paris, 1987).

8 There is a new and valuable study by Katia Béguin, *Les Princes de Condé: Rebelles, courtisans et Mécènes dans la France du Grand Siècle* (Seyssel, 1999).

9 J. Boucher, 'L'évolution de la Maison du Roi: des derniers Valois aux premiers Bourbons', *XVIIe Siècle*, 137 (1982), 359–79; E. Griselle, *Etat de la maison du roi Louis XIII…1601–1665* (Paris, 1912), gives details of the composition of other households. For the following century there are the less detailed *Almanachs*.

10 *Versailles et les tables royales en Europe, XVIIe–XIX siècles*, exh. cat. (Versailles, 1993), esp. B. Saule, 'Tables royales à Versailles, 1682–1789', pp. 41–68.

11 For the hunt see P. Salvadori, *Chasseurs d'ancien régime* (Paris, 1996).

12 J. Chagniot, in *Dictionnaire de l'ancien régime*, pp. 783–4.

13 M. Benoit, *Versailles et les musiciens du roi, 1661–1733*, 2 vols. (Paris, 1971).

14 For the queen's Household in the time of Marie de Médicis, see L. Batiffol, *La Vie intime d'une reine de France au XVIIe siècle* (Paris, 1906), pp. 134–91.

15 See, for example, D. Parrott, 'A "prince souverain" and the French crown: Charles de Nevers, 1580–1637', in R. Oresko, G. C. Gibbs and H. M. Scott (eds.), *Royal and Republican Sovereignty in Early Modern Europe, c.1450–1650* (Cambridge, 1997), pp. 149–87.

16 For the du Plessis in the later sixteenth century, see Joseph Bergin, *The Rise of Richelieu* (New Haven and London, 1991; French trans., Paris, 1994).

17 K. Malettke, 'The crown, *ministériat* and nobility at the court of Louis XIII', in R. G. Asch and A. M. Birke (eds.), *Princes, Patronage, and the Nobility: The Court at the Beginning of the Modern Age* (Oxford, 1991), pp. 415–39.

18 Madame de Motteville, *Mémoires* (Paris, 1831; Collection de Mémoires de l'Histoire de France, 24), pp. 50–55.

19 H. Duccini, *Concini: grandeur et misère du favori de Marie de Médicis* (Paris, 1991).

20 G. Chaussinand-Nogaret, *La Vie quotidienne des femmes du roi, d'Agnès Sorel à Marie-Antoinette* (Paris, 1990), and S. Bertière, *Les Reines de France au XVIIe siècle* (Paris, 1996).

21 J. M. Constant, *Les Conspirateurs: le premier libéralisme politique sous Richelieu* (Paris, 1987); and A. Jouanna, *Le Devoir de révolte: la noblesse française et la construction de l'état moderne* (Paris, 1989).

22 M. Antoine, 'La monarchie française de François Ier à Louis XVI', in E. Le Roy Ladurie (ed.), *Les Monarchies* (Paris, 1986), pp. 185–208; and *Le Conseil du Roi sous le règne de Louis XV* (Geneva, 1970). See also his *Le Gouvernement et l'administration sous Louis XV: dictionnaire biographique* (Paris, 1978).

23 D. Dessert, *Argent, pouvoir et société au grand siècle* (Paris, 1984), esp. pp. 311–68. For the first half of the century see F. Bayard, *Le Monde des financiers au XVIIe siècle* (Paris, 1988).

24 This is the irresistible and thought-provoking question which arises from reading Dessert, *Argent, pouvoir et société*, p. 362. In its apparent political defeat, the élite was in fact financially triumphant.

25 J. Bergin, *The Making of the French Episcopate, 1589–1661* (New Haven and London, 1996).

26 J. Boutier, A. Dewerpe and D. Nordmann, *Un Tour de France royal: le voyage de Charles IX, 1564–1566* (Paris, 1984).

27 Louis XIV, *Manière de montrer les jardins de Versailles*, ed. S. Hoog (Paris, 1982), pp. 19–20.

28 J. F. Dubost, *La France italienne: XVIe et XVIIe siècles* (Paris, 1997).

29 M. Laurain-Portemer, *Une Tête à gouverner quatre empires: études Mazarines*, 2 vols. (Nogent-le-Roi, 1997), I, pp. 745–57.

30 L. Bély, 'Souveraineté et souverains: la question du cérémonial dans les relations internationales à l'époque moderne', *Annuaire-Bulletin de la Société de l'Histoire de France* (1993), 27–43.

31 *Charles Le Brun, 1619–1690: le décor de l'Escalier des Ambassadeurs à Versailles* (exh. cat. Versailles, 1990).

32 However, for formal personal presentation to the king, the requirements in terms of noble ancestry became steadily more exacting under Louis XV: F. Bluche, *Les Honneurs de la cour* (Paris, 1957).

33 The *Mémoires* of Brantôme, and his *Dames Galantes*, paint a lively picture of court life in the later sixteenth century; see his *Oeuvres complètes*, 11 vols. (Paris, 1864–82). On duelling, see F. Billacois, *Le Duel dans la société française des XVIe–XVIIe siècles. Essai de psychosociologie historique* (Paris, 1986). For a later period there is a fine gallery of portraits in Tallemant des Réaux, *Historiettes*, ed. A. Adam, 2 vols. (Paris, 1960–61).

34 D. Potter, 'An Englishman's View of the Court of Henri III, 1584–1585: Richard Cook's *Description of the Court of France*', *French History*, 2 (1988), 312–44.

35 The *lever* is described in B. Saule, *Versailles triomphant: une journée de Louis XIV* (Paris, 1996), pp. 32–45.

36 M. McGowan, 'La fonction des fêtes dans la vie du cour au XVIIe siècle', in N. Hepp (ed.), *La Cour au miroir des mémorialistes* (Paris, 1991), pp. 27–41; M. C. Moine, *Les Fêtes à la cour du Roi Soleil, 1653–1715* (Paris, 1984); and S. du Crest, *Des Fêtes à Versailles: les divertissements de Louis XIV* (Paris, 1990).

37 M. F. Christout, *Le Ballet du cour de Louis XIV, 1643–1672* (Paris, 1967).

38 M. Fumaroli, *L'Age de l'éloquence: rhétorique et 'res literaria' de la renaissance au seuil de l'époque classique* (Geneva, 1980), pp. 233–56.

39 An account of the concept of glory can be found in O. Chaline and G. Ferreyrolles (eds.), *La Gloire dans l'Europe moderne* (Paris, 1999).

40 J. R. Armogarthe, 'Gloire du ciel, gloire des hommes', in C. Continisio and C. Mozzarelli (eds.), *Repubblica e virtù: pensiero politico e monarchia cattolica fra XVI e XVII secolo* (Rome, 1995), pp. 457–63.

41 La Bruyère, *Les Caractères*, 'De la Cour', no. 74, observes of the Chapel Royal, in which the courtiers faced each other in the stalls while between them the king faced towards the altar, 'it seems as though the people worship the prince while the prince worships God'.

42 A. Maral, 'Autour de la chapelle royal de Versailles: le cadre archéologique et institutionel de la cérémonie religieuse sous Louis XIV', *Positions de thèses des élèves de l'Ecole nationale de Chartres* (1994), pp. 129–33. P. Steib is currently engaged under the supervision of J. C. Waquet on a thesis on religious life at the court of Henri IV.

43 N. Elias, *The Court Society* (Oxford, 1983).

44 After years of a tardy and somewhat undiscriminating enthusiasm for Elias's sociological theories, it is now time for a more critical approach, in France as elsewhere, see J. Duindam, *Myths of Power: Norbert Elias and the Early European Court* (Amsterdam, 1995). The author accepts that the court was, at times, the model for 'good manners', but remains unconvinced by Elias's attempt to combine the Weberian understanding of monopoly with the Freudian concept of civilization as the repression of impulses. See also the critique of Elias in John Adamson's Introduction, above.

45 A. Couprie, 'Courtisanisme et christianisme au XVIIe siècle', *XVIIe Siècle*, 132 (1981), 369–91.

46 The atmosphere of the Catholic Reformation was favourable to the role of women in religion, and the queens and ladies of the court supported the new female orders, essentially imports from Spain and Italy.

47 A. Couprie, 'La cour et l'idéal de l'honnêteté', in J. Truchet (ed.), *Le XVIIe siècle: diversité et cohérence* (Paris, 1992), pp. 179–87. M. Fumaroli, 'La conversation', and N. Hepp, 'La galanterie', in Nora, *Les Lieux de mémoire*, III/2, pp. 679–743, 745–83.

48 O. Ranum, 'Courtesy, Absolutism and the Rise of the French State, 1630–1660', *Journal of Modern History*, 52 (1980), 426–51.

49 See P. de l'Estoile, *Mémoires-Journaux*, ed. G. Brunet et al., 3 vols. (Paris, 1875), especially the volumes from the reign of Henri III.

50 O. Chaline, 'Port-Royal et la gloire', in O. Chaline and G. Ferreyrolles (eds.), *La Gloire dans l'Europe moderne* (Paris, 1999).

CHAPTER THREE

1 For the best introductions to politics and organization of the early modern English court, see David Starkey (ed.), *The English Court from the Wars of the Roses to the Civil War* (London, 1987) and Simon Adams, 'The Court as an Economic Institution: The Court of Elizabeth I of England (1558–1603)', in Maurice Aymard and Marzio A. Romani, *La Cour comme institution économique* (Paris, 1998), pp. 127–58.

2 Statutes of the Realm, 28 Hen. 8, c. 12; Simon Thurley, *The Royal Palaces of Tudor England* (New Haven and London, 1993), p. 54.

3 British Library [hereafter BL], Lansdowne MS 736 (Survey of Whitehall, 1688–9), fo. 18; Gregorio Leti, *Del teatro Brittannico, o vero historia dello stato…della Grande Brettagna*, 2 vols. (London, 1683), I, p. 120; and Simon Thurley, *The Whitehall Palace Plan of 1670* (London Topographical Society, 1998).

4 Elizabeth I, for example, visited Windsor annually from 1563, usually in late summer, either as part of a progress, or as a refuge where 'we make our abode during plague times': warrant, 25 Feb. 1575, quoted in H. M. Colvin (ed.), *The History of the King's Works, III, 1485–1660, Part I* (London, 1975), p. 322n.

5 For an example, see W. J. Tighe, 'Country into Court, Court into Country: John Scudamore of Holme Lacy (c.1542–1623) and his

Circles', in Dale Hoak (ed.), *Tudor Political Culture* (Cambridge, 1995), pp. 157–78.

6 In practice, the number attending at any one time would have been substantially fewer, as many offices were held 'quarterly', by rotation: three months on, nine months off. I am grateful to Sir John Sainty for a discussion on this point; see also G. E. Aylmer, *The King's Servants* (rev. edn., London, 1974).

7 See, for example, the 1610 household ordinances of Henry, Prince of Wales, in *A Collection of Household Ordinances and Regulations for the Government of the Royal Household* (Society of Antiquaries of London, 1790), pp. 319–38.

8 Roy Strong, *Henry Prince of Wales and England's Lost Renaissance* (London, 1986), pp. 71–137.

9 The Household was administered by the Board of Green Cloth; see Adams, 'The Court as an Economic Institution', p. 130. For an excellent introduction to the personnel of the court departments, Penry Williams, *The Later Tudors: England, 1547–1603* (Oxford, 1995), pp. 124–35.

10 M. M. Reese, *The Royal Office of Master of the Horse* (London, 1976), pp. 128–203.

11 Edward Chamberlayne, *Angliae Notitia: or the Present State of England* (16th edn., London, 1687), Part I, p. 197.

12 Felicity Heal, *Hospitality in Early Modern England* (Oxford, 1990), Ch. 2, 'Hospitality in the Great Household'. Chamberlayne, *Angliae Notitia*, I, pp. 194–6.

13 Chamberlayne, *Angliae Notitia*, I, p. 197.

14 Bodleian Library, Oxford, [hereafter Bodl. Lib.], MS Clarendon 80, fo. 189: [Duke of Ormond] to Charles II, Dublin, 9 Sept. 1663. (I owe my knowledge of this letter to Dr Andrew Barclay.)

15 Alan Young, *Tudor and Jacobean Tournaments* (London, 1987), p. 23.

16 R. W. Hoyle, 'Introduction: Aspects of the Crown's Estate, c.1558–1640', in idem (ed.), *The Estates of the English Crown, 1558–1640* (Cambridge, 1992), Table 1.1, pp. 10–11.

17 R. Malcolm Smuts, 'Art and the Material Culture of Majesty', in idem (ed.), *The Stuart Court and Europe: Essays in Politics and Political Culture* (Cambridge, 1996), pp. 92–3; Paula R. Backscheider, *Spectacular Politics: Theatrical Power and Mass Culture in Early Modern England* (Baltimore and London, 1993), p. 13; John Ogilby, *The Entertainment of…Charles II in his Passage through the City of London to his Coronation* [1662], ed. Ronald Knowles (Binghampton, NY, 1987), p. 17.

18 Quoted in Stephen Greenblatt, 'Invisible Bullets: Renaissance Authority and its Subversion', *Glyph*, 8 (1981), 57.

19 Robert Latham and William Matthews (ed.), *The Diary of Samuel Pepys*, 11 vols. (London, 1972–83), II, p. 74.

20 Marc Bloch, *The Royal Touch: Sacred Monarchy and Scrofula in England and France* (London and Montreal, 1973), pp. 181–92.

21 BL, Add. MS 71009, fo. 16.

22 Leti, *Del Teatro Brittannico*, II, p. 541.

23 BL, Sloane MS 1494, fo. 83v; Fiona Kisby, 'The Royal Household Chapel in Early Tudor London, 1485–1547' (unpub. Ph.D. diss., University of London, 1996).

24 See BL, Sloane MS 1494, fos. 86v–87: 'Observations for St George's Feast as now it is kept, 1610'.

25 BL, Add. MS 71009, fo. 15v; BL, Sloane MS 1494 (Household orders), fo. 39v. The use of the *cortina* (or curtained booth for the king near the altar) at the sixteenth-century Castilian Chapel Royal has been studied by Juliet Glass of Johns Hopkins University, to whom I am grateful for information on this subject.

26 Peter McCullough, *Sermons at Court: Politics and Religion in Elizabethan and Jacobean Preaching* (Cambridge, 1998), pp. 11–42.

27 BL, Add. MS 71009, fo. 15; Chamberlayne, *Angliae Notitia*, I, pp. 135–6.

28 Chamberlayne, *Angliae Notitia*, I, p. 136; Samuel Pegge, *Curalia: or an Historical Account of Some Branches of the Royal Household* 3 parts (London, 1791), I, p. 21n.

29 BL, Add. MS 71009, fo. 12; see also 'Ritus celebrandi Missam', in *Missale Romanum ex Decreto…Concilii Tridentini Restitutum* (Salamanca, 1688), sig. C5[v].

30 BL, Sloane MS 1494, fos. 11–13, 'The ancient order of the Kings dyning abroad in State'.

31 BL, Harl. MS 4931, fo. 8; Kevin Sharpe, 'The Image of Virtue: The Court and Household of Charles I', in Starkey, *The English Court*, p. 243.

32 BL, Stowe MS 562, fos. 3v, 5v; Thomas Birch (ed.), *The Court and Times of Charles I*, 2 vols. (London, 1848) I, p. 24: Joseph Mede to Sir Martin Stuteville, 25 July 1629.

33 BL, Sloane MS, 1494, fo. 16. Cf. M. St Claire Byrne (ed.), *The Lisle Letters*, 6 vols. (London and Chicago, 1981), V, pp. 468–525, 262–75.

34 BL, Sloane MS 1494, fo. 16.

35 For the Jacobean revival, see *Calendar of State Papers, Venetian, 1603–7*, p. 46; E. K. Chambers, *The Elizabethan Stage*, 2 vols. (Oxford, 1923), I, p. 15.

36 G. R. Potter and E. M. Simpson, *The Sermons of John Donne*, 10 vols. (Berkeley, 1953–62), I, p. 223.

37 C[alybute] D[owninge], *A Discourse of the State Ecclesiasticall of this Kingdome* (Oxford, 1633), p. 46.

38 John Guy, 'The Rhetoric of Counsel in Early Modern England', in Hoak, *Tudor Political Culture*, pp. 292–310.

39 Colvin, *History of the King's Works*, V, p. 183.

40 Both quoted in G. W. Groos (ed.), *The Diary of Baron Waldstein: A Traveller in Elizabethan England* (London, 1981), p. 42n.

41 For Whitehall, Colvin, *History of the King's Works*, III, p. 130; IV, p. 329; for Salisbury, see Lawrence Stone, *Family and Fortune: Studies in Aristocratic Finance in the Sixteenth and Seventeenth Centuries* (Oxford, 1973), p. 91.

42 R. Malcolm Smuts, 'The Court and its Neighbourhood: Royal Policy and Urban Growth in the Early Stuart West End', *Journal of British Studies,* 30 (1991), 117–49.

43 Donald King, 'Textile Furnishings [of Charles I]', in Arthur MacGregor (ed.), *The Late King's Goods: Collections, Possessions, and Patronage of Charles I in the Light of the Commonwealth Sale Inventories* (London and Oxford, 1989), p. 313.

44 For James and Mortlake, see David Howarth, *Images of Rule: Art and Politics in the English Renaissance, 1485–1649* (London, 1997), p. 254; for the estimate of Charles I's expenditure I am indebted to Dr Thomas Campbell, of the Metropolitan Museum of Art, New York.

45 Alvin Kernan, *Shakespeare, the King's Playwright: Theater in the Stuart Court, 1603–13* (New Haven and London, 1995).

46 Anne Barton, *Ben Jonson: Dramatist* (Cambridge, 1984); Blair Worden, 'Ben Jonson among the Historians', in Kevin Sharpe and Peter Lake (eds.), *Culture and Politics in Early Stuart England,* (London, 1994), pp. 67–89; Kevin Sharpe, *Criticism and Compliment: the Politics of Literature in the England of Charles I* (Cambridge, 1987), pp. 136–9, 162–5, 176.

47 I owe this point to Dr David Starkey; see his 'Intimacy and Innovation: The Rise of the Privy Chamber, 1485–1547', in idem, *The English Court*, pp. 74–5.

48 Diarmaid MacCulloch, *Thomas Cranmer: A Life* (New Haven and London, 1996), p. 275; see also David Starkey, *Henry VIII: Personalities and Politics* (London, 1985), pp. 129–33.

49 John Murphy, 'The Illusion of Decline: The Privy Chamber, 1547–58', in Starkey, *The English Court*, p. 130.

50 Pam Wright, 'A Change in Direction: The Ramifications of a Female Household, 1558–1603', in Starkey, *The English Court*, pp. 150, 152. For an important revision, see Stephen Alford, *The Early Elizabethan Polity* (Cambridge, 1998).

51 Simon Adams, 'Eliza Enthroned? The Court and its Politics', in Christopher Haigh (ed.), *The Reign of Elizabeth I* (London, 1985), pp. 55–77; and idem, 'Favourites and Factions at the Elizabethan Court', in Ronald G. Asch and Adolf M. Birke (eds.), *Princes, Patronage, and the Nobility: The Court at the Beginning of the Modern Age, c.1460–1650* (Oxford, 1991), pp. 265–87.

52 Wright, 'A Change in Direction', p. 170.

53 Sir Robert Naunton, *Fragmenta Regalia: or Observations on Queen Elizabeth: Her Times and Favourites*, ed. John S. Cerovski (Washington, 1985), p. 69.

54 Christopher Haigh, *Elizabeth I* (London, 1988), p. 87; and Simon Adams, 'La noblesse et la cour sous Elisabeth, in André Stegmann (ed.), *Pouvoir et institutions en Europe au XVIe siècle* (Paris, 1987).

55 Mervyn James, 'At the Crossroads of the Political Culture: The Essex Revolt, 1601', in idem, *Society, Politics and Culture: Studies in Early Modern England* (Cambridge, 1986), pp. 416–65.

56 Keith Brown, 'The Scottish Aristocracy, Anglicization, and the Court, 1603–38', *Historical Journal,* 36 (1993), 543–76.

57 Philippa Glanville, 'The Court Plate of James I', in *Sotheby's Art at Auction, 1990–91* (London, 1991), pp. 17–23; eadem, *Silver in Tudor and Early Stuart England: A Social History and Catalogue of the National Collection, 1480–1660* (London, 1990).

58 Neil Cuddy, 'The Revival of the Entourage: The Bedchamber of James I, 1603–1625', in Starkey, *The English Court*, p. 188.

59 Cuddy, 'The Revival of the Entourage', p. 197.

60 Quoted in Roger Lockyer, *Buckingham: The Life and Political Career of George Villiers, First Duke of Buckingham, 1592–1628* (London, 1981), p. 209.

61 'The Journal of Sir Roger Wilbraham', *Camden Miscellany X* (London, 1902), p. 57. Taking grants of royal bounty to the peerage during the entire period between 1558 and 1641, 29 individuals received some 75 per cent of all crown gifts; of these, ten received their perquisites as members of James's Bedchamber: Cuddy, 'The Revival of the Entourage', p. 198; Lawrence Stone, *The Crisis of the Aristocracy, 1558–1641* (Oxford, 1965), pp. 470–76, 774–6.

62 Historical Manuscripts Commission, *MSS of the Duke of Portland,* IX, p. 113. (I owe my knowledge of this reference to Dr Cuddy.)

63 Linda Levy Peck, *Court Patronage and Corruption in Early Stuart England* (London, 1990).

64 Kevin Sharpe, *The Personal Rule of Charles I* (New Haven and London, 1992), pp. 209–35; Peter W. Thomas, 'Charles I: The Tragedy of Absolutism', in A. G. Dickens (ed.), *The Courts of Europe, 1400–1800* (London, 1977), pp. 191–211.

65 Elias Ashmole, *The Institution, Laws and Ceremonies of the Most Noble Order of the Garter* (London, 1672), pp. 570–72; Adamson, 'Chivalry and Political Culture in Caroline England', in Sharpe and Lake, *Culture and Politics*, pp. 165–85.

66 Conrad Russell, *Parliaments and English Politics, 1621–29* (Oxford, 1979), pp. 267–322.

67 Caroline M. Hibbard, *Charles I and the Popish Plot* (Chapel Hill, NC, 1983), Ch. 3.

68 John Adamson, 'The Baronial Context of the English Civil War', *Transactions of the Royal Historical Society*, 5th ser., 40 (1990), 93–120.

69 *A Deep Sigh Breath'd through the Lodgings at Whitehall… Deploring the Absence of the Court* ([4 October] 1642), sig. A3; quoted in Sean Kelsey, *Inventing a Republic: The Political Culture of the English Commonwealth, 1649–53* (Manchester, 1997), p. 29.

70 Scottish Record Office, Hamilton MS GD 406/1/2105: Duke of Hamilton to [Sir Robert Moray], 7 Dec. 1646; Hamilton MS GD 401/1/2239: Earl of Lauderdale to the Duke of Hamilton, 27 April 1647.

71 David Sturdy and Abigail Brueggman, 'British Gardens 1590–1740 and the Origins of the Museum', *Apollo*, Sept. 1997, pp. 3–6; Kelsey, *Inventing a Republic*, p. 31. For the Whitehall Privy Garden as part of the Privy Chamber, see Pegge, *Curalia*, p. 69.

72 Roy Sherwood, *Oliver Cromwell: King in All But Name, 1653–58* (London, 1997), pp. 50–51.

73 Roy Sherwood, *The Court of Oliver Cromwell* (Willingham, 1977).

74 Edward Hyde, Earl of Clarendon, *The Life of Edward Earl of Clarendon, Written by Himself*, 2 vols. (Oxford, 1760), I, p. 366.

75 Pepys, *Diary*, II, p. 74, entry for 13 April 1661.

76 Jane Roberts, *Royal Landscape: The Gardens and Parks of Windsor* (New Haven and London, 1997), Ch. 2.

77 R. O. Bucholz, 'Introduction' to J. C. Sainty and Bucholz (eds.), *Officials of the Royal Household, 1660–1837: Part I, Department of the Lord Chamberlain and Associated Offices* (London, 1997); A. P. Barclay, 'The Impact of King James II on the Departments of the Royal Household' (unpub. Ph.D. diss., University of Cambridge, 1993), pp. 69–71.

78 Colvin, *History of the King's Works*, V, p. 271.

79 Barclay, 'The Impact of James II', pp. 63–4.

80 John Dryden, *His Majesties Declaration Defended in a Letter to a Friend* (London, 1681); BL, Stowe MS 562 (Household Ordinances, c.1662), fo. 11.

81 BL, Stowe MS 562 (Household Ordinances, c.1662), fo. 5; see also Gregorio Leti, *Il ceremoniale historico e politico*, 6 vols. (Amsterdam, 1685), VI, p. 218.

82 BL, Stowe MS 562 (Household Ordinances, c.1662), fo. 11v.

83 Nancy Klein Maguire, 'The Duchess of Portsmouth: English Royal Consort and French Politician, 1670–85', in Smuts, *The Stuart Court and Europe*, pp. 247–73, quotation at p. 266; Leti, Il *ceremoniale historico*, VI, pp. 51–2.

84 John Ogilby, *The Entertainment of…Charles II* [1662], II, p. 186; Pepys, *Diary*, II, p. 86 and nn.

85 Keith Thomas, *Religion and the Decline of Magic: Studies in Popular Beliefs in Sixteenth and Seventeenth Century England* (London, 1971), p. 206.

86 Pepys, *Diary*, II, p. 74.

87 Bloch, *The Royal Touch*, pp. 219–20.

88 Sharpe, 'The Image of Virtue', p. 260.

89 Andrew Swatland, 'The Role of Privy Councillors in the House of Lords, 1660–81', in Clyve Jones (ed.), *A Pillar of the Constitution: The House of Lords in British Politics, 1640–1784* (London, 1989), pp. 51–77; Tony Claydon, *William III and the Godly Revolution* (Cambridge, 1996), pp. 198–9, 205–13.

90 *Claydon, William III*, pp. 76–7; Sainty and Bucholz, *Officials of the Royal Household*, p. 97 (fig. 5).

91 Groos, *Diary of Baron Waldstein*, p. 42n.

92 R. O. Bucholz, *The Augustan Court: Queen Anne and the Decline of Court Culture* (Stanford, CA, 1993); J. C. D. Clark, *Revolution and Rebellion: State and Society in England in the Seventeenth and Eighteenth Centuries* (Cambridge, 1986), p. 80 (for quotation). For the early Hanoverians, see J. M. Beattie, *The English Court in the Reign of George I* (Cambridge, 1967).

93 Average annual issues to the royal household rose steadily throughout the eighteenth century, from around £240,000 p.a. under Anne to over £430,000 under George IV: Bucholz, 'Introduction', fig. 6, p. xcviii.

94 Claydon, *William III*, pp. 3–4, 71–7, 91–100, 227–37.

CHAPTER FOUR

1 C. W. Fock, 'Teruggevonden ontwerpen voor de tapijtreeks De Nassause Genealogie', *Jaarboek Oranje-Nassau Museum* (1995), p. 39. For a general survey, see also Herbert H. Rowen, *The Princes of Orange: The Stadholders in the Dutch Republic* (Cambridge, 1988); and Marika Keblusek and Jori Zijlmans (eds.), *Princely Display: The Court of Frederik Hendrik and Amalia van Solms* (Washington, 1998).

2 Dom António was driven into exile in 1581 after a Spanish army under the Duke of Alba conquered Portugal for Philip II; but he continued to claim to be the country's legitimate ruler.

3 J. L. J. van de Kamp, *Emanuel van Portugal en Emilia van Nassau* (Assen, 1980), pp. 65–6, 199.

4 K. W. Swart, *Willem van Oranje en de Nederlandse Opstand, 1572–1584* (The Hague, 1994), pp. 149–52.

5 A. T. van Deursen, 'Maurits', in C. A. Tamse (ed.), *Nassau en Oranje in de Nederlandse geschiedenis* (Alphen aan den Rijn, 1979), pp. 86–8.

6 Ibid., 'Maurits', p. 86.

7 Van de Kamp, *Emanuel van Portugal*, pp. 187–8; P. Lekkerkerk, *Paleis Noordeinde* (Zutphen, 1991), p. 15. Dom Manoel I (c.1568–1638) was an illegitimate son, and the legal heir, of Dom António, and successor to the latter's claims to be King of Portugal.

8 J. I. Israel, *The Dutch Republic: Its Rise, Greatness, and Fall, 1477–1806* (Oxford, 1995), pp. 465–74.

9 See Heinz Schilling, 'The Orange Court: The Configuration of the Court in an old European Republic', in Ronald Asch and A. M. Birke (eds.), *Princes, Patronage, and the Nobility: The Court at the Beginning of the Modern Age, c.1450–1650* (Oxford, 1991), pp. 444–6; also Olaf Mörke, 'Souveränität und Autorität. Zur Rolle des Hofes in der Republik der Vereinigten Niederlande in der ersten Hälfte des 17. Jahrhunderts', *Rheinische Vierteljahrsblätter*, 53 (1989), 130, 133, 139.

10 Van Deursen, 'Maurits', p. 86. In this characteristic, they were like their older Catholic brother, Philips Willem, who had succeeded their father as Prince of Orange in 1584, and held the title until his own death in 1618. Philips Willem had remained a bachelor until, at the age of fifty-two, he married Eleonore Charlotte de Bourbon at Fontainebleau in 1606. J. Ph. S. Lemmink, 'Philips Willem Graaf van Buren, Prins van Oranje in Spanje 1568–1595', *Jaarboek Oranje-Nassau Museum* (1995), pp. 28–33.

11 A. C. Snoukaert, 'Voorschriften betreffende de Hofhouding van Prins Maurits', *De Nederlande Heraut*, 7 (1897), 6–8; M. E. Tiethoff-Spliethoff, 'De Hofhouding van Frederik Hendrik', *Jaarboek Orange-Nassau Museum* (1989), pp. 43–53; see also Olaf Mörke, 'De hofcultuur van het huis Oranje-Nassau in de zeventiende eeuw', in Peter te Boekhorst et al. (eds.), *Cultuur en maatschappij in Nederland, 1500–1800* (Meppel, 1992), pp. 45–9.

12 Exeter College, Oxford, MS 48 (Edward Davenant's diary), fo. 4v. (I owe this reference to the kindness of Dr Anthony Milton.)

13 Mörke, 'Hofcultuur van het huis Oranje-Nassau', pp. 54–8.

14 Martin Royalton-Kisch, *Adriaen van de Venne's Album in the Department of Prints and Drawings in the British Museum* (London, 1988), pp. 105–12.

15 Royalton-Kisch, *Adriaen van de Venne's Album*, p. 112.

16 J. I. Israel, *Dutch Primacy in World Trade, 1585–1740* (Oxford, 1989), pp. 121–56.

17 J. I. Israel, 'Adjusting to Hard Times: Dutch Art During its Period of Crisis and Restructuring (c.1621–c.1645)', *Art History*, 20 (1997), 456–83.

18 J. J. Terwen and K. A. Ottenheym, *Pieter Post, 1608–1669* (Zutphen, 1993), pp. 46–56.

19 Ibid., pp. 35–8.

20 Ibid., pp. 38–43; Lekkerkerk, *Paleis Noordeinde*, pp. 22–5.

21 Terwen and Ottenheym, *Pieter Post*, pp. 38, 42; K. Ottenheym, 'Architectuur', in J. Huisken, K. Ottenheym and G. Schwartz (eds.), *Jacob van Campen: Het klassieke ideaal in de Gouden Eeuw* (Amsterdam, 1995), pp. 174–6.

22 S. Groenveld, *Verlopendgetij: De Nederlandse Republiek en de Engelse Burgeroorlog, 1640–1646* (Dieren, 1984), p. 234.

23 P. J. Blok, *Frederik Hendrik, Prins van Oranje* (Amsterdam, 1924), pp. 188–9.

24 Ibid., p. 189; J. J. Poelhekke, *Frederik Hendrik, Prins van Oranje: Een Biografisch Drieluik* (Zutphen, 1978), p. 545.

25 Poelhekke, *Frederik Hendrik*, p. 474.

26 Blok, *Frederik Hendrik*, pp. 232–3.

27 Terwen and Ottenheym, *Pieter Post*, pp. 56–72; see also H. Peter-Raupp, *Die Ikonographie des Oranjezaal* (Hildesheim, 1980).

28 Israel, *Dutch Republic*, pp. 700–13.

29 H. H. Rowen, *John de Witt, Grand Pensionary of Holland, 1625–1672* (Princeton, NJ, 1978), pp. 380–400.

30 Ibid., pp. 442–8.

31 Lekkerkerk, *Paleis Noordeinde*, pp. 31–2.

32 K. H. D. Haley, *the British and the Dutch: Political and Cultural Relations through the Ages* (London, 1988), pp. 130–33.

33 J. I. Israel, 'The Dutch Role in the Glorious Revolution', in J. I. Israel (ed.), *The Anglo-Dutch Moment: Essays on the Glorious Revolution and its World Impact* (Cambridge, 1991), pp. 1–5, 62; idem, *Conflicts of Empires: Spain, the Low Countries and the Struggle for World Supremacy, 1585–1713* (London, 1997), pp. 361–73.

34 Israel, *Conflicts of Empires*, pp. 362–4.

35 Bob Haak, *The Golden Age: Dutch Painters of the Seventeenth Century* (London, 1984), pp. 38–46.

36 J. G. van Gelder, 'The Stadholder-King William III as Collector and "Man of Taste"', in *William and Mary and their House* (exh. cat., New York and London, 1979), p. 29.

37 Ibid., p. 32.

38 Ibid., pp. 30–32.

39 Israel, *The Dutch Republic*, pp. 991–2.

40 Van Gelder, 'Stadholder-King William III as Collector', p. 39.

41 A. J. C. M. Gabriels, 'Het hof van prins Willem V in 1768: een momentopname', *Jaarboek Oranje-Nassau Museum* (1995), pp. 109, 123.

42 G. J. Schutte, 'Willem IV en Willem V', in Tamse, *Nassau en Oranje*, pp. 209–15; Van Gelder, 'Stadholder-King William III as Collector', p. 40.

43 Schilling, 'The Orange Court', p. 454.

CHAPTER FIVE

The author wishes to thank Dr John Adamson, Brian Murphy, Dr Deborah Howard, Professor Olwen Hufton and especially to Dr Caroline P. Murphy for their help and advice.

1 The standard history of the papacy remains, Ludwig von Pastor, *The History of the Popes from the close of the Middle Ages, 1305–1800*, 40 vols. (London, 1891–1953); see also the account by Eamon Duffy, *Saints and Sinners: A History of the Popes* (New Haven and London, 1997). There is, as yet, no comprehensive study of the papal court in the early modern period. In the meantime, among the best introductions to the politics of the papal court is Wolfgang Reinhard, 'Papal Power and Family Strategy in the Sixteenth and Seventeenth Centuries', in Ronald G. Asch and A. M. Birke (eds.), *Princes, Patronage and the Nobility: The Court at the Beginning of the Modern Age c.1450–1650* (Oxford, 1991), pp. 329–56; and Gianvittorio Signorotto and M. A. Visceglia (eds.), *La corte di Roma tra cinque e seicento: 'Teatro' della politica europea* (Rome, 1998).

2 Paolo Prodi, *The Papal Prince, One Body and Two Souls: The Papal Monarchy in Early Modern Europe* (Cambridge, 1982), pp. 45–6.

3 F. Gregorovius, *Geschichte der Stadt Rom in Mittelalter vom V. bis zum XVI. Jahrhundert*, ed. W. Kampf, 4 vols. (Munich, 1978), III, pp. 3, 51.

4 Quoted in Prodi, *The Papal Prince*, p. 58.

5 The Tomb of Julius II was completed (incorporating the Moses figure) in an altered state in 1545 at San Pietro in Vincoli, the titular church that was given to Cardinal Giuliano della Rovere in 1471.

6 John W. O'Malley, *Praise and Blame in Renaissance Rome: Rhetoric, Doctrine, and Reform in the Sacred Orators of the Papal Court, c.1450–1521* (Durham, 1979).

7 Prodi, *The Papal Prince*, pp. 165–6; Garrett Mattingly, *Renaissance Diplomacy* (London, 1955).

8 Reinhard, 'Papal Power and Family Strategy', pp. 329–56.

9 Herbert Norris, *Church Vestments: Their Origin and Development* (London, 1949), p. 113.

10 For descriptions of the Roman court, see G. F. Commendone, *Discoro sopra la corte di Roma*, (1554), ed. C. Mozzarelli (Rome, 1966) and Girolamo Lunadoro, *Relatione della corte di Roma* (Padua, 1635, and numerous other editions); for a comparison with the Roman aristocracy, see Patricia Waddy, 'The Famiglia', in her *Seventeenth-Century Roman Palaces: Use and the Art of the Plan* (Cambridge, 1990).

11 For a comprehensive account of the papal administration, see Peter Partner, *The Pope's Men: The Papal Service in the Renaissance* (Oxford, 1990).

12 Léon Dorez, *La Cour du Pape Paul III* (Paris, 1932), p. 36.

13 Dorez, *La Cour du Pape Paul III*, pp. 53–63.

14 Dorez, *La Cour du Pape Paul III*, pp. 45–8.

15 Alessandro Ferrajoli, *Il ruolo della corte di Leone X, 1514–1516*, ed. Vincenzo de Caprio (Rome, 1984).

16 Dorez, *La Cour du Pape Paul III*, pp. 37–41.

17 Lunadoro, *Relatione della corte di Roma*, pp. 4–5.

18 For the master of the Sacred Hospice, see [Christophorus Marcellus], *Sacrarum Cerimoniarum sive Rituum Ecclesiasticorum Sanctae Romanae Ecclesiae* (Rome, 1560), fo. 19r–v.

19 Dorez, *La Cour du Pape Paul III*, pp. 48–52.

20 Herbert M. Vaughan, *The Medici Popes* (London, 1908), pp. 197–8.

21 The sixteenth-century meaning of the Italian word *segreto* is ambiguous; it can refer to something that is secret, private or segregated.

22 Ferrajoli, *Leone X*, pp. 558–61.

23 Vaughan, *The Medici Popes*, pp. 173–4.

24 Vaughan, *The Medici Popes*, p. 171.

25 Vaughan, *The Medici Popes*, p. 172.

26 Dorez, *La Cour du Pape Paul III*, pp. 54–8.

27 Lunadoro, *Relatione della corte di Roma*, pp. 78–9.

28 For a synthesis of these events and the numerous law suits that ensued, see Evert Volkerzs, *The Orsini Family Archive* (UCLA special collections manuscript) (Los Angeles, 1967), pp. 3–12.

29 Richard Bonney, *The European Dynastic States, 1494–1660* (Oxford, 1991), p. 479.

30 For the building history of the Vatican palaces, see Franz Ehrle and Hermann Egger, *Der Vaticanische Palast in seiner Entwicklung bis zur Mitte des XV. Jahrhunderts* (Vatican City, 1935); Deocletio Redig de Campos, *I Palazzi Vaticani* (Bologna, 1967); Carlo Pietrangeli (ed.), *Il Palazzo Apostolico Vaticano* (Florence, 1992).

31 For issues concerning the recovery of the Antique, see Roberto Weiss, *The Renaissance Discovery of Classical Antiquity* (Oxford, 1969); Howard Burns, 'Quattrocento Architecture and the Antique: Some Problems', in R. R. Bolgar (ed.), *Classical Influences on European Culture, A.D. 500–1500* (Cambridge, 1971), and Ingrid D. Rowland, *The Culture of the High Renaissance, Ancients and Moderns in Sixteenth-Century Rome* (Cambridge, 1998).

32 Peter Partner, 'The Restoration of the Papal State under Martin V', in Peter Partner, *The Papal State under Martin V: The Administration and Government of the Temporal Power in the Early Fifteenth Century* (London, 1958), pp. 42–94.

33 Leon Battista Alberti (trans. Joseph Rykwert, Neil Leach and Robert Tavernor), *On the Art of Building in Ten Books* (Cambridge, 1988), Bk. I, Ch. 10.

34 The papacy moved to Avignon in 1309, a period that came to be known as the 'Babylonian Captivity'. For a comprehensive history of the Papal Palace at Avignon, see L.-H. Labande, *Le Palais des Papes et les monuments d'Avignon au XIVe siècle*, 2 vols. (Aix and Marseilles, 1925).

35 John Shearman, 'The Chapel of Sixtus IV: The Fresco Decorations of Sixtus IV', in Carlo Pietrangeli et al. (eds.), *The Sistine Chapel: The Art, the History, and the Restoration* (New York, 1986), pp. 22–87. It sits on an earlier chapel known as the Cappella Magna or Great Chapel, which can be identified in a detail of Piero de Cosimo's painting, *The Madonna and the Sleeping Christ Child*, dating from the 1490s.

36 Shearman, 'The Chapel of Sixtus IV', p. 28.

37 For a description of the Avignon palace as Guiliano della Rovere may have known it, see Yves Renouard, *The Avignon Papacy, 1305–1403* (London, 1970); Labande, *Le Palais des Papes*.

38 For Sangallo see Gustave Clausse, *Les San Gallo: Architectes, peintres, sculpteurs, médailleurs, XVe et XVIe siècles*, 3 vols. (Paris, 1900–02); for Bramante see Arnaldo Bruschi, *Bramante architetto* (Bari, 1969); for Michelangelo, see Johannes Wilde, *Michelangelo: Six Lectures* (Oxford, 1978); for Raphael, see Roger Jones and Nicholas Penny, *Raphael* (New Haven and London, 1983).

39 [Marcellus], *Sacrarum Cerimoniarum*, fos. 44–5, 99v.

40 Later in the sixteenth century the success of this window design was popularized by the architect Sebastiano Serlio (1475–1554), who was the first to illustrate it in his *Architettura* (1537), and Andrea Palladio (1508–80), who used it extensively in his building designs. Bramante's window would even be referred to as Serliana or Palladiana, although during the early decades of the century it would have been identified as solely Bramantesca.

41 Catherine Wilkinson-Zerner, *Juan de Herrera: Architect to Philip II of Spain* (New Haven, 1993), pp. 107–8; John Summerson, *Inigo Jones* (Harmondsworth, 1966), p. 61.

42 Henry Fernández and Barbara Shapiro, 'La Scala di Bramante e Raffaello nei Palazzi Vaticani', and 'La Cordonata di Bramante e Raffaello', both in Fabrizio Mancinelli et al. (eds.), *Raffaello in Vaticano* (Milan, 1984), pp. 136–47.

43 Rolf Quednau, *Die Sala Die Costantino im Vatikanischen Palast* (Hildesheim, 1979), pp. 44–69; John Shearman, 'The Apartments of Julius II and Leo X', in Guido Cornini et al. (eds.), *Raphael in the Apartments of Julius II and Leo X* (Milan, 1993), p. 35, n. 32.

44 John Shearman, 'The Vatican Stanze: Functions and Decorations', *The Proceedings of the British Academy*, 57 (1971).

45 For a history of the Pauline Chapel, see Christoph L. Frommel, 'Antonio da Sangallos Cappella Paolina, ein Beitrag zur des Vatikanischen Palastes', *Zeitschrift für Kunstgeschichte*, Jahrgang (1964), 1–42.

46 On the history of Gian Lorenzo Bernini's design for the piazza, see Timothy K. Kitao, *Circle and Oval in the Square of St Peter's* (New York, 1974), 19–22.

47 On the Scala Regia and its history, see T. A. Marder, *Bernini's Scala Regia at the Vatican Palace: Architecture, Sculpture and Ritual* (Cambridge, 1997).

48 Jack Freiberg, *The Lateran in 1600: Christian Concord in Counter-Reformation Rome* (Cambridge, 1995).

49 Pöllnitz, *Memoirs*, II, p. 24; Hook, 'Urban VIII', pp. 219–20.

50 For a description of the Villa Madama, located on Monte Mario, and the way it may have functioned in the sixteenth century, see John Shearman, 'A Functional Interpretation of Villa Madama', *Romisches Jahrbuch für Kunstgeschichte*, 20 (1983).

51 Joseph A. Jungmann, *The Mass of the Roman Rite: Its Origins and Development*, trans. Francis A Brunner, 2 vols. (Westminster, 1992), I, pp. 135–9.

52 Jungmann, *Roman Rite*, I, p. 136. This figure excludes octaves.

53 Josepho Catalano, *Sacrarum Caeremoniarim*, 2 vols. (Rome, 1750–51); Gregory Martin, *Roma Sancta* (1581), ed. George B. Parks (Rome, 1969), p. 99.

54 Martin, *Roma Sancta*, pp. 99–100.

55 Marder, *Bernini's Scala Regia*, p. 241.

56 Joaquim Nabuco (ed.), *Le Cérémonial apostolique avant Innocent VIII: Texte du manuscrit Urbinat latin 469* (Rome, 1966), pp. 15–40

57 Prodi, *The Papal Prince*, p. 45.

58 Nabuco, *Le Cérémonial apostolique*, pp. 15–40.

59 J. O'Malley, 'Fulfilment of the Christian Golden Age under Pope Julius II: Text of a Discourse of Giles of Viterbo, 1507', *Traditio*, 25 (1969), 265–338.

60 B. Mitchell, *Italian Civic Pageantry in the Renaissance: A Descriptive Bibliography of Triumphal Entries and Selected Other Festivals for State Occasions* (Florence, 1979).

61 Nabuco, *Le Cérémonial apostolique*, 'Introduction'.

62 Prodi, *The Papal Prince*, pp. 42–3; and for a description of a procession of Corpus Christi that began in the Sala Regia, see Margaret A. Kuntz, 'Antonio da Sangallo the younger's Scala del Maresciallo: A Ceremonial Entrance to the Vatican Palace', in Renata L. Colell et al., *Pratum Romanum, Richard Krautheimer zum 100 Geburtstag* (Wiesbaden, 1997).

63 Marder, *Bernini's Scala Regia*, p. 227; see also Maurizio Fagiolo dell'Arco, *Effimero Barocco*, 2 vols. (Rome, 1977–8).

64 The processional canopy, with its royal associations, has a long history dating back to ancient Assyrian times; see 'The Imperial Ciborium', in E. Baldwin Smith (ed.), *Architectural Symbolism of Imperial Rome and the Middle Ages* (Princeton, 1956).

65 Marder, *Bernini's Scala Regia*, p. 234.

66 Geoffrey Parker (ed. and trans.), *At the Court of the Borgia, being an Account of the Reign of Pope Alexander VI written by his Master of Ceremonies Johann Burchard*, (London, 1963), pp. 138–40.

67 William Roscoe, *The Life and Pontificate of Leo the Tenth*, 2 vols. (London, 1846), I, pp. 294–5.

68 For a description of Leo X's possesso, see Francesco Cancellieri, *Storia de' solenni possessi de' Sommi Pontefici* (Rome, 1802), pp. 60–84; Marcello Fagiolo and Maria Luisa Madonna, 'Il possesso de Leone X. Il trionfo delle prospettive', in Marcello Fagiolo (ed.), *La Festa a Roma dal Rinascimento al 1870* (exh. cat., Turin, 1997), pp. 42–49.

69 For an exception, when the Emperor Charles V entered by the Porta San Sebastiano, see Maria Luisa Madonna, 'L'ingresso di Carlo V a Roma', in Fagiolo, *La Festa a Roma*, pp. 50–65.

70 [Marcellus], *Sacrarum Cerimoniarum*, fo. 113v. Marcellus is describing the usage of the papal court as it was settled by the reign of Leo X.

71 Gregorio Leti, *Il ceremoniale historico e politico*, 6 vols. (Amsterdam, 1685), VI, p. 707; [Marcellus], *Sacrarum Cerimoniarum*, fo. 113v.

72 Marder, *Bernini's Scala Regia*, p. 241; and for a brief descriptive history of the Sala Regia and its ceremonial function in the Vatican palace see Loren Partridge and Randolph Starn, 'Triumphalism and the Sala Regia in the Vatican,' in Barbara Wisch and Susan Muunshower (eds.), '*All the World's a Stage*': *Art and Pageantry in the Renaissance and Baroque* (Papers in Art History, Pennsylvania State University) 6 (University Park, 1990), pp. 22–82.

73 *Memoirs of Charles-Lewis, Baron de Pollnitz*, 2 vols. (London, 1737), II, p. 55. He describes an audience of Clement XII in 1731; but the protocol had not changed materially in two centuries. Cf. Marder, *Scala Regia*, pp. 224–6.

74 Anna Lo Bianco (ed.), *Pietro da Cortona, 1597–1669* (Milan, 1997), pp. 305–6.

75 Dorez, *La Cour du Pape Paul III*, pp. 224–32.

76 Margaret Murata, *Operas for the Papal Court, 1631–1668* (Ann Arbor, 1981).

77 Prodi, *The Papal Prince*, pp. 48–51.

78 Reinhard, 'Papal Power', p. 333.

79 See John A. F. Thomson, 'The College of Cardinals', in John A. F. Thomson, *Popes and Princes 1417–1517: Politics and Polity in the Late Medieval Church* (London, 1980), pp. 57–77.

80 Charles L. Stinger, *The Renaissance in Rome* (Bloomington, 1985), p. 95. Stinger points out that 27 of the 38 in the conclave that chose Julius II, 18 of 25 in Leo X's conclave, and 34 of 39 in Clement VII's election were Italian.

81 Prodi, *The Papal Prince*, p. 83.

82 Count d'Elici, *The Present State of the Court of Rome, Containing the Life and Characters of the late Pope Clement XI* (London, 1721), pp. xvi–xvii.

83 d'Elici, *The Present State of the Court of Rome*, pp. vi–vii.

84 G. L. Moncallero, *Il Cardinale Bernado Dovizi da Bibbiena, umanista e diplomatico, 1470–1520* (Florence, 1953).

85 Cf. R. Reinhardt, 'Köntinuität und Diskontinuität. Zum Problem der Koadjutorie mit dem Recht der Nachfolge in der früh-neuzeitlichen Germania Sacra', in J. Kunisch (ed.), *Der dynastische Fürstenstaat. Zur bedeutung von Sukzessionsordnungen für die Entstehung des frühmodernen Staates* (Berlin, 1982), pp. 115–55.

86 Giacinto Gigli, *Diario Romano, 1608–1670*, ed. Giuseppe Ricciotti (Rome, 1958), p. 264.

87 Lunadoro, *Relatione della corte di Roma*, pp. 91ff.

88 Detlef Heikamp, 'Vicende di Federigo Zuccaro', *Rivista d'Arte*, 3rd ser., 32 (1957), 175–232. I am grateful to Dr Caroline P. Murphy for this information.

89 Reinhard, 'Papal Power', p. 339.

90 Wolfgang Reinhard, *Freunde und Kreaturen. 'Verflechtung' als Konzept zur Erforschung historischer Führungsgruppen: Römische Oligarchie um 1600* (Munich, 1979).

91 Kathleen Weil-Garris and John F. D'Amico, 'The Renaissance Cardinal's Ideal Palace: A Chapter from Cortesi's *De Cardinalatu*', in Henry A. Millon (ed.), *Studies in Italian Art and Architecture 15th through 18th Centuries* (Cambridge and London, 1980), pp. 45–123; and Christoph Luitpold Frommel, *Der Römische Palastbau der Hochrenaissance*, 3 vols. (Tübingen, 1973).

92 Gregorio Leti, *Il ceremoniale historico e politico*, 6 vols. (Amsterdam, 1685), VI, p. 714; [Marcellus], *Sacrarum Cerimoniarum*, fo. 45.

93 Janet Southorn, *Power and Display in the Seventeenth Century: The Arts and their Patrons in Modena and Ferrara* (Cambridge, 1988), p. 103.

94 Gigliola Fragnito, 'Cardinal's Courts in Sixteenth-Century Rome', *Journal of Modern History*, 65 (1993), 38–39.

95 Prodi, *The Papal Prince*, pp. 88–89.

96 For Cesare Borgia, see Parker, *At the Court of the Borgia;* for della Rovere, Christine Shaw, *Julius II: the Warrior Pope* (Oxford, 1993); for the Farnese, Claire Robertson, '*Il Gran Cardinale': Alessandro Farnese, Patron of the Arts* (New Haven, 1992).

97 Reinhard, 'Papal Power', p. 334.

98 Giovanni de Luca, *Theatrum veritatis et iustitiae*, 18 vols. (Venice, 1734), XV/2, p. 242. (The work was first published in Rome, 1669–73.)

99 Prodi, *The Papal Prince*, p. 95.

100 Reinhard, 'Papal Power', pp. 335–6.

101 Reinhard, 'Papal Power', pp. 343, 347; for case studies, see Paulo Prodi, *Il Cardinale Gabriele Paleotti, 1522–1597*, 2 vols. (Rome, 1959–67); V. Reinhardt, *Kardinal Scipione Borghese (1605–1633). Vermögen, Finanzen und sozialer Aufstieg eines Papstnepoten* (Tübingen, 1984).

102 Irene Fosi, *All'ombra dei Barberini. Fedeltà e servizio nella Roma barocca* (Rome, 1997).

103 Renata Ago, *Carriera e clientele nella Roma barocca* (Rome, 1990).

104 For Urban VIII, see Judith Hook, 'Urban VIII: The Paradox of a Spiritual Monarchy', in A. G. Dickens (ed.), *The Courts of Europe: Politics, Patronage and Royalty, 1400–1800* (London, 1977), pp. 213–31.

105 Prodi, *The Papal Prince*, p. 52.

106 Duffy, *Saints and Sinners*, pp. 191, 193.

107 Pöllnitz, *Memoirs*, II, pp. 21–2.

108 Pöllnitz, *Memoirs*, II, p. 24; Hook, 'Urban VIII', pp. 219–20.

109 Antoni Maczak, *Travel in Early Modern Europe*, trans. U. Phillips (Cambridge, 1995), pp. 209–12.

CHAPTER SIX

The author wishes to express his thanks to Professor R. J. W. Evans for reading and commenting upon the first version of this text, and to Kate Delaney for correcting it. A longer version of the chapter is published in *Mitteilungen der Residenzenkommission der Göttinger Akademie der Wissenschaften* (1998).

1 Charles Patin, *Relations historiques* (Amsterdam, 1695) p. 3; *Mémoires de Charles-Louis Baron de Pöllnitz*, 2 vols. (Amsterdam, 1734), I, p. 287.

2 Casimir Freschot, *Mémoires de la Cour de Vienne* (Cologne, 1706), pp. 4–5; Johann Basilius Küchelbecker, *Allerneueste Nachricht vom Römisch-Kayserl. Hofe* (Hanover, 1732), esp. pp. 213–19. Edward Brown, *A Brief Account of Some Travels* (London, 1687), offers an exception.

3 Pöllnitz, *Mémoires*, I, p. 304.

4 The literature on the Austrian Habsburg court is meagre. Eduard Vehse, *Geschichte der deutschen Höfe seit der Reformation*, 8 vols. (Hamburg, 1851–60), and Thomas Fellner, Heinrich Kretschmayr, *Die österreichische Zentralverwaltung* (Vienna, 1907), are still indispensable. Ivan Zolger, *Der Hofstaat des Hauses Österreich* (Wiener staatswissenschaftliche Studien 14, Vienna and Leipzig, 1917), is the only extensive study focusing on the court. Among recent works, R. J. W. Evans's publications stand out: *Rudolf II and his World: A Study in Intellectual History* (Oxford, 1973); 'The Austrian Habsburgs: The Dynasty as a Political Institution', in A. G. Dickens (ed.), *The Courts of Europe: Politics, Patronage and Royalty, 1400–1800* (London, 1977), pp. 121–45; *The Making of the Habsburg Monarchy, 1550–1700: An Interpretation* (Oxford, 1979); Volker Press's works have contributed much to a better understanding of the relations between emperor and nobles throughout the Habsburg territories: 'The Habsburg Court as a Center of the Imperial Government', *Journal of Modern History*, 58 (1986), suppl., 23–45; 'Josef I. (1705–1711) – Kaiserpolitik zwischen Erblanden, Reich und Dynastie', in R. Melville and C. Sharf (eds.), *Deutschland und Europa in der Neuzeit*, 2 vols. (Stuttgart, 1988), I, pp. 277–97; 'Österreichische Grossmachtbildung und Reichsverfassung: Zur kaiserlichen Stellung nach 1648', *Mitteilungen des Instituts für österreichische Geschichtsforschung* (hereafter *MIÖG*), 98 (1990), 131–54; 'The Imperial Court of the Habsburgs: From Maximilian I to Ferdinand III, 1493–1657', in R. G. Asch and A. M. Birke (eds.), *Princes, Patronage, and the Nobility: The Court at the Beginning of the Modern Age, c.1450–1650* (Oxford, 1991), pp. 289–312; 'Kaiser und Reichsritterschaft', in R. Endres (ed.), *Adel in*

der Frühneuzeit: Ein regionaler Vergleich (Bayreuther Historische Kolloquien 5, Cologne and Vienna, 1991), pp. 163–94; 'The System of Estates in the Austrian Hereditary Lands and in the Holy Roman Empire: A Comparison', in R. J. W. Evans and T. V. Thomas (eds.), *Crown, Church and Estates: Central European Politics in the Sixteenth and Seventeenth Centuries*, (London, 1991), pp. 1–22. Hubert Ch. Ehalt, *Ausdrucksformen absolutistischer Herrschaft: Der Wiener Hof im 17. und 18. Jahrhundert* (Vienna, 1980), mainly extends Norbert Elias's model to the Austrian court. John P. Spielman, *The City and the Crown: Vienna and the Imperial Court, 1600–1740* (West Lafayette, Ind., 1993), is the most recent major contribution to the history of the court. Charles Ingrao, *The Habsburg Monarchy, 1618–1815* (Cambridge, 1994), is an excellent general introduction.

5 Zolger, *Hofstaat*, pp. 1–7.

6 Ibid., pp. 13–27; *Österreichische Zentralverwaltung*, II, pp. 100–39; see also the concise description in Rousset and Du Mont, *Le Cérémonial diplomatique des cours de l'Europe*, 2 vols. (Amsterdam and The Hague, 1739), I, pp. 679–80.

7 Spielman, *City and the Crown*, gives ample information on this aspect of the marshal's task.

8 Zolger, *Hofstaat*, pp. 56–7 gives examples; for the imperial kitchen, see Ingrid Haslinger, *Küche und Tafelkultur am Kaiserlichen Hofe zu Wien* (Bern, 1993).

9 Küchelbecker, *Allerneueste Nachricht*, pp. 159–62; E. G. Rinck, *Leopold des Grossen Röm: Kaysers wunderwürdiges Leben und Thaten* (Cologne, 1713); *Österreichische Zentralverwaltung*, II, pp. 139–236; Ehalt, *Ausdrucksformen*, pp. 56–62.

10 L. Baur, 'Berichte des Hessen-Darmstädtischen Gesandten Justus Eberhard Passer', *Archiv für Österreichische Geschichte*, 37 (1867), 273–409, esp. 308, 312, 330; Vehse, *Geschichte*, VII, pp. 28–9.

11 Paul-Joachim Henig, 'The Court of Emperor Frederick III', in Asch and Birke, *Princes, Patronage, and the Nobility*, pp. 150–51; Ehalt, *Ausdrucksformen*, pp. 214–16.

12 Spielman, *City and the Crown* p. 59; Ehalt, *Ausdrucksformen*, p. 57; Paula S. Fichtner, 'To Rule Is Not To Govern: The Diary of Maximilian II', in Solomon Wank, Heidrun Maschl, et al. (eds.) *The Mirror of History* (Santa Barbara and Oxford, 1988), p. 262, n. 30; Evans, 'Dynasty as a Political Institution', p. 123; *Österreichische Zentralverwaltung*, II, docs. 10 and 12.

13 Rinck, *Leopold des Grossen*, pp. 201–35; Küchelbecker, *Allerneueste Nachricht*, pp. 172–4.

14 Küchelbecker, *Allerneueste Nachricht*, p. 159.

15 Ehalt, *Ausdrucksformen*, pp. 57–9; Jean Bérenger, *Finances et absolutisme autrichien dans la seconde moitié du XVIIe siècle* (Paris, 1975).

16 Henry Frederick Schwarz, *The Imperial Privy Council in the Seventeenth Century* (Cambridge, Mass., 1943).

17 Harry Kühnel, *Die Hofburg zu Wien* (Graz and Cologne, 1964); and his 'Forschungsergebnisse zur Geschichte der Wiener Hofburg im 16. Jahrhundert', *Anzeiger*, 93 (1956), 255–71; 'Beiträge zur Geschichte der Wiener Hofburg im 16. und 17. Jahrhundert', *Anzeiger*, 95 (1958), 290–97; Moriz Dreger, *Baugeschichte der K. K. Hofburg in Wien bis zum XIX. Jahrhunderte* (Vienna, 1914).

18 Matthaeus Merian, *Topographia Germaniae: Österreich* (Frankfurt, 1649–56; repr. Kassel, 1963), p. 45. See also Freschot, *Mémoires,* pp. 4–5; Pöllnitz, *Mémoires*, I, p. 304; A. F. Pribram (ed.), 'Aus dem Berichte eines Franzosen über den Wiener Hof in den Jahren 1671 und 1672', *MIÖG*, 12 (1891), 270–96, 273, 295; and Alphons Lhotsky, 'Kaiser Karl VI. und sein Hof im Jahre 1712–13', *MIÖG*, 66 (1958), 52–80, 57.

19 Montesquieu, *Voyages*, in *Oeuvres complètes* (Paris, 1964), pp. 211–12; *Mes pensées*, pensée 6 and 47, in ibid., pp. 855–6; Pöllnitz, *Mémoires*, I, pp. 307–9.

20 Oskar Raschauer, *Schönbrunn: Eine denkmalkundliche Darstellung seiner Baugeschichte* (Vienna, 1960).

21 Küchelbecker, *Allerneueste Nachricht,* pp. 222–49; Elisabeth Kovacs, 'Kirchliches Zeremoniell am wiener Hof des 18. Jahrhundert im Wandel von Mentalität und Gesellschaft', *Mitteilungen des Österreichischen Staatsarchivs* (hereafter *MÖSTA*), 32 (1979), 109–42; Anna Coreth,

Pietas Austriaca: Ursprung und Entwicklung barocker Frömmigkeit in Österreich (Vienna, 1959).

22 See the unreliable *Mémoires du maréchal duc de Richelieu*, ed. M. F. Barrière, 2 vols. (Paris, 1868–9), I, p. 209; Vehse, *Geschichte*, VI, pp. 287–9.

23 'Berichte…Passer', pp. 278–9; Küchelbecker, *Allerneueste Nachricht*, pp. 257–62.

24 'Berichte...Passer', pp. 289, 370.

25 Küchelbecker, *Allerneueste Nachricht*, pp. 219–49.

26 'Berichte…Passer', p. 349. See also Zolger, *Hofstaat*, p. 90; Franz Hadamowsky, *Barocktheater am Wiener Kaiserhof: mit einem Spielplan (1625–1740)* (Vienna, 1955), p. 24.

27 Pribram, 'Berichte eines Franzosen', pp. 275, 294; Rousset, *Cérémonial diplomatique*, I, pp. 680–82; Vehse, *Geschichte*, V, pp. 156–62.

28 Lhotsky, 'Kaiser Karl VI. und sein Hof', pp. 60–61; 'Berichte…Passer', p. 375.

29 Küchelbecker, *Allerneueste Nachricht*, pp. 254–7, 262–3.

30 Oswald Redlich, 'Das Tagebuch Esaias Pufendorfs, schwedischen Residenten am Kaiserhofe von 1671 bis 1674', *MIÖG*, 37 (1917), 541–97, 568.

31 Th. G. von Karajan, 'Kaiser Leopold I. und Peter Lambeck', *Almanach der Kaiserlichen Akademie der Wissenschaften*, 18 (1868), 103–56.

32 Zolger, *Hofstaat*, pp. 153–60; Vehse, *Geschichte*, V, pp. 156–60; VI, pp. 281–303; VII, pp. 27–30.

33 Magdalena Hawlik-van de Water, *Der schöne Tod. Zeremonialstrukturen des Wiener Hofes bei Tod und Begräbnis zwischen 1640 und 1740* (Vienna, Freiburg and Basle, 1989); Liselotte Popelka, *Castrum Doloris oder 'Trauriger Schauplatz'. Untersuchungen zu Entstehung und Wesen ephemerer Architektur* (Vienna, 1994); Karl Vocelka, *Habsburgische Hochzeiten, 1550–1600. Kulturgeschichtliche Studien zur manieristischen Repräsentationsfest* (Vienna, Cologne and Graz, 1976).

34 'Berichte…Passer', p. 335.

35 Pöllnitz, *Mémoires*, I, pp. 292–3.

36 Vehse, *Geschichte*, VII, p. 287; Küchelbecker, *Allerneueste Nachricht*, p. 221.

37 *Küche und Tafelkultur*, pp. 8–19; Pöllnitz, *Mémoires*, I, pp. 290–92; Vehse, *Geschichte*, VI, pp. 289–90.

38 'Berichte…Passer', p. 337.

39 Brown, *A Brief Account*, p. 152; 'Berichte…Passer', pp. 321, 323, 337.

40 *Küche und Tafelkultur*, p. 14.

41 Rousset, *Cérémonial diplomatique*, pp. 680–81.

42 Hugh Murray Baillie, 'Etiquette and the Planning of State Apartments in Baroque Palaces', *Archaeologia*, 101 (1967), 169–99; Samuel John Klingensmith, *The Utility of Splendor: Ceremony, Social Life, and Architecture at the Court of Bavaria, 1600–1800* (Chicago, 1993).

43 Oskar Raschauer, 'Die kaiserlichen Wohn- und Zeremonialräume in der Wiener Hofburg zur Zeit der Kaiserin Maria Theresia', *Anzeiger*, 95 (1958), 283–91; Hadamowsky, *Barocktheater*, pp. 39–40.

44 'Berichte…Passer', pp. 308, 311; Freschot, *Remarques historiques et critiques*, I, pp. 110–11; idem, *Mémoires*, pp. 113–15; Pöllnitz, *Mémoires*, I, pp. 287–90.

45 Louis de Clermont-Gallerande, Comte de Cheverny (d.1722) first came to Vienna in 1673 after the death of the empress to present his condolences to Leopold; in January 1684 he returned as envoy extraordinary.

46 Saint-Simon, *Mémoires*, ed. A. de Boislisle, 41 vols. (Paris, 1879–1930), VI, pp. 369–70.

47 Pribram, 'Berichte eines Franzosen', pp. 294–5; Küchelbecker, *Allerneueste Nachricht*, pp. 250–53, 266–7; Pöllnitz, *Mémoires*.

48 'Berichte…Passer', pp. 335, 336, 348 370–71, 379.

49 Brown, *A Brief Account*, p. 152.

50 'Berichte…Passer', pp. 355–6; Lhotsky, 'Kaiser Karl VI. und sein Hof', pp. 58–9; Sebastian Brunner (ed.), *Die 'hoechst vergnueglichste Raiss' des Churfürsten Carl Albrecht von Bayern nach Mölk 1739* (Vienna, 1871), pp. 35, 40.

51 Zolger, *Hofstaat*, pp. 47–63, 79–91, 91–104.

52 Hadamowsky, *Barocktheater*, p. 24; Zolger, *Hofstaat*, p. 155.

53 Pribram, 'Berichte eines Franzosen', pp. 276–7.

54 See my critique of Norbert Elias and Jürgen von Krüdener's 'functionalist' approach, *Myths of Power: Norbert Elias and the Early Modern European Court* (Amsterdam, 1995).

55 This is masterfully described and analysed in Evans's *Making of the Habsburg Monarchy*.

56 Robert Bireley, *Religion and Politics in the Age of the Counter-Reformation: Emperor Ferdinand II, William Lamormaini S. J., and the Formation of Imperial Policy* (Chapel Hill, 1981).

57 James van Horn Melton, 'The Nobility in the Bohemian and Austrian Lands, 1620–1780', in H. M. Scott (ed.), *The European Nobilities in the Seventeenth and Eighteenth Centuries* (London, 1995), II, pp. 110–43, esp. p. 113.

58 Schwarz, *The Imperial Privy Council*, pp. 226–8; Thomas Winkelbauer, 'Krise der Aristokratie? Zum Strukturwandel des Adels in den böhmischen und niederösterreichischen Ländern im 16. und 17. Jahrhundert', *MIÖG*, 100 (1992), 328–53, esp. 349–50.

59 Klaus Müller, 'Habsburgische Adel um 1700: die Familie Lamberg', *MÖSTA*, 32 (1979), 78–108.

60 Georg Heilingsetzer, 'Prinz Eugen und die Führungsschicht der österreichischen Grossmacht 1683–1740', in Erich Zöllner and Karl Gutkas (eds.), *Österreich und die Osmanen: Prinz Eugen und seinen Zeit* (Vienna, 1988), pp. 120–37, esp. 124; Schwarz, *Imperial Privy Council*, pp. 323–5.

61 Bérenger, *Finances et Absolutisme Autrichien*; van Horn Melton, 'Nobility in the Bohemian and Austrian Lands', pp. 125–8, 133.

62 Paula Sutter Fichtner, *Ferdinand I of Austria: The Politics of Dynasticism in the Age of Reformation* (New York, 1982), pp. 28–30; Christiane Thomas, 'Von Burgund zu Habsburg: Personalpolitische und administrative Verflechtungen in den Herrschaftskomplexen des Hauses Österreich'; Elisabeth Springer and Leopold Kammerhofer, (eds.), *Archiv und Forschung: Das Haus-, Hof- und Staatsarchiv in seiner Bedeutung für die Geschichte Österreichs und Europas* (Vienna and Munich, 1993), pp. 35–48.

63 Pribram, 'Berichte eines Franzosen', p. 275; Spielman, *City and the Crown*, pp. 99, 118, 119.

64 G. von Antal, J. C. H. de Pater (eds.), *Weensche Gezantschapsberichten van 1670 tot 1720*, 2 vols. (The Hague, 1929–34), II, pp. 541–2; Lhotsky, 'Kaiser Karl VI. und sein Hof', p. 65. Hadamowsky, *Barocktheater*, p. 46.

65 Theo Gehling, *Ein europäischer Diplomat am Kaiserhof zu Wien: François Louis de Pesme, seigneur de Saint-Saphorin, als englischer Resident am Wiener Hof 1718–1727* (Bonn, 1964).

66 *Weensche Gezantschapsberichten*, I, pp. 494–9; Pribram, 'Berichte eines Franzosen', p. 277; Redlich, 'Tagebuch Esaias Pufendorfs', p. 570.

67 Gehling, *Europäischer Diplomat*.

68 Merian, *Topographia Germania*, pp. 44–5.

69 Vocelka, *Rudolf II. und seine Zeit* (Vienna, Cologne and Graz, 1985), pp. 158–9.

70 Evans, *Rudolf II and his World*; Vocelka, *Die politische Propaganda Kaiser Rudolfs II.* (Vienna, 1981); Thomas DaCosta Kaufmann, *Variations on the Imperial Theme in the Age of Maximilian II and Rudolf II* (New York and London, 1978).

71 Thomas DaCosta Kaufmann, *Court, Cloister and City: The Art and Culture of Central Europe, 1450–1800* (London, 1995), pp. 185–203.

72 Herbert Haupt, 'Kultur- und Kunstgeschichtliche Nachrichten vom Wiener Hofe Erzherzog Leopold-Wilhelms in den Jahren 1646–1654', *MÖSTA*, 33 (1980), 346–55; see also his 'Kunst- und Kultur in den Kameralzahlamtsbüchern Kaiser Karls VI.: die Jahre 1715 bis 1727', *MÖSTA*, 12 (1993), 7–186.

73 Hadamowsky, *Barocktheater*, pp. 16–17.

74 Richard Alewyn and Karl Sälzle, *Das Grosse Welttheater: Die Epoche der höfischen Feste in Dokument und Deutung* (Hamburg, 1959).

75 'Berichte…Passer', p. 321; Hadamowsky, *Barocktheater*, pp. 20, 43, 56.

76 Kaufmann, *Court, Cloister and City*, pp. 298–300.

77 Hadamowsky, *Barocktheater*; Lhotsky, 'Kaiser Karl VI. und sein Hof', p. 55.

Chapter Seven

1 For a survey with references to the most important literature, see Dieter Albrecht, in Max Spindler (ed.), *Handbuch der bayerischen Geschichte*, II, Part 2 (Munich, 1988), pp. 699ff. A good outline of the cultural and scientific aspects can be found in A. Schmid, 'Der Hof als Mäzen. Aspekte der Kunst- und Wissenschaftspflege der Münchner Kurfürsten', in V. Schubert (ed.), *Rationalität und Sentiment (Wissenschaft und Philosophie)* (St Ottilien, 1987).

2 The results are documented in H. Glaser (ed.), *Kurfürst Max Emanuel. Bayern und Europe um 1700* (Munich, 1976); and idem (ed.), *Um Glauben und Reich. Kurfürst Maximilian I. Beiträge zur Bayerischen Geschichte und Kunst, 1573–1657* (Munich, 1980).

3 On this, see V. Bauer, *Die höfische Gesellschaft in Deutschland von der Mitte des 17. bis zum Ausgang des 18. Jahrhunderts* (Tübingen, 1993).

4 E. Straub, *Repraesentatio Maiestatis oder churbaierische Freudenfeste. Die höfischen Feste in der Münchner Residenz von 16. bis zum 18. Jahrhundert* (Munich, 1969).

5 Samuel John Klingensmith, *The Utility of Splendor: Ceremony, Social Life and Architecture at the Court of Bavaria 1600–1800* (Chicago and London, 1993).

6 'Inter urbes, quae ducales Principum reges clarent amplitudine, elegantis mundicie excellit atque enitet'.

7 Berndt Ph. Baader, *Der Bayerische Renaissancehof Herzog Wilhelms V. (1568–1579). Ein Beitrag zur bayerischen und deutschen Kulturgeschichte des 16. Jahrhunderts* (Leipzig and Strasbourg, 1943).

8 J. Stockbauer, *Die Kunstbestrebungen am bayerischen Hofe unter Herzog Albrecht V. und seinem Nachfolger Wilhelm V.* (Vienna, 1874).

9 W. Boetticher, *Orlando di Lasso und seine Zeit* (Munich, 1958).

10 For a comprehensive account, see Baader, *Renaissancehof.*

11 The most recent treatments are A. Kraus, *Maximilian I. Bayerns Grosser Kurfürst* (Graz, Vienna and Cologne, 1990) and D. Albrecht, *Maximilian I. von Bayern, 1573–1651* (Munich, 1998). On his youth, see H. Dotterweich, *Der junge Maximilian. Jugend und Erziehung des bayerischen Herzogs und späteren Kurfürsten Maximilians I. von 1573 bis 1593* (Munich, 1962).

12 H. Dollinger, *Studien zur Finanzreform Maximilians I. von Bayern in den Jahren 1598–1618. Ein Beitrag zur Geschichte des Frühabsolutismus* (Göttingen, 1968).

13 A. Schmid, 'Geschichtsschreibung am Hofe Kurfürst Maximilians I. von Bayern', in H. Glaser (ed.), *Um Glauben und Reich. Kurfürst Maximilian I. Beiträge zur Bayerischen Geschichte und Kunst, 1573–1657* (Munich, 1980), pp. 330–41.

14 D. Breuer, '*Princeps* und *poeta*. Jacob Baldes Verhältnis zu Kurfürst Maximilian I. von Bayern', in Glaser, *Um Glauben und Reich*, pp. 341–53.

15 On this, see Kraus, *Maximilian*, p. 322; R. Heydenreuther, 'Der Magistrat als Befehlsempfänger. Die Disziplinierung der Stadtobrigkeit 1579 bis 1651', in R. Bauer (ed.), *Geschichte der Stadt München* (Munich, 1992).

16 M. Schattenhofer, 'München als kurfürstliche Residenzstadt', *Zeitschrift für bayerische Landesgeschichte*, 30 (1967).

17 Cited in Straub, *Repraesentatio Maiestatis*, p. 169.

18 Cited in Schattenhofer, 'München als kurfürstliche Residenzstadt', p. 1219.

19 C. Häutle (ed.), 'Die Reisen des Augsburgers Philipp Hainhofer nach Eichstädt, München und Regensburg in den Jahren 1611, 1612 und 1613', in *Zeitschrift des Historischen Vereins für Schwaben und Neuburg*, 8 (1881); see also F.V. Reber, *Kurfürst Maximilian I. als Gemäldesammler* (Munich, 1892); M. Meyer, *Geschichte der Wandteppichfabriken des wittelsbachischen Fürstenhauses in Bayern* (Munich and Leipzig, 1982); G. Goldberg, 'Dürer-Renaissance am Münchner Hof', in Glaser, *Um Glauben und Reich*, pp. 318–23; M. Bachtler, 'Goldschmiedearbeiten im Auftrag Herzog Maximilians I. von Bayern', in ibid., pp. 323–30; B. Volk-Knüttel, 'Maximilian I. von Bayern als Sammler und Auftraggeber', in H. Glaser (ed.), *Quellen und Studien zur Kunstpolitik der Wittelsbacher vom 16. bis zum 18. Jahrhundert* (Munich, 1980), pp. 83–128; and A. Schmid, 'Maximilian I. und Venedig. Ein Beitrag zur Hofkultur des Frühabsolutismus', in B. Roeck, K. Bergdolt, A. J. Martin (eds.), *Venedig und Oberdeutschland in der Renaissance. Beziehungen zwischen Kunst und*

Wirtschaft (Sigmaringen, 1993).

20 R. von Bary, *Henriette Adelaide von Savoyen, Kurfürstin von Bayern* (Munich, 1980).

21 See Straub, *Repraesentatio Maiestatis*, p. 21.

22 P. Volk, 'Die bildende Kunst am Hofe Max Emanuels', and U. Krempel, 'Max Emanuel als Gemäldesammler', in Glaser, *Kurfürst Max Emanuel*, pp. 125–42, 221–39.

23 Bauer, *Die höfische Gesellschaft in Deutschland*, p. 121. For an analysis of the Bavarian court under Max Emanuel that draws closely on the arguments of Norbert Elias but tends towards over-abstraction, see Jürgen von Krüdener, 'Hof und Herrschaft im Absolutismus – und in Bayern unter dem Kurfürsten Max Emanuel', in Glaser, *Kurfürst Max Emanuel*, pp. 113–24.

24 Straub, *Repraesentatio Maiestatis*, p. 43; cf. P. C. Hartmann, 'Luxuseinkäufe des Münchner Hofes in Paris', *Francia*, 1 (1972), 350–60; idem, 'Zur Ökonomie des höfischen Luxus in Frankreich und Kurbayern', in Pankraz Fried, Walter Ziegler (eds.), *Festschrift für Andreas Kraus zum 60 Geburtstag* (Kallmünz, 1982).

25 Cited in Krüdener, 'Hof und Herrschaft im Absolutismus', p. 124.

26 On Karl Albrecht, see P. C. Hartmann, *Karl Albrecht-Karl VII.: Glücklicher Kurfürst, unglücklicher Kaiser* (Regensburg, 1985).

27 Figures given in M. Lanzinner, *Fürst, Räte und Landstände. Die Entstehung der Zentralbehörden in Bayern, 1511–1598* (Göttingen, 1980), p. 22.

28 R. A. Müller, *Der Fürstenhof in der Frühen Neuzeit* (Munich, 1995), p. 30, calculates that the Viennese court establishment numbered around 530 persons in 1576.

29 Standard editions in A. Kern (ed.), *Deutsche Hofordnungen des 16. und 17. Jahrhunderts*, 2 vols. (Berlin, 1905–7), and H. Föringer, 'Anordnungen über den Hofhaushalt in München im 16. Jahrhundert', *Oberbayerisches Archiv*, 31 (1871), 238–63; important material can also be found in M. J. Neudegger, *Die Hof- und Staatspersonaletats der Wittelsbacher in Bayern, vornehmlich im 16. Jahrhundert* (Munich, 1889), Lanzinner draws on unpublished material to offer a more extensive analysis. See also F. Kramer, 'Zur Entstehung und Entwicklung von Hofordnungen am Münchner Hof in der zweiten Hälfte des 16. Jahrhunderts', in H. Kruse and W. Paravicini, *Europäische Hofordnungen des Mittelalter und der Frühen Neuzeit* (Sigmaringen, 1998) pp. 383–399.

30 R. Heydenreuther, *Der Landesherrliche Hofrat unter Herzog und Kurfürst Maximilian I. von Bayern, 1598–1651* (Munich, 1981). On the partial overlap between the court and the state administration, see also D. Stievermann, 'Southern German Courts around 1500', in R. G. Asch and A. M. Birke (eds.), *Princes, Patronage and Nobility: The Court at the Beginning of the Modern Age, c.1450–1650* (Oxford, 1991), pp. 157–72.

31 Heydenreuther, *Der Landesherrliche Hofrat*, p. 44.

32 Ibid., p. 23.

33 Lanzinner, *Fürst, Räte und Landstände*, p. 23.

34 Ibid., p. 45.

35 Cited in ibid., p. 53.

36 On the seventeenth and eighteenth centuries, see also the references in Schattenhofer, 'München als kurfürstliche Residenzstadt', pp. 1229ff.

37 According to Lanzinner (*Fürst, Räte und Landstände*, p. 22), the size of the court household was 711 in 1573, 754 in 1586, and 700 in 1591.

38 H. Föringer, 'Hofstat oder Beschreibung aller unnd jeder der frstl. drtl. Unnsers genedigsten herrn herzog Maximilian in Mayern etc. hoher unnd anderer Offizier unnd Diener etc…anno 1615', *Oberbayerisches Archiv*, 31 (1871), 238–63.

39 L. Hüttl, *Max Emanuel, der Blaue Kurfürst, 1679–1726. Eine politische Biographie* (Munich, 1976), p. 572, reports (without citing a source) a total of 450 persons at the end of the war. See also Klingensmith, *The Utility of Splendor*, p. 14.

40 Krüdener, 'Hof und Herrschaft', p. 120.

41 All figures taken from Klingensmith, *The Utility of Splendor*, p. 14.

42 See for example Müller, *Fürstenhof*, p. 30.

43 M. H. Dausch, 'Zur Organisation des Münchner Hofstaats in der Zeit von Albrecht V. bis zu Kurfürst Maximilian' (Ph.D. diss., Munich, 1944). See also Heydenreuther, 'Der Landesherrliche Hofrat', pp. 42ff, quotation at p. 49.

44 Dausch, 'Zur Organisation des Münchner Hofstaats', pp. 148ff.; on the court service of noblewomen in the household of the duchess, see also M. Ksoll, *Die wirtschaftlichen Verhältnisse des bayerischen Adels, 1600–1679* (Munich, 1986), pp. 53ff; idem, 'Der Hofstaat der Kurfürstin von Bayern zur Zeit Maximilians', *Zeitschrift für bayerische Landesgeschichte*, 52 (1989), 59–69.

45 Klingensmith, *The Utility of Splendor*, pp. 8ff.

46 J. Turmair (Aventin), *Sämtliche Werke*, 6 vols. (Munich, 1880–1908), IV, Part 2, p. 43.

47 Evidence for the sixteenth century is in Lanzinner, *Fürst, Räte und Landstände*, pp. 198, 202.

48 See Heydenreuther, *Der Magistrat*, pp. 198ff.

49 See Ksoll, *Die wirtschaftlichen Verhältnisse des bayerischen Adels*, pp. 48ff.

50 B. Stenger, 'Fürstliche Stadt München (1530) – Fürstliche Hauptstadt (1575): Ein sozialtopographischer Beitrag zur Geschichte Münchens im 16. Jahrhundert', *Blätter für deutsche Landesgeschichte*, 123 (1987), 127ff.

51 Schattenhofer, *Residenzstadt*, p. 1211.

52 Kramer, 'Zur Entstehung und Entwicklung von Hofordnungen'; Lanzinner (*Fürst, Räte und Landstände*, p. 148) mentions, for example, the particular role of the Habsburg court at Graz in the further refinement of the Spanish-Burgundian court ceremonial in Munich during the 1680s which can be traced in the correspondence between Duke Wilhelm V and his sister, Maria, who was married to Archduke Karl II of Inner Austria.

53 See for example Lanzinner, *Fürst, Räte und Landstände*, p. 232.

54 On the Spanish court ceremonial in general, see C. Hofmann, *Das Spanische Hofzeremoniell, 1500–1700* (Frankfurt and Bern, 1985).

55 On this, see Klingensmith, *The Utility of Splendor*, pp. 155ff.

56 For the Ritterstube and its various functions, see below.

57 Klingensmith, *The Utility of Splendor*, pp. 159ff.

58 See Adalbert Prinz von Bayern, *Als die Residenz noch Residenz war* (Munich, 1967); also Klingensmith, *The Utility of Splendor*, pp. 19ff.

59 H. H. Stierhof, 'Zur Baugeschichte der Maximilianischen Residenz', in Glaser, *Um Glauben und Reich*, pp. 269–278.

60 P. Diemer, 'Einrichtung und Ausbau der Kammergalerie Maximilians I. von Bayern', in Glaser, *Quellen und Studien*, pp. 129–174.

61 In 1611, the Augsburger Philipp Hainhofer, who served the Bavarian duke as his art agent, left a vivid description of the regulation of access to Maximilian's quarters: 'One proceeds to His Highness through two rooms. In the first 100 lackeys are seated on two sides with halberds in long, Old German trousers in blue and white and in short jackets, also decorated in blue and white stripes. In the other room (in the upper part of which various episodes of Bavarian history are depicted in paint) there are 100 guards on two sides with partizans in their hands…From this room, one enters into a great hall, the Ritterstube, in which there is a fine oven, also the long table under the baldachin at which His Highness dines'; see C. Häutle (ed.), 'Die Reisen des Augsburgers Philipp Hainhofer', pp. 59ff. The Ritterstube, in the sense of a generic space performing the same functions, could also be found at the Viennese Hofburg, and probably at all major German courts; Klingensmith, *The Utility of Splendor*, p. 129.

62 Klingensmith, *The Utility of Splendor*, p. 35.

63 Ibid., p. 38; see also Daniel Chapuzeau, *Relation de l'estat présent de la maison électorale et de la cour de Bavière* (Paris, 1673), and Ranuccio Sforza Pallavivino, *I trionfi dell'architectura nella sontuosa Residenza di Monaco* (Munich, 1667).

64 Cited in K. Gallas, *München. Von der welfischen Gründung Heinrichs des Löwen bis zur Gegenwart: Kunst, Kultur, Geschichte* (Munich, 1978), p. 175.

65 Saint-Simon, *Mémoires*, ed. Arthur de Boislisle (Paris, 1879), I, p. 71.

66 Straub, *Repraesentatio Maiestatis*, p. 271.

67 The ordinance is transcribed in Klingensmith, *The Utility of Splendor*, p. 222. The wording of art. 21 suggests that the practice of conceding access to court members without title or of lower rank was a novelty: 'Although his electoral Highness has gracefully allowed those gentlemen and persons of noble estate who, although they are not electoral chamberlains, are nonetheless permitted to enter the electoral antechambers to frequent the so-called *appartements* as well, they should nevertheless refrain not only from participating in games, but also from entering the innermost chamber where the highest sovereign persons are accustomed to play'.

68 Klingensmith, *The Utility of Spendor*, p. 174.

69 G. Hojer, 'Die Münchner Residenzen des Kurfürsten Max Emanuel: Stadtresidenz München, Lustheim, Schleissheim, Nymphenburg', in Glaser, *Kurfürst Max Emanuel*, pp. 147–70.

70 Häutle, 'Die Reisen des Augsburgers Philipp Hainhofer', p. 129.

71 Klingensmith, *The Utility of Splendor*, p. 70.

72 Häutle , 'Die Reisen des Augsburgers Philipp Hainhofer', p. 277.

73 Straub, *Repraesentatio Maiestatis*, p. 246 with references.

74 Klingensmith, *The Utility of Splendor*, p. 76.

75 A wooden model dating from 1725 shows that Effner was reluctant to relinquish the (ultimately) unrealized plan to construct a three-winged complex.

76 G. Imhof, *Der Schleissheimer Schlossgarten des Kurfürsten Max Emanuel. Zur Entwicklung der barocken Gartenkunst am Münchner Hof* (Munich, 1978).

77 Among the rare examples of contemporary bathing pavilions, Klingensmith mentions the Residence of Saverne designed by Robert de Cotte and that of Prince Conti in the Palace of Issy.

78 D. Görgmaier, 'Gartenfeste Versailler Prägung unter Max Emanuel and Karl Albrecht' (Ph.D. diss., Munich, 1973).

79 Straub, *Repraesentatio Maiestatis*, p. 313.

80 Bauer, *Die höfische Gesellschaft in Deutschland*, p. 113.

81 Karl Ludwig von Pöllnitz, *Mémoires*, 2 vols. (Amsterdam and London, 1735), II, pp. 20ff.

82 J. Berns, 'Die Festkultur der deutschen Höfe zwischen 1580 und 1730. Eine Problemskizze in typologischer Absicht', *Germanisch-Romanische Monatsschrift*, 65 (1984), 295f.

83 Cited in Straub, *Repraesentatio Maiestatis*, p. 146.

Chapter Eight

1 Friedrich Carl von Moser, *Teutsches Hof-Recht*, 2 vols. (Frankfurt and Leipzig, 1754–55), I, p. 1.

2 John C. Röhl, *Kaiser, Hof und Staat: Wilhelm II. und die Deutsche Politik* (Munich, 1987); Eng. trans., *The Kaiser and his Court: Wilhelm II and the Government of Germany* (Cambridge, 1995).

3 In accordance with the central importance of these questions, at first 'Brandenburg Ceremonial' was exclusively ambassadorial ceremonial, see *Ceremoniale Brandenburgicum* (Dortmund, 1691) and Gottfried Stieve, *Europäisches Hoff-Ceremoniel* (Leipzig, 1715), pp. 131–4.

4 See Eckhard Müller-Mertens, 'Die landesherrliche Residenz in Berlin und Kölln 1280–1486: Markgrafenhof, Herrschaftsschwerpunkt, Residenzstadt', *Zeitschrift für Geschichtswissenschaft*, 36 (1988), 138–54, esp. p. 151.

5 Ulrich Schütte, *Das Schloss als Wehranlage: Befestigte Schlossbauten der Frühen Neuzeit* (Darmstadt, 1994), pp. 118–30.

6 See Werner Hegemann, *1930: Das Steinerne Berlin* (4th edn., Brunswick and Wiesbaden, 1988), p. 28.

7 Peter-Michael Hahn, *Struktur und Funktion des Brandenburgischen Adels im 16. Jahrhundert* (Berlin, 1979), p. 143.

8 Hahn, *Struktur und Funktion*, p. 189. All the same, the court of Elector Joachim II did include 763 people; see Martin Hass, *Die Hofordnung Kurfürst Joachims II. von Brandenburg* (Historische Studien, 87, Berlin, 1910).

9 In his introduction, Heinz Ladendorf, *Der Bildhauer und Baumeister Andreas Schlüter* (Berlin, 1935), paints a sobering picture of the situation with regard to records concerning Berlin (pp. 2–4).

10 Arthur Kern, *Deutsche Hofordnungen des 16. und 17. Jahrhunderts*, 2 vols. (Berlin, 1905–7); see also Holger Kruse and Werner Paravicini (ed.), *Höfe und Hofordnungen, 1200–1600* (Sigmaringen, 1998).

11 Franz Genthe, 'Die preussischen Oberjägermeister: Ein Beitrag zur Geschichte des Oberjägermeister-Amtes von 1579–1825', *Hohenzollern-Jahrbuch*, 10 (1906), 261–74.

12 Eduard Vehse, *Geschichte des preussischen Hofs und Adels wie der preussischen Diplomatie*, 6 vols. (Hamburg, 1851), I. This work, which is unfortunately as yet irreplaceable, does contain errors and careless mistakes, but is sometimes very 'modern' in the way in which it formulates its questions.

13 Edgar von Ulbisch, 'Eine Rüstung des Kurfürsten Joachim II. Hektor (1505–1571)', *Hohenzollern-Jahrbuch*, 3 (1899), 92–103.

14 Ludwig Keller, 'Die Hohenzollern und die Oranier in ihren geistigen, verwandtschaftlichen und politischen Beziehungen', *Hohenzollern-Jahrbuch*, 10 (1906), 221–60.

15 Leopold von Ledebur, *Schauplatz der Thaten oder Aufenthalts-Nachweis des Kurfürsten Friedrich Wilhelm des Grossen* (Berlin, 1840). Thus on 18 December 1679 the court moved from Potsdam to Berlin, 'not without the great joy of the inhabitants, because the court had not been there for so long'; see Vehse, *Geschichte des preussischen Hofs*, I, pp. 250–86.

16 Matthäus Merian, *Topographia Germaniae: Beschreibung Brandenburgs* (Frankfurt am Main, 1652); on p. 28 he emphasizes the use of rooms for the Chancellery, Chamber, and Treasury, but also already mentions a large silver-room.

17 John Toland, *Relation von den Königlich Preussischen und Chur-Hannoverischen Höfen* (Frankfurt am Main, 1706), pp. 29–31.

18 *Der Grosse Kurfürst 1620–1688* (exh. cat., Staatliche Schlösser und Gärten Potsdam-Sanssouci, Potsdam-Sanssouci, 1988), pp. 119–26; Albert Geyer, 'Zur Baugeschichte des Königlichen Schlosses in Berlin. I. Der Festsaal des Grossen Kurfürsten; II. Die Kapelle Friedrichs I.', *Hohenzollern-Jahrbuch*, 1 (1897), 146–62, 162–73. In 1728, the statues were erected in a different form in the newly built 'Weisser Saal' (White Hall) and are now at the Neues Palais in Potsdam.

19 One finds a description of the patriarchal and time-honoured court style in Veit Ludwig von Seckendorff, *Teutscher Fürsten-Staat* (Frankfurt and Leipzig, 1695), Book III, Ch.. v, pp. 524–98: 'Von Bestellung und Verfassung einer Fürstlischen und derglichen Hoff-Stat'. In a later edition of this famous work, the court is even described entirely from the point of view of the household, and not at all as a universal sphere.

20 Paul Seidel, 'Der Einzug des Grossen Kurfürsten in Berlin am 12 Dezember 1678', *Hohenzollern-Jahrbuch*, 6 (1902), 246–53. A description of the entry was published in the *Dritter Pommerischer Kriegs-Postillion* (Leipzig, 1679), with illustrations of the eight gates of honour and all the inscriptions. As a piece of printing, however, this *Postillion* is of very poor quality.

21 Vehse, *Geschichte des preussischen Hofs*, I.

22 Gregorio Leti, *Ritratti historici, politici, chronologici e genealogici della casa serenissima ed elettorale di Brandeburgo* (Amsterdam, 1687).

23 The combined construction of palace and town was repeated when it came to setting up the sons of the Great Elector's second wife, Dorothea (1636–89). For the cadet line of the Margraves of Schwedt (1689–1788), a palace was built from 1670, and from 1680 a grid-shaped planned town; Gerd Heinrich, 'Festung, Flüchtlingsstadt und Fürstenresidenz: Zur Entwicklung und Raumfunktion brandenburgisch-preussischer Neustädte', *Abhandlungen der Pädagogischen Hochschule Berlin*, 1 (1982), 137–77, esp. p. 146.

24 The 'master of Sanssouci' gives the following judgement in drawing historical parallels between the Great Elector and Louis XIV, 'Mémoires [pour servir a l'histoire] de la Maison de Brandebourg', in *Oeuvres de Frédéric le Grand* (Berlin, 1846), I, p. 94: 'En fait de galanterie, de politesse, de générosité, de magnificence, la somptuosité française l'emporte sur la frugalité allemande; Louis XIV avait autant d'avance sur Frédéric Guillaume, que Lucullus en avait sur Mithridate'. See also Jeroen Duindam, *Myths of Power* (Amsterdam, 1995), pp. 13–34.

25 'Mémoires de la Maison de Brandebourg', p. 229.

26 A room such as the 'Wappensaal' (Heraldic Hall) in the upper floor of the palace (completed, after the Great Elector's death, *c*.1695) is not only one of the few Brandenburg state rooms from the seventeenth century to have survived, but also a testament to the ruler's striving to turn his territories into both a legal and, among its great families, a genealogical unity. The heraldic hall unites twenty-five coats of arms of the Brandenburg lands into a representative unity. It was here, in 1730, that the court sat to judge the attempted flight, which constituted high treason, of the then crown-prince, Friedrich.

27 The authoritative edition of the coronation was published by the master of ceremonies, see Johann von Besser, *Preussische Krönungs-Geschichte* (Cölln an der Spree, 1702; 2nd edn. 1712, with illustrations, reprinted Berlin, 1901).

28 'Wan ich alles habe was zur Königlichen würde gehöret auch noch mehr als andere Könige warumb sol ich dan auch nicht trachten den Nahmen eines Königs zu erlangen': essay by the Elector Friedrich III in his own hand, written in 1699; printed in Ernst Berner, 'Die auswärtige Politik des Kurfürsten Friedrich, König Friedrich I. in Preussen', *Hohenzollern-Jahrbuch*, 4 (1900), 60–109, esp. at 105–9.

29 Carl Ludwig Freiherr von Pöllnitz, *Mémoires zur Lebens- und Regierungsgeschichte der vier letzten Regenten des Preussischen Staates mit einem berichtigenden Anhange*, 2 vols. (Berlin, 1971), I, pp. 326–7.

30 Arnold Berney, *König Friedrich I. und das Haus Habsburg* (Munich and Berlin, 1927), pp. 215ff. The so-called *Ceremoniale Brandenburgicum* (two impressions, 1691 and 1700) is, incidentally, an unauthorized work which, as handwritten insertions in copy Sx 7473a in the Staatsbibliothek in Berlin reveal, was immediately banned on publication.

31 Hans Philippi, *Landgraf Karl von Hessen-Kassel* (Marburg, 1976), pp. 294–5.

32 Moser, *Teutsches Hof-Recht*, II, pp. 203–4.

33 The members of the order were placed above the rest of the court in listings of rank; see *Das jetztlebende Königlich Preußische und Chur-Fürstliche Brandenburgische Haus* (n.p., 1704), the first ever calendar of court and state in Prussia which has survived.

34 Pöllnitz, *Mémoires*, I, p. 332.

35 Jean-Baptiste Broebes, *Vue des Palais: Prospect der Palläste und Lust-Schlösser seiner Königlichen Mayestätt in Preussen* (Augsburg, 1733). When the first king died, there were apparently twenty-four furnished palaces and pleasure-houses; see Carl Hinrichs, 'Der Regierungsantritt Friedrich Wilhelms I', in Gerhard Oestreich (ed.), *Preussen als historisches Problem* (Berlin, 1964), pp. 91–137, esp. p. 114.

36 Goerd Peschken, *Das königliche Schloss zu Berlin*, 2 vols. (Berlin, 1993); C. Keisch, *Das Grosse Silberbuffet aus dem Rittersaal* (Berlin, 1997).

37 Margarete Kühn, *Schloss Charlottenburg* (Berlin, 1955); Susan Prösel and Michael Kremin, *Berlin um 1700: Die Idealstadt Charlottenburg* (Berlin 1984).

38 Philippi, *Landgraf Karl von Hessen-Kassel*, p. 287.

39 Vehse, *Geschichte des preussischen Hofs*, II, pp. 145.

40 A.F. Riedel, *Der brandenburgisch-preussische Staatshaushalt* (Berlin, 1866), p. 42.

41 Wolfgang Ribbe (ed.), *Geschichte Berlins*, 2 vols. (Munich, 1987); Helga Schulz, *Berlin 1650–1800: Sozialgeschichte einer Residenz* (Berlin, 1992).

42 The above in based on Hinrichs, 'Der Regierungsantritt Friedrich Wilhelms I', pp. 99–105.

43 These figures are derived from Friedrich Förster, *Friedrich Wilhelm I., König von Preussen* (Potsdam, 1834), which examines the Prussian royal household for 1711 and 1712; ibid., pp. 59ff. This documentation as a whole has many gaps and must be treated with scepticism on some points.

44 'Mémoires de la Maison de Brandebourg', p. 230: 'Les beaux-arts, enfants de l'abondance, commèrcerent à fleurir: l'Académie des Peintres, dont Pesne, Werner, Weidemann et Leygebe étaient les premiers professeurs, fut fondée; mais il ne sortit de leur école aucune peintre de réputation'.

45 Lorenz Beger, *Thesaurus Brandenburgicus Selectus*, 3 vols. (Cölln, 1696–1701).

46 Paul Seidel, 'Die bildenden Künste unter König Friedrich I.', *Hohenzollern-Jahrbuch*, 4 (1900), 255. The essay by Margarete Kühn,

'Zum Antikenverständnis am Berliner Hof von Kurfürst Joachim II. bis zu König Friedrich dem Grossen', *Berlin und die Antike* (exh. cat., Berlin, 1979), pp. 23–42 is of central importance. After the interruption under Friedrich Wilhelm I, Friedrich II again turned strongly to antiquity. His approach is an individual one, however, since he was accustomed to interpret the classical models in the French style.

47 There is ample evidence of the second king's feverish travelling-activity in *Kurtzgefasste Lebens- und Regiments- Geschichte König Friedrich Wilhelms I* (n.p., 1743).

48 Otto Krauske, 'Vom Hofe Friedrich Wilhelms I.', *Hohenzollern-Jahrbuch*, 5 (1901), 173–210.

49 In this a clear distinction was made between pure representation and genuine fighting strength. Only fighting strength was truly representative, as was noted on the occasion of a visit to the Saxon camp at Radewitz; 'Mémoires de la Maison de Brandebourg': 'Le roi de Pologne, qui était venu à Berlin l'an 1728, voulût à son tour étaler sa magnificance aux yeux du Roi, en lui donnant des fêtes militaires. Il rassambla ses troupes dans un camp auprès de Radewitz, village situé sur l'Elbe; les manoeuvres qu'il fit faire a son armée étaient un image de la guerre des Romains, mêlée aux visions du chevalier Folard. Les connaisseurs jugèrent que ce camp était plûtot un spectacle théâtral, qu'an emblème véritable de la guerre.'

50 Moser, *Teutsches Hof-Recht*, I, Bk. III, Ch. III, section 6.

51 Reinhold Koser, 'Vom Berliner Hofe um 1750', *Hohenzollern-Jahrbuch*, 7 (1903), 1–37; Vehse, *Geschichte des preussischen Hofs*, III.

52 *Schloss Charlottenburg* (Fondation Paribas, Museés et Monuments de France, 1995); the king housed one of his five identical libraries at the Berlin palace.

53 Horst Drescher and Sibylle Badstübner-Gröger, *Das Neue Palais in Potsdam* (Berlin, 1991), pp. 24-42.

54 Friedrich Nikolai, *Beschreibung der Königlichen Residenzstädte Berlin und Potsdam*, (3rd edn., Berlin 1786, partly reprinted Berlin, 1987).

CHAPTER NINE

1 This article is based on archival sources housed at the Biblioteca Reale, Turin (Miscellanea Storia Patria 720–26), and at the Archivio di Stato di Torino (Cerimoniale). As most of this material consists of court regulations, which were not always strictly followed, a form of control in the grey area between rule and practice, what *ought* to be done as distinct from what actually *was* done, has been provided by the eyewitness accounts of the French diplomatic representatives at Turin, preserved at the Archives du Ministère des Affaires Étrangères, Paris: Correspondance politique, Sardaigne. The standard survey of the political history of the Sabaudian realm during the period covered in this chapter is now the deeply flawed Pierpaolo Merlin, Claudio Rosso, Geoffrey Symcox, Giuseppe Ricuperati, *Il Piemonte Sabaudo: Stato e territori in età moderna* (Turin, 1994).

2 Martha Pollak, *Turin, 1564–1680: Urban Design, Military Culture and the Creation of the Absolutist Capital* (Chicago and London, 1991); Giuseppe Ricuperati, *Storia di Torino*, III: *Dalla dominazione francese alla ricomposizione dello Stato (1536–1630)* (Turin, 1998).

3 Geoffrey Symcox, 'From commune to capital: The transformation of Turin, sixteenth to eighteenth centuries', in Robert Oresko, Graham Gibbs, H. M. Scott (eds.), *Royal and Republican Sovereignty in Early Modern Europe: Essays in Memory of Ragnhild Hatton* (Cambridge, 1997).

4 Pierpaolo Merlin, *Emanuele Filiberto: un principe tra il Piemonte e l'Europa* (Turin, 1995); Cristina Stango, 'La corte di Emanuele Filiberto: organizzazione e gruppi sociali', *Bollettino storico-bibliografico subalpino*, 85 (1987).

5 Vittorio Amedeo Cigna-Santi, *Serie cronologica de' cavalieri dell' ordine supremo di Savoia* (Turin, 1786).

6 Of the enormous literature on the Shroud, the exhibition catalogue Ada Peyrot (ed.), *La Sindone nella collezione di Umberto II* (Turin, 1998), offers an important analysis of its ostension.

7 Pierpaolo Merlin, *Tra guerre e tornei: la corte sabauda nell' età di Carlo Emanuele I* (Turin, 1991); Franca Varallo, *Il duca e la corte: cerimonie al tempo di Carlo Emanuele I di Savoia* (Geneva, 1991).

8 On the Nemours–Genevois establishment, see the sequence of articles in *Annesci*, 12 (1965).

9 Vittorio Viale (ed.), *Guarino Guarini e l'internazionalità del barocco* (Turin, 1970); Harold Meek, *Guarino Guarini and his Architecture* (New Haven and London, 1988).

10 The career of Maria Giovanna Battista awaits scholarly attention, although a collection of essays edited by Giovanni Romano, *Torino, 1675–1699: strategie e conflitte del barocco* (Turin, 1993) provides an entry for cultural politics during her regency. See also Louis Mallè, *Palazzo Madama* (Turin, 1970).

11 Robert Oresko, 'The Glorious Revolution of 1688–9 and the House of Savoy', in Jonathan Israel (ed.), *The Anglo-Dutch Moment: Essays on the Glorious Revolution and its world impact* (Cambridge, 1991).

12 Robert Oresko, 'Bastards as Clients: The House of Savoy and its Illegitimate Children', in Charles Giry-Deloison and Roger Mettam (eds.), *Patronages et clientélismes, 1550–1750* (Lille, 1995).

13 Robert Oresko, 'Le repas princier à la cour de Turin pendant le règne di Vittorio Amedeo II', in Catherine Arminjon (ed.), *Tables et festins de cour en Europe* (Paris, forthcoming).

14 Enrico Stumpo, 'I ceti dirigenti in Italia nell' età moderna: due modelli diversi: nobiltà piemontese e patriziato toscano', in Amelio Tagliaferri (ed.), *I ceti dirigenti in Italia in età moderna* (Udine, 1984); Stuart Woolf, 'Studi sulla nobiltà piemontese nell' epoca dell' assolutismo', *Memorie dell' Accademia delle Scienze di Torino* (Turin, 1963). Toby Osborne, *Dynasty and Diplomacy: The Court of Savoy and the Thirty Years War* (Cambridge, forthcoming), sheds much light on the Scaglia di Verrua clan.

15 G. de Léris, *La comtesse de Verrue et la cour de Victor-Amédée II de Savoie* (Paris, 1881).

16 Francesco Gianazzo di Pamparato, *Famiglie e palazzi, dalle campagne piemontesi a Torino capitale barocca* (Turin, 1997).

17 Isabella Massabò Ricci and Claudio Rosso, 'La corte quale rappresentazione del potere sovrano', in Giovanni Romano (ed.), *Figure del Barocco in Piemonte* (Turin, 1988).

18 The cult of the Sabaudian court hunt stands at the heart of the exhibition catalogue, Michaela Di Macco and Giovanni Romano (eds.), *Diana Trionfatrice: arte di corte nel Piemonte del Seicento* (Turin, 1989).

19 Franco Mazzini, *L'Armeria Reale di Torino* (Busto Arsizio, 1982).

20 Giovanni Romano (ed.), *Le collezioni di Carlo Emanuele I di Savoia* (Turin, 1995).

21 Mercedes Viale Ferrero, 'Essai de reconstruction idéale des tapisseries ayant apparentues à la Maison de Savoie', *Het Herfsttij van de Vlaamse Tapijtkunst* (Brussels, 1959).

22 Vera Comoli Mandracci, *Torino* (Bari, 1983); Augusto Cavallari Murat (ed.), *Forma urbana ed architettura nella Torino barocca* (Turin, 1968).

23 Robert Oresko, 'The House of Savoy in Search of a Royal Crown', in Oresko, Gibbs and Scott, *Royal and Republican Sovereignty*.

24 Marie-Christine has attracted considerable biographical attention, most recently Giuliana Brugnelli Biraghi and Maria Bianca Denoyé Pollone, *Chrestienne de Francia, Duchessa di Savoia, Prima Madama Reale* (Turin, 1991).

25 Marziano Bernardi, *Il Palazzo Reale di Torino* (Turin, 1959) and 'Vicende construttive del Palazzo Reale di Torino', in Vittorio Viale (ed.), *Mostra barocco Piemontese*, 3 vols. (Turin, 1963), essential for understanding court patronage in Turin.

26 Costanza Roggero Bardelli, Maria Grazia Vinardi, Vittorio Defabiani, *Ville sabaude: Piemonte 2* (Milano, 1990) is the outstanding and definitive source for these questions.

27 Maria Luisa Tibone, Giuliana Biraghi, Luciano Tamburini, *Venatio Regia: delizie e caccie nella Real Venaria* (Turin, 1990).

28 Gregorio Leti, *L'Italia regnante* (Geneva, 1674–6), II.

29 Gianfranco Gritella, *Stupinigi, dal progetto di Juvarra alle premesse neoclassiche* (Modena, 1987).

30 See the exhibition catalogue *La Maison de Savoie à Nice* (Nice, 1988).

31 Mercedes Viale Ferrero, *Feste delle Madame Reali di Savoia* (Turin, 1965); Margaret McGowan, 'Les fêtes de cour en Savoie: l'oeuvre de Filippe d'Aglié', *Revue de l'histoire du théâtre*, 22 (1970).

32 John Beldon Scott, 'Seeing the Shroud: Guarini's Reliquary Chapel in Turin and the Ostension of a Dynastic Relic', *The Art Bulletin*, 77 (1995).

33 Nino Carboneri, *La Reale Chiesa di Superga di Filippo Juvarra (1715–1735)* (Turin, 1979).

34 Geoffrey Symcox, *Victor Amadeus II: Absolutism in the Savoyard State, 1675–1730* (London, 1983).

35 Gianfranco Gritella, *Filippo Juvarra, l'architettura* (Modena, 1992); Andreina Griseri and Giovanni Romano (eds.), *Filippo Juvarra a Torino: nuovi progetti per la città* (Turin, 1989).

36 Giancarlo Ferraris, with Alvar Gonzáles Palacios, *Pietro Piffetti e gli ebanisti a Torino, 1670–1838* (Turin, 1992).

37 Sandra Pinto (ed.), *Arte di corte a Torino da Carlo Emanuele III a Carlo Felice* (Turin, 1987).

38 See the exhibition catalogue *Il tesoro del principe: titoli, carte, memorie, per il governo dello stato* (Turin, 1989); also, for the decoration of the private court archives, Arabella Cifani and Franco Monetti, *Il piacere e le grazie: collezionismo, pittura di genere e di paesaggio fra Sei e Settecento in Piemonte* (Turin, 1993).

39 Alberto Basso (ed.), *L'arcano incanto: il Teatro Regio di Torino, 1740–1990* (Turin, 1991); Marie-Thérèse Bouquet-Boyer, *Il teatro di corte dalle origini al 1788* (Turin, 1976), vol. I of the *Storia del Teatro Regio di Torino*.

40 Alessandro Baudi di Vesme, 'Sull' acquisto fatto da Carlo Emanuele III re di Sardegna della quadreria del Principe Eugenio di Savoia', *Miscellanea di storia italiana*, 2 (1886).

41 Andreina Griseri, Giovanni Romano and Giovanni Bertolo, *Porcellane e argenti del Palazzo Reale di Torino* (Sonzogno, 1986).

CHAPTER TEN

1 M. Fantoni, *La corte del granduca: forma e simboli del potere Mediceo fra cinque e seicento* (Rome, 1994). General works include F. Diaz, 'Il Granducato di Toscana: I Medici', in *Storia d'Italia*, XIII/I (Turin, 1976); *Firenze e la Toscana dei Medici nell'Europa del Cinquecento*, 3 vols. (Florence, 1980); and K. Langedijk, *The Portraits of the Medici: Fifteenth–Eighteenth Centuries* (Florence, 1981). Still useful as a source of biographical information on individual members of the Medici family is G. Pieraccini, *La stirpe dei Medici di Cafaggiolo*, 3 vols. (Florence, 1924–5).

2 K. Lankheit, 'Firenze sotto gli ultimi Medici', in *Gli ultimi Medici: Il tardo barocco a Firenze, 1670–1743* (Florence, 1974), p. 20.

3 J. R. Hale, *Florence and the Medici: The Pattern of Control* (London, 1977), p. 155.

4 On the European dimension of the Florentine court, especially in the sixteenth century, see *Firenze e la Toscana*.

5 G. de Angelis D'Ossat, 'La Francia: l'architettura delle monarchie', in *Il potere e lo spazio: la scena del principe* (Florence, 1980), pp. 119–132; D. Marrow, *The Art Patronage of Maria de' Medici* (Ann Arbor, 1982); R. Millen, *Heroic Deeds and Mystic Figures: A New Reading of Rubens' Life of Maria de' Medici* (Princeton, 1989), and S. Mamone, *Firenze e Parigi: due capitali dello spettacolo per una regina: Maria de' Medici* (Milan, 1987).

6 I. Hyman, 'Notes and Speculations on San Lorenzo, Palazzo Medici, and an Urban Project by Brunelleschi', *Journal of the Society of Architectural Historians*, 34 (1975), 98–120; and C. Elam, 'Lorenzo de' Medici and the Urban Development of Renaissance Florence', *Art History*, 1 (1978), 43–66.

7 L. G. Satkowski, *Vasari: Architect and Courtier* (Princeton, 1993). On the Palazzo Vecchio, see also R. Starn and L. Partridge, *Arts of Power:*

Three Halls of State in Italy, 1300–1600 (Berkeley, 1992), and U. Muccini, *Il Salone dei Cinquecento in Palazzo Vecchio* (Florence, 1990).

8 L. Baldini Giusti, 'Una "casa di granduca" sulla collina di Boboli', *Antichità Viva*, 19 (1980), 40; also L. Satkowski, 'The Palazzo Pitti: Planning and Use in the Grand-Ducal Era', *Journal of the Society of Architectural Historians*, 42 (1983), 336–49.

9 M. Chiarini and S. Padovani (eds.), *Gli appartamenti reali di Palazzo Pitti: una reggia per tre dinastie: Medici, Lorena e Savoia tra granducato e regno d'Italia* (Florence, 1993).

10 Cf. F. Diaz, 'Cosimo I e il consolidorsi dello stato assoluto', in E. Fasano Guerini (ed.), *Potere e società negli stati regionali italiani del '500 e '600* (Bologna, 1973), pp. 75–97.

11 J. R. Hale, 'The End of Florentine Liberty: The Fortezza da Basso', in N. Rubinstein (ed.), *Florentine Studies* (London, 1968), pp. 501–32; and M. Gianneschi and C. Sodini, 'Urbanistica e politica durante il principato di Alessandro de' Medici, 1532–37', *Storia della Città* (1979), 5–34. On the Medicean impact on the urban fabric of Florence, see G. Fanelli, *Firenze* (Bari, 1981), and F. Borsi, *L'architettura del principe* (Florence, 1980).

12 M. B. Hall, *Renovation and Counter-Reformation: Vasari and Duke Cosimo in Santa Maria Novella and Santa Croce, 1565–77* (Oxford, 1979).

13 U. Baldini, *La Cappella dei Principi e le pietre dure a Firenze* (Milan, 1979).

14 G. Spini (ed.), *Architettura e politica da Cosimo I a Ferdinando I* (Florence, 1976).

15 G. Spini, 'I Medici e l'organizzazione del territorio', in *Storia dell'arte italiana*, III/V, *Momenti di architettura* (Turin, 1993), pp. 163–212.

16 B. Ammannati, *La città: appunti per un trattato*, ed. M. Fossi (Rome, 1970), and G. Vasari il Giovane, *La città ideale: Piante di chiese (palazzi e ville) di Toscana e d'Italia*, ed. V. Stefanelli (Rome, 1970).

17 Even before Vasari and Ammannati, the need to harmonize practice with theory had already been felt in the field of military engineering. G. B. Belluzzi, *Il trattato delle fortificazioni di terra*, ed. D. Lamberini, in Franco Borsi et al. (ed.), *Il disegno interrotto: trattati medicei di architettura*, 2 vols. (Florence, 1980), pp. 373–513.

18 The personnel of the Medici court may be precisely reconstructed to 1540 thanks to the so-called 'ruoli', the lists of salaried employees conserved in the *fondi* of the Guardaroba, Miscellanea Medicea and Mediceo del Principe at the Archivio di Stato di Firenze.

19 F. Angiolini and P. Malanima, 'Problemi di mobilità sociale a Firenze tra metà cinquecento e primi decenni del seicento', *Quaderni Storici*, 26 (1991), 875–99; S. Berner, 'The Florentine Patriciate in Transition from Republic to "Principato"', 1530–1609', *Studies in Medieval and Renaissance History*, 9 (1972), 3–15; and B. R. Litchfield, *Emergence of a Bureaucracy: The Florentine Patricians, 1530–1790* (Princeton, 1986).

20 Gregorio Leti, *Il ceremoniale historico e politico…*, 6 vols. (Amsterdam, 1685), V, pp. 230–33.

21 The volumes of the *Diari di Etichetta* and *Ceremoniale* are found in various *fondi* of the Archivio di Stato di Firenze, in particular Guardaroba and Miscellanea Medicea.

22 M. Fantoni, 'L'abito, le resole e la trasgressione: usi e simbologie delle livree alla corte medicea', in A. G. Cavagna and G. Butazzi (eds.), *Le trame della moda* (Rome, 1995), pp. 95–107.

23 Biblioteca Nazionale Centrale di Firenze, Magliabechiano II/I, 284, fo. 219: D. M. Marmi, 'Norma per il Guardarobba del Gran Palazzo della Citta di Firenza'.

24 An example of these is Biblioteca Nazionale Centrale di Firenze, fondo G. Capponi, n. 261:1–2, 'Diario e Ceremoniale della Corte Medicea, tenuto de Cesari di Bastiano Tinghi, ajutante di Comere del Gran Duca Ferdinando I' (22 iuglio 1600– 9 novembre 1623).

25 Archivio di Stato di Firenze, Miscellanea Medicea, 438, fo. 97r.

26 M. Fantoni, 'Il culto dell'Annunziata e la sacralità del potere Mediceo', *Archivio Storico Italiano*, 147 (1989), 771–93.

27 E. Borsook, 'Art and Politics at the Medici Court II: The Baptism of Filippo dei Medici in 1577', *Mitteilungen des Kunsthistorischen Institut in Florenz*, 13 (1967–8), 95–114.

28 R. Gaston, 'Liturgy and Patronage in S. Lorenzo, Florence, 1350–1650', in F. W. Kent and P. Simons (eds.), *Patronage, Art and Society in Renaissance Italy* (Oxford, 1987), pp. 111–33. On the funeral rites of the grand dukes, see S. Pietrosanti, *Sacralità Medicee* (Florence, 1991), and E. Borsook, 'Art and Politics at the Medici Court I: The Funeral of Cosimo de' Medici', 'Art and Politics at the Medici Court III: Funeral Décor for Philip II of Spain', and 'Art and Politics at the Medici Court IV: Funeral Décor for Henry IV of France', *Mitteilungen des Kunsthistorischen Institut in Florenz*, 12 (1965–6), 31–54; 14 (1969–70), 91–114, 201–34.

29 M. Fantoni, 'Il bigottismo di Cosimo III: da leggenda storiografica ad oggetto storico', in M. Verga, V. Bergagli and F. Angiolini (eds.), *La Toscana nell'età di Cosimo III* (Florence, 1993), pp. 389–402.

30 E. Albéri (ed.), *Relazioni degli ambasciatori veneti al senato* (Florence, 1839–63), III/1, p. 271.

31 Peter Brown, *Society and the Holy in Late Antiquity* (London, 1982), p. 249.

32 P. Ricasoli, *Orazione dell'offizio del principe, fatta nell'occasione dell'esequie del Serenissimo Gran Duca di Toscana, Cosimo II* (Venice, 1622), p. 45.

33 *Maestri toscani del secondo Cinquecento: The Painters of Palazzo Vecchio and the Studiolo, the Founders of the Accademia* (Florence, 1976); J. Cox-Rearick, *Dynasty and Destiny in Medici Art: Pontormo, Leo X, and the two Cosimos* (Princeton, 1984); and L. J. Feinberg, *From Studio to Studiolo: Florentine Draftsmanship under the First Medici Grand Dukes* (Oberlin, Allen Memorial Art Museum, 1991).

34 P. W. Richelson, *Studies in the Personal Imagery of Cosimo I de' Medici, Duke of Florence* (New York, 1978); K. W. Forster, 'Metaphors of Rule: Political Ideology and History in the Portraits of Cosimo I de' Medici', *Mitteilungen des Kunsthistorischen Institutes in Florenz*, 15 (1971), 65–104; R. A. Scorza, 'Vincenzo Borghini and *Invenzione*: the Florentine *Apparato* of 1565', *Journal of the Warburg and Courtauld Institutes*, 44 (1981), 57–75.

35 *Curiosità di una reggia: vicende della guardaroba di Palazzo Pitti* (Florence, 1979); *Le arti del principato mediceo* (Florence, 1980), and P. Barocchi and G. Gaeta Bertelè, *Collezionismo mediceo: Cosimo I, Francesco I, e il Cardinale Ferdinando* (Modena, 1993).

36 S. Bertelli, 'Egemonia linguistica come egemonia culturale e politica nella Firenze cosimiana', *Humanisme et Renaissance*, 38 (1976), 249–83. On the Etruscan myth, see G. Cipriani, *Il mito etrusco nel Rinascimento fiorentino* (Florence, 1980).

37 Cf. M. Plaisance, 'Affirmation de la politique de Côme Ier', and 'Culture et politique à Florence de 1542 à 1551: Lasca et les Humidi aux prises aves l'Académie Florentine', in *Les Ecrivains et le pouvoir en Italie à l'époque de la Renaissance*, 3 vols (Paris, Université de la Sorbonne, 1973), II, pp. 361–438; III, pp. 149–242.

38 S. Berti, *Il principe dello studiolo: Francesco I de' Medici e la fine del Rinascimento fiorentino* (Florence, 1967).

39 For some of Pietro da Cortona's designs for the Pitti Palace during the 1640s and for a new high altar for the church of the knights of Santo Stefano in Pisa, see Anna Lo Bianco (ed.), *Pietro da Cortona, 1597–1669* (Milan, 1997), pp. 463–5.

40 Cf. *Il seicento fiorentino: arte a Firenze da Ferdinando I a Cosimo III* (Florence, 1986); E. Micheletti, *Masterpieces of the Palatine Gallery and the Pitti Palace* (Florence, 1969); M. Campbell, *Pietro da Cortona at the Pitti Palace: A Study of the Planetary Rooms and Related Projects* (Princeton, 1977); E. L. Goldberg, *After Vasari: History, Art, and Patronage in Late Medici Florence* (Princeton, 1988); idem, *Patterns in Late Medici Art Patronage* (Princeton, 1983).

41 *Sustermans: sessant'anni alla corte dei Medici* (Florence, 1983).

42 M. Mosco (ed.), *Natura viva: Animal Painting in the Medici Collections* (Florence, 1986).

43 See A. M. Cummings, *The Politicized Muse: Music for Medici Festivals, 1512–1537* (Princeton, 1992); A. Solerti, *Musica, ballo e drammatica alla corte medicea dal 1600 al 1637* (Florence, 1905); G. Gaeta Bertelà and A. Petrioli Tofani (eds.), *Feste e apparati medicei da Cosimo I a Cosimo II* (Florence, 1969); M. Fabbri, E. Garbero Zorzi and A. M. Petrioli Tofani (eds.), *Il luogo teatrale a Firenze: Brunelleschi, Vasari, Buontalenti, Parigi* (Milan, 1975); A.M. Nagler, *Theatre Festivals of the Medici: 1539–1637* (New Haven, 1964); R. Strong, *Splendor at Court: Renaissance Spectacle and the Theater of Power* (Boston, 1973), pp. 169–212; L. Zorzi, *Il teatro e la città: saggi sulla scena italiana* (Turin, 1977), pp. 61–234; J. M. Saslow, *The Medici Wedding of 1589* (New Haven and London, 1996).

44 *Theater Art of the Medici* (Hanover, NH, Dartmouth College Museum and Galleries, 1980), p. xv.

45 See M. Biagioli, *Galileo, Courtier: The Practice of Science in the Culture of Absolutism* (Chicago, 1993).

46 See 'La rinascità della scienza' and 'Astrologia, magia e alchimia', in *Firenze e la Toscana*, pp. 123–244, 309–434.

CHAPTER ELEVEN

1 Rudolf Cederström, *De svenska riksregalierna och kungliga värdighetsstecknen* (Stockholm, 1942). For the court in general, see Fabian Persson, *Servants of Fortune: The Swedish Court between 1598 and 1721* (Ph.D. diss., Lund University, 1999).

2 Nils Edén, *Under den äldre Vasatiden, 1523–94* (Ph.D. diss., Uppsala University, 1899).

3 Gustaf Upmark, *Gustaf Vasas hof* (Stockholm, 1912); Birgitta Odén, *Rikets uppbörd och utgift* (Ph.D. diss., Lund University, 1955).

4 Nils Edén, *Om centralregeringens organisation* (Uppsala, 1899), p. 139.

5 Riksarkivet [hereafter RA], Kungliga Arkiv, Överkammarherreinstruktion 1653.

6 Uppsala Universitetsbibliotek [hereafter UUB], Bengt Rosenhane Collection: Gabriel Gabrielsson Oxenstierna to Bengt Rosenhane, n.d. [1670]. Karl X Gustav's Court Law (1655), section 9; and Karl XI's Court Law (1687), sections 14 and 15; in Johan Schmedeman (ed.), *Kongl stadgar, förordningar, bref och resolutioner, ifrån åhr 1528 intil 1701*, 2 vols. (Stockholm, 1706).

7 Martin Olsson et al., *Stockholms slotts historia: Det gamla slottet*, I, (Stockholm, 1940).

8 Carl Magnus Stenbock (ed.), *Lorenzo Magalotti: Sverige under år 1674* (Stockholm, 1912), p. 9.

9 Guy Miège, *A Relation of Three Embassies from his Sacred Majestie Charles II…in the Years 1663 and 1664* (London, 1669), p. 352; William Carr, *Remarks on the Government of Several Parts of Germany, Denmark, Sweden* (London, 1727), p. 133; A. F. Payen, *Les Voyages de Monsieur Payen, Lieutenant General de Meaux* (2nd edn., Paris, 1667), p. 87.

10 Jan Samuelson, *Aristokrat eller förädlad bonde? Det svenska frälsets ekonomi, politik och sociala förbindelser under tiden 1523–1611* (Ph.D. diss., Lund University, 1993).

11 For a general overview of the early modern Swedish nobility, see A. F. Upton, 'The Swedish Nobility, 1600–1772', in H. M. Scott (ed.), *The European Nobilities in the Seventeenth and Eighteenth Centuries*, 2 vols. (London, 1995), II, pp. 11–40.

12 Ingvar Elmroth, *För kung och fosterland: Studier i den svenska adelns demografi och offentliga funktioner, 1600–1900* (Lund, 1981).

13 RA, Kungliga Arkiv, Queen Christina's *Hovordning* (court ordinance) of July 1653.

14 RA, Riksrådsprotokollet (Council Minutes), 7 Dec. 1669.

15 For fireworks, see Gunilla Dahlberg, '"Snart sprutar Draken Eeld, snart seer man Örnen flechta": om 1600-talets lustfyrverkerier', in Sten Åke Nilsson and Margareta Ramsay (eds.), *1600-talets ansikte* (Lund, 1997).

16 See the engravings by C. C. Eimart, after Ehrenstrahl, in *Certamen Equestre Caeteraque Solemnia* (Stockholm, 1685); Lena Rangström, *Karl XIs karusell 1672* (Stockholm, 1995).

17 Printed in Fredrik Wilhelm von Ehrenheim (ed.), *Tessin och Tessiniana* (Stockholm, 1819); at the end of the sixteenth century Duke Karl also had his meals announced by kettledrums and fanfares: see also his Court Ordinance of 1590, Section 18, in Schmedeman, *Kongl stadgar*.

18 S. Hallberg (ed.), *Från Sveriges storhetstid: Charles Ogiers dagbok under ambassaden i Sverige 1634–5* (Stockholm, 1914), pp. 102–3.

19 Henry Reeve (ed.), *A Journal of the Swedish Embassy in the Years 1653 and 1654…by the Ambassador Bulstrode Whitelocke*, 2 vols. (London, 1855), I, pp. 223–4; see also Stenbock, *Lorenzo Magalotti*, p. 115.

20 See Gustaf Floderus (ed.), *Johan Hultman Annotationer öfver Konung Carl XIIs Hjeltebedrifter* (Stockholm, 1819), p. 68.

21 RA, Riksregistraturet, 22 March 1673, fols. 354v–355v.

22 Folke Lindberg, 'En Stockholmsskildring från Karl XI's tid: Olaus Bodinus' dagboksanteckningar från 1686 års riksdag', in Nils Ahnlund (ed.), *Studier och handlingar rörande Stockholms historia* (Uppsala, 1938), I, pp. 33.

23 David Lindqvist, 'Hovförsamlingens liturgiska tradition 1614–1693', in *Lunds Universitets Årsskrift*, n. s., 41 (1945).

24 Ibid., p. 10.

25 Johannes Wendel Bardili, *Des Weyland Durchl: Printzens Maximilian Emanuels Hertzogs in Würtemberg u. Obristen über ein Schwedisch Dragoner-Regiment Reisen* (Stuttgart, 1730), p. 123.

26 Schmedeman, *Kongl stadgar*, p. 35.

27 Ibid., pp. 1150–52.

28 Lindqvist, 'Hovförsamlingens liturgiska tradition', p. 43.

29 Olaus Ekman, *Siönödz-löffte aff två deelar* (Stockholm, 1680), p. 136.

30 John Granlund and Gösta Holm (eds.), *Oeconomia eller Hushållsbok för ungt adelsfolk* (Lund, 1971).

31 *Reyncke Fosz* (Stockholm, 1621), p. 8. Religion at the Swedish court is, however, a subject on which further work is needed.

32 Gustav Vasa's Court Ordinance of 1544; printed in *Konung Gustaf den förstes registratur, XVI [1544]* (Stockholm, 1895); published in *Handlingar rörande Sveriges historia*, 1st ser. p. 113.

33 Barbro Hovstadius, *Svenskt silver: Från renässans till rokoko* (Stockholm, 1990).

34 M. Lindgren., 'Måleriet', in *Signums svenska konsthistoria: Renässansens konst* (Lund, 1996).

35 Her grandson, the future Karl XII, named the miniaturist 'the monkey'. L. Looström, 'Andreas von Behn', in *Svenskt Biografiskt Lexikon* (Stockholm, 1922), III, p. 65.

36 Nicolas Millich from Antwerp can be considered the leading sculptor in Sweden during the 1670s and 1680s. He was closely associated with the building activities at Drottningholm Palace, just as the French sculptor, Bernard Foucquet (father of Jacques), worked almost exclusively at the royal palace in Stockholm (from around 1700).

37 I. Estham, 'Textilkonsten', in *Signums svenska konsthistoria*.

38 For tapestries, see also Johan Fredrik Böttiger, *Svenska Statens samling af Väfda Tapeter*, 4 vols. (Stockholm, 1895–8).

39 Åke Nisbeth, 'Glas i Sverige intill 1900', in Märta-Stina Danielsson (ed.), *Svenskt glas* (Stockholm, 1995).

40 Torbjörn Fulton, *Stuckarbeten i svenska byggnadsmiljöer från äldre Vasatid* (Ph.D. diss., Uppsala University, 1994).

41 Astrid Tydén-Jordan, *Kröningsvagnen* (Stockholm, 1985).

42 Sten Karling, *Trädgårdskonstens historia i Sverige intill Le Nôtrestilens genombrott* (diss., Göteborg University, 1931); M. Olausson, 'Trädgårdskonsten', in *Signums svenska konsthistoria*.

43 Göran Alm, 'Arkitekturen', in *Signums svenska konsthistoria*.

44 Bo Bennich-Björkman, *Författaren i ämbetet: Studier i funktion och organisation av författarämbeten vid svenska hovet och kansliet, 1550–1850* (diss., Stockholm University, 1970); Kurt Johannesson, *Polstjärnans tecken* (diss., Uppsala University, 1968).

45 Erik Kjellberg, *Kungliga musiker i Sverige under stormaktstiden: Studier kring deras organisation, verksamhet och status, c.1620–c.1720*, 2 vols. (diss., Uppsala University, 1979).

46 Allan Ellenius has described the use of paintings for similar ideological purposes: Ellenius, *Karolinska bildidéer* (Uppsala, 1966).

47 For travelling actors at the court, see Gunilla Dahlberg, *Komediantteatern i 1600-talets Sverige* (Stockholm, 1992).

48 Nils Sjöberg (ed.), *Johan Ekeblads bref*, 2 vols. (Stockholm, 1911).

49 John Robinson, *An Account of Sweden, as it were in the Year 1688* (London, 1694), p. 80.

50 Paul Bonnefon (ed.), *Mémoires de Louis Henri de Loménie Comte de Brienne, dit le jeune Brienne*, 2 vols. (Paris, 1917), II, p. 250.

51 Sjöberg, *Johan Ekeblads bref*, I, p. 284.

52 At least there was one cost that was not included in the court budget: for reasons that remain unclear, the maintenance of Tre Kronor Castle was covered by a budget specifically earmarked for the maintenance of royal residences.

53 In 1693, for example, the court used 60,993 tallow candles, 18,462 wax candles and 1,224 wax torches; Slottsarkivet, Stockholm, Hovförtäringsräkenskaper (1818), Kungl. Majts. hov 1693, I/A/123.

54 Max Hein, 'Christoph von Brandts relationer om den svenska staten under Karl XI', *Karolinska Förbundets Årsbok* (1920), 56–7.

55 Robinson, *Account of Sweden*, p. 82.

56 Reeve, *Journal of the Swedish Embassy*.

57 RA, Reduktionskollegium Reduktionsprotokoll D/IV/1: General-Extract öfver Donationema.

58 UUB, Bengt Rosenhane MS Collection: Ulf Bonde to Bengt Rosenhane, Stockholm, 26 July 1676.

59 UUB, Rosenhane Collection: Åke Ulfsparre to Bengt Rosenhane, 1672.

60 UUB, Rosenhane Collection: Anna Maria Clodt to Bengt Rosenhane, Stockholm, 1 November 1673.

61 Jesper Swedberg, *Gudz Barnas heliga Sabbats Ro*, 2 vols. (Skara, 1710–12), I, p. 304.

62 Fabian Persson, 'Dog utlefwad cammarfröken: Det svenska hovfruntimret under stormaktstiden', in Eva Österberg (ed.), *Jämmerdal och fröjdesal: Kvinnor i stormaktstidens Sverige* (Stockholm, 1997).

63 Granlund and Holm, *Oeconomia*, p. 32.

64 Kungliga Biblioteket, Stockholm [hereafter KB], Carl Maximilian Adlerfelt's Journal, 1715.

65 KB, I/X/5: with annotations by the page Johan Teet, 1697.

66 Norbert Elias, *The Court Society* (Oxford, 1983).

67 Elmroth, *För kung och fosterland*, p. 42

68 By 'new nobility' I mean those who had held noble status for only one or two generations.

69 RA, Riksregistraturet: Queen Christina to Ingeborg Gyllenstierna, 19 August 1606.

70 Christopher Grubb, *Penu proverbiale* (Linköping, 1665), p. 447.

71 For the chancery, see Svante Norrhem, *Uppkomlingarna: Kanslitjänstemännen i 1600-talets Sverige och Europa* (Ph.D. diss., Umeå University, 1993).

72 KB, Carl Gustaf Tessin's Åkerödagbok, 31 May 1758, p. 615.

73 Johan Adler Salvius to Magnus Gabriel de la Gardie, 30 June 1649; in A. B. Carlsson, 'Adler Salvius såsom rådgifvare åt Magnus Gabriel De la Gardie', *Personhistorisk Tidskrift*, 12, Parts 3–4 (1910), 151.

CHAPTER TWELVE

1 A concise account of the rise of Moscow is Robert O. Crummey, *The Formation of Muscovy, 1304–1613* (London, 1987). M. Pliukhanova, *Siuzhety i simvoly moskovskogo gosudarstva* (St Petersburg, 1995), pp. 15–19, argues that the 'Third Rome' theory has been given undue prominence in discussions of Muscovite ideology; nevertheless, see D. Stremoukhof, 'Moscow the Third Rome: Sources of the Doctrine', *Speculum*, 28 (1953), 84–101; Gustav Alef, 'The Adoption of the Muscovite Two-Headed Eagle', *Speculum*, 41 (1966), 1–21.

2 See Robert O. Crummey, *Aristocrats and Servitors: The Boyar Elite in Russia, 1613–1689* (Princeton, 1983).

3 Nancy S. Kollmann, *Kinship and Politics: The Making of the Muscovite Political System, 1345–1547* (Stanford, 1987); Crummey, *Aristocrats and Servitors*; see also G. Alef, *Rulers and Nobles in Fifteenth-Century Muscovy* (London, 1983); Ann Kleimola, 'Status, Place and Politics: The Rise of Mestnichestvo', *Forschungen zur Osteuropäischen Geschichte*, 27 (1980), 195–214. On the rhetoric of ritual abasement, see N. S. Kollmann, 'Concepts of Society and Social Identity in Early Modern Russia', in S. H. Baron and N. S. Kollmann (eds.), *Religion and Culture in Early*

Modern Russia and Ukraine (DeKalb, 1997), pp. 34–51.

4 See N. S. Kollmann, 'The Seclusion of Elite Muscovite Women', *Russian History*, 10 (1983), 170–87; L. Hughes, *Sophia, Regent of Russia, 1657–1704* (New Haven, 1990), pp. 16–22.

5 See Arthur Voyce, *The Moscow Kremlin: Its History, Architecture and Art Treasures* (Berkeley, 1954); J. Raba, *The Moscow Kremlin: Mirror of the Newborn Muscovite State* (Tel Aviv, 1978); W. C. Brumfield, *A History of Russian Architecture* (Cambridge, 1993), pp. 92–106. The most detailed Russian studies are I. E. Zabelin, *Moskva v eia proshlom i nastoiashchem*, 12 vols. (Moscow, 1910–17); S. P. Bartenev, *Moskovskii Kreml' v starinu i teper'*, 2 vols. (St Petersburg, 1912–18).

6 These frescoes were repainted in the 1650s 'exactly as they were', to emphasize dynastic continuity; see David B. Miller, 'Creating Legitimacy: Ritual, Ideology, and Power in Sixteenth-Century Russia', *Russian History*, 21 (1994), 312; Michael Cherniavsky, 'Ivan the Terrible and the Iconography of the Kremlin Cathedral of the Archangel Michael', *Russian History*, 2 (1975), 3–28.

7 The most detailed descriptions of the palace can be found in the works of I. E. Zabelin, see n. 5, and *Domashnii byt russkikh tsarei v XVI i XVII stoletiiakh. I. Gosudarev dvor, ili dvorets* (repr., Moscow, 1990). On access, see Grigorii Kotoshikhin, *O Rossii v tsarstvovanie Alekseia Mikhailovicha* (St Petersburg, 1906). A visual reconstruction of the palace is problematical. No plans of the building survive from the seventeenth century; one has to rely entirely on descriptions and to some extent on the parts of the building extant today, but still closed to the public.

8 Miller, 'Creating Legitimacy', pp. 304–5.

9 Paul Bushkovitch, 'The Epiphany Ceremony of the Russian Court in the Sixteenth and Seventeenth Centuries', *Russian Review*, 49 (1990), 1–18.

10 R. O. Crummey, 'Court Spectacles in Seventeenth-Century Russia: Illusion and Reality', in D. C. Waugh (ed.), *Essays in Honor of A. A. Zimin* (Columbus, OH, 1985), p. 138.

11 Valerie Kivelson, *Autocracy in the Provinces: The Muscovite Gentry and Political Culture in the Seventeenth Century* (Stanford, 1997), p. 38.

12 Richard Wortman, *Scenarios of Power: Myth and Ceremony in Russian Monarchy*, 2 vols. (Princeton, 1995), I, p. 30. See also Daniel Rowland, 'Biblical Imagery in the Political Culture of Early Modern Russia: The Blessed Host of the Heavenly Tsar', in M. Flier and D. Rowland (ed.), *Medieval Russian Culture*, 2 vols. (Berkeley, Los Angeles and London, 1994), II, pp. 182–212.

13 Miller, 'Creating Legitimacy', p. 294; M. Cherniavsky, 'Ivan the Terrible as Renaissance Prince', *Slavic Review*, 27 (1968), 195–211; N. S. Kollmann, 'Pilgrimage, Procession, and Symbolic Space in Sixteenth-Century Russian Politics', in Flier and Rowland, *Medieval Russian Culture*, pp. 163–81.

14 Palace records were published as *Dvortsovye razriady*, 4 vols. (St Petersburg, 1852–5) and *Vykhody gosudarei tsarei i velikikh kniazei Mikhaila Fedorovicha, Alekseia Mikhailovicha, Fedora Alekseevicha, vseia Rusii Samoderzhtsev* (Moscow, 1844). See also *Treasures of the Czars from the State Museums of the Moscow Kremlin* (London, 1995); *Gosudarstvennaia Oruzheinaia palata Moskovskogo Kremlia* (Moscow, 1969).

15 Michael S. Flier, 'Breaking the Code: The Image of the Tsar in the Muscovite Palm Sunday Ritual', in Flier and Rowland, *Medieval Russian Culture*, pp. 213–42; L. Hughes, 'Did Peter I Abolish the Palm Sunday Ceremony?', *Newsletter of the Study Group on 18th-Century Russia*, 24 (1996), 62–5.

16 Pliukhanova, *Siuzhety i simvoly*, p. 233.

17 Philip Longworth, *Alexis, Tsar of All the Russias* (London, 1984). On the seventeenth-century background, L. Hughes, 'The Seventeenth-Century "Renaissance" in Russia', *History Today*, February 1980, 41–5.

18 S. Karlinsky, *Russian Drama from its Beginnings to the Age of Pushkin* (Berkeley, 1985); C. R. Jensen, 'Music for the Tsar: A Preliminary Study of the Music of the Muscovite Court Theatre', *The Musical Quarterly*, 79 (1995), 368–401.

19 Longworth, *Alexis, Tsar of All the Russias*, pp. 118–20.

20 E. Mozgovaia, 'Obraz Petra I-imperatora v proizvedeniiakh tvorchestva Bartolomeo Karlo Rastrelii', *Monarkhiia i narodovlastie v kul'ture prosveshcheniia* (Moscow, 1995), p. 4; Wortman, *Scenarios of Power*, pp. 42–4.

21 Quoted in L. Oliva, *Peter the Great: Great Lives Observed* (Englewood Cliffs, 1970), p. 108.

22 See L. Hughes, 'Between Two Worlds: Tsarevna Natal'ia Alekseevna and the "Emancipation" of Petrine Women', in Maria Di Salvo and L. Hughes (ed.), *A Window on Russia: Papers from the V International Conference of the Study Group on Eighteenth-Century Russia, Gargnano, 1994* (Rome, 1996), pp. 29–36; and Hughes, 'From Caftans into Corsets: The Sartorial Transformation of Women during the Reign of Peter the Great' (forthcoming).

23 See James Cracraft, *The Petrine Revolution in Russian Architecture* (Chicago, 1990), and *The Petrine Revolution in Russian Imagery* (Chicago, 1997); also L. Hughes, *Russia in the Age of Peter the Great* (New Haven and London, 1998).

24 *Polnoe Sobranie Zakonov Rossiiskoi Imperii*, V (St Petersburg, 1830), no. 3241, pp. 597–8.

25 See John Fennell, *A History of the Russian Church to 1448* (London, 1995), p. 21.

26 G. Vilinbakhov, 'K istorii uchrezhdeniia ordena Andreia Pervozvannogo', *Kul'tura i iskusstvo petrovskogo vremeni* (Leningrad, 1977), pp. 144–5; A. I. Andreev, 'Petr I v Anglii v 1698', in *Petr Velikii: Sbornik statei* (Moscow and Leningrad, 1947), p. 87.

27 Sermon delivered on 23 Nov. 1718 by Archbishop Feofan Prokopovich, 'Slovo v den' sviatogo blagovernago kniazia Aleksandra Nevskago', in Prokopovich, *Sochineniia*, ed. I. P. Eremin (Moscow and Leningrad, 1961), pp. 94–103; see also N. A. Sindalovskii, *Legendy i mifi Sankt-Peterburga* (St Petersburg, 1994), pp. 24–5.

28 *Polnoe Sobranie Zakonov*, VII, no. 4241, pp. 74–5 (4 June); H. Bassewitz, 'Zapiski grafa Bassevicha, sluzhashchie k poiasneniiu nekotorykh sobytii iz vremeni tsarstvovaniia Petra Velikogo (1713–1725)', *Russkii arkhiv*, 3 (1865), 251–2; M. Cherniavsky, *Tsar and People: Studies in Russian Myths* (New York, 1961), pp. 84–5; Wortman, *Scenarios of Power*, p. 62.

29 See 'The Story of the Ship's Boat, which gave his Majesty the Thought of Building Ships of War', in James Cracraft (ed.), *For God and Peter the Great: The Works of Thomas Consett, 1723–1729* (Boulder, 1982), p. 210.

30 'Pokhodnyi zhurnal 1723 goda', *Kamer-furerskii zhurnal, 1721–1726* (St Petersburg, 1855), 15 (these court journals replaced the Muscovite *razriady*; see n. 14).

31 Bassewitz, 'Zapiski grafa Bassevicha', p. 233.

32 'Pokhodnyi zhurnal 1723 goda', 18–19.

33 *Polnoe Sobranie Zakonov*, VII/4562, p. 345 (2 Sept. 1724). For the boat's political role up to the present day, see M. Sarantola-Weiss, 'Peter the Great's First Boat, "Grandfather of the Russian Navy"', in Di Salvo and Hughes, *A Window on Russia*, pp. 37–42.

34 See Stephen Baehr, *The Paradise Myth in Eighteenth-Century Russia* (Stanford, 1991), pp. 1–13; I. M. Lotman and B. A. Uspensky, 'Echoes of the Notion "Moscow as the Third Rome" in Peter the Great's Ideology', in Ann Shukman (ed.), *The Semiotics of Russian Culture* (Ann Arbor, 1984), pp. 53–64.

35 *Pis'ma i bumagi Imperatora Petra Velikogo*, 13 vols., continuing (St Petersburg, Moscow and Leningrad, 1887–1992), V, p. 61 (Jan.–Feb. 1707): letters and papers of Peter the Great. In November 1709, Peter again wrote to Menshikov, on the eve of St Andrew, from 'this holy land', *Pis'ma i bumagi Imperatora Petra*, VIII, p. 469.

36 Texts of the Table are in *Polnoe Sobranie Zakonov*, VI/3890, pp. 486–93 (24 Jan. 1722). See also Brenda Meehan-Waters, *Autocracy and Aristocracy: The Russian Service Elite of 1730* (New Brunswick, 1982).

37 Short biographies can be found in the relevant volumes of *Modern Encyclopedia of Russian and Soviet History* (Gulf Breeze, 1977–).

38 See *200-letie Kabineta ego imp. velichestva, 1704–1904* (St Petersburg, 1911), pp. 258–9. Also S. F. Platonov, *Petr Velikii. Lichnost' i deiatel'nost'* (Paris, 1927), pp. 123–4; V. V. Kvadri, *Svita Petra Velikogo* (St Petersburg,

1902); N. I. Pavlenko, *Ptentsy gnezda petrova* (Moscow, 1989).

39 Pavel Miliukov, *Gosudarstvennoe khoziaistvo Rossii v pervoi chet. XVIII St i reforma Petra Velikogo* (St Petersburg, 1905), p. 665 and appendix, p. 150.

40 Kvadri, *Svita Petra Velikogo*, p. 39. See also N. E. Volkov, *Dvor russkikh imperatorov v ego proshlom i nastoiashchem* (St Petersburg, 1900).

41 L. Hughes, 'The Petrine Year', in K. Friedrich (ed.), *Feste Feiern Wie Sie Fallen: Festival Culture in Germany and Europe* (forthcoming).

42 *Polnoe Sobranie Zakonov*, VI, pp. 444–8, 453.

43 Prokopovich, *Kratkaia povest'*, pp. 29–30; and see the picture in V. Iu. Matveev, 'K istorii vozniknoveniia i razvitiia siuzheta "Petra I, vysekaiushchii statuiu Rossii"', *Kul'tura i iskusstvo Rossii XVIII veka: Novye materialy i issledovaniia* (Leningrad, 1981), p. 35.

44 On 'new beginnings', see Baehr, *Paradise Myth*, Ch. 3; on titles, Isabel de Madriaga, 'Tsar into Emperor: The Title of Peter the Great', in R. Oresko et al. (eds.), *Royal and Republican Sovereignty in Early Modern Europe* (Cambridge, 1996), pp. 351–81.

45 Descriptions were published in *Opisanie koronatsii e. v. Ekateriny Alekseevny* (St Petersburg, 1724; Moscow, 1725); see also Wortman, *Scenarios of Power*, pp. 72–3, and Friedrich von Bergholz, *Dnevnik kammer-iunkera Berkhgol'tsa, vedennyi im v Rossii v tsarstvovanie Petra Velikogo s 1721–1725 g.* (3rd edn., Moscow, 1902–3), pp. 32–42.

46 *Opisanie poriadka derzhannogo pri progrebenii blazhennyia vysokoslavnyia i vernodostoineishiia pamiati vsepresvetleishago derzhavneishago Petra Velikago* (St Petersburg, 1725, Moscow, 1726); F. Prokopovich, *Kratkaia povest' o smerti Petra Velikogo Imperatora i Samoderzhtsa Vserossiiskogo* (St Petersburg, 1831).

47 *Pis'ma i bumagi Imperatora Petra*, I, p. 162.

48 J.-G. Korb, *Diary of an Austrian Secretary of Legation at the Court of Czar Peter the Great*, trans. and ed. Count MacDonnell, 2 vols. (London, 1863, repr. 1968), pp. 195–6.

49 *Pis'ma i bumagi Imperatora Petra*, I, p. 424 (29 Jan. 1701), the tsar's pseudonym often appears written in Latin script; ibid., II, p. 159; ibid., IX (1), pp. 227–8, 242–3, 983; J. Juel, 'Iz zapisok datskogo poslannika Iusta Iulia', *Russkii arkhiv* (1892), 130. Visitors to Romodanovskii's home were greeted by a bear with a glass of vodka, which ripped off the hat or wig of anyone who refused a drink: F. C. Weber, *The Present State of Russia*, 2 vols. (London, 1722), I, pp. 5, 137.

50 See R. Zguta, 'Peter I's "Most Drunken Synod of Fools and Jesters"', *Jahrbücher für Geschichte Osteuropas*, 21 (1973), 18–21.

51 'Pokhodnyi zhurnal 1721 goda', 59–75. See also the wedding of Nikita Zotov in 1715, Weber, *The Present State of Russia*, I, 89–90;

M. I. Semevskii, *Slovo i delo, 1700–1725: Ocherki i rasskazy iz russkoi istorii XVIII veka* (St Petersburg, 1884), pp. 319–20.

52 'Pokhodnyi zhurnal 1710 goda', 23; *Pis'ma i bumagi Imperatora Petra*, X, pp. 270–71. See also descriptions in *Exacter Relation von der…neu erbauten Festung und Stadt St Petersburg…von H. G.* (Leipzig, 1713), and Juel, 'Iz zapisok datskogo poslannika Iusta Iulia', pp. 39–41. Weber's much-quoted account (*Present State of Russia*, I, pp. 285–9) is, in fact, borrowed, with amendments, from the Leipzig account (but Weber may be the author of both).

53 'Pokhodnyi zhurnal 1724 goda', 37–8; Bassewitz, 'Zapiski grafa Bassevicha', pp. 243–4; Bergholz, *Dnevnik kammer-iunkera Berkhgol'tsa*, 1724, pp. 13–14.

54 See N. Aristov, 'Pervonachal'noe obrazovanie Petra Velikogo', *Russkii arkhiv*, 13 (1875), 473.

55 Weber, *Present State of Russia*, I, p. 109; Juel, 'Iz zapisok datskogo poslannika Iusta Iulia', p. 37.

56 Bergholz, *Dnevnik kammer-iunkera Berkhgol'tsa*, pp. 52–3.

57 M. S. Anderson, 'Peter the Great': Imperial Revolutionary?', in A. G. Dickens (ed.), *The Courts of Europe: Politics, Patronage and Royalty, 1400–1800* (London, 1977), p. 276.

58 Korb, *Diary of an Austrian Secretary*, II, p. 155; G. Grund, *Bericht über Russland in den Jahren 1705–1710 (Doklad o Rossii v 1705–1710 gg.)*, trans. and ed. Iu. N. Bespiatykh (St Petersburg, 1992), p. 126. See also Weber, *Present State of Russia*, I, p. 210.

59 *Sbornik imperatorskogo rossiiskogo istoricheskogo obshchestva*, 148 vols. (St Petersburg, 1866–1918), XLIX, pp. 344, 350–51 (hereafter, *SIRIO*): letters to Dubois, 11 and 13 June n.s.

60 See L. Hughes, 'Peter the Great's Two Weddings: Changing Images of Women in a Transitional Age', in Rosalind Marsh (ed.), *Women in Russia and Ukraine* (Cambridge, 1996), pp. 31–44.

61 G. Bogdanov, *Istoricheskoe, geograficheskoe i topograficheskoe opisanie Sanktpeterburga, ot nachala zavedeniia ego s 1703 po 1751 god.* (St Petersburg, 1779), pp. 54–5.

62 *SIRIO*, XL, pp. 273–4: letter to Louis XV, 3 Sept., n.s., 1723.

63 'Oration at the funeral of…Peter the Great (1725)', in M. Raeff (ed.), *Peter the Great Changes Russia* (Lexington, 1972), p. 42.

64 Wortman, *Scenarios of Power*, Ch. 3.

65 Volkov, *Dvor russkikh imperatorov*, pp. 50–51; *Polnoe Sobranie Zakonov*, VIII/5878.

66 James Keith, *A Fragment of a Memoir of James Keith written by Himself, 1714–1734* (Edinburgh, 1843).

67 Sarantola-Weiss, 'Peter the Great's First Boat', pp. 410–11.

LIST OF ILLUSTRATIONS

(Photographic sources are in brackets, if different from the original source.)

ENDPAPERS: Orazio Scarabelli, *The Naumachia at the Pitti Palace*, 1589. Gabinetto dei Disegni e delle Stampe, Uffizi, Florence (Scala).

1 'Så lever man vid hovet', from Schering Rosenhane, 'Hortus Regius', MS *c.*1645. Courtesy of the Royal Library, Stockholm.

2 Anon., *Louis XIII and the Infante Felipe at the Bidasoa River in 1615*. Convent of the Incarnation, Madrid (Institut Amatller d'Art Hispànic).

6 Sir Peter Paul Rubens (1577–1640), *The Debarkation of Marie de Médicis at Marseilles, 3 November 1600, c.*1622–5. Musée du Louvre, Paris (Lauros Giraudon).

13 Jean-Michel Chevotet (1698–1772), *L'escalier des ambassadeurs*, engraving, from L. Surugue, *Grand escalier du château de Versailles, c.*1725. Bibliothèque Nationale, Paris (Giraudon).

17 Jacques Callot (*c.*1592–1635), *Catafalque*, from A. Ademari, *Esequie…Principe Don Francesco de' Medici*, 1614. British Library, London.

18 French School, *Henri III and the Knights of the Saint-Esprit, c.*1578–84. Musée Condé, Chantilly (Giraudon).

22–3 Flemish School, *David and Bathsheba, c.*1530. Marylebone Cricket Club, London (Bridgeman Art Library, London/New York). The editor is grateful to Mr Roger Stephens for this reference.

31 Antonio Joli (*c.*1700–77), *Naples: La Festa dei Quattro Altari, c.*1757. By kind permission of the Duke of Buccleuch and Queensberry KT.

32 Wenceslaus Hollar (1607–77), *Charles II at the Garter Feast*, from Elias Ashmole, *Institutions of the Most Noble Order of the Garter* (London, 1672). (Fotomas Index).

35 Antonio de Pereda (1611–78), *Vanitas* (detail), *c.*1635. Kunsthistorisches Museum, Vienna.

36 Giovanni Paolo Pannini (1691–1765), *View of the Base Landing and Scala Regia from the North Corridor, c.*1730. Bibliotheca di Archeologia e Storia d'Arte, Rome (Bibliotheca Hertziana, Rome).

39 See above, **2**.

42 Dioscorides, *Acerca de la Materia Medicinal [De Materia Medica]* (Antwerp, 1555), title page. Biblioteca Nacional, Madrid (Institut Amatller d'Art Hispànic).

49 Spanish School, seventeenth century, *Casa Real del Pardo*. Copyright © Patrimonio Nacional.

51 Spanish School, seventeenth century, *The Alcázar and Bridge of Segovia, Madrid*. Caylus Anticuario, Madrid (Bridgeman Art Library, London/New York).

53 Gómez de Mora, *Plan of the Alcázar at Madrid*, 1626. Biblioteca Apostolica Vaticana (Institut Amatller d'Art Hispànic).

54 Spanish School, seventeenth century, *Bird's-eye view of El Escorial*. Musée du Louvre, Paris (Giraudon).

55 Jusepe Leonardo, *Panoramic view of El Buen Retiro*, 1636–7. Royal Palace, Madrid (Institut Amatller d'Art Hispànic).

58 *An auto-da-fé in the Plaza Mayor, Madrid*, from Bernard Picart (1673–1733), *The Ceremonies and Religious Customs of the Known World*, 7 vols. (London, 1733–9). Mary Evans Picture Library.

60 Schematic plan of the Chapel Royal of the Alcázar, Madrid, after a plan of 1667. Copyright © Weidenfeld and Nicolson, London.

62 Francisco Rizi, *The auto-da-fé in the Plaza Mayor, Madrid, 30 June 1680*, 1683. Museo del Prado, Madrid (Institut Amatller d'Art Hispànic).

63 Claudio Coello (*c.*1642–93), *The Adoration of the Holy Eucharist*, 1685–90. Monasterio del Escorial, Madrid (Institut Amatller d'Art Hispànic).

64 Gonzalo Fernández de Oviedo y Valdes, *La historia general de las Indias* (Seville, 1535), title page. Biblioteca Nacional, Madrid (Institut Amatller d'Art Hispànic).

66 French School, seventeenth century, *Louis XIV followed by the Grand Dauphin on Horseback, passing the Grotto of Thetis at Versailles, c.*1680. Château de Versailles et de Trianon (RMN-D. Arnaudet, Gérard Blot).

71 French School, *Antoine Macault Presenting his Translation of the First Three Books of Diodorus Siculus to François I, c.*1530. Musée Condé, Chantilly (Giraudon).

74 Jacques Tortorel (*fl.*1560–90) and Jacques Perrissin, *The Assassination of the Duc de Guise at Blois, 23 December 1588*. Bibliothèque Nationale, Paris, Cabinet d'Estampes (Giraudon).

75 Fredrik de Moucheron (1633–86), *A Hunting Party at Fontainebleau*, 1650. Private Collection (photograph courtesy of Raphael Valls Gallery, London).

78 French School, seventeenth century, *Madame de Lansac and the Royal Children, c.*1643. Château de Versailles (Giraudon).

79 Flemish School, *Louis XIV's Coach Crossing the Pont Neuf, c.*1665. Musées de la Ville de Paris, Musée Carnavalet (Giraudon).

80 Anon., *The Carrousel in the Place Royale*, Le Roman des Chevaliers de la Gloire, *in 1615, c.*1615. Musée Carnavalet, Paris (Phototèque des Musées de la Ville de Paris).

82 Studio of Jean Mozin, *The Marriage of Louis XIV and Marie-Thérèse, at Saint Jean de Luz, 9 June 1660*, Gobelins tapestry, 1665–80. Château de Versailles et de Trianon (RMN-Jean Shormans).

83 Pierre-Denis Martin the younger (1663–1742), *View of the Church of the Invalides: The Visit of Louis XIV and his Court in August 1706, c.*1706. Musées de la Ville de Paris, Musée Carnavalet (Giraudon).

86 Pierre-Denis Martin the younger, *The Château and Pavilions of Marly*, 1723. Château de Versailles, Grand Trianon (Giraudon).

90 Pierre Patel, *The Château and Gardens of Versailles*, 1668. Château de Versailles (Giraudon).

91 Pierre-Denis Martin the younger, *The Château of Versailles from the Place d'Armes*, 1722. Château de Versailles (Giraudon).

92 Jean de Saint-Igny (?–*c.*1645), *Louis XIII, Anne of Austria and Cardinal Richelieu watching the Ballet* The Triumph of French Arms *at the Palais Cardinal*, 1641. Musée des Arts Décoratifs, Paris.

93 Israël Silvestre (1621–91), *Fireworks and the Burning of the Palace of Alcina at Versailles*, from *Les Plaisirs de l'Ile Enchantée*, 1664. Fotomas Index.

94 Antonio Canale, il Canaletto (1697–1768), *Whitehall and the Privy Garden from Richmond House* (detail), *c.*1747. Goodwood House, Earl of March and Kinrara and the Trustees of the Goodwood Collection.

97 Georg Höfnagel, *View of Nonsuch Palace, c.*1590, from Georg Braun (1541–1622) and Franz Hogenberg, *Civitates Orbis Terrarum* V (1597). Fotomas Index.

98 Plan of Whitehall Palace, *c.*1670, based on H. M. Colvin (ed.), *The History of the King's Works*, III–V (London, 1975–6). © Weidenfeld & Nicolson, London.

101 Anon., *Elizabeth I's Coronation Procession, 1559*. British Library Egerton MS 3320, fo. 5.

102 Lucas Hornebolte (?–1544) and assistants, *Henry VIII in his Traverse*, from the *Liber Niger of the Order of the Garter* (detail), *c.*1534. Reproduced by permission of the Dean and Canons of Windsor.

103 Robert Peake (*c.*1557–1619), attrib., *The Collar-Day Procession (Eliza Triumphans), c.*1601; Private Collection, courtesy of Mr and Mrs John Wingfield-Digby.

107 Studio of Daniel Mytens, *George Villiers, 1st Duke of Buckingham*, c.1630 (detail). Christie's Images, London.

110 Maker's mark WI, London 1604–5, silver-gilt water jug; Moscow Kremlin Armoury Museum.

111 Hendrijk van Steenwijk the younger (*c.*1580–1649) and others, *Charles I as Prince of Wales*, c.1620. Den Konglige Maleri- og Skulptursamling, Statens Museum for Kunst, Copenhagen.

114 Dirck Stoop (*c.*1610–*c.*1685), *Coronation Procession of Charles II to Westminster from the Tower of London*, 1661. Museum of London (Bridgeman Art Library).

115 Leonard Knyff (1650–1721), *Panoramic View of Hampton Court Palace*, *c.* 1720. Royal Collection © Her Majesty the Queen.

118 Theodoor van Thulden (1606–69), *Allegory of the Transfer of the Survivance to Willem II*, c.1641. Royal Collections, The Hague.

123 Adriaen van de Venne (1589–1662), *A Hunting Party of the House of Orange*, c.1620. Rijksmuseum Paleis Het Loo, on loan from the Geschiedkundige Vereniging Oranje Nassau (photograph: A. W. W. Meine Jansen).

124 Jan Matthysz (*d.*1710) after Pieter Post (1608–69), *Huis ten Bosch*, plan, *c.*1655. Collection Royal House Archives, The Hague.

127. Dirck van Delen (1605–71), *The Great Hall of the Binnenhof during the Great Assembly of 1651*, c.1651. Rijksmuseum, Amsterdam.

128 Solomon Savery after Simon de Vlieger, *Water Revels for Marie de Médicis in Amsterdam, 1638*. Bodleian Library, Oxford. Douce Prints Portfolio.

131 Jan Mijtens (1614–70), *The Marriage of Louise Henriëtte to Friedrich Wilhelm II, in the Oude Hof, 1646*, 1647. Musée des Beaux Arts, Rennes (Giraudon).

132 Pieter Philippe (*c.*1635–*c.*1701) after Jacob Toorenvliet (*c.*1635–1719), *Dinner in the Mauritshuis for Charles II, 1660*. Stichting Atlas van Stolk, Historisch Museum, Rotterdam.

133 Daniel Marot the elder (1663–1752), *Willem III and his Consort at a Ball in the Oranjezaal, Huis ten Bosch, 1686*, 1686. Stapleton Collection (Bridgeman Art Library).

134 Caspar Netscher (1639–84), *Prince Willem III in Armour*, 1677. Rijksmuseum, Amsterdam.

137 Romeyn de Hooghe (1645–1708), *View of Het Loo*, c.1690. Paleis Het Loo, National Museum, Apeldoorn (photograph: R. Mulder).

139 Hendrick de Meyer (*c.*1600–1690) and Pieter Bout (*c.*1658–1702), *The Arrival of Willem III of Orange at Dordrecht*. Galerie de Jonkheere, New York and Paris.

140 S. de Peracco, *Mass before the Pope in the Sistine Chapel*, 1578. Biblioteca Apostolica Vaticana, Riserva Stragr. 7, fo.116.

143 Pietro da Cortona (1597–1669), *Prince Paulo Savelli's Audience with Pope Paul V, 1620*, c.1630. Schloss Rohrau, Graf Harrach'sche Familiensammlung.

147 Plan of the Vatican Palace before 1521, from a plan by Henry Dietrich Fernández; © Weidenfeld & Nicolson, London.

148 Etienne Dupérac (*c.*1520–*c.*1607), *Coronation of Cosimo de' Medici as Grand Duke of Tuscany in the Sala Regia on 18 February 1570*, c.1570. Biblioteca Apostolica Vaticana (Archivio Fotografico Riserva Str. 7).

151 Giovanni Paolo Pannini (1691–1765), *The French Ambassador to the Holy See, the Duc de Choiseul, leaving St Peter's Square, Rome*, c.1757. Staatliche Museen zu Berlin, Preussischer Kulturbesitz, Gemäldegalerie (photograph: Jorg P. Anders).

152 Leonard von Matt, *Pope Pius XII on the* Sedia Gestatoria *with canopy*, 1939, photograph. Gemeinnützige Stiftung Leonard von Matt, Buochs, Switzerland.

155 Giorgio Vasari (1511–74), *Pope Leo X returning to Florence, 1515*, 1555–62. Palazzo Vecchio, Florence (Scala).

159 Andrea Sacchi (1559–1661), *Urban VIII and Cardinal-Nephew Antonio Barberini at the Gesù, 1640*, c.1640–41. Galleria Nazionale d'Arte Antica, Rome (Scala).

163 Joseph Wright of Derby (1734–97), *The Girandola at the Castel Sant' Angelo in Rome*, c.1775. Birmingham Museums and Art Gallery.

164 *The Oath-taking in the Ratstube, 1654*, from *Der Erbhuldigung für Ferdinand IV* (Vienna, 1654), reprinted in Moriz Dreger, *Baugeschichte*

der K. und K. Hofburg in Wien bis zum XIX. Jahrhunderte (Vienna, 1914), plate 137.

170 Lucas van Valkenborch (1530–97), *Emperor Rudolf II taking the Waters at a Spa near Prague*, c.1590. Kunsthistorisches Museum, Vienna.

172 Franz van den Stein, *The Battle of the Elements in the Courtyard of the Hofburg, 1667*. Historisch Museum der Stadt Wien. Direktion der Museen de Stadt Wien.

175 After Martin van Meytens II (1695–1770), *The Coronation Dinner of Joseph II, 1765*, copy *c.*1790. Schloss Schönbrunn, Vienna (Bridgeman Art Library, London/New York).

179 After van Meytens II, *The Arrival in Vienna of Isabella of Parma, 1760*, copy *c.*1790. Schloss Schönbrunn, Vienna (AKG, London).

180 Franz Gessels, *A performance of* Il Pomo d'Oro *before Leopold I, 1668, showing the interior of the theatre designed by Giovanni Burnacini*, c.1668. Reprinted in Dreger, *Baugeschichte* (see **164**), plate 117.

183 Bernardo Bellotto (1720–80), *View of Vienna from the Upper Belvedere Palace*, c.1760. Kunsthistorisches Museum, Vienna.

184 J. A. Delsenbach, engraving after Johann Bernhard Fischer von Erlach (1656–1723), *Projected Design for a Palace and Terraced Park at Schönbrunn*, c.1695, from J. B. Fischer von Erlach, *Entwurff einer historischen Architektur* (Vienna, 1721), Book IV, plate II.

187 Bernardo Bellotto (1720–80), *Schloss Schönbrunn from the Gardens*, c.1759–61. Kunsthistorisches Museum, Vienna.

188 *Florus Anglo-Bavariae* (Liège, 1685), frontispiece. Cambridge University Library.

191 Antonio Zanchi (1631–1722), *Altarpiece for the Theatinerkirke (St Cajetan's), Munich*, 1662. Alte Pinakothek, Munich (AKG, London).

195 Michael Wening (*fl.*1701–26), *The Munich Residenz, looking East*, c.1700. Bayerische Verwaltung der Staatlichen Schlösser, Gärten und Seen, Munich (hereafter BVSGS).

196 *A Tournament in the Brunnenhof of the Munich* Residenz, from Wilhelm Peter Zimmermann, *Beschreibung von Kurtze radierte entwerff und der fürstlichen Hochzeit* (Augsburg, 1614). British Library, London.

198 Hans Georg Beuerl, Agraffe of Maximilian I of Bavaria (Augsburg), 1603. Residenz München, Schatzkammer (BVSGS).

199 Hans Reimer, Display goblet made for Duke Albrecht V of Bavaria and his wife, the Archduchess Anna. Residenz München, Schatzkammer (BVSGS).

201 Plan of the principal floor of the Munich *Residenz*, c.1630–58; based on Samuel John Klingensmith, *The Utility of Splendor: Ceremony, Social Life, and Architecture at the Court of Bavaria, 1600–1800* (Chicago and London, 1993), Plan A. © Weidenfeld and Nicolson.

203 Peter Jakob Horemans (1700–76), *The Electoral Families of Bavaria and Saxony*, 1761. BVSGS.

207 Friedrich Sustris (*c.*1540–99) and Hans Scheich, attrib., Reliquary of St George, 1586–97. Residenz München, Schatzkammer (BVSGS).

209 Matthias Diesel, *The Grottenhof of the Munich Residenz*, 1720. Staats- und Stadtbibliothek, Augsburg.

210 Lucas Cranach the younger (1515–86), *Elector Joachim II Hektor*, c.1570. Schloss Grünewald, Berlin (AKG London).

213 Johan Gregor Memhardt (?–1678), *Berlin*, c.1650–51, from Matthäus Merian and M. Zeiller, *Topographia Electoratus Brandenburgici*, Berlin, 1652.

215 Anton Mozart (1573–1625), *The presentation of the* Kunstschrank *to Duke Philip II of Pomerania-Stettin*, 1617?. Staatliche Museen, Berlin, Preussischer Kulturbesitz, Kunstgewerbemuseum (Bildarchiv Preussischer Kulturbesitz, hereafter BPK).

218 Daniel Nikolaus Chodowiecki (1726–1801), *Allegory of the Great Elector Friedrich Wilhelm receiving the Huguenot Refugees in 1685*, 1782. BPK.

223 Jean-Baptiste Broebes (*c.*1660–*c.*1720), *Idealized View of Royal Berlin*, c.1702–3, from his *Prospect der Palläste und Lust-Schlösser Seiner Königlichen Mayestaat in Preussen* (Augsburg, 1733). (BPK).

227 Johann Stridbeck (1666–1714), *The* Residenz *at Cölln*, 1690. Staatsbibliothek zu Berlin Preussischer Kulturbesitz (BPK).

228 Peter Schenck (*fl.*1700–22), *View of the Entrance Façade of the Potsdam* Residenz, 1702. Neues Palais, Potsdam, Plankammer. Stiftung Preussische Schlösser und Gärten, Berlin-Brandenburg.

230 Giovanni Battista Bagnasacco, *The* Salone *of Stupinigi, c.*1780. Palazzo Chiablese, Torino (Filippo Gallino).

233 Giovanni Tommaso Borgognio, (*c.*1632–1692?), *Bird's-eye view of Turin.* Musei Civici di Torino.

234 Giovanni Tommaso Borgognio, *The ballet* Il dono del Re dell' Alpi a Madama Reale, 1645. Biblioteca Nazionale, Turin ris.Q.V. 60.

237 Antonio Tempestà (1555–1630), *View of the Piazza del Castello, Turin, during the ostension of the Holy Shroud,* 1613. Biblioteca Reale, Turin BRT Inv. IV. 23.

239 Carlo Bossoli (1815–84), *King Vittorio Emanuele II, Cavour, and courtiers descending the Scalone of the Palazzo Madama,* 1853. Musei Civici di Torino.

246 Jan Miel (1599–1663), *La Curea,* 1661. Musei Civici di Torino.

247 Vittorio Amedeo Cignaroli (1730–1800), *La Curea,* 1773. Castello di Stupinigi, Turin (Filippo Gallino).

250 Anon., eighteenth century, *Interior of the Teatro Regio, Turin.* Museo Civico d'Arte Antica e Palazzo Madama, Turin (Scala).

251 Giovanni Paolo Pannini (1691–1765), *An Idealized View of the Castello di Rivoli.* Castello di Racconigi, Turin (Filippo Gallino).

254 Justus Sustermans (1597–1681), *Cosimo II with his Wife Maria Maddalena of Austria and his Son Ferdinando II.* Galleria degli Uffizi, Florence (Scala).

257 Cornelius Cort (1533–78), *Genealogical Tree of the Medici,* 1589. Graphische Sammlung Albertina, Vienna.

258 Bernardino Gaffurri and Jacques Bylivelt (*fl.*1570–89), *The Piazza della Signoria, pietre dure* and gold. Museo degli Argenti, Florence (Scala).

259 Map of Florence, *c.*1580, from Stefano Buonsignori, *Nova pulcherrimae civitatis Fiorentinae topographia accuratissime delineata* (Florence, 1584). Museo Firenze com'era, Florence (Scala).

260 Diacinto Maria Marmi, *Plan of the Piano Nobile of the Pitti Palace.* Biblioteca Nazionale, Florence (photograph: Pineider).

262 Jan Frans van Douven, *Elector Johann Wilhelm of the Palatinate dancing with his wife, Anna Maria Luisa de' Medici,* 1695. Galleria Palatina, Florence (Scala).

263 Alessandro Fei, il Barbiere (*c.*1540–92), *The Metalworkers' Studio c.*1590. Palazzo Vecchio (Studiolo), Florence (Scala).

267 Anon., *Tournament in the Piazza del Campo, Siena, from the Tavoletta di Biccherna, c.*1607–10. Archivio di Stato, Siena (Scala).

268 *The* Argonautica *on the River Arno, 1608,* from Camillo Rinucci, *Descrizione delle feste fatte nelle reali nozze de[i] Serenissimi Principi di Toscana* (Florence, 1608). British Library, London.

270 Pseudo-Marcuola, *Cosimo Riccardi visiting Grand Duke Gian Gastone de' Medici,* 1735. Museo degli Argenti, Florence (Scala).

273 Jacques Callot (*c.*1592–1635), *The first* intermezzo *of* La

Liberazione di Tirreno, *with sets by Giulio Parigi,* 1617. Gabinetto dei Disegni e delle Stampe, Galleria degli Uffizi, Florence (Scala).

274 Willem Boy (1520–92), *King Gustav I Vasa, c.*1550. Courtesy of the Nationalmuseum, Stockholm.

277 Jean le Pautre (1618–82) attrib., *The Inner Court of the Tre Kronor Castle, Stockholm,* engraving, *c.*1692, after a drawing by Erik Dahlberg (1625–1703), *c.*1670, from *Suecia Antiqua et Hodierna* (Stockholm, 1692). Courtesy of The Royal Library, Stockholm.

281 Hieronymus Nutzel, *Johan III lying in State at Tre Kronor Castle, with his Funeral Procession of 1592 in the Background,* 1593. Courtesy of The Royal Library, Stockholm.

282 Enamelled gold pendant depicting King Gustavus Adolphus, *c.*1630. Rijskmuseum, Amsterdam.

283 Ruprecht Miller (*fl.*1606–23), Fittings for the Coronation Saddle of Charles IX, 1607. Royal Armoury, Stockholm (Livrustkammeren).

286 Jurian Ovaens (Jürgen Ovens) (1623–78), *The Bedding Ceremony of King Karl X Gustav and Hedvig Eleonora von Gottorp, 1654, c.*1654. Courtesy of the Nationalmuseum, Stockholm.

287 Anon., seventeenth century, *Queen Christina of Sweden with Courtiers and Men of Learning.* Château de Versailles (Bridgeman Art Library, London/New York).

288 Willem Swidde (*fl.* 1660–70), *Drottningholm Palace,* engraving, after Erik Dahlberg (1625–1703), from *Suecia Antiqua et Hodierna* (Stockholm, 1692). Courtesy of the Nationalmuseum, Stockholm.

291 Anon., *The Tre Kronor Castle, Stockholm, c.*1650. Uppsala University Kontsamlingarna.

294 Anon., *The Coronation of Tsar Mikhail Federovich,* 1625, from the MS 'Book Describing the Chosing of the Tsar' (1672–3), printed 1856. Courtesy of Motovun Publishing, Lucerne.

297 'The Kremlin: The Palm Sunday procession, 10 April 1636', from Adam Olearius (1599–1671), *Vermehrte Newe Beschreibung der Muscowitschen und Persichen Reise* (Schleswig, 1656), p. 132a. (Fotomas Index).

298 Map of Moscow as it appeared at the end of the fifteenth century, from Georg Braun (1541–1622) and Franz Hogenburg, *Civitates Orbis Terrarum,* V (1597). (Fotomas Index).

299 Anon., *Tsars Ivan V, Peter I with the Tsarevich,* engraving, *c.*1690. British Library, London (Fotomas Index).

303 Anon., seventeenth century, *The Murder of the Tsarevich Dmitri Ivanovich at Uglich in 1591.* Private Collection, Paris (Giraudon).

305 Bernard Picart (1673–1733), *Peter I's Triumphal Entry into Moscow, 1710.* British Museum, Prints and Drawings (Fotomas Index).

306 *Map of St Petersburg,* from Schutz, *A Description of the City of St Petersburg and the Town and Castle of Cronslot,* I (1723). The British Library (Fotomas Index).

309 *The Tsaritsa Natalia Driving Out in State,* from O. Palmquist's *Album,* 1674. National Archives, Sweden (photograph: Kurt Eriksson).

311 Jean-Marc Nattier (1685–1766), *Tsar Peter I,* 1717. Hermitage Museum, St Petersburg (Bridgeman Art Library, London/New York).

INDEX